SCOTLAND FOR THE HO.

SCOTLAND FOR THE HOLIDAYS

A History of Tourism in Scotland, 1780–1939

Alastair J. Durie

TUCKWELL PRESS

First published in Great Britain in 2003 by
Tuckwell Press Ltd
The Mill House
Phantassie
East Linton
East Lothian, Scotland

Copyright © Alastair J. Durie 2003

ISBN 1 86232 121 3

British Library Cataloguing-in-Publication Data
A catalogue record is available
on request from the British Library

Typeset by Hewer Text Ltd, Edinburgh
Printed and bound by Bell and Bain Ltd, Glasgow

To Ruth and Alex, who often wondered why their holidays took them within range of so many local libraries.

CONTENTS

List of Illustrations   viii
Preface and Acknowledgements   ix
Introduction: Why Study Tourism?   1

1. The Discovery of Scotland   21
2. Transport and Tourism, 1800–1850   44
3. To the Seaside   65
4. The Search for Health   86
5. The Sporting Tourist   109
6. The Promotion of Scotland   129
7. Transport and Tourism, 1850–1914   150
8. The First World War and Tourism in Scotland   171

Postscript: The Interwar Years   192
Index   198

LIST OF ILLUSTRATIONS

1. Steamboat with excursionists on the Clyde, 1818.
2. Moffat Well, c. 1890.
3. North Berwick Station, 1914.
4. 'The shooting of the last grouse'.
5. 'A grouse battue'.
6. 'It's an ill wind . . .'
7. Sabbath Observance, 1884.
8. Arrivals at the Union Hotel, Inverness, 1843.
9. The *Bridge of Allan Journal and Spa Directory*, 1853.
10. Postcard from North Berwick, 1907.
11. George Washington Wilson view of the West Bay, North Berwick, 1893.
12. Moffat Hydro, c. 1910.
13. Moffat: Official Guide, 1920s or '30s.
14. *Tourist's Guide to the Picturesque Scenery of Scotland*, 1832.
15. *Shearer's Guide to the Trossachs and Loch Lomond*, 1915.
16. Mixed bathing.
17. The height of the season at Prestwick.
18. The Last Boat from Dunoon.
19. Monday morning at the Coast.
20. Portobello.
21. MacBrayne's *Summer Tours in Scotland*, 1884.
22. 'If you're run down, come to Pitlochry.'
23. LNER holiday season ticket, 1937.

Preface and Acknowledgements

It was Robert Louis Stevenson, who himself features in this book, who said that it was better to travel hopefully than to arrive. It is agreeable to have finished this study, but it has certainly been a pleasure to work it up, and en route I have incurred a great many obligations to those who have not only produced material of which I was aware, but have gone out of their way to draw my attention to other sources. It is perhaps invidious to single out any individuals amongst the many archivists and local studies librarians who have been of help, but some were of special significance. George Dixon of Central Regional Archives was the person who persuaded me of the value of tourism as a research subject, and Professor Tony Slaven of the Centre for the Study of Business History in Scotland did much to shape the academic thrust of the study. Murdo MacDonald of the Argyllshire and Bute County archives at Lochgilphead introduced me to a whole range of sources from auction records to burgh records, which I have tapped. Other archives and local history holdings, which I have used, and to whose custodians I am grateful, include those of the University of Aberdeen, Glasgow City, Dundee University, Dundee City, Edinburgh Public Library, Dumfries, Moray and Inverness, Fort William, Fife and Perth, Dumbarton, Ayr and Bute. The East Lothian Local History section, in the persons of Chris Roberts and Veronica Wallace, have as elsewhere gone far beyond what could reasonably be expected by way of service, as have Steve Dolman and Elma Lindsay of Stirling Library Services, and Graeme Wilson at Elgin. The National Archives of Scotland – still the SRO to my vintage – have had their usual wealth of holdings but much is held elsewhere. The County Record Offices of Durham, Northamptonshire, Worcestershire and South Yorkshire have supplied valuable journal and diary evidence. My own university of Glasgow's Special Collections has a remarkable amount of pamphlet and other material. Support with travel and photocopying has come from the Transport History Trust, and the University of Glasgow. Some sections have been tried out at seminars, at the universities of Lancaster, Leeds and Stirling, and amongst the academic community Neil Tranter and John Walton have been constantly encouraging.

Elements of this study have been taught at undergraduate level, and several students have produced dissertations of very real value and originality, including Barry Gardner, Ann Cameron, Kirsten Lang, Gillian Cooke and Jenny Cronin. The course of the research has been much furthered by the vacation work undertaken by Anna Gillies and Fiona McKean, and the neatness and care in the presentation of their findings in local newspapers and the like. My wife Kate has read and re-read drafts to the point of being able, or so she swears, to repeat them in her sleep, and Margaret Green has reviewed them with an eye to detail and grammar which I do not possess. But to no one do I owe more than to the late Professor Jack Simmons, whose knowledge of Victorian railways in all their aspects was without peer. His discussions, enquiries and prompting pushed this study on, even though his considered view was that the obstacles in the way of the study of Victorian tourism seemed insurmountable. He might have still thought so, but perhaps something of a start has been made.

INTRODUCTION: WHY STUDY TOURISM?

If statistics are to be believed, tourism is now the most important economic activity in the world, ahead even of oil, with scarcely any part of the globe unaffected. Tourists get everywhere, even to quite unsafe locations, as recent experience in the Yemen, Uganda and Egypt have demonstrated, and do so for quite a range of motivations. Some are traditional – for culture, antiquities, scenery, or 'sun, sand and sex'; some are new niche activities – whale watching, wreck diving, the roots experience, or whatever. Tourist money powers resort development, and, critics would argue, can corrupt and corrode traditional societies via, for example, the temptation to provide tourists with the images they want to find, regardless of whether they are current or genuine. The Scots promotion of Scotland as a land of heather, the kilt and whisky fits this model precisely: a dash of truth, a splash of history and a good deal of manufacture and manipulation! Tourism is therefore a very significant and important economic and social phenomenon of the present day.

Yet the study of tourism and its development in Britain and elsewhere has been relatively neglected until recently, and nowhere more so than in Scotland: a rather surprising lacuna, given both its current and past importance to the country over the last two hundred years. An article (1993) in the journal, *Scottish Economic and Social History*, by Professor George Peden of the University of Stirling observes that while tourism is the second most important industry in Scotland after oil, virtually nothing has been done on its history. 'It deserves more attention than it has had from economic historians of the twentieth century', and indeed from historians of the nineteenth century. As we shall see, the picture is not perhaps quite as bleak as he suggests, yet there remains some substance to his assertion. There has been in the last few years a major sea change in the literature of tourism. Quite a number of substantial studies have been published on the history of tourism on the Continent and in Britain. Amongst the most important are Harvey Levenstein, *Seductive Journey: American Tourists in France* (1998); John Pemble, *The Mediterranean Passion: Victorians and Edwardians in the South* (1985); Jeremy Black, *The British Abroad:*

The British and the Grand Tour (1985) and Christopher Hibbert, *The Grand Tour* (1987). England, of all parts of the United Kingdom, has been best served by M. Andrews, *The Search for the Picturesque* (1989); John Urry, *The Tourist Gaze* (1990), and Ian Ousby's *The Englishman's England: Taste, Travel and the Rise of Tourism* (1990). Coastal tourism has been especially considered by John Walton with *The English Seaside Resort, A Social History, 1750–1913* (1983), *The Blackpool Landlady* (1978) and most recently *Blackpool* (1999). Other excellent regional studies include John Travis' *The Rise of the Devon Resorts, 1750–1914* (1993). The study of tourism in Scotland lags behind, though ahead of that for Ireland, on which nothing of significance has yet emerged. There has been the recent excellent short study by Eric Simpson, *Going on Holiday* (Edinburgh, 1997) and J. & M. Gold's *Imaging Scotland: Tradition, Representation and Promotion in Scottish Tourism since 1750* (Aldershot, 1995). Local and transport historians have made useful contributions on the steamer and railway companies' tourist business, and individual resorts, such as Millport and Aberdour, have been described. There are a number of relevant articles in the periodical literature, notably those by T.C. Smout, R.W. Butler and K. Haldane. The focus of all three has been on the Highland experience. What is yet lacking, and what this book addresses, is the broad integrated picture of the rise of tourism in Scotland which gives due weight to developments elsewhere.

There is certainly no denying the significance of tourism in a Scottish context, and three reasons for studying tourism stand out. The first is the degree of reliance on tourism experienced by many parts of Scotland, not perhaps Airdrie, but in the Borders, the Trossachs, the Highlands, and the Clyde. From very modest beginnings in the later eighteenth century, tourism grew to become by the later nineteenth century the mainstay of some communities and localities. Oban is a good example. As a contemporary attested in 1881, 'Oban exists simply for tourists'. The same could have been said of quite a number of other places, inland and coastal, southern and northern, from Crieff in the Central belt to Strathpeffer in Ross-shire to Carnoustie or North Berwick in the East and Rothesay and Dunoon in the West. Such local economies rested on tourism just as much as other towns relied on a single activity such as coal, steel or wool. This degree of dependence, of course, was not unique to resorts and localities in Scotland. In England there were places like Brighton, Blackpool and Scarborough, in Wales Llandudno, on the Isle of Man Douglas and Ramsay. There were an ever-increasing number of tourist destinations on the Continent – the spas of Germany and

Belgium, the health resorts of the Riviera, the cultural meccas of Italy: Venice and Rome – all increasingly accessible thanks to the growing rail network.

A second point is that income from tourism did filter down to almost all layers of Scottish society other than the poorest. Critics of tourism today argue that much of the revenue generated by tourism ends up in the pockets of the moneyed elite of the receiving country who control the hotels and leisure facilities on offer. In Scotland, the income seems to have much been much more widely spread. Certainly landowners benefited from the leasing of their moors for deerstalking or grouse shooting, hoteliers from the influx of visitors, railway and steamship companies from transporting visitors, their staff and their luggage. Seventeen trunks of clothing and accessories was considered par for the course for a visiting American lady in Europe, and while many a porter must have groaned at their arrival, the tip may well have compensated him. In tourist areas, the takings may have been surprisingly high. The keepers of castles, monuments and battlefields reaped a harvest from visitors, through their tours, spiels and the sale of souvenirs. The enterprising custodian of Doune Castle, a former soldier, in the 1880s prepared and sold his own guidebook, which went into several editions; and when the Gallows tree at the Castle was damaged by fire, he bought what was usable to make into tourist 'knick-knacks'. In England where, according to Lord Gower, more and more the finest places were being left 'to solitude, tourists and the charge of a housekeeper', with its generally bigger numbers the returns could be very substantial. When the Earl of Warwick's housekeeper died in 1834, she was said to have left no less than £30,000 earned from tourists' tips. Warwick Castle had at least 6,000 visitors in 1825–1826, forcing an end to the practice of serving polite visitors with tea. It was very popular with honeymooners and Americans: when Hariet Beecher Stowe visited in 1853, she found the castle so infested with tourists that she considered it had become 'a public museum and pleasure-grounds for the use of the people'. Yet as tourism grew and spread, the effects were seen quite widely beyond the great houses and historic sites. In 1867 the Bank of Scotland considered a proposal for a new agency at Dalmally and asked their agent at Aberfoyle to assess the prospects. In general he was sceptical as to the possibilities in such a thinly populated area, but he did qualify his pessimistic remarks: 'In passing through the district you would not think that a small shopkeeper in a thatched cottage would have two or three thousand in a bank or that a *Post Boy had saved £1,400*' [my italics]. Was not some of this prosperity the result of tourist spending and tips?

Employment was generated for beaters and ghillies on the moors, porters at the stations, cooks, waiters and servants in the hotels, entertainers and vendors of ice-cream at the beaches, and so on. Two cyclists camping out at Loch Katrine in 1904 met up with a tinker family. During the winter they stayed in Perth, but in the summer they migrated to this favourite tourist locality, with father dressed up in bonnet and trews playing the pipes 'to the "gents" arriving from the Trossachs by steamer'. Admittedly some of this work was only seasonal, and would fluctuate with the state of tourism, but it was an asset. And then there was the income from house-letting, whether apartments at the seaside or big houses in the more fashionable resorts such as Bridge of Allan and North Berwick. Even croftholders were able to cash in by letting their properties to tourists during the summer, themselves moving out temporarily to outhouses or bothies for the duration, as did lodging-house landladies at the seaside. An account of Helensburgh in 1880 said that no-one ever saw the land-*lords*: 'they were relegated to some outhouse or cellar, where they lived in secrecy and silence, allowing their wives full control'. This widespread practice of subletting in the countryside and at the coast even led to friction between some landlords and their tenants, the former considering that it was their right to put up the rent charged in the light of this summer income. Several cases came to the Scottish Land Court for resolution. One in August 1914 involved Malcolm MacGregor of MacGregor and eight of his crofter tenants at Balquhidder. It was agreed at the hearing that the crofters had been letting their properties to visitors during July and August for £5 a month, no small addition to their income, given that their rents were in the order of £11–£12 per annum. The landlord's attempt to raise the rents failed, as it had done earlier in the year in a similar case from Arran. The Court Assessors observed that

> [letting] has become by general custom a use which is reasonable in itself, and contemplated by both landlord and tenant, except when forbidden by contract . . . The practice has become general amongst all classes of farmers, clergymen and schoolmasters for many years. Indirectly it is an advantage to the landlord, because tenants who desire to attract summer visitors or boarders or pupils improve their houses and keep them in more thorough repair than would otherwise be required. The main advantage to the tenant is that he gets ready money for payment of his rent and necessary expenditure on the holding. On the other hand, the small tenant and his family, in the case of letting the dwelling-

house have to remain on the holding for its cultivation and therefore suffer the inconvenience of having to live in an extra cottage or often in a part of the steading or a makeshift building during the period of letting.

A third point to be aware of is just how tough and competitive the tourism business was. It is today, and was equally so in the nineteenth century. Tourism was subject both to long-term changes in direction, influenced by a complex of factors – taste and fashion, access and amenities – and quite violent short-term swings, caused by bad weather or the outbreak of war or economic conditions. And unlike areas of manufacturing industry where competition was muted by cartel agreements or protection offered by tariffs, the tourist business was highly competitive, resort against resort, locality against locality, country against country. New resorts with new attractions came on stream in Britain and the Continent. Monte Carlo converted itself in the 1870s from a health resort for invalids to a highly popular centre for gambling, an example followed by Nice and Cannes. Railway and steamship companies promoted their favoured destinations, even to the point of building their own hotels complete with golf course, as did the Great North of Scotland Railway at Cruden Bay near Aberdeen in 1899. Some resorts, particularly the smaller and more elite, could rely on a loyal clientèle which returned year after year, a pattern only to break down in Britain in the 1960s. But the majority found they had to invest in new or additional facilities to retain their appeal and place in the market. Piers, towers, marine gardens and amusement parks all had a part to play, as did local scenery and sights. Amenities such as adequate clean and safe water supplies, sewage systems and the like had to be provided to complement private investment in hotel and other accommodation. The requirement for communities to provide from local taxation proper facilities for the summer populations, swollen as they might be by visitors to three of four times their normal size, was something that generated tension. On the one hand were ratepayers who had to finance this provision, and on the other, those hoteliers and others who primarily benefited. However, those resorts that did not invest ran the risk of slipping off the tourist map, as some indeed did. And if growth was not easy to sustain, even with investment and promotional campaigns, decline was and remains even harder to arrest. One of the key questions we need to ask is what were the selling points for Scotland and its resorts as against its competitors, what its strengths and weaknesses were.

But, despite the reasons for taking tourism in Scotland seriously as an economic phenomenon and integral part of economic history, the reality remains that until comparatively recently the history of tourism had taken a back seat on the academic agenda and the field had been left largely to either popular writers or local studies historians, good though some of these studies were. And just as some people look down on 'tourists', the academic community has tended to have a low view of tourism. Indeed when the possibility of teaching a course on the history of tourism was raised at one university, there was a blunt reaction that 'tourism was not a real subject'. Fortunately that was not the majority view, but it did demonstrate a position that many have held, though perhaps not as bluntly. Why was there, and still perhaps lingers, this negative response? It can be suggested that there are three reasons.

There has been a longstanding fascination with the sinews of the economy, the manufacturing sector, centred on textiles and the heavy industries, production as against consumption, work as against play; and while banking has been scrutinised, the service sector in general has been until relatively recently under-researched and written up. A second major problem has been the nature of the subject, which hinders analysis. Tourism is, as we shall see, an umbrella term, which covers a very diverse range of experiences. The term 'tourist' was originally applied in the seventeenth century to those who made a tour, in Britain or on the Continent, following an established schedule to see the sights of antiquity and scenery. This tourism was cultural in motivation and confined to the elite with money and time to spare. But over time, tourism was to change in numbers, broaden in motivation, and as a term come to cover not just upper-class visitors on a leisurely tour, but a much broader constituency. There were also the professional and upper middle classes on their two-month summer break and the artisan excursionist travelling on a fixed budget and schedule, plus the working-class day tripper. Motivation became much more complex; for some, scenery, culture and health – constants in the tourist world – for others, sport and recreation. In Scotland the appeal of activities such as golf, fishing, hill-walking and shooting was particularly significant. Some of the driving forces were relatively short-lived such as the Victorian passions for geology and botany or fern-collecting or for the haunts of popular writers; others permanent – the fascination with the Roman and the Greek world. But the complexity of what appears at first sight a straightforward term is a problem. An issue fought over, incidentally, is the distinction which is drawn forcibly by some between a 'traveller' and a 'tourist'. A 'traveller', it is argued, is someone who ventures – often alone or with a very few companions – into new and uncharted territory in search of the undiscovered and unfamiliar. By contrast, a tourist is someone who tends to travel in company along routes and to places made familiar by those who have gone before. Tourism is something made possible by mass transportation, by the work of travel companies, guide books and other tools which partially at least familiarise the visitor with what they are about to see. Tourism rises at the expense of exploration, and after the travelling of the few has made the initial inroads.

A third deterrent relates to the sources for the study of tourism. It is a subject which suffers both from too few and too many resources. There is a wide range of primary and secondary sources to tap, as will be discussed below. But a critical deficiency, for some, is the lack of quantitative data which would enable the scale and direction of tourism to be charted in the same ways as other economic activities. Even today, the official data collected are far from perfect, and for earlier periods much more spasmodic and inconsistent. The census in Britain between 1851 and 1911 was taken too early in the year, usually at the end of March or the beginning of April, to be of much service, except at the spas where the season began rather earlier than was true of the resorts. Passports for entry to Britain were not required prior to 1914, no parliamentary investigation was ever undertaken into tourism, nor were foreigners required to register with the police, as was the case in France. This has led historians of the eminence of Professor Jack Simmons (*The Victorian Railway*, 1994) to conclude that 'the history of Victorian tourism has not been studied much. The obstacles in the way of any full investigation of it seem insurmountable'. While conceding that there is some validity in this judgement, it is perhaps too pessimistic. There is no simple source for the number of visitors to Scotland in any given year, or how they were distributed, or the duration of their stay. No easily accessible long-run series is available for the number drawn to the principal attractions. Nor do the railway and steamship company returns offer much help, other than to show how passenger traffic increased during the summer. There are some snippets of statistical information, usually to be found in the local or national press, and occasionally elsewhere, as to the numbers going on railway excursions or passing through the turnstiles of the Clyde steamer piers. It was reported in August 1913 that over 123,000 people had passed through those at Dunoon Pier during the previous week of the Glasgow Fair, 'a record'. The numbers of visitors to Bannockburn, according to the keeper's book at the Borestone, rose from 2928 in 1895 to 4252 in 1898, but fell away sharply thereafter for reasons which are not clear, other than that there was little or nothing to see. We have some figures for a few other calling places for tourists where registers of visitors have survived and can be used to generate totals: Burns' Monument at Ayr from 1845 to 1860, and Burns' Cottage at Alloway from 1860 to 1864. The Wallace Monument at Abbey Craig, with its central location, Hall of Heroes and magnificent views, attracted large numbers (Table 1) of tourists in, or passing through, Stirling.

Unfortunately there are no comparable returns for Stirling Castle, which was more popular with visitors, to put these from the Wallace Monument in perspective, but it was well ahead of Bannockburn, showing the superiority of a manufactured draw as against an authentic but unenhanced historic site. The most complete series is that for Abbotsford House, whose visitors' books are complete from 1833 onwards (Table 6.1, see page 139), which shows a surge in numbers from the 1840s onwards, holding around the 6–7,000 mark for the next half-century. This can be put in context by a comparison with those for the key English attractions. According to Peter Mandler, *The Fall and Rise of the Stately Home* (1997), the most-visited private house in England before the First World War was Chatsworth, with 80,000 visitors a season. At the great show houses in England, some dozen were drawing over 10,000 a year by the 1870s.

TABLE 1.   WALLACE MONUMENT VISITORS, 1876–1905.

1876	15,873
1884	10,080
1886	12,340
1887	9,135
1897–1901 *average per annum	36,293
1901–1905 *average per annum	30,942

Visitors' books and hotel registers, where they survive – and not many have – can be of great service as can the lists of visitors (discussed below) which local papers carried during the tourist season in the more exclusive resorts. They have their limitations but are better than nothing. So, although the quantitative picture is very imperfect, there is not a total blank, and enough data to indicate some numbers and trends. Even the much-maligned census data have some use. As already indicated, these were held too early in the year to be of any service for the summer resorts. What the enumerators' books do indicate for places like Helensburgh and North Berwick are the number of houses either empty or manned only by a skeleton staff awaiting the summer. There are growing numbers of people describing themselves as lodging-house keepers. But in the spa resorts there was already by the end of March – depending on when Easter was – an influx of 'temporary residents', a category that covered visitors, construction workers and vagrants. However, the bulk of the 1,100 temporaries in Bridge of Allan in 1871 would have been in first category. In 1881 the census noted 553 temporary visitors, and the local enumerators added the comment that most were 'visitors at the Hydropathic Institute' or 'Just here for the sake of their health'. There seems to have been a reclassification in 1891 with those merely staying overnight being classified as *boarders*. Note, however, the comment of Norman Kemp in April 1931, acting as the census enumerator for the third time for the Waverley Hydropathic Hotel at Melrose:

> We have lost a great many visitors this week. We are all of the opinion that the census is sending many of the guests home: particularly some of the elderly ladies, who may not wish such intimate matters as age etc to be revealed to me.

If there is a shortage of quantitative data on tourism, there is no shortfall in other kinds of source. There are a multitude of primary sources for the study of the history of tourism, from printed accounts, diaries, letters and journals, newspapers and periodicals, guidebooks (both national and local), prospectuses for hotels, paintings, photographs and postcards, town council, business and legal records. Even police regulations come into play. The County's Chief Constable, James Fraser, framed the Argyllshire Constabulary's Orders in 1894. General Order no 12 (just after one about dog licences and the worrying of sheep) relates to tourists and others refusing to pay their hotels bills because they allege they have been overcharged. There had been more than one recent complaint, resulting in troublesome correspondence and reflection. Fraser urged caution where the parties appeared to be respectable, and had given their names and addresses, the hotelier after all retaining the luggage of doubtful lodgers until their bills were paid.

A prime source, and one already much quarried, is obviously that of travellers' accounts. Scotland as a tourist destination and experience has been much written about. There are any number of published accounts of travel in Scotland by English, American and Continental visitors, written from a variety of perspectives. Some are, or pretend to be, factual and descriptive, others humorous such as Toddles' *Highland Tour* (London, *c.* 1865) or A'Beckett and Linley Sambourne's *Our Holidays in the Highlands* (London, 1876). Some are broad surveys; others more tightly focused by area or a particular enthusiasm for fishing or walking or geology. Amongst the last category are accounts of botanical excursions. A paper was read in December 1876 to the Manchester Botanists' Association and subsequently published in the *Transactions of the Oldham Microscopical Club*. 'An Excursion to the Grampian Mountains' is an account of a two-week tour to look for rare Scottish alpine plants, specimens of which were brought back. It is interesting not just for where the party went and what they found, but how they travelled, their accommodation and the people they met, including a party of three young men from Aberdeen on a holiday ramble. The journeys of Johnson and Boswell are well known, though in many respects of much less service to the historian of tourism than those of Mrs Sarah Murray of Kensington or the Wordsworths. Amongst other notables to leave a record of their visit to Scotland are Harriet Beecher Stowe, Felix Mendelssohn, Jules Verne, Nathaniel Hawthorne and Theodore Fontane. One whose writing deserves more recognition is J. M. Bailey, a newspaperman from Connecticut whose wry observations are still enjoyable, such as 'We reached Glasgow at four p.m. but commenced to smell it at a quarter past three'. Or while in Edinburgh, where he was shocked – for all his flippancy – by the level of dirt and poverty, and the number of boys, many begging:

> There are about two million boys in Edinburgh, whose ages range from twelve to fifteen years; and all but nine of them wear Scotch bonnets, either of Glengarry or other pattern (*England from a Back Window*, Boston 1879).

For many nineteenth-century middle- and upper-class people and even some artisans, the keeping of a daily journal or diary was standard practice, but especially so if on tour, whether on business or pleasure. A rich source is that of Lord Cockburn's *Circuit Journeys*, which covers his travels in Scotland as a judge between 1838 and 1854 and is full of sharp observations relating to travel and tourism. Early in September 1843 his duties took him to Rothesay:

> At this season, on a fine day, enjoyment seems to be the sole business of the inhabitants. Going in cars, boating, sitting on the rocks or at open windows, bathing, sewing or reading on the shore, looking through telescopes, or basking in luxurious idleness – these are the occupations of a community composed of strangers who resort there for pleasure, and of natives who let their houses to them.

The more gifted might illustrate their jottings with sketches of the

scenery and sights. Some were designed right at the outset for publication; others were published after an interval, as Cockburn's was;
others were merely retained for perusal by friends and family. Unpublished accounts, of which an increasing number have come to
light, of tours in Scotland, or collections of letters, are held in record
offices throughout Britain and abroad, local history libraries, and
indeed private hands. An example of the last is a *Journal of a Tour
from St Andrews to Loch Maree* undertaken in June and July 1857 by
one Thomas Allan, a St Andrews graduate later resident in Glasgow
where he was secretary to the Clyde Navigation Trust. Thirty pages
long, it is full of useful observation, and the 9th of July, for example,
finds him on the way to Corpach:

> Invergarry Castle in ruins is one of the picturesque objects on this
> part of the journey. It is only too symbolical of the present
> condition of Highland lairds and chieftains; but the curtain fell
> here in the shape of rain, and little else was visible besides the
> steamer, and her cargo and the banks of the canal until we
> arrived at Corpach Inn. Ben Nevis was as usual half-shrouded in
> mist and the evening continued rainy. Were it not for the ben, this
> place would be as dreary as the middle of the moor of Rannoch.
> The inn was tolerably full, having English, French and German
> Tourists in the company. They were very quiet and at ten I left
> them all reading or sleeping or drinking toddy, and retired to a
> crib and a bed apparently intended for ancient wights of small
> stature and not for modern Britons of ordinary size. However, I
> slept till five in the morning when a series of solid thumps on all
> the bedroom doors in the long passage intimated that they who
> were going by the morning boats had better be moving. An
> hour's bustle followed . . .

What in Thomas Allan's view saved Loch Maree from development,
which would have spoiled it, was its distance from Edinburgh and
Glasgow so that 'neither Lords of Session nor fortunate merchants can
conveniently build modern palaces here'. The weather, accommodation, service and food, as well as the company found, are frequent
topics of comment for Allan as are contemporary issues such as
emigration. There are two questions to ask of such a source. First,
for whom was the writing intended? Was it just as a personal reminder
and for recollection, in the same way as later generations were to
compile photograph albums? For an anxious mother or wife or
children? Or a wider readership of friends and acquaintances back
home? Fellow religious or political enthusiasts? Second, what factors –

upbringing, religious or political or cultural or class or age or gender –
may have affected the way writers described the scenes they viewed?
The world they saw they did not see through plain glass, and the
modern reader has to recognise the challenge of viewing through their
lens, and allowing for possible biases or distortions. How far, for
example, did the temperance convictions of many American visitors
colour their view of Scotland? Not all writers were upper-class, male
and moneyed. A recent discovery on Tayside has been the diary for
1864–65 of a Dundee millwright. John Sturrock, like many other
respectable working men, chose to spend some of his leisure time in a
day away from the city. Saturday the 24th of June 1865, as his diary
records, finds him spending his annual holiday at Perth, Pitlochry and
the battlefield of Killiecrankie, a day that highly pleased him. Many
others were finding the same experience, even if little record has been
left of their outings. And not all tourists and sightseers were adult.
John Gullane, a teenage Edinburgh boy, kept a diary which describes
his summer holiday in 1846: to Portobello for a bathe, and then to St
Boswells for a longer stay during which he and a friend visited
Abbotsford. Having got a lift to Melrose, they walked to the house,
and hung around until a lady and gentleman arrived. They went into
the house with them, and after an hour's tour, put their names down in
the visitors' book (their signatures are there yet) and came away. In the
Lamb Collection at Dundee is a 47-page manuscript, very neatly
written by John Young, of a two-week pedestrian tour in late August
1855 from Dundee by way of Blairgowrie to Ben Macdhui and back,
undertaken by 'three merry boys with knapsack and staff'. Young, an
entrepreneurial youth, sold a digest of their travels, including an
account of their getting lost overnight in the Grampians, to the
Dundee Weekly News, like other papers always on the lookout for
lively stories.

   Few sources offer more to the historian of tourism than the national
and local press. Indeed, without tourism the latter would have been
hard pressed to fill its columns. Big city papers, *The Glasgow Herald*
and *The Scotsman*, for example, and nationals such as *The Times* by
the later nineteenth century were carrying much of relevance. There
were reports from resorts, news about sporting tourism, 'the prospects
for the grouse', lists of hotels, hydros and other accommodation to
rent in the country or at the seaside, and travel advertisements. But the
local press is a mine of unique information. Freed from tax and duties
in the 1850s, virtually every community or locality came to have its
own paper, which was usually a weekly issue. Their staffs were small
and some indeed were one-man shows, but they are invaluable for

accounts of excursions from and to the area, organised by churches, temperance and other organisations – the masons, factories and works, antiquarian societies, and the railway companies themselves. As we see later, the day-trip or excursion became a feature of travel for leisure, thanks to the steamship and the railway, in the nineteenth century, and was seized upon with enthusiasm. The *Stirling Journal and Observer* reported on 4 August 1848 that

> a most numerous and respectable party of the inhabitants of Stirling and others residing in the neighbourhood, left here yesterday for Perth and Dundee at greatly reduced fares. The train which left early in the morning consisted of thirty-four carriages, and appeared like a huge serpent coiling its way along the curves of the line as it passed between Stirling station and Lecropt. The day was passed most pleasantly.

In the early days, it was the experience of travelling, and the sights en route, that were as much the package as the destination. A sense of the sheer enjoyment, despite the wet weather, runs through this account of the Innerleithen Holiday excursion of 11th July 1884. Leaving by special train at 5.45 a.m., and calling at various local stations, some 550 set off, one group for Edinburgh and Leith to enjoy a sail, or Portobello for bathing, and the other to Stirling:

> We arrived in Stirling a few minutes past nine, and marched in a body to Mr R. Wooley's Caledonian Restaurant where we had engaged a hall for dancing etc. After the band had finished their tune, we made for the various places of interest around Stirling viz. Bannockburn, Bridge of Allan, Wallace's Monument, Menstrie, Alva, Dollar etc. On our return we engaged in dancing, and kept up our sport until the time arrived when we had to leave viz. 6.30. With the band in front we marched to the station, and all getting seated, we arrived in Edinburgh in time for the train to start for Innerleithan at 8.20, reaching Innerleithan at 10 p.m. It may be stated that the whole body behaved themselves in gentlemanly and lady-like manner, and seemed highly pleased with their trip.

One of the first Scottish local papers was *The Bridge of Allan Journal and Spa Directory*, first published for this rising resort in 1853, every second Wednesday during the season. It carried a mix of local intelligence, national news, and advertisements for excursions in the locality by rail, steamer or coach. Shopkeepers, merchants, booksellers and hoteliers amongst others publicised their businesses, and much of this was aimed at new arrivals. Such newspapers and their columns give a real flavour of summer life in tourist resorts, and illustrate what local merchants and others hoped would appeal to visitors. *The Strathspey News and Grantown Supplement* in July 1891 carried two pages of advertisements directed at tourists: the local bee farm, the services of photographers for picnics and other gatherings, the hire of camp beds, perambulators and clothing, both for outdoor activities and evening functions. A. G. Grant of the Caledonian House Drapery assured his numerous lady customers that 'arrangements for the tourist season were so complete that Visitors entrusting him with orders, as well as his regular customers, could depend on having their commands promptly executed'. Local papers also tended to carry verbatim accounts of town or burgh council proceedings relating to the provision of tourist amenities, letters of complaint, and even the occasional enthusiastic endorsement from a satisfied visitor. What also appear – and they are difficult to find elsewhere – are details of accidents to visitors: deaths while bathing or boating, fatalities while motoring or climbing. It is in *The Haddingtonshire Courier* of 12th September 1873 that we find an account of the tragic drowning of two servant girls from England, part of the staff of a London family staying for the summer at North Berwick. Bathing at low tide amongst the rocks, it appears that they fell into a deep gully, and though a third member of the group was revived, the other two succumbed. What this sad episode underlines is that going away on holiday was an experience shared by servants and staff, though they have left little record of their time.

One of the most important sections of these local papers is the lists of visitors that were published during the tourist season as to who was staying where. They have their limitations; by definition only people staying for some time – at least a week – would be included, and the lists tend to include only the adults, with children and servants seldom mentioned though the occasional nurse (and even an ayah) does feature. All resorts of any social pretension had these up to *c.* 1914. They can be used, as Chapters 3 and 4 show, to get an indication of changes in numbers, and the origins of visitors. Local hotels might or might not publish in the newspaper register a list of visitors in residence. They were sometimes coy about divulging how full or empty they were, but certainly not slow to publicise, either in the list or in their advertising, the residence of any nobility, however minor, as did the George Hotel at Melrose in 1872:

J. Menzies [the proprietor] begs to call the attention of Strangers visiting Melrose to the comforts of this Establishment, being the only hotel in Melrose patronised by the Royal family and the Empress of the French etc., etc. (Black's *Picturesque Tourist of Scotland*, 19th edition, Edinburgh, 1872).

All hotels, country houses, castles, abbeys and the like would have kept registers of visitors staying or visiting. But alas, very few of these have survived, either thrown out or cut apart for the signatures of the famous. Amongst the lots sold at auction in Edinburgh in February 1878, the property of the Rev. D.T.K. Drummond, was the Visitors' book for Dryburgh Abbey covering the years 1821 to 1835, with the signatures of Sir Walter Scott and 'many other famous persons'. If it still exists, its whereabouts are presently unknown. Emily Pankhurst left her signature in the John o' Groats Hotel on 17 September 1910, along with a verse about a young man who wore a top hat and seventeen coats: 'He explained he had sworn that such clothes should be worn, till the day when all women have votes!' One of the most unusual runs of surviving books is for the hotel at the summit of Ben Nevis, open from June to September and able to accommodate twelve guests. As might be expected, the most common – and unoriginal – comment is 'missed the view and viewed the mist'. The registers for Tibbie Shiels' Inn, a fishermen's haunt at St Mary's Loch near Selkirk, are complete for the years 1866 to 1922, and are full of comments and illustrations as well as claims as to how many fish and of what size visitors had caught. Marginalia do add interest: the Brodies of Lilliesleaf in July 1911 stated that they had cycled 26 miles to the inn, and hoped to meet with Colonel Cody's biplane. There were aeroplane races between London and Scotland that month, which aroused considerable excitement, with crowds turning out to watch their passing. Cyclists were not slow to leave their mark: the Atholl Arms at Dunkeld's book for May 20th 1872 carries a sixteen-line description of a cycling tour of 106 miles from Perth to Pitlochry and Killiecrankie filled in on his return by one George J. Cayley Smith. He was proud of his exploit: 'wonderful'; others were less impressed. 'Fools are communicative' was one blunt comment. Other places keeping registers which visitors would have signed include country houses, museums and even some industrial works which were on the tourist trail, like New Lanark. But one has to be careful. Did everyone sign? The answer is probably 'yes' at the places where admission was supervised, but less so perhaps at those places frequented by the less polite. And there are always the humourists who adopt a pseudonym to forge a celebrity's signature. The reading room at the Birnam

Institute, established in 1883, which was for the use of visitors and locals alike, had a visitors' book which can still be inspected. Salted in amongst the quite genuine signatures of Lady Millais and Beatrix Potter are several fakes, all in the same hand: those of Robert Louis Stevenson on 6th October 1885, Rudyard Kipling and Christabel Pankhurst.

The role of photography in the promotion of Scotland is fully discussed in Chapter 6. Photographs both shaped where people might go, and were bought as souvenirs of what tourists had seen and where they had been. Of great value to the study of tourism, popular as well as elite, is the postcard, produced in very great numbers from the 1890s onwards. These have a double value: the views portrayed and the messages sent. Many are humdrum, of the 'having a nice time' school. But others stand out, or intrigue. What did L.G. imply, whose card from Leven was posted on 14th August 1914 to a friend: 'Was here at Largo this morning on the look out for flounders but got none. Mary knows what I mean'. Postcards can raise more questions than can be resolved. An American visitor to Edinburgh in June 1909 sent back a card to a friend at the Post Office, Kansas City, enthusing over the delightful time she was having and wishing that all the P[ost] O[ffice] Clerks could have 'as fine a holiday as I am having this summer'. What this suggests is that she herself was a Post Office employee, and that transatlantic tourism had indeed broadened in social and economic terms.

In fact tourism has left its mark across a wide range of material, and the range of sources only appears narrow at first glance. There are frustrating gaps, as in the railway and steamship company records, and isolated items. On display at Culzean Castle is a pass for the grounds issued by the factor's office at Maybole on 19th August 1895 for a party from Helensburgh who wished to visit on the following Wednesday. It carries a warning that the Porter had written instructions to stop all picnic parties on the premises. What one would like to know is how many such passes were issued, and on what criteria. Yet, for all the deficiencies, there are some unexpected compensations. The Lands Valuation Court would not seem a promising source, hearing as it did appeals against the rating placed on properties by county and burgh assessors. Yet quite a high proportion of the cases it heard in the 1880s, for example, do have a bearing. There are the Hydro hotels at Glenburn and Pitlochry appealing against their rating – the first successfully, the second not so – and in the process having to produce a good deal of hard commercial evidence as to their business, and their clientèle. When asked whether the cost of maintenance was high,

Andrew Philp of Glenburn replied that it was considerable: 'we have a great many young people who rollick about, and they create a good deal of wear and tear'. Particularly valuable is the use of expert witnesses, and the leading of detailed evidence about the scale and nature of operations. MacDonald, the proprietor of the Atholl, based his case largely on the fact that his hydro, unlike the others, was not open all year round but during the summer only. He stated that it had been found to be much more profitable to close the establishment during the winter, a common problem for Highland hotels. Amongst the other appeals submitted to the valuation judges were several relating to deer forests, another as to how much of the revenue from the admission of visitors to Abbotsford – £419 in the previous year – should be regarded as 'rental income', and two from station book-stalls, at Callander and Tayport, where much turned on how reliable their summer income was.

Shortage of material is not, therefore, a problem. And there are also some useful analytical tools. This study does not want to dip deep into the theoretical side of tourism, as annexed by economists and sociologists. But it is useful to examine two models, which are of service to our understanding of the dynamics of tourism: those of R. W. Butler (*Canadian Geographer*, 24, 1980) and Schmoll (*Tourist promotion*, 1977). We know that resort areas go through periods of growth, and then perhaps experience stagnation or decline. What Butler suggests is a four-stage Tourist Area Life Cycle of DISCOVERY, DEVELOPMENT, CONSOLIDATION, and STAGNATION, to which some would add a fifth, DECLINE or REJUVENATION. This framework has been refined and reworked by others, particularly at the third stage. B. Goodall (*Progress in Tourist Recreation*, 1992) has stressed the importance of resorts adding to their portfolio of *natural* attractions (scenery, beaches, walks and views), man-made and purpose-built crowd-pullers such as piers, towers and the like. This model remains a useful tool, although, as critics have pointed out, it is not watertight. How, for example, does one identify when a locality passes from one phase to the next? On numbers alone? And in a country like Scotland, is there not a complex of life cycles at work at different levels? There is that of the hotel or night-club which is 'in' one year but drops out of favour the next; or the resort which manages to retain its clientèle generation after generation whereas its neighbour loses its place in the sun, e.g. the contrast between Elie, still a holiday haunt of the Edinburgh professional classes, and Burntisland, once very popular, but now largely a caravaners' haunt. The life cycle also operates at regional level; one of the most popular destinations in Scotland in the nineteenth century was Ayrshire, 'the Land of Burns'. It still has a presence but not to the same extent.

Schmoll's model identifies four factors of significance to the tourist flow: [1] the importance of travel stimuli provided by travel agencies, literature, advertising and word-of-mouth reports; [2] those things that shape the ability and willingness of the individual or group to travel; [3] external variables; the degree of risk and uncertainty involved; and [4] the characteristics of the destination which are important, key amongst which are the cost of living and the range of amenities. These are all relevant to tourism both in the present and the past. In the nineteenth century, there developed quite sophisticated advertising through posters and special promotions. What was it that persuaded people to undertake their first tourist trip? Some would point to the role of the Great Exhibition of 1851 which drew large excursions to London, or in a Scottish context Queen Victoria's tours in the Highlands, and the purchase of Balmoral that conferred royal warrant on the Highland experience. Once the desire was implanted, what factors shaped the capacity to travel: income, age, gender, class, family group, legislation? Which factors affected the timing of holidays: Fair days and schools? What determined which group went where? All these, and others, are questions we need to have in the back of our minds as we start to examine the history of tourism in Scotland.

Finally there is a remarkable constancy to the tourist experience, to the pleasures and disappointments of the visitor, and to the response of the receiving communities. Not everyone is enthused by the descent of the tourist, particularly as the discerning few give way to the mass hordes. This letter from an Argyllshire schoolteacher to the County Clerk in June 1932 would have received sympathetic nods from many others on the receiving end elsewhere:

Dear Sir,
   It has been a customary thing for numerous charabancs to find parking spaces between the Shire Bridge and The Rest and Be Thankful. We do not mind this but the occupants of these charabancs and numerous bands of cyclists are making themselves a public nuisance and a menace to the moral welfare of the children. The inhabitants of the district cannot walk along the public highway but they get all manner of insolent remarks and filthy language shouted after them. Men and women in various states of undress parade about the road and hillsides. Men, absolutely naked, stand on the banks of the River Croe and do their utmost to attract the attention of passers by whilst all

sorts of immorality are practised on the lower slopes of the hill-sides and in full view of the public and of young children.

Throughout my stay here I have seen things go from bad to worse, till I and the other people of Glencroe have become thoroughly disgusted with the outrageous behaviour of these visitors. I do hope, if only for the sake of the young children and their future outlook on life that something will be done to prevent this lovely countryside from becoming a den of iniquity.

What we are doing in this study, therefore, is as much a traveller's journey as a tourist trip, going into territory some of which is mapped, some not. Much of the material which will be presented is work in progress to which undergraduate students and others have contrib-uted over the years. And it is remarkable what they have managed to unearth. A Danish undergraduate was interested in Hans Christian Andersen's visit to Scotland in August 1847. While in Edinburgh, Andersen went to Heriot's Hospital (now School) where he was moved to find that his name was recognised and his stories were known. The register with his signature, and those of the others in his party, is prized and preserved yet, as she found. That is proof, if any were needed, of how rich the resources are for the history of tourism in Scotland.

FURTHER READING

Sir Arthur Mitchell's 'List of Travels, Tours, etc relating to Scotland', *Proceedings of the Society of Antiquaries of Scotland*, 1901–1910, is still of great use. There is as yet no comprehensive Scottish equivalent to *The Observant Traveller* (edited by Robin Guard, London, 1989), which lists diaries of travel in England, Wales and Scotland held in the County Record Offices of England and Wales. The use of the keywords 'tourist, travels', etc will, however, open an increasing number of archive holdings: National Archives of Scotland, Glasgow City etc. The Scottish Records Association Journal, *Scottish Archives*, 1996 carried several papers on tourism, including A.J. Durie, 'Sources for the study of tourism in Nineteenth Century Scotland', A. Hiley, 'Scotland's name is poetry to our ears: German Travellers in Scotland *c.* 1800–1860' and P.G. Vasey, 'Visitors and Voyages: A personal selection of travel diaries and related material in the Scottish Record Office'. Amongst local studies, of which there are many, is Eric Simpson, 'Aberdour: the Evolution of a Seaside resort', in *A Sense of Place: Studies in Scottish Local History*, ed. G. Cruikshank (Edinburgh, 1988), and J.R.D. Campbell, *Millport and the Cumbraes* (Glasgow, 1975). The experience of the Highlands has been well assessed by, for example, T. C. Smout, 'Tours in the Scottish Highlands from the Eighteenth to the Twentieth Century', *Northern Scotland* (1985); R.W. Butler, 'The Evolution of Tourism in the Scottish Highlands', *Annals of Tourism*, 12 (1985), and K. Haldane, 'Tourism and the Idea of the Skye Crofter: Nature, Race, Gender and the Late Nineteenth Century Highland Identity', *Victorian Institute Journal* (25, 1997). Transport studies abound, and will be dealt with more fully in Chapters 2 and 7, but as indicators see A. J. S. Paterson, *The Victorian Summer of the Clyde Steamers* (1972), and Andrew M. Hadjducki, *The North Berwick and Gullane Branch Lines* (1992). A good introduction to the study of tourism as a discipline is C. Cooper *et al, Tourism: Principles and Practice* (1993).

1

THE DISCOVERY OF SCOTLAND

It is now become fashionable to make a tour into Scotland for some weeks or months . . .

(*The Weekly Magazine*, January 1772)

All the world is travelling to Scotland or Ireland. People are coming north at a great rate, it seems.

(Elizabeth Diggle, July 7, 1788)

When did tourism, as opposed to the intrepid travelling of the few, start to be significant in Scotland? Unfortunately, we have no reliable statistics for this period such as might have been generated by the issue of passports, or tourist tickets, or hotel registers. We are thrown back on a range of travellers' accounts, of which much use has already been made. Indeed they have been the primary and almost the only source to be tapped in the quest for the early roots of tourism in Scotland. As Nenadic has shown, the number of accounts mushroomed in the later eighteenth century from a handful each decade until the 1780s to several each year by the turn of the century:

TABLE 1.1. NUMBER OF TOURS AND TRAVELS IN SCOTLAND PUBLISHED BETWEEN 1730 and 1819.

Decade in which published	Published in England or Europe	Published in Scotland	Total
1740–49	3	–	–	3
1750–59	5	–	–	5
1760–69	5	1	1	7
1770–79	10	2	2	14
1780–89	14	5	2	21
1790–99	10	2	14	26
1800–09	21	9	16	46
1810–19	15	14	24	53

Source: S. Nenadic, 'Land, the Landed and Relationship with England', in *Conflict, Identity and Economic Development in Scotland and Ireland*, ed. S.J. Connolly, R. A. Houston and R. J. Morris (Preston, 1995).

As one early nineteenth-century reviewer complained in the *Quarterly Review* (February, 1806), when faced with yet another 'Tour through Scotland':

There is Johnson's Philosophic Tour, Pennant's Descriptive
Tour, Gilpin's Picturesque Tour, Stoddart's Sketching Tour,
Garnet's Medical Tour, Mrs Murray's Familiar Tour, Newte's
Nautical Tour, Mawman's Bookselling Tour, Campbell's Crazy
Tour, Lithie's Insipid Tour, and Boswell's fantastic Tour . . .
From collating these, the curious may learn without straying
from the sound of Bow bell, the depth of the unfathomable Loch-
Ness, the four wonders of Loch Lomond, the height of Fingal's
cave, and all those Caledonian memorabilia which the more
desperate visit in person . . .

There are problems for the historian in trying to assess their role. How
far did people consult a work such as *Pennant's* – perhaps the most
important of the early accounts, particularly when Sir Joseph Bank's
description of Staffa and Fingal's Cave had been added – in order to
merely *inform* their curiosity about the North without necessarily
motivating them to travel? Or was their perusal designed to *shape*
their schedule of what they must see? How widely read were these
travel proto-prospectuses or brochures? There are important but
irresolvable questions of print-run, reprinting, circulation, constituency (armchair or potential traveller?). These accounts and the associated illustrations, with Stoddart's coloured prints being of particular
merit, are important in showing and shaping the growing interest in
Scotland, but how influential they were it is impossible to determine.
They clearly played some part. They do show what the nature of the
appeal of the North was – scenery and landscape, geology, literature,
legend or whatever. To them can be added published journals and
letters written by tourists such as those of Diggle, which may actually
have more authenticity, if not necessarily more influence, as they were
not designed for a public market. And all need to be read with an
awareness of whose eyes the experience is being seen through, and
with which preconceptions, prejudices, romantic notions and cultural
baggage they were travelling. Different readers had and still have
differing favourites, but while Johnson's and Boswell's is the best-
known and Pennant's was the most influential at the time, Mrs Sarah
Murray's *The Beauties of Scotland* has the highest merit. Well-written
and accessible, it is eminently practical in its advice. And she was
certainly known and her work talked about: something that ensured
her a warm welcome on Mull. On enquiring of her whether she was
the person who had written about Scotland, and having been assured
by her that she was, the inn-keeper at Auchnacraig lent her a horse and
a lad for as long as they were needed. 'See', she remarked, 'what an

advantage it is to have written a book.' News travelled surprisingly fast in remote districts. A clergyman who showed her the great yew at Fortingall had already heard talk of her being in the adjoining district some forty miles away.

Yet essential as these accounts are to an understanding of the early growth of tourism in Scotland, there are some other indications of when tourism was first beginning to make a mark. Three can be singled out: the increasing number of guides, the use of visitors' books or registers, and the building or refurbishment of inns and hotels to cater for better-off travellers. The appearance of guides with a set patter – to the key attractions, natural or man-made – was a very significant step, which had started on the Continent and in England. One enterprising guide in North Wales, Ralph Edwards, was producing handbills in the 1790s to advertise himself and his services to tourists. Some of the guides were casual – waiters, lodge-keepers, gardeners, gamekeepers – merely pressed into service, and sometimes reluctant or even forbidden to accept tips. Lord Breadalbane's were instructed not to accept gratuities. Elizabeth Diggle commented with some surprise that the servants who showed the houses at Queensferry and Kinross refused the accustomed fees. But as the numbers of tourists grew, so they became a recognised source of income, with in some places the guides supplementing their tips by the sale of souvenirs and handbooks. An English visitor to Dunkeld in the 1860s noted with approval that the guides to the grounds there were all family retainers too aged to work. The fees charged – 1/- per head – went to pay their wages: 'this seems fair, as it would be scarcely just to impose on the Duchess a tax for the enjoyment of visitors'. The system was to develop far more as tourism grew. Towns such as Stirling and Perth appointed burgh guides, castles and abbeys acquired their keepers, as at Doune, Melrose and Elgin; great houses organised tours of their interiors under the direction of the housekeeper, and of their grounds using outside workers. Disputes over the division of tips were not unknown: Patrick Cadell has described how a falling-out between the keepers of the various parts of the palace at Holyrood led to the case going to both the Sheriff and the Abbey courts. Guides were not just money-grubbers, and some were genuinely interested in the properties of which they were in charge. The guide at Elgin Cathedral, John Shanks, did much to preserve the ruins there and clear away spoil and rubbish; Cockburn wanted a memorial erected to this 'worthy, garrulous body' in recognition of his services. But their routine inevitably became hackneyed: Heron was not much enthused by the statue of a fowler in the grounds at Blair Atholl, which he was supposed to take for a madman recently escaped and at loose. To the natural attractions of estates were added paths, bridges and views, and at Blair Atholl was to be found, as Heron did, the exhibit of the unfortunate eagle, a pretty poor rival to the menageries of some English great houses: Longleat, for example, had lions. Twenty years later, an eagle – presumably not the same one – was still one of the attractions at Blair and Thomas Baxter from Dundee was impressed: 'What enormous claws!', he marvelled. Not all guides were reliable, as one foreigner discovered when climbing Ben Lomond. His guide, having first of all dropped him in an icy stream when trying to carry him across, then consumed far too much whisky on the way to the top and, in the pouring rain, Custine was obliged to take charge of the descent. Half dead with cold and fatigue, they only just made it back to safety.

Not surprisingly, given its importance to the flow of tourists, the system of guiding was first formalised at Dunkeld. There the Duke of Atholl's factor issued in 1814 (see Appendix) a set of regulations for the guides to the grounds – not the house – of whom there were three, later increased to five. Each had to wear a badge, to make sure that parties signed the book at the porter's lodge, and to accompany tourists around the policies. Parties were not to be allowed to wander unsupervised, as experience showed that, left to themselves, some tourists were not be trusted. The collection of souvenirs – flowers and leaves, for example – had already begun to cause concern. And besides, the tip would have been lost, the gratuity at Dunkeld being graduated according to the status of the guide doing the showing. The outside guides, as opposed to the house servants, were under the control of the head gardener, who would on occasion – if he adjudged them sufficiently important (and therefore profitable) – conduct tourists himself. When two Americans, on a walking holiday, visited Dunkeld in 1801, posing as sailors, their poor clothing excited only his disgust, and they were sent off with one of the lesser guides:

A man in a pigtail and powdered head came, and after surveying us minutely with expressions of very great contempt, told us that he was an Englishman, and no less a personage than my lord duke's head gardener, and that he would not think of showing the grounds himself, but would send one of his underlings. Saying which he strutted off with great consequence, and also with some precipitation, lest anyone should detect him in the unworthy act of stooping to converse with two such wretched and dismally-looking vagabonds as we were.

The level of income derived is not known, but must have been considerable. Between 1815 and 1842 some 60,000 people (of whom nearly 4,000 were foreigners) visited the grounds – over two thousand a year. At sixpence each – which may be too high an honorarium – that would represent just over £800 annually to be split three ways. And whatever the earlier practice, by the first quarter of the nineteenth century the guides were active in their pursuance of the tips, as Cockburn complained. He was greatly irritated by the way that the guide or *showman*, 'impatient for his wages', dictated every step of their tour and would not tolerate any deviation. Such income was very welcome in the North. The dismal poverty of the boatmen on Loch Tay, according to Bristed, was relieved only in the summer when travellers visited the area. If unchecked, tourists, as well as taking souvenirs, did quite literally leave their mark behind, sometimes in the form of initials carved on some suitable rock or tree, or, on Staffa, on the columns at the entrance to Fingal's Cave. Burns' use of windows, as at Carron and Inveraray, in inns where he had lodged, is well known. Another poem was 'written with a pencil over the Chimney piece in the Parlour of the Inn at Kenmore'. Ironically, one at least of these mementoes was itself pilfered by a visitor. A French traveller, Charles Nodier, found in July 1822 that travellers who stayed at the Luss Inn on Loch Lomondside 'seldom fail to write their names on the wall and wainscot'. He was very surprised to find that some acquaintance of his had put up his name. On a window in the inn at Tarbet, there was some rhyming verse to be found in 1817, dated 5th October 1777, of advice to those thinking of climbing Ben Lomond. 'Don't attempt too adventurous a pace' was firmly urged by the writer, one Thos. Russell:

> Stranger, if over this pane of glass perchance
> Thy roving eye shoulds't cast a casual glance
> If taste for grandeur and the dread sublime,
> Prompt thee Ben Lomond's fearful height to climb
> Here gaze attentive nor with scorn refuse
> The friendly rhymings of a tavern muse.

(Glasgow City Archives, TD 637, Journal of a Tour to the Highlands, September 1817)

A second indicator of the growing scale of tourism is the introduction to Scotland of visitors' books, which would scarcely have been kept had there not been some traffic. These in the later eighteenth century became general at the key attractions. Robert Heron, for example, on his journey in 1792, visited Taymouth Castle, as did virtually everyone, it being described – with some accuracy – by the local minister in the *First Statistical Account* (1798) as one of those places to which every foreign tourist hastens on his arrival in Scotland, 'nor does he return disappointed'. Heron noted that

> An Album is kept at the house of Taymouth in which visitors who are admitted to see it are required to insert their names. Looking over the list of the names of those whose visits to Taymouth were there recorded, I saw here and there a sentence added, expressive of the high delight with which the subscriber had viewed the house, and surveyed the surrounding grounds. (*Observations*, 1793, p. 242)

This book, and its partners, have long since disappeared, as has that provided by Lord Gardenstone, a noted eccentric, in the inn at Laurencekirk, entitled 'The Album to be given to Strangers'. So 'everybody amuses themselves with writing what they like – isn't it very droll?' – thought Elizabeth Diggle, in 1788.

There survives one late eighteenth-century visitors' register covering the period August 1795 to October 1799 for New Lanark, where David Dale's cotton mills, and the nearby Falls of Clyde, made a very convenient stop for tourists and other travellers passing north, or returning home. The first register starts abruptly on the 7th of August 1797, and from the sameness of the hand for the first three pages it would appear that initially this is a fair copy made from an earlier book. Comments of any kind are almost entirely absent, but at least as a general rule the names, date of visit and addresses are given. Occasionally the entry is very sparse, as on June 6th, 1796 when all that is to be found is a line noting '2 gentlemen from London'. By contrast, when Alexander Naismyth of Edinburgh called in the following August, he described himself as 'landscape painter'; his fellow-citizen, James Clepham, added 'cabinet-maker' in the Canongate. Another visitor, John Ainslie, was a 'land surveyor'. Parties of ladies without male escort were not uncommon, though these tended to be from the locality rather than further afield. There were occasional visitors in what might be called the off-season. But – as elsewhere – the great bulk (around 90% in 1796 and 1797) came between May and the end of October, with August and September consistently both the most popular months and the ones with the largest number of visitors with addresses outside Scotland.

TABLE I.2.   NUMBER OF VISITORS TO NEW LANARK, 1796 to 1799.

Year   Signatures

1796   750
1797   751
1798   660
1799   678*

* In this year the book breaks off at the 4th of October. The total for the year
has been rounded up by the addition of an allowance for the missing months
based on the numbers in the same period in the previous two years. Three pages
appear to have been torn out.

(University of Glasgow Archives, Gourock Ropework Mss, UGD 42/7/1/1)

As well as the signatures of the great and the good – James Watt,
Henry Brougham and the like – it is interesting also to look at the
geographical origins of the visitors. Most were Scottish, and of the
others the English were the largest group, including on 25th July 1796
the Revd James Plumptre of Clare Hall Cambridge, and a colleague.
Plumptre was an avid traveller in many parts of Britain during the
1790s and was to return in 1799 – though not to New Lanark – as
part of what Ousby rightly describes as an extraordinary four-and-a-
half-month tour through Scotland, the Lakes and North Wales,
covering 2,236 miles, 1774¼ of them – according to his addition –
on foot. There were some Continental visitors including a Mr Jacobi
from Düsseldorf, and an occasional American such as James Speed of
Kentucky in late August of 1796. If that year and the following are
typical, visitors from outwith Scotland constituted between one in
seven or one in eight of all callers, the proportion and numbers alike
being highest, not surprisingly, in the popular travelling months of
high summer. And while a few may have been travelling on political or
other business, the great majority were almost certainly tourists,
though their motives for seeing New Lanark were complex, many
being interested in the social regime there. Industrial sites, factories,
mills and works were a source of interest. Carron Ironworks was
another much-visited locality, though the proprietors were liable to be
careful over whom they admitted. The French visitor Faujas St Fond in
1784, though armed with letters of introduction and not declaring his
official position within the French government as an inspector of
cannonry, was debarred from the gun-making workshops. Washington Irving on his tour in September 1817 was not allowed access, but
without any explanation being given: his journal simply records 'Pass
by Carron works – no Admittance – beautiful scenery in the neighbourhood of the works'. By contrast, Elizabeth Diggle saw as much as
she wanted to see of this 'Dominion of Vulcan':

Heavens! We are escaped from the infernal regions. Imagine the Carron Ironworks, a whole town of smoke and fire, & a thousand people at work; furnaces blazing on all sides, half seen through a black smoke; beings whose appearance I leave it to you to imagine, pouring liquid fire into caldrons, hammering red hot iron etc & an engine working that absolutely overpowered me by a louder noise than I had ever heard before and that had wakened me at the inn in the morning with an idea that it thundered.

A third indicator of the development of tourism is the growing number of inns and specialised accommodation for travellers. The early flow of visitors, moneyed as they were, largely stayed with local proprietors, using letters of introduction. While numbers were small, this presented no problem, though Lord Breadalbane's forbearance was stretched to the limit even as early as 1773, as he told his daughter:

We have had a good deal of company here this summer, sixteen often at table for several days together, many of them from England some of whom I knew before, and others recommended to me, being on a tour thro' the Highlands which is becoming le bon ton, but sometimes a little troublesome. Being always in a crowd is not agreeable.

A decade and a half later Elizabeth Diggle used a private residence, Murthly Castle near Little Dunkeld, as a base for several days of travelling in the vicinity of Perth, Dunkeld and Blair. She commented that since returning to Murthly:

we have had several additions to, and changes in the family party, for people come here to visit their neighbours, & stay a day or two at a time without any previous notice; a very agreeable circumstance in a remote place with a large house and quite in the style of ancient hospitality before inns were invented.

Guests could sing for their supper with news and gossip, and entertainments were laid on for their amusement. 'In the evening we dance reels, and I got great credit for my performance here.'

The calibre of Scottish inns, and the roads alike, were the subject of considerable debate. It is clear that the best were very good, the worst terrible. One has to have considerable sympathy for the problems of hotel and innkeepers in the more remote areas. There were long periods when few travellers of any kind were to be expected, or at best they would be drovers or packsmen, whose needs were very basic. And then there would be sudden, unpredictable influxes of travellers, who wanted a much higher standard of accommodation and service for themselves and their horses. It could be difficult, indeed, should tourists arrive at the same time as the circuit judge and his retinue, important persons to whom priority had to be given. This was St Fond's experience not once but twice during his travels at Luss and Inveraray in September 1787. Fortunately for him and his companions, letters of introduction to the Duke of Argyll secured them a stay at the Castle. Earlier in the same year Robert Burns had not been so fortunate at Inveraray, the castle being full, and the overflow displaced to the inn. He vented his spleen at the deference being shown by the innkeeper to the Duke's guests – a party from the British Fisheries Society of which the Duke was President – in an epigram:

> Who'er he be who sojourns here,
> I pity much his case,
> Unless he come to wait upon
> The Lord their God, his Grace.

> There's naething here but Highland pride,
> And Highland scab and hunger:
> If providence has sent me here,
> 'Twas surely in an anger.

Small wonder that the better-organised tourists sent ahead to reserve beds and rooms, and give advance notice so that appropriate food, as well as fresh bedding, could be laid in. To travel on speculation was bold, but unwise, as Bristed and his companion found when they called in at the Inchture Inn in August 1801 en route to Perth from Dundee. The breakfast that they were grudgingly offered consisted of addled eggs, dirty and rancid butter, stomach-turning bread and undrinkable tea. Their scruffy appearance did nothing to help, and elsewhere on their tour they fared very badly. At the Duke's Inn near Pitlochry – the exact location is not specified – they could secure a room with only the most meagre furnishings. There was no glass in the windows, the dirt floor was entirely bare of anything other than a bed, and in the corner was a box bed for the post-coach driver, who was due to arrive in the early hours of the morning. The bed-linen was foul. But the landlady's son, 'in whom the beauty of the baboon was united with the wisdom of the ass', slapped down their complaint, saying that the sheets were pretty cleanish, 'for that only two foot passengers and a carrier had slept in them since they were last washed'.

But even the best-organised traveller could run into difficulties. One of the worst experiences for Mrs Murray came when she found herself at Tyndrum early in September 1796. She arrived just early enough on a wild night to get the best room and its two beds for herself and her maid before numbers of drovers on their way back from Falkirk took every other corner and outhouse. Her servant had to sleep in the carriage, the horses were almost crushed to death in the stables, and to cap it all, two chaises came to the door at eleven p.m. There was no other local accommodation, and in any case the horses were exhausted after their twenty-five-mile haul from Lochearnhead, and so everyone had to crush up yet further. A complication that threw out the schedules of some southern travellers, and meant an arrival much later than they had anticipated, was that the Scots mile was 10% longer than its English counterpart. Mrs Murray exaggerated somewhat when she thought the Scots mile to be double the English, but that may have been how it felt towards the end of a long day on the road. Also unhelpful was the absence of signposts in the Highlands, and locals, even if well meaning, could be vague both as to direction and distance. Packsmen, peddlers and drovers were better informed but not always to hand when needed.

There were, however, increasing numbers of road guides available such as Taylor & Skinner's roads map of Scotland, which was surveyed in 1775. Diggle follows this, and it went through many editions. Another aid was *The Travellers' Guide Through Scotland and Its Islands* (Edinburgh, 1806), which had a series of maps, exact tables of distances, topographical detail as to what was to be seen to left and to right and vantage points at which to stop and view sights. Later editions added a supplement containing six pleasure tours in Scotland and significantly began to indicate which inns were available where, and of what calibre. Cairndow's Inn, for example, was described as neat and comfortable. Hotels had the highest charges, especially in Edinburgh, of which St Fond complained. His bill at Dun's Hotel was double what he had paid at the best and dearest inns on the road, and to add insult to injury the rapacious landlord had even added an itemised charge of three English pence for half-a-sheet of writing paper. 'We return no more to Dun's Hotel' was St Fond's verdict. It was by all accounts a very high-class establishment with a superb salon and every magnificence, which greatly surprised and delighted other visitors, such as the La Rochefoucauld brothers on a Scottish tour in 1786, they having been warned to expect nothing but inns which were dirty and bad. Inns on the beaten tourist track – or 'tour' – could and did charge more than those elsewhere. The Wordsworths were surprised at how little the bill was at remote Bonawe in Argyllshire where they were charged only seven shillings and sixpence for the whole-horse, liquor, supper, and the two breakfasts. We thought they had made a mistake, and told them so, for it was only just half as much as we had paid the day before at Dalmally, the case being that Dalmally is in the main road of the tourists.

In the back of her journal Elizabeth Diggle made a list of the ratings she would award to the various inns and hotels in which she had stayed during her tour. Some thirty-two are noted, most of which were either good or at least tolerable. Six were very good, and two excellent: the recently opened New Inn at Stirling, with upwards of thirty rooms, stables and coach houses to match, and Walker's Hotel in Edinburgh. By contrast five were 'bad' or 'very bad', with those at Luss and Dalmally particularly damned. Yet Robert Heron some four years later found the latter quite acceptable, with decent accommodation and civility of attention. Even quite good premises could be marred by poor service, which is not an unfamiliar problem today. Knox complained that at Inverary, where there was a very good inn with excellent stables provided by the Marquis of Argyll, the servants, though willing, were too few in number. By contrast, years later the Wordsworths found it an inn 'over-rich in waiters and large rooms'. At Killin, the standard of service was excellent. Significantly, this inn, as elsewhere in the Highlands, was the property of the local landowner and was leased to a carefully selected tenant, sometimes a former household retainer, often English rather than a Scot, a move perhaps prompted by the desire to raise standards to match those south of the Border. Heron enthused over the calibre of care here:

> The servants are indeed Highlanders, and the waiters wear fillibegs, but are not less cheerfully and actively attentive than the supercilious and foppish attendants at the inns and taverns in great cities.

If accommodation was one problem, by far the greatest was that of travel. The roads of Scotland attracted much criticism from contemporary writers, and no doubt in many places, particularly in the Highlands, they were no better than beaten tracks or horse paths, and sometimes not even that. The mosses of Caithness were impassable except on foot and with a competent guide. Faujas St Fond found the Killin road as 'dismal as it was monotonous'. Yet there were better stretches of road in the North. Both Knox and Heron, who thought that 'the highways in the Highlands were indeed excellent', spoke approvingly of the roads constructed by Wade and his successor Caulfield, some 1000 miles, between 1725 and 1767. Others agreed:

one English traveller, R.L. Willis, en route to Elgin in 1790, confided to his journal that he was surprised both at the high quality of the inns and of the roads, built at the expense of the government. Though some lengths fell into disuse, many a tourist used these military roads and the associated bridges, such as, for example, that over the Tay at Aberfeldy.

If some of the roads in the North were better than is often allowed, some of the poorest were elsewhere in Scotland in more populous and supposedly developed areas. Elizabeth Diggle thought Fife roads the worst in Scotland. Dorothy Wordsworth's highest praise was for the road at Callander and that between Tyndrum and Crianlarich ('excellent'); her harshest words were for the old road at Crawfordjohn (both 'steep and bad', and 'stony and rough'). She was very pleasantly surprised by the smoothness of the road at Portnacroish near Appin on Loch Linnhe, which was more like a gravel walk in a gentleman's grounds than a public highway. But one has to be careful. Travellers' accounts were liable to be coloured by such factors as the weather, the calibre of their driver and transport, their mood and the night before. The same road, therefore, can invite quite different judgements. Garnet, for example, thought that the Crawfordjohn road so disliked by Dorothy Wordsworth was 'by no means unpleasant'; Elizabeth Diggle that it was 'a romantic track'.

But in the later eighteenth century there were improvements afoot on both the statute roads and the turnpikes. In Aberdeenshire alone, above 300 miles of turnpike roads were completed between 1795 and 1811. Travelling by road was still a challenge in late eighteenth-century Scotland, but becoming less so. It was still good sense, if you were touring in your own carriage or chaise, to follow Mrs Murray's advice to the traveller and to take a strong carriage with well-corded springs, plus a well-stocked repair kit. 'Have also a stop-pole and strong chain to the chaise. Take with you linch pins, and four shackles, which hold up the braces of the body of the carriage: a turnscrew, fit for fastening the nuts belonging to the shackles, a hammer, and some straps.' A hundred years later bicyclists and motorists in the North were equally well advised to come prepared, given the demands of road surfaces and the shortage of repair facilities in some localities. Pedestrianism had its devotees, and continued to do so, provided that the social niceties were preserved. Diggle recorded that 'We just now met [near Hamilton] a gentleman walking a journey with two footmen behind him'. But while cheaper, more leisurely, more fashionable and healthy – especially amongst young men – and in the eyes of some participants offering far more opportunity for men (it was not recommended for ladies) to see the countryside and talk with its people, there were disadvantages which deterred some from knapsack travelling. What about wet days, and the need for not one but several changes of clothing, and decent footwear? Where could the journal, sketching book, eyeglass and other necessaries of the trip be stowed? An umbrella, which could double as a walking stick, was essential, or so Stoddart considered.

It can be argued that no travel account is really complete without some accident or near-disaster. While Scotland was amazingly safe for the traveller, highway robbery being almost unknown, road travel in Scotland did have its hazards. Tourists got lost – even Queen Victoria on one famous occasion in the hills near Dunkeld – carriages overturned, horses went lame. St Fond and his companions, despite the benefit of a local schoolmaster, Patrick Fraser of Dalmally, who acted as their guide and interpreter, went badly astray during the night in a thunderstorm between Bonawe and Oban. They were rescued by a party of Highlanders who could not conceive how their carriages could have got down into such a place without being broken to pieces. It required all the address and strength of these athletic men to draw them out, which they did by making a kind of road with pick-axes and '. . . lifting up the carriages on their shoulders'. Elizabeth Diggle got a scare when her horses failed near the summit of a sharp incline near Blair and 'down we went, chaise, horses and all, backwards; & I was frightened to death, but no[t] otherwise killed for a tree stopt us after a time'.

Getting horses, and skilled drivers, was not always easy. In the central belt, hotels and inns did keep horses for hire, but north of Perth things were much more problematic. Mrs Murray, who had had to make do with the last two horses available from the inn at Langholm, both of which were broken-down nags which only just made it to Hawick, was delighted to recommend the Salutation Inn at Perth for horses, and the driver she secured there: 'I thought myself safe with James Allen and his steady black horses'. Thirty years earlier, Thomas Gray, who said that no regular post-chaises were to be found north of Edinburgh, had given a similar endorsement to a driver, John Black from Edinburgh: 'he is worth any money'. Accidents there were, but no fatalities seem to have occurred, even with the much more heavily laden coaches. The Glasgow to Perth stagecoach Rapid overturned just north of Dunblane in June 1844: two of the outside passengers – more vulnerable than those inside – 'travellers from the south' (my italics) were injured rather severely, but made a full recovery.

If travel on land had its hazards, far more dangerous was the water.

And if travellers to Scotland were spared the rigours of the Channel crossing which those bound for Europe had to endure, the geography of Scotland compelled the equally disquieting use of any number of ferries and boats. The crossing of the Firth of Forth was for some terrifying. The poet, Thomas Gray, found the experience so unnerving in September 1765 that on his return from the North he took the longer land route round via Stirling, 'being a foe to drowning'. Not surprisingly, his recommended tour in Scotland omitted the Queensferry passage from the schedule. It was not just the tourists who found the water-crossings worrying. Chaises and coaches could be swung on board and off by capstan, but that was not something that the horses enjoyed. They could be swum across in some places, but if forced on to a small, unsteady boat, a horse could panic. The Wordsworths' horse, an aged but stout and spirited animal, was so badly used by the ferrymen at Connel that he was left with a terror of water that nearly resulted in catastrophe the following day. There were no drownings of tourists, but some close-run shaves, particularly on the West Coast, such as that of Johnson and Boswell. The trip to Staffa was especially dangerous, given the smallness of the boats and the changeability of the weather, and it was not uncommon for travellers to wait for days for fair weather. Some took one look and turned back. Stoddart met one traveller who intended to visit, he having heard that 'there was something curious to be seen there', but the sea 'was blowing great guns' so he abandoned the venture. It was probably a very sensible decision. Knox describes the narrow escape of three Scottish gentlemen en route back from Staffa in August 1787 when their boat struck an uncharted rock; fortunately for them, the weather was flat calm, and they got off unscathed. Some friends of St Fond were forced by rough seas to take shelter on Staffa for the best part of three days until the boatmen were able to get them off. They returned to Mull covered in lice, which the locals alleged – to the amusement of St Fond – to have been imported to the area by Sir Joseph Banks in 1771.

By the third quarter of the eighteenth century, therefore, Scotland was beginning to become a destination of some significance for travellers. 'The tour of the Highlands of Scotland has become fashionable' was Heron's verdict in 1793. Admittedly, outside Edinburgh and the Lowlands, the numbers were probably not great. Smout guesses that, at the turn of the century, the Highlands were seeing at best a few hundred visitors annually, although this was an increase on the numbers thirty years previously. Travellers' accounts tend to confirm this picture of a region penetrated only by a handful, a number of

whom were female, travelling with a companion or relative, as in
Elizabeth Diggle's case. Mrs Murray said that she was the ninth female
visitor to Staffa in the year, but the only one travelling alone (apart
from four boatmen and a lad as her interpreter). Meeting with other
travellers, by chance or otherwise, because they were so few, stood out
in their memory and in their journals. Andrews points out that Dr
Garnet met not a single other traveller during the first three weeks of
his tour in the Highlands during July 1798, though this was the height
of the travelling season. St Fond had chanced across a fellow-French-
man, M. de Bombelles, at Killin, who was on his way to Ireland,
having undertaken a short Highland tour. Mrs Murray encountered
by the side of Loch Katrine John Leyden, who was himself the author
of a journal based on his experiences when accompanying two
sprightly youths through the Highlands, one of whom was the brother
of a traveller from Germany she had met four years previously. He for
his part recalled how she guided him to a scenic viewpoint, 'Murray
Point, named from herself the discoverer', a practice reminiscent of a
European explorer in Africa. She elsewhere retails an anecdote told to
her by Leyden of having climbed Cruachan on a hot day, and reaching
the summit, having the misfortune to drop his precious bottle of thirst-
relieving cider, which smashed to pieces.

Account after account emphasises the growing significance of Scotland for tourists, travellers and sportsmen. But why was there this
developing interest? It has to be emphasised that the Scottish experience was not unique, and that other areas of Britain – North Wales,
the Lakes and Cumberland – were also gaining recognition. Yet
Scotland does seem to have been making ground, albeit from a very
low base. At work were a number of factors. The logistics of travel
were made reasonably simple by a good postal service and financial
network. And the more accounts came back from the North, the less
forbidding travel there became. The ignorance and prejudice about
Scotland that was apparently commonplace about North Britain in
mid-century began to fade. There had been some vagueness as to its
actual location. One Londoner asked Smollett whether the weather
was good when he crossed the sea from Scotland!

Most importantly, the general reputation of Scotland was becoming
established in contrast to parts of Europe or even Ireland, not as a
home to barbaric and hostile inhabitants but as both a respectable and
a safe destination. It was a place where young men would not fall into
sexual temptation, thanks to the rule of the Kirk, and travellers were
very unlikely to be mugged or robbed. The latter was an image that
would have come as a great surprise to outsiders even a generation or

two earlier in the century. The land of the rebellious had become the land of the respectable, where rain rather than rapine was the main concern. Black (*The British Abroad*, 1992) has argued that crime was not all that serious a problem for the Continental traveller and 'a tourist was more likely to suffer from food-poisoning than a stiletto'. But, as modern tourism has found, even a few incidents can very adversely affect the appeal of a locality, such as the attack by highwaymen in 1787 on Adam Walker in Belgium. What is striking is how peaceable and crime-free the North was, even in the most remote areas. Highway robbery or theft aggravated by violence ('*stouthrief*') was almost unknown north of Perth, and the victims in the Lowlands were mostly drunken farmers and tradesmen on the way back from market. There were occasional murders in the Highlands of travellers, such as a peddler in Assynt in the summer of 1830, but none of tourists. What stands out is the honesty of the locals. There was the innkeeper's wife from Dunkeld sending on – despite her obvious hankering after it – an eyeglass which Bristed had left behind: 'a very commendable specimen of honesty'. At Taynuilt the Wordsworths were given a cup to return that a previous visitor had left behind. Unfortunately, they in their turn left it at the next stop. Bristed, who was the victim of a night-time rifling of his property, was asked by one very doubtful character whether he wasn't afraid of trouble. 'He supposed that if we are gentlemen and travelling about for pleasure, that we carried a good deal of money with us and were worth robbing.' Bristed replied that were he and his companion to be bothered, they would knock the brains of any intruder out; in the event all he did was to make enough noise to deter an entry to their room. A similar enquiry was put to them at Kenmore:

> were we not afraid to travel over such a desolate country by night, when we might be so easily murdered, and no one be the wiser for it? 'No,' [responded Bristed], 'When we travelled in Spain, in Italy, and in Germany, we were obliged to carry pistols that we might shoot or be shot in case of necessity; but in the Highlands we entertained no fear, because we knew the people to be kind, generous, hospitable, and honest.'

A French traveller in 1810 found it remarkable that travellers' heavier baggage remained on their coaches outdoors all night, yet without risk. 'All the treasures contained in a trunk of clothes do not tempt people who have scarce a shirt to steal it!'

This more favourable image of Scotland was only strengthened by political disturbances in Europe, and war alike which played an important part in diverting some of those who would otherwise have gone on a Grand Tour to the Continent. The Seven Years' War had an impact: Lord Breadlabane noted in 1759 how many English visitors there were in the Highlands that year, 'I suppose because they can't go abroad', and much the same occurred during the American Revolution. On both occasions, however, once peace was concluded, tourism resumed with redoubled vigour. The French Revolution had a major impact because it blocked off many of the most popular parts of the Continent for so long. Moneyed travellers, whose coaches, servants and dress marked them out, found out very quickly that they were not welcome. The Burnett family from Crathes Castle in Aberdeenshire met real hostility in 1791 on a tour through France:

> We met a party of soldiers who came up to the coach and called out English aristocrats. Sometimes in villages or towns when we are walking, little children of 3 or 4 years will run after us, calling us Aristocrats. (Mrs Burnett, Journal, 1791)

It is probably no coincidence that the number of visitors during the peak season of the summer substantially increased in the early 1790s at key tourist attractions in Scotland such as Inveraray. The parish minister there reported that whereas in 1790 there had been at most a hundred visitors a week to the pleasure grounds and plantations, two years later the number had doubled. The duration of the troubles was a real bonus. 'Since the Continent has been shut against us, Edinburgh is as much visited by every dashing citizen who pretends to fashion as Margate or Tonbridge', said a writer in the *Quarterly Review* in 1809. Scott took a similar view in 1810: 'Every London citizen makes Loch Lomond his washpot and throws his shoe over Ben Nevis'. War abroad certainly benefited Scotland.

But it is important not to view Scotland merely as a diversionary destination, a fallback when more favoured options were blocked off. There is weight in the view that tourism in the form of a trip or journey for education, amusement or health was becoming part of the established routine of those who could afford the money and time, and would go somewhere each year. What was to be decided was where, not whether. The British upper and propertied classes had acquired a taste for travel to look at scenery, enquire into antiquities and ruins, and pursue interests in botany, geology and natural history:

> The extreme partiality of our countrymen for travelling is a subject which has often excited the surprise of foreigners . . . No sooner is the season of fashionable gaiety concluded in London

than the roads are covered with tourists and travellers, who issue
from the metropolis in every direction. Some, who are contented
with the humblest portion of itinerary fame, record their delights
and their dangers in an excursion to the Isle of Wight, or to the
mountains of Wales: others, better directed, or more courageous,
explore the wilds of our beloved Scotland, and risk their safety
on the shores of the Hebrides; while others, still more ambitious,
cross the tempestuous channel, trust their persons to Hibernian
post-chaises, and wade for pleasure, or for glory, through the
bogs of Ireland. (*The Edinburgh Review*, July 1806)

But to characterise Scotland as merely a second-choice destination
would be unfair, though Heron did think that part of the reason why
summer and autumn tours to Scotland had become so fashionable
'within these last ten or twelve years' was that people had become
bored with resorts in England. But he did add that there were a
number of factors at work to make Scotland particularly appealing
and favoured: the writings of Johnson and Pennant, good roads and
accommodation, and enthusiasm for the wonders of the Scottish
landscape. Explanations for the rise of touring and tourism in Scotland in the later eighteenth century have tended to focus on this last
element, the shift in cultural taste in which two strands were significant. There was the cult of the picturesque – Wordsworth writes of
'prospect hunters and picturesque travellers' – and secondly the
associated enthusiasm for Ossian. What was the picturesque? It
was a change in taste – a change which took place for reasons not
entirely clear – which turned the rugged mountainous landscapes of
the North from a liability, a place of horror, into an asset; a scenery
which drew (not repelled) the tasteful and artistic eye, and won the
plaudits of the educated observer as 'sublime', even if still terrifying.
To the appeal of mountains was added that of lakes, lochs and
waterfalls. Nature could be improved upon by a judicious retouching
and enhancement by walks, avenues, viewpoints and hermitages, and
as at Dunkeld, a mirrored room with coloured glass to cast a dazzling
kaleidoscope of light. Mrs Drummond of Perth provided some wicker
huts at the side of Loch Katrine to shade travellers while they paused
to view the scene. Garnet describes how tourists from Callander used
these as refreshment shelters in wild weather.

One of the first writers to tune into this new appreciation of the
Highlands, which applied equally to the Alps, was the poet Thomas
Gray. A trip to Glamis in 1765 opened his eyes to what he called the
'ecstatic mountains' of the Highlands: 'none but those monstrous

creatures of God know how to join so much beauty with so much horror'. Other writers were to develop the theory of the picturesque, and the proper aesthetic response to landscape. Smout sees the writings of the Reverend William Gilpin as especially significant. Allied to this shift in cultural values was the fascination with Ossian, the Gaelic warrior hero and his poetry. This was a myth – in every sense of the word – that exercised a level of appeal rivalled perhaps only by that of Prester John for the Victorians or the Arthurian legend at Glastonbury. The search for Ossian preoccupied many an early visitor to Scotland from the 1760s onwards when James Macpherson first published what he claimed were extracts from the long-ignored original texts. He created what some called an elaborate fraud, but it was a literary sensation in Europe, the poems being translated into many languages. The follow-up was immediate and sustained: in 1800, for example, John Leyden dined at Inveraray Castle with Sir John MacGregor Murray, who was on his way to collect evidence as to the authenticity of the poems, so as to resolve the controversy one way or another. He himself did his best to trace the whereabouts of any Ossianic manuscripts. The net effect was to put places such as Staffa, with its Fingal's Cave, firmly on the itinerary of serious tourists provided that they had sufficient time to allow for the weather. A partial proxy for those who could only manage the so-called Short Tour, as defined by Knox in 1784, was to visit what Heron called the land of Ossian's heroes, in and around Dunkeld. To play to this fascination the Duke had had the Hermitage, which had been built in 1757 above the falls, revamped as 'Ossian's Hall', complete with a painting of the hero. Some visitors were impressed, others not.

By the later eighteenth century, the visitors to Scotland were following a variety of schedules, depending on their time and individual preferences. Most travelling north up the West Coast would take in the Falls of Clyde en route to Glasgow, and then make for Loch Lomond and Inveraray via Dumbarton; cut across by Dalmally to Taymouth, Blair, Dunkeld and Perth ('the short tour'). The Edinburgh area offered much to see in the City itself, and the surrounding countryside: Roslin Chapel, Carron Ironworks, and to the west Stirling, with the nearby battlefield of Bannockburn. Leyden confessed to approaching that rather unremarkable site with such vivid feelings of patriotism 'that had an Englishman presented himself I should have felt strongly inclined to knock him down'. But the basic tour schedule could be augmented by a foray to Staffa and Iona, or up the East Coast to Aberdeen, Elgin and Inverness. Burns' Highland Tour in late August and early September 1787 took in Castle Cawdor, where he saw the bed in which tradition held that King Duncan was stabbed. The Falls of Foyer drew a poem from him ('Amongst the healthy hills and the ragged woods, the roaring Foyers pours his mossy floods') and also Culloden Muir, although his reflections there have not survived. Some went to the very far North: the Wordsworths met an Edinburgh drawing master on a pedestrian tour to John O'Groats.

But important though the appeal of Scotland's scenery was, both natural and man-made, the value of its history and antiquities, and the pull of tradition and literary association, there were other holdings in Scotland's tourist portfolio. The Highlands by the turn of the century were already acquiring a reputation as a sporting playground. Heron (1793) speaks of the impact of the flow of visitors to the North: 'the frequent resort of gay company to the North, for the purpose of pursuing game or viewing its scenery, has . . . rendered the state of this country better known'. Proprietors were beginning to preserve their muir-fowl and deer, or more accurately to reserve them for their own pleasure or to be let out to visiting sportsmen. At Dalnacarroch, near Dalmally, Mrs Murray on the 18th of August 1800 – significantly just after the start of the grouse-shooting season – found that the scene was enlivened by the attendants and horses of sportsmen, 'who were come to the Highlands to shoot'. This was a male preserve, and mostly younger men at that. To lack any interest in field sports was to miss out on one of the most enduring ingredients in the passion that many Southerners from the upper drawer of society came to feel for Scotland. Some visitors were unenthused. The Londoner Mawman, whose *Excursion to Scotland* appeared in 1805, was honest enough to admit that Scottish country life was not to his liking. Fishing, shooting and hunting left him cold. But his was a minority perspective. One of Queen Victoria's chaplains in Scotland, Dr Norman MacLeod, recalled a dinner in London in 1855 with a party of English parsons: 'correct manners, large hearts, middling heads, and knowing nothing of Scotland except as a place in the Islands from which grouse come'. The groundwork for that perception was already firmly in place half a century earlier.

Inevitably, perhaps, the main focus of this chapter has been on the experience of travellers in Scotland, English and Continental. Yet Scots were themselves beginning to discover their own country. Travel for health was a long-established tradition, whether taking the waters at Moffat or one of the other spas, or drinking goat's milk at Dunkeld or Brodick or Blairlogie, or sea-bathing at Peterhead or South Queensferry. There was the start of what became an annual summer exodus of the urban professional and middle classes to the seaside or the country. Heron talks of the way in which Edinburgh by the middle of August was 'commonly deserted by all the migratory parts of its inhabitants whether people of gaiety or study or business'. Prompted by the enthusiasm of other travellers, Scots began to venture into parts of their own country hitherto unknown to them. The nineteen-year-old Henry Cockburn made a sight-seeing trip with the other lads to Inverness in 1797 or 1798. Thomas Handyside Baxter of Dundee and two companions went on a Highland *jaunt* in August 1811 and were astonished by the fineness of the prospects at Taymouth 'where I had always thought there was nothing but Poverty and Barrenness'. Scottish tourism was stirring, and beginning to move away from its initial small base in the moneyed elite to involve a much wider constituency.

APPENDIX

A set of regulations for the guides employed by the Duke of Atholl. Blair Castle Charter Room, Atholl MSS, Bundle 721, 1814.

First Guide. Duncan Ritchie to have two assistants to be approved of by Mr Palliser. Peter Murrary Inver one, and James Chalmers, Dunkeld.

A distinguishing badge to be worn so as at a distance to be sure that one of the three guides is with every company.

Duncan Ritchie to have charge and to be answerable for himself and Guides, and a written direction to be left at Smyttan's and Crerars' where each is to be found.

Duncan Ritchie will immediately forfeit his situation if the following rules are neglected or omitted.

First. If Company's names calling for a Guide are not put down either at the Porter's Lodge or at Crerar's Inn, where books for that purpose must be kept.

Secondly. If Dogs with Companies are admitted.

Thirdly. If any Flowers, Shrubs, etc are pulled; or Persons go wantonly off the walks.

Fourthly. If Gates, Doors, & of which Keys are entrusted to the Guides, are left open by any of them.

If any Companies mention being acquainted with the Duke or Dutchess, the Guide who they are with will report it to the Principal Servant in the House.

Guides must call if unemployed at two o'clock, four o'clock and six o'clock afternoon at one or other of the Inns.

If any of the guides are seen or Reported to be in Liquor, That Guide be he the first, second or third will be immediately dismissed.

Duncan Ritchie will give a letter stating that he enjoys the situation of First Guide only during the Duke's pleasure and Subject to be immediately dismissed, if neglecting or acting contrary to any of the foregoing orders, or such further orders as he may receive from the Duke or Mr Palliser.

When meeting any of the Family they are to step aside out of the walk or take another.

Locks spoiled or the least damage done or the Room at the Hermitage dirtied will immediately be made good at the expence of Duncan Ritchie unless he can clear himself or Guides of having done any mischief to the satisfaction of Mr Palliser. The Gardens are not included under Duncan Ritchie's shew. And Ross is not to be applied to shew them except in a very special case when permission must be asked by Letter to the Gardener.

Source: Ann Cameron, 'The development of Tourism at Dunkeld and Birnam', undergraduate dissertation, the University of Glasgow, 1997.

FURTHER READING

There is an extensive literature on the picturesque but of especial value are Malcolm Andrews, *The Search for the Picturesque: Landscape Aesthetics and Tourism in Britain, 1760–1800* (Stanford, 1989) and Lynne Whitney, *Grand Tours and Cook's Tours* (Aurum, 1997), Chapter 2, 'Touring in Search of the Picturesque'. On great houses, see Adrian Tinniswood, *A History of Country House Visiting* (Oxford, 1989) and Peter Mandler, *The Fall and Rise of the Stately Home* (New Haven and London, 1997). The growing artistic enthusiasm for Scotland is very well covered in James Holloway and Lindsay Errington, *The Discovery of Scotland. The Appreciation of Scottish Scenery Through Two Centuries of Scottish Painting* (Edinburgh, 1978). Of the various travellers, particularly recommended are the accounts of Mrs Murray, Lord Cockburn, Robert Heron and the Wordsworths. (*Recollections of a Tour Made in Scotland*. By Dorothy Wordsworth. Edited by Carol Kyros Walker, Yale 1999; *James Plumptre's Britain. The Journals of a Tourist in the* 1790s, edited by Ian Ousby (London, 1992)). T.C. Smout's important article, 'Tours in the Scottish Highlands from the Eighteenth to the Twentieth Century', *Northern Scotland*, 5.2, 1983, draws heavily on William Gilpin, *Observations relative to Picturesque beauty, made in the year* 1776 *on several parts of Britain, particularly the Highlands of Scotland* (London, 1792). Raymond Lamont Brown, *Robert Burns's Tour of the Highlands and Stirlingshire* (Ipswich, 1973), gives a full text of Burns' journal and letters, with detailed commentary.

2

Transport and Tourism, 1800–1850

> Conveyance by steam has been as signal in its effects in our
> Northern localities as elsewhere – annihilating distance and
> pouring a tide of living energies through scenes heretofore ex-
> cluded.
>
> (*Anderson's Guide to the Highlands*, 3rd edition, 1850)

During the nineteenth century Scotland passed from being the preserve of a few moneyed and culturally motivated tourists, well
defined by education and status, to becoming a mass destination
for all levels of society. There remained the literary tourists, particularly from abroad, with North Americans especially prominent,
still drawn to the land of Scott and of Burns, some coming on their
own or in family groups, others with organised parties and college
study tours. These were to be found in the Borders, visiting historic
houses such as Abbotsford, or castles in and around Edinburgh, or
calling at Burns' Cottage in Alloway. Many made their way through
the Trossachs on a whistlestop tour of Rob Roy country. But there
were also the sportsmen, up in the Highlands from London and
elsewhere in the South for the grouse-season, salmonfishing or
deerstalking, whose luggage, servants, and dogs cluttered up the
station platforms of the Northern lines. The yachtsmen for the Clyde
regattas, the golfers for the summer medals at the East-Coast links,
hill-walkers and climbers to the Skye hills, the tennis-players and
croquet enthusiasts: all found a place in Scotland. Some came for
their health, to health resorts in medically approved areas such as
Strathspey, Deeside and Upper Lanarkshire, others to the spa resorts
of Moffat and Strathpeffer, others for the pleasure of the seaside, to
the select smaller resorts of Elie and North Berwick, or to the popular
destinations of the Firth of Clyde.

But increasingly tourism was no longer a middle- or upper-class
preserve; works outings, special trips and Sunday school outings
poured increasing numbers into the countryside and coast, perhaps
only for an afternoon or a weekend. Some critics, indeed, were
beginning to complain that tourism was spoiling the countryside,
that it was getting more and more difficult to find the 'happy
combination of comparative seclusion with easy access to great

centres'. The same writer in *The Strathearn Herald* (6 August 1881), not perhaps entirely innocent of special pleading, went on to press the virtues of St Fillans as a peaceful place off the beaten tourist track. The only excitement there, apart from the arrival of the daily coach from Crieff, was the appearance of an unexpected angler or stray bicyclist. Nowhere, and at no time, was the summer exodus more pronounced than during the Glasgow Fair, when the city emptied of all who could escape, by train, steamer, tram, horse-bus, bicycle or on foot. Tourism was overwhelmingly concentrated in the months of June, July and August when the resort communities could be swollen to three or four times their normal size. But this season, however compressed, was vital to many. As one Rothesay local replied, or so J.C. King reported (*Bute and Beauty*, 1881), when asked what supported his community: 'What do you live on in the winter? Tatties and herring. And in the summer? We're all right then; we live on the Glasgow folk'.

Tourism, therefore, was transformed in scale and composition in the nineteenth century. In this change a number of factors were at work. There was firstly the growing ability, and supporting levels of disposable income, of more and more people to take the time to travel whether for their health, education or amusement. There was also an increasing awareness of what Scotland had to offer, and an increasing diversity of attractions on offer. There were the pleasures of the seaside and of the hills, which increasing numbers enjoyed. To what might be called 'natural assets' were added others which were manufactured, or at least enhanced. The appeal of inherited antiquities, caves, castles and abbeys, was set in a landscape and culture endorsed by royalty. The presence of the past was preserved for profit, rather than plundered for stone, and judiciously enhanced by man-made artefacts, evocative of past personages and episodes. There were battlefield cairns as at Culloden, renovated graves as, for example, that of James III at Cambuskenneth, and the Wallace and Glenfinnan Monuments. Thirdly, and fundamental to growth, were ever-improving means of transport, which allowed access for some to the most remote parts and for the many to places near at hand.

It is an interesting question, when tourism in Scotland crossed the watershed from an elite experience to a more general one. As we have seen, the Continental Wars had done something to turn attention away from Europe and to the North. But the effect of the publication of Scott's *Lady of the Lake* in May 1810 (by coincidence rather than purpose just before the tourist season set in) was dramatic. It sold 20,000 copies in the year and triggered a rush of visitors to the locality

in which Roderick Rhu's ruffianly doings were set, to use the place to recreate the drama for themselves. For the Trossachs the results were immediate and startling. It was an area already known and made familiar by Mrs Murray and other writers, but Scott's poem led to its rising to the head of places to see for those of literary pretensions. Mrs Anne Grant of Laggan went in mid-September of that year to Callander to meet some English friends and to accompany them 'to these same Trossachs to which all the world are going to disturb the wood nymphs and emulate Walter Scott. How much we owe to Burns and Walter Scott'. In early November Sir John Sinclair wrote to Scott to congratulate him on increasing the number of visitors to Loch Katrine and the Trossachs beyond measure: 'My carriage was the 297th in the course of this year and there never had been above 100 before in any one season'. Sinclair urged Scott – without success – to consider a sequel to be entitled *The Mermaid*, or *The Lady of the Sea*, to be set in his native Caithness, in the hope of inspiring a similar tourist boom there. But what Scott did for the Trossachs was to be repeated in many other localities to greater or lesser extent. There was Scott's View at the Wicks of Baiglie near Perth, the exact site of which was disputed but whose location gave hours of pleasure to Victorian visitors equipped with the *Fair Maid of Perth*. Even an otherwise insignificant fishing village such as Auchmithie near Arbroath was able to reap benefit from the link to 'Mu⌐ ⌐ Craig' of Scott's *Antiquary*. Jenny Dean's Cottage was onlv   nany *Heart of Midlothian* associations in Edinburgh   being listed in essential guides to
Scotland, such   f Murray's *Handbook* issued in
1907. Scr⌐   ially, more slowly in the case of
overs⌐   t was extraordinarily important to   part of a century. No-one
played a   of Scotland as a place of
romance ⌐   ther literary figures had
their devote   her had the generalised
impact, or st⌐   ⌐g places on the map of the
literary tourist.   ware of the continuing interest in
Ossian, to whici⌐   usceptible, and himself visited Burns'
house in Dumfrie⌐   utumn of 1844. He thought it a 'shame to Scotland that that h⌐ use is not bought and preserved'. But he was in no doubt as to the overriding importance of Scott. When he visited Oban in early September 1840, he found there an astonishing number of travellers, some foreign but chiefly English, who had (in his judgement) been drawn there 'by scenery, curiosity, superfluous time and wealth and the fascination of Scott'.

Without Scott, or perhaps a lesser literary light, a locality could struggle to attract visitors. It was said of St Andrews that its relative neglect, despite the castle, beaches and other attractions, was due to its having been ignored by writers:

> Had it been written into popular notice by Burns, Byron or Scott, it would have been drawing far more wealth from the visits of fashionable visitors . . . But by a strange popular caprice, it continues until quite recently to be totally neglected.
>
> (*The Scottish Tourist*, 1852 edition)

The year 1810, therefore, has a real claim to be one of the decisive dates in the development of Scottish tourism.

But there was another event of great significance, the bringing into commercial service of the world's first paddle steamer, Henry Bell's *Comet*, on the Clyde in August 1812. It marked the start of what later generations were to recognise as 'A Perfect revolution effected in Favour of the Tourist'. The phrase is that of Scott Moncrieff Penney, editor of the late nineteenth-century Murray's *Handbooks for Travellers in Scotland*. The improvement of transport, whether on land or on water (and in the twentieth century by air) has always played a major part in shaping tourism. What matters is the quality, reliability and cost of access. Poor transport links in terms of irregular service and unreliability deter some travellers, and prevent any mass flows developing. Cost constricts choice and filters out many destinations, as does the constraint of journeying time. In the nineteenth century transport changes broadened options for all levels of society as the communications network improved, both nationally and abroad. There was both opportunity – and more competition. That transatlantic travellers, thanks to the new steamer services, could much more easily reach Britain was good for Scotland; but the growth of the Continental rail network strengthened the appeal of the South of France and elsewhere to Scots and others. Better transport, though not sufficient to guarantee growth, was necessary for tourism to develop.

The coming of the steamship was of particular significance to Scotland, opening up as it did tourism in the Clyde estuary, and to a lesser extent in the East of Scotland. Bell's initial venture was a regular, three times a week, steam passage between Glasgow, Greenock and Helensburgh. It left at about midday from the Broomielaw, depending on the state of the tide, without too precise a commitment to arrival times. The possibilities of special sailings must soon have become apparent. When the *Comet* was through at Bo'ness for a refit in May 1813, Bell took the opportunity to run an excursion to Leith.

The paddle-steamer, small, slow and not entirely reliable, did offer all sorts of opportunities for regular and special services, especially in the more sheltered waters of the Firth of Clyde as well as inland on Lochs Lomond and Katrine. The range of operations soon extended from sailings down the river to Greenock, to Rothesay in 1814, to Tarbet, Campbeltown and Inveraray in 1815. Loch Lomond acquired its first steamer, the *Marion*, in 1816, which ran full-day excursions during the summer months from Balloch round the Loch, calling at Tarbet, Luss and various islands. Amongst the sights on the route, as helpfully indicated by the letters 'R.R.' painted on the rocks below, was Rob Roy's Cave. Most tourists loved the *Marion*, but not all were enthusiastic: Lord Jeffrey agreed that it was very strange and striking to hear and see the boat 'hissing and roaring', but felt that 'it vulgarised the scene too much'. So intense was competition for the loch trade, as it was called, that at one point the competing companies offered free food and drink.

Confidence in the steamers, both for business and tourist travel, soon gathered. James Cleland, Superintendent of the Public Works and a statistician of Glasgow devoted to the chronicling of the city's life and growth, noted how much their patronage was increased. In less than four years the volume of passenger traffic between Glasgow and Greenock had risen tenfold

> Owing to the novelty and the dangers of the passage in the Firth below Dumbarton, the numbers of passengers were at the outset but small. The public, however, having gained confidence by degrees, the watering places all along the coast have been crowded with company beyond all former precedent, in consequence of steam conveyance.
>
> (James Cleland, *Annals of Glasgow* (1816))

The artist, William Daniell, sketched one of the very early steamboats, a barge-like vessel with a tall but very spindly funnel, on the Clyde near Dumbarton. As it is a fine day, the upper deck is crowded with a well-dressed company of ladies and gentlemen out for a day's pleasure. The parasols would have been useful protection against the sparks from the funnel. There is no evidence of the chairs and benches which Daniell said were set out on the roof – nor, and this, one hopes, was merely artistic licence – any sign of guard-rails. He took some care to find out more about the boats: the principal cabins were equipped with draughts, chessboards and backgammon to help pass the time, and cheaper accommodation was available next the mast and engine ('steerage') at half the full fare. Another view of an early steamboat is that of the *Marion*, shown in Fred. Walker, *The Song of the Clyde* (1984), the original of which is in the Mitchell Library. It shows an open-decked boat, with benches but no salon cabin. There are parties of tourists, ladies with parasols and several gentlemen using telescopes to allow them to inspect the scenery. The slightness of these early craft makes it understandable why captains had to ask their passengers not to crowd to one side lest they 'disturb the equilibrium of the vessel'. They were not capable of any great speed and must have struggled in adverse seas and contrary winds: six miles an hour was the best the Rothesay boat could manage in 1814. By 1840 they could achieve eleven or twelve m.p.h., which meant marked savings in voyage times. Yet even in the early days they could already match the mail-coach for speed on the run between Glasgow and Greenock, and travellers preferred the boats, as Daniell found:

> One of them has been known to carry 247 persons at a time; and in fine summer weather from five to six hundred have gone from Glasgow to Port Glasgow and Greenock and returned the same day. This has induced many persons to make this a mere excursion of pleasure: and the bathing places below Greenock furnishing an unexceptionable apology for a trip of this kind are beginning to be much frequented.
> (William Daniell, *A Voyage Round Great Britain undertaken in the year 1813* (London, 1818))

What the Firth of Clyde experienced was soon felt elsewhere. Speed and reliability improved, as did landing and boarding facilities. And though in many places passengers on embarking still had to face the risky transfer from a skiff or small boat to the steamer, proper piers were built at the larger ports. One of the most impressive was the 750-foot-long Suspension Pier at Newhaven near Edinburgh, opened in 1821 primarily for the use of steamer traffic. Owned by a private company, in which the Stirling Steamboat Company had shares, it charged a toll of a halfpenny on each passenger boarding or landing there. A lawyer, John Burns, travelled from his native Falkirk to St Andrews in July 1840. His journey began by canal passage-boat to Edinburgh, horse-coach to Newhaven and thence onwards by the Largo Steamboat; his landing in Fife was much less comfortable than his embarkation at the chain pier, as he was put on shore by small boat. On his return to Newhaven, he found that there were many vehicles waiting for passengers to Edinburgh. After being approached by a number of drivers, he agreed with a small party of three, a man and two women – 'decent looking people' – to share transport in a 'Minibus which we filled'.

The returns on steamer traffic – eight per cent was not an un-common dividend – were sufficient to stimulate the construction of many new boats and the development of new routes. The Prussian architect, Schinkel, found on his visit to Glasgow in 1826 that there were no fewer than 60 to 70 steamboat advertisements posted up in George Square, most of which were offering pleasure trips either to the Scottish lochs or to Staffa and Iona. Schinkel, who was impressed by the range of tours on offer, and their efficient organisation, started his Highland journey by a trip by water down to Dumbarton in company with a large number of English, French and Italians. He commented on what he called the civilising role of the steamships: 'These boats are always full of people, Scots going South to have a look at the new splendours of Glasgow and Edinburgh, or Southerners seeking the Highlands out of curiosity'. Oban, which he reached by road in a little cramped carriage from Inveraray, was the centre of a network of tourist sailings by the mid-1820s, offering a twice-a-week service to Staffa during the summer; travellers from Glasgow could also reach Skye and Mull via Oban.

Publishers of guides were quick to respond to the need to provide information to potential travellers about what was available where. In 1825 appeared the first edition of the *Scottish Tourist and Itinerary*, which carried 'A description of the Principal Steam Boat Tours'. It identified six main routes: Edinburgh to London, Leith to Stirling, Leith to Aberdeen, Glasgow to Inveraray, Glasgow to Fort William and Inverness, and finally Glasgow to Arran. Dedicated to Sir Walter Scott, the introduction referred to the way in which tours of Scotland had 'of late' become so fashionable, and to the role played by steamboats, which had laid open to thousands scenes of 'uncommon grandeur'. The last comment is highly significant. It suggests that the clientèle of the steamboats, small in number though they were, were both more numerous and less socially exclusive – though still respect-able – than the carriage- and chaise-travelling contingent; and that, like their railway counterparts, the excursionists, they were made less welcome. One English visitor from Warrington complained in late August 1818 of his reception at the inn at Inveraray, after arriving off the steam-packet. He found it uncomfortable and very dirty, the waiters haughty, and the accommodation very cramped. But he did make some allowance for his treatment:

> It was not much to be wondered at that in a house of this description, Steam-Boat Passengers should not receive a very civil reception or that those visitors only should be welcome who

brought their families, their servants, their chariots and their horses.
(Glasgow City Archives; Journal of a Tour to the Highlands, 1818)

In no part of Britain was the coming of coastal steamboat services so important for tourism as it was in Western Scotland. Other areas had their steamer services on inland waters, notably the Lakes. There were canal cruises in the Midlands, and the Forth & Clyde carried sufficient passenger custom for it to be worth the issue in 1823 of a specific handbook, *A Companion for Canal Travellers Between Edinburgh and Glasgow*, which listed all the sights to be seen on either side. It also indicated how much pleasure there was to be gained from watching one's fellow-passengers, 'a motley group'. The coming of the steamship was significant everywhere; in England river steamers went down the Thames and excursion boats crossed the Bristol Channel from South Wales to North Devon.

But the impact on Scotland was greater: within a relatively short time the steamboat opened up the Firth of Clyde and the West Coast of Scotland for longer-distance travellers and commuters from their summer quarters alike, for seaside vacationers, scenic prospectors, and a whole variety of tourists. Elsewhere in Scotland the railways were to play the critical role as transport agents in the development of tourism, alone or in conjunction with steamer services. In the West it was the steamers which led the way, and they were to continue to play a vital role, in the hands of those thrusting entrepreneurs, J. & G. Burns, David Hutcheson, and of course, MacBraynes. Visitors were impressed by what was on offer. The English banker, J. E. Bowman, who toured Scotland in the summer of 1825, enjoyed the company he found on what he termed ships of *pleasure*, numerous and respectable, 'some indeed of superior understanding and manners, many of them English, but chiefly Scottish or Hebridean'. He thought the travelling delightful, thanks to the sudden contrasts in scenery and atmospheric conditions. The conversation was good, the locals hospitable and the sound of the bagpipes 'melodious', the piper being used as a kind of ship's bell to announce meals, times of departure, lights out and the like. Not everything, however, went smoothly. When the *Ben Nevis* steamer arrived at Oban, on which he and his companion had intended to sail to Fort William, it was so overcrowded, with a double contingent of no less than 280 passengers on board, that the paddle-wheels rocked out of the water. The captain was extremely drunk, which drove Bowman and some others to the alternative strategy of renting a wherry. It took longer, and cost more, but in the circumstances was decidedly safer.

The distinguished English surgeon, W. C. Dendy, has left a delightful, if somewhat caustic, description in *The Wild Hebrides* (London, 1859) of the kind of summer clientèle to be found aboard the Skye steamers in the later 1850s. There were Highland lairds, and travellers of every description and standing:

> There sit a brace of the true devotees of beautiful nature . . . close to them stands their contrast, the mere holiday tourist, gazing around like an automaton, looking at everything and seeing nothing. And there is a very spicy sot, incessantly plying at his flask of Glenlivat, yet no more inspired by the blue hills of Lorn, that rise in majesty before him than with the russet molehill of Primrose in front of his London villa. There is the petit-maitre from London, the mere routine excursionist, decked out in all the exuberant fashion of Regent Street; now with lacklustre eye, poring over the dirty leaves of his itinerary, and teasing the man at the helm with idle enquiries. There is the desecrating vagrant, boasting of his immortal name done in black paint on Schloss Drachenfels: and now his highest pride is to carve his initials on one of the holy tombs on Iona, chip off a morsel of moulding from the prentice pillar in Roslin, and filch one of Macalister's stalactites in the spar cave of Strathaird.

Added to the cast are a wandering fisherman and his tack, a geologist with hammer ready to 'pummel the side of Ben Nevis for pebbles', a fly-catcher complete with green net, and a botanist, tin basket at the ready. Civic magnates from London find themselves next to girls escorted by dowager aunts, and young gallants with an eye for mischief. All that is missing is a clergyman or a honeymooner, both species much in evidence on the Western circuit. John Fell of Uxbridge wrote to Henry Pease, Darlington, in August 1854 that he had been at Glasgow but not on the West Coast, and added, 'which way does WP take his bride for the wedding tour?'

Another list, which overlaps with Dendy's, is that of Frederick Fag (James Johnson) in a delightful account entitled *The Recess, or Autumnal Relaxation in the Highlands and Islands* (London, 1834). Fag adds, amongst others on the steamer from London bound for Scotland, Boarding School Misses, Judges, Barristers and Doctors, Bankers and Political Economists, Cantabs 'with their tutors going to study spherics in the Isle of Eigg', and Oxonians 'to collate Greek and Gaelic in the monumental inscriptions of Iona'. In short, 'tourists of all characters and calibres; some to make a tour simply, some to write a tour badly; but the greater number to talk of a tour incessantly afterwards'. Another group to be found in the North during the late summer in ever-increasing numbers from the 1830s was the university reading party, from Oxford or Cambridge, complete with tutor or 'bear-leader'. Lord Cockburn had come across one group at Callander in 1837 and another at Inveraray, complete with their books. He conjectured that the amount of Greek they took in was doubtful, 'but they can do nothing better for their minds or bodies than breathe such air, in such scenes'. Such reading parties made frequent appearances in the local press. One group with their professor fell foul of the Duke of Atholl's gamekeepers in Glen Tilt, in 1847, trespassing, as they were, onto his ground during the shooting season. Another party of Oxford students, who had been staying at the Lochearnhead Hotel for two months, under the tutelage of the Rev. Dr Rogers, a controversial Stirling figure – best known for his role in the promotion of the Wallace Monument – organised a supper and free ball for the locals. Held on the eve of their departure in early September 1850, it was attended by at least 200, including several sportsmen from Liverpool, who were also staying at the hotel. Two turned out in full Highland dress; 'their manly and truly Celtic appearance was much admired'.

As the reach of the steamboats lengthened, along with passage times, so the provision of catering became an important element for those fortunate enough to be unaffected by seasickness, and the steamship companies competed hard in this respect. 'You are feasted on salmon and white herrings', reported one travel-writer, William Howitt, en route to Staffa from Glasgow. The steamer is a 'kind of floating kitchen' or 'cake house', said Chauncey Hare Townshend. The supply of food and drink was generally let to a steward, and it was alleged that on occasion passages were lengthened to promote his sales. This could be a highly profitable part of the steamboat business, though the question of the supply of spirits could be vexatious, and the catering on the Alloa and Newhaven steamer was let in the early 1820s at an annual rent of no less than £100. But there were poor seasons, and stewards did come to grief financially. *The Callander and Oban Advertiser* recorded in July 1885 the bankruptcy of a steward on a Loch Lomond steamer.

In the early days, steamboats anchored at night, and this added a trying element to longer-distance voyages. Those quickest off their mark, or with local contacts, might find lodgings on shore, as at Tobermory where there was no hotel; the rest had to make do with what was available on board. To the claustrophobia of the cabin – on the first generation of boats the best that could be provided by way of accommodation were sofas – was added the lack of privacy. Charles Weld, on his way north in the summer of 1832 to Staffa, found himself kept awake by his fellow-passengers: one snored, another tweaked the sofa, and a third talked in his sleep. Another en route from Liverpool via the Isle of Man found his crib excessively warm, but did manage some refreshing sleep.

But the discomfort of travellers was nothing new and coach passengers suffered just as badly as those on the boats. Both forms of transport had points for and against. Argument over which was better was common. Frederick Fag, who considered himself experienced in these matters, felt that on balance the steamer had the advantage, 'whether we view it with reference to economy, comfort, society, or health'. Good though the box seat ('outside') of the coach was on a fair day, when it rained it was no pleasure to have your neighbours' umbrellas dripping down your neck. Nor was the discomfort of a steamboat cabin quite as bad as that of the very cramped interior of the stage, where you were liable to be annoyed by passengers from whose conversation you could not escape; or those who insisted on the windows being shut in the hottest weather because they had a cold; or conversely those with asthma who wanted all the fresh air possible, regardless of the temperature.

The differential, incidentally, for travellers by steamer or boat was almost identical whether going outside or steerage, or inside or cabin: usually somewhere between a third and a half more for the supposedly better accommodation. In August 1838 the new Stirling to Callander coach, *The Highland Chieftain*, advertised its fares as 3s. per person for outside and 4/6d for inside. In the same year the steamboat ticket from Stirling to Edinburgh was 1/- for steerage and 1/6d for cabin, plus the pier charge at Newhaven. The 'expense of travelling' from Glasgow to Staffa given in Anderson's *Guide* was for steerage and back, and was very much cheaper than going cabin – 8s as against 25s. But the lack of cabin cover on such a long voyage must have been very testing, and this premium does appear to have been quite exceptional. A complaint often heard from visitors was the requirement to tip the coachmen and drivers, but the steamer companies firmly forbade any such douceurs. Nevertheless there were always pierhead porters to please, and it was usually better to keep them sweet than risk the consequences of their ill temper.

There were also marked changes in land transport. Coach services were being extended, becoming more regular and frequent. Some were explicitly run only during the summer season – normally June to

September – to cater for the tourist trade, such as the *Queen of Beauty*, a light post coach between Dunkeld and Callander, brought into operation for the first time in the late 1830s. Others linked with the loch steamers or in the West with the sailings for the Western Islands. The capacity of these coaches was not great: four inside and sixteen or twenty outside, boarding by ladder. The movement of 113 passengers from Stirling to Callander one Thursday in late August 1852 required the use of eight or nine coaches, though this was partially in consequence of the arrival of a large pleasure party from England, perhaps one of Thomas Cook's tours. Luggage and dogs were a further complication, and Fontane, for one, marvelled how the conductor and driver managed to pack everybody in. Also available for use were open omnibuses; the enterprising coach-proprietor, James Grant of Stirling – nicknamed the 'omnibus man' – even managed to run a vehicle drawn by five horses to Bridge of Allan for the Strathallan Games capable of carrying eighty passengers in first, second and third class. This was merely a short-distance service, however. Also improving was the availability for hire of chaises with hoods, open cars, phaetons and gigs, as well as horses. These were kept at hotels and posting inns in the Highlands, with Oban, Perth, Dunkeld, Inverness and Stirling major centres for the tourist.

The supply of accommodation was increasing; indeed by the 1840s one guidebook – perhaps not entirely disinterestedly – considered that it was almost universally good, in some places excellent, and at worst respectable. Some were old premises enlarged; others were built from new. Innkeepers were alert to the possibilities of the tourist trade. The experienced Dugald Paul at Cairndow found it worth his while to advertise in the Glasgow press in July 1825 – without falling into any danger of understating the calibre of his establishment, a trait still common to his craft. 'Steam-boat travellers', he said, could 'depend on excellent beds, fresh provisions, and choice liquors, as well as onward transport by light cart or boat'. The hotel at Balloch was extensively remodelled in the late 1830s to cater for tourists to Loch Lomond, and amongst the advertised facilities were a posting department with vehicles of every type and careful drivers, new stabling and lock-up coach houses, pleasure boats for the loch, and an omnibus service to and from Dumbarton. There was a stock of the best wines, large and elegantly fitted up parlours and bedrooms for those who wished to stop over. In the larger tourist centres, the arrival of the tourist boats (or later the trains) set off a frenzy of competition between the scouts of the rival hotels, anxious to snap up the uncommitted traveller and indeed to mislead the unsure. Visitors to Edinburgh were urged by the lessee of the Royal Hotel in Princes Street to be careful that 'they were not taken by cabmen or porters to another establishment, as it has caused great annoyance'. The secret was to secure the luggage; the tourist would tend to follow. Hence, as one seasoned traveller observed, 'it is among the baggage train that words frequently proceed to blows, and pitched battles are fought for a trunk or a band-box'. The mixture on the island steamers of commercial freight and tourist accessories was astonishing, as Fag found: 'the contents of the steamers [are] men, women, children, sheep, poultry, pigs, salmon, herrings, casks, trunks, bags, baskets, hampers, books, portfolios, maps, guns, fishing tackle, and thousands of other articles'. It can have been no easy task to reclaim your own, particularly if rushing to make an onward connection.

But there was an acute problem that was to handicap the supply of transport and accommodation alike, and was never to be satisfactorily resolved. Intense though demand was in the summer months, there was a much longer period in the Highlands and the Borders, particularly in the late autumn, winter and spring, when there was no tourism and little or no other trade. In high season demand far outstripped supply for vehicles and beds. Bowman in early August of 1825 found a stream of sportsmen heading north on the Inverness Road, with their horses, dogs and servants: 'coaches in that direction were so loaded that ordinary passengers could not be forwarded'. The provision of accommodation at times was simply swamped in the smaller localities, and sometimes in the large as well should there be any exceptional attractions in the vicinity. Anne Porter from Worcester arrived in Inverness on 19 September 1849. Not only was the annual meeting of the Highland Games being held, but also the first stone for a cairn commemorating the battle at Culloden was due to be laid. The result was that the town was full, all hotel beds were 'bespoken', and her group were obliged to take lodgings at a dressmaker's at what she considered an exorbitant rate: six pounds for the three days of the festivities. At least hot water and clean linen were provided. To travel without sending ahead, as the more provident did, to reserve rooms, was highly risky. The small inn at the west end of Loch Katrine was already full when one English traveller and his party arrived one evening in August 1839, but somehow they were found beds. The next group who came in were obliged to sleep in the parlours and passages, and the final arrivals late in the night had to go on a further ten miles to Callander, not that they were certain of any luck there. The previous year Cockburn had witnessed for himself the problem at such a popular destination. The

Trossachs Inn could, he thought, put up perhaps a dozen, or at most two dozen people:

> But last autumn I saw about one hundred apply for admittance; and after horrid altercations, entreaties and efforts, about fifty or sixty compelled to huddle together all night. They were all of the upper rank, travelling mostly by private carriages, and by far the greatest number strangers. But the pigs were as comfortably accommodated. I saw three or four English gentlemen spreading their own straw on the earthen floor of an outhouse, with a sparred door and no fireplace or furniture. And such things occur every day there.

Cockburn was no happier with the situation eight years later at the same place:

> [Tourists] all arrive from Loch Lomond, Callander, and other quarters, expecting accommodation at the wonderful and expensive place called Stewart's Inn, and except the twelve or the twenty-four, are all daily, or rather hourly destined to be disappointed. On our return to Callander from that place we counted about fifty people returning from Stewart's Inn in vehicles. There had been above one hundred people at that inn that day.
>
> (*Circuit Journeys*, p. 187; 8th September 1846)

The Trossachs Hotel was rebuilt in 1849 to provide ten private parlours and about 70 beds.

Bigger hotels might be built, but what of the off-season? There was no easy solution which made financial sense. What was true of the inn at Tarbet held with equal economic force elsewhere: 'this inn is very good, but far too small for the resort in summer, and far too large for the want of resort in winter'. One response was to shut from October to March, as many Highland hotels did, but what then of the staff, the idle facilities and horses? Some Highland hotels and carriage hirers, it appears, were in the habit of auctioning off horses at the end of the season. In October 1888 at the cattle market in Glasgow Buchanans the Auctioneers sold some 110 Highland coach and post horses. Their owners included The Glasgow and Inverary Steamboat Company, whose horses were 'well-seasoned and just withdrawn from the Dunoon and Loch Eck Coaches', Donald MacPherson, Coach Proprietor and Post-master at Oban, Mr D. Fraser of Dalmally, and Mr R. P. Dayton of the Loch Earnhead Hotel. It is an interesting question who wanted to buy horses at that time of year: farmers for carting over the winter, perhaps? Charles Weld found himself on the last coach of the season from Banavie to Loch Lomond via Glencoe, and it was a lively affair:

> At every place between Bannavie and Loch Lomond where we stopped, we took up various articles belonging to the coach establishment: brushes and buckets, horse-cloths and harness, with an enormous quantity of whisky contained in living barrels, said barrels being the ostlers. The fact is, the coach was returning to its winter quarters to be laid up in ordinary until the ensuing season: and as no passengers were expected, everybody considered that he had full licence to get drunk. How the coach got through Glencoe is a mystery to me. I walked.
> (*Two Months in the Highlands, Orcadia and Skye* (London, 1860, p.402))

To put charges up during the summer, in order to compensate for the very lean pickings during the off-season, was inevitable but attracted much criticism.

By the 1830s and 1840s, therefore, the impact of growing tourism was beginning to be evident, fed as it was by the developing network of steamer services, and improved road transport facilities. New inns and hotels were being built, with those at Edinburgh and Glasgow fully the equal of their London counterparts, posting and guiding being provided. Innkeepers, coach- and gig-hirers, shopkeepers and others, such as the schoolmaster on Iona who was handsomely tipped for showing visitors over the ruins, were receiving some benefit. But a downside was already apparent. There was the problem of begging, which worried both Scots and visitors alike. The preferred image, much talked up in journals and accounts, was that of the hospitable poor, willing to share what little they had, and reluctant to take any recompense. Some argued – and this was disturbing – that tourism created begging. It might be thinly disguised by the sale of souvenirs – children on Iona besieged tourists with the offer of pebbles for a penny – and it was no new problem, not confined to Scotland, nor even at its worst there. Everywhere in Britain, where there was a sight to see, beggars were in attendance, as one French traveller observed in 1810, when visiting the Wye valley: 'They are attracted, indeed created' by tourists was his view. Fleecing wealthy visitors was acceptable, but in Scotland mendicancy was not. Then there was also the tendency of tourists to despoil what they came to see. Chauncy Townshend, touring Scotland in the early 1830s, was appalled at the destruction being wrought by tourists on the Spar Cave on Skye:

The abomination, not of desolation, but of visitation is upon it. Steam-boats come here, and vomit forth their gaping multitudes, who burn torches, and even set on fire tar barrels till its own snowy surface is in many places blackened even to London blackness.

(A *Descriptive Tour in Scotland*, London, 1833)

Even amenities especially provided for tourists were not immune. On Ellen's Isle on Loch Katrine, Lord Willoughby had erected a rustic windowed shelter for visitors. But his generosity was rewarded by their either scribbling 'indecencies' on the walls, or cutting strips off the parchment wall-coverings to take home as a memento. In 1837 the entire building was burnt down by accident, thanks to the carelessness of some tea-making tourists. Other owners who opened their grounds to visitors endangered their flowers and shrubs, and at Dollar Town-shend noticed a sign of the times: he and his friends were shown over the castle by an elderly, half-blind woman, who insisted that before they left, they sign the visitors' book. Or, to be exact, flatteringly *not* the lesser book:

> ye must na' gang before ye' ha' written yere names in the Buik, the gentelfolk's buik. I keep twa'; ane for the gentles and ane for the rabblement.

If tourism in the early stages of development was beginning to disturb Scottish life, the coming of the railways was greatly to accelerate its impact. It was not so much that they led to the opening up of virgin areas for tourism, save perhaps in the Southwest of Scotland. Nearly all of the main Scottish tourist destinations were already known and accessible by steamship or coach, whether the resorts of the Clyde, the islands of Skye, Iona and Staffa, the spas of Moffat and Strathpeffer, the sporting grounds of the Highlands, or the cities and burghs of historic Scotland. What the railways did was greatly to transform the scale and composition of tourism. Whereas the coaches could carry dozens of passengers at a time, and the steamboats a few hundred, the railways could move much greater numbers; and move them more quickly, with greater regularity and at less cost for those prepared to accept the spartan conditions of third-class travel. The savings in time were very significant to the longer-distance tourist from the South, but even more important to the middle- and working-class traveller, limited both by time and pocket. The railways did not create excursionism. The steamship companies in the Firth of Clyde and elsewhere had already developed that. In July 1835, for example, a steamer trip was offered from Glasgow to the Western Isles, by way of the Giant's Causeway and Londonderry. For this five-day excursion, the fare was two guineas, exclusive of refreshments, to be furnished by the steward 'on the most moderate terms'. But the railways did build it into a social institution of major importance for every level of society. Travel firms emerged to stimulate and serve the growing appetite for travel to seaside or inland resorts, for a week's or fortnight's tour in the Highlands or the Borders, some even offering a schedule tailored to the last five minutes and to an exact budget.

Railways fanned tourism through promotion and the provision of facilities. They also fed off it, some lines, particularly in North, more than others. In good years, the railways' passenger (and luggage) receipts benefited, but should there be a downturn in tourism – through bad weather, for example, or a failure of the grouse-shooting – then their profits suffered badly. This degree of interest in tourism was not anticipated in the early days of the railways, whose prime concern in the 1820s and 1830s was the movement of freight: coal above all else. Yet it was not long before passenger traffic did start to make its mark, and the potential of railway travel for pleasure, as well as on business or in search of work, quickly became apparent. There was already a proven and increasing demand for the seaside. The steamboats had shown that this coastal business could pay. An example of this was the Glasgow, Paisley & Greenock Railway. Promoted in 1837, it had its eye on bringing travel to a number of Clyde resorts into its hands. It hoped to attract not just weekend traffic, or families going down to Clyde and Ayrshire coast resorts for the summer months, but commuting traffic, the head of the household returning at the beginning of each week to his business in Glasgow. And this they did very successfully, though the financial returns were somewhat diluted by the middle-class unwillingness to travel first- or even second-class, preferring third. The line to Greenock, from which steamer services could take passengers on to Rothesay and other resorts, opened in March 1841, and by the summer the Saturday trains from Glasgow were being well patronised, as were the Monday morning return services, regularly crowded with sea-bathing folk. Their mood is well caught in this contemporary song (1843) entitled 'The Railway' about the weekend travellers coming back from Dunoon on the steamer for Greenock where they were to catch the train:

> The steam was up, the wind was high,
> A dark cloud scoured across the sky,
> The quarterdeck was scarcely dry

Of the boat that meets the Railway;
Yet thick as sheep in market pen,
Stood all the Sunday watering men,
Like growling lions in a den,
With faces inches five and ten;
Some were hurrying to and fro,
Others were sick and crying, oh!
Whose wooden peg's that on my toe?
In the boat that meets the Railway.
Rushing, crushing, up and down,
Tipping the cash to Captain B–n;
O what a hurry to get to town
Upon the morning Railway.

(*Source:* Chambers' *Edinburgh Journal*
(1846), p.224. The original is to be found
in Park's *Songs for All Seasons* (Glasgow, 1843))

Holiday traffic was particularly heavy: the GP & G ran out of engines during the August Paisley holiday in the first year of its operation, but still managed to carry over 8,000 passengers in the one day. Glasgow Fair Week traffic, nearly all of it for pleasure, generated 21,980 passengers in July 1841, and 33,887 the next year, an increase of 50 per cent. Similar stories about the growth of pleasure traffic were to be heard elsewhere in Scotland, and it is not surprising that when the bill to authorise the Scottish Central Railway was scrutinised by a Parliamentary Committee in March 1845, an important question was what watering places and spas the project might serve.

A related development was the growth of excursionism, which the railways did much to promote. As we have already seen, this innovation had been pioneered in Scotland by the steamboat companies, but it was seized upon both by the railways and the travelling public. As early as 1834, the Glasgow & Garnkirk ran what was in Robertson's judgement probably the first *British* excursion train. Later excursions were to rely on special trains to popular destinations and cheap fares but, initially at least, the G & G provided only first-class coaches and set a single fare with no concessions. The train ran non-stop from Glasgow to what is now Coatbridge, with only an hour allowed for sightseeing at Gartsherrie, which may have been more than adequate, and the total duration of the trip was only two hours. Much of the pleasure must have been the experience of travelling and the wayside views. Places were strictly limited:

This arrangement is intended to obviate the objections made by many to the crowds in the ordinary trains, and to the stoppages for passengers in the intermediate places on the line of Railway. Genteel Parties will find the trip an agreeable and healthful mode of spending part of the day.

(Handbill advertising *Railway Pleasure Trips*, 10 June 1835)

By the later 1830s excursion traffic had become a feature of the spring and summer traffic of many lines and not just in the West of Scotland, but also around Edinburgh and Dundee. There were limiting factors: the availability of motive power and rolling stock was a problem, made only worse by the Scottish Sunday Observance that ruled out Sunday as suitable for outings, something that also bedevilled the operations of coach and steamboat companies.

But excursionism, whether organised by the railway companies themselves, or by others, grew by leaps and bounds, and by the 1840s the scale of excursion traffic, aided by cheap fares, was so large as to cause serious concern on safety grounds. Masonic parades, Sunday schools, works outings and others found their special trips subscribed to the limit. In July 1843 a temperance society took such a large contingent of teetotallers to Ayr that not all could get inside: some were apparently clustering outside like 'bees'. While excursion trains could be divided into more manageable smaller workings, this was not always possible and more difficult to police. One outing of 1500 people to Linlithgow from Glasgow in 1842 went in three trains but was brought back in a single monster compilation of five locomotives and 110 carriages. Small wonder that such trains were described, as noted already of the expedition from Stirling to Perth on 4 August 1848, as appearing like 'huge serpents coiling their way along the curves of line'. Amongst those organising outings in Scotland was Thomas Cook, whose first excursion in England was a temperance trip from Leicester to Loughborough in July 1841. In the mid-1840s, however, his attention was to turn north to Scotland. His first sortie across the Border, after a successful venture to Wales, came in the summer of 1846. His party of 350 travelled by steamer from Fleetwood to Ardrossan, and by train thereafter. It was to be the first of many such 'Tartan Tours'.

Day-trips, weekend trade, and longer-distance travel all began to fall into the hands of the railways. In some areas their grip was total, with coaching reduced to a purely feeder and support role. Those who could switch from sea to land by and large did so without delay and in some cases even before the new routes were complete. The Quaker ironmaster, Edward Pease, travelled by rail up the East Coast to Edinburgh in early August 1847. 'The railroad from Berwick is new, and in some places we pass over glens of great depth upon wooden piles. But the beauty is great so that we in degree forget our rather frightful position.' Once the cross-Border routes were complete from the later 1840s, long-distance coaching died, and even the steamships struggled to compete. In other localities, notably the Clyde, there was a partnership with the steamers, and in a few cases, as on Loch Lomond, joint-ownership. But for the traveller for pleasure, of whatever class other than the poorest, the period saw a remarkable transformation in what was on offer and the range of options that the transport network could provide. The Saturday of the Glasgow Fair in 1850, when the July holiday brought virtually all business in the city to a standstill, saw a mass exodus. Thirty-five steamers left the Broomielaw for the coast, with – it was thought – some 20,000 passengers. As many left by train to Greenock, Ayr, Hamilton and Edinburgh. A special excursion to Perth and Aberdeen, returning at midnight, carried no less than 3,000 passengers in 62 carriages, drawn in three divisions with six engines. The inhabitants of smaller burghs, of which Stirling is an example, benefited equally. On Saturday the 24th of July 1852, according to the local paper, the first group away were a steamer party of 500 down the river to Fife. They were followed, also before breakfast, by those ('a large portion of our people') whose families were already at the seaside. The railway took another 396 to Perth, and 250 to Bridge of Allan. The Strathallan Highland Games at Bridge of Allan attracted large numbers, some walking, but others – perhaps 1200–1500 – went by horse bus. In all, something like a third of the town's population was away, some just for the day, others for longer, leaving behind, as the writer observed with a mild degree of exaggeration, only the bed-ridden and those who had to work. There was partial compensation with an influx of excursionists from Aberdeen, some of whom had come on a 'grand monster' excursion organised by Messrs Murray, and others from Bathgate and Kirkcaldy.

Transport was being revolutionised, so also was tourism, and few parts of Scotland, urban or rural, were untouched. Some communities sent tourists – the large cities, mining communities and textile towns; others received them, such as the seaside resorts and scenic inland communities; a third group acted as both source and destination for tourism, with some leaving and others arriving. In this last category were places like Edinburgh, Perth and Stirling, where the balance may well have been level. Once the taste for travelling for pleasure was implanted, it became an addiction, part of an accepted pattern of life.

FURTHER READING

This section draws on John Thomas, *Regional History of the Railways of Great Britain*, Vol. 6: Scotland, The Lowlands and the Borders (Newton Abbot, 1971), esp. Chapter vii, 'The River Clyde and Loch Lomond'. Also of major importance is C. J. A. Robertson, *The Origins of the Scottish Railway System, 1722–1844* (Edinburgh, 1983). Peter Marshall, *The Scottish Central Railway* (Oakwood, 1998) has material of relevance. On the provision of steamer services and facilities, see Ian Brodie, *Steamers of the Forth* (Newton Abbot, 1976), Ian McCrorie and Joy Monteith, *Clyde Piers: A Pictorial Record* (Inverclyde, 1982), Ian McCrorie, *Steamers of the Highlands and Islands: An Illustrated History* (Greenock, 1987), and Donald MacLeod, *Loch Lomond Steamboat Companies* (Dumbarton, 1889). For travelling experiences, J.E. Bowman, *The Highlands and Islands; a nineteenth century tour* (Sutton, 1986), Karl Friedrich Schinkel, *The English Journey: Journal of a Visit to France and Britain in 1826*, eds. David Bindman and Gottfried Rieman (Yale, 1993), Theodore Fontane, *Across the Tweed: Notes on Travel in Scotland, 1858* (London, 1965), Chauncy Hare Townshend, *A Descriptive Tour in Scotland* (new edition, London 1847). William Howitt, *Visits to Remarkable Places, Old Halls, Battlefields and Scenes Illustrative of Striking Passages in English History and Poetry* (London, 1840) has an account of a visit to Staffa and Iona. The full title of Frederick Fag's work is *The Recess or Autumnal Relaxation in the Highlands and Lowlands being the home circuit versus foreign travel, a tour of health and pleasure. A Serio-Comic Tour to the Hebrides* (London, 1834). Unpublished but of great value are the Pease letters in Durham Record Office; Charles Weld's 'Highland Journal 1832' in the Dorset Record Office; Anne Porter's letters in the Worcester Record Office; and the Leete MSS in the Northamptonshire Record Office.

3

TO THE SEASIDE

Everyone seems to have money to go to go to the seaside.
(The Saturday Review, 8 August 1863)

By the third quarter of the nineteenth century, the annual pilgrimage
to the seaside had become established as one of the great institutions of
Victorian life. Professional and moneyed people either owned or
rented houses at the coast, which were occupied for the summer.
Middle-class and artisan families rented cottages or lodgings for up to
a month, and many working-class Scots, if unable to manage a week in
a seaside apartment, at least sallied to the coast for a holiday weekend,
some sleeping rough if need be. Though Scotland never developed any
mass resorts on the scale of Blackpool or Scarborough, the numbers in
high season were still very substantial. It was claimed in 1891 of
Rothesay that during the Glasgow Fair Week, the resident population
of 9,000, already increased by another 700 families resident for the
summer, was further swollen by no fewer than 30–40,000 weekend
visitors. Pressure on water supplies and sewage was considerable, and
not surprisingly, accommodation was at a premium, with in one
instance no fewer than twenty-one people sharing a single room
and a kitchen. And what was true of resorts along the Clyde and
Ayrshire coast also held for places at the sea in East Lothian, Fife,
Angus, Aberdeenshire, Nairn and Ross-shire. Some resorts were more
exclusive than others, with a steady, respectable clientèle, and settled
culture of leisure and recreation, in which golf was the central element.
But all places, inland and coastal, were liable to the challenge of
working-class day-trippers, some of whom were well behaved, others
of whom were not. Descending by train or steamer, they were liable –
women as well as men – to be rowdy, drunk and indifferent to local
conventions about separate bathing, for example. Their incursions
provoked a steady stream of complaints, except from the shopkeepers,
innkeepers and others who welcomed their custom. The columns of
local papers were filled with complaints on similar lines to this from
Dunoon in June 1871:

> On Saturday last, a number of excursion parties landed here
> from various steamers. One or two of them, accompanied by

bands of music, paraded about the streets. We regret to say a large amount of drunkenness was visible, many of the gentler sex being in that respect no better than those they were keeping company with, with riotous and disorderly conduct so much in keeping with too many of the excursions of the present day to Dunoon.

(The Argyleshire Standard, 28 June 1871)

When, and why, did coastal tourism start to become significant in Scotland? The evidence suggests that, as with other types of tourism, its roots lie firmly in the later eighteenth century, and that a very important ingredient was the discovery of the therapeutic value of salt water. Bathing, or, more strictly, ducking in the sea, perhaps (in the better resorts) with the aid of an attendant and from a bathing machine, was a key element in the therapy; to this could be added drinking seawater, and massage with seaweed. For those who were frailer, the treatments could be administered at purpose-built baths. Cold (or hot) saltwater treatment was held to be good for a whole variety of ailments, particularly gout, scrofula and rickets, to give young girls the right constitution, and to correct depraved or indulgent living habits. But dipping was only part of the day's schedule, and just as at the spas, other activities had to be found to fill the long day. Among these were the exploration of the beach and shoreline with its rock pools and other attractions, excursions and walks in the locality, promenades and discussions.

Sea-bathing was rather later in achieving recognition in Scotland than in England, where Brighton, Deal and Scarborough were major centres by the mid-eighteenth century, and the habit had spread well north by the 1780s. Elizabeth Diggle observed that when she passed through Tynemouth in late April 1788, it was too early in the season for the bathing machines to have been moved to the beach. A salt water bath, which may well imply that the practice of sea-bathing was already established there, was built at Peterhead in 1762 to augment its existing mineral spring treatments. In July 1772 a list of some forty visitors at the waters there was published in *The Aberdeen Journal*. They were a select group of local gentry, headed by the Duke and Duchess of Gordon. Ten years later the number had grown substantially, and the catchment area was much wider, with several from Edinburgh and Glasgow. Peterhead, perhaps understandably, failed to build on this early start, and had not added either warm baths or bathing machines, to the regret of its parish minister in 1793. But the idea that sea-bathing was healthy, and the seaside good as a tonic began to catch on, and received medical endorsement. The highly popular and influential medical writer, Dr William Buchan, whose *Domestic Medicine, Or A Treatise on the Prevention and Cure of Diseases* (first edition, 1769) was much consulted, added a chapter on 'Seabathing' in the ninth edition which was published in 1786. He highly recommended sea-bathing for those suffering from skin complaints but also as a preservative of general health. Buchan's advice was followed. The young and rather sickly Walter Scott was sent in 1778 to take advantage of the local bathing at Prestonpans, which became, like a number of places near Edinburgh, a popular resort in the summer. Children seem to have been particular beneficiaries. Elizabeth Grant records in her *Memoirs of a Highland Lady* the sending of a cousin 'who was very delicate' to the seaside.

The increasing popularity of the seaside is evident in reports from several localities contained in Sir John Sinclair's Statistical Account of Scotland. Those within easy range of Edinburgh benefited; it was already a town which the better-off deserted in the summer in order to go to some fashionable 'watering place'. Elie in Fife, with its sheltered bay and good beach, was one favourite, as was South Queensferry, where accommodation for sea-bathing was described as 'excellent', and much resorted to of late for that purpose. Of all the east-coast resorts, Portobello developed fastest, as John Stewart has shown. Close to Edinburgh – within walking range – it had a good sandy beach and matching facilities. In 1795 bathing machines were being advertised for hire during the summer months, and hot and cold water baths were opened sometime in the next decade. A three-times-a-day coach service was provided in 1805 for those not able or wishing to walk.

It was significant that by the turn of the century the seaside was becoming a place not just for invalids but for an individual or family holiday. It was medical therapy for some, but recreation and amusement for the majority. Those who could afford it were beginning to think in terms of a retreat at the coast. One English visitor to the Brodie House at Elgin in the summer of 1790 was able to join the family at their Lossiemouth property, which was kept for the restorative benefit of sea-bathing. Broughty Ferry had its enthusiasts: George Dempster of Dunnichen sent his children there each year for a few weeks at the seaside in the hope that their constitutions would benefit from the combination of sea-air and sea-bathing. Adam Bald, a Glasgow merchant, kept a journal of some of his holiday excursions over the period 1791 to 1833, part in prose, latterly mostly in verse of very limited virtue. As a sample, here is a verse from a lengthy poem inspired by a visit to Dunoon in the summer of 1826:

> Along the Coast in gaudy steamer paddling
> Some to the Isles, some nearer home doth bend
> Amongst vulgar crowds or gay parades to seek
> Some for retirement in some cozy glen.

His trips in the 1790s included an equestrian trip to Edinburgh, a pedestrian tour to Gartness, an ascent of Ben Lomond, a ramble to the Campsies, and a sea voyage to Liverpool. Several of his expeditions were to the coast. He was an inveterate early morning bather when-ever the opportunity offered, a practice that he recommended to all visitors as a preventative to the 'itch' which they risked by the absence of clean bed clothes in ferry houses. One such outing in July 1791 took him to Greenock, and then on to visit some relatives at Gourock, whom he describes in a very significant phrase as having '*been seized with the saltwater mania*' (my italics). The strength of interest in the coast, and the change in those there, is evident in the opening passage of his account:

> It was the custom for valetudinarians in the inland parts of the country to repair for the summer to the Sea coast, with the expectation of confirming a state of convalescence and purifying their constitutions from the Morbifick influence of a winter blast. For this purpose every spot on the seashore was crowded with the diseased and emaciated part of mankind, but now the scene is dramatically changed. Instead of the cadaverous looking sojour-ner, you meet now the plump and jolly, sauntering the rocky shore, or climbing the heathery hill, full of health and spirits, while the sickly race are confined to their gloomy chambers, driven from their summer retreats . . . Nought now will satisfy either married or unmarried or the aged and young but a trip for the summer to the Sea coast.'
> (Glasgow City Archives: commonplace book of Adam Bald)

With two companions Bald carried on to Inveraray where they visited the Castle, the Duke's family being so civil as to shift rooms ahead of them so as to allow all the apartments to be seen, and then returned to Glasgow by passage boat. On subsequent trips Bald had his full share of problems with inns, ferries and boats, but considered his time away necessary in 'diverting the mind from the anxious concerns of the mercantile world'. Others in increasing numbers shared this view. What helped, of course, was better transport and access. A family intending to spend the summer in Rothesay in 1778 had to hire a special boat. It was, Senex recalled, no mean undertaking then to go to

Bute. Houses were available and were cheap, but getting there was the problem for a big household and its servants, laden as they were with luggage, pets and supplies:

> It is so easy nowadays to proceed to the coast by railways and steamers . . . that many of your younger readers will scarcely believe how serious a matter it was to transport a large family of children to the coast, nor the shortage of lodgings, particularly for a dozen or so individuals.
>
> (Senex, *Glasgow Past and Present*, Glasgow, 1894)

In 1822 an Episcopalian minister from Paisley, W.M. Wade, issued a guide to the spas and watering places of Scotland, in which he described the attractions of a number of seaside resorts. His list is not comprehensive, but it is none the less interesting, including as it does some from the West Coast (Ardrossan, Campbeltown, Gourock, Helensburgh, Largs and Rothesay), others from the East (St Andrews, Elie and North Berwick) and Fraserburgh in the North-East, the last doubtless to the chagrin of its neighbour and rival Peterhead. Wade's is not just a descriptive account, but also analytical. His general assessment was that Scottish resorts lagged behind their counterparts in England because of a later start, less of a population base, and a more cautious pattern of expenditure. They had developed much less in the way of seaside amenities and culture – 'the showy theatre, the gay assembly, the brilliant parade, the dazzling repository of dress and decoration'. Nor were facilities anything like comparable to those at the English resorts. Leith was exceptional for its bathing machines, as yet all too rare elsewhere. Lord Cockburn was to complain twenty years later of Ardossan that while there were all of three to be found at that popular resort, only one was ever in use, and two were stored in the back court of a local inn. Perhaps the problem was lack of demand, though that was to alter; or perhaps less in the way of cultural inhibitions, though as we shall see the proprieties of sea-bathing were to be the subject of much controversy.

Scottish resorts, therefore, had to rely on what might be called their natural attractions, as at Elie: fine sea air, a good beach, adequate accommodation, cheap provisions, agreeable walks in the vicinity, views and sights, and boats for aquatic excursions. A coffee room, music chamber and subscribing library were assets for wet days, as were covered baths. But even these did not guarantee success, as the experience of St Andrews showed. It appeared to Wade, with its fine sands and range of antiquities, to have everything necessary to attract visitors, summer and winter. There had been considerable investment in elegant baths and in suites of apartments intended for letting to the influx of 'company during the bathing season', but the uptake had been less than anticipated. Access was in his view the Achilles heel, for it lacked adequate coastal services and good roads. By contrast, what made places like Rothesay and Largs so popular was the steamboat service from Glasgow, to which Wade devoted a full section. Road transport also played its part in the visit to the 'sawt water', by coach, chaise, car and cart for the purpose of carrying 'papas, mammas, masters and misses to the chosen Watering Place'. Portobello and Leith were doing extremely well, thanks to their close proximity to Edinburgh. What Wade drew attention to was the growing addiction of the mercantile and professional classes – families, as he termed them, above the lower ranks – to a summer at the seaside for themselves and their families, but only at such a distance as allowed paterfamilias to return to his office and practice during the week. This might be on the Monday, as already seen on the Clyde, or even in the case of Edinburgh's resorts on a daily basis. According to Wade, this pattern was well established at Portobello:

> Hither oft, when summer is scarcely begun, does the professional or mercantile citizen of Edinburgh bring his family; here place them, and here after the fatigue of the day in the busy town is over, nightly rejoin them, deriving at once pleasure and health from his morning and evening walks between the two places.

It was to become, and still to some extent remains even today, a feature of the Scottish professional classes' way of life. Elie in Fife was described by one later nineteenth-century guide as 'Edinburgh by the sea', a title which it still retains. The summer exodus of the better-off became firmly established by the middle of the nineteenth century. 'There never was a city', remarked one writer of an article called 'Glasgow down the Water' in *Fraser's Magazine* in November 1856, 'whence the annual migration to the seaside is universal or so protracted as it is in Glasgow.' But, as Fife and East Lothian could attest, Edinburgh's well-to-do also moved out each summer.

The emphasis throughout Wade's work is on how it was the upper and professional classes – the genteel – who were colonising the seaside resorts. For them facilities were provided, accommodation built, property made available for rent. Even the clergy found summer letting profitable: the parish minister at Largs built himself a neat cottage, and rented out the manse from June onwards. Advertisements began to appear in the Scottish press for 'Sea-bathing quarters', which were clearly intended for whole households rather than individuals or couples. A farmhouse, with a parlour, three bedrooms, a nursery with four beds, and a kitchen, at Ascog on Bute was offered in July 1835 for rent at 25 shillings per week. Stabling for horses and carriages was also available if required. In terms all too familiar to the tourist trade, the delights of the property were talked up. Well-situated, it commanded delightful views across to the mainland, and a beach, 'which is admirably adapted for bathers', was less than five minutes' walk away. The same issue of *The Glasgow Herald* carried another advertisement for a five-bedroomed house at Fairlie, where the sea-bathing was good and '*retired*' (i.e. secluded), a variety of good walks was at hand, and a good steamer service was available to and from Glasgow. But the supply of holiday lodgings, reflecting increased demand, became increasingly geared to the provision of smaller and cheaper accommodation. In Helensburgh in 1834–5 more than half of the burgh's householders were willing 'for a consideration to take in lodgers and do for them'. The majority was not, however, single room [Table 3.1].

TABLE 3.1.   ROOMS FOR RENT AT HELENSBURGH, 1834–5.

Rooms per let	Number available	Rooms	Number available	Rooms	Number available
1	12	6	12	11	3
2	11	7	5	12	3
3	7	8	7	13	1
4	17	9	6	14	1
5	35	10	6		

Note. 126 households of a town total of 217 had rooms to let out.

Source: Donald Macleod, *A Nonagenarian's Reminiscences of Garelochead and Helensburgh* (Helensburgh, 1883), citing Fowler's *Helensburgh Directory*.

The prospects promoted resort development and the building of piers to allow steamer services at all states of the tide. At Hunter's Quay, near Dunoon, a jetty constructed by an enterprising merchant and local estate owner in 1828 led to the building of substantial villas in the vicinity as summer homes for the moneyed class of Glasgow. This development remained select and was chosen as the headquarters of the Royal Clyde Yacht Club. But not all resorts were as fortunate, for all their pretensions to elite status. The growth of tourism created tensions, strains which became so severe as to allow John Walton, the social historian, recently to call the seaside 'a crucible of conflict' between classes and lifestyles. There were disagreements within communities over who should pay for the provision of additional water and sewage facilities for the summer visitors. Hoteliers, lodging house and shopkeepers benefited, but why should other residents, particularly those retired or without any involvement in tourism, be held responsible? What about the growing problem of rowdyism, which was especially associated with the day-tripper or weekender? The growing numbers of working-class excursionists posed problems everywhere in Britain for communities which wanted to retain a respectable tone. The resorts of North Devon, for example, as Travis has shown, had their troubles with parties of miners from South Wales. A visitor to Torquay was shocked in August 1887 when a number of working-class men, who had just arrived by train, whisked off their trousers and ran like savages to the sea. Some visitors to the seaside were very well behaved and no trouble at all, such as those organised by Industrial or Sunday schools and other religious organisations. The philanthropist and temperance enthusiast John Hope organised several Juvenile Pleasure Excursions in the later 1840s, which involved hundreds of children aged 9 to 14, outings that were closely supervised and marked by the best behaviour. Several large parties, numbering three hundred or so, visited Stirling by special steamer from Fife each year in the early 1850s and there were no complaints about their conduct. But other outings were not as decorous, as the police and magistrates of many communities, coastal and inland, could attest.

Respectable Scottish society's sensibilities were liable to be offended in a number of ways, apart merely from the cheerful behaviour of the visiting masses. Three points of conflict stand out: the way in which some visitors flaunted the proper conventions of the beach, by mixed bathing and improper dress – or undress – the day-trippers' tendency to excessive drinking, and the growing indifference to Sunday observance, a particular flashpoint in Scotland. There was a vocal and powerful lobby for whom Sunday travel was unacceptable, and travel for pleasure even less so. People like Peter Drummond of Stirling conducted unabated campaigns against Sunday trips by coach or steamer, and others harried the railway companies.

It did not take long for the resorts to feel the impact of less restrained visitors. During the Glasgow Fair weekend – always a pressure point – in July 1852, steamers landed hundreds of visitors at Helensburgh, some in a state of 'beastly intoxication', many without lodgings, who then slept rough, and stripped off on the front to bathe without any modesty. The report agreed that people had to change somewhere, and that a sensible response would be to provide either some bathing machines or shelters. Similar reports came from elsewhere. In 1859 Jules Verne enjoyed a day at Portobello, though the water was, as ever, very cold. There were mobile beach huts there which carried mothers and misses alike some distance beyond the water's edge, the men bathing a short distance away. But what astonished Verne was that while he and his companion could hire a bathing machine, they were quite unable to procure a costume! Men bathed stark naked and then waded back to the beach, 'quite oblivious of the misses, mistresses and ladies on shore' (*Voyage en Angleterre et en Ecosse*, 1859). The French, in considerable embarrassment, backed into their changing hut. Portobello seems to have had a bad reputation. Cockburn said that it was the most immodest spot in Scotland, with the bathing machines where people changed far too close together for the women to be quartered at a respectable distance. Elsewhere, as at Ardrossan, he was critical of the practice of ladies changing after their bathe on the beach, shielded only by their maid's efforts:

> I never saw bathing performed by ladies in Scotland even with common decency. Why the devil can't they use bathing machines, or go into retired places, or wall or pale off enclosures?

Bathing for health was perfectly respectable. Bathing in the buff, though reckoned by some medical authorities to be the best way to benefit from a sea dip, was not acceptable to the new morality of Victorian Britain. But the question of what was respectable garb was a ticklish one. Resorts, or at least those with any pretensions to respectability, moved to tackle the problem of mixed bathing. In some places – in both Scotland and England – the answer, as at St Andrews, was separate beaches. The men were banished to the West Sands, and the ladies were given their own bathing place on the Castle Sands, complete with changing hut. North Berwick went for an alternative solution, that of separate times. In 1871 public notices were posted to regulate a proper segregation of the sexes: 'Gentlemen are requested to bathe before eight a.m. If after that hour, they must go to the West of the March wall, or east of the Mill Burn'. This prescription attracted objection: 'if we are clad in proper lineaments, should we not bathe en famille?', asked one critic. Millport went for a comprehensive solution in 1900. Bathing boxes had to be used at some bathing places, a list of male only beaches was set out, and it was sternly stipulated that 'no female persons shall bathe at any of the above places specified for male bathing'. But while burghs could pass regulations, how successful they were in enforcing them is doubtful. Mostly, one suspects, it was a matter of common sense. Unless the beach was very crowded, the males, if requested, would simply move. One party of English visitors went for a morning dip at Oban in 1868:

Just as we were prepared for a dive, some ladies sent a request we would remove a little further up to enable them to have a dip. We requested their patience for a few minutes, plunged in, soon dressed and left the ladies, who quickly followed our example. (Glasgow University Archives, Dougan 109, 'Tour in Scotland, Autumn 1868')

At South Queensferry, there was by the 1850s a clear understanding of who went where. Females and children had the full range of the beach, and gentlemen had to move off further afield. And to prevent any temptation, such as happened at Portobello, with what W.W. Fyfe called its 'almost promiscuous bathing' from machines in full view of spectators lounging on the sands, there were admirable facilities for undressing. At Rothesay *The Buteman Guide* recommended in the early 1880s that separate changing rooms be provided by the magistrates, something 'certainly necessary so long as men go into the water almost in a state of nudity, and the ladies in ugly bathing dresses which still obtain in this country'. The author looked forward, on both moral and aesthetic grounds, to the arrival of the American and Continental fashion of 'gay' costumes.

The conventions of bathing were one sensitive area. Another source of offence was the state of many of the weekend visitors or day trippers, whether arriving by train or by steamer. Nor was their return necessarily in any better condition. A day trip to Lochgoilhead in April 1861 ended in tragedy when drunken excursionists swamped the rowingboat which was trying to take them ashore at Govan: six drowned. But what concerned the resorts was what happened when the day-trippers arrived. The great fear in places like Dunoon and Helensburgh was that they would lose their respectable summer clientèle, their regulars who stayed for a week or longer and whose custom was steady. They would be driven away, it was thought, and once a resort lost its reputation there was no easy way to regain it. The Saturday excursion trade would ruin their tourism. There was no denying what tended to happen at any resort – inland or coastal – within reach of the parties from the cities or the mining communities. The correspondence columns of the Scottish press bore ample witness to the aggravation caused. A letter was published in *The Scotsman*, on 1 July 1872, allegedly from an Indian visitor, and dubbed by the sub-editor 'A Hindoo on Scotch Excursion Parties'. He had gone to Scotland to see the nature that produced Scott – Sir Walter Scott. 'I go to the Trossachs – I pass through a village of Callander on Saturday past. I see many persons in its streets, and many in a grass compound near to the station. There is no decency in their conduct. They speak loud – they stagger about – they are, or many of them are, drunk. I have been told that they are excursionists.' This experience was repeated in many other places, as at North Berwick in July 1873:

> Saturday after Saturday there are poured into the streets excursion parties, the members of which have no other idea of passing a holiday than of swilling strong liquor . . . the results are the beautiful links invaded by bands of shouting inebriates: pugilistic encounters at every corner, and our ordinary quiet streets converted into a miniature Donnybrook Fair.

Saturday visitors, with some justice, were all tarred with the same brush. The American Baptist J. H. Coghill travelled on a Saturday evening from Tarbet to Glasgow in September 1868 and disapprovingly observed that at every landing place:

> We took in large numbers of travellers, apparently mechanics and workmen who as I had learned had come down in the morning to spend the day. Every inch of the deck was occupied and apparently every other man was intoxicated. Singing, swearing and fighting were the favourite amusements, and we were glad to get away from such a crowd, at 7.30 p.m. Saturday is a bad day for travelling in the vicinity of Glasgow.
> (*Journal of a Tour Through Great Britain and the Continent*, New York, 1868)

But for all the unpleasantness resulting from some of the Saturday incursions, perhaps the effect was not too serious, but rather akin to living next to a football stadium with one or two lively crowds a year. What did begin to test the endurance of residents and the loyalty of their steady summer lodgers was when the Saturday excursions became more frequent, and the hold on Sunday travelling started to ease. Glasgow Fair holidays, which were beginning to lengthen from a weekend to a week or longer, were always the worst period. One party of English visitors staying at Oban in early August 1868 went to look at the ruins of Dunolly Castle, normally open three days a week. Ignoring various warning signs telling them not to trespass, they clambered over a dyke, only to be stopped by a gentleman whom they later found to be the owner, Captain McDougall. He was not pleased but cooled down when they admitted they were in the wrong, and apologised for the closure which had only been temporary. 'Glasgow Fair had lately been held and so many excursionists invaded the place causing all kinds of damage.' By way of compensation they got a personal tour of the old keep. The same group later encountered at Fort William a large party of 400 excursionists complete with their own brass band ('very bad'), not a few of whom had imbibed freely. They were cheerful and noisy but no more, but at the English party's request, the Captain of the Fort Augustus boat kept them at the front of the steamer, away from the rest of the passengers.

The growing use of Sundays for excursions was salt in the wounds of respectable Scotland, and the combination of excessive drink and abuse of the Sabbath was highly inflammatory. Sunday was always a bit of a problem for visitors, especially those from cultures and countries with a more relaxed approach. Some found sermon-tasting a perfectly enjoyable, educational and instructive way of passing the day. Churches at the resorts, particularly Episcopalian to which Anglicans might go, tended to have their best attendances during the summer season, engaging, if they could, a big-name or popular preacher, glad of a spell away from his city parish. Others were bored. The German traveller, Theodore Fontane, found a Sunday in Scotland 'like a thunderstorm at a picnic. You get wet, you can't go on, and all your humour vanishes'. Not all Scots were committed to a severe view of the Sabbath, and some sympathised with the needs of the working class to use what little free time they had as they wanted. One Rothesay minister, the Rev. Hutchison of St Brendan's Church, went as far in June 1897 as to say that he had not a word to say against Sunday steamers, Sunday golf and so on. He knew many fine young people serving in grocers' shops in Glasgow who were behind the counter all week and until midnight on Saturday 'to whom the Sunday steamer must be a blessing, and the golf too' (quoted in *The Clyde Programme. A Summer Paper for the West Coast.* 2nd year. Number 11, Week ending 12 June 1897). Most Scots, however, fell into line, some out of conviction, others from expediency, though it was a standing joke that scruples were liable to melt when a boatman or innkeeper met with an opportunity on a Sunday. But there was strong and protracted resistance to Sunday travel, whether on business or for pleasure – not entirely dead today – and this opposition was strengthened by legislation in the Forbes-Mackenzie Act of 1853. Intended to control drinking on a Sunday, it stipulated that only *bona fide* travellers could be sold alcohol. Quite how far someone had to travel was never decided, though there was a popular notion that three miles was the qualifying distance. But there could be no better way, or so some enterprising steamboat proprietors concluded, of complying with the act and satisfying the drouthy, than by running special Sunday excursions. Within a week of the legislation coming into force, the *Emperor* steamboat was put on the Clyde specifically to offer Sunday trading. Its first cruise on the 22nd of August from Glasgow to the Gareloch was met with firm resistance. The local landowner at Garelochhead had the pier barricaded with boxes, barrels and whatever else was at hand, and a pitched battle ensued, with coals, potatoes, and bottles flying. The locals were affronted; the more so as this all took place during divine worship and one lady onlooker, it was reported, fainted three times. There was eventually further legislation in 1882, the Passenger Vessels Licences (Scotland) Act, which put an end to Sunday sales, but there were always hip-flasks, and by that time the reputation of the west-coast Sunday excursionist was firmly fixed. It is no coincidence that in Glasgow patois even today, to be steaming is to be intoxicated.

The problem, or so contemporary opinion thought, was at its worst in the West, but was to be found elsewhere, as Fife and Stirling could attest. The small South Fife resort of Aberdour, for example, had also been in the firing line from the 1850s onwards for Sunday traffic, including sailings from Leith in the *Garibaldi*, a ship nicknamed the 'floating shebeen'. The Sabbath Observance Committee of the Free Church produced a report in 1867 which alleged that every Sunday saw hundreds of pleasure seekers landing in Aberdour, many of whom were in various stages of inebriation. Sceptics thought the report an exaggeration. Of course, some did drink en route, but the great majority of visitors were decent and sober, more likely to be found patronising Kinnaird's Tearoom than the Star or any other of Aberdour's hostelries. The issue of working-class behaviour did continue to cause concern:

> We lament to say that very many Scotch people of the working class seem incapable of enjoying a holiday without getting drunk and uproarious. We do not speak from hearsay but from what we have ourselves seen. Once or twice we have found ourselves on board a steamer crowded with a most disagreeable mob of intoxicate persons, amongst whom, we grieve to say we saw many women. The authorities of the vessel appeared entirely to lack both the power and the will to save respectable passengers from the insolence of the roughs.
>
> (Letter to *The Scotsman*, 15 July 1873)

Clearly there was no simple solution. Many of the smaller resorts lacked any police presence, and even if there had been any, one man was scarcely likely to be of much use. But matters do seem to have improved in the later nineteenth century. The Glasgow Fair of 1879 was marked by an unusual degree of decorum at Dunoon: 'both on shore and afloat there was a noticeable improvement in demeanour'. The provision of drinking fountains and other amenities may have helped, as perhaps did growing familiarity with the day out or holiday away. Time may simply have taken the edge off outrage, though stepping over the line as to what was deemed permissible on the Sunday invited criticism regardless of who was involved. A walk was just within bounds; boating, sailing or golf were desecration in the eyes of the purists. It is clear that the summer influx of working-class holidaymakers did not, as was feared, destroy the middle-class clientèle which resorts counted on and preferred. The July masses were an overlay which was tolerated and accepted. They wanted to attract and retain the custom of the more affluent, longer-stay visitor in preference to the day-tripper, who often stayed long enough only to create a nuisance. To be forced to rely on casual working-class tourism was quite literally in economic terms the last resort. Loyalty to the same locality was not a preserve of the better-off; Cronin has drawn attention to the way that a Mrs Colville *c* 1908 was letting one room in her Mill Row tenement in Campbeltown to the same Glasgow family of four every year during Fair Week. This was no doubt unremarkable. Truly extraordinary, however, is that her eleven children, plus father, decamped to the kitchen for the week.

Portobello was perhaps a lost cause, given its proximity to Edinburgh. One observer thought it shaded even Rothesay on Fair Saturday. An onlooker (*The Clyde Programme*, 13 August 1898) reported that he had been there during the Edinburgh holiday, and a tougher crowd he had never seen. The sight of fat women buckling up their skirts and petticoats, and waddling in the waves was 'gruesome, sir, gruesome'. Some resorts remained elite and exclusive throughout the summer, with little or no excursionism to trouble their order and social programme. Into this category would fall places like Elie in Fife, Nairn and North Berwick. Others would change character at weekends and during the holiday season for works and factories in July and early August. An interesting indicator of respectability is the Lists of Visitors published during the season in the local press on a weekly or monthly basis for many Scottish resorts in the later nineteenth century. They relate only to those in residence for some time, usually a minimum of a week, and exclude therefore the day-tripper or weekend excursionist. The names, said the editor of *The Haddington Courier*, are not those of casual visitors, but those 'parties who have taken up residence for the season or part of it'. This practice, which had originated at the English spas in the eighteenth century, and was quite widespread at the more fashionable resorts in Britain and the Continent, not only sold local newspapers but had a number of other functions as well. The first was that of information: to act as a kind of summer directory, to let people in the locality know who was staying where and to encourage those thinking of coming with the news that they would find friends and acquaintances on arrival. The list acted also as a social register to help with the planning of visits and events. It was a medium of advertising: local tradesmen would look up the list for new arrivals to whom they could send their card to invite custom. Social climbers sought inclusion:

> It is an historical event for the Bugginses of Peckham to be commemorated in the same type and on the same sheet as marchionesses and earls, and you can be sure that several copies are dispatched by post to dazzle friends in the country while another two pence is spent on procuring one for preservation in the family archives at home
>
> (*The Saturday Review*, 11 October 1873)

The lists could be abused. Some found it amusing to send in false entries for the unwary editor to publish. Newly-weds acquired families, bachelors wives, and servants became guests. The format was not always consistent, and all too often the detail was lacking or incomplete. Nor was their collection always reliable. Forms for completion were distributed to the hotels, lodging-houses and house-tenants themselves but in some places it was left up to them to return the completed slips. When the newspapers sent round a lad, the level of return was much higher. At best, the entries, grouped by where people were staying, listed all the members of a family or group, said how many servants there were, and of what kind – nurse or governess, for example – where they came from, and gave some indication of occupation or profession. Ministers stand out, but the frequency with which the Kintyre lists in the later 1880s include 'artists' is striking: William MacTaggart, McGregor Wilson and Wellwood Rattray were part of a colony there, one of several on the West Coast. *The Helensburgh and Gareloch Times* noted in August 1881 that there were a considerable number of artists at Kilcreggan touching up the various studies they intended to forward to the approaching exhibitions at Glasgow. At Corrie on Arran, some little huts had been observed in the hills amidst the heather. Enquiries revealed that some London artists, including Mr. John Pettie, had fixed themselves up there for the season.

The value of these lists to the historian of tourism in the second half of the nineteenth century is considerable. At their best they show how many visitors there were, their status and background, what distance they had come, the duration of stay, fluctuations over the summer season, and from year to year. In an important study Jennifer Watson has shown what can be done with the data. She has examined the lists for Dunoon as published in the local paper – *The Dunoon Herald and Cowal Advertiser* – over the period 1876 to 1914, focusing on the third week of August. After making due allowance for the common tag 'and family', the numbers of visitors staying were never fewer than the 421 in 1883. For several years the lists pointed to a visiting population well over the thousand mark, with the highpoint being 1421 in 1900, an astonishing figure, given the town's resident population of 6472 in March 1901. Some variations may simply have been due to the care with which the lists were compiled, but others can be tied to factors such as the weather: 1883 was a poor damp year and the effects were felt widely, as we shall see. Watson has also examined visitors' addresses to see whether Dunoon's catchment area was regional or national. The results are consistent: roughly half came from Glasgow but one fifth from England, with a few from further afield – Ireland, the Continent and the Colonies. Comparisons have yet to be made, but the proportion of English visitors for somewhere like North Berwick might be much higher and does show a marked increase in the later nineteenth century. The largest single contingent at the Marine and Royal Hotels there in September 1881 was from England, with Scottish addresses in a distinct minority:

TABLE 3.2.   VISITORS RESIDENT IN DUNOON, AUGUST 1880–1900, percentages from various parts.

Year	Glasgow	Clydeside	Scotland Other	Britain	Europe	Other	Not given
1880	47	7	15	21	1	2	6
1885	43	14	14	18	1	3	5
1890	52	14	17	6	2	2	9
1895	52	15	14	14	1	2	3
1900	49	20	14	14	[0.3]	[0.6]	2

These lists, some more complete than others, exist for a dozen or so inland localities – Grantown-on-Spey, Crieff and Moffat, for example – and a further fifteen to twenty Scottish coastal resorts including, in East Lothian, Dunbar and North Berwick; in Fife, Elie and Earlsferry, Pittenweem, Largo and Crail; on the Moray Forth, Lossiemouth and Nairn; in the West, Dunoon, Helensburgh, Rothesay and Campbeltown. It is not surprising that Portobello does not feature in this roll call, as it was by this period very much a day-trippers' resort, and very much looked down upon by some. The compiler of the North Berwick list for mid-August 1870 remarked that it would be understood that the 'names are not those of casual visitors but those parties who have taken up residence for the season, or part of it'. Oban's appearance is rather more intriguing, as it was a place that people tended to pass through, hence its nickname 'The Charing Cross of the Highlands'. In 1865 Alexander Smith said of it that:

> a more hurried, nervous, frenzied place than Oban during the summer and autumn months it is difficult to conceive. People seldom stay there above a night. The old familiar faces are the resident population. The tourist no more thinks of spending a week in Oban than he thinks of spending a week in a railway station. When he arrives, his first question is after a bedroom; his second as to the hour at which the steamer from the south is expected.

> (*A Summer in Skye*, Edinburgh 1865)

Yet a local publisher of guides and timetables, Thomas Boyd, thought it worth his while in the late 1880s to prepare a register of Oban Visitors, which appeared weekly during the summer. The register, which cost one penny, carried advertising for local tours and excursions, for whisky and mineral waters, fishing and yachting supplies, and information about what to see in the vicinity. There was a large hotel population, of over 900 in the principal establishments, much of which was transient, and the addresses given show that the visitors were from every part of Britain, with quite a number of Americans and Continentals also present. Truly, as Smith observed, all kinds of pleasure seekers were to be found in the town or passing through: sportsmen, reading parties from Oxford, elegant ladies and military men:

> Sportsmen in knickerbockers stand in groups at their hotel doors: Frenchmen chatter and shrug their shoulders; stolid Germans smoke curiously curved meerschaum pipes, and individuals who have not a drop of Highland blood in their veins flutter about in the garb of the Gael.

But, as the register makes clear, as does its counterpart for Rothesay, there were those who were in residence for a month or longer during the summer at a villa or in a lodging-house, of which there were over one hundred and twenty. The Tarbets, a family of seven from Liverpool, arrived at the beginning of August 1890 and were still in residence at Albion Villa at the end of September. The presence of a summer community even in resorts which were not exclusive in the way that some were, or wished themselves to be, is a check to the labelling of some places as merely mass or popular. They were at times, perhaps, but not all season.

What the lists do confirm is the degree of loyalty shown by visitors, many of whom seem to have come back season after season; some of them started by renting and graduated to ownership of a summer retreat. Mr George Blanchard, a wine merchant from Leith, first brought his family to North Berwick in 1863, and they returned every summer for the next ten years. The Ford household was to be found at Ebenezer Villa every July and August from 1876 to 1885. At Dunoon, Colonel Bouverie-Campbell and party from Winchester were in residence at Glengarr, Bullwood each summer from 1887 to 1898. The same pattern can be found everywhere in Scotland. Though the summer season was always busy for the railway companies, it was the changeover days at the end of each month, with some arriving and others departing, that stretched resources to the full, despite additional seasonal staff. It was not just the number of families in transit but their piles of luggage, sporting equipment and pets. North Berwick station was busy all day, the local newspaper reported, with the 'arrival of ladies, ladies' maids, pretty children, pet poodles, and the miscellaneous impedimenta by which a sojourn at the seaside is nowadays rendered additionally pleasant'. The station was allowed an additional guard, porter and parcels deliverer, but even then they could not cope; one newly arrived girl complained that their luggage had not come from the station for ages, and 'father had had to go up to the station about it'. Other resorts had exactly the same difficulty. Passenger receipts at Elie for the late 1880s and early 1890s show the impact of summer travel. They averaged between £40 and £50 a month off-season but leapt to £150 to £250 or more in the three months from July, with daily receipts notably at their highest at the end of the month. For the railway companies, shopkeepers, hoteliers and others the problem was what happened after the season ended. 'We must all take our homeward way, nor after August longer stay.' The late autumn and winter months were lean ones indeed, and in the view of many locals not just quiet but empty. As *The East of Fife Record* observed on 4 October 1872: 'The summer visitors almost all have left for their respective homes, and Elie and Earlsferry have again assumed their dull ordinary aspect'.

The picture of the Scottish seaside in the later nineteenth century is a healthy one for the resorts and those who visited them. Most would have been known at the beginning of the century, but a few others, thanks to better transport, did make an appearance. The Hotel at Uig on Skye, with its sea-views, boating and fishing, was billing itself in the later 1880s as a new summer and health resort, the 'future Brighton of the West'. Others which had made a promising beginning, such as Broughty Ferry, failed to develop as much as might have been anticipated: 'it is a place by the sea, but not what I would call a summer resort', was one judgement in 1913. Some resorts catered for a mixed clientèle, others remained more exclusive, and this was reflected in the range of attractions they offered. Some had piers, to which large numbers of holidaymakers were daily drawn, which offered facilities to concert entertainers, swimmers, fishermen, and promenaders, and a place to watch steamer arrivals and departures. The special holiday granted in 1871 to celebrate the centenary of Sir Walter Scott's birth brought no fewer than 2,500 to pay their one penny admittance charge to the newly opened Portobello Pier. Bandstands, gardens, swimming pools, bowling and putting greens, with libraries and reading rooms for wet days, added to the resorts' natural attractions, and travelling entertainers, bands and dancing bears made their appearance. Sandcastle competitions attracted and diverted the young, as did exploring rock pools and catching crabs. And almost everywhere in Scotland, the appeal of the coast was complemented by that of the links – and above all golf. 'There is one thing we all do', said a visitor to Elie in 1873. 'We golf.' 'What is there to do at North Berwick?', asked one Glaswegian who in 1881 had found it otherwise rather dull, lacking as it then did a band and some of the other facilities deemed essential in the West. 'The reply is easy, and a single word explains all – golf.' It was a potent and distinctive part of the Scottish seaside resorts' range of attractions, but especially those on the East and North-East coasts. For many visitors, particularly the better off, the control and respectability of a place like Nairn was what they wanted:

And in the summer season, it's a very popular place
And the visitors from London and Edinburgh find solace,
As they walk along the yellow sand inhaling fresh air;
Beside there's every accommodation for ladies and gentlemen
    there.
Then there's a large number of bathing coaches there,
And the climate is salubrious, and very warm the air,

And every convenience is within the bathers' reach,
Besides there's very beautiful walks by the seas beach.
And there's ornamental grounds, and lovely shady nooks,
Which is a great advantage to visitors while reading their books;
And there's a certain place known as the Ladies' beach,
So private that no intruder can them reach.
And there's many neat cottages with gardens very nice,
And picturesque villas, which can be rented at a reasonable price;
Besides, there's a golf course for those that such a game seeks,
Which would prove a great attraction to the knights of clubs and
    cleeks.

William McGonagall, *More Poetic Gems*
(Dundee, 1976 edition; originally *c.* 1880)

FURTHER READING

John Walton, 'The Demand for Working Class Seaside Holidays in Victorian England', *Economic History Review*, May 1981; and *The English Seaside Resort: A Social History, 1750–1914* (Leicester, 1983), Ch. 8, 'Styles of holidaymaking: Conflict and Resolution'. John Travis, *The Rise of the Devon Seaside Resorts, 1750–1900* (Exeter, 1993), 120–121. W.M. Wade, *Delineations, Historical, Topographical, and Descriptive of the Watering and Sea-Bathing Places of Scotland* (Paisley, 1822). According to the title page, Wade had written two previous tourist guides: *Walks in Oxford* (Oxford, 1817), and *A Tour of Modern, and Peep into Ancient Glasgow* (Glasgow, 1822). J. Verne, *Backwards to Britain* (Edinburgh, 1922) was originally entitled *Voyage en Angleterre*. Verne had Scots ancestry and based a number of his novels in Scottish settings. W.W. Fyfe, *Summer Life on Land and Water At South Queensferry* (Edinburgh, 1852), Ch. 3, 'Bathing'. Fyfe urged the construction of public baths – warm, tepid, cold, shower and plunge, in connection with a reading and promenade room, as at Moffat spa. Irina Lindsay, *Dressing and Undressing for the Beach* (Hornchurch, 1983). A.J. Durie, 'The Development of Scottish Coastal resorts in the Central Lowlands, *c.* 1770–1870', *The Local Historian*, xxiv, No. 4 (1994) pp. 206–216.

J.E. Cronin, 'The development of Tourism in Kintyre', Glasgow University Undergraduate dissertation, 1993–4. A.J. Durie, 'The better-off tourist in Victorian Scotland. The value of Visitors' Lists', *The Scottish Local Historian*, 26 July 1992, pp. 26–27. J. Watson, 'The development of Tourism in Dunoon, *c.* 1800–1914', University of Glasgow, Honours Dissertation in Economic History, 1996. John M. Stewart, 'The Architectural Development of Portobello in the early 19th century', Portobello District Local History Society, 1990, pp. 5–12. A typical publication laying emphasis on the therapeutic value of the seaside is *Sea-Air and Sea-Bathing*, Ward Lock's Long Life Series (London, *c.* 1880). On this development in a European context, see Alain Corbin, *The Lure of the Sea: The Discovery of the Seaside* (Penguin, 1994), especially Chs. 3 and 11.

4

THE SEARCH FOR HEALTH

The whole land frae Maiden-kirk to John O' Groats is one great
Health Resort for summer.
(Dr Thomson, *The Health resorts of Britain*
and How to profit by Them (London, 1860))

We now turn to an important ingredient of Victorian tourism, namely
the search for health, either by way of a cure or at least a tonic to the
system for those feeling jaded. Health was a very important part of the
impulse behind travel and tourism. Some travelled, as had been the
practice for many centuries, either to recuperate or to seek a cure at a
place of healing; others to find a climate better suited to their needs, or
to enjoy the tonic of new surroundings, scenery, and company.
Scotland became a major centre for those who needed their health
and their spirits revived. Some stayed at one of the many Scottish
resorts and localities recommended as healthy, thanks to their climate
and air; others received treatment at spas, of which Scotland had a
few, though only Strathpeffer could rival the competition elsewhere in
Europe. Hydropathic establishments and their 'water cure', as at
Peebles, Crieff and Rothesay, drew an increasing number of visitors.
And, of course, there was the therapy of a change of air and exercise;
activities such as golf, fishing and grouse shooting were central
elements in the promotion and perception of 'Scotland for health'.

In 1885 the then Professor of Therapeutics at the University of
Glasgow, M. Charteris, wrote a *Guide to Health Resorts at Home and*
Abroad in which he identified three principal kinds of resort in Britain
and on the Continent. There were *sea-bathing* health resorts, including
Blackpool, Brighton, Bilbao and Trouville-sur-Mer. Sea-bathing, or
dipping, had a long pedigree in Scotland as a therapeutic instrument.
The ailing and debilitated Robert Burns was advised by his medical
friends in July 1795 to visit the sea-bathing station at Brow on the
Solway. It relieved his rheumatism, but did nothing for his general
health, and indeed may have hastened his death. Others were more
fortunate, as the growing popularity of the coast confirms. Whether
for the bathing, or the sea-air, the seaside could not be rivalled for its
benefits to young and old, or so many Victorians thought; 'much
health, comfort and amusement are to be picked up in a three or four

weeks' residence', one authority concluded. But even the day-trip had its positive effect, while the value of a longer stay for those recovering from illness or surgery was recognised by the foundation of quite a number of seaside convalescent homes.

In Charteris' next category were what he called *climatic* health resorts such as Bournemouth, Cannes, Davos and Torquay, where what mattered most was good fresh and clean air, not too much wind, a mild climate and a steady temperature. In Scotland, Rothesay, with its gentle winters, was one such resort. A Dr. Morison, who arrived on the island in 1808, is credited with making known the virtues for all seasons of the local climate. By the 1830s, when a good sulphuretted spring had been brought into use, Bute was being frequented by 'consumptive invalids' as an alternative to travelling to the Continent. Other places which made much of their advantages of climate included the Upper Ward of Lanarkshire, West Aberdeenshire, and Speyside, which by the later nineteenth century had a distinct reputation as a healthy district. It was described by a local guidebook (*Romantic Badenoch*, 1909) as well suited to be the sanatorium of Scotland. Pitlochry had its supporters. It was after all recommended by no less than Queen Victoria's physician, Sir James Clarke, who prescribed a period of residence there as a cure to a number of his patients. Endorsements from people of his standing mattered. Health was big business; and specialist publications like *The Holiday Whitaker: A Guide to the Holiday and Health Resorts of the United Kingdom* (1908 edition) were much thumbed, listing as they did essential details on the climate, drainage, temperature, water supply and so on. Nairn was particularly praised, being dubbed – bizarrely – the Stonehenge of Scotland, 'enjoying as it does an exceptionally dry and bracing climate (beneficial for lung diseases), very low rainfall and excellent facilities for sea-bathing'. It was thought to be an ideal resort for 'overwrought brain workers' and convalescents: Fortescue Fox recommended it with its dry climate and invigorating air as ideally suited for a period of 'after-cure' following a stay at Strathpeffer Spa.

In Charteris' third category were places where an additional *curative* dimension was added. This might be through special diets often based on goat or cow's whey as at Gais in Switzerland. Good quarters for the drinking of goat's whey were being advertised at Brodick on Arran as early as 1759. Callander, Blairlogie (near Stirling) and Moffat were other centres for this particular enthusiasm, which was quite widespread. Elizabeth Diggle noted in June 1788 of Dunkeld that

People come into this neighbourhood to drink goats' whey and ride on horseback for their health, here are pretty good accommodations at a house prettily situated on the other side of the river for such temporary inhabitants & such summer lodgings are advertised in various parts of the Highlands.

Another form of cure, one which could trace its origins to pre-Christian times, was the use of salt, spring or mineral water, for washing, bathing or drinking. In some places the taking of the waters, and associated routines, became the raison d'être of a spa resort, and because the treatment was not miraculous, as it had been in medieval times, but scientific and took time to work, local interests acted to provide not just accommodation for visitors but a culture of entertainment and amusement. Amongst the best known of the many Continental spas by the later nineteenth century were Baden-Baden, Carlsberg, Vichy and Monte Carlo, with their casinos and racetracks. Tens of thousands of British visitors went each year across the Channel, some to escape the British winter, others to take the waters and enjoy the life of these resorts. They might go for specific ailments such as gout, tuberculosis, rheumatism or bronchitis, or for a general rest and tonic. Many benefited, such as Robert Louis Stevenson, but there were exceptions: Eric Simpson has drawn attention to the number of graves in the so-called English section of the Old Cemetery at Mentone. The twenty-two-year-old Andrew Faill, son of a businessman, who died in 1890, is but one of a number of Scots to be found there. The oldest spa in England was at Bath, but other major centres included Buxton, Cheltenham and Malvern: Hembry has identified over one hundred either founded or enlarged between 1700 and 1815. There developed on the Continent in the 1820s and 1830s a new and popular water-based therapy, the brainchild of an Austrian peasant, one Vincent Priessnitz, a therapist without any medical training whatsoever. His system involved a range of water-based treatments, including wrapping patients in cold wet sheets, sweating them, plunging and soaking them. It was demanding, but less harsh than many of the remedies of orthodox medicine, and as effective, or so many thought. Hydropathy came to Britain in the early 1840s, to Malvern, Ben Rydding and a number of other places, and took root nowhere deeper than in Scotland. The large purpose-built hydropathic establishment, as at Crieff or Peebles or Pitlochry, became a feature of the Scottish landscape, catering for a moneyed and respectable clientèle.

It is surprising that the spa movement never achieved the same degree of success in Scotland as hydropathy, with which there was a substantial overlap. There were plenty of mineral wells, some sulphurous (or 'stinking'), others saline or chalybeate ('iron'), but, despite attempts, few developed commercially to more than minor spa status. The distinguished chemist, Dr Francis Home, was engaged in 1751 to analyse the waters at a well in Duns, which seemed to him to be of proven value for stomach complaints: one local lady, Mrs. Murdoch of Ayton, was drinking a bottle each morning. But neither Duns nor Dunblane nor Pannanich near Ballater, nor a dozen other springs, made the transition to a wider clientèle, though St Ronan's Well at Innerleithen at least achieved recognition by Scott in a novel. Pitkeathly at Bridge of Earn near Perth did establish itself on a modest scale by the early nineteenth century, with some thirty beds available locally at the estate mansion-house for visitors. This business was eventually bought over by Schweppes in 1919, who sold bottled table water from there as a 'healthful and agreeable diluent for wines and spirits', a commercial venture then being currently emulated in a number of places. The overall picture, as one observer writing in *Blackwoods Magazine* in September 1862 argued, was not encouraging: 'Somehow', he said, 'the Scottish spas have failed in attracting that class of visitors who in the summer season congregate so thickly at the famous baths of Germany'. He blamed this in part on the calibre, or lack of it, of the Scottish waters, but levelled his sharpest criticism at the 'utter vileness' of Scottish cookery.

There were three Scottish spas that rose above the general run: Moffat, Strathpeffer, and Bridge of Allan. For a long period Moffat in the Scottish Borders was the foremost. A mineral well had been discovered there in the early seventeenth century. A favourable analysis of the medical waters, said to be as powerful in purging as those of Scarborough, was published by Dr Plummer, Secretary to the Philosophical Society of Edinburgh, which led to increased patronage by gentry such as Sir John Clerk of Penicuik, who complained in 1748 that:

> As the well is quite open day and night, there is a number of diseased, scrofulous, leprous people lying about it who seem to be waiting for an opportunity to wash their sores unseen by the two keepers.

Things were tightened up, better accommodation was built, the facilities were enlarged and Moffat became a highly successful health resort, much visited during the summer vacation of the law courts at

Edinburgh. But as well as its clientèle drawn from the better-off in society, there were also some whose stay was paid by charitable funds and bodies. The Town Council of Stirling provided five shillings through their Cowane's Trust to allow a Margaret Stirling, the daughter of a local blacksmith, to travel 'to Moffat Wells for recovering her health' in March 1755. The treatment does not seem to have helped as she was still on their books for charitable relief in the following year. Important to its development was the support of the local landowner, the Duke of Buccleuch and Queensberry, who himself, or so it appears, preferred to take the waters at Bath! He made a proper road to the newly discovered Hartfell springs and erected a building to cover them so that patrons could take the waters under shelter. In the 1760s, Lord Hopetoun, another Scottish noble who himself patronised an English spa, this time at Buxton, had two inns built to provide very superior accommodation for the class of invalid whom he hoped to attract to Moffat. The outcome was satisfactory: a painting by David Allan of the Mineral Well in 1795 shows several well-dressed parties at the wellhouse: one purchasing his draught, another quaffing his glass and a third having his leg washed. Mawman in 1805 estimated that there were no fewer than two hundred and fifty invalids in the burgh for the air and the waters. Moffat continued to expand in the nineteenth century, thanks in part to the railway, with the four-times-a-day omnibuses from the Caledonian Railway's Beattock Station absolutely packed in high season, and visitors being turned away for lack of lodgings, or so the *Whitehaven Herald* reported in 1857. A branch line to Moffat was later opened on 2nd April 1883 at a cost of £22,000. Its Baths Company advertised hard at Torquay and other English resorts, stressing Moffat's appeal as a watering-place to the 'gay lounger, the fashionable invalid, and the tourist and idler'! In addition to the 'Scotch service', an Episcopalian clergyman was available to minister to English visitors of the Anglican persuasion. During June, July and August the town was full: it was generally reckoned, and with some justice, that there were as many visitors as residents during the summer. On offer, as there had to be, given the seasonal growth in this community of just over 2,000 according to the 1871 census (see Table 4.1), was an ever-expanding range of summer accommodation. There were numerous apartments and cottage parlours, whole villas and big houses, as well as rooms at the Star, Annandale and other hotels, to which was added a large hydropathic establishment opened in 1878.

TABLE 4.1. NUMBER OF VISITORS RESIDENT AT MOFFAT IN THE MIDDLE OF
           AUGUST, 1866–69, 1872–78.

Year	Number	Year	Number
1866	1177	1873	1575
1867	1072	1874	1539
1868	1078	1875	1632
1869	1159	1876	1689
****	****	1877	1722
1872	1535	1878	2149

Source: Fairfoul's Guide to Moffat (2nd edition, Moffat, 1879), p.12.

There was also a full portfolio of attractions, walks and excursions.
New churches were built in the 1860s, such as the United Presbyterian, existing ones were enlarged, and for the Episcopalians – or
Anglicans from England on holiday – services were held 'every
Sabbath during the visiting season'. To occupy and amuse the visitor
on both good and wet days there was the pumproom, which doubled
as a concert hall and ballroom, baths, a circulating library, shops, a
bowling green, croquet grounds and a band, the last a requirement for
any spa. It is clear that Moffat catered for quite a varied clientèle, not
all of whom were wealthy. The tariff in 1870 for drinking at the well
was 6d per week for Ladies and Gentlemen, but half that rate for
tradespeople of Moffat, servants and labourers. But by the later
nineteenth century the town was attracting fewer people who were
ill, and more who merely enjoyed the place as a holiday centre. There
were still those who came to quaff the waters, either bottled and
delivered to their lodgings, or in person at the well, up to four or five
tumblers – a quart each – at a time, with perhaps several visits in the
day. But the old emphasis on cure was fading in favour of a tonic to
the system:

> Of the company at the well, many can certainly be seen drinking
> there for health, some in the period but not the bloom of youth,
> struggling to attain to miserable age; others already old making
> the vain attempt to renew their youth. But the majority are
> manifestly drinking for pleasure, and are by no means of the
> invalid class.
> (William Wallace Fyfe, A Guide to the Scottish Watering Places:
> A Visit to Moffat, Its Spas and Neighbourhood (Edinburgh
> 1853), p.30)

Moffat's visitors were mainly drawn from Central Scotland, with only
about one-fifth from further afield, and those mostly from the North
of England. By contrast the most northerly of Scotland's spas, Strath-

peffer, came to attract support from much greater distances. It was already well known by the later eighteenth century, and there had been various attempts in the early nineteenth century to further exploit its waters: a wooden pump room had been built in 1819. When visitors first arrived, they signed the book at the counter, and paid 2/- a week for the waters and the services of an attendant. As elsewhere, the poor were not charged, a tradition carried on for many years. In the 1890s paupers, providing they could produce supporting certificates from the minister and medical officer of their parish, were supplied gratis: it is not clear how they were able to finance either their travel or their accommodation. According to *The Aberdeen Journal* of 11 August 1819, the list of company at the wells numbered just over a hundred, the great majority from the North of Scotland. Six weeks was recommended as the minimum period of stay, with a regime of early to rise and early to bed; three or four tumblers in the morning, a like quantity in the afternoon, and one by way of nightcap. But things stagnated thereafter, and the spa was neither a commercial success nor looked like becoming so. It was the Duke of Sutherland who was to set in train the transformation of Strathpeffer by embarking in the 1860s on a major programme of investment. The local agent, who was not enthusiastic, remarked that

> A sum of about £2,500 is to be laid out on the pump room, and in building a wellkeeper's house, and a set of shops and a post office and postmaster's dwelling house. Building is rather a hobby of the young Duke's as it was of his Father. It is less foolish than gambling or racing.
> (Cited in Eric Richards and Monica Clough, *Cromartie Highland Life, 1650–1914* (Aberdeen, 1989), 'Strathpeffer Spa', pp. 269–283)

Spas required investment in facilities and promotion in what was a highly competitive market, and were under threat from established Continental, English and Welsh rivals. A German chemist was brought in to give his endorsement of the medical quality of the waters, new springs were found, local treatments provided such as Peat and Pine Baths and massage, a pavilion and Ladies' baths were built, and walks and sporting facilities were provided. By the mid-1880s, when the railway reached Strathpeffer by a branch line from Dingwall, it was firmly established as a spa of some reputation ('the Harrogate of Scotland'). It had some sixty lodging houses, about a third of which were small private hotels with over ten bedrooms and inside toilets. There were high-quality hotels, able to attract the

English invalid, such as the Spa Hotel, complete with Hungarian Band, which called itself 'The Sporting Hotel of the Highlands' (*Black's,* 1882 edition). Its guests were offered shooting, fishing, boating and tennis, and it even catered for the apprentice bicyclist, with a professional available to give lessons. But the best, or so visitors thought, was the Ben Wyvis, a handsome building opened in 1879 at which Robert Louis Stevenson stayed the following summer. Though he liked the surrounding country, he was not enthused by Strathpeffer, 'a beastlyish place, near delightful places, but inhabited alas by a wholly bestial crowd'. It was the company, and its invalid state, that irritated him most:

ON SOME GHASTLY COMPANIONS AT A SPA
That was an evil day when I/To Strathpeffer drew anigh
For there I found no human soul,/But ogres occupied the whole
They had at first a human air/In coats and flannel underwear
They rose and walked upon their feet/And filled their bellies full
    of meat
They wiped their lips when they had done -/But they were ogres
    every one;
Each issuing from his secret bower./I marked them in the
    morning hour.
By limp and totter, list and droop,/I singled each one from the
    group
I knew them all as they went by -/I knew them by their blasted
    eye!
(*R.L. Stevenson's Letters to Charles Baxter*, edited by DeLancey
Ferguson and Marshall Waingrow (London, 1973), p.79)

Others were much more enthusiastic. The veteran Scottish minister, Dr Boyd, spent two successive summers in the early 1890s at Strathpeffer as a visiting preacher, times that he greatly enjoyed. He and his wife stayed at the Spa Hotel, which he described as 'homelike', with about 130 in residence, 'amongst whom were many especially pleasant people, mainly from England', including quite a number of Anglican clergy. What he enjoyed was the routine, the company and the countryside, the last surveyed from a unique boat-carriage, a coach which could be lifted from its wheels and launched on lochans or rivers:

Each morning, early, the piper of the establishment was heard in the distance approaching: and in a little the piercing sound went round and round the house effectually waking all sleepers. At 7

AM the handsome omnibus was at the door, to carry all comers down to drink the awful water, and to undergo various baths. Everything looked thriving. The horses were plump and handsome. The driver was as intelligent and obliging a man as you could easily see. One pleasant feature of that great hotel was that you were waited upon at table by bright pretty young women, so neat and trim in dress that it was a pleasure to look at them. They were all girls of the surrounding country: patterns of good behaviour, and the gentle refined Celtic voice was always there. (A.K.H.Boyd, *The Last Years at St Andrews* (London, 1896))

The treatments, or so publicists insisted, did work. Dr. Fortescue Fox, a leading spa specialist and enthusiast, published an illustrated guide to the spa in 1889 and included by way of encouragement a list of fifteen recent cases where recovery had been seen. The patients ranged in age from 17 to 71, suffered from conditions such as eczema, gout or rheumatism, and stayed between two weeks and two months, some returning subsequently for further courses of preventative treatment. Spa treatment was helpful rather than severe, and spa society sufficiently pleasant for an annual visit to become addictive. A representative case was that of a forty-five-year-old lady, who had returned home from tropical South America in ailing health:

Subject to recurring internal chills, diarrhoea, and general weakness. She was stout, very anaemic, nervous with frequent indigestion, headaches and flying pains. For nearly four weeks this lady took the Chalybeate, usually hot, and latterly to the extent of forty-five ounces daily. With this were combined occasional Douches, Sulphur Baths, and Massage, which contributed to a striking improvement in nervous, muscular and digestive tone. (Fox, *Strathpeffer Spa*, 'Illustrative Cases', p.87)

Its northern location, and the cost of travel, kept Strathpeffer exclusive, and of all the Scottish spas, it alone attracted and retained a superior clientèle, as the lists of visitors published each Friday in the *Ross-shire Journal* confirm. Quite what the death in early August 1912 – due, it was said, to a chill caught on his journey north – at the Ben Wyvis Hotel of Sir Joseph Dinsdale, former M.P. and ex-Lord Mayor of London, did for Strathpeffer's reputation as a health resort is uncertain. But it did show what kind of person came. Indeed, in 1911 the Highland Railway built its own hotel at Strathpeffer, and a weekly service – the Strathpeffer Spa Express – was run every Tuesday during the summer, with through coaches from London. The journey had taken seventeen hours in the mid-1880s but was shortened by the opening of the Forth Railway Bridge in 1890 to a still taxing but not unmanageable fourteen by 1910. The great problem for Strathpeffer, and for all northern resorts, was that its season lasted only from May to September or October. Attempts were made to promote Strathpeffer as a 'Bracing Winter Resort' to rival the Swiss but with little success. A small meteorological station set up locally to monitor the weather did do its best to provide helpful evidence as to how mild, dry and relatively fog- and frost-free the climate was – better than Cambridge or London or Buxton – but southern customers were not convinced. And some critics found Strathpeffer dull. Dr Charteris – himself a Scot – described it as a place which presented only the 'sterner features of austere country life, the gossip on the arrival of the trains, and demure questionings as to the nationality and pedigree of fresh visitors'.

TABLE 4.2. VISITORS IN RESIDENCE AT BRIDGE OF ALLAN, 1865–1905

[end of each month]

	Jan	Feb	Mar	Apr	May	June	July	Aug	Sept	Oct	Nov	Dec
1865	150	150	200	500	800	650	500	500	650	550	250	250
1875	350	450	550	800	900	600	550	600	680	660	450	350
1885	250	400	300	700	800	550	400	700	600	450	330	300
1895	250	350	300	680	550	380	350	380	370	350	200	190
1905	275	150	230	300	310	250	250	200	250	250	200	190

Source: A. J. Durie, 'Bridge of Allan: "Queen of Scottish Spas": Its Nineteenth Century Development as a Health Resort', *Forth Naturalist and Historian*, Vol. 16, 1994, p.103.

The rise of Bridge of Allan in Central Scotland is one of the great success stories of Scottish tourism. In the 1790s it had been only a small village beside the bridge over the Allanwater; 'a wayside inn, a smithy, with a few hovel-looking huts constituted the sum and substance of the place'. A century later it had become a fashionable resort of some substance, and one of the favourite inland watering places of Scotland, according to Baddeley's *Thorough Guide* (1903), with several large hotels – the Queen's, the Royal and the Masterton. There was a Hydropathic, opened in 1866, scores of lodging houses and grand villas, a library and reading room, a bowling green and of course churches: enough to earn it in the view of one guidebook – admittedly local and therefore partisan – the title 'the Queen of Scottish spas'. Though not in the first division of British spas, it did attract large numbers of visitors (Table 4.2), some of whom were resident for quite long periods. Unlike Strathpeffer and Moffat, its season was not limited to the summer months. At times in good years the resort was so full in the spring that those who turned up on spec were turned away. *The Ayr Advertiser* on 30th April 1864 reported that 'at present Bridge of Allan is so crowded that apartments have to be engaged for weeks previous to occupation, and several parties who arrived last week without that precaution had to return to Stirling'. Though the numbers of visitors, even if generous allowance is made for day-trippers, may not have been as high as the 30,000 claimed for the resort in 1853, they were certainly substantial for a place with a resident population of only 1803 in 1861 and 3004 in 1891. But how substantial?

As we have already seen, Lists of Visitors were printed in the local newspapers of many leading upper-class resorts in England. Bridge of Allan was one of the earliest in Scotland to follow suit, with its first register appearing in May 1853, something that underlines both the nature of its existing clientèle and its aspirations. The lists were collected systematically and published almost every week for the next sixty years. They demonstrate by way of the addresses given where people were coming from; most were from either Glasgow or Edinburgh – the Stevenson family for example – though some were from further afield. But the overall monthly figures show interesting changes during the year, and from year to year.

Some caution must be shown about the reliability of the lists, but two important findings do emerge from Table 4.2. The first is that Bridge of Allan's peak season was the spring rather than the summer. Spas were rather different to seaside resorts in this respect, and indeed Bridge of Allan appears to have had some claim to being an all-year-round resort, in which it differed markedly from other Scottish spas. Moffat's season began at best in early May and was dead by the end of September. The burgh was, as one correspondent ('Solitaire') of the local paper, *The Moffat Guide*, asserted in an article on 30th July 1864, entitled 'Winter Papers. Moffat in Winter versus Moffat in Summer', 'a bustling watering-place in summer, and in winter a secluded village known only to its inhabitants'. There is also some evidence as to longer-term trends. It is of course dangerous to build on the experience of single years which may be atypical, but it does look as if Bridge of Allan was beginning to decline in popularity by the turn of the century, and other evidence confirms this. The numbers in May 1905 were one-third of what they had been thirty years earlier, for reasons which we will explore later.

For once, however, census data are of some value in providing a cross-check on the reliability or otherwise of the visitors' lists. As already indicated, the census in the nineteenth century was taken either on the last weekend of March or the first of April, and therefore was too early in the year for the majority of resorts. But, as Table 4.2 shows, Bridge of Allan did have visitors in residence by then and the enumerators recorded their presence. In the 1871 census, taken on Sunday 2nd April, there was a category in the returns of 'temporarily resident', which included visitors, vagrants and construction workers. Whereas North Berwick had a mere seven, Bridge of Allan had no fewer than 1,129 in this category, the majority of whom must have been visitors, such as William Troup, a retired university librarian at Hart Villa in Charlton Road. In April 1881, 553 temporary residents were counted and the enumerators specifically noted that most were visitors at the Hydropathic establishment, 'here for the sake of their health' or 'here for a change of air'. In 1891, however, only 43 were listed in this category, probably because the enumerators had been instructed to include only those who were literally on an overnight stay; the rest were reclassified as boarders, of whom there were 150 staying at the Hydro, for example.

The census enumerators' returns for individual lodgings and hotels are of further value in fleshing out the profile of those in residence. At the Hydro in 1871 there were 83 guests, whose occupations included surgeon, stockbroker, publisher, minister and merchant. At Aboukir Villa in Well Road, Margaret MacRae was looking after sixteen visitors including the Steels from Glasgow, who according to the visitors' list for that week were a Mr. & Mrs. Steel, 'and fam'. The census reveals that he was a Lanarkshire wine merchant, and that the family consisted of three sons aged 13, 11 and 3. There is a profitable, if time-consuming, seam to be worked on the cross-correlation between these two key sources. What the census enumerators' returns also show – and this would be true for many other resorts – is the number of house-owners, most of whom were women, listing their occupation as that of 'letting apartments'. The schedules for North Berwick show quite a number of houses shut up for the winter, or with only a skeleton staff; the structure of the property market in Bridge of Allan was rather different.

What were the reasons for the growth of Bridge of Allan as a health resort? There was, obviously, an existing and growing enthusiasm for spa treatment. There were good mineral springs in the immediate locality, a necessary but not sufficient condition for growth. Clearly the location in Central Scotland, within easy range of Edinburgh, Glasgow and Perth, was an advantage as against somewhere like Strathpeffer or even Moffat. It had a large urban and professional clientèle within close range, a position only enhanced by transport changes, the coming of the steamships in the 1820s and the railways in the 1840s, and the provision of a tram service in 1874 from Stirling to supplement the hotel buses. The patronage of local landowners was also significant, not that it was altruistic. What they hoped to get out of the rise of tourism was income from feuing and the sale of land. At Bridge of Allan what set matters under way in 1820 was Sir Robert Abercrombie's initiative. He had been 'moved by the success of mineral springs elsewhere'. Following established practice, he had the waters of the worked-out copper mines at Airthrey analysed by Dr Thomson, Professor of Chemistry at Glasgow University, an exercise which showed their medicinal value, and in the following year a well house was opened. A new pump room with hot, cold and shower baths was fitted up, and there was some success: by the early 1840s, customers were coming in their hundreds to drink the waters. Another local landowner to make an important contribution was Major Henderson of Westerton, both by funding various improvements and by allowing his grounds to be open for visitors to walk in.

Also very important was resort promotion by way of favourable newspaper and periodical articles, some of which were undoubtedly planted. There was, for example, an encouraging piece in *The Scotsman*, entitled 'A few days at Bridge of Allan', which shows how popular and fashionable the place had become:

> Just now it is chiefly filled with visitors from the west – the Belles of Glasgow and the Beaux of Greenock. In a month after it will be gay with all the glitter that Fife can bestow, and in August the folk of Edinburgh will taste of its waters. The hour of assembly is about 7 am; the Hygeian goddess holding levee between that hour and 9 a.m. After the morning scene at the wells, friends form themselves into parties for walks, drives or angling during the day.
>
> (*The Scotsman*, June 13 1846)

The finest example of an advertising and publicity brochure, commissioned by Major Henderson for £20, was that of the journalist, writer and historian, the Reverend Charles Rogers, a 400-page work entitled *A Week at Bridge of Allan*. The first edition of 1000 copies appeared in 1851 and ten more were to follow. There is no modesty about it, nor was there any about the man (dismissed by some as a charlatan) who later claimed to hold an LL.D from Columbia University in New York; but it was effective. Rogers praised the local climate of what he called 'the Montpelier of Scotland', the quality of the spa's regime, the excellence of the local facilities, and the range of excursions available in the neighbourhood. Rogers was also active in persuading local shopkeepers and others to subscribe to a fund for advertising Bridge of Allan in English provincial journals and in the very widely used railway guides. His other services to tourism in the area, tapping the growing interest in Scottish history, included acting as Secretary to the Committee and principal fund-raiser for the construction of the national monument to Wallace at the nearby Abbey Craig, completed in 1869. The Wallace Monument seems to have drawn consistently more visitors than Bannockburn, where of course there was very little to see, merely a hut and flagstaff at the Borestone. The Wallace Monument averaged over 36,000 visitors a year in the 1890s; Bannockburn less than 4,000.

The final ingredient in the rise of Bridge of Allan was the essential provision of amenities, amusement and entertainment. In the 1850s a German band was hired at a cost of £4 a week, and a piper was engaged, who played lively tunes on the bagpipes every morning at six o'clock. A talented musician, he then switched to the violin when people drank at the wells, and rounded off the day with a further bagpipe recital. There was provision for both dry and wet weather: sporting facilities such as the tennis courts, a bowling green ('The Airthrey Spa Club'), and later the golf course laid out by Tom Morris in 1895. For the less active there were the reading rooms and library, local walks, and excursions to scenes of historic interest such as Bannockburn, Stirling Castle and Cambuskenneth Abbey. These factors, the patronage of landowners, the effective promotion and provision of a full range of amenities, may account for the rise of Bridge of Allan. What, however, of its apparently fading popularity around the turn of the century?

By the last decade of the nineteenth century complaints were being voiced in the local press about falling numbers of visitors. One critic felt that despite the recent provision of new facilities such as the golf course, the village was in danger of falling behind; other resorts were catering much more lavishly for the visitor, something that a vigorous advertising campaign could not reverse. The Hydro continued to attract good numbers, though it was felt that enthusiasm for the hydropathic regime was in retreat; a break and exercise was what it offered. Scottish spas generally were losing ground. The shops, hotels and lodging houses were feeling the pinch of declining numbers. Increasingly they turned, or had to turn, to taking in retired people and annuitants, which further dampened the atmosphere of the place, and made it less attractive to younger visitors with families. Bridge of

Allan was set on a downward spiral from which it never recovered. Perhaps the Town Council should have done more, but Bridge of Allan's experience was not exceptional. The Central Region as a whole seems to have been feeling the impact of changed patterns of travel and taste. The custodian of the Wallace Monument wrote to the Custodiers' Committee of Stirling Council in November 1906 to point out that the numbers there – and his takings – were down by over 5,000 a year in the last five years. This meant substantial losses to him in the form of admission money, sales of souvenirs, tobacco, teas and ginger beer. 'Each year', he said, 'less and less: the numbers are not coming to Stirling.' He blamed the cost of railway fares; also:

> all the specially conducted trips brought by Cook, Lindsay, Mackay, The London Polytechnic Company etc are leaving out a visit to the Monument. They are taken to the Castle, the Churches, a few to the Borestone and then off by train to Callander or Aberfoyle. Before there was more time given and they were brought up to the Monument but this is all gone now. (Central Regional Archives, SB 10/1/2; William Middleton to the Town Clerk of Stirling, 28 November 1906)

The popularity of resorts does rise and fall, as the experience of Bridge of Allan illustrates. And despite the best efforts of the Town Council and other interested parties, its decline proved impossible to reverse, something that other destinations have found.

The spa movement was never of more than minor significance in Scotland. By contrast, interest in hydropathy as a system of cure went much deeper and was sustained longer. From modest beginnings in the early 1840s, this enthusiasm, which many in conventional medicine regarded as quackery, became a mania in the later 1870s when quite a number of these large centres for hydropathic treatment ('hydros') were opened. As one contemporary, the publisher William Chambers, remarked in September 1878 on his return from laying the foundation-stone of yet another hydro, this time at his native Peebles:

> Scots who are pretty cautious in their undertakings have plunged in a surprising manner into enterprises connected with Hydropathic Establishments. Within a very few years a dozen of these health resorts have sprung up in various parts of Scotland, north and south.

The movement overreached itself, and many of the new companies went into liquidation in the early 1880s. But others moved in to revive the ventures, and the hydros were to remain a very important part of the business of health in Scotland until, and in some cases beyond, the First World War.

The starting point for hydropathy, as we have already seen, lay on the Continent. News of Pressnitz's water cure system, which linked both traditional ideas of long standing about the value of water treatments with a new pattern of practice, reached Scotland in the early 1840s by two routes. There were amateur crusaders like Captain Claridge of the Middlesex militia, who gave a series of well-attended lectures in various parts of Britain and visited Glasgow in 1843; an influential organisation, the Glasgow Hydropathic Society, was formed as a result. But also promoting the water cure were qualified physicians who had actually visited Grafenburg, and seen the medical and commercial advantages of Pressnitz's regime. In 1842 Drs Gully (an Edinburgh graduate in medicine) and Wilson established the first hydropathic establishments in Britain at Malvern; in Scotland in the following year Dr Paterson set up a small hydropathic practice, which was primarily a consulting surgery, at Argyle Place in Rothesay, already a recognised health resort. Four years later he moved to Glenburn House, where there were residential facilities for patients. Others followed his lead, including Rowland East at Dunoon in 1846.

The choice of location, as in the case of Rothesay, was significant. East believed in hydropathy, and published a list of cases of rheumatism, gout and nervous exhaustion treated successfully. But he argued that the sea air would also help, something which was generally agreed, as would the many excursions by land or sea possible in the area. The cure was not instant but took weeks, patients had a lot of time on their hands, and what better way to occupy them, if they were fit enough, than a trip to Loch Lomond, or Inveraray? Sea-bathing was another option; Professor J.S. Blackie, who spent five weeks at Dunoon Hydro in 1846, thought that 'a dip in the briny billow' was the way to give a 'finishing-off to the perfectly hydropathised frame'. The need for hydros to be centres of recreation and amusement as well as cure was strengthened by the presence of friends and relatives, staying to keep the patients company. It is no accident that from the 1860s onwards places in good tourist locations like Seamill, Melrose, Peebles, Crieff and Moffat were chosen as hydropathic centres. And those which had started in, or close to, the larger cities, moved out, as at Aberdeen and Glasgow. Quite a number of the early hydropaths were lay enthusiasts. At Gilmorehill, Archibald Hunter (who had been an upholsterer) had had a two-storey mansion capable of accommodating some thirty residents, as well as others on an out-patient basis. Some could continue with treatment at home, providing they had adequate facilities, especially plenty of water. Charles Darwin did so after a stay at Malvern, and in 1876 Hunter was to publish a well received book, which went through thirteen editions in twenty years, entitled *Hydropathy: Its Principles and Practice for Home Use*. It was a useful and helpful compendium of advice for mothers with young children, and others. Its remit ranged widely from treatments for fevers to how best a clergyman should prepare his voice before preaching. But the growing numbers of those seeking a residential cure, and the willingness of wealthy backers to assist him, prompted Hunter to move in the mid-1860s to Bridge of Allan, to larger premises and a better location at what was to advertise itself as 'The Scottish Grafenburg'. Significantly, while the management was left to Hunter and his formidable second wife, ownership passed to a limited company. Investors had scented that profits could be made out of hydropathic institutions, whether as centres of cure or of relaxation. And in the period 1865 to 1882 no fewer than sixteen hydros were opened, none of them small, and some very large or 'palatial' indeed: Moffat, for example, could accommodate over 300 guests. The magnificent Athole at Pitlochry, with its 40 acres of grounds, cost £80,000, much of that coming from shareholders, some of whom were small investors – a bank teller, a forester and local schoolmaster – all of whom lost their money when the first company went into liquidation. The movement temporarily overreached itself in the early 1880s and had to retrench. No new hydros were built after 1882, and two projects at Oban and Morningside in Edinburgh were aborted.

The venture which marked the transition to the new order was that at Cluny Hill near Forres, which was opened in August 1865. It was a purpose-built property with ninety rooms, baths and other equipment, financed by a circle of investors, some local, some not, drawn in by the new legal protection for limited liability companies. It drew on a clientèle from much further afield: amongst those in residence in June 1875 were visitors from Newcastle and elsewhere in England. There was even a group from Gibraltar. But what was of critical importance was the change in the guests and their interests. Fewer came for a cure, more for a break in pleasant surroundings with good company. There were still those who looked to the therapeutic side of hydro operations. An early visitor to Forres in September 1866 was the prominent Glaswegian clergyman, Dr. Norman Macleod, whose preaching Queen Victoria so much enjoyed. He put himself through the full treatment:

> Here I am in a state of perpetual thaw, ceaseless moisture, always under a wet blanket, and constantly in danger of kicking the

bucket – 'water, water, everywhere'. I have been stewed like a goose, beat on like a drum, battered like a pancake, rubbed like corned beef, dried like Finnan haddock, and wrapped up like a mummy in wet sheets and blankets. My belief is that I am in a lunatic asylum – too mad to be quite sure about it.
(*Memoir of Norman Macleod, D.D. By his brother* (London, 1876), vol. 2, p.206)

The hydros increasingly catered not for those who were seriously ill, but for professional people who had simply being overdoing things, 'had become fagged with labour and worry, and [stood] much in need of holiday rest'. A growing number came just for a break in congenial surroundings. The change in focus and function is well caught in an extraordinary accident at Forres in October 1869 when the Managing Director, James Calder, was shot dead in the grounds of the Hydro. A guest who was clearly not an invalid, the well-known English naturalist, Mr. George Notman, was trying to dispose of a local cat, which was regarded as a pest. His rifle shot grazed the cat, which survived, ricocheted to hit Calder, who did not, and Notman was later to be charged with manslaughter. But the point stands. Increasingly, what mattered to the hydros was not the cure, but the food and amenities; not the calibre of the resident hydropathic doctor, but the enthusiasm of the 'Lady Entertainers' who organised the social programme. The peak times for the hydros came to be Christmas and Easter, when a full week of entertainments was planned. The highest ever number of guests recorded at Crieff pre-1914 came one year on the first of January when, according to James Caw, the House Steward, no fewer than 399 visitors were in residence, with about seventy staff sleeping under the same roof. Some kept the old traditions going longer than others, but even Peebles by 1908 found that its takings from the medical or cure department were less than 10% of its total revenue. The downside was that while the patients had tended to stay for a month or two, the new leisure clientèle was in residence for a week or even less.

These signs of change, that 'visitors were beginning to crowd out patients', as one journalist described it, were apparent in the 1870s, ironically just as hydropathy was becoming more respectable as it toned down its claims. Thomas Meikle, the founder of Crieff Hydro which opened in 1868, insisted that hydropathy was not magic or a panacea and that expectations should not be too high: cures took time, not a few days. And what was also part of the package, in addition to a carefully tailored programme of treatment, was a carefully arranged system of diet, fresh air and exercise. It was the latter that attracted more and more visitors. While baths remained important, golf courses, tennis courts, bowling greens and croquet lawns became essential, as were conservatories and greenhouses, well laid-out grounds and good local walks. There was an increasing emphasis on the quality of the cuisine, and the way that ladies could be freed from the cares of managing their household. The hydros became holiday rest centres for the better-off, their charges being about one-third higher than the general run of first-rate family hotels. What added to the appeal of the hydros in Scotland, as investors recognised, was their respectability, and their close association with the temperance cause, then gaining real momentum. Hydropaths such as Archibald Hunter denounced alcohol as a poison, to be dealt out only in emergencies. 'Water is best' was their motto, whether for external application or internal consumption. There was a widespread assumption that all the hydros were temperance institutions, and their advertising stressed that no spirituous liquors or intoxicants were available. Andrew Philp, the owner of Glenburn and Dunblane Hydros, was a close friend of Thomas Cook, and like him a firm supporter of the temperance movement. Crieff Hydro was to continue 'dry' until the 1970s. The reality was, of course, rather different from the image, and one or two hydros right from the outset seem to have taken a less severe line. Peebles had a Glasgow wine merchant amongst its directors, and Moffat allowed guests to bring wine bottles to their table. And there was always evasion, with surreptitious supplies smuggled in, or refuelling at licensed premises in the vicinity. A fictionalised account, but one with the feel of authenticity, describes the visit of two men to Glenburn Hydro at Rothesay for a weekend early in January to recover from their New Year celebrations. They paused on arrival for some refreshment at the Bute Arms, being in no hurry to reach the 'watter institution' as the 'cars' [tramcars] were stopped by snow, and the landlady was instructed that

> As we're gaun awa' tae a place where we'll get naething but watter, ye'll better fill oor pistols and this waulking stick with the 'Auld Kirk' an mak us ready a guid stake tae help keep up the edifice.
> (James Rae, *The Jeems papers* (Stirling, c. 1890), 'Jeems at the Hydropathic')

The temperance tag was important in the building and retention of a respectable image, critical to the attraction of the right clientèle, which was largely drawn from the professional and middle classes: mer-

chants, architects, solicitors and, of course, ministers. The management at Crieff did have available – and continues to have – generous
endowment funds to subsidise the holidays of ministers, missionaries
and church workers, and the remarkable missionary Mary Slessor of
Calabar may well have been a beneficiary. On her visit to Crieff while
on leave in 1889 she brought with her four of her African girls. Other
hydros offered special terms to ministers, who could sing for their
supper by saying grace, or by conducting Sunday morning worship.
Adding to the air of religious decorum was the practice adopted by
wealthy patrons of sending over-tired Christian workers for a break at
their expense: John Hope's temperance agents, for example. The Frys
of Bristol, the Rowntrees of York and William Booth of the Salvation
Army were amongst the philanthropic and religious figures on the
guest lists at Scottish hydros. A consequence was that Sundays at the
hydros were very strictly policed, with at best a concert of sacred
music permitted. Some visitors, and especially those from outside
Scotland, chafed at the dullness of the Sabbath, and golfers in
particular formed a vociferous pressure group in favour of Sunday
play. However much sympathy there may have been from some of the
directors, there could be no relaxation for fear of alienating a substantial section of both their clientèle and their shareholders. A report
in April 1896 that two gentlemen had had a Sunday game on the
Dublane Hydro course produced an instant denial from the directors
that it had happened with their knowledge or consent. The local paper
commented wryly that:

> This Golf Course is in connection with one of these unimpeach-
> able institutions known as Hydropathic establishments. They are
> patronised by the 'unco guid' of all denominations. Alcohol is
> forbidden. Until lately sinful games were barely tolerated and
> anything like halfpenny nap would be scowled down at once.
> Our readers can understand how absolutely necessary it is for the
> proprietor of this Golf Course to disclaim all complicity with
> these Sabbath breakers.
> (*The Bridge of Allan Reporter*, 25 April, 1896)

The tone, more than the treatments, was the hydros' key selling point.
They were places where respectable people could be sure of meeting
their own sort. In 1881 George Walker, a bookseller in Aberdeen, and
his wife Jane took a holiday at Crieff Hydro. They had intended to
take a trip up the Rhine, but she was not well enough, and so they
went instead to Crieff. Rather to their surprise, they enjoyed themselves. Walker's journal records the excursions, conversations and

company, but despite his wife's ill-health, there is almost no reference to any therapy. Jane did try a warm bath, but it proved too much for her: 'she nearly fainted', and that was the end of that. There was plenty to do and see during the day, and the evenings passed very pleasantly thanks to a programme of music, charades, mock trials, elections and *tableaux vivants*, one of which they had photographed as a memento. So pleased were they that they returned the next year for a change of scene and air with a recently bereaved neighbour, and found once more 'choice good company'. 'We felt it to be a second home', wrote Walker. The clientèle was made cohesive by cost and the ethos of the hydropathic establishment. But there were those who did not fit in the eyes of their fellow guests. One spat in 1906 went all the way to the Court of Session. It was between a lady from Bruntsfield in Edinburgh, and a couple from Lilybank Gardens in Glasgow – similar areas – who were staying at Clunyhill Hydropathic. The Robertsons took against Mrs Mackenzie, and called her a 'low woman' and 'unfit to be a guest at the hydropathic'. She sued, and won substantial damages of £400 for slander.

A journalist on *The Times* in September 1878 spotted the significance of the cultural role of the hydro in Scotland, both for those who were comfortably professional and middle-class, and for those who had aspirations that way for themselves or their children, an integration eased by shared values such as religious commitment and temperance. He thought that:

> The system offers an opportunity of participating in a certain kind of social life for persons who have no other chance from year's end to year's end of mixing with those who are, in externals at least, better than themselves. In the spacious and luxuriant furnished drawing room at Moffat, or Melrose or Wemyss Bay, or Pitlochrie, the forlorn bank clerk or the provincial shopkeeper may hobnob with the railway director or city clergymen, and the small farmer or rural manufacturer may have his ambition warmed by seeing his wife and daughters share couches and exchange civilities with real ladies.

To his eye – and there is some truth in this – a prime function of the hydros was their role as a marriage mart. He advised any planter or colonial administrator in search of a wife to spend two or three months in making a round of the Scottish hydropathic establishments.

By the later nineteenth century the hydros, therefore, were providing a range of services beyond their original therapeutic role. There was still a physician, though he might be visiting rather than resident.

There were still baths and equipment at most. When Kyles of Bute Hydro was rebuilt after a disastrous fire in December 1909 – a hazard to which a number of establishments fell victim – the new premises included what was described as a 'splendid group of baths including Turkish, Russian, plunge, spray and swimming ponds, all supplied with hot and cold, fresh and salt water'. But hydros were increasingly high-class leisure and tourist hotels, rather than therapy centres, and as such they were highly successful once the problems of too rapid expansion in the early 1880s had been put behind them. Visitor numbers climbed. Over the period 1888 to 1894 Shandon's rose by a third. Moffat saw its daily average of guests double between 1898 and 1901. The clientèle were happy, and so were the shareholders. Crieff never paid less than a 9% dividend in the 1890s, and Forres reached 12½%. The hydropathic movement in Scotland was a success. And it was a movement in which Scotland had a disproportionately large stake. In 1906 there were, or so one authority concluded, fifteen hydropathic establishments in Scotland as against fifty in England, with its much larger population, and only one in Ireland.

TABLE 4.3.   VISITORS TO SHANDON HYDROPATHIC IN 1881 (by Country of Origin).

Country	Number	Percentage
Scotland	1575	76
England	371	18
Ireland	76	4
Wales	8	0.4
Other	32	1.6

The hydros' importance to Scottish tourism was that they offered a high-class alternative to those who might well have travelled to a Continental resort or spa, and drew in appreciable numbers of visitors from England and further afield. Shandon's experience illustrates the point. In 1881, just over 2,400 names feature in the lists of visitors. Most appeared only once in the weekly lists, but there were those who stayed much longer. The Hendersons from Glasgow were in residence from the beginning of January to the end of March. Their presence would have been welcome indeed in February, always the dullest month for Scottish hotels. The breakdown of the clientèle by address is interesting. The most common entry gave Glasgow (668), then Edinburgh (428), London (123), Dublin (49) and Dundee(38). Table 4.3 shows the origins by country; the 'others' category includes some from the USA, Chile and Canada. Three-quarters were from Scotland, but a significant minority was not, and their cost of travel and spending increased their economic impact.

The business of health was good business indeed, and a very important part of Scottish tourism. It was achieved in the face of established competition from elsewhere in Britain, on the Continent and even further afield. Resorts in North America, South Africa and even New Zealand were beginning to make their presence felt.

Further reading

On the general background, see M. Charteris, *Health Resorts at Home and Abroad* (London, 1887) and T.D. Luke, *The Spas and Health Resorts of the British Isles* (London, 1919). On spa resorts in England, Phyllis Hembry, *The English Spa, 1560–1815: A Social History* (London, 1990), is comprehensive, though Frederick Alderson, *The Inland Resorts and Spas of Britain* (Newton Abbot, 1973) is livelier. Contemporary accounts of Scottish spas include Dr William Horsburgh, *Observations on Hartfell Spa* (Edinburgh, 1754) which gives a detailed list of 27 cases, mostly local, where a cure had been effected by these waters, Francis Home, M.D., *An Essay on the Contents and Virtues of Dunse Spaw* (Edinburgh, 1751), and Fortescue Fox, *Strathpeffer Spa: Its Climate and Waters* (London, 1889). For an account of the enterprising Charles Rogers and his role at Bridge of Allan, see Malcolm Allan, 'Who was Charles Rogers?', *Forth Naturalist and Historian*, Vol.13, 1989. On hydropathy, an entertaining account is given by E. S. Turner, *Taking the Cure* (London, 1967), Chapters 11 to 13. James Caw, *Reminiscences of Forty Years on the Staff of a Hydro* (Crieff, 1914) is worth reading. For first-hand accounts of life at the hydros, there are Aberdeen Central Library, George Walker Journals, Vol. 4, pp. 458–474 and J. S. Blackie, *The Water Cure in Scotland: Five Letters from Dunoon* (Aberdeen, 1846). More recent academic work includes J.Bradley, M.D.Dupree and A.J.Durie, 'Taking the Water-cure: the Hydropathic Movement in Scotland, *c.* 1840–1940', *Business and Economic History*, 26, 1998. A reminder of the migration of the sick to the Continent is given by Eric Simpson, 'Grave Thoughts from Abroad', *Scottish Local History*, 26, July 1992. The same author's *Going on Holiday* (Edinburgh, 1997) has much useful material, especially Chapters 5, 'Health-Cure Fads' and 8, 'Hydropathics, Fresh-Air Fanatics, and Summer Camps'.

5

THE SPORTING TOURIST

During the week the passenger traffic to the Highlands has been
very great, and it will probably reach its flood-mark today, when
all who intend to be out on the moors tomorrow will reach their
shooting quarters. The arrivals from London this morning will be
in excess of any that have been recorded in the annals of Highland
Railway travelling. The usual night mail from London will be
preceded by six, if not seven special express trains, all of which
bear parties for the shooting lodges.

(The Inverness Courier, August 11, 1911)

One of the major forces behind the nineteenth-century development of
Scotland as a tourist destination was the range of sporting activities
which it came to offer the visitor. Sport, rather than scenery or history,
became a key factor in the popularity of Scotland, a change reflected in
the later nineteenth-century editions of the standard guidebooks such
as Murray's *Handbook for Scotland*. The early editions in the 1860s
and 1870s had dwelt long and lovingly in their introductions on
general information about travel arrangements and accommodation,
charges at inns, the luggage to be taken, the need to be respectful of the
rigour of the Scotch Sabbath, to be patient with the weather, to be
sensitive to Scottish humour, and to endure the midge. They listed
amongst the antiquities worth seeing lake dwellings, brochs, round
towers, Roman remains, castles, abbeys and other historic ruins. A full
section was devoted to that great Victorian passion, the geology of
Scotland, the heights of its mountains and the origins of its place
names, Gaelic or otherwise, with little or nothing for the sporting
traveller. The fourth edition in 1875 did provide hints for yachtsmen
intending to sail on the West Coast, but otherwise there was little or
nothing of significance to the sporting tourist. But decade by decade,
the sporting information became much fuller. Advice to cyclists and
mountaineers was added by the time of the sixth edition in 1894,
motoring in the seventh, and the eighth edition in 1903 devoted a full
section to angling centres, with associated hotels, and another to
golfing links: 'there are few summer resorts where there is not a golf
course of some kind'.

This change in focus underlines just how important sporting tourism had become by the later nineteenth century in Scotland, and how in many eyes Scotland had become a sporting playground. There are a number of Scottish outdoor sports that in this context bear examination, from fishing to yachting or deerstalking or mountaineering, all of which had their devotees amongst visitors, as well as tennis, bowls and even cricket, which helped to entertain holidaymakers. Mountaineering, for example, had a long pedigree in Scotland. The path to the top of Ben Lomond was well trodden already by the 1790s, and each year saw enthusiasts foraging further afield, with Ben Nevis and the North-West particularly popular. Blackwood's *Edinburgh Magazine* in September 1862 remarked that the increase in this 'mania for mountain climbing was quite remarkable', even though it was critical about the physical condition of some participants, with every year some elderly gentleman, whose ambition had outstripped his constitution, having to be rescued from the hills. The provision of an excellent pony track to the top of Ben Nevis and the erection in the 1890s of a Temperance Hotel at the summit, where refreshment and overnight accommodation could be obtained, made Ben Nevis the most frequently climbed peak of any in Britain, except perhaps Snowdon. The emergence of much better prepared enthusiasts found expression in the *Scottish Mountaineering Journal*, which was published three times a year from 1890. A growing interest in rock and winter climbing, fostered for many in the Alps, led to Henry Lunn acquiring the Atholl Hotel at Pitlochry in the summer of 1914 as a Scottish all-year sporting resort centre. The Highland Railway had plans in the same year for running winter weekend services from Perth to Speyside for ski-ing, curling and skating, but the outbreak of war put a stop to that.

Climbing, walking and rambling attracted growing numbers of visitors in the later nineteenth century. Fishing, practised at all levels of skill, was a bigger attraction earlier. Catherine Sinclair – Sir John's daughter and a well-known novelist in her own right – complained in 1840 that the inn at Alford on Deeside, where she and her companions had intended to stay, could offer only a curtainless, carpetless and dingy apartment, which was in any case already occupied by sportsmen for fishing. She noted how many of those 'wielding the rod' were ladies. Theodore Fontane, a German visitor to Scotland in 1858, reported that 'at the beginning of summer hundreds and thousands of Englishmen make for the Highlands of Scotland, there to spend two, three, or four weeks on a kind of angling campaign'. In the height of the angling season, that is from March till June, it was said that every cottage on Tweedside was occupied by 'some piscatory amateur'. The prime focus was trout rather than salmon, which was mostly reserved

1. A well-dressed party of early excursionists on a steamboat on the Clyde near Dumbarton. From William Daniell, *Voyage Round the Coast of Great Britain* (1818).

THE WELL, MOFFAT.

2. Moffat Well, c.1890: two ladies on their morning walk. This modest building underlines that Moffat, popular though it was, was no rival to Bath or Baden.

"THE HEIGHT OF THE SEASON"
—NORTH BERWICK STATION.

3. The height of the season: North Berwick Station. Wives, chauffeurs and coachmen meet golfers off the early evening train from Edinburgh, after their day at the office. From the 1914 edition of the *North British Railway Official Tourist Guide.*

THE SHOOTING OF THE LAST GROUSE.
AN ALARMIST'S VISION OF A.D. 1900.

4. 'The shooting of the last grouse'. Some were worried that supply could not keep up with demand. But in fact weather and disease were more of a threat. From *Punch*, August 1882.

5. 'A grouse battue'. The reality was usually very different from this fanciful 'valley of death'. Southern sportsmen had to endure instead a long hot walk, or a long cold wait. From *Punch*, 1883.

6. 'It's an ill wind ... '. The outbreak of war in early August put an almost complete stop to the grouse season due to start on the 12th. From *Punch*, August 1914.

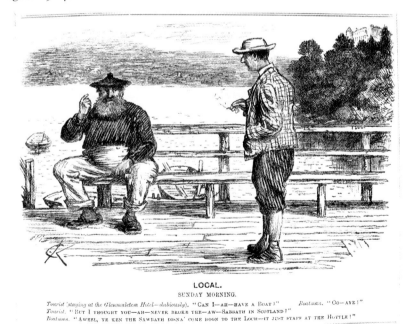

LOCAL.
SUNDAY MORNING.

Tourist (staying at the Glenmuletem Hotel—dubiously). "CAN I—AH—HAVE A BOAT?"   *Boatman.* "OO—AYE!"
Tourist. "BUT I THOUGHT YOU—AH—NEVER BROKE THE—AW—SABBATH IN SCOTLAND?"
Boatman. "AWEEL, YE KEN THE SAWBATH DISNA' COME DOON TO THE LOCH—IT JUST STAPS AT THE HOTEL!"

7. Sunday Morning. Strict though Sabbath Observance was, tourists could find that some of the locals were flexible. From *Punch*, September 1884.

ARRIVALS AT THE UNION HOTEL.

His Grace the Duke of Marlborough, and the Lord Adam Loftus, on their way to the shootings of Killin ; the Right Hon. Lord Bollingbroke ; Mrs and the Misses Dennistoune, and Miss Campbell, Circus Place, Edinburgh, on their way to Strathpeffer ; L. Palk, Esq., on his way to Phoiness House ; Major Shirreff, on his way to shooting quarters ; E. Mackinlay, Esq., and Lady, and Miss Scrymegeour, Buenos Ayres, on a tour ; Captain Innes and Lady, St Germains ; G. Dick Lauder, Esq., and Miss M. Dick Lauder, on their way to shooting quarters, Rannoch ; J. Murray Grant, Esq. of Glenmoriston, Miss Grant, and Miss Macdonell, Scothouse, to Invermoriston House ; Hugh Rose, Esq. of Kilravock, and Mrs Captain Rose, on their way to Nairn ; C. Webster, Esq., Lady, and Party, Denham House, on their way north ; Mr and Mrs Borthwick, do. ; G. Ebrington, Esq., R.N., and Lady, on a tour ; H. Henderey, Esq., and Son, on a shooting excursion ; Mr and Mrs Morris, and the Misses Morris, on a tour ; E. Wilkinson, Esq., and Lady, and the Misses Duncombe, on their way north ; T. B. Browne, Esq., and Party, on their way south ; J. S. Wainman, Esq., on his way south ; J. Ackers, Esq., M.P., Lady, and Family, Heath Ludlow, on their way to shooting quarters ; W. Collier, Esq. of Newington Park, on his way south ; G. Deans, Esq., Lady, and Family, on a tour ; J. L. Adamson, Esq., and Lady, on a tour ; G. S. Blair, Esq., on his way north ; Geo. Hogg, Esq., Lady, and Family, on their way to London ; J. Todd, Esq., on his way south ; G. Small, Esq., on his way south ; Frederick L. Templemore, Esq., on his way north ; G. Dunbar, Esq., on his way south ; G. L. Murray, Esq., on his way south ; T. H. Harrison, Esq., on his way to Skye ; G. S. Lyall, Esq., on his wny south ; G. Ingleton, Esq., Lady, and Family, on their way north ; H. J. Coddell, Esq., on his way south ; G. S. Dick, Esq., on his way south ; G. Robertson, Esq., and Party, on a fishing excursion ; J. M. Jones, Esq. ; G. A. Goldie, Esq., on his way south ; — Binney, Esq., Lady, and Family, on their way north ; F. Leslie, Esq., on his way north ; J. E. Forrester, Esq., do. ; T. Miller, Esq., on a tour ; J. A. Morris, Esq., Lady, and Family, do. ; C. Bell, Esq., do. ; T. Duncan, Esq., do. ; J. A. Ingram, Esq., on his way south ; G. S. Cavendish, Esq., on his way to Brocket Hall, Pembrokeshire ; R. Spencer, Esq., on his way south ; F. Bower, Esq., on a tour ; W. Beatson, Esq., on a tour ; R. Somerville, Esq., on a tour ; J. Sawyers, Esq., do. ; R. Oliver, Esq., do. ; G. Seyton, Esq., on his way south ; G. Dealtey, Esq., and Party, on their way to shooting quarters ; J. Whitehurst, Esq., on his way south ; F. A. Brown, Esq., on a tour ; H. Wiseman, Esq., on his way south ; G. Scott, Esq., on a tour ; the Hon. W. Percy and Friend, do. ; F. Rogers, Esq., do. ; R. Milligan, Esq., on his way south ; G. Dornington, Esq., and Friend, on a tour ; J. Currie, Esq., and Party, on their way south ; — Cumming, Esq., on a tour ; — Merryweather, Esq., on his way south ; G. Blackwood, Esq., on his way north, from Brook Street, London ; F. W. Erskine, Esq., on his way to Horsley Common, Sussex ; R. King Wylie, Esq., on his way to Hanbury Hall, Worcestershire ; E. Montgomery, Esq., on his way to Roynal Park, Northamptonshire ; A. Houston, Esq., Lady, and Family, on their way south ; A. Guinston, Esq. of Gliside, Durham, on his way north ; P. Ramsay, Esq., on his way south ; A. Walker, Esq., on his way to Glenavin, Berwickshire ; H. J. Cardow, Esq., on a tour ; G. A. Montieth, Esq., on a tour ; J. Clements, Esq., on his way south ; A. Lloyd, Esq., Lady, and Family, do. ; Robert Allison, Esq., do. ; J. C. Watt, Esq., do. ; R. S. Stewart, Esq., and Party, on a tour ; H. M. Peacock, Esq., do. ; G. H. Crampton, Esq., on a botanical excursion ; W. Hawkins, Esq., and Lady, on their way to Touley, Lancashire ; James Smyth, Esq., on a tour ; J. A. Adam, Esq., on his way south ; H. M. Mowbray, Esq., on a fishing excursion ; G. T. Latimore, Esq., on his way south ; S. Harvey, Esq., and Friend, on their way north ; J. Hawes, Esq., on his way south ; G. Kelly, Esq., on a tour ; F. Elphinstone, Esq., and Lady, do. ; H. Trecoott, Esq., do. ; R. N. Clarke, Esq., on his way south ; T. Greenfield, Esq., on a tour ; G. Dawson, Esq., on his way south ; G. J. Archbold, Esq., do. ; — Wilkinson, Esq., do. ; H. Roberts, Esq., Lady and Family, on their way to Torquin, Llandaff ; A. Anderson, Esq., on his way south ; J. Craigie, Esq., on a tour ; G. Haines, Esq., on a pleasure excursion ; R. Wise, Esq., on a tour ; W. Hunter, Esq., and Friend, do. ; A. Henderson, Esq., on his way south ; Rood, Esq., on a tour ; C. Dixon, Esq., on his way north ; — Sheridan, Esq., on a tour ; A. Lyster, Esq., Mrs and Miss Lyster, do. ; J. Harthill, Esq., do. ; G. Cairncross, Esq., and Family, do. ; A. Blackmore, Esq., and Friend, on their way south ; T. Blair, Esq., on a tour ; A. Fraser, Esq., on his way north ; E. Napier, Esq., do. ; J. B. Allan, Esq., on a tour ; — Morton, Esq., and Lady, on his way south ; J. Arnott, Esq., and Lady, do. ; — Archer, Esq., on a tour ; W. Thomson, Esq., on his way south ; S. Neil Talbot, Esq., on his way south ; J. Wickham, Esq., on his way to Culmakyle House ; — Ewart, Esq., on a tour ; — Mackenzie, Esq., on a tour ; H. Penfold Wyatt, Esq., and G. G. P. Wyatt, Esq., on their way north ; Miss Chapman and Party, Scottin Rectory, Lincolnshire, on a tour ; E. Thompson, Esq., Lady, and Party, on a tour ; C. M. Levy, Esq., and Friend, on a fishing excursion ; L. Wigram, Esq., Queen's Counsel, and Friend, on a tour ; — Lindsay, Esq., and Party, on their way north ; Mr and Mrs Tattershall, on a tour ; E. Ellice, Esq., M.P., Lady, and Miss Balfour, from Cawdor Castle, on their way to Glenquoich ; Wm. Gibson Craig, Esq., M.P., and H. B. Vivian, Esq., Swansea, from Beaufort Castle, on their way south ; W. Mackenzie, Esq. of Muirton, W.S., Lady, and Miss Mackenzie, on their way to Muirton House ; — Moore, Esq., on a tour ; Sir Philip de Grey Egerton, from Lancashire, on his way to shooting quarters, Tolly, Sutherlandshire ; — Hodges, Esq., on a tour ; W. B. L. Baker, Esq., and Friends.

8. Arrivals at the Union Hotel, Inverness. Many were returning south from a Highland tour, others were bound for Strathpeffer for the waters, others were en route to shooting quarters, and some were on botanical or fishing excursions. From *The Inverness Courier*, September 1843.

BRIDGE OF ALLAN JOURNAL,
And Spa Directory.

File Copy 450 printed

No. 9.   WEDNESDAY, 31st AUGUST, 1853.—Published every alternate Wednesday.   Price 3d

The Dunfermline Races

TAKE place at EASTER GELLET, on THURSDAY, 1st September, 1853, at Twelve o'clock noon.

The ORDINARY after the Races to be in the Commercial Inn, Douglas Street.

TO TOURISTS.

ROBERT S. SHEARER,

BOOKSELLER, STATIONER, and LIBRARIAN,

19, King Street, Stirling.

OPPOSITE GIBB'S HOTEL.

STRANGERS will find a very Large and Complete Assortment of Guide Books, Scottish Views, Maps, Time Tables, &c. Tourists' Companions, and other Fancy and Useful Articles, especially adapted for Souvenirs of Scotland.

A General Stock of all New Works, Magazines, &c.; also, a Superior Selection of Bibles, Prayer-Books, &c. in morocco bindings.

New Books added to Library as Published.

OBSERVE NAME AND ADDRESS,
ROBERT S. SHEARER,
19, KING STREET,
STIRLING.

Directly opposite Gibb's Hotel.

Feuing at Bridge of Allan,

ON THE LANDS OF WESTERTON.

THE Proprietor is ready to dispose of any of the Unfeued portions of the Grounds for the Erection of Houses or Villas, on liberal terms. The proposed Annual Feu Duties, or permanent ground rents, are, for the upper grounds of Dunsyle, *Eight Pounds* per Imperial Acre, when a whole acre or more is taken; *Nine Pounds* for Half an Acre, or *Three Pounds* for a quarter of an Acre; and for the lands or low grounds *Twelve Pounds* per Imperial Acre, when a whole acre or more is taken; *Seven Pounds* for Half an Acre and *Four Pounds* for a Quarter of an Acre.

The Feu Duties or Ground Rents will not be charged till after the expiry of the first year, so as to allow time for laying out the grounds and erecting the houses, and there will be no restrictions as to the style or elevation of the houses or villas, provided they have a neat appearance, as more particularly explained in the Conditions of Feu.

The Lands are well supplied with excellent water; and the Village is illuminated with Gas.

The feus extend to the limits of the original title, will be about Nine Cottages.

Further particulars as to the Feuing can be procured by applying to Mr William Hutton, writer, Stirling; Mr John R. Forman, W.S. 8, Heriot Row, Edinburgh; or to Mr Alex. Ridgway, Notary and Conveyancer, 28, Royal Exchange, and 12, Leicester Square, London.

A Large Feuing Plan of the property may be seen at Westerton.

Bridge of Allan, June, 1853.

POWER OF PRAYER
AND
POWER OF THE PRESS.

IS NOT THE CHURCH ASLEEP, AND THE ENEMY WIDE AWAKE?

Why should we not persevere in treating the power of Prayer, and pointed Tract Distribution, in arousing the whole Country from its alarming Slumber?

STIRLING TRACT ENTERPRISE. Commenced 1848. Eighth Million far advanced, and being sent out daily to all directions, to order and gratuitously. Prices from 6d. to 2s. 6d. per 100.

THE BRITISH MESSENGER, in the Newspaper form, started in March last, and published Monthly, in connection with the Enterprise, price 1½d. Twenty-fifth Thousand in progress. Sixteen copies go by post for 6d. and 32 for 1s. as postage.

(A specimen copy will be sent gratuitously by post, on receipt of two penny stamps for postage.)

GRATUITOUS DISTRIBUTION. The Subscriber has already issued upwards of Three Millions of Tracts gratuitously, at an outlay of above £1900, and to assist which about £330 have been already thankfully received. Donations, however...

LADIES' FANCY BAZAAR,
IN AID OF THE
Funds of the Dunfermline Female Beneficent Society.

THIS SALE of LADIES' WORK, &c. &c. will take place in the MUSIC HALL, Dunfermline, on TUESDAY, 13th SEPTEMBER next, commencing at Eleven o'clock forenoon, under the Management of

Mrs Hunt, Logie House.
Mrs Kerr, Abbey Park Place, Dunfermline.
Mrs Beveridge, Prior's House.
Mrs Carr, Bank of Scotland.
Mrs Duncanson, Abbey Park Place.

Mrs Kidd, Viewfield Place.
Mrs Kno??, Buchanan Street.
Miss M'Diarmid, St Margaret Street.
Mrs Inglis, Viewfield Place.
With the assistance of other Ladies.

Contributions of Fancy Work, &c. will continue to be received by the above-named Ladies till the day of Sale.

The Music Hall will be Decorated for the occasion, and an INSTRUMENTAL BAND will be in attendance.

ADMISSION.—From Eleven A.M. till Three P.M. One Shilling; from Three P.M. to Close of Sale, Sixpence.

N.B.—The Prices of Articles Exposed to Sale will be marked upon them, and will be regulated as nearly as possible by the actual value.

ABERFOYLE INN.

ROBERT BREWSTER, with his sincere and cordial acknowledgements to the Public for the patronage bestowed upon his Hotel, begs to intimate, that by an enlargement of the Hotel and extension of his premises, he will now be enabled to provide for the increased conveniences, and still more comfortable accommodation of those who may honour him with their countenance.

The Inn of Aberfoyle is situated within the distance of a short walk from the singularly picturesque and celebrated angling Lake of Loch-ard, and within six miles of the admirable scenery of the Trosachs and Loch Katrine.

N.B. will be happy to point out the various interesting localities to Tourists, and to afford them every information connected with the portion of their route. Well aired Beds are now fully provided, and every attention bestowed on the comforts of those residing in the Hotel.

Breakfasts, Dinners, and Refections, got ready on the Shortest Notice.

WINES and SPIRITS, PORTER and ALES of the First Quality.

Vehicles for Hire, and suitable Stabling.

THE RAVENSCRAIG
CHEMICAL COMPANY
AND PREPARERS OF THE
ASPHALTE WORK,
Of every description, for Home or Export.

THEIR position enables them to produce the best Materials at the most moderate cost, and skilful Workmen will ensure satisfaction to their Employers. As the advantages and appliances of ASPHALTE are not generally known, these may with propriety be stated:—

...no, any sand properly manufactured Land floor is form a Cheap and Durable Pavement, but its imperviousness to Damp and Vermin recommends it as the best sort of Flooring for dwelling-houses, Cellars, Flat Warehouses, Grain Mills and Granaries, Barns, Stables, Dairies, &c. &c.

Builders and Contractors who prefer laying Asphalte themselves, may be supplied with BITUMEN of the best quality, on the most liberal terms.

Apply at the Works; or to
JAMES BOGIE, Manager, Kirkcaldy.

Highland and Agricultural Society's Show,

WESTERN DISTRICT OF PERTHSHIRE.

COMPREHENDING the Parishes of Callander, Kilmadock, Kincardine, Comrie, Dunblane, Aberfoyle, and Port of Monteith, with that part of the District of Drumblane, comprising Glendochy, Glenfinlarig, and Glenfalloch, will be held at Callander, on Thursday, the 29th day of September next, when the following Premiums will be awarded:—

AYRSHIRE BREED.

1. For the best Bull, not exceeding eight years old, belonging to a Proprietor or Farmer—The Silver Medal.

2. For the best Bull, calved before the 1st January, 1851, and not exceeding eight years old, belonging to a Tenant or Proprietor farming who rents his own lands—Eight Sovereigns.

3. For the second best—Four Sovereigns.

4. For the best Bull, calved after the 1st January, 1851, belonging to a Tenant or Proprietor farming the whole of his own lands—Five Sovereigns.

WEST HIGHLAND BREED.

1. For the best pair of heifers (of three years old), calved after 1st January, 1850, belonging to a Tenant or Proprietor farming the whole of his own lands—Five Sovereigns.

2. For the second best—Three Sovereigns.

The Highland Society's Rules will be strictly adhered to, and no Money Premiums will be adjudged unless there are three Lots established, and not more than one half unless there are six. A competitor may exhibit two Lots in each class. For the Silver Medal two Lots authorise an...

Scottish Central Railway.

Pleasure Trip to Aberdeen.
On SATURDAY, 3d September.

A SPECIAL TRAIN WILL LEAVE
Stirling, ... At 6 A.M.
Bridge of Allan, ... At 6.10 "
The Return Train will leave Aberdeen at 6.30 P.M.

Passengers may remain in Aberdeen until the following Monday, and return by any Train according to the Class of Carriage.

Fares to Aberdeen and Back—
4s 6d. Third Class—6s. First Class.
To ensure Conveyance, early application is necessary.

SATURDAY EXCURSION TRAINS.

EVERY SATURDAY, until further notice, a SPECIAL TRAIN will Leave
Stirling at .... 7 P.M.
Bridge of Allan, ... 7.10 P.M.
Arriving in Perth at .... 8.45 P.M.

THE RETURN TRAIN
Will leave Perth at .... 7.30 P.M.
And Arrive at Bridge of Allan, 9.5 P.M.
" Stirling, 9.15 P.M.

FARES.
Stirling, or Bridge of Allan, to Perth & back,
Third Class, ... One Shilling.
First Class, ... Two Shillings.

These Tickets enable the holders to leave and join the Excursion Trains at any of the Intermediate Stations.

By Order.

Farm in Stirlingshire to Let.

THE Farm of Frossanbine, in the Parish of Balfron, on which there is a good Steading, consisting upwards of 80 Scotch Acres of excellent Arable Land, a considerable part of which is thoroughly drained. The Farm lies in the immediate vicinity of Fintry, and at the Balgair Cattle Markets, and will be Let for such term of years as may be agreed upon. Entry at Martinmas.

There are several hundred Larch Trees, suitable for Railway Sleepers, on the Estate, for Sale.

For particulars as to the Farm, apply to A. G. Spiers, Esq. of Culcreuch, the Proprietor, or James Kerr, writer in Stirling; and as to the Trees, application may be made to Rt. Strachan, Forester in Culcreuch.

August, 1853.

TO LET,

For such number of years as may be agreed upon, with entry at Martinmas, 1853,

THE following FARMS and INN in the Parish of Port of Monteith, and County of Perth:—

The Farm of Ballingrew, as at present possessed by Mr Archd. Dow, containing 150 acres Scots or thereby, of which about 140 are arable, the remainder good moor pasture.

The present Tenant is not to be an offerer.

The Farm of Lochend, containing 140 acres Scots or thereby, of which about 130 are arable, the remainder good meadow and pasture land.

The whole Farm is at present under grass, and would be much benefited by draining, to which an enterprising Tenant would be assisted. Also, to Let, the New Inn and Stables, &c. at Port of Monteith. The Inn will present many advantages, on account of the beauty of the surrounding...

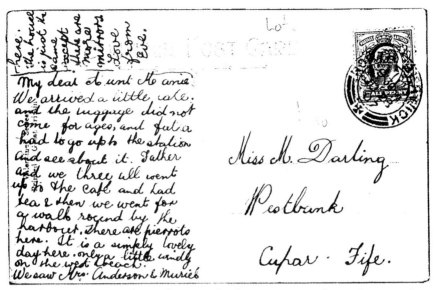

10. The attractions of North Berwick, from a postcard sent in 1907 (see page 82).

11. A George Washington Wilson postcard view of the West Bay, North Berwick, c.1893, with bathing huts at the beach.

MOFFAT HYDROPATHIC 2572

12. Moffat Hydro, from a postcard c.1910. One of the largest Scottish hydro hotels, Moffat was to burn to the ground in June 1921, and was never rebuilt.

MOFFAT *The* OFFICIAL GUIDE WITH MAP

13. Moffat: The Official Guide. By the 1920s every tourist resort in Scotland of any consequence had an official guide, usually published by E. J. Burrows of Cheltenham, which was available either free or at a nominal charge from the Town Clerk.

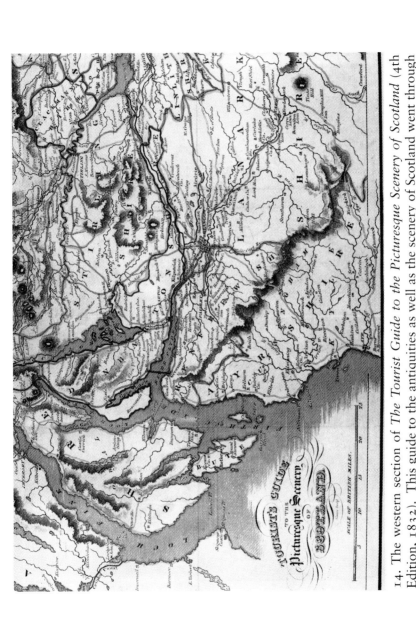

14. The western section of *The Tourist Guide to the Picturesque Scenery of Scotland* (4th Edition, 1832). This guide to the antiquities as well as the scenery of Scotland went through several editions and included details of steamboat tours from Leith and Glasgow.

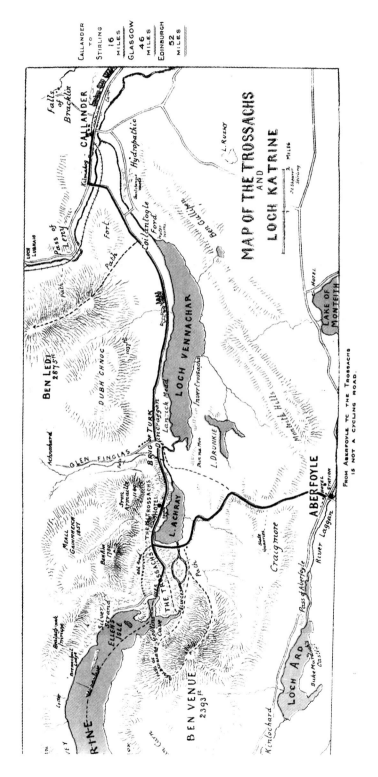

15. Map of the Trossachs and Loch Katrine, from *Shearer's Guide to the Trossachs and Loch Lomond* (1915 edition). Tours, as this map shows, were to be undertaken by a combination of train, coach and steamer.

MIXED BATHING

16. Mixed bathing. The sort of scene that flouted every convention of proper seaside behaviour.

17. The height of the season at Prestwick. Overcrowding during the peak of the summer season was endemic at all resorts, especially if the sun shone.

18. The Last Boat from Dunoon. Steamers to and from the coastal resorts were packed during the summer and especially during the Glasgow Fair. Many, of course, had to get back to their work. 'Very right', adds the sender of this card in August 1911.

Monday morning at the Coast – "Good bye" to the Boys 15/8/04

Is this you weeping I don't think so

19. Monday morning at the Coast. Many professional families took houses at the coast for the summer, with the fathers commuting back during the week to their city offices. Waving 'goodbye to the boys' on the Monday morning was perhaps a familiar scene. Perhaps the husbands were not missed as much as they might have wished: 'Is this you weeping? I don't think so' is the tag added in pen by the sender.

ESPLANADE AND SANDS, LOOKING E., PORTOBELLO.

20. Portobello Esplanade and Sands. A crowded beach and packed promenade at this popular resort. Everyone is well covered up, even those paddling, due to the stiff east wind as much as conventions of proper beach dress.

21. The front cover of David MacBrayne's Official Guide (1884). Not surprisingly, this features the caves of Staffa and the Abbey at Iona, key destinations for MacBrayne's summer outings.

IF YOU'RE RUN DOWN,
COME TO PITLOCHRY

22. 'If you're run down, come to Pitlochry'. The coming of the motor car brought mobility for the monied few, but made main streets hazardous for the locals during the touring season, as here c.1910.

UNLIMITED RAIL TRAVEL WITH

WEEKLY HOLIDAY SEASON TICKETS

1st APRIL to 31st OCTOBER 1 9 3 7

UNLESS OTHERWISE SHOWN

EDINBURGH
THE LOTHIANS
BERWICKSHIRE AND
LAND OF SCOTT

23. A weekly holiday season ticket (LNER 1937). The railways in the 1930s were still a major force in Scottish tourism. Billed as 'the cheapest way to travel', these tickets allowed you to travel anywhere in the given area. In this instance the Borders are still being called the Land of Scott.

for more moneyed visitors. Numerous guides for fishermen appeared
to cash in on this growing market, some advising on tackle, dress and
technique on well-known waters such as Loch Leven, others publicis-
ing the possibilities in Sutherlandshire and the far North. An early one
to appear was that of the Borders expert, Thomas Stoddart of Kelso,
The Angler's Companion, (first edition 1850) which covered the
stream, river, loch and estuary fishing in Scotland from the Solway
to Caithness. Another writer was Robert Blakey, a philosopher and
logician to trade, whose guide was published at Glasgow in 1854.
Blakey argued that no country in Europe was better for angling than
Scotland. This was because of the ease of access: 'impediments resulting from exclusive reserves and pet waters are but of rare occurrence,
and the fair and gentlemanly sportsman will experience but little
interruption'. Stewart's *The Practical Angler*, which went through
several editions in the 1850s and 1860s, agreed: 'trout-fishing in
Scotland is within reach of all'. Hotels in the Highlands and elsewhere
made a point in their advertising of stressing whether they had fishing
and boats available. Tibbie Shiels' Inn at St Mary's Loch was one very
popular Borders hostelry for anglers, some of whom left a record of
their prowess in the visitors' books. One claim, which may have been
liable to the usual exaggeration, made on 7th June 1869 by a Lasswade
expert, that he had caught three dozen splendid trout averaging from 1
to 3 pounds each, drew a scornful comment – 'The above is a load of
tosh'. It was certainly worth hotels doing what they could to encourage
the sport: John M'Fadyen at Cuilfail Hotel ('take yer rods and yer
reels') near Oban in the 1880s had several local lochs stocked with
Loch Leven trout, and kept steady boatmen to take guests deep-sea
fishing. It was not unknown for local angling associations to take
advantage of visitors' ignorance, and their enthusiasm. It was agreed at
the AGM of the Speyside group in January 1916 that it was a little
unfair to charge two guineas for a salmon permit for April, a month in
which not a fish had been caught for years.

Fishing and some other sports have had considerable attention
already. The focus here, however, is on two activities drawn exclu-
sively from supposedly opposite ends of the social spectrum. The first
is grouse shooting, an upper-class preserve, and the other golf, a sport
which in Scotland has always been held to be a democratic game,
enjoyed by all sections of society, rather than as in England just the
economic elite. Both were long-established activities, but, owing in no
small measure to their place in Scottish tourism, were greatly to be
reshaped in the nineteenth century.

Grouse shooting, as in the case of salmon fishing, was reserved for and by the economic and social elite. Indeed it became the sport par *excellence* for many southern sportsmen. It was remarked by the editor of *The Field* in 1872 that 'If you could throw a net over the Highlands in August, you would catch nine-tenths of the genius and glory of Britain'. It was a group rather than an individual activity, unlike deerstalking. Orr has shown how deer forests were formed in increasing numbers from the 1830s onwards, a process accelerated in the later nineteenth century by the fall in sheep prices and the flow of southern money, particularly new money coming north. As one contemporary remarked in 1892, 'as soon as a man has amassed a fortune in any way, his first desire seems to be to buy or hire a deer forest in Scotland and there to gather his friends to enjoy hospitality and sport'. There was the quip of J.S. Blackie that 'London brewers shoot the grouse, and lordlings the deer'. Amongst the tenants of Scottish deer forests were Sir Alfred Bass, Samuel Whitbread and others. Rents soared, more and more land was put into forest; and whereas in 1883 16% of the land in the crofting counties had been devoted to deer stalking, by 1911 the proportion had doubled to 34%. Roads, fences, paths and lodges were built at considerable expense, keepers, ghillies and stalkers taken on. Deerstalking was big business; George Malcolm, an expert in Highland matters, estimated that between 1843 and 1883 about £4.5 million had been spent on Scottish deer forests. But, important though deer forests were in revenue generation, the income (rental and expenditure) from grouse moors, according to contemporary expert evidence in 1909, was five times that of the deer forests, at £1.5 million from just over 3,000 grouse shootings as against £300,000 from 197 deer forests. A number of Highland estates – some deer, some grouse – were by 1893 highly dependent on sporting income to balance their books, with nearly 50% of their income coming from this source. In Mrs Tweedie's novel, *Wilton QC: Or Life in a Highland Shooting Box* (London, 1895), the attractive Lorna Stracey is told by Mr Fraser, her Highland host, that 'Were it not for the grouse, and the possibility of letting the moors, many an owner would be utterly penniless'.

Rises in rentals during the nineteenth century were substantial; not just a few percent but very much higher depending on the past bags, the facilities and the proximity of a moor to the railway. Evidence gathered in 1865 showed rises of between three- and tenfold in rentals for shootings as against the situation in the 1830s. Some moors made even more: the shootings of Glen Urquhart were let for £100 in 1836, and in 1864 – less than thirty years later – for about £2000. The rise seems to have been general: the rental of Aberarder in Aberdeenshire had increased from £70 p.a. in the 1830s to £400 in the mid-1860s; that of an estate on Harris from a mere £25 in 1833 to £2,000 in twenty years. Such was the impact of southern demand. Contemporaries regarded the income from sporting rents as a golden stream of no small magnitude and one which benefited all classes alike. The proprietors, of course, had running costs to meet and had to spend money on providing accommodation, shooting lodges and the like. At the top end of the market, Lord Abinger spent some £40,000 on Inverlochy House, near Inverness, in the 1880s, and others were not far behind. The role of the gamekeepers, of whom there were 609 in 1836 and 1,060 in 1868, was and remains very important. Moors where there is no burning nor any control of vermin and predators tend to carry many fewer grouse than keepered ground, as recent research has confirmed. The head keeper was a figure of great authority to those who were new and inexperienced, barely respectful to their face, out of earshot often scathing about their deficiencies.

Though grouse shooting reached its zenith in the later nineteenth century, it seems probable that the flow of southern sportsmen north, after fish or game, was probably already established on some scale in the later eighteenth century, rather earlier than has been allowed, though the evidence is very fragmentary. There was the instruction of the local laird to the innkeeper at Aviemore in 1792 to give preference in accommodation to genuine travellers as against southern sportsmen. What helped greatly to publicise the North was the famed, indeed notorious, tour of the Yorkshire squire Colonel Thornton, so sharply criticised by Walter Scott. This was supposedly undertaken in c. 1784 when he shot and fished his way across the Highlands, safari-style, with servants and supplies to match. His caravan included 11 dogs, six falcons, four servants and a housekeeper, tents, three months' supply of food and drink, spirits, rum and porter ('the latter being a necessary I had great want of'). His book, which was actually a composite of several tours and a regular rental of a shooting lodge on Speyside, was published in 1804. It was only the first of a series of publications that served to whet southern appetites for the North as a sporting destination, and to promote the notion of the Highlands as a place where sportsmen could hunt, shoot and fish, apparently without charge or hindrance. Thornton did not pay for his sport, nor did others. Migratory shooters and fishers, who were gentlemen, merely sent their card ahead, and as the game they sought was abundant and had little or no value, they were granted permission to hunt it, much as present-day landowners would allow anyone to chase midges. That the English believed access was free in Scotland, and the preservation of game not as constricting a factor as elsewhere in Britain, is shown, according to Catherine Sinclair, by the arrival in Scotland in the 1830s of parties of English sportsmen disembarking at Aberdeen or Dundee to shoot their way across country in the (misguided) belief that no-one could or would stop them. In the South of Scotland, where there were also good grouse moors, things were very different: as early as the 1770s proprietors were advertising that their land, whether low or hill ground, was closed to unauthorised gentlemen, and gamekeepers were appointed to enforce such a policy. But as the news spread about the Highlands, and its abundance of game apparently there for the taking, interest was growing: William Paul of London and his nephew came north in 1816 to shoot the Mains of Cluny in Aberdeenshire, to which the tenant, one Macpherson, objected strongly. In 1817 the prowess of two Highland proprietors on the Mar Estate was reported in Scottish newspapers: the Marquis of Huntly's party shot upwards of 1100 brace of grouse, and another group had 821 brace, 'besides red deer, roes and ptarmigan'. This account smacks rather of the medieval battue, rather than what was to develop – the careful cropping of a commercial gamebird.

The 1830s have traditionally been seen, by the Earl of Malmesbury amongst others, as the decade when southern sportsmen started to come north in number rather than in penny lots to fish and shoot, and to pay their way rather than merely relying on Highland proprietors' hospitality. Grouse shooting was beginning to acquire status: one of the exiled Charles X's ministers, the Baron D'Haussey, found himself invited to shoot in the Highlands. He seems to have enjoyed it but little: 'fatiguing and the weather miserable' was his diary entry. But he did recognise that the invitation was a mark of respect and acceptance in society. An American tourist, Nathaniel Willis, complained in 1835 about the way in which the Caledonian Canal boats were so crowded with sportsmen and their ladies. There were dogs of every kind; some, like the terriers and pointers, were working dogs, others merely ornamental, 'chained to every leg of a sofa, chair, portmanteau and fixture in the vessel'.

Why may this decade have been so significant in marking the transition of grouse shooting to a commercial sport? There was legislation in 1831 which extended the right to shoot game to anyone who had bought a game licence and had permission to shoot. It also legalised the sale of game, something which became of increasing significance as the steamships and railways pushed north; grouse and venison could now reach southern markets fresh. But the growth of sporting tourism in Scotland in the 1830s was due not to legislative change but to a combination of two factors. There was the greater knowledge of Scotland through writings such as those of Thornton and his many successors who wrote on sporting matters, and first-hand reports spread by word of mouth from sportsmen who had been north. Easier access afforded first in the 1820s by the steamships, and then increased in the 1840s by the railways, also helped. More and more sportsmen found their way north, to fish or shoot. The visitors' books for the Atholl Arms at Dunkeld in Perthshire contain the signatures of many southern sportsmen; for example on August 28th 1840, Col. Lewis Coker and Capt. G. Longman stayed 'on return from shooting quarters'. Lord Cockburn, the circuit judge, in the same year observed that 'attracted by grouse, the mansion houses of half of our poor devils of Highland lairds are occupied by rich and titled southrons'. In September 1846 he noted that he had found a party of Irish grouse shooters at Glenshee; he remarked that:

> this autumnal influx of sporting strangers is a very recent occurrence in Scotch economy. Almost every moor has its English tenant. They are not to be counted singly or in pairs, or in coveys but by droves or flocks.

A sign of the growing commercialisation of field sports in the High-lands was the issue in 1837 by the Inverness gunsmith Snowie of his first list of shootings available for rent. Snowie was, in the words of one contemporary, 'a perfect mine of information about sport in the Highlands' and was to build a remarkable position as the intermediary between Highland proprietors and Southern sportsmen. He was the 'pivot on which all shooting business and information turned in the Highlands between 1835 and 1875', spending a month each year in London, where he could give first-hand advice. His first list in 1837 contained but eight moors; thirty years later it had several hundred entries, and was issued quarterly. There were grouse moors in the Scottish Lowlands and in North Yorkshire, but, good though these were, they were already sewn up and relatively few were available to rent. The Highlands essentially offered fresh pastures to the southern sportsmen. Under financial pressure, some Highland proprietors wanted to sell, others to let out part or all of their ground for sport. Southern demand, both to purchase or to rent, was steadily growing. The Highlands were an ever more popular area which, thanks in part to Queen Victoria, and Albert's enthusiasm for northern sports, forced itself on to the fashionable calendar. 'A summer excursion to the Highlands is now become what a trip to Paris or a tour in Switzerland was formerly', said the *Quarterly Review* in 1865, and enterprising middlemen cashed in on this. A successor to Snowie was the Perthshire journalist, J. Watson Lyall. His guide, which first appeared in 1873, listed hundreds of shootings and fishings, with considerable detail. Other firms were to follow, including E. Paton & Son of St James' Street, London (Scottish Shooting, Fishing and Estate Agents), Robert Hall of *The Highland Sportsman*, and the Glasgow-based firm, Walker, Fraser & Steele of *The Scottish Register of Grouse Moors, Deer Forests, Fishings and Mansion Houses*. The last found them-selves involved in a most embarrassing case in 1899 over the rental of an estate by a southern sportsman, Sir Benjamin Brodie of Surrey, who had rented the Aros Castle estate and fishing on Mull on the strength of the description in their handbook. When the baronet arrived, complete with family, five servants and a butler, he found that he had been badly misled. The castle was a run-down farmhouse, with rats in the kitchen, no furniture for the servants, and dreadful drains; the six miles of fine exclusive fishing turned out to be less than three and shared with scores of others, all of whom seemed to have permission. He successfully sued the owner, one MacLachlan, a shifty Oban draper, who had supplied the misleading description, and won hefty damages. Walker, Fraser & Steele escaped formal liability, but the whole matter can have done their reputation no good. It would never have happened in Mr Snowie's day, as he recommended nothing that he had not personally inspected. There was certainly a need for scrutiny. It was a constant theme of Victorian literature that the southern sportsman needed to be careful or he would be fleeced. A highly popular novel by Thomas Jeans which appeared in 1864, *The Tomniebeg Shootings*, narrates the misfortunes of two gullible young London clubmen, rather under the weather, who are recommended to take a moor by a Scots doctor: 'It's bracing air ye require'. They fail to appreciate the finely phrased wording of 'no more than eight hundred brace of grouse to be killed in the season', and get rooked left, right and centre over the dogs they rent, the equipment they are sold, the furnishings and provisions that they need but which are not supplied except at a steep price by the factor of the estate, the cupiditous McSnail. Fortunately, love in the person of a local landowner's daughter saves the day for Mr Peter Fribbles. Most scams had no such favourable outcome for the victims.

What added to the appeal of grouse shooting was the way in which it acquired a social distinction or cachet as against ordinary game shooting, parallel to the gap between salmon and trout. For a sports-man to be able to say that he had shot grouse confirmed his position in sporting society, hence many Scottish moors were taken by people on the make, who wished to be able to invite their friends and business acquaintances. Syndicate leasing, as was increasingly the practice on English pheasant shoots, seems to have been very unusual pre-1914 where grouse moors were concerned. The majority of people who shot grouse were in fact guests; Evan Mackenzie estimated in 1895 that 5,000 out of the 6,000 or so who travelled north incurred no expenditure other than their rail fare. Such were the Hittaways, of Trollope's *The Eustace Diamonds* (1882), he being a medium-rank civil servant. When they went to Scotland, as they endeavoured to do every year:

> it was very important that they should accomplish their aristo-
> cratic holiday as visitors at the house of some aristocratic friend
> . . . So well had they played their cards in this respect that they
> seldom failed altogether [and] went to delicious shooting lodges
> in Ross and Argyleshire. Part of the secret of their success was
> that he could handle a gun, and was clever enough never to shoot
> a keeper.

If the steamship began in the 1820s the process of easier access from the South, the trans-Border railways were greatly to enhance it. Even prior to the opening of the Highland Railway north of Perth to Inverness in the mid-1860s, the flow of southern traffic north by rail and road was already well established. *The Perth Courier* reported in mid-August 1845 that in

> the previous eight days the stream of sportsmen, tourists and
> travellers had set in strongly to the north, and in the current week
> a continuous line of private carriages and vehicles of all kinds
> had passed through Perth, independent of those conveyed by
> four daily stage coaches to the Highlands. From the East of
> Inverness there were four steamships in the course of three days –
> two from London and two from Leith, all freighted with the
> muniments of a deer-stalking and grousing campaign.

The prospect of sporting traffic, much of it travelling first-class, was one which attracted railway promoters. The prospectus of the Ding-wall & Skye Railway in 1864 drew attention to the potential revenue to be generated by sportsmen: 'The country which the proposed line will traverse is of a most picturesque character, abounding in the finest scenery and stocked with game, so that tourists and sportsmen will both benefit by such a district thrown open to them and the pleasure traffic is likely to form an important ingredient in the success of this scheme'. When the West Highland line was being considered in the late 1880s, one of the local agents suggested that there was no point in holding a meeting in the area until August when the sportsmen would be in the county; they, rather than the local proprietors, had the necessary capital. Sporting revenue, all ˙ largely concentrated in two months, was an important element ˙ ˙nances of many northern railway companies, with Perth ? ˙tre of traffic. Of course the relationship could turn ˙ companies. The half-yearly meeting of the Hig¹ ˙er 1873 heard that the passenger traffic

usually so goc   ˙ejudicially
affected by the ˙   shooting
traffic suffered a he   he grouse
this season in the H₁

Why did grouse shooting b   ˙tter and high-status activity for the Victorian s₊   ˙mber of factors were significant. First there was the   ˙ the quarry. The grouse – *lagopus Scoticus* – and the blac˙ ˙e, unlike those staples of the shooting fraternity, the pheasant, the partridge and the duck, cannot be bred on any scale, though attempts were made in the 1890s. The biggest of all the grouse family, the capercailzie, was successfully reintroduced in the 1860s from Norway, but the failure to develop grouse breeding successfully was something that led to acute concern when diseases like the worm or the tick reached epidemic proportions. There was even a high-powered landowners' Committee on Grouse Disease, chaired by Lord Lovat, which began work in 1905. It produced in 1911 a two-volume report entitled *The Grouse in Health and Disease*. Challenged by the tick, the weather, the burning of heather ('muirburn') and predators, there were years when stocks were so low the grouse could not be shot, or at least the number of days had to be sharply reduced. The return of grouse bags on one Lanarkshire moor at Douglas over the period 1858 to 1887 showed several low years with just a few hundred shot and yet others with three, four or even five thousand. Perhaps the starkest contrast on this particular moor was between 1866, a remarkable season with 5942 brace, and the following year with a mere 208. There was a similar collapse in 1873 after a good summer the previous year. The reason was not overshooting but disease. The degree of uncertainty heightened the expectation of the southern sportsman. No columns were pored over more anxiously than those entitled 'prospects for the Twelfth', which appeared in June and July in the national press. The grouse was not like the pheasant, where rearing could supply any shoot with a superfluity; this was a wild bird. This reality imposed on landowners and lessees alike the need for a longer-term perspective which clashed with the practice of annual letting, which offered no security to the responsible tenant who wished to cancel a season's shooting because of a shortage of birds. There was indeed some concern by the later nineteenth century as to whether grouse were in danger of being shot out: *Punch* in August 1882 carried an apocalyptic cartoon entitled 'The Shooting of the Last Grouse. An Alarmist's Vision of A.D. 1900', of a solitary bird surrounded on all sides by southern sportsmen. Allied to the wildness of the quarry, which made the quest for the grouse an expedition rather than a weekend sortie, were the distances involved and the exclusiveness of participating sportsmen. The time involved, and cost, kept the hoi-polloi away, and afforded relief and protection to harassed politicians. When the crusading Florence Nightingale returned from the Crimea in August 1856, she was unable to gain access to the Secretary at War, Lord Panmure, because he was grouse-shooting in Scotland.

The chronology of the season also played a major role. The timing of the opening of the season fitted nicely with August and the English holidays, when the law courts and Parliament alike were normally out of session. The Preservation of Game Act (1772) Scotland had set the seasons: 12th August to 28th December for grouse. Grouse was (and remains) the first of the British game birds to come into season, partridge not until Sept 1st, pheasant a month later on October 1st. The eve of the Glorious Twelfth saw monster trains wending their way north. The 7.50 a.m. train from Perth north in the first week of August set records year after year. On 8 August 1888 a thirty-six carriage train set forth, including carriages from nine companies from the London & Brighton to the Highland Railway: saloons, luggage cars, horse boxes and carriage trucks, all traffic assessed in 1890 by the railways expert W. M. Acworth as 'Splendidly profitable'. Dogs, of course, abounded; something that was caught well by the novelist Ian McLaren in his description of the fictional Muirtown station on the eve of the Twelfth:

> Along the edge of the Highland platform stretches a solid mass of life, close-packed, motionless, silent, composed of tourists, dogs, families, lords, dogs, sheep-farmers, keepers, clericals, dogs, footmen, commercials, ladies, maids, grooms, dogs waiting . . . (*Kate Carnegie*, London, 1896)

This timetable could be thrown askew should the parliamentary year overrun. Gilbert used a powerful argument in *Iolanthe* (1882) when

the Fairy Queen threatened to prolong the life of Parliament into
August and September. 'You shall sit, if he sees reason, through the
grouse and salmon season'; cries of 'No, No, Spare us' from the peers.
It happened in 1909, thanks to Lloyd George's Budget. As early as
June of that year, *The Times* was wondering whether there would be
the same rush for moors that season: 'Alas for the weary legislators
who see no prospect or release from Budget woes and strife. Is it not
probable that many who have hitherto been accustomed to rent a
shooting may hesitate and turn their thoughts to more rigid economy
in view of the heavy burdens which are threatened on all sides'. The
article went on to refer to the consequences for all sections of the
Highland community: 'Railway companies, hotel proprietors, farmers, crofters, moor proprietors . . . every class depends on the harvest.
The moors are to the Englishman what "les eaux" are to the Frenchman or the Alps to an Italian'. The worst did indeed come to pass in
that year; Parliament sat on through August, and although there were
some extra trains on the eve of the Twelfth, railway traffic from
London was much quieter than in normal years. The implications for
the North were serious. In Perthshire alone some £5,000 worth of
rented moors, or roughly 1 in 12 of the locality's moors and forests,
were unlet, and others were leased at very reduced rents. The reason,
which all understood, was obvious: 'Parliament is still sitting, and a
large number of members who come north for shooting are detained
with their Parliamentary duties'.

The value of grouse shooting as a recreation which restored the
jaded mind and body of the professional man also counted greatly in
its favour. It was seen as a healthy pursuit, undertaken in a healthy
environment, clean air, empty hills and the like. W. Grant Stewart, for
example, in his book *Highlands and Highlanders*, which appeared in
1860, talks of the way in which competition for good grouse moors
had brought both high rents to proprietors, and benefits to the takers:

> Behold the Saxon sportsman proceeding to his moors on the eve
> of the great day, the twelfth of August; his pale parchment
> physiognomy perhaps rendered still more cadaverous by hirsute
> appendages of Crimean fashion, his trembling feeble steps, still
> breathing from his pulmonic cells a store of miasma imbibed
> from the putrid Thames, like a spectre escaped from the church-
> yard – and then returning to his metropolis home with expanding
> cheeks suffused with the bloom of health.

What was the place of women and families? There is some evidence to
suggest that whereas in the early days northern forays had been a male

preserve, this pattern changed during the latter part of the nineteenth century. MacKenzie observed that 'the shooting lodges are now more luxurious and accessible and bachelor parties have to give way to family ones, occasioning treble the expense of transfer'. Game books for the grouse moors do show that women did occasionally shoot, as happened in low-ground sport. There was a range of alternative occupations other than shooting for them: fishing, picnicking, sightseeing, sketching and so on to fill the time, and, of course, letter-writing and churchgoing to pass the Sabbath, on which no sporting activity was permitted. The arrival of families and of marriageable daughters is held to have been instrumental in developing an evening circuit of balls and dances, 'le apres-grouse'. 'Grouse are', said Catherine Sinclair in 1840, 'the unconscious benefactors of Scotland. They gather the best company round them, as without their attractions we should be almost entirely deserted.'

Two other factors were of major significance in the later nineteenth century when grouse shooting came to attain its fullest popularity. Firstly there were significant advances in the technology of shooting, in particular changes to guns and cartridges. Breach loading was introduced in the 1860s, and the use of smokeless cartridges in the 1870s was also a major advance; both of them made it possible to shoot faster, if not better. Another consequence of the new, lighter guns was that they allowed the older shooter to continue with his sport longer than had been possible with the heavy muzzleloaders. Horatio Ross, M.P., one of the most notable grouse shots of the century, is recorded in his mid-70s as having shot 86 birds with 89 shots, shooting over dogs on the 12th of August 1875. Secondly there was an important organisational development: the introduction on northern moors of the technique of driving grouse over butts, which required an elaborate system of keepers, beaters, and flagmen. It allowed both bigger bags and an opportunity for less fit or active sportsmen to participate. With dogging, using pointers and setters, the shooters went to the birds; under driving the birds came to the shots. By 1900 roughly half the grouse were falling to driving rather than dogging. Prince Albert did much in the 1850s to confirm the status of deer stalking; Edward VII did the same for grouse driving. He had been a keen walker-up and stalker in his youth, but as he got older, and bulkier, the sheer physical exertion would have ruled these activities out. In any case, his commitments to Cowes and Doncaster Races meant he got to Balmoral too late in the season for walking up, as the birds were too wild by then. Driving was a godsend to him, and his endorsement and that of his son, the Prince of Wales, did much to enhance the popularity of driven grouse. Both methods had their devotees and season; there was ground which could be driven, and some that could not. And many younger shots enjoyed the walking-up days on the margins or tops of the moors.

Sometimes tourism, or some types of it, does not benefit the local population. While Highland proprietors did well from the sporting interest in grouse, was this shared by those crofters whose year-round livelihood depended on sheep and other traditional forms of land-use? Deerstalking was controversial and several flashpoints existed between sheep and deer. The taking of ground for deer forests was a very sore point, as the working of sheep and stalking did not mix, and the winter raiding of deer on crops was much resented. Crofters were not the only group to be put out by deer preserves; the general public, walkers and mountaineers complained vigorously about being barred entry to Highland estates. Correspondents to *The Times* in 1866 complained that tourists were being denied access to a number of desirable points, including Ben Macdhui. Powerful denunciation of the feudal power of proprietors was voiced: 'In these secluded glens, oppression may silently and ruthlessly crush the poacher and the poor hospitable harbourer of the poacher. The same submissive deference cannot surely be expected from travellers'. The American millionaire, W. L. Winans, was especially unpopular with locals and other sportsmen, thanks to his revival of deer driving where his keepers brought the beasts to him rather than stalking them himself, and to his treatment of anyone disrupting his deer preserves. He is said to have had thrown off his ground a Glasgow naturalist who was collecting flies on his heather. Even more controversially, in 1885 he tried, and failed, to prevent one of the cottars on his rented estate from letting his pet lamb stray onto the unfenced part of his deer forest across the road.

Deer have a firmly established place in the debit sheet of Highland land management, but much less controversy arose over grouse, though sheep and grouse do not always mix well. Control of predation by keepers did not worry sheep farmers; rather the reverse in the case of foxes. Burning did create strain: farmers inclining, or so keepers said, to burn too much and to let their sheep overgraze the young heather, thus preventing its regeneration. Some of the sporting income from grouse found its way into local pockets. Perhaps, whereas the deerstalking generated little or no call for additional labour, as many as 10,000 or even more beaters were required in the Highlands during the season. Alexander Fenton has shown from the account book of a day labourer in Glenesk how much difference the arrival of commercial grouse shooting in the 1820s made to him. His normal wage was 1/3d to 1/6d for cutting grass, but when acting as a ghillie on walking-up days for wealthy visitors he could earn from 3/- to 5/- a day in wages. Tipping, particularly after a good day, to keepers, pickers-up and loaders involved substantial sums. The merchants of the larger centres benefited by many of the lodges buying in everything for the season: lock, stock and barrel (or piano). Amongst the Perth businesses advertising in one popular sporting publication in 1882 to supply shooting parties were McIntyre and Stewart, Pastry, Biscuit and Bread Makers, the Perth Coach Hiring Establishment, and McKendrick, Family Butcher. Gunsmiths and fishing-tackle shops in Scotland, whose sales reached a crescendo in July and August, doubled in number in the second half of the nineteenth century. Scottish-made double-barrelled shotguns, Martins and Dicksons, became popular, though many English visitors brought their Purdeys or Lancasters, some matched pairs. The sale of cartridges, clothing and footwear brought in additional income.

Grouse shooting was a sport enjoyed by the relatively few. Golf reached a much wider sporting constituency. It had a long history in Scotland, played on the East Coast and in the North both by the elite and the general populace; the parish minister reported in 1795 that the fishwives of Musselburgh on holidays frequently played at golf on the local links. Indeed, a special prize of a new creel and shawl was created in 1810 for their New Year's Day competition. There were exclusive clubs, such as that of the Honourable Company of Edinburgh Golfers at Muirfield, but golf steadily became more and more popular, and people of all ages and ranks took up the game, with a strong artisan representation. Dirleton Castle Golf Club in East Lothian, founded in 1854, had a playing membership which included local farmers, tradesmen (including the village's butcher and shoemaker), a commercial traveller and a horse trainer. Their secretary was the landlord of the appropriately named Golf Tavern. Amongst the first winners of the Patron's medal, presented by a local landowner, was a railway worker. This participation was thanks in part to the development from the 1840s onwards of a replacement for the expensive golf featherie by the gutty ball, which was much cheaper and therefore opened the sport to a wider clientèle, especially the novice or wild hitter. Every resort had its shops at which equipment could be bought, and local boys discovered a useful sideline in the recycling of lost balls. Golf clubs, cleeks and irons were made by an ever-growing number of small firms. St Andrews had the Auchterlonies and the Forgans, North Berwick Ben Sayers, Dumfries George

Fernie, and even Monifieth could show two: James Smith and James Watson.

Golf was already well established by the mid-nineteenth century at Aberdeen, St Andrews, Perth, Edinburgh and North Berwick, but there was to be an extraordinary boom thereafter with as many as 200 courses opening between 1870 and 1914 in and around the cities, and at every holiday destination of any significance from Aberfeldy to Uist. *The Golfer's Annual* for 1888 listed 73 courses for Scotland – more than the combined total for England, Ireland and Wales. Ten years later there were three times as many. As Baddeley's *Thorough Guide* remarked in 1912, 'in Scotland, a place is not a place without its 'gowf''. Some of the courses, not all of which were 18 holes in length, were new: others, as at St Andrews, reconstructions or additions to old links courses. Most were privately financed, but some were municipally funded, of which a good example is that of the Braid Hills in Edinburgh opened in 1890. Within a few years a penny charge had to be introduced as in the summer 5000 golfers a week were using the course. Troon had three municipal courses, patronised by both locals and visitors. Railway companies also played a part; the Great North of Scotland Company opened a prestigious golfing hotel at Cruden Bay in March 1899; six years later the Glasgow and South Western Railway Company followed suit at Turnberry in Ayrshire. The building of the Caledonian Railway's luxury complex at Gleneagles was brought to a halt by the outbreak of the First World War. Special services, and 'golfers' fares', were provided by a number of railway companies on a Saturday to get golfers to and from their course, with supplementary trains provided for the big competitions such as the autumn medals at St Andrews and Dunbar. The Aberlady, Gullane and North Berwick Railway, which served a number of East Lothian courses, was dubbed 'The Golfers' Line'.

While golf was an all-year-round sport in Scotland, many courses were busiest during the summer. Visitor demand was a key element behind the foundation of courses in resort areas everywhere in Britain from Alnmouth to Westward Ho! But nowhere more so than in Scotland. Professionals and businessmen from the towns were influential in the creation and initial support of golf courses in resorts that they could reach at weekends or during the long summer evenings, when in any case their working day finished at about 4 p.m., time enough for a quick round at the coast or in the country. When a course was opened at Burntisland in 1898, many of its out-of-town players came by steamer from Leith. At nearby Kinghorn, of the 234 members enrolled, more than 135 had Edinburgh addresses, and only 31 were from the burgh itself. Though tennis, bowling, swimming and sailing had their devotees, it was golf that interested most active holiday-makers, whether young or old, male or female. Golf equipment was relatively cheap, and old wooden-shafted clubs could be cut down for children. For many, the seaside came to mean both the beach and the links. 'What is there to do at North Berwick?', asked one Glaswegian visitor in 1881, whom we have already quoted. He had found this much-praised resort rather lacking (to his West-coast eyes) in musical and other entertainment:

> The reply is easy, and a single word explains it all – golf! The royal game is the autocratic absorber of the attention of nine-tenths of the gentlemen who reside here. There is scarcely a man who is not an authority on 'tees', 'drives', 'putts' and the other paraphernalia of the game. The very laddies are educated up to golf.

A holiday visitor to the Fife resort of Earlsferry in September 1894 sketched in a typical day there: an early morning bathe, followed by two rounds of golf before lunch, and another bathe; an afternoon rest and a few holes in the early evening, with perhaps a little fishing or gentle walk to round off the day. Golf could be played in most weather and could be enjoyed by fathers and sons, husbands and wives, young men and ladies alike. True, there were some separate courses for ladies, as at Lundin Links, founded in 1890. At Carnoustie, the ladies were excluded from the main championship course, it being considered by male authority that they could not manage the full distance, and that holes of seventy to eighty yards were quite taxing enough. Cruden Bay had a nine-hole ladies' course. But in most places and on most days families could play together. At some, indeed, as at Callander, women were allowed to compete in the club championships. There was segregation of the sexes, at the beach but not on the links. Indeed, mixed golf became quite an established part of the holiday, and added to the delight with many clubs holding weekly mixed foursomes as well as summer tournaments and boys' competitions. Another asset was that, thanks to the handicapping system, people of quite different abilities and experience could have a game on reasonably level terms. In Scotland these seem initially to have been set by the clubs themselves on a reasonably *ad hoc* basis. The committee at one East Lothian course based them both on actual scores and potential: a young player from a golfing family always had his set lower. For those who wanted or needed to improve, there was the local professional or golf instructor, or the caddie's advice, solicited or not. The trials of the caddie with a wealthy novice on the links paralleled the vexations of his counterpart, the keeper, on the grouse moor.

Inland resorts were not slow to follow the lead given by the coast, and by the turn of the century no Scottish holiday centre anywhere was without a course of some kind, and some had several. Arran acquired no fewer than seven, beginning with one at Lamlash in 1889. Aberfoyle, Edzell, Moffat, Crieff, Forres and Dunblane were just some of the other courses which had tourist use firmly in their sights. In the north, at Dornoch, where the links were amongst the oldest in Scotland, golf became the centrepiece of the town's attractions. In 1881 Professor J. S. Blackie described its golfing ground as 'second to none in Scotland', a view endorsed by amateurs and professionals alike: 'There canna be better found for gowf', said Tom Morris. Edward VII endorsed the calibre of Dornoch in 1906 when he awarded the club the title of 'Royal'.

Not to have a course was a major handicap to a resort in Scotland, for which other amenities – boating ponds, parks, and the like – could not compensate. Callander is a case in point. Prompted by Mr A. L. Bruce, a summer visitor from Edinburgh, who was himself a keen golfer, Callander formed a committee in the spring of 1890 to add a golf course to the burgh's attractions. Local business interests were enthusiastic as they felt that fishing and walking were no longer enough, and that golf was undoubtedly the most popular game in Scotland and 'also in England now'. But while the course was well laid out, and it was advertised that strangers who were golfers would be welcome, it was two miles away, accessible not on foot but by bus or some other means of transport. Only when it was moved to a site much closer to the railway station did the club begin to thrive. It was extended from nine to eighteen holes in 1913, the short course having become seriously congested during the summer season. This development was deemed essential by the Town Council if Callander were to preserve its status as a leading health resort and tourist centre. At the opening of the lengthened course in June 1914, one of the speakers, who had been a moving spirit behind the original course, referred to the way it had begun:

It was about the year 1890 that golf became so popular and fashionable in Scotland. Previous to that time, the only golf courses in existence were those at St Andrews and the seaside resorts of Fife and on the coast of Ayrshire, but, owing to courses becoming so general, courses were springing up at every important summer inland resort. A few citizens who still had a grain of public spirit left in them felt that if Callander was to maintain its reputation as a summer resort, some effort should be made to provide a course.

Expenditure on golf courses could be justified not just by the tourist business that they attracted, but by the way that the summer income underpinned club finances. Essentially, while local golfers might be inconvenienced during the tourist season, and have to queue on the starting tee, for the rest of the year they had the course to themselves. Summer income kept their annual subscriptions low. At Callander, the golf club terms were 1/- for daily visitors, 5/- per week, 10/- a month and 27/6 for a family ticket. A year's membership, taken out in January, cost a local only 10/- in all. In 1919, the income from visitors' fees was double that from year-round membership, a pattern that held true for many courses. This goes far to explain why there was so little friction on the golf course (and bowling green or tennis courts) between regulars and visitors. In many resorts, friendly matches were organised every year between residents and summer arrivals. In August 1914, despite the outbreak of war, Dunbar Golf Club played a team of visitors in a 22-man-a-side match, and lost. What also helped to ease relations was the practice of visiting worthies presenting cups and prizes for club competitions. At Grantown-on-Spey, the summer trophy was gifted by Mr and Mrs Miller from Liverpool: the entry rules required that players had to be members of not less than two weeks' standing. Nor could wealthy visitors always insist on preferential treatment. At Dornoch (and elsewhere) during the summer there was a ballot each morning to determine the order of play:

> To the comparatively poor man there are few things in golf more galling than to observe the plutocrat who only arrived on the last train the night before, going off the first tee jauntily at 10.9, while your time, a visitor of some weeks is 11.56. We all know how this is done. It is not done here. As well might you cry for the moon as for a 'wangled time' at Dornoch.

Sport and tourism in Scotland were interwoven. Sport drew visitors to Scotland, and tourist centres in Scotland did what they could to provide attractions for all ages. None fitted the bill better, year in, and year out, than golf. The grouse might fail, but the courses, whatever the climate and conditions, were always playable. Small wonder, therefore, that in the chaos of Perth Station in mid-August as painted by George Earl, there are amongst the gun cases, and other luggage, golf clubs aplenty. Adding a further touch of spice to its attractions was the way that golf could bring the great and the good back to earth. Nothing sums this up better than a newspaper report of Mr A. J. Balfour's misfortunes on one occasion at North Berwick, where he was a frequent visitor: 'The Premier made an unfortunate start, put his ball on the rocks, and took eight to the first hole'. At least on the grouse moor there were no journalists or casual bystanders.

FURTHER READING

Murray's *Handbook for Travellers in Scotland*, 8th edition, ed. Scott Moncrieff Penny (London and Edinburgh, 1903) contains sections on various sports. For golf there is a vast literature, but see for example *A History of Golf in Britain*, eds. B. Darwin, G. Campbell *et al* (London, 1952); G.Pottinger, *Muirfield and the Honourable Company* (Edinburgh, 1972); P. Ward-Davis, *The Royal & Ancient Club of St Andrews: A History* (St Andrews, 1980). While most authorities hold firmly to the democratic nature of golf in Scotland, for a very different assessment see John Lowerson, 'Golf and the Making of Myths', in *Scottish Sport in the Making of the Nation*, ed. G. Jarvie and G. Walker (Leicester, 1994), pp.75–90. On salmon fishing, see Augustus Grimble, *The Salmon Rivers of Scotland* (London, 4 vols., 1899–1900) and Crawford Little, *The Salmon and Sea-Trout Fisheries of Scotland* (Newton Abbot, 1990). For deerstalking, see Duff Hart-Davis, *Monarchs of the Glen: A History of Deer-stalking in the Highlands* (London, 1978). W. Orr, *Deer Forests, Landlords and Crofters* (Edinburgh, 1982) is essential for context. The best account of grouse and grousing is Ronald Eden, *Going to the Moors* (London, 1979). Life on a Highland sporting estate is well caught in John Kerr's study of the Atholl Estates, *The Living Wilderness* (Perth, 1996). For mountaineering there is *The Scottish Mountaineering Journal*, published three times a year since 1890, and W. D. Brooker (ed.), *A Century of Scottish Mountaineering* (Aberdeen, 1989). There is abundant contemporary literature in the periodicals. *Blackwood's Edinburgh Magazine* (Vol. 146, 1889) carried an article by T. Pilkington White, 'Camped out under the Cuillins', which describes a climbing and fishing holiday on Skye. *The Badminton Library of Sports and Pastimes* (London, 1886–1902) includes volumes on *Fishing*, *Big Game Shooting*, *Golf*, and *Yachting*.

6

THE PROMOTION OF SCOTLAND

> . . . Toddles and his friend went out to do Inverness in proper
> tourist fashion. After going to a stationer's shop, where Toddles
> bought a newspaper and a packet of views of the places they had
> seen, they strolled into MacDougall's tartan warehouse, where
> Richard again spent his money on heaps of tartan knickknacks.
>   (Richard Toddles, *Toddles' Highland Tour* (London, 1864))

By the later nineteenth century, for an increasing number of people the
question was not *whether* they would have a holiday, but *where* and
for how long. Income and time would be significant constraints on the
degree of choice. Not all were in the carefree position of this lady, an
experienced traveller, who confided to her journal in 1863:

> What an anxious question this annual holiday is now becoming!
> Everyone here has been to Scotland. Some of us had done Land's
> End, Ireland is not everybody's choice, the International Exhibi-
> tion had tired us all of London, Scarborough is only suitable for
> invalids and children, the Lake district done years ago, and
> Fleetwood is worse than Scarboro'; where shall we go next?
> (*Miss Jemima's Swiss Journal*, London, 1863)

She opted for a Cook's tour to Switzerland with the Junior Alpine
Club, a trip that included an ascent of Mont Blanc. We are looking
now at some of the factors which in the nineteenth century helped to
promote Scotland as a tourist destination for the tourist with choice.
There was a context of rising demand, but also growing competition,
and there was no guarantee that Scotland would benefit. The Continent had always had its devotees on the grounds of health or culture,
and better long-distance transport was opening up all sorts of other
options further afield. Tourism was becoming a highly competitive
business; resort against resort, region against region, country against
country, and unlike nowadays there was no government-sponsored
strategy. Though some legislation had a bearing, such as the Sunday
licensing laws, the British State remained aloof and uninterested
except at the margin. The promotion of Scotland, as elsewhere in
the United Kingdom, was left in private hands, to those parties and
individuals whose financial self-interest was served by growing tour-

ism. It was the pursuit of profit that led companies, especially those in transport and the service sector, to become involved in advertising and promotion, as it did town councils and landowners. The tourism industry was an area of the economy in which the initiative and vision of individuals was highly significant, tourism throwing up entrepreneurial figures just as thrusting – perhaps even more so – as in any other sector of British business. We focus on the activities of two important figures in the development of tourism in Scotland: Thomas Cook, the excursion agent, and George Washington Wilson, the photographer, both of whom played a part in putting Scotland on the tourist map. Successful marketing depends on having a product (in this case decent hotels, recreational services, and the like), on the packaging of the product ('Scotland, the land of the mountain and the flood' was one slogan much favoured) and on promotion. As tourism grew, it was no longer self-directed but increasingly influenced in direction and scale through advertising and image. Several factors shaped tourism: cost was one; fashion another; promotion a third. The best form of promotion, of course, then as now, was that of satisfied customers. Word of mouth played an important, if unquantifiable, role, as did newspaper articles, letters and later postcards.

As the second half of the nineteenth century progressed, the flow of tourist publications about Scotland and its favoured localities became a flood. Specialist publications were produced, as previous chapters have shown, for those interested in fishing, shooting, yachting, mountaineering and other activities. Railway and steamship companies published their own guides. Amongst these were the West Highland Railway's *Mountain, Moor and Loch*, the North British's *The Beauties of Scotland*, the Great North of Scotland's *Three Rivers Tour* (the Dee, the Don and the Spey), the Glasgow & South-Western's *Summer Tours in the Land of Burns*, and MacBrayne's *Summer Tours in Scotland*, 'Glasgow to the Highlands, The Royal Route'. The Photochrom Company of London, already much involved in the issue of albums of views, took a further step in 1910 with the publication of *Bonnie Scotland*, an East Coast Route Official Publication, jointly with the North British Railway Company, the first of 'The Imperial Series' – whose companion volume was entitled 'Twixt Thames and Tweed'. A full list of the Company's 74 tours in Scotland was given, along with prices from either Edinburgh or Glasgow, details of hotels and a medley of advertisements, including one – rather inappropriately – for granite memorial headstones. Montrose, calling itself a 'Garden City by the Sea', took a full-page spread: the selection of photographs included a view of a well-attended sandcastle competition on the beach, and a dull picture of the suspension bridge over the Southesk. Attractively produced in both black & white and colour, well written and beautifully illustrated, such guides served both to inform and to whet the appetite. Resorts could not sit back on their traditional strengths, and town councils increasingly began to realise the importance of advertising. By the end of the century many had publicity committees – usually with a strong representation of local merchants – and were issuing their own guides, either free or at minimal charge. Initially the Town Clerk or some other worthy drafted these, but increasingly there was a move to the use of advertising firms such as E. J. Burrows & Co of Cheltenham. Their *Official Guide to Bridge of Allan* (1915) was number 628 in their Pocket Guides Series; *Crieff* was number 612. Another very active group were local printing and publishing firms, whose business owed much to the tourist trade. An example of this is Daniel Mackay of Oban, bookseller and publisher. In the frontispiece to the Duke of Argyll's *Iona* (1913), Mackays described themselves as the Leading Book, Bible, Stationery and Photographic Warehouse in the locality. They offered maps and guides to Oban and district, models of Iona Cathedral, a list of furnished houses and apartments in the district and – for the use of householders – an ample supply of cards with the headline 'Lodgings to Let'. Newspapers – local, regional and national – were highly influential by the early twentieth century, carrying as they did extensive advertising, reports of excursions, and news of attractions, bazaars, and sports days, as well as weather forecasts. In some resorts – Oban, Rothesay and North Berwick, for example – special summer supplements were issued for visitors. Indeed, so significant was tourism to the local press that one wonders what these papers carried in the winter months. Hotels, apartment keepers, and letting agencies advertised in the national guides and newspapers such as *The Scotsman* or *The Glasgow Herald* which from the Spring onwards carried lists of accommodation to let, and reports from the various resorts as to weather and the attractions.

We have already seen that a complex of attractions drew visitors to Scotland: the search for health, and for sport, scenery and geology, history and literature. The last was particularly significant in the age of the well-read, educated traveller, inclined to visit literary shrines such as Scott's Abbotsford or Burns' Cottage at Ayr. Many of the attractions were permanent features of the tourist landscape, but sometimes nature was enhanced by walks and landscaping, or judicious embellishment. There were also one-off or occasional attractions such as the Glasgow International Exhibition of 1888 which attracted some 5.7 million visitors, including, it was said, many Americans, and indeed Queen Victoria for only her second visit to Glasgow. It was followed by another twenty years later. But whatever draws people to a given destination, there has still to be a significant offering, i.e. an experience of value, or the first visit could be the last. Should a resort get a reputation for dirt, disease and danger, none but the bold will go there, regardless of its natural attractions. It was important to Scotland, therefore, that in addition to its natural resources, the provision of transport, accommodation and facilities was so dramatically improved during the later nineteenth century. Amenities were provided, often with ratepayers' money: better water and sewage provision, golf courses, boating ponds and tennis courts. The building of hotels or their enlargement represented a significant investment; some 190 were built in the period 1840–1900 in the Highlands alone. The capital involved was very considerable. The Marine Hotel at North Berwick, opened in 1880 at a cost in excess of £25,000, was reckoned one of the leading hotels of its type, and the sixteen hydro hotels built in the 1870s required the investment of something like £1/2 million. Most expensive of all was the palatial Atholl Hydropathic at Pitlochry, which cost no less than £80,000 to build and equip. Obviously employment, both permanent and seasonal, was created. According to the 1901 April census, which is far from precise, there were in Scotland over 7,000 inn-hotel keepers, and wine and spirit merchants, but only 4,500 employees in hotels, lodgings and eating places, a figure which takes no account of summer employees. This expansion was obvious everywhere in Scotland, but nowhere more than at Oban, with allegedly more hotels in proportion to its size than Edinburgh. By 1894, 15 hotels were open, plus numerous temperance hotels and lodging houses: some 40 in all, as against a dozen or so thirty years previously. These had been built, as one advert said, stressing the obvious, expressly for 'summer visitors'. Some were very large; at least eight could accommodate over a hundred people. The Marine Hotel, which called itself a high-class *temperance* house, had 100 rooms in 1906: 'On esplanade. Magnificent Sea-view. Moderate tariff. Cook's Coupons'. Patronage by royalty was important to hotels in putting them on the map. The Imperial Hotel in Edinburgh proclaimed in 1881 that it had been 'personally patronised by their royal highnesses, the Duke of Edinburgh, and Prince Frederick William of Prussia'; its advertisement added that it had 'magnificent lavatories with no stairs to climb'! The Royal Hotel at Cupar had been 'patronised by H.R.H. Prince Leopold'; the Balloch Hotel had been visited by the Empress Eugénie, and the Udny Arms at Newburgh had been frequented by the

Crown Prince of Siam. These were what commercial circles knew as titled decoy ducks to lure investors and guests alike. The Royal Hotel at North Berwick, financed by a consortium of local businessmen and the North British Railway Company, was so called after the visit of Prince Albert Edward there in 1859. It was just one of many to play on a royal connection. None made more of its endorsement by royalty than the Palace Hotel at Aberdeen, in the ownership of the Great North of Scotland Railway Company and much used for breakfasts by those travelling on the Royal train to Ballater for Balmoral. It had been personally patronised, its advertising trumpeted in 1903:

> by their Majesties the King and Queen, The Prince and Princess of Wales, The late Empress Frederick of Germany, The Duke and Duchess of Connaught, Princess Christian and Princess Victoria, Princess Henry of Battenberg, Prince and Princess Charles of Denmark, H.S.H. The Duke of Teck, H.I.H. The Princess Eugenie, H.R.H. The King of Portugal, The Prince and Princess Dolgorouki, Grand Duke and Grand Duchess Serge, Grand Duke Paul of Russia, and many distinguished visitors.

What mattered (and still matters) to the visitor was not just the provision of accommodation, but the quality of service. There were certainly complaints about various things: Lord Tennyson, on a visit to the Western Isles in August 1853, complained to his wife that she 'could not possibly conceive the stew and bore of this little hotel crammed to suffocation, dinners, teas and suppers going on altogether which makes it impossible to write'. The grievance most frequently voiced was about the charges imposed and the tips expected in Highland hotels; something which surfaced from time to time in the press. One correspondent to *The Times*, Sept 1st 1869, complained of a constantly growing system of petty extortions – drivers' fees, pier dues, and tips which were driving tourists away from Scotland. He particularly drew attention to the cost of beer: everywhere when a pint was ordered, a mere glass was served, though he specifically exempted good Lowland hotels from this practice. Highland inns were again the subject of a swingeing attack in 1871 by *The Saturday Review* and again in 1883 by an American visitor. Kenneth Bellais thought the food at the smaller inns off the beaten track 'detestable', with no fruit, or any vegetables other than potatoes, to be seen. And even where the hotels were excellent, as at Oban, Aberdeen and Inverness, they were 'terribly dear'. The defence made, and it was made *ad nauseam*, was that the season in the Highlands was a very short one: 'Highland inn-keepers must make their hay in a very short season of sunshine'. Knowledgeable authorities such as Murray tended to take the hotel-keepers' side: 'even if accommodation is rather expensive, it must be remembered that for eight months in the year, the hotel with all its outlay is virtually tenantless'. The short nature of the season – three or four months at best – was a serious problem, though not unique to Scottish hotels. Swiss establishments had exactly the same problem, and were equally criticised. The notion of off-season breaks is a relatively new one, and was scarcely feasible for the more remote locations. There was a busy summer season: June through September, some fishing or sporting men at other times, but mostly October through to May was a dead time for the great majority of Scottish hotels. Some guides did try to persuade tourists to come early and avoid the unpleasantnesses of overcrowding in the height of the season; Baddeley advised that there was no better month than June: 'even so far south as Oban you can read the paper by daylight at 10PM'. But there seems to have been relatively little response.

It is extremely interesting to see how the image of Scotland was massaged in the nineteenth century for tourist consumption. For many visitors, especially from overseas, it was the land of Scott, of Burns, of Ossian and of Barrie. Literary tourism attracted people to places mentioned in the literature which could be either fictional (Jeanie Dean's Cottage) or real (the Trossachs) or actual places associated with the writers, such as their birthplaces or residences: Abbotsford, Burns' Cottage near Ayr, Barrie's birthplace in Kirriemuir. Historical association was also important, particularly with such romantic figures as Mary, Queen of Scots. Increasingly, localities began to manufacture such connections on the merest rumour, a tendency noticed by the American visitor and journalist J. M. Bailey in 1879. He observed how, in the Borders:

> there are nearly five hundred castles in this vicinity. Queen Mary was imprisoned in all of them. That unfortunate must have been in jail about four-fifths of the time. What I now want, what I really pant after, is a ruin that wasn't her prison, that Sir Walter Scott hasn't written about, and that Queen Victoria didn't visit in 1842. But I don't know where to look for it.
>
> (J.M. Bailey, *England from a Back Window*, p.284)

Localities without such literary associations suffered. As has already been noted, it was said of St Andrews in 1852 by *The Scottish Tourist* that it owed its relative neglect, despite its history, ruins and beaches, to the fact that no writing of any standing had been based in or around it. That there is a spin-off from literary-type or media tourism is still noticeable: according to *The Sunday Times* (4 Feb 1996):

> Admissions to the Wallace Monument at Stirling have increased three-fold in the four months after the release of *Braveheart*, and passenger numbers on the SS *Walter Scott* on Loch Katrine in the heart of Rob Roy country were up 25%.

If literature was important, so also was *visual* appeal: railway posters, which showed a Scotland of amiable, welcoming tartan-clad shepherds. In a provocative study, the sociologist Grant Jarvie, in *Highland Games: the Making of a Myth* (1991), has argued that the expansion of Highland Games was part of the Balmoralisation process, by which loyalty, royalty and Highland dress and customs became inextricably linked in Romantic myth. Landscape painters also played their part in the popularisation of Scotland and the projection of a carefully selected image of it, of which Sir Edwin Landseer's *The Monarch of the Glen*, which was painted in 1851, is the most familiar. Perhaps a picture that sums up his part best is an earlier one, based on a Scott poem, of a Scottish terrier faithfully waiting beside his shepherd master's body, killed in a fall. Such faithfulness would bring a tear to every Victorian eye. One of the most fascinating stories is that connected with the artist Millais and the sage Ruskin, writer on aesthetics and cultural values. Ruskin had just got married in 1853, and persuaded Millais to join him and Effie on their honeymoon in the Trossachs where Millais painted him beside the river at Bridge of Turk. Unfortunately, Ruskin's marriage was a disaster, and had not been consummated. Not surprisingly, the attractive Effie was not going to hang around, and fell in love with Millais. There was a divorce and a great scandal.

Photography also played a very important part. Firms such as Wilson's of Aberdeen had a significant role to play in the development of tourism. As tourism grew, so demand for guides, views and scenes soared, either to inform visitors about what was ahead or to serve as reminders of a pleasant time. Photographic businesses everywhere in Scotland did what they could to respond to the demands of visitors, and while George Washington Wilson was one of the largest operators in this area of the market, rivalled only by Valentine of Dundee, there were many other, if mostly local, firms. It is extraordinary how quickly by the end of the century they could respond to local events by turning out postcards. Within a week of Peebles Hydro burning to the ground on the night of July 7th 1905, picture postcards of the scene were on sale locally. Some were, it has to be said, merely old photographs, touched up clumsily by the addition of flames and smoke. George Washington Wilson (GWW) was one of the first Scottish photographers to show an awareness of the potential of the tourist market. As early as 1856 he had determined the course his work was going to follow: primarily he was going to appeal to tourists. An emphasis on the tourist market was to run right throughout Wilson's career, as he and contemporary reviewers recognised. It was not his only source of income: there was a thriving portrait section to his business.

The firm's advertising, as for example, in Paterson's 1881 *Tourist's Hand-guide to Scotland*, laid stress on the availability of pictures in and of 'every noteworthy district visited by Tourists'. Wilson, his sons and staff photographers were active in photographing and retaking popular views especially during the summer. In June 1882 there was a serious fire at the Aberdeen works, but none of the photographing apparatus had been destroyed, 'a good deal of it being at the time away in the country along with the operators'. *The British Journal of Photography* in July 23rd 1875 observed that a photographer's cab had been seen at work in Edinburgh for some weeks and that it had turned out to belong to Mr Wilson of Aberdeen, whom they described as having a 'jolly, genial, good-natured face'. The report added that 'already we have the result in a volume, very recently published, of Edinburgh and its Surroundings which just appears in the nick of time, *when tourists do most abound*' (my italics). That the summer visitor was the key potential customer in mind is evident also in the way that GWW's products were sold through a retailing network of 'Agents on all the Tourist Routes'. Railway station bookstalls carried his views sold in albums or separately as scraps for pasting into journals. In a brief history of the Photographic Publishing Trade published as a foreword to the firm's 1903 catalogue, GWW & Co claimed to have published in 1880 no less than 100,000 shilling albums. One wonders how many of them were of Edinburgh, then, as now, the major destination within Scotland for tourists. Given the price of his views and albums – between 12/- and 10 guineas in the 1870s – it was the better-off tourist with means at whom Wilson aimed his products in the early years. Later on, the firm was to move down market with 1/- albums, published at such a cheap rate 'as to bring them within the reach of all classes'.

A key question is the extent to which GWW and his fellow-photographers may actually have shaped the flow as opposed to merely cashing in on it when established. Claims have been made for GWW's major contribution to the development of tourism in

Scotland during the latter part of the nineteenth century. David Hutcheson, whose West-Coast steamers carried ever-increasing numbers of tourists, is said often to have told Wilson that 'with his camera he had as effectively opened up the Highlands as the steamboats had done'. GWW's friend, George Walker, claimed that 'he had done more for opening up Scotland generally than Sir Walter Scott had done for the Trossachs'. But GWW mostly followed the existing tourist routes, if only because it was there that he could be sure of sales. In the tourist business he was less of a promoter of new ventures than a publicist of existing attractions. And the calibre of his work was recognised. In 1865, when the Princess of Wales visited Stirling, she was presented with a very elegantly bound copy of *The Lady of the Lake*, with illustrations by G.W. Wilson. Another local souvenir of renown, which other distinguished visitors received, was an edition of Scott, bound – or so it was alleged – in Bannockburn Wood and with a small GWW photo of Stirling Castle inserted in the front cover.

We can certainly agree, however, that Wilson's coverage does show which areas were on the beaten track for tourists and also reflects their preferred taste, whether for castles, abbeys or landscapes. It is clear that the popularity of the Western Isles, for example, was already well established with tourists before photography came on the scene, but they did become favourite hunting grounds for the scenic photographers, particularly after Royal visits there as elsewhere had conferred social cachet. In 1865 Alexander Smith recorded several meetings in Skye with a photographer, 'bearded as all artists at the present-day are', who might have been Wilson himself. That GWW was to be keenly interested in the area is predictable, and he was to be found in and around Oban during the summer of 1858. The next year he was on Staffa and Iona, a pairing which was to merit an early album of choice views. It was a locality to which he was to return often, even as late in his career as September 1882 when the boat with his assistant capsized; GWW is said to have saved him by his umbrella. A secondary form of evidence of the areas in demand, given the slowness of the printing process, is the number of plates of those views most popular with the market, such as the Pass of Killiecrankie or Ellen's Isle on Loch Katrine. Study of the firm's catalogues, particularly those from 1863 onwards (1877, 1893 and 1903), reveals not only which localities were covered when, but which remained unphotographed or were only included much later. To borrow a phrase from R. N. Smart's study of the Valentines of Dundee, the Wilson catalogues provide both 'a map and an index of the popularity of the tourist destinations of Scotland'. It is not perhaps surprising that neither Cowdenbeath nor Airdrie features in any catalogue. What takes more explanation is why coverage of East Lothian, Angus and Fife, for example, was so limited until the last decades of the century. But this does seem to tie in with their rise to popularity much later than Edinburgh, or the Trossachs, or the West Coast, which were already firmly established tourist destinations when GWW began his scenic operations in the late 1850s. In broad terms his coverage reflected existing tastes and only moved into new areas when demand showed some prospect of expanding. Angus, for example, was relatively neglected until the 1890s when a major drive was undertaken in the county; the 1877 catalogue listed only a few views of Arbroath Abbey. It took Barrie to put Kirriemuir on the map, and golf to establish Edzell, and as one might expect, the numbers of views in Angus rose sharply in the 1890s to over 300. St Andrews is another case in point. It too was relatively ignored by GWW until the final decades of the century. While we are primarily concentrating on the relationship with tourism in Scotland, it is worth noting that Wilson's work outside Scotland may also have had considerable significance. It is no accident that he showed an early interest in Stonehenge, which was a major tourist attraction in England, and which he photographed in May 1860. One of his sons claimed that his work had a wider significance for tourism than just in Scotland, though that was where GWW's work and impact may have been most concentrated; his tours were by no means confined to the Highlands: he was the first to make the public acquainted with the beauties of the English cathedrals, the first to supply artistic photographs of the Lake District; the 'distressful country' (Ireland) too received his attention, and 'the earliest sun pictures of the Giant's Causeway were his'. Taylor puts the persuasive point that Wilson was himself a tourist and quotes him as saying, 'I often do not know the evening before I start, for what place I may chance to take my railway ticket on the morrow. There are so many places which I am told I ought to visit, and so many beautiful scenes in this beautiful country of ours, that I often have difficulty in deciding whether I ought to go to the seaside in search of clouds and shipping, to the English cathedrals for picturesque interiors, or to the mountains and lochs for rocks and foliage and calm water'. One is inclined to take with a touch of salt this implied notion of the photographer as thistledown, ready to be blown hither and thither. But what we should really understand from his language is the sense of how many commercial possibilities there were for him and his camera. 'I have to study popular taste as well as my own, and must try not only to get a pleasing picture of a place, but one also that can be recognised by the public.' And by public recognition, Wilson had in mind sales.

TABLE 6.1.   VISITORS TO ABBOTSFORD HOUSE, 1833–1913.

1833	1422	1873	6892
1838	2387	1878	7890
1843	2581	1883	6543
1848	1364	1888	6559
1853	1016	1893	6214
1858	5013	1898	7004
1863	4693	1903	7288
1868	6229	1908	7857
		1913	9019

As has already been explained, there are no simple statistical series that show which areas and attractions were most popular with visitors to Scotland. There are no figures for Edinburgh Castle, say, or of visitors to Iona. But the Visitors' Books at Abbotsford House, home of Sir Walter Scott, are complete from 1833 onwards and do give a clear picture of the changes in numbers over the eighty years to 1913.

The house had already attracted visitors during Scott's lifetime, but after his death it became a kind of literary shrine, to which a stream of admirers made their way. Amongst the more prominent visitors were Charlotte Brontë, Charles Dickens, the German traveller Theodore Fontane, Harriet Martineau and Oscar Wilde. A signature of particular significance in the history of photography is that of Henry Fox Talbot in company with James Donaldson of Edinburgh and George Wight of Morpeth on the 24th of October 1844 when he took the earliest known views of the house. What added to the pull of the locality were the abbeys at Melrose and Dryburgh, which could be visited in the same day. Quite when Wilson made his first visit to Abbotsford cannot be precisely established. His signature is to be found, along with that of George Walker, on the 9th of July 1875, but he had photographed there and in the vicinity many years earlier. Views of Abbotsford were listed in the 1863 catalogue, and the *British Journal of Photography* on the 9th of December 1864 praised them as 'beautiful in point of execution and deeply interesting from their association with our greatest novelist. It is fortunate for tourists that Mr Wilson has been able to give them such a series of views – gems of photographic art – to say nothing of the attraction the subjects must possess over mere landscape views'. One of these views hangs to this day in the entrance hall at Abbotsford. The house itself did nothing in the way of promotion or advertising other than to indicate when it would be open. It was Scott's reputation that drew people there, whetted perhaps by prints and views of the area. Elihu Burritt, an American pacifist, who called on the 9th of September 1863, said of the ruins of Melrose Abbey that they 'stand thus in pictures hung up in the parlours of thousands of common homes in America, Australia and India'. Though we know very little about the extent of the firm's sales overseas, GWW's reputation was firmly established in Canada. Yet it is possible that GWW prints may have been yet another influence in increasing the flow of Americans to Scotland, their numbers increasing sharply after the end of the Civil War, as reflected in the flow to Abbotsford (Table 6.2). There were sharp fluctuations, as in 1893, but the broad trend was one of growth from the end of the Civil War and a plateau in the decade immediately before the outbreak of European war in 1914.

In the context of both the Western Isles and Abbotsford, it is proper now to introduce another name important in the promotion of Scottish tourism, namely that of the pioneer of excursionism, Thomas Cook of Leicester. It is intriguing to speculate whether Cook and GWW ever met. They might well have done so at Fingal's Cave, perhaps, which Cook visited no less than 50 times over the period 1847 to 1860, or at Edinburgh or elsewhere on the beaten tourist track. They certainly had friends in common such as David Hutcheson. There is even the remote prospect that when GWW visited Egypt in 1878, taking not his camera but his painting palette, he may have come into contact with a Cook, not Thomas but John Mason, his son, who was responsible for that branch of the firm's tour activities.

TABLE 6.2.   VISITORS TO ABBOTSFORD HOUSE FROM THE UNITED STATES OF
             AMERICA, 1833–1913.

1833	28	1838	105
1843	110	1848	144
1853	232	1858	449
1863	290	1868	995
1873	1743	1878	2077
1883	1613	1888	2194
1893	772	1898	1224
1900	3116	1903	2383
1908	2915	1913	2362

Note: there were also appreciable numbers of visitors from Canada: 375 in 1913.

Cook's great contribution to tourism in Scotland and elsewhere is that he was able to organise tours with all the travel and accommodation planned down to the last detail. Time schedules and costs alike were carefully calculated in advance, something of real significance to those of lesser means and limited free time who wished to travel. He negotiated deals with the railway and steamship companies, and with coach hirers established a network of hotels willing to guarantee beds for his tour parties and to take coupons rather than cash. One of his closest commercial relationships was with Andrew Philp, with whom Cook shared an enthusiasm for the temperance cause. Philp, who became a close friend, acted as Cook's Edinburgh agent, and his Cockburn Hotel, near Waverley Station in Edinburgh, was Cook's headquarters when he brought parties to Scotland. On one occasion in August 1877 the firm was asked at very short notice to arrange a tour of Scotland for Prince Heinrich of Prussia and some fifty naval cadets and officers, but neither Cook nor his son was free. The party was instead conducted by Philp's older son, James, who himself was to become a hotelier in London. Cook's genius was to open up Scotland (and elsewhere) to a much wider constituency than hitherto. Moneyed people did travel with Cook for the comfort of his arrangements. But by providing tours which were costed down to the last penny, run methodically and run to a tight schedule, Cook opened Scotland to those whose time and money were alike limited, and gave confidence to those who had little or no experience of longer-distance travel. Cook treasured a tribute to himself from another expert in the business, whom he merely calls a Highland Steamboat Commander, but who may have been either George or James Burns, owners of one of the most important steamship companies in the West:

> I have been on these boats for many years, and have seen the great change that has come over the circumstances of our traffic. For a long time we had few, except the wealthy, many of whom came thousands of miles, from almost all parts of the world to see the wonders of Fingal's cave and Staffa, and the interesting island of Iona. But now I see large numbers of the middle and humbler class of society coming out this way, and they will constitute the grounds of future success to the proprietors of these boats. (*Cook's Scottish Tourist Official Directory and Guide* (London, 1861))

He issued briefing notes which were clear and persuasive, to help those who were travelling for the first time, and he made it quite clear that it was entirely 'safe and proper' for ladies to join his Highland tours. (He did however draw the line at children.) The Thomas Cook publication, *Travelling and its requirements, a few words of advice* (the first edition of which appeared in 1875), stressed how important, for example, a waterproof tweed jacket was, with hood and sleeves to cover the frock entirely. Women seem to have been particularly appreciative of the services provided by Cook. One of his strongest supporters was Lydia F. Fowler of 337 The Strand, London, a minor authoress and Professor of Obstetrics at a New York College, whose publications included a series of lectures (*Why, when and where to sleep*) and a book intriguingly entitled *Woman: her destiny and maternal relations, or hints to the single and married*. She provided this testimonial for him in 1865:

> Mr Cook, Dear Sir, Those who have puzzled over Bradshaw, hoping to make the most of their time in travelling, can appreciate your efforts in planning of excursions by which they can travel over a large extent of country without losing an hour of time or missing a train. I shall never forget the delightful excursion with you to the Highlands of Scotland, to classic Iona and the world-renowned Island of Staffa. England has many great men and philanthropists and Thomas Cook of Leicestershire is one of them. You will be remembered as having afforded facilities by which the people have been enabled to get away from their daily toil and cares of business to visit remote parts of the country, which action has improved their health, enlarged their minds, and invigorated their spirits. You are the King and Father of excursions.

> (Thomas Cook Archives)

Cook's first excursion venture had been on July 5th, 1841, with a temperance trip from Leicester to Loughborough and back, 12 miles only each way, but the success of this and similar ventures led him to look further afield, to Liverpool and Wales. Thomas Cook's first sortie across the Border came in the summer of 1846, after reconnoitring there some months previously. He took 350 people from Leicester to Fleetwood, via steamer to Ardrossan, special train to Glasgow where they got a civic reception and then to Edinburgh where an even more lavish reception was held. There were problems: too many first-class passengers had been booked for the available accommodation, but the precedent had been set. Thereafter Scotland was to be a favourite haunt for Cook. He was to be found there two or three times each season, and even the Scottish railway companies, who would have liked to take over his business entirely, had to admire his acumen. John MacLaren, General Manager of the North British Railway Company, who was nobody's fool, said in 1865 that he could speak from personal experience about the success that invariably attended Cook's excursions over his railway between Scotland

and England during the previous eighteen years. *The Railway News* (Sept. 8 1866) was equally complimentary: 'This week Mr Cook has brought 3000 excursionists from the Midland towns on a visit to Scotland. The Leicester printer is a great man in his way, and he generally manages things with great success. Looking to the large numbers he has to marshal and provide quarters for, it is wonderful how few hitches occur, and how few letters appear in the newspapers'. There were other entrepreneurs around – Marcus, Gaze *et al* – but none to challenge him in Scotland. His agreements with hotels such as the Dreadnought at Callander and the Royal Hotel at Portree, and with coach hirers (Macara at Rumbling Bridge and Aird at Kilmarnock being two regularly used) held and coped apparently without strain.

Much of the success was due to due to Cook's first-hand knowledge, and care. He was himself a regular visitor to Scotland:

> For fifteen summers, exempting the year of the great Exhibition, I have spent about two months of every season in Scotland, heralding and conducting Excursionists and Tourists. I have gone over the Highlands about fifty times; have been in Fingal's cave about 45 times, and have as oft trod the hallowed soil of venerated Iona. I calculate that I have taken by special trains nearly 40,000 visitors to Scotland, about 4,000 of whom have accompanied me to the Western Isles, while at least 10,000 have promenaded the decks of the Lochlomond steamers. Many of these visitors have been so pleased with Scotland and my Scottish excursions that they have made annual visits; while others have gone two, three or four or more seasons within the time of which I am writing.

In a later assessment of his life's work, he recalled that 'From every part of England visitors came to the Midland Counties to join in with my Scottish excursions, immense numbers falling in with me en route. I had generally to take two and sometimes three special trains from Newcastle'. In 1864 in an interview with the magazine *All The Year Round* he spoke of the way in which the destination of his excursions determined both the numbers and the social classes from which the parties were built up. The trips to Edinburgh, which might be only two-day affairs, and the shorter excursions in England attracted, or so he observed, tradesmen and their wives, merchants' clerks away for a week's holiday with their knapsack, and 'swart mechanics'. It is clear, incidentally, that while many did travel on a conducted tour with Cook himself, his son, or a Cook's courier like W. E. Franklin of

Newcastle, there were many more who merely took the excursion train to Scotland and then went their own way. Over a million passengers had travelled under his care on the Scottish and English railways by 1864, or so he claimed. A proportion of these were, of course, Scots travelling south.

Where did he, or his couriers, go? One is struck by the variety and complexity of the options in Scotland that he put on offer to the travelling public: seven-day or 14-day tours from various starting points such as Glasgow, Edinburgh, Oban, Inverness and even Newcastle where their agent and conductor, Edward Franklin, was based. He prepared an *Itinerary for the Trossachs and over the Royal Route in Scotland*, which was very detailed as to what could be seen during train journeys to the right and left, what to visit when in Stirling, Oban, and Inverness, and how much to tip guides and drivers. He recommended when in Edinburgh the taking (cost 4½ d) of a tramcar from the East End of Princes Street out to Morningside: 'if your ladies are not too sensitive, you will obtain an immense advantage by mounting up to the roof'. Dunkeld was a favourite stopover point for his tours in the 1870s, and Franklin's signature, with those of his Cook's parties, is to be found two or three times a year in the hotel register of the Atholl Arms at Dunkeld. The group of 24 who signed in there on the 8th of September 1880 were drawn from London, Birmingham, Manchester, Leicester and North Shields, and also included an American and a German in their number; there were four married couples, and two unaccompanied ladies. The shape of Cook's tours was little changed from the schedule fixed in the early days, although adjustments were made in timing as rail and coaching services improved.

In 1849 Edward Chatfield undertook what could be described as the core itinerary, the details of which come from a diary, the original of which, alas, has since been lost. He, his brother and a friend left Derby for a week-long tour to Scotland on Tuesday the 24th of July. After various mishaps – for example the train couplings parting at Berwick – they arrived in Edinburgh that evening. The next day Cook himself organised them into parties of 50, to start sightseeing, the guide being paid 1/- per head or £4 2/-; no mean salary for a day's work. Their subsequent itinerary took in Linlithgow, where they sang 'God Save the Queen' from the Palace roof, Stirling, Glasgow, and in the same day Ayr, to visit Burns' birthplace. Friday and Saturday were spent on an excursion down the Clyde, Saturday at Loch Lomond, Sunday a walk to Callander, Monday to Stirling, and then a steamer to Edinburgh. 'On return to our hotel we found that some Scotchmen had joined our party, for the purpose of bidding goodbye, and both English and Scotch were all singing like so many larks, full merry enough too. All sorts of invitations were given to all Scotland and all England to call upon them at their respective houses. However, we were soon off to bed, for the last time in Scotland'. And the next day, they duly departed, arriving back in Derby, having travelled a thousand miles in 207 hours for an expense of £5 10/-.

There were critics of Cook's excursionism: a leader in *The Times* on October 8th 1861 commented on the Excursion mania and expressed scepticism as to its value:

> Scotland or Ireland seen in six days is a feat; it is looked back upon with proud satisfaction and the vivid consciousness of trains caught at the last moment, and a surpassing fit of hours and half-hours such as never yet fell to the lot of mortal man. We doubt whether Nature submits with so much readiness to be sold by contract.

The Helensburgh and Gareloch Advertiser in May 1881 repeated this kind of criticism, describing a party of *Cookites* 'doing' an art gallery in Venice in five minutes flat before being marched out again. Yet Cook not only introduced Scotland to many new travellers; he also helped Scots and others to travel overseas; his party of 29 to Palestine in April 1872 included seven Scots. Robert Brown, Provost of Paisley, joined a Cook's party to the Continent in the early spring of 1866. Their group numbered about 40, amongst whom were a number of females, and they visited Paris, Rome (where they were blessed by the Pope) and Naples. He was one of a small number to go to the top of Vesuvius, which he climbed with great ease: the sand was so hot that the guides cooked eggs in it for their lunch. There were various alarms – a bolting horse frightened by a train, an avalanche at Mount Simplon, and the rough Channel crossing, which made him very sick – but it was an interesting and educational experience. And everywhere there was a first-class guide, provided by Cook's, to point out and describe everything of importance.

High on the agenda of every educated tourist, Scottish, English or foreign, in Victorian Scotland was Abbotsford, home of Sir Walter Scott. Not surprisingly, Thomas Cook often incorporated a stop there, and at nearby Melrose and Dryburgh abbeys, as part of his tours in Scotland, taking advantage of the ever-expanding railway network. Melrose, a short horse-carriage trip away from Abbotsford, lay on the Edinburgh to Hawick line, opened in 1849. The completion of the North British Railway Company's Waverley line in 1862 was a further bonus to travellers from the South. In 1858, for example, Cook organised a special train to the 'Land of Scott' for the Ladies Temperance Association of Newcastle, a cause in which he was personally interested, and the Visitors' Book at Abbotsford records for June 14th 1858 no fewer than 118 signatures of people in his party. It was drawn from the whole of the North-East: Tynemouth, Sunderland, Bamburgh, Glanton and Hexham feature amongst the addresses. In the next year, each of his three Scotch Campaigns saw a party at Abbotsford; the first on June 29th, which included his wife and daughter, numbered 65. The second (August 9th) and third (September 5th) both mustered 80, which must have stretched the resources of the house and its guides. The Cook connection to Abbotsford, then, was substantial and significant. Almost too much so, in the view of John Henry Newman, a friend of the family, who complained bitterly in July 1872 about the intrusiveness of such visitors:

> There are these excursionists again – Cooke's – walking past the windows. Yesterday men of that kidney were before the windows at 6 o'clock in the morning, and they go on all day.
> (Ian Ker, *John Henry Newman, A Biography* (Oxford, 1988))

A contingent who were especially interested in viewing Abbotsford were the Americans, whose numbers rose from a few hundred each year in the 1850s to over a thousand by the later 1860s. They included some very famous names: the novelist Harriet Beecher Stowe, the abolitionist William Lloyd Garrison, ex-Confederate President Jefferson Davis, and so on. Scott seems to have been part of the essential reading of the educated classes in the United States. It is not surprising, therefore, that when in 1873 Cook came to plan his first Educational Tour of Britain and Europe for American teachers 'and those engaged in Educational Pursuits', a slot was made in their hectic programme for a visit to Melrose Abbey and Abbotsford. The party numbered 150, of whom many were teachers or ministers. They were certainly given a royal welcome, these tourists by wholesale as *The Times* dubbed them. When they reached Scotland after a brief stop to see the Giant's Causeway in Ireland, they landed at Glasgow, and hastened on via the Trossachs to Edinburgh where they were given a civic reception. Their photograph was taken in Princes Street Gardens on the 5th of July. All the big guns of the city turned out to a conversazione in the Museum of Art and Science. It was not a total success: 'The Lord Provost presided and made a lame attempt at a welcome, and Dr Witherspoon made one of the grandest speeches of

the kind that I ever heard'. That was the verdict of the Rev. F. W.
Hooper of Lynchburg, Virginia, in Samuel Watson, *A Memphian's
Trip to Europe with Cook's Educational Party* (Nashville, 1874). The
evening was concluded with bagpipe music and several Scottish songs.
Sunday found them in church – where else? – and the Monday took
them to Abbotsford en route to Alton Towers. Hooper was much
more complimentary about Abbotsford than he had been about the
reception in Edinburgh, 'one of the grandest old places in Scotland', as
were others. Thomas Cook himself signed the register there on Monday, July 7th: 'Thomas Cook, London with a party of 137 American
Teachers'.

Cook was to repeat the tour in the following year with less
numerical success. But the value of the first tour should not be
underestimated. The numbers of Americans visiting Scotland, and
Abbotsford in particular, continued to grow, and this may well have
been due in part to Cook's influence and that of his first party. As *The
Scotsman* newspaper noted, out of the ladies and gentlemen there were
between 40 and 50 correspondents of newspapers in America. Scotland may, in fact, have benefited more than Cook's from the fostering
of the American connection. In addition to increasing numbers of
private American visitors to Abbotsford, who travelled independently
– over 2000 a year by the late 1870s – American colleges began to
organise study tours in Britain with Scott's residence as one of their
cultural stops. In August 1898, for example, the house received as part
of a British tour a party of ladies from Pomona College in Los Angeles.
The Abbotsford connection illustrates that if Scott had every claim to
be the father of tourism in Scotland, Cook had no mean role as that of
midwife.

In this survey of the Cook-Scotland connection, one further episode
deserves mention. 1893 was a bleak time for the Scottish tourist
industry, with a dramatic shortfall in American visitors. In Edinburgh,
during what should have been high season, many hotels found
themselves with unlet rooms, with less than one-tenth of the usual
numbers. The Scottish correspondent of *The Railway News* reported
in September 1893 that

> there appears to be a very great falling off, principally in the
> number of Americans travelling North. In some of the larger
> Scottish hotels the diminution in the number of sleepers varied
> from 1,000 to 2,000 a month during June and July. Even the
> great Forth Bridge is at a discount with the coaches leaving with
> but a single tourist. Nor does Edinburgh alone suffer from this

collapse. If the state of matters is bad here, it must be still worse for the provincial and Highland hotels, which are still more dependent than Edinburgh on the tourist traffic.

All the tourist agencies had an exceptionally slack season, the worst, it was considered, for 15 years as Thomas Cook & Son themselves confirmed in an end-of-season review. Their magazine, *The Excursionist*, explained that American visitors had been kept at home more than usual, in particular by the Chicago Exhibition, organised to celebrate the 400th anniversary of Columbus' discovery of America. What recently unearthed printing accounts for Thomas Cook & Son reveal is how strenuous a campaign the firm, under the direction of Thomas' son, John Mason Cook, had mounted in 1892 and 1893. They tried very hard to offset the anticipated loss of American business in Europe and Scotland by promoting the Chicago Exhibition in Britain. 101,400 Chicago pamphlets were printed in November 1892, along with posters, maps and hotel guides. Circulars were sent to newspaper editors and directors of railway companies, advertisements were placed in guidebooks and Continental timetables. Over £1500 was spent in what would nowadays be termed a saturation advertising campaign. The accounts reveal that Cook's attempts met with some success. Each member of a Cook's party was issued with a printed list or card showing their fellow travellers. It can therefore be inferred from the number of cards printed prior to their departure by the SS *Majestic* on May 30th, or subsequent sailings, to Chicago that the first party from the Society of Arts, and there were other groups, numbered as many as two hundred. Other groups were even larger; one thousand cards were printed for the first-class Scottish parties on the 11th of July, which sailed on SS *City of Rome*, and in all Thomas Cook & Son handled the travel arrangements for some 2,500 visitors from Britain. 1893 was one of the few years when American travellers to Scotland may have been balanced, or even exceeded, by those from Scotland travelling to America. Cook's maintained their American connection with success, and in 1913, for instance, there were apparently so many American visitors in Ayr that Thomas Cook & Son appointed a special local guide for the Burns district.

The firm of Thomas Cook lasted much longer than that of George Washington Wilson. Thomas Cook was pushed acrimoniously aside by his son in 1878 whereas Wilson gave way amicably in the later 1880s, as his health failed, to his three sons. But while the Cook business flourished, the Wilsons' faltered. They did invest heavily and to some effect in postcards, black & white, sepia and coloured, and at the final liquidation in July 1908 some 200,000 cards were amongst the remaining assets to be sold. But, thanks to the cinema, sales of lantern slides were in decline. Above all, the arrival in the later 1890s of the hand-held camera, of which the Box Brownie is the best known, cut ever deeper into the market for views. People took their own holiday snaps. But Wilson's work had made its contribution to the promotion of Scotland.

FURTHER READING.

J. & M. Gold, *Imaging Scotland: Tradition, Representation and Promotion in Scottish Tourism since 1750* (Aldershot, 1995) contains much of relevance, as does Alan Sillitoe, *Leading the Blind: A Century of Guide Book Travel* (London, 1995). On George Washington Wilson, see R. Taylor, *George Washington Wilson: Artist and Photographer* (Aberdeen, 1981), and *By Royal Appointment. Aberdeen's Pioneer Photographer. GWW Centennial Essays* (Aberdeen, 1996), also A. J. Durie, 'Tourism and Commercial Photography in Victorian Scotland: The Rise And Fall of G. W. Wilson & Co., 1853–1908', *Northern Scotland*, 12, 1992, 89–104. On their great competitors, R. N. Smart, 'Famous throughout the World: Valentine & Sons Ltd., Dundee', *Review of Scottish Culture*, IV, 1988, 77. There is an extensive literature on Thomas Cook, of which Edmund Swinglehurst, *Cook's Tours: The Story of Popular Travel* (Blandford Press, Dorset, 1982), 88–101, and Piers Brendon, *Thomas Cook: 150 Years of Popular Tourism* (London, 1991) are of especial value. The visiting clientèle at Abbotsford is described in A.J. Durie, 'Tourism In Victorian Scotland: The Case of Abbotsford', *Scottish Economic and Social History*, 12, 1992, 42–54.

7

TRANSPORT AND TOURISM, 1850–1914

> The country which the proposed line will traverse is of a most
> picturesque character, abounding in the finest scenery and
> stocked with game so that tourists and sportsmen will both
> benefit by such a district thrown open to them and the pleasure
> traffic is likely to form an important ingredient in the success of
> this scheme.
>
> (Prospectus of the
> Dingwall & Skye Railway Company, 1864)

The development of tourism and the growth of transport went hand in
hand during the second half of the nineteenth century. At the heart of
affairs were the railways, though the steamer services were vital to the
expansion of travel on the West Coast, and pleasure sailings were an
important feature of many inland lochs. According to Ransom,
steamer services began on Loch Awe in 1861, Loch Tay in 1882
and Loch Shiel about 1893. Longer-distance travel by road was
displaced, except in the remote North-West, and so little traffic
was there on the Perth to Inverness route that grass was reported
to be growing over the carriageway at Dalwhinnie. A party of visitors
travelling north to Scotland in the late 1880s stayed overnight at a
once busy coaching inn near Carlisle. The stalls, which had held forty
horses, were empty, and no regular meals were offered. The elderly
ostler told them why: 'It was the railway that had done it'. Yet
coaching from hotels and stations was still vigorous and increasing,
and during the tourist season farmers' carts and other normal users
found themselves almost literally pushed to one side by tourist brakes,
buses and traps. The summer excursion traffic from Oban in the early
1880s strained the local road system to its limits: 3,500 each month by
coach tour or private trap to Melfort, 2000 to and from Ballachulish,
others to Glencoe. The Trossachs saw equally heavy traffic, mostly
originating from Callander. But from the 1870s a new feature of the
roads was the bicycle or tricycle, and the 1890s saw the arrival of the
motor car, George Johnstone bringing in the first from the Continent
to Leith in October 1895, and the petrol bus. The former was the
preserve of the wealthy elite; the other increasingly patronised by all
other classes of society. Motor cars, many of which were tourers, were

in penny numbers to start with, but sufficient to warrant the foundation of the Scottish Automobile Club in 1899. When vehicle registration was first introduced in December 1904, some 1,700 cars and 1,600 cycles were recorded, rising sharply in the next nine months. Motoring was launched, and while doctors and landowners used theirs for professional purposes, motoring for pleasure was very much in vogue. And providing a real challenge in the early days – where to get petrol, for one? – as well as opening up all sorts of possibilities for the urban day tourer, as well as the longer-distance motorist.

The expansion of the railway network in the middle decades of the nineteenth century in Scotland was remarkable. There were the cross-Border routes which brought so much traffic north, constructed in the 1840s and 1850s: East-Coast from Berwick, West-Coast from Carlisle and the Waverley by Hawick, the last of which was only completed in 1862. There were the lines linking the major cities, including the Highland Railway finally opened through to Inverness in 1863, and the many branches which brought every community of any size and significance into the system from Moffat to Crieff, to Ballater and Dornoch. To have the railway did not guarantee growth for a mainland community, but to be without was to be certain only of stagnation and decay. Not surprisingly, local merchants and hoteliers were prominent in advocating and subscribing to railway companies which promised a connection to their burgh or locality. The relationship between the railways and tourism was significant in many areas, and very close indeed in some. It took a variety of forms. Tourism did much to shape which companies were promoted where, and played a key role in determining the financial viability of many ventures. Prospectuses made much of the possibilities, drawing on the success of summer and excursion traffic experienced by many lines everywhere in Britain (and referred to in Chapter 2). The Dingwall & Skye tempted its investors in 1864 with the prospect of a lucrative trade to Strathpeffer, so 'famous for its mineral waters', and forecast a large tourist traffic throughout its entire length during the autumn and summer months. One English traveller in 1875, enjoying the lovely scenery – grand trees, glorious skies and soft lakes – of this line, described it as 'purely a tourist's line'. He added that, if reports were to be believed, the engineers were more anxious for views than for anything else and had gone out of their way to secure a picturesque route. Railway enthusiasts tended to anticipate that where tourists were already making their presence felt, their numbers would only be increased by the provision of railway services, and in many cases they were proved right. The surge of holiday traffic which came to Oban when the Callander & Oban arrived in 1880 exceeded all expectation, causing, or so *The Oban Telegraph* said, a 'surfeit of custom' for local hotels, lodging houses and shops. It was estimated in 1881 that in the previous summer, the six months from May to October had seen 65,000 visitors to Oban, of whom 26,000 had come by steamer, 37,000 by rail (in the first year of its operation) and only 2,000 by coach. Much of this traffic was tourist, and many of the visitors were new to the area.

But sometimes promoters proved over-optimistic, and lines were built which never generated enough traffic to justify their existence; the Invergarry & Fort Augustus was a spectacular example. Opened in 1903 at a cost of £339,000 to tap, amongst other things, the tourist traffic on the Caledonian Canal and Loch Ness, it was a financial disaster and lasted a mere seven years. The Galloway port of Garlieston, reached by the Portpatrick & Wigtonshire Joint Railway in 1876, was intended as an excursion port for traffic to the Isle of Man, but the tidal nature of the Solway made that chancy. The odd special was run successfully – 750 passengers took a day trip to Douglas in August 1897 -- but others missed the tide, and all passenger services were withdrawn in 1903. But other lines, such as that to the Clyde and Ayrshire resorts, as we have already seen, did generate immense and continuing tourist business. The majority of tourist lines succeeded, and succeeded well. It was no coincidence that the engineer-in-charge of the Highland Railway was forced against his better judgement by his Directors to open the final section at Dunkeld prematurely in early September 1863 because they 'wished to catch the tourist traffic of that season'.

If there were some ventures that turned out badly, there were others that never came to fruition, sometimes because so much time and money had been squandered in debate and parliamentary litigation. Some were far-fetched, such as the schemes mooted in the late 1880s and early 1890s for a network of tourist lines radiating from Fort William which would make that town another Perth or Carlisle for 'Cockney tourists in great numbers'. Or for funicular or mountain railways on the Swiss model up Ben Nevis, surveyed in 1889, or (most improbably) Arthur's Seat. The Isle of Man acquired one for Snaefell, and Wales another for Snowdon; Scotland none. A network of cross-country express tramways, as in the Isle of Man, was one Dunoon solicitor's suggested solution in 1910 to the transport problems of Argyllshire. An intriguing proposal, first aired in the early 1870s and then with more seriousness in 1882, was a Trossachs railway to run through prime tourist country from Callander by Loch Vennachar to

Loch Katrine. The idea had the whole-hearted support of the owner of the recently extended Trossachs Hotel at Loch Achray, Robert Blair, who offered to subscribe £4,000. Keenly interested was John Anderson, Secretary to the Callander and Oban Railway, whose line relied heavily on excursion and tourist business. Anderson did everything in his power to promote tourism; a key question which he asked himself was, 'What can we do to attract the multitudes to this unsurpassed scenery?' His many initiatives included writing promotional material which offered excursionists from Glasgow a trip to Glen Ogle, or as he dubbed it, the 'Khyber Pass of Scotland'! A weather station was set up at Strathyre, to show how mild the climate was there. An instruction was issued by him, and duly complied with, to the hotel-keeper at Crianlarich to provide a guide on arrival of the first train from the South for those wishing to climb the 3,384-foot Ben More, five miles away. Anderson liked the idea of a Trossachs Railway, and was prepared to landscape the line so as to minimise the impact on the scenery. Special coaches would be designed, with roofs removable in good weather, and to keep costs down and add to the enjoyment, speeds would never exceed 12 m.p.h. Given that there was no prospect of any freight, or even a commercial traveller or two, the line would be closed off-season, common practice for many steamer services which were suspended from the beginning of October until April, but without precedent for a railway. It was to be purely and simply for tourists. The scheme might have been viable, but the Caledonian Railway, which would have been called upon for capital, was doubtful, having had its fingers burnt on a number of occasions. What sealed matters was that while one great landowner, Lady Willoughby d'Eresby, was agreeable, the other in the area, the Earl of Moray, dithered and then categorically refused to consider the proposal. And so it fell.

The attitude of landowners in rural and Highland areas was important as they were a key source of finance, and because their properties would be directly affected. Their rentals would rise, especially from sporting tenants, and land could be feued for summer residences but their amenity might suffer. A proposal was made in 1897 for a light railway from Dalmally to Inveraray, which had strong support from local hoteliers, and steamship and coaching interests, who saw its potential for developing their summer tourist traffic as well as the area's sheep and cattle trade. John Anderson of the Callander and Oban argued in evidence that its introduction would benefit everyone: 'by introducing the holiday traffic, that is what helps the crofter and fisherman because it introduces money'. But the Duke of Argyll would have none of it because of the damage that would be done to the grounds of Inveraray Castle, and the scheme foundered, which with hindsight was probably no bad thing. But the decision did condemn the community to the status of a backwater. 'Inverary is', remarked one motorist in 1909, 'a place that has been.' Dealing with the landed interest, promoters had to be diplomatic, and prepared to make concessions. When in 1860 Joseph Mitchell was surveying the line from Perth to Inverness, he found the Duke of Atholl initially hostile. His Grace, however, was won over when the route was adjusted by bridging the Garry in such a way so as not to spoil the pleasure-walks and view of the falls. By contrast Lord Seafield made no objection, nor did the chief of the Macintoshes. Some landed figures were very positive in their support for railway and tourist-related development. There was the Duke of Montrose's private toll-road between Aberfoyle and Loch Katrine built at the Duke's expense through his lands in the mid-1880s. He received financial support from three railway companies, including the North British, and the tenants of the Trossachs and Aberfoyle Hotels, all of whom would stand to benefit from the increased traffic. The Marquis of Breadalbane took 2000 £20 shares in the Callander and Oban, when the company was struggling to finance its construction, and without his support in cash and in kind the Killin branch would never have been built. In the summer the line paid its way, with visitors coming to the falls, or on the Loch Tay steamers. In the winter, traffic was thin, except for schoolchildren en route to Callander, but the line and its passenger services did survive the death of their patron in 1922 for several decades.

If tourism played an important part in the creation of the railway network in Scotland, the railway companies in turn did what they could to promote tourism, in conjunction with steamship companies, coaching firms and hotels, and in competition (sometimes cut-throat) with each other. Free or cheap travel was offered to newspaper correspondents who would write up a railway and its locality. D. W.Logie, a lawyer and travel writer, went on the West Highland line to Fort William in August 1895 where he climbed Ben Nevis. This was a demanding but rewarding experience which he encouraged others to follow, pointing out at the conclusion of his article that the return rail ticket from Glasgow to Fort William cost only two and ninepence, 'a sum well within the reach of anyone desirous of seeing the heart of the Western Highlands'. Special villa or building tickets were issued to those with summer retreats, passes to the directors of the big hydro-pathic hotels, and advertising programmes were worked out with local town councils. The railway companies' pockets were not bottomless, however, and sometimes they declined proposals. The North British Railway Company in July 1860 refused to assist in the erection of a water fountain on the Marine Parade at Portobello. But they could be quite innovatory. The Callander and Oban Hotel Express, introduced in 1905, from Edinburgh and Glasgow offered a long weekend service. Travellers could chose accommodation and full board at any one of a number of hotels at Oban or Ballachulish or other centres in the area. During the summer, tours and excursions were a feature of every company's timetable. Fanned by cheap fares and publicity, these were highly popular. The last Friday in July 1889 saw a special train organised from Peebles to mark the burgh's annual holiday by the Caledonian Railway Company to Gourock. Marshalled by the town's Local Constables, three hundred passengers of all ages made their way in procession to the station for a 6.05 a.m. departure. On arrival at Gourock at 8.50 most went on to Rothesay, others to Arran, while a third group stayed in the town where a hall had been booked for a dance in the afternoon. Despite a sumptuous dinner in the Bute Arms, and an enjoyable hour thereafter in the refreshment rooms, everyone seems to have made it back to Gourock station in time for the return train, which arrived back in Peebles at 10.35 p.m. It is small wonder that the town, with a resident population of only 4,800, had a very dull and deserted appearance when it is considered that the North British Railway Company was also running cheap fare outings that day to Edinburgh, Glasgow and Perth, and took over seven hundred away. The same story would have been true of many cities, towns and villages.

The railways promoted tours, cheap days away and excursions, and such business kept many a rural and coastal line busy during the summer. And local traders and shopkeepers benefited. Amongst those pressing for a new station at Whistlefield, eventually provided by the North British in 1896, was the baker at Garelochhead. He wanted facilities there 'in consequence of the approaching season for picnic, excursion parties, Sunday school picnic parties and the like' for which he had been invited to purvey. But was it profitable to the companies? They thought so, but, after all, there was the off-season when the rolling stock, or much of it, lay idle, and the timetable was cut back to a minimum. But the track still had to be maintained. And the demands of the tourist season did require the provision of accommodation, staff and facilities, with complaints being made every year about the handling of luggage and the availability of porters. Baggage and belongings could be sent ahead, and the steamship companies had special luggage boats, but some confusion was inevitable at the changeover days in the summer as one lot of monthly visitors left and others arrived. Eve Darling sent a postcard from Canty Bay to her aunt in Cupar on 28th July 1907, explaining that they had arrived a little late at North Berwick and that their luggage did not come for ages: 'father had to go up to the station and see about it'. Such tales were commonplace. The most serious and sustained problems were at Edinburgh and Perth, which were overwhelmed by the volume of summer traffic. Waverley Station at Edinburgh was sharply criticised as 'hopelessly inadequate' by Acworth in 1890, swamped as it was by suburban, local, Glasgow and English traffic, a situation only worsened by the opening of the Forth Railway Bridge in March of that year. Heavy investment by the North British Railway Company in the 1890s created a station second in Britain only to Waterloo in terms of its platform accommodation. The new North British Station Hotel (or NB) became the dominant feature of the east end of Edinburgh's principal thoroughfare, Princes Street. The problems at Edinburgh eased, but Perth remained a pinch point for travellers, with rather less excuse. Even outwith the second week of August when sporting traffic to the North reached a crescendo, any change at Perth in the summer was liable to be an ordeal. The Rev. Boyd and his wife returned from Strathpeffer to St Andrews at the end of July 1894, and had to change at Perth for Dundee:

> The miserable disorganisation of Perth Station at such a time must be seen to be understood. The staff of porters was sadly deficient. Not one could be had, even by liberal bribery. One or two men set in authority were quite the stupidest human beings I have ever seen. The train, of course, was much too late. And when my wife had pitifully struggled over the bridge to the Dundee train, carrying a weight for which she was quite unequal, my hands much more than full too, it was to see the train move off. I trust I may never see that deplorable station nor its bemuddled servants in this world again.

By contrast Inverness, despite its very awkward layout, seems to have coped remarkably well, even despite the extraordinary levels of traffic at the start of the shooting season. The two or three days before the Twelfth saw all the regular day and sleeper services packed, plus the extra trains that were laid on, and the companies had to send empty carriages back to London and the South to meet demand. On the Thursday and Friday nights of the second week of August 1912 the Highland express from Euston was run in five portions, and that from

King's Cross in four. For some travellers Inverness was where they left the train, to motor on to their shooting lodges, but others – and their dogs, servants and luggage – carried on north or west to Skye. The sorting out of parties was no easy task, but somehow, thanks to the experience and skill of the officials, it was mostly managed without too much delay, or so one seasoned observer thought. But there was not much to spare at the best of times, and any mishap, due for example to a broken-down freight train as happened on one occasion, could throw the timetable into chaos.

Steamer services, inland and coastal, were also very significant in the movement of tourists, and there was considerable collusion and co-operation between railway and steamship companies. A whole variety of combination tours were developed, which were tightly timetabled, starting either from Gourock, Glasgow or Oban, the 'Charing Cross of the Highlands'. While most tourists stuck to the Clyde and Argyllshire coast, bolder spirits could venture further afield: to the Orkneys or Shetland, or even to St Kilda, reachable by fort-nightly sailings from Glasgow during the summer. Landings there were 'W.P.', weather permitting (the more pious would add, *D.V.*, God permitting). D.W. Logie took passage there in the third week of August 1889 on the S.S. *Hebridean* from Oban with a party of 31, some of whom were Scots, others from Manchester. The St Kildans he found to be of 'slow and listless demeanour', but grateful for presents from the visitors which were divided out. The poverty of these islanders was apparent, and disturbing. Thomas Cook's tourists had had a similar experience on Iona in the late 1850s. Besieged, as all visitors were, by children selling pebbles, which is all they had to offer, and moved by the wretchedness of the populace, Cook's travellers had subscribed funds for the purchase of several properly equipped fishing boats, one of which was called 'The English Ex-cursionist'. The arrival at Iona of the daily steamers, with their cargo of tourists for a flying visit, had become the major event of the day there, and elsewhere, for the locals and for the growing number of summer holiday-makers on the island. The first saw the chance of profit, the second amusement.

A favourite tour offered by David MacBrayne's in the 1890s, which cost for Cabin and first class 21/-, or Steerage and third class 10/-, was a two-day sortie from Glasgow to Oban via the Crinan Canal and back through the Trossachs on the Callander and Oban Railway. What fare people chose seems in part on the shorter trips to have been shaped by the weather as much as anything else. One wealthy family from Durham, taking the *Fusilier* from Oban to Fort William in late

September 1905, opted for third-class tickets, and because it was windy, decided not to pay the extra for the upper deck as there was more shelter on the lower. Those who had more time could take the five-day special circular tour by the *Columba* to Oban, the *Gael* to Portree and Gairloch, coach to Achnasheen, train to Inverness and swift steamer via the Caledonian Canal to Oban and Glasgow. Of all the sailings, that from Oban to Iona and Staffa was the most popular with visitors. The handsome *Grenadier* sailed daily from 31st May until 30th September, with MacBrayne's providing boats and guides – stout and active-looking Highlanders in Company livery – to let tourists inspect Fingal's and the other caves at Staffa. This part of the excursion could be quite unnerving in anything other than a flat calm, just as it always had been. James Wilson's description in 1842 would have rung bells with people fifty years later:

> We could see the not altogether undismayed indulgers in the picturesque descending the vessel's side, then hovering in the mid air for a few brief moments of suspense, and finally and fearfully wedging themselves into the tossing boat, the skirt of an occasional surtout hanging into the liquid main.

Malcolm Ferguson in 1894 reported that the walk along the causeway was quite slippery, which posed problems even for sprightly young girls, whose fashionable footwear was far from suitable – 'thin soled and ridiculously high-heeled boots and shoes'. The climb by a 150-foot wooden ladder to the summit was also a challenge. Yet accidents on this or any other excursion seem to have been few: the odd mishap or drenching, delays due to bad weather or fog, but no fatalities. And what added spice to any voyage was the company. Arthur A 'Beckett and the artist Linley Sambourne travelled on the *Iona* in September 1875:

> It was a perfect little town. The crowd was constantly changing. As we stopped at the various piers, heaps of old people disembarked and allowed their places to be taken by heaps of new people. Every hour it seemed that the dinner-bell was sounded for the benefit of fresh comers. On the raised deck close by the paddle boxes and near the steering cabin was a large bookstall at which all sorts of publications could be purchased. From morning to night the boat was crowded with passengers. There were peals of laughter and any amount of flirtation. The deck was covered with children, who played about to their hearts' content . . . [there were] fat manufacturers, smug tradesmen, worthy

parsons and dignified dandies . . . members of Parliament on board and popular barristers, and London journalists, and reading parties from Oxford and Cambridge and smart young surgeons: ladies who looked as if they were born to be the helpmates of men as good mothers and excellent wives, and ladies who seemed to be intended as the curse of Adam – who you knew would have a great deal to say about the Income Tax and Woman's Rights . . . In fact, the Iona was a kaleidoscope, with its deck for a focus and its passengers for pieces of bright metal and worthless glass.'

(*Our Holidays in the Highlands* (London, 1875))

The bay at Oban during the season was full of steamers and private yachts, some racing, others cruising and socialising. The week of the Oban Games and the Argyllshire County Ball in the second week of September 1890 saw 78 yachts, schooners and cutters in the bay, and amongst the large company at the Gathering Hall was Lady Brown and her party from the steam yacht *Lyra*. There were those wealthy enough to take a cruise through the Western Isles in their own boats, or well enough connected to be invited as a guest. Colonel Henry Platt, owner of the steam yacht *Erne*, ran cruises during the months of April to September, each week picking up parties of 30 at Oban. But for those of lesser resources, the steamship companies provided week-long tours in the Hebrides. But these might be disrupted by commercial needs, as the Sladden family from Worcester found. They sailed at the end of August 1911 on the London & Edinburgh Shipping Company's *Chieftain*, acquired by MacBrayne's in 1907, from Oban to Stornoway, a voyage that they enjoyed thanks to the scenery and the three meals a day, and despite very rough weather in the Minch. But the return trip was disrupted by a recall for the *Chieftain* from Lochalsh where they transferred to a small but – in their view – quite comfortable paddle steamer, the *Gael*. The change had been forced, they gathered, by a summons from Stornoway, where there had been heavy landings of herring, to collect urgently by fast boat several hundred fish girls, returned by train by the West Highland Railway from some other fish centre. Such episodes, for some tourists, only added to the appeal of steamer travel in the Isles.

Though no overall statistics exist of how many tourists travelled by steamer, it is clear that the numbers were very considerable. The Glasgow & Inverary Steamboat Company alone carried during the summer months of 1896 some 65,000 passengers on its route, the great majority of whom were away for the day only. The steamers were used by all classes of people, and, while tourists from further afield or excursion parties would have booked ahead, there were many who would have made up their minds only on the day. Good weather – not that the Glasgow Fair always seemed to enjoy that – made for queues, and there must have been disappointed travellers, but mostly everybody got away, and found their way back, though the last boats were often packed to the gunnels. When the Glasgow storekeeper James Allison was given some time off ('got released from his duties') one Thursday in mid-July 1881, it seems as if it was only the beautiful weather on the Friday that decided him, and his wife, to go to Lochgilphead. Despite the piers being thronged with pleasure-seekers, they had no difficulty in getting on the 10.30 sailing of the *Edinburgh Castle*. The only slight irritation was that, even so early in the day, a few 'mistaken souls' were already tipsy. But that was nothing new.

On the Saturday, the Allisons went walking, and Mary's journal records that they observed a good many people riding on bicycles. 'They were generally in pairs, and as nothing but good bicyclists would be likely to venture so far from the city, they went along very swiftly.' Her line drawing shows them to have been penny-farthings. Touring by bicycle – or tricycle – had become a widespread enthusiasm in Britain during the 1870s with cycling clubs to be found in many parts of the country; that at Falkirk, for example, was founded in 1877. While some enjoyed racing, and others the pursuit of long-distance records, the first Land's End to John O' Groats rider arriving in June 1873, large numbers of middle-class and artisan cyclists became interested in touring. Local authorities passed bye-laws for 'velocipedes', to regulate the carrying of lamps at night, meeting or overtaking wagons or led animals, and conduct generally. There were frequent complaints about the dangers to pedestrians from furious riding, and the fright caused by fast riding to horse-draw transport. The County Road Boards of Fife and Perth jointly approached the Secretary of State for Scotland in October 1901 to urge him to introduce a system of registration and number plates for bicycles so that offenders (of whom there were many) could be identified and prosecuted. The cyclists were to escape such regulation; motorists did not.

In 1878 a Bicyclists' (later Cyclists') Touring Club was established with 600 members, annual subscription 2/6d (later 3/6d). Five years later the CTC had over 10,000 members, including some ladies, and in 1900, 56,000. Many short-distance pleasure-riders did not bother to join, but to any serious touring cyclist the CTC's services were of great value. It was the CTC that pioneered so many of the features that the motoring organisations, the AA and the RAC, were later to adopt. There was set up a network of recognised hotels, approved repairers, route maps and danger signs. One suggestion, made by a veteran Scottish rider, was however vetoed. He wanted a notice board erected on the Lockerbie to Crawford road to warn riders that there was no pub for thirty miles! The CTC lobbied for better roads, and pursued County Clerks to keep them in good order. A circular was sent in 1897 to every authority in Britain to ensure that hedge-clippings and thorns, for example, were properly swept up. The condition of the surfaces, as the secretary E. R. Shipton pointed out in a letter to Argyllshire County Council, was not just in the interests of cyclists and their tyres, but sheep, cattle and dogs. Another issue was that of steep gradients, and hairpin bends: Gall & Inglis' first cyclists' road book for Scotland, which appeared in 1900, was appropriately entitled *The Contour Book of Scotland*. It provided profile diagrams for no fewer than 399 routes to show which were stiff, steep or heavy – above a 1 in 15 grade. Inside the front cover was an insert page, 'Riding Summary', for the user to note the date, route and distance of their outings. A companion volume was available, the 'Safety' map of Scotland, which showed at a glance the calibre of roads in any locality. The worst in the country was generally reckoned to be that through Glencoe, and of the stretch from Dalwhinnie to Struan on the Inverness road, the advice was simply that it was 'best done by train'.

The trade of riders seems to have benefited quite a few country hostelries. The visitors' book for Tibbie Shiel's contains several signatures of Cycling Club members from the Borders and Edinburgh area – including a sketch of one cyclist measuring his length in the mud. The Hawick Club who visited on May 20th 1879 left a written request that a licence for the sale of whisky should be obtained as 'beer is abominably cold'. Writing in 1904 in his *Scottish Reminiscences*, Sir Alexander Geikie thought that a distinct revival of the wayside inn in Scotland could be traced to the wide spread of bicycle riding:

> Wheelsmen appear to be drouthy cronies who are not sorry to halt for a few minutes at an inviting change-house; but many of them take up their quarters for a night at such places, and this demand for sleeping room has led to the resuscitation of little inns that had almost gone to decay.

By the time of the 1899 edition of the CTC handbook, no fewer than 343 hotels (some temperance) and another 108 farmhouses or lod-

gings were listed for Scotland from Wigton to Shetland. Prices were
agreed and published: a standard tariff was single bed 2/-, breakfast
1/6d, but an extra 3d would bring a supplement to the standard tea or
coffee and eggs of ham, chops, steak, cold joint or fish. As important
to the touring cyclist was the availability of repair facilities. Tyres,
chains, brakes and frames were all at risk, as the experience of Dr
Gordon Stables in 1881 showed. An Aberdeen University graduate,
Stables had had a colourful career, including serving in an anti-slavery
patrol ship off the Mozambique coast before becoming a prolific
author of boys' books, and medical columnist for *The Stirling Observer*. An enthusiastic caravaner in later life, and first Vice-President
of the Caravan Club on its formation in 1907, at the age of forty he
undertook a 69-day tour of Scotland by tricycle, subsequently published as 'Nauticus in Scotland'. In the course of his 2,462 miles, he
was beset by mechanical problem after problem, necessitating stoppages at local blacksmiths, some of whom were helpful and others
completely baffled, as well as by wind, rain and stretches of very bad
roads. He in fact wore out one machine and had to have a replacement
'Cheylesmore' tricycle sent north from Coventry to Strome Ferry,
which he immediately crashed, the steering gear jamming as he tried to
avoid an old woman. Only by cannibalising a wheel from the old
machine could he continue. Stables' experiences, even allowing for a
degree of exaggeration, do underline the challenge to the early cyclist,
particularly if travelling in the more remote areas. But cycles became
more reliable, and groups combining cycling and camping became a
familiar sight in country areas, permission to camp being seldom
refused, providing no damage was done or litter left. The railway
companies, although they said that they did not like bicycles and
detested tricycles, made provision for carrying cycles and their equipment. The Great North of Scotland was the first company in Britain to
introduce cycle vans in 1902, and in 1905 the Caledonian had bicycle
racks fitted in the guard's compartment of its trains from Edinburgh
and Glasgow to Aberdeen. What was much complained of by cyclists
was the hazard of ferry crossings by small boat, especially in the North
of Scotland, and level of charges for carrying cycles made by Mac-
Braynes and the other steamer companies. The CTC brought pressure
to bear and these latter exactions were halved in 1900, but they were
still far too high, or so cyclists thought. The service given by ferries in
Scotland, and the ferrymen, were often the subject of indignant letters
to the county authorities. The behaviour of the men at the North
Connel crossing in Argyllshire, a short but tricky passage at the best of
times, was particularly bad. An excursionist from Edinburgh missed

his train back to Oban in September 1890 because the two ferrymen would not be diverted from unloading a cargo of flour. A month later, three young ladies found a rough passage made far worse by the drunken state of the only boatman available. Had they not taken over the oars, they would not have made the far shore. The Council should have intervened in everybody's interest, whether local resident or tourist, but by some legislative omission in the Local Government Act of 1889, had no powers to do so. What changed the situation was the opening in 1903 on the Callander and Oban's Ballachulish branch of a railway bridge at Connel. But crossing was not free: people on foot had to buy a passenger ticket to cross.

It is relevant to ask how far cycling for pleasure, whether short-distance or touring, was open to people of lesser means. The early machines were expensive, but as cycles became mass-produced, with their price falling from £20 or so in the 1870s to £4–£5 in the mid-1890s, and as more became available second-hand or for hire, as at Millport, it became cheaper and cycling broadened its appeal. People rode to work, and for pleasure, sometimes even on a Sunday. The October meeting in 1889 of Glasgow Presbytery of the United Presbyterian Church received a report from the Sabbath Observance Committee that during the summer the Clyde resorts were full on the Sunday mornings with bands of young men with their bicycles, bent on an excursion for the day. *The Scottish Cyclist*, founded in March of the previous year, held that a man could cycle on a Sunday, and not infringe any commandment, providing that his object was health rather than frivolity, and that he had been to church first:

> The poorest city clerk, the apprentice mechanic, or the struggling student, can enjoy a week's or a fortnight's wandering by lake and river, mountain and valley, storing up health for the struggles and studies of another season or session at less cost than that entailed in a "Saturday to Monday" trip to the Coast, or a "Weekend" at a popular hydropathic.'
> (*Cycle, Camp and Camera in the Highlands*, 1905)

But another form of transport was to make its appearance on Scotland's roads, one that was to have a profound effect within a relatively short time on travel and tourism alike. This was the motor car – and its fellows, the motor cycle and the motor bus – a development about which other road users were far from enthusiastic. One pair of touring cyclists (*Two on a Tour*, by Walter Munsell, Paisley 1909) on their way north to Loch Maree from Edinburgh found their journey blighted on the Perth to Inverness stretch:

The one and only drawback to the Tour was the motors. These were innumerable and intolerable. What with the stink of their petrol, the bray of their hooters, the pother of their dust, and the illimitable lordliness of their occupants, they added appreciably to the terrors of life. There is something so infernally aggressive and provocative about them.

If there had been complaints from the general public about cyclists riding too fast and recklessly, these were as nothing to the stir that the growth of motoring caused. There was the usual curiosity when these vehicles first made their appearance. The arrival at Tarbert on Tuesday 21st July 1898 of a motor car from Lochgilphead with a party of excursionists created, or so *The Campbeltown Courier* reported, a great sensation in the village, a large crowd turning out to inspect the vehicle. But interest soon became tempered by concern. It was not just the dangers to other road users, pedestrians and animals, that aroused concern, it was the damage done to the roads by this traffic, throwing up dust in the summer and mud in the wet seasons. And who was to pay for better road surfaces? Or for the replacement of the old hump-backed bridges, or the straightening of the dangerous 'S' bends? In what way could touring traffic, growing every year, be made to contribute, or was it to be left to the residents? Merchants and hoteliers benefited from tourist traffic, but farmers and others did not. Why, then, should they pay? This was a very real issue, not least in those districts where touring was popular but the local population thin, and its traffic light. Ratepayers in Inverness-shire complained about the responsibility for the upkeep of the county roads falling on them when in the summer only one in eleven cars was local. There was a real dilemma, as Lord Lovat pointed out to a conference of Highland County Councils held in Perth 1908. Northern areas already depended on the income from summer visitors, and anything that deterred touring motorists, such as reining in their speed by means of traps, would hurt those areas remote from the railways. Better roads and bridges, which had to be paid for, were essential to attract these high-spending motorists, even if it was their cars, heavily laden and travelling at speed, that did the most damage. Yet even they would complain if their tyres – worth £20 apiece – were shredded by poor surfaces, the roads around Tyndrum having an especially bad reputation. Something had to be done, and the need got only greater as traffic increased. Sir John MacDonald, himself a keen motorist, visited Pitlochry in the summer of 1904, and found 'the place crawling with autocars, one every minute and half for the whole time I was there, for two or three hours'. Inverness and Perth were no better. The Roads Surveyor for Stirlingshire reported in 1908 how there had been a marked increase in motor traffic in his area:

> especially in the autumn months coming from the east coast route, and passing on through the district to Stirling and the North, and to Glasgow and the West. These are principally heavy touring cars, with steel-studded tyres, and often been driven at a high rate of speed, they no doubt cause an excessive strain on the surface of the road. It is this kind of traffic that is doing harm and breaking through the crust of weaker roads.

It was not just the volume of traffic that created friction, but the speed and lack of consideration that motorists showed to other road users. The 'Toad of Toad Hall' species of driver was all too common. Prosecutions for speeding or dangerous driving multiplied, and Mr Graham of Ardencaple was only one of several motorists convicted; his offence in July 1906, for which he was heavily fined' was to drive through Helensburgh at the incredible speed of 47mph, or so the police alleged. That this transgression was on a Sunday merely aggravated the crime. Accidents involving pedestrians, livestock and other vehicles rose sharply, and bad roads and the inexperience and incompetence (there being no driving test) of many drivers combined to make them a hazard to others and themselves. A couple on holiday in the Aberfeldy district were killed in early August 1911 when their driver lost control after his brakes failed on a steep descent. Some, as they had done, employed others to drive their own or hired vehicles; it was considered that 'Scotland is in most respects an admirable touring ground for the *chauffeur*'. Others did not. A young Irish lady drove a party of ladies and gentlemen in an Arrol-Johnston car from Land's End to John O'Groats in the early autumn of 1903. This was an impressive feat made all the more remarkable by the fact that she had never driven until a few weeks previously, and had had less than a dozen driving lessons. What tended to make matters worse was that while touring was at its peak during the summer, motorists from the cities began to range quite widely at other times of year when road conditions were much more difficult. A picture published in *The Motor World* in April 1905 showed an immobilised Albion car on a trial being towed through thick snow by a team of horses.

To protect the interests of motorists the Scottish Automobile Club (SAC) was formed in December 1899, motto 'Gang Warily'. It was to play an important part in lobbying government and local authorities alike over where speed limits should be imposed, and in resisting the demands in some areas for roads to be closed entirely to motor traffic, as happened on Arran. In Perthshire there was pressure for the closure of quite a number of roads, but the only one eventually shut was the route from Callander to the Trossachs. It was, as all agreed, a dangerous road because it was narrow with falls of twenty feet or so on both sides and was much used by horse-drawn tourist traffic: 'large brakes taking twenty and thirty people up'. There were prosecutions for the illegal use of this road: in November 1912 a chauffeur from Ireland was fined 4 guineas for driving on it. His plea that owing to the dull, wet and foggy nature of the weather that morning, he had failed to observe the notices at the start of the road won no sympathy. The SAC liaised with the London-based Auto-mobile Club over matters such as a recognised list of hotels in Scotland, first published in 1903. It organised club runs and trials, of which an expedition in April 1902 from Glasgow to London was an early example, and arranged for signposts to indicate not just directions and distances, but where care was needed because of dangerous bends or steep hills. Other signs included Dangerous Cross Roads, School – Please Drive Slowly, and Be Careful of Sheep. It did what it could to promote courteous driving, to discourage what was called 'scorching', and sent letters to members who were seen exceeding the speed limit by ominously named 'special agents'! This rather cut across the work of the Automobile Association whose Scottish office had been set up in 1908, and whose patrolmen were stationed primarily to warn members where speed traps were ahead, a role resented by the police. In 1910 the AA issued its first guide, *Scotland for the Motorist*, planned very much with the needs of the touring motorist in mind, and largely written for the first-time traveller from the South, or indeed, the Continent or America. Sketch maps and descriptions were given for all the main routes, and details of ferries and their charges, hotels and garages listed. The beats of the patrolmen – 'practical men able to render assistance in case of minor roadside affairs' – were identified, and whether they were full-week, weekend or summer only, as the Aboyne to Ballater was. The registration of cars had been introduced in January 1904, and one of the resulting features, which gave delight to generations of road travellers and car watchers, was the number plate lettering which identified where a vehicle was from – SA was Aberdeenshire, SY Midlothian. Lanarkshire, with V was the odd one out in the Scottish list of 1910 as carried by the guide.

TABLE 7.1. TRAFFIC IN ARGYLLSHIRE, 1911.

Census point	Dates	Ordinary Cycles	Motorcycles	Motor cars*	Horse-drawn
Connel Ferry	17–23 May	411	7	80	219
	7–13 Aug	1102	25	422	287
Pass of Brander	17–23 May	16	1	73	23
	7–13 Aug	79	13	193	7
Inveraray	22–28 May	769	32	282	669
	28 Aug-†	898	47	482	873
Lochgilphead	22–28 May	1169	33	845	1149
	28 Aug†	1194	61	929	1125
Sandbank	19–25 May	1284	17	158	1420
	8–14 Aug	2645	106	291	2626
Inellan	19–25 May	747	19	115	1091
	8–14 Aug	1807	10	314	1801
Tarbert	22–28 May	241	28	105	1364
	7–13 Aug	1035	54	371	2281

* 'Motor cars' includes traction engines.
† Monday 28th August to 3rd September; Friday May 19th.

That touring was greatly on the increase in the years before the First World War, no one doubted, least of all the county authorities who had to maintain the roads. The number visiting the Highlands, many with English number plates, was particularly noticeable. Pausing for a quarter of an hour near Tyndrum one day in early August, a touring motorist and his party saw five cars and three motor cycles pass. Bystanders hated the dust and dirt that the cars threw up. And then there was the smell and the noise. 'You cannot hear the kirk bells for the hooting of horns', complained one correspondent to *The Motor World*. The impact was out of all proportion to the numbers involved as cars were still expensive; the Argyll Company's Streamline Torpedo cost £575 in 1912, the Rover Twelve £350 and even the Ford Touring car, £220. Censuses of weekly traffic on the roads taken in 1911 for May and August underlined how little there was outside the major towns, and most of the summer increase in motor traffic, which was much more substantial than that for horse-drawn traffic, was of visiting vehicles.

What is also revealing is the detailed information on a daily basis. The leap in the amount of traffic on the Tyndrum to Dalmally road, whether motor or horse-drawn, on the eve of the Glorious Twelfth – Saturday the 12th – is corroboration of the influence in that locality of the grouse season. In her column, 'Woman's Sphere', in *The Motor World* for August of that year, Helen Maxwell wrote of the popularity of the motor car in the North. It was a double asset, allowing not just the sportsmen to reach the grounds with ease, but also enabling the ladies of the house party to join the men for lunch. And land agents reported that numerous shootings and fishings were being let better and more easily because they could be reached by motor. Conversely, a shooting tenant at Glenfinlas, near Brig o' Turk, had given up his lease, because 'he could not get his cars up', the Trossachs road being closed to motor traffic.

TABLE 7.2.   TRAFFIC ON THE DALMALLY TO TYNDRUM ROAD.

(Wed 17 May – Tuesday 23 May: Monday August 7 – Sunday August 13, 1911. Taken at the Farm House at Arivean.)

DAY		One	Two	Three	Four	Five	Six	Seven	Total
Cycles	May	2	1	–	5	2	1	–	11
	Aug	5	2	9	9	11	11	12	59
Cars	May	1	3	6	3	9	9	1	32
	Aug	12	11	14	24	28	17	12	118
Horse vehicles	May	3	–	3	1	–	3	–	10
One-horse	Aug	6	4	6	14	4	7	2	43
Motor cycles	May	–	4	–	–	–	–	–	4
	Aug	1	1	1	–	5	–	5	13

(No motor omnibuses, lorries or horse omnibuses were recorded.)

The numbers of touring cars, though increasing, may not have been very great, but there is no doubt that their effect was already being felt by the early years of the twentieth century. Near the cities, and perhaps especially on a Sunday, there was the drive for the day – or post-church – outing. It was good news for many hotels and inns, both near to the large cities and in the more remote areas, which found their business appreciably increased. High-class establishments equipped themselves with garages and inspection pits, facilities which were quickly incorporated into their advertising, and some acquired their own charabancs to collect guests and run local excursions. Peebles Hydro bought two Argyll cars for hiring out in April 1908 but neither proved reliable and they were soon sold. But while the touring motorist was welcome, there was a growing tendency which caused some concern: their mobility made them less inclined to settle in the one spot, and more inclined to move on after only a short stay. 'We detest fixed programmes when touring' was one tourer's comment in 1912. And the railway companies began to feel the pinch as those who would have travelled first class now came north under their own steam. The Highland Railway, understandably, was greatly worried. Its shareholders were told in 1904 that

The more extensive use of the motor car by visitors from the south is making serious inroads into the receipts of the Highland railway from first-class fares. A large number of people who used to visit the Highlands by train, and travelled first-class, have during the present year arrived in the Highlands by motor car, and have moved about the country by the same means, instead of taking train and travelling first-class from station to station as they used to do.

But the problem was a real one, and only to become worse. The announcement of the Invergarry and Fort Augustus Railway's closure to passenger traffic in January 1911 was greeted by *The Manchester Guardian* with the headline 'A Highland Railway to be Abandoned. Business Taken Over by Motor Cars'. It had never been a viable project, but other lines and services that had been kept solvent began to experience a decline in receipts, if not numbers. The railway companies fought back. Starting in 1904, the Great North of Scotland Railway ran its own motor services from Ballater, some of which were seasonal and designed to tap tourist business. The Callander & Oban took shares in a motor car company running trips between Dalmally and Inveraray. It also introduced a car-shuttle service in 1909 on the Connel Bridge. Robert Dollar, a rich and successful American shipping magnate, who had emigrated from his native Falkirk half a century earlier, was taken on a motoring tour of the West Highlands in August 1912. At Connel their motor was put on what he called a 'railroad car' and transported across the bridge, while they sat in a motor-rail charabanc. More than 500 motors, or so he was told, had already been carried that summer. But enterprising local firms were not slow to move into the business of offering day-trips, tours and excursions catering for those with less spare time and money than the motoring clientèle. By 1908 Hendersons of Stirling were offering for 4/6- a head a series of day-long popular motor tours to places of interest around Stirling – Crieff, Aberfoyle, Dollar, and Doune – as well as evening runs for a shilling. Quite which bus company was the first to offer the 'Mystery Tour' is not known. But the bus offered much more flexibility of route and destination than the train or the tram. And its reliability, which had made early outings less a question of where than whether, did improve.

In November 1905, Sir John MacDonald, who was giving evidence to the Royal Commission on Motor Cars, was asked what he saw as the advantages of motor transport. There were several, but amongst the key benefits were

> a means of healthy recreation and health restoration to dwellers in crowded cities, they being able to travel many miles into the

country easily and cheaply. A revival of road touring on a grand scale, and consequent revival of the decayed country inn.

MacDonald was right on both counts. But the full impact of motor transport on tourism was to come after the First World War.

FURTHER READING

On the history of cycling and Cyclists' Touring Club, see J. T. Lightwood, *Cyclists' Touring Club, Being the Romance of Fifty Years' Cycling* (London, 1923). The early editions of *The Contour Road Books of Scotland* and *Scotland For The Motorist* are very revealing as to what the traveller faced. The challenges to the motorist are caught in Piers Brendon, *The Motoring Century, 1897–1997, The Story of the Royal Automobile Club* (London, 1997) and *Gang Warily: The Jubilee History of the Royal Scottish Automobile Club, 1899–1949* (Glasgow, n.d.). A.J. Durie, 'The Impact of Motor Transport on the Roads System of Central Scotland c. 1896–1919', *Scottish Economic and Social History*, 17 (1997) looks at the problems generated for the upkeep of roads and in striking a balance between motorists and other road users. For canal and inland water transport, see P.J.G. Ransom, *Scotland's Inland Waterways* (Edinburgh, 1999). Of the railway histories, while many contain material relevant to tourism, use has been made here in particular of John Thomas, *The Callander & Oban Railway*, in *The History of the Railways of the Scottish Highlands*, vol. 4 (Newton Abbot, 1966) and also John McGregor, *The West Highland Railway* (East Linton, 2003).

8

THE FIRST WORLD WAR
AND TOURISM IN SCOTLAND

The War has had a very injurious effect on the visitor season in Strathearn.

(*The Strathearn Herald*, 8 August 1914)

Though almost every aspect of the outbreak of the First World War in August 1914 has been studied in depth, there remains one area which has been relatively neglected. War broke out at the height of the tourist season in Europe. What immediate impact did it have on tourism in Scotland? To what extent did those holidaying in Scotland abandon their break and return home? What about those many Scottish tourists who were abroad on the Continent? What happened to the many seaside or inland resorts and service industries dependent on tourism whose season was ruined? In the longer run how quickly, and to what extent, did tourism revive, as the war that was supposed to be over by Christmas dragged on year after year? A key question that emerged was to what extent could the loss of American custom be redressed in Scotland by increased numbers of British tourists who in peacetime would have taken a Continental holiday at a German spa or French resort? Some tourist destinations in Britain appear to have done quite well out of the War. Brighton's hotels and boarding-houses were crowded out, as Clunn has shown, thanks to a combination of leisured people unable to get abroad, others escaping the air raids in London, and officers convalescing from war wounds. A final significant issue is, given that so many men were away on war service, what changes the war years may have seen in the composition and nature of tourism: more women with money from munitions work holidaying on their own, fewer young men and more elderly visitors.

Any downturn in tourism, for whatever cause, put the prosperity and employment of many in Scotland at risk, from hoteliers to lodging-house keepers, tearoom girls, ice-cream vendors, tourist guides and excursion tour organisers. The Scottish tourist industry was, of course, no stranger to fluctuations caused by factors over which it had little or no control, and which could lead either to an upturn in trade or depression. Prime amongst these was the weather, which could lead to people either staying longer or cutting back on their time away. By the mid-1850s, during the summer the newspapers, under pressure from people such as John Hope, were extending their coverage of the weather from the big cities to the resorts, and a bad forecast must have had some effect on the impulse traveller. But equally many day-trippers, whose opportunity was so very limited, carried on regardless, determined to enjoy their outing come what may. Golfers tended to be indifferent, but one sector of sporting tourism that was distinctly vulnerable, as Chapter 5 has shown, was the grouse shooting. A combination of a cold spring, disease and wet summer made 1873 one of the worst years on record for sporting tourism in Scotland. The Highland Railway's half-yearly shareholders' meeting in November of that year was told that revenues from passenger traffic in July and August were badly depressed

> by the wet and uncongenial weather, while the shooting traffic suffered a heavy diminution from the failure of the grouse this season in the Highlands.
>
> (*The Railway News*, 8 November 1873)

Economic conditions also played a part. The depression of the early 1880s, following the collapse of the City of Glasgow Bank in 1878, led to the insolvency of several large Scottish hotel ventures. Several schemes were abandoned which were virtually complete, such as that for a hydropathic hotel at Oban where the roofless building was to be a local landmark for decades. Transport developments, which opened up new localities, promotional campaigns run by the tour companies, and changes in fashion could all shape where tourists went in a particular season, whether drawn from Britain or further afield. The number of American tourists visiting Scotland in 1893 was less than one-tenth its normal level, to the great dismay of the industry in Scotland. Edinburgh hoteliers blamed a combination of problems on the Continent where there was a cholera scare, and the attractions of the Columbian Exposition in Chicago which kept many Americans at home. Political factors played an important part. The stability and security of Scotland was normally a distinct asset, particularly in time of political upheaval or actual war on the Continent. The so-called 'Crofters' war' on Skye in the early 1880s, a series of land disputes which included a battle between locals and 50 police officers drafted in from Glasgow, had only a marginal impact on tourism in the area at the time, and no lasting effect. By contrast the Franco-Prussian War of 1870–71 and the unsettled state of Ireland in the early summer of 1914 alike greatly benefited tourism in Scotland. And a general

European war was bound to have an unrivalled impact. But would this war lead to further development, or to decline?

Before assessing the immediate and longer-term impact of the war, it is relevant to ask how well tourism in Scotland was doing in the last months of peace. There is no one simple source on which a judgement can be based, but if newspaper reports are to be believed, 1913 had been a good year, and all the indications were that 1914 was going to be even better. A valuable source of information is the weekly column which was carried in *The Glasgow Herald* during the summer months, variously entitled 'Mountain and Sea', or 'Land and Sea', which covered both Scottish and other British resorts including Llandudno and Southport. One has, perhaps, to be a little cautious; the local correspondents who were supplying the information, usually on a fortnightly basis, were not likely to underplay the charms of their resort. But the picture everywhere – despite cold and boisterous weather – was very positive, as it had been since the start of the season in May. Blairgowrie reported an immense influx from Dundee in the last week of July with every room in the district let; Fort William that it was so thronged with visitors that boarding accommodation was taxed to its limit; North Berwick was very busy with golfers in their hundreds; and Elie was so much in demand that the Galloway Company steamers from Leith had been unable to carry all who had wished to travel. The municipal concerts at Helensburgh were attracting very large audiences, as were the performances at the shore bandstand of the banjoist Olly Oakley. The Glasgow Fair, despite the poor weather, had seen large numbers of holidaymakers, excursionists and day-trippers leave the City either by steamer from the Broomielaw or by train. Some were bound for Blackpool and other English resorts; others for the Isle of Man or Ulster, with no fewer than twelve special trains being run on the first Thursday evening of the holiday to Ardrossan for Belfast and Portrush. Many found their way to Arran or Bute, with 60–70,000, it was thought, intending to spend the weekend in Rothesay. The trades' holidays of other Scottish cities also made their impact; some 20,000 left Aberdeen at the weekend of the 18th–19th July, some for Deeside, and others for Fife and Ayrshire. Overseas visitors were much in evidence, including one touring American of Scottish extraction, a New York silk importer, who was convicted and fined heavily for the theft of a bureau handle from Burns' Cottage at Alloway, which he had taken as a souvenir. That he had been drinking heavily at the Tam O'Shanter Inn in Ayr beforehand was no excuse in the Sheriff's eyes, and he narrowly escaped a prison term. Abbotsford House, Sir Walter Scott's home, was receiving nearly as many American and other overseas visitors as in any normal year: the Visitors' Books show that up until the end of July some

1,200 visitors with addresses in the USA had called as against 1,300 in the same period the previous year. There was more good news for the tourist industry in the Highlands: after a poor year in 1913, the prospects for the grouse season, thanks to good weather and no disease, were confirmed as being the best for many years. The letting of moors went on briskly throughout the spring and early summer. The last list of tenants for the coming season appeared in *The Times* on the 24th of July, and included Dunvegan Castle ('one of the oldest inhabited residences in the Kingdom') and its 15,000 acres of shooting, taken by Mr. Geoffrey Lubbock of London. He was lucky to secure such prime ground, which also included good fishing, as late in the year. In short, the Scottish tourist business, whether inland or coastal, sporting or recreational, mass or select, appeared to be almost universally healthy.

But the increasing likelihood of war did start to make an impact towards the end of July; a party of 500 German excursionists bound for the Trossachs cancelled their visit. Not all German visitors were so prescient: a Dr August Schmidt and his wife from Berlin, who were touring Scotland, were at Abbotsford on 28 July, a week before war was declared on August 4; one wonders whether they got home in time. A Mr. Sauer from Cologne was still in residence at the Hydropathic in Moffat in the second week of August. In the frenzy of the opening weeks of war German nationals were rounded up: 28 sailors, for example, from two ships detained at Alloa and Grangemouth and six waiters from Oban. Others arrested included bandsmen and the odd tourist, 'all who were liable to be called back to the Fatherland for service in the Army' as *The Stirling Journal* of 13th August reported. There were those who had not kept in touch with the latest developments. *The Glasgow Herald* on 18th August carried the news of the arrest of a luckless German schoolmaster who had been in Britain on a walking holiday since early July. Completely ignorant of the state of war between Britain and Germany, he had been apprehended near the Glasgow waterworks at Loch Katrine, The spy mania caught some quite innocent travellers, including a young American, on a bicycle tour 'doing the beauties of Scotland', who was detained by the police at Perth in early September.

Particularly hard-hit in the first month or two of war were hotels, many of whose staff were foreign. In Edinburgh, for example, it was estimated that no less than sixty percent of hotel workers were foreign. A large proportion of these were either German or Austrian, and therefore liable to internment had they not left in time. Some did not move quickly enough, and were sent under escort to Redford Barracks. An additional problem was that hotel employees who were either French or British

Territorial reservists were liable to call-up: one Edinburgh hotel was reported to have lost 20 of its staff to military service by the 4th of August, with more expected to be mobilised shortly. Peebles Hydro lost two of its men, a night porter and a masseur, both of whom were German nationals and military reservists. They tried to get back to Germany, but failed and apparently returned to Peebles where they were arrested without resistance. Perhaps that was in their own best interest as they were spared the carnage of the western front. At Grantown-on-Spey, a less hysterical approach was taken to alien workers; the chief chef at the Grant Arms, a German, was not arrested until the third week of October, *after* the tourist season was over.

If the outbreak of war caught German tourists in Britain, there were also Scottish and English tourists on the Continent, some of whom were in Germany, and neutral Americans in Europe. What happened to these people? As we have seen already, the instinct of both sides was to intern unlucky visitors if they belonged to the other party, especially if they were male and of military age. In the last days of peace there was a desperate exodus of British visitors from Germany in particular. Some press accounts reported rough treatment of British nationals in Germany, an allegation specifically denied by an Edinburgh University student who had been in Germany; he and his friend had experienced much assistance in their trip from Hamburg to Denmark. Their acknowledgement of some German kindness got them into trouble; 'pro-German' was the label applied. One notable trapped in Germany was the Principal of Glasgow University, Sir Donald Macalister of Tarbert, a distinguished medical man whose general ill health had taken him (and his wife) to the German spa town of Ems, where he was receiving treatment for his rheumatism. They had heard in late July rumours of impending trouble, but did not finally decide to leave until 1 August, which was almost too late. They eventually got a passage on a Dutch barge from Cologne down the Rhine, leaving behind their entire luggage and a volume of proofs of *British Pharmacopoeia*, which Sir Donald had been checking. These belongings were retrieved only in 1919. Local Scottish newspapers carried all sorts of accounts of those who had got away, and those who had not. A 62-year-old Scottish minister, the Rev. John Munro, was shot dead on the Belgian frontier, as he and a group of fellow refugees tried to make good their escape from Germany.

Travel companies, such as Thomas Cook and George Lunn of Polytechnic Tours organised missions to retrieve British tourists in neutral Switzerland, who had either been holidaying in that country or had managed to make their way there. It was estimated that there were 8–10,000 in Berne alone. There were large numbers of Scottish tourists in other neutral countries who found it no easy matter to get back. One such group was a party of Good Templars, who had been attending an International Convention in Norway. They had booked a return trip by steamer, but the expectation of a North Sea battle between the British and German navies led to a suspension of all sailings of British shipping. The situation was retrieved for them and other stranded tourists only by the Norwegian government laying on a special ship – the SS *Haakon VII* – from Bergen to Newcastle. All the berths were allocated to ladies, and some 200 males had to find whatever deck space they could. There were also large numbers of American tourists, as many as 100,000 to 150,000, in Europe at the beginning of August. They faced a variety of problems, the first of which was financial. Many banks refused anything but their own paper or letters of credit. As a result many wealthy tourists found themselves penniless, holding temporarily worthless travellers' cheques. There was also the problem for the Americans of getting back home. Shipping services were severely disrupted, both for Americans in Britain and on the Continent. 'Several Americans', remarked *The Peeblesshire Advertiser* in mid-August, 'who are staying in Peebles, have been unable at present to proceed across the 'herring pond'.' But, thanks to initiatives by travel companies such as American Express and help from the American government and its consular officials, by mid-September the crisis was over; those who wanted to get home had done so, even including a party of Negro minstrels who had been performing in London. There was still the problem of their motor cars and luggage: American Express alone had to arrange for the passage back to the States of no less than 15,000 cases and trunks.

A Scottish relief committee to provide both funds and accommodation for stranded Americans was set up on 10th August by a Mrs. Malcolm Bruce Milne of Dowanhill. It helped Americans until shipping could be arranged. Three ships, the *Cameronia*, the *Athenia* and the *Grampian*, left Glasgow for Canada on 15th August carrying 2,800 Americans and Canadians, in 'scenes', *The Glasgow Herald* reported, 'reminiscent of the boom days of emigration'. The North Americans, and other overseas tourists, went away like swallows in the autumn of 1914, but they were not to return until 1919, a serious blow to tourism in Scotland and elsewhere. Whereas Abbotsford had received nearly 2,500 North American visitors in 1914, the following year – when the USA was still neutral – saw a mere 28, and not until 1919, other than a few visitors on leave from military duty, was there any real recovery. One effect of the War was, therefore, adverse, in that it blocked a key flow of relatively high-spending tourists to Scotland for several years.

On the other hand, there was some compensation, it was anticipated, to be gained from those British tourists who in peacetime would have gone to the Continent. Some hoped for more touring. *The Motor World* and other motoring journals were optimistic that 1915 would turn out to be a bonanza year for the North of Scotland. 'There is no doubt that the Highlands will attract more motor tourists this year than ever. Many motorists who generally tour the Continent will come to Scotland instead this year.' Others commentators were alert to the potential prospects for British spas and hydropathic hotels. Bath launched an advertising programme in mid-September 1914 to capture business that would previously have gone to Germany. Over 4000 guides outlining the virtues of Bath as a health resort were sent out to British doctors with some success, and a special folder was prepared for the French market. Dr. Fortescue Fox pushed a similar line with respect to Buxton and Strathpeffer in a lecture (subsequently published) to the Royal Society of Medicine in June 1915.

Of all the Scottish regions, the Highlands seem to have suffered worst in 1914, and for a longer time: 'The first few days after war was declared saw an exodus south, especially of those who were touring by motor-car and residing at hotels and hydropathics'. Hotels which catered for short-term tourists passing through a locality as part of a tour in Scotland were especially hard-hit. At Callander, a stopping place for many exploring the Trossachs, the fall in numbers at the Dreadnought and Ancaster Hotels became more severe as August wore on, and September's figures were disastrous. Some lessening of business was usual as the season wore on, but not the loss of three-quarters.

TABLE 8.1.   VISITORS AT THE DREADNOUGHT AND ANCASTER HOTELS,
         CALLANDER, SUMMER OF 1914

Date*	Dreadnought	Ancaster	Total	Americans
25 July	36	60	96	33
1 Aug	67	57	124	13
8 Aug	60	45	105	20
15 Aug	58	45	103	9
22 Aug	29	23	52	15
29 Aug	39	22	61	18
5 Sept	26	18	44	9
12 Sept	9	13	22	3
19 Sept	13	14	27	3
26 Sept	12	8	20	2

* These returns were published in the Saturday edition of *The Callander Advertiser*, but were collected two days previously and relate to those staying on the Thursday. They would include only those who were booked in for more than one night's stay, and exclude casual trade.

Moreover, and this had major implications for both the Highland and the Borders economies, there was a nearly universal cancellation of grouse shooting for the season. To cite just one example, army officers and others who had taken shooting quarters in the Callander district sent instructions that no servants or ghillies were to be engaged on their account. There was very little shooting elsewhere despite the fact – ironically – that the birds were for once plentiful and strong. *The Bath Register* noted sadly what good sport some keepers had had, taking a turn over the moors themselves in the absence of the normal parties. One team of Americans at Balnakeilly near Pitlochry did bag 52 brace on the Twelfth, but mostly moors went unshot, with all the knock-on effects that this meant for local employment and income. And where there *was* some shooting, there was little enthusiasm. Subsequent years provided no real recovery. Too many of the young men, and the beaters and keepers, were occupied elsewhere, though some did volunteer to fill their place, in the name of not sport but national service. A Mr. Irvine from Drumgoon Manor in Ireland wrote to *The Times* on 7th September 1915 to offer his assistance to save the moors from overcrowding and spare the owners the expense of having them shot by paid men: there is no record of any response. It has to be said that the weather, as much as the war, was to blame in 1916. A hard winter meant an almost universal cancellation of shooting. Nor was the next year much better. Though the opening of the season was again brought forward by a week – to provide 'our wounded soldiers with a delicacy' – the Fifth proved inglorious. There was excellent weather and some coveys, but sportsmen and cartridges alike were in short supply, and one Glasgow game-dealer could not lay his hands on a single bird. Not till after the War did sporting income seriously revive, and even then bags were almost universally poor, with birds much scarcer than in pre-war days.

Other resorts and localities in Scotland did not suffer as badly or for as long as the Highlands. The immediate, and understandable, impact of the declaration of war in August 1914 was to sharply reduce holidaymaking. Many resorts reported, as Ayr and Dumfries did, that 'a good many people who had proposed visiting the town this month have cancelled their rooms'. The *Peeblesshire Advertiser* noted how hard hit were the many thrifty housewives in the town 'who had been wont to make hay while the sun shines in August' by letting rooms. The report continued that:

> At this time of year Peebles usually receives its best class of visitors, but since the war fever spread their numbers have

diminished, many leaving the town in a panicky mood which filled them with a desire to be in their own homes when the Germans arrived . . . 1914 will be a lean year in the esteemed landlady's coffers.

(*The Peeblesshire Advertiser*, 15 August 1914)

From Edzell came the gloomy report that the outbreak of war had practically ruined the August season there. There were no enquiries at Elie for September property lets. One sympathetic observer pointed out how hard hoteliers and lodging-house keepers were being hit by cancellations, and urged that some compensation be paid. But not all resorts were as badly off; Dunbar said its golf course continued to be well patronised by hundreds of players. Professional families from Edinburgh who had taken lodgings for the month were perhaps less likely to abandon their holidays then those from further afield. What was hurt was the September constituency. In many localities those who had taken hotel or lodging accommodation for the month of August left, but were not replaced. The two main hotels at Grantown-on-Spey, the Grant Arms and the Palace, saw virtually no change in their numbers in the first three weeks of the War, but September arrivals were few indeed, and their combined business fell by over half. Other places reported that though things had been bad for a week or so, visitors were returning. Girvan was as busy in the third week of August as it had ever been, with a stream of heavily laden charabancs and wagonnettes setting out each day on tours in the locality. Some railway companies restored their excursion fares, as did the Portpatrick and Wigtonshire in the Stranraer area, and the Great North of Scotland Railway began to run again its Wednesday and Saturday cheap outings to Ballater and Deeside. A visitor to the Firth of Clyde cheerfully scribbled a message to a friend that

now the scare has died down, things are nearly normal. I wrote W.H. that Loch Lomond Tour was off but since found that it was only the Caledonian: North British running as usual was on Monday anyway. Hasn't it been a time for fairytales, Germans everywhere.

(Robert Preston, *Days at the Coast*, Ochiltree, Ayrshire, 1994)

But even when the initial panic had died down, there was not an easy return to a pre-war normality. What posed problems for Scottish tourism was first a series of constraints on transport, accommodation and amenities. What compounded the difficulties of all resorts, whether

Scottish or elsewhere, was the withdrawal by railway companies of cheap tourist and excursion tickets. Just as serious was the loss of steamer services, although nowhere in Scotland was as severely hit as the Isle of Man, which had been a very popular pre-war destination for Scottish visitors. It was estimated that in 1916 tourism in Douglas was one-tenth of its peacetime level. Travel to Ireland was also restricted, though not as badly. But there was severe dislocation of coastal services as the Admiralty requisitioned steamers for service as minesweepers, guardships and other duties. All the excursion boats of the Galloway Company working on the Firth of Forth were taken over, with compensation eventually being paid, and none were to return. Two, the *Edinburgh Castle* and the *Lord Morton*, were blown up to avoid capture in September 1919 while serving as hospital ships in the White Sea in the campaign against the Bolsheviks. Others fell victim while on active service to mines, the first being the Caledonian Steam Packet Company's *Duchess of Hamilton* in November 1915. The shortage of shipping was especially serious in the West of Scotland. By 1917 only one steamer – *The Lord of the Isles* – was left to service sailings to Dunoon and Lochgoil from Glasgow's Broomielaw, and on Fair Saturday the following July, despite its carrying 1,200 passengers, as many again were left behind. Demand far outstripped supply everywhere. The popular Largs-Millport service in 1916 was subject to huge waits at peak periods of up to ten hours for many families. These problems seem to have worked to the benefit of those resorts accessible by rail, and one which particularly benefited from the difficulties of the Clyde and the Isle of Man was Blackpool, which established a popularity with Scottish visitors during the War that was to last for many decades.

While the arrival of refugees and the billeting of troops helped to compensate some for the loss of their tourist lets, and provided valuable income in the off-season, the tourist business was further handicapped by the requisitioning of hotels and lodgings for military or medical purposes. The War Office had asked the Royal Society of Medicine in April 1915 to find out what accommodation might be available at health resorts in Britain for military patients, and Moffat was one of several Scottish places approached. The Town Council assured Dr Park that the community would do what they could, including making available the mineral baths, but only after residents and visitors had first use. Though many country houses and town properties were volunteered, the mounting number of casualties forced the acquisition of more and more premises suitable for adaptation as hospitals. The hydropathic hotels, with their baths and medical facilities, were particularly suited to such use. Peebles Hydropathic, for example, was taken over in 1916 as a convalescent home for naval officers. Dunblane Hydro was closed as a hotel in 1918, and all the hydro furnishings were sold off in a three days' sale, with the baby grand piano fetching the highest individual price for any single item of £61. It reopened in the early summer as a hospital for shell-shocked cases. The first batch of 126 patients arrived in June, and it was reported that they were speaking highly of the kind treatment they were receiving, and that they were making rapid improvement. The first statement may have been true; the second is much more doubtful, as recent studies of the evolution of psychiatry have shown. Craiglockhart Hydropathic's military clientèle during the war included such well-known figures as Siegfried Sassoon and Wilfred Owen.

Nor was the business of those hotels that remained in operation easy. The records of Cluny Hill Hydropathic near Forres (now in Elgin Public Library) show quite clearly the problems posed there by shortages of staff, rising running costs, and uncertainty over visitor numbers. With increasingly heavy losses being incurred as the war went on, no dividends being paid and increasing calls being made on the reserves created pre-war, economies had to be made where possible. When their experienced manager secured in 1916 an equivalent position at Craiglockhart Hydro, which was a promotion for him in career terms, a manageress on a lower salary replaced him. The Directors advised her in February 1917 that they 'would have to lower their sights somewhat and run the house more as a boarding house than a hydropathic establishment'. Later in the same year they approached Alexander Grant of the Edinburgh firm Messrs. McVitie & Price (bakers) for a loan to tide them over till better times came:

Owing to the War, our visitors, as you are aware have fallen away and costs of everything have gone so high that we have not been making a profit. We have hitherto done well and it is really the exceptional circumstances caused by the War which have affected our revenue.

TABLE 8.2. FORRES CLUNY HILL HYDROPATHIC RETURNS, 1913–1919.

Year Ending 31 Dec	Receipts from Visitors (£)	Profit (Loss) (£)
1913	£7,376	£1,166
1914	£6,169	£204
1915	£6,050	£270
1916	£4,743	(£1,350)
1917	£4,352	(£1,238)
1918	£6,507	(£321)
1919	£9,761	(£243)

Moffat Hydro found itself equally embarrassed. When war broke out, it had been virtually full with over 280 guests in residence, and the number of visitors remained high during August. In September, however, there was a sharp fall to a mere 117, with arrivals failing totally to compensate for departures. In the next year, as the Annual Report for 1916 reported, things were slightly better. Numbers had fallen seriously in the early months of the War, but 'Fortunately a high class English school for young ladies was secured as tenants for two terms until July 1915'. After the school, St Felix's from Southwold in Suffolk, had vacated the premises and returned south, the scare of German naval raids having abated somewhat, the Hydro resumed normal business. Numbers in August 1915 were down on the pre-war years by about a third, but September was better than twelve months previously. Though there were a few Continental visitors, including three ladies from Paris, most of the shortfall, not surprisingly, was in visitors from England, and this situation only worsened in 1916. On the 11th of August, at what had once been the height of the summer season, there were only 125 guests in residence. Receipts, which had fallen by a third, fell yet further and any prospect of a dividend for the 188 shareholders vanished. It is difficult to escape the conclusion that the war years fatally undermined the Hydro's financial viability and that the Directors were perhaps quite glad when the buildings were requisitioned in 1917 by the Army Medical Services. Parties of convalescing officers became a familiar sight in the area. Five, drawn from a mix of regiments, visited that favourite pre-war haunt of tourists from Moffat, Tibbie Shiels' Inn at St Mary's Loch, on the 17th of February 1918. They were followed a few days later by another group, one of whom simply signed himself as 'Scott H of Paschendale Ridge'. The Hydro was handed back by the War Office in mid-1919, and compensation paid for 'Delapidations etc.' of £1750, every penny of which was needed to put the place back in order.

Yet for some places the reduction in competition through the requisitioning of large hotels as military hospitals was actually an asset to those remaining in business, as was the absence of any new competitors. Work on the Caledonian Railway Company's luxury hotel at Gleneagles, with its two fine golf courses designed by James Braid, was suspended late in 1914 for the duration, and building did not restart until 1922, the complex not finally opening until September 1923. The possibilities of profitable trading for some tourist operations during the war years were reflected in the quiet success of the few. The Directors' Report for Melrose Hydropathic Company commented in August 1919 that they had enjoyed 'for the last eighteen months or so virtually a monopoly of Hydropathic business south and east of Crieff', but with peace that was about to end.

The region of Scotland hardest hit during the war years by a reduction in tourism was the Highland area. It had been doing exceptionally well, as one commentator enthused:

> The summer of 1913 will long be remembered as an ideal season; we will have to go back many years to find its equal. For some months now sunshine has flooded the hills and valleys, and even the cities are gay with the long spell of fine weather. The touring season in Scotland has in consequence been an exceptionally busy one. Hotels, especially in the Highlands, find it difficult to cope with the demand for accommodation from all quarters, and inquirers for rooms meet with the usual reply 'full up'. This year the trek to the North has been phenomenal. English and American visitors have invaded the country in their cars by the hundreds . . . Trade in Scotland has in consequence had a record year.
>
> (*The Motor World*, 14 August 1913)

It was caught by a combination of factors. Access was much less easy whether by rail or steamer or road. The touring motorist had been an important part of pre-war tourism in the North, with the great majority of cars in the area during the summer coming from the South. Restrictions on the availability of petrol, pressure to reduce pleasure motoring, and taxation alike restricted touring. A survey of privately wned cars in Edinburgh carried out in April 1916 found that over a third were laid up for financial reasons or because their owners were on active service; others were being used by doctors or on Red Cross business to convey the wounded. Only a tiny proportion – 6% – were still being used for pleasure. *The Motor World* observed in August 1916 that the number of visiting cars to be seen in the Highlands was much below the normal, and that since the start of the War the Highland season had been very badly affected. In evidence to the Royal Commission on Motor Cars in November 1906, the Secretary to the Scottish Automobile Club had spoken of an inn in a remote part of the North-West of Scotland – 25 miles from the nearest railway – which had seen its trade grow from virtually nothing, thanks to the motor trade which was bringing it 80 persons a week during the season. It, and others like it, must have seen their business wither. Car-hirers were also suffering from the downturn in traffic: one northern firm had had no fewer than fifty cars available pre-war for hire on a weekly basis. Other outdoor activities, such as fishing, hill-walking and mountaineering, were also much restricted. *The Cairngorm Mountaineering Club Journal* of July 1915 stated that one in five of its membership was already on active service, and that opportunities for days on the hills were fewer: 'men, horses, or motor cars were .unobtainable: the war had removed them'.

If the mainland was hard hit, the islands were even worse off. Skye found the reduced and uncertain steamer services a severe handicap to tourism and the local economy. Bad summers contributed to pushing up the cost of living, and the absence of hill-walkers in the Cuillins added to the loss of sporting revenue. The absence of shooting tenants meant lost work and wages. As already noted, the virtual suspension of game-shooting, and a parallel fall in fishing, was a serious loss to the Highland economy, and so also was the absence of American tourists. Their numbers fell, as has already been seen, at Callander, and the impact of this loss is further well illustrated by the experience of two other big tourist hotels in the Trossachs. The first, the Stronachlachar, was a new hotel built at the turn of the century. Situated at the west end of Loch Katrine, its primary purpose, though it did offer some fishing, was to cater for tourists during the summer season on a circular tour through the Trossachs. If its Visitors' Book is to be trusted, the clientèle was overwhelmingly moneyed and foreign, with Americans accounting for over half of its visitors in 1913, and much the same level in 1914. There were some Continental visitors, including travellers from Germany, one of whom arrived as late as the 28th of July, a lady from Leipzig.

TABLE 8.3.   VISITORS TO STRONACHLACHAR HOTEL, 1912–1917.

Year   Number

Year	Number
1912	957
1913	1039
1914	742
1915	330
1916	165
1917	10

Source: Glasgow City Archives, TD20248: Stronachlachar Hotel Visitors' Book, 2 July 1911 to 10 October 1925.

The last groups of Americans – and Canadians, South Africans and others from abroad – were recorded in September of that year. Thereafter business went into sharp decline, the numbers of visitors halving in 1915 and falling yet further in 1916. The loss of foreign custom was fatal, with domestic tourism unable to make up the shortfall, and with the suspension of the once-popular Loch Katrine to Loch Lomond tour by steamer and coach in May 1917, the hotel itself was forced to close. The proprietrix, Mrs. Ferguson, retired, and all the coaching stock was sold off in June 1918. Eleven coaches and brakes each designed to carry from 15 to 24 passengers fetched between £4 and £9, with waggonettes realising up to £18. Waterproof covers, harness and the hotel's 13 rowing boats were also disposed of. Not very far distant from Stronachlachar and serving the same tourist constituency was the Baillie Nicol Hotel at Aberfoyle. The tenant there, an experienced hotelier whose family controlled several hotels in the area, was Alexander Blair. He had the ill luck just to have taken a fresh lease of the premises in the spring of 1914. His annual rent of £700 included an allowance valued at £250 for the free use of the Duke of Montrose's private seven-mile road north from Aberfoyle to Loch Katrine, on which a toll was normally charged on all traffic from bicycles to horse buses. At one shilling per head, the Duke reaped a fine harvest from the 12,000 or so tourists who annually used this road in pre-war years. But Blair's operations turned sour as the War blighted his custom, turnover fell, and he had to sell off his horses. The Duke successfully sued in 1918 for the rent which Blair would not or could not pay. His counsel argued that a contract was a contract whatever the commercial outcome. The defence pled – unsuccessfully – that it was unreasonable to expect payment

> on the ground mainly that the coach route was of no use now, and because there was no steamer on Loch Katrine at present. The larger part of the traffic on the road consisted of people who were not natives of this country, and since the unrestricted U-boat warfare even the Americans had not come.
> (*The Callander Advertiser*, 25 May 1918)

Blair survived this setback, and successfully rebuilt operations after the War. By the early 1930s the Bailie Nicol, the Loch Achray, the Inversnaid and the Trossachs Hotels were in the Blair family portfolio. Many other hotels in the Highlands, or in the Borders and South-West, must have had a parallel wartime experience to that of Stronachlachar. A number, if they did not close, could only survive by offering, as the Woodbank Hotel at Dumfries did, reduced terms during the War. There was some hope that the War might offer some compensation by way of the 'creation of a new class of excursionists', soldiers from the Colonies who were of Scottish stock, and who wished to visit their roots. In 1917 Abbotsford did receive some military visitors, who were serving with either Australian or Canadian regiments, although their numbers were far from adequate to make up the shortfall in foreign visitors.

But it would be a mistake to think that domestic holidaymaking ceased everywhere in 1914 for the duration of the four years of war. Certainly, as we have already seen, some hotels and hydropathic establishments were requisitioned; access to some training areas, notably north of Inverness, was restricted or prohibited; steamer services were sharply reduced; and the railways were heavily absorbed in the war effort.

A survey of Scottish local newspapers confirms that although tourism may have been reduced, it did not by any means come to an end, though there was a change in direction, and in the social and age composition of the clientèle. What helped restore confidence in 1915 and subsequent years was the absence of any coastal raids as were suffered by some English east-coast resorts. There had been worries about German naval sorties from the start, and the Town Council of Scarborough, a prime destination for holidaymakers from Scotland, had been forced to take out advertisements in August in the Scottish press to deny the rumours that raids were imminent: 'foolish and groundless', they insisted. But Scarborough and Whitby were shelled, and the bombardment in December 1914, which shattered the upper stories of the Grand Hotel, led to an immediate exodus of some 6000 well-to-do people. Some Scottish resorts were to make a virtue out of their location: Rothesay insisted that it was 'the safest resort in Britain'; 'sixty miles inland', Callander Hydro underlined in its advertising. 'Safety and comfort' was Moffat's slogan, and this resort, as well as drawing St Felix's Ladies School north, continued to attract a steady and loyal clientèle, a pattern aided by continuing publicity in the Scottish and North of England press. The advertising firm of E. & J. Burrows of Cheltenham, who saw in the War an opportunity for British spas to take over custom that would pre-viously have gone to the Continent, made several approaches to the Town Council including a proposal for a new town guide in March 1917. The Caledonian Railway continued its advertising of Moffat through posters and in its timetables, the cost of which was shared with the burgh, and in October 1914 offered to include a view of Moffat Public Park amongst the photographs that were hung – and long remained hanging – in their passenger coaches. The Council were doubtful that this kind of advertising would be of much value, but at 3s 4d per 100 photographs, thought that not much would be risked by trying it.

It is noticeable, however, that although there were some families in the summer lists for Moffat and other Scottish resorts in 1916, 'Misses', 'Mrs. and Miss' or 'Mrs. and Family' feature more often than single males or even men as heads of household. The girls of the town, or female visitors, may well have noticed a serious shortage of fit young male company. There was quite a heated exchange in the columns of the local paper for months over the conduct of some young ladies during the sojourn of the Yeomanry in the town in May 1915. What made their behaviour worse was that the alleged misconduct, the nature of which was not specified, took place on the Golf Course on a Sunday. And there was a feeling that the growing number of what was dubbed 'the tripper excursion element' was lowering the general tone. While no one would deny the hard-working man or woman, one correspondent wrote, a pleasant day's outing, the beauties of the local scenery and sights would be wasted on the 'mind of the rough factory hand or trade worker'. He continued:

> Moffat, which has always been the resort of the cultured, refined and educated, will do well if in these days of democratic trend she bend all her energies to the keeping intact the character she has hitherto maintained of a secluded, select and sylvan spot – a character of which she must be justly proud.
> (*The Moffat News and Annandale Herald*, July 16, 1915)

Moffat was far from being the only resort to feel the impact of a change in its clientèle. Indeed, the evidence suggests that the working class may actually have benefited (those not at the front) by the full employment and enhanced hours in munitions and other war-related work. There was some disruption of Trades Holidays, particularly in 1916 during the Somme offensive when the Unions agreed to a postponement for a month to the third week of August for munitions workers and miners of the traditional holiday arrangements in the West of Scotland. Compensation had to be paid for the agreements which had to be broken for the letting of holiday apartments. In the following year no such alteration was made, and the volume of Fair Holiday traffic reminded observers of days before the War. The cost of travelling, and the shortage of rolling stock, meant that people did not go as far afield as previously, which benefited Ayrshire and Fife resorts. The following year traffic was even heavier, and more widely distributed. *The Callander and Killin Observer* (20 July 1918) commented on how busy, and not just in and around Crieff, the Glasgow Fair weekend of 1918 was as against pre-war years, despite much reduced railway services:

The rush to coast and country of which it was the culmination
has altogether been of extraordinary dimensions . . . [and re-
flects] the prosperity of the industrial community. The excursionists have shown in many cases that they possess the means to
support a disposition to spend freely.

The Editor concluded that traffic was not just 'unprecedented for
wartime, but . . . exceeded the Fair Saturday activity of pre-war
years'. Other reports confirmed this view, with the railway companies
laying on numerous relief trains and specials – 50 from St Enoch
Station alone to the Ayrshire coast. There was heavy steamer traffic
for Dublin, Belfast and Londonderry. The turnstiles at Rothesay's
pier did record business: 51,093 passed through them in the four
principal days of the Fair, as against 46,491 the previous year. And
for some middle-class and professional families life went on as before,
lodgings being taken for the summer in such favoured resorts as Elie
and North Berwick. Seaside landladies found their trade revived.
Indeed, there was a very interesting dispute in March 1918 which
forced a Government enquiry and intervention over the provision of
housing at Troon, Saltcoats and Largs for shipyard workers. They
had been accommodated over the winter in lodgings, but received
notice to quit as their accommodation was wanted for letting to
summer visitors, who were prepared to pay more than the workers
thought was reasonable. It was an indication of the strength and
solvency of summer tourism.

But with so many men away on military service, what was significantly different was the gender and age composition of tourism.
The visitors to the hydros and hotels tended to be older; those to the
beaches, particularly the day-trippers, either females with children or
girls on their own. At Largs an unofficial census in September 1915
found two-thirds of the visitors there to be female, and in the
following year another estimate suggested that in some resorts there
were as many as 20 women to every young man. This gender
imbalance reflected the number of men away at the front, but also
perhaps how much money was in the pockets of working-class
women. Amenities at the resorts were maintained at some level,
although there was always tension over how much drink should be
available. The local paper at Helensburgh, which regarded itself as a
cut above 'tawdry Dunoon' or 'the Bedlam that is Rothesay', complained bitterly in the summer of 1917 about the way the tone of the
place was being lowered:

Last week there were very painful scenes, which show the need that exists for prohibition during the war at least. Many of the victims were young men, between twenty and forty, evidently engineering and munitions workers with plenty of money in their pockets, and behaving in a foolish way as if no war was going on. They managed mostly to keep out of the hands of the police, but all the same it was disgraceful, and such scenes should be put down with a firm hand.

(*The Helensburgh Gazette*, May 16, 1916)

The supply of food and other goods was also a problem. In the countryside eggs, vegetables and meat were obtainable without paperwork. Elizabeth Malloch's biography, *An Ordained Life* (Edinburgh, 1995), records how her middle-class family took rented rooms in Crail each summer during the War, 'times of amazing treats, especially the luxury of foods city dwellers couldn't get'. Visitors to resorts were advised to take sugar and tea with them. In 1918 a proper system of rationing was introduced in the West of Scotland, which catered for holidaymakers by allowing them to register temporarily for supplies. Helpful though this was, it still could not resolve the problem of sudden influxes of day-trippers on sunny weekends. Despite the difficulties of supply, the menu at Crieff Hydro, however, was still very impressive. A medical missionary on leave there in September 1918 made a hearty breakfast of two plates of porridge, fillet of fish, and then bacon and eggs, a roll and butter, and toast and marmalade. Dinner was not stinted: roast beef and chicken, pudding and coffee followed salmon and cucumber soup. Shopkeepers everywhere did have their difficulties in balancing the demands of their regulars with those of the tourists, although there was widespread suspicion about how well they were doing. They did have problems in getting regular supplies, and retaining staff: 'message boys, even at fancy wages, are almost unobtainable, and the utmost difficulty is experienced in the delivery of goods'. Shortages of servants, and the higher wages required to retain labour, were the subject of complaint by many hoteliers and house agents. What the resorts offered was also under pressure and there was a series of petty regulations to observe. All boats, even small rowing or motor boats, had to have an official identification number for coastal defence purposes. Guests at hotels had to register, and fines were imposed for failure to comply. Photography at the coast was restricted, and postcards of sensitive areas were confiscated. Some entertainment was still provided, with a greater use of home-grown talent. But there was generally less on offer, and one indication of the increasing demands of war, and the

loss of visitor income, was the closure of some golf courses, as at
Tobermory because of a shortage of players. The golf complex at
Cruden Bay lost money heavily from 1915 onwards, though paradoxically the hotel receipts moved into the black. At Grantown-on-
Spey receipts from membership and the sale of daily tickets to the
course were down in 1915 by nearly half on what they had been
before the War. Many of the locality's younger men were away on
military service, and there were far fewer visitors. It became difficult to
keep the course in order when the greenkeeper went off to better-paid
munitions work at Alexandria. Other courses were taken over for
military or agricultural purposes. None of this loss of amenities,
however, seems to have been a serious deterrent to those who could
still holiday.

   Although tourism in peacetime was quick to regain pre-war levels,
there was a legacy nevertheless. Portobello, near Edinburgh, never
regained two of its pre-war key attractions, the Marine Gardens and
the Pier. The first was taken over for military billets and suffered
accordingly, though the ballroom was reopened post-war. The 50-
year-old Pier, from which excursion sailings had regularly departed
pre-war up the river Forth to Stirling or across the Firth to Fife, was
damaged by storm in 1917. Unrepaired, it was demolished, as was its
near neighbour, the chain pier at Newhaven. Some of the requisitioned
hotel properties never reopened post-war; the military tended not to
be very careful of buildings and grounds in their keep. Others such as
Moffat Hydropathic Hotel made only a brief reappearance; destroyed
totally by fire in June 1921, it appears that its finances were already in
disarray. The Directors had just tried to sell the building to Glasgow
Corporation's Health Department for conversion into a tuberculosis
hospital. The run-down Craiglockhart Hydropathic, infested by bee-
tles and rats, became a Roman Catholic teacher training college in
1920. But others came back into successful commercial operation.
After renovation, Stronachlachar Hotel was re-opened in 1920, as was
Shandon Hydro after its return by the Admiralty.

   To conclude, by and large the severest dislocation to Scottish
tourism came in 1914, and much of that can be put down simply
to panic. Tourism did not disappear, and some resorts did surprisingly
well. Dunoon, for example, with its good rail links, saw a rise in visitor
numbers during the War. The Highlands were probably the hardest-
hit area within Scotland, thanks to the transport situation, but there
was no Scottish equivalent of the Isle of Man, where the drastic
curtailment of steamer services led to a dramatic downturn in tourism,
with very serious effects on the local economy. While during the War

tourism had been dislocated seriously in some areas, it still was a significant element in the Scottish economy, and was to become once again a central component in the inter-war years. One of the more serious losses may have been in a hæmorrhage in the kind of steady clientèle on whom respectable resorts pre-war had been able to count year after year. The Grantown paper noted in November 1914 the death of a London man in his seventies, Mr. A. P. Watt, literary agent to, amongst others, Marie Corelli and Rudyard Kipling, who had been coming for the previous 15 years to various houses on Speyside, including the Inverallan manse. That generation of loyal summer visitors passed away and was not, it appears, ever replaced quite to the same extent.

FURTHER READING

J. K. Walton has explored the topic of the War and tourism in 'Leisure Towns in Wartime: The Impact of the First World War in Blackpool and San Sebastian', *Journal of Contemporary History*, vol. 31, 1996, pp. 603–619. An important assessment of the impact of war on resorts in the South of England is to be found in Harold Clunn, *Famous South Coast Pleasure Resorts Past and Present* (London, 1929). On the impact on Skye, see J. A. MacCulloch, *The Misty Isle of Skye* (3rd edition, Edinburgh 1922), p. vii. Two recent undergraduate dissertations at the University of Glasgow have made excellent use of the local press in Scotland for the war years: K. Lang, 'The Effects of the First World War on Scottish Tourism' (1998) and G. Cooke, 'Helensburgh, 1914–1920: War and its Impact on Tourism' (1999). The experience of American tourists in Europe is covered in Harvey Levenstein, *Seductive Journey: American Tourists in France from Jefferson to the Jazz Age* (London, 1998), Chapter 15, pp. 217–232. The role of Craiglockhart Hydropathic as a military hospital is discussed in Wendy Holden, *Shell Shock: The Psychological Impact of War* (London, 1998), pp. 59–65. The letter from Dr Peter Sturrock about the meals at Crieff is from Eric Simpson's private collection, Letter from Dr. Peter Sturrock to his daughter, 24 September, 1918.

> Have you seen the hotel since it was renovated? There's trans-
> formation!
>
> (Advertisement for Shandon Hydropathic, July 1922)

Given the impact of the First World War, and its cost in human, social
and economic terms, it is perhaps rather surprising how quickly tourism
returned to its old patterns, and built on the trade that had continued
during the War. There was indeed a period of renewal as steamer and
railway services were mostly restored to their pre-war levels, though
there were some gaps as several of the east-coast piers, as at Newhaven
and North Berwick, were unserviceable or in very poor condition.
Resorts had to make good the years of relative neglect in housing and
facilities, and in the case of those hotels requisitioned by the military,
had to remedy the abuse they had suffered. Shandon Hydro, for
example, was handed back by the Admiralty after some considerable
delay, and reopened after a complete refurbishment only in July 1922.
The return to peace did mean that the Isle of Man was once more fully
accessible to Scottish holidaymakers, and many Scots found their way
there summer after summer, or to Scarborough or Blackpool, especially
during the Glasgow Fair when all accommodation in the Clyde area
was full to overflowing. Travel to the Continent revived, with a new
emphasis for the well-to-do on winter sports in the Alps. A legacy of the
War was the provision of tours of the battlefields and cemeteries of the
Western Front organised by Thomas Cook and other tourist agencies:
an eight-day guided tour to Bruges and Ypres in July 1920 cost £9 for
travel and accommodation. It would be interesting to know how far the
uptake came from those who had fought there or the bereaved, or those
who were just curious. Another question would be what proportion
were the relatives of other ranks as well as the kith and kin of officers.

The picture for tourism of all kinds was reasonably prosperous in the
1920s. Middle- and upper-class families had returned in strength to the
Scottish resorts to which their parents had taken them before the War
and indeed during it. The Daiches family from Edinburgh – father was a
Rabbi – were in Crail during seven successive summers from 1927, and
this pattern was typical of many professional families. This kind of
tourism was very deep-rooted; and the census of 1921, which was taken

in June on the weekend of the 19th–20th rather than as usual in the early spring, showed many localities already benefiting from an influx of early summer visitors. The increase in recorded population was most marked for Bute, an 85% increase as against the previous figure for 1911, nearly all of which was accountable in terms of the timing of the census. When the 1931 census returned to its traditional time, order was restored, most strikingly in the case of Millport, where the population had apparently trebled between 1911 and 1921.

TABLE.   THE POPULATION OF LEADING SCOTTISH HOLIDAY RESORTS
         (according to the census of 1911, 1921 and 1931)

	1911	1921	1931
Millport	1614	5834	2083
Rothesay	9299	15218	9347
Bridge of Allan	3121	3579	2897
Moffat	2079	2426	2006
North Berwick	3304	4524	3473
Elie and Earlsferry	1014	2252	1098
Oban	5557	6344	5759

Had the 1921 census been taken in late July at the height of the tourist season, the results would have been even more revealing. But as it is, the figures are confirmation of the health of tourism, especially at the seaside resorts.

Another indication of health was the investment in the early 1920s in new hotels and facilities in various parts of the country. The loss of Craiglockhart Hydro through sale to a Catholic training order, and its counterpart at Moffat through fire, was more than conteracted at the top end of the market. There was the post-war completion of Gleneagles Hotel and the conversion of Taymouth Castle to a high-class country club, or hotel super-excellent as it called itself, complete with golf course, riding track and 400 acres of grounds. Though not all of the hydro hotels were as successful, Crieff and Peebles went through the decade with high annual dividends. What helped them and other hotels was the return of the American visitor. Abbotsford House's overall numbers rose from 7,500 in 1919 to just over 11,000 in 1925; and the American contingent increased fivefold from 548 to 2,479. Yet to retain their custom was not easy, as the Managing Director of Melrose Hydro, Norman Kemp, recognised. The Americans, he noted, might make an exception for a few places which because of their age and atmosphere were regarded as 'quaint', but normally insisted on hot and cold running water in their hotel rooms, not jugs and basins.

Hotels had to invest in the upgrading of their facilities, en-suite bathrooms, electric rather than gas lighting, and the like. Those that did modernise, as Peebles Hydro did, reaped their reward.

What held true for the private sector, that there had to be more and better amenities, held also for the public. Aided by legislation passed in 1921, the Health Resorts and Watering Places Act, town councils everywhere embarked on vigorous advertising, which was charged to the rates. Town guides became available for any place with a foothold in the tourist business from Annan to Wigton, and considerable effort was put into the provision of visitor amenities. Golf courses, tennis courts and putting greens, boating ponds and paddling pools, band-stands and promenades, esplanades and walks all became part of the minimum range of attractions, and there could be more. The town councils of St Andrews and Leven, for example, provided ground to local quoiting clubs on condition that they made sure that visitors were welcome. If a seaside resort was to hold its own, there had to be a good swimming pool or lido, which might be outdoor or covered, salt or freshwater. But none – and this remained true for decades – was heated. Troon's open-air pool, designed by the Burgh Engineer, and opened in the mid-1930s at a cost of £20,000, was typical of the grander examples. Its main pond was 180 feet by 90, the shallow end 2½ feet, the deep only six (but there was a separate diving pool), and it was equipped with springboards, rafts and chutes. For the bathers 160 changing cubicles were provided as well as rest and ambulance rooms. The Pond was used for swimming galas, fireworks displays and picturesque tableaux, and had seating accommodation for some 4000 spectators. Helensburgh, Prestwick and other resorts had to match this level of provision, and Edinburgh projected in 1937 a comprehensive redevelopment of Portobello with a new open-air swimming pool, replacement pier and promenade and other attrac-tions. But this scheme was largely thwarted by the outbreak of war in 1939 though the pool, with its wave machine, was built.

The Scottish seaside resorts seem to have done reasonably well throughout the interwar years. Some of the more select places did complain that there was a change in their clientèle as fewer families could afford the servants required to staff the big villas, or indeed to leave them empty for nine months in the year. Walter Ferrier, minister in North Berwick for over 25 years, reported that after the War quite a number were either scaled down by subdivision or sold off for conver-sion into boarding houses. His colleague at Dunbar confirmed this trend:

After the war, with the economic confusion attendant on it, the

increase in the number of motor cars, and the rise of bus companies and day trippers, many of the house owners sold their property to prospective boarding house keepers.
(*The Third Statistical Account of Scotland: East Lothian* (Edinburgh, 1953))

The managers of the hydros were also worrying about the shortage of younger visitors, that theirs was an ageing clientèle. Most concerned of all were the spa resorts, which seem to have experienced a genteel decline. There was no one specific cause, just a steady loss of ground, which proved irreversible. Determined efforts were made in the 1920s by the British Spas Federation to promote the medical case for places like Strathpeffer, and a major attempt was made to reconstruct and recondition the facilities at Bridge of Allan. The Spa was reopened on 30 October 1930, with an electro-therapeutic department to add to the bathing and the douche room, and high hopes were held out for a revival of the resort as a health centre. This does not seem to have materialised, though there were some moments of encouragement as when the Spa Hotel reported in July 1932 that it was having a highly successful season, with large numbers of American and South African visitors, as well as a large party of doctors from the Royal Medico-Psychological Association. During the inter-war years, no new Scottish tourist resorts came into being, and none disappeared from the map, but Bridge of Allan was undoubtedly amongst the weaker runners.

What made matters far harder, of course, was the onset of economic depression in 1929. There were other factors at work such as the changes in transport, but these were broadly neutral, or even beneficial to tourism. Motor tours, on a day- or week-long basis, became firmly established, and coach services began to cut into the passenger receipts of many railway lines, something to which a number of coastal and inland branches were very vulnerable. The isolated Campbeltown-Machrihanish service was one of the first casualties in 1931. The LNER's Gullane line lost its passenger service in September 1932 after a steady haemorrhage of business to the buses from Edinburgh. Predictably there were complaints the following year about the impact on tourism, and a village plebiscite overwhelmingly demanded the restoration of the trains. The railway company were unconvinced. Even if they were to run a summer only service, it would be at a loss, and they preferred to let the station buildings to campers, which at least brought in a clear income. Similar debates were taking place elsewhere. But times were so hard, given the loss of freight business as well, that the companies had to take a hard line. The Cruden Bay Hotel, once the pride of the Great North of Scotland, after years of mounting losses, was converted to a railway laundry in the 1930s. Yet the railways did not give up. Both the LNER and the LMS ran vigorous advertising programmes, offering a wide variety of holiday season tickets, and to some effect.

The Depression affected all levels and types of tourism, making the 1930s as difficult a decade for Scottish tourism as the 1920s had been a good one. There was the loss of American custom, which was felt everywhere in Europe. The arrival in July 1932 of a party of 500 American Scots, members of the Scottish Club of America on the liner *Caledonia*, was welcome indeed, and fully deserving of a warm reception by provost and pipers. But there were all too few groups, and their absence was a sore loss. At Abbotsford, for example, the number of American visitors fell from two or three thousand a year during the mid-1920s to a mere 215 in 1932. A note in the Visitors' Book inserted by General Maxwell-Scott simply observed that there had been few USA or Dominion visitors 'owing to the depressed times in which we live'. Nor was there much recovery prior to the outbreak of War in 1939.

Equally, the Depression and the level of long-term unemployment experienced in many parts of industrial Scotland greatly handicapped domestic tourism. The West of Scotland was particularly hard-hit. The Glasgow Fair Week of 1932 called forth the gloomy response from the Dumbarton paper that 'we are a town mostly existing on the dole, and a great many of us have had too many holidays'. Yet somehow many do seem to have managed a day or two, or even more, away. Though more investigation is needed, the level of holidaymaking seems to belie the scale of unemployment. Some might have had their children taken to the coast by a church or charitable or political organisation, but others found the resources from somewhere. Rothesay maintained its established routine: 'invalids came in the spring, Glasgow folk in July and the English in August' was one view. In the East, despite the terrible condition of its staple industries of coal and textiles, Fife held its place: one estimate suggests that 150,000 visitors came in the summer of 1933. Over 350 special trains were run that summer to places such as St Andrews, Leven, Crail and Kirkcaldy, many of which came from the West of Scotland. Special cheap holiday tickets, and the very good weather that summer, led to exceptional railway traffic to English resorts also, notably Scarborough, Whitley Bay and Blackpool. It is true that withdrawals from the Glasgow Savings Bank for the Fair Holidays fell appreciably from their pre-Depression levels of about £875,000 in 1928 and 1929, but they were still over £700,000 in 1932 and 1933 when things were at their worst. But observers did note one clear difference, that it was the young who were the keenest to get away:

Everyone connected with transport [has been] surprised at the
volume of holiday traffic. In the local aspect, however, one
noticed that there was not the old going-off of family parties.
It was the younger people without encumbrances who were able
to spend the money on a trip to the holiday resorts.
(*The Lennox Herald*, 29 July, 1933)

The summer break had become a key element in the culture of the
young, as indeed it remains.

The state of tourism induced a highly significant change in the attitude
of the state. For the first time, and on a very modest scale, central
Government began to provide financial support, concerned about the
contribution of inwards tourism to Britain's balance of payments. A
number of voluntary, private-sector organisations to promote tourism
had been formed in the 1920s, including one body called 'The Come to
Scotland Association'. In 1929 the Government made available a grant
to the Travel Association of Great Britain and Ireland, and the Scottish
Office provided support for a new organisation called the Scottish
Tourism Development Association. It was a small change – a mere
£346 in the case of the STDA – but one with major implications in the
longer term. So also was the extension of the practice of holidays with
pay, a long campaign which culminated in 1938 with a Holidays With
Pay Act, that doubled the number of workers provided with this right.
The summer of 1939 was to be the last at peace for six years, and yet
again tourism in Scotland was greatly affected, much more severely than
during 1914–1918, with many beaches out-of-bounds, hotels requisitioned, and transport and facilities in very short supply. The exploration
of this period is yet to be undertaken, territory as unfamiliar in some
respects as Scotland was to the early tourists of the later eighteenth
century, with whom we began.

FURTHER READING

A good general account is given in Stephen G. Jones, *Workers at Play: A
Social and Economic History of Leisure, 1918–1939* (London, 1986).
Amongst contemporary accounts of travels in Scotland, H.V. Morton, *In
Search of Scotland* (London, 1929) and *In Scotland Again* (London, 1933)
are still worth reading. Some of the issues raised here have been explored in
Alastair Durie, 'The Scottish Seaside Resort in Peace and War, c. 1880–
1960', *International Journal of Maritime History*, IX, June 1997.

A'Beckett, Arthur 9, 158–9
Abbotsford 12, 17, 44, 131,
 139–140, 146–7, 173, 176, 193,
 196
Aberarder 113
Abercrombie, Sir Robert 98
Aberdeen 5, 39, 63, 114, 135
Aberdeenshire 113
Aberdour 2, 77
Aberfeldy 124
Aberfoyle 2, 126, 154, 169,
 185
Abinger, Lord 113
Accidents 33, 165; drownings 14,
 74; shooting 103
Accommodation 5, 14, 16,
 sporting lodges 113, 115–6, 121,
 landladies 78, private hospitality
 28, 117, seabathing quarters
 70–1
Accommodation-letting income 5
Acworth, W.M. 119, 156
Airdrie 138
Albert, Prince 121
Alexandria 190
Alford 110
Allan, David 90
Allan, Thomas 11
Allison, James 160
Alloa 53, 174
Alloway 8, 44, 173
Alnmouth 124
Alton Towers 147
Andersen, Hans Christian 19
Anderson, John 153
Andrews, Malcolm 35
Annan 194
Appin 32
Arbroath 138
Ardencaple 176

Ardrossan 62, 69, 73, 142
Argyll, Duke of 29, 31, 131,
 154
Arran 50, 79, 126, 155, 166
Ascog 71
Assynt 36
Atholl, Duke of 53
Attractions–Bannockburn 7, 99,
 Burns' Cottage 8, 44, 173,
 Carron 27–28, Culloden 40, 45,
 56, Doune Castle 3, 23, New
 Lanark 15, 26–27, Wallace
 Monument 8, 100
Auchmithie 46
Auchnacraig 22
Aviemore 113
Ayr 8, 62, 131, 148
Ayton 89

Baden-Baden 88
Bailey, J.M. 134
Bald, Adam 67–8
Balfour, A.J. 128
Ballachulish 150
Ballater 89, 133, 166, 169
Balloch 48, 55, 132
Balmoral 18, 121, 135
Balquhidder 4
Banavie 58
Banks, Sir Joseph 22
Bannockburn 7, 99
Barrie, J.M. 46, 134, 138
Bass, Sir Alfred 112
Bathgate 63
Bath 88, 90, 177
Battlefield tours 192
Baxter, Thomas 24
Baxter, Thomas Handyside 41
Begging 58
Belgium 36, 175

Bell, Henry   47
Bellais, Kenneth   133
Ben Lomond   24–25, 68, 110
Ben Macdhui   12, 122
Ben More   153
Ben Nevis   11, 37, 52, 110, 152, 154
Ben Rhydding   88
Bergen   176
Berlin   174
Berwick-on-Tweed   62, 144
Bilbao   86
Birnam   15
Black, Jeremy   36
Black, John (driver)   33
Blackie, J.S.   101, 112, 126
Blackpool   65, 86, 173, 180, 192, 196
Blair Atholl   23–4, 42
Blair, Alexander (hotelier)   185
Blair, Robert (hotelier)   153
Blairgowrie   173
Blairlogie   87
Blakey, Robert   111
Blanchard, John   82
Bo'ness   47
Bombelles, M. de   35
Bonawe   30, 33
Booth, William   104
Bouverie-Campbell, Col.   82
Bowman, J.E.   51, 56
Boyd, Rev. A.K.H.   93–94, 156
Boyd, Thomas   81
Braid, James   124, 182
Breadalbane, Earl of   28, 37, 154
Bridge of Allan   9, 13, 55, 95–100, 102, 195
Bridge of Earn   89
Brig O'Turk   135, 168
Brighton   66, 83, 86, 171
Bristed, John   25, 129, 136
Bristol   51, 105
British Fisheries Society   29
British Spas Federation   195
Brodick   40, 87
Brodie, Sir Benjamin   116
Brontë, Charlotte   139
Broomielaw   47

Brougham, Henry   27
Broughty Ferry   67
Brow (Solway)   86
Brown, Robert   145
Bruce, A. L.   126
Buccleuch, Duke of   90
Buchan, Dr William   67
Burnett family   37
Burns, J. & G.   51, 141
Burns, John   49
Burns, Robert   29, 39–40, 86
Burntisland   17, 125
Burritt, Elihu   140
Bute   87, 193
Butler, R.W.   17, 132
Buxton   88, 95

Cadell, Patrick   23
Cairndow   30
Cairngorms   184
Caithness   111
Calabar   105
Calder, James   103
Caledonian Canal   114, 152
Callander   32, 38, 46, 53, 56, 74, 87, 125–127, 143, 150, 166, 177–178, 186
Cambridge   27, 53, 95, 159
Cambuskenneth   45, 99
Cameron, Ann   42
Campbeltown   69, 78, 81, 195
Campsies   68
Canada   176
Cannes   5, 87
Canongate   26
Canty Bay   156
Carlisle   150
Carlsberg   88
Carnoustie   125
Carron   25, 27–28
Caw, James   103
Cawdor Castle   39
Census 7–9, 193; Bridge of Allan 9, 96–97; road traffic 167–8
Chambers, William   100
Charteris, Dr. M.   86–7, 95
Chatfield, Edward   144–5
Chatsworth   8
Cheltenham   88, 131

Chicago   148, 172
Claridge, Captain   101
Clarke, Sir James   87
Cleland, James   48
Clepham, James   26
Clerk, Sir John   89
Clyde   47–49
Clyde, Falls of   26
Coatbridge   61
Cockburn, Lord   10, 25, 41, 46,
   53, 56, 69, 73, 115
Cody, Colonel   15
Coghill, J.H.   75
College study tours 147
Cologne   174–175
Comet 47
Commuting 60, 70
Complaints 34, 62–63; calibre of
   inns 28–31, 55–56, 133–134;
   hotel charges 30; ferries 162;
   service 28–29; tipping 133–134
Connel 163
Connel Bridge 169
Connel Ferry   162; 169
Cook, Thomas 55, 62, 140–149;
   and the Continent 129–130,
   145, 175; Egypt 140; North
   America 146–148
Cook, Thomas Mason   140, 148
Coventry   162
Cowes   121
Craiglockhart Hydro 181, 190
Crail   189, 192, 196
Crathes   37
Crawfordjohn   32
Crianlarich   153
Crieff   45, 86, 103–105, 131, 169,
   182–183, 189
Crinan Canal 157
Cronin, J.   78
Cruden Bay   5, 125, 190, 195
Cuillins   184
Culloden   40, 56
Culzean Castle   16
Cumberland   35, 138
Cupar   132, 156
Custine, A., Marquis   24
Cycling 160–4; Cyclists' Touring
   Club 160–161

D'Haussay, Baron   114
Daiches family   192–3
Dale, David   26
Dalmally   3, 30, 33, 40, 153, 167,
   169
Dalnacarroch   40
Dalwhinnie   150
Daniell, William   48–49
Darlington   52
Darwin, Charles   102
Davis, Jefferson   146
Deal   66
Deeside   44
Dempster, George of
   Dunnichen   67
Dendy, W.C.   52
Depression, the 196
Derby   144–145
Devon   2, 72
Dickens, Charles   139
Diggle, Elizabeth   21, 22, 27–28,
   32, 35, 66, 87
Dingwall   92, 117
Dinsdale, Sir Joseph   94
Dirleton   123
Dollar   59, 169
Dollar, Robert   169
Dornoch   126–127
Douglas (Lanarkshire)   118
Douglas, Isle of Man   180
Doune   3, 23, 169
Drinking – Forbes Mackenzie Act
   76
Drummond, Mrs   38
Drummond, Peter   72
Drummond, T.D.K.   15
Dryburgh   15, 41, 139
Dumbarton   48, 55
Dumfries   46, 123, 178, 185
Dunbar   124, 127, 179, 194
Dunblane   89, 105, 181
Dundee   13, 41, 114, 135
Dunkeld   15, 23–24, 33, 36, 38,
   40, 87, 115, 144
Dunolly Castle   75
Dunoon   7, 65, 74, 78, 80, 101,
   180, 188, 190
Duns   89
Dunvegan Castle   174

Durham 157
Düsseldorf 27

Earl, George 128
East, Dr Rowland 101
Edinburgh 30, 56, 63, 124, 132, 141, 141–143, 147–148, 156, 172, 174, 183, 194
Edward VII 121, 126
Edwards, Ralph (guide) 23
Edzell 126, 138, 179
Egypt 140
Eigg 52
Elgin 23, 32, 67
Elie 17, 44, 67, 69–70, 82, 125, 173, 179
Ems 175
Eugénie, Empress 133
Excursions 13, 61–63, 65–66, 74–75, 150–151, botanical 10, Cook's 142-3, motor tours 169, special 63, 72, 196, temperance 62, 722

Fag, Frederick 52, 56
Faill, Andrew 88
Fairlie 71
Falkirk 160, 169
Fenton, Alexander 122
Ferguson, Malcolm 158
Ferguson, Mrs (proprietrix) 185
Ferrier, Rev. Walter 194
Fingal's Cave 39
Fleetwood 142
Fontane, Theodore 10, 55, 76, 110, 139
Forres 102–103, 107, 181
Fort Augustus 76, 169
Fort William 76, 152, 154, 157
Forth Railway Bridge 95, 156
Fortingall 23
Fowler, Lydia 142
Fox, Dr Fortescue 87, 94, 177
Foyer, Falls of 40
Franklin, W.E. 143-4
Fraser, D. 57
Fraser, James 9
Fraser, Patrick 33
Fraserburgh 6

Fyfe, W.W. 74

Gairloch 158
Gardenstone, Lord 26
Garelochhead 77, 155
Garlieston 152
Garnet, Dr 32
Garnkirk 61
Garrison, William Lloyd 146
Gartsherrie 61
Geikie, Sir Alexander 161
Germany 35
Giant's Causeway 60, 138
Gilmorehill 101
Gilpin, Rev. William 39
Glamis 38
Glasgow 7, 48, 60, 61, 63, 101, 131, 142, 173
Glasgow Fair 45, 61, 63, 72, 74, 77, 78, 160, 173, 187–188, 192, 196
Glasgow Savings Bank 196
Glen Ogle 153
Glen Tilt 53
Glen Urquhart 112
Glencoe 58, 150
Glencroe 19
Gleneagles 124, 182, 193
Glenesk 122
Glenfinnan 45
Goats' whey 40, 87–88
Gold, J. & M. 2
Gordon, Duke and Duchess of 66
Gourock 155
Gower, Lord 3
Graham, R. 165
Grant, A.G. 14
Grant, Alexander 181
Grant, Mrs Anne of Laggan 46
Grant, Mrs Eizabeth 67
Grant, James of Stirling 55
Grantown-on-Spey 127, 175, 179, 190
Gray, Thomas 33–34, 38
Greenock 60, 68
Guidebooks 50–51, 54, 81, 109, 130–131, 141, 161, 166
Guides 3, 23–25, 42; Cook's conductors 143–145; mountain 24, 153

Gullane   195
Gullane, John   12
Gully, Dr. W.   101

Hall, Robert   116
Hamilton   32
Harris   113
Hawick   33, 145, 151, 161
Hawthorne, Nathaniel   10
Health Resorts and Watering
   Places Act   194
Hebrides   159
Helensburgh   4, 69, 71–72, 80,
   173, 188, 194
Hembry, P.   88
Henderson, Major, of
   Westerton   90
Heron, Robert   25–26, 31, 38–39,
   41
Highland Games   135
Holidays with Pay Act   197
Holyrood Palace   23
Home, Dr Francis   89
Hooper, Rev. F.W.   147
Hope, John   72, 105
Hopetoun, Lord   90
Hotels 32–36, 81–83, 94–95, 185–
   186, 192–194; construction 132,
   153; off season 17, 57, 134;
   patronage 132–133; during
   WW1 184–185
Howitt, William   53
Hunter's Quay   71
Hunter, Archibald   101–102, 104
Huntly, Marquis of   114
Hutcheson, David   51, 137, 140
Hutchison, Rev.   76
Hydropathy and hydros 101–102,
   163, 195; culture and clientèle
   101–107; finance 102;
   temperance emphasis 104–105;
   wartime hospitals 180–182

Innerleithen   13, 89
Inveraray   29, 37, 39, 50, 68,
   153–154, 169
Invergarry   11, 152
Inverlochy   113
Inverness   56, 113, 156–157

Iona   50, 52, 58, 140, 142–143,
   158
Ireland   130, 138, 146, 172, 178
Isle of Man   54, 180, 190, 192

Jacobi, Mr   27
James III   45
Jarvie, Grant   135
Jeans, Thomas   116
Jeffrey, Lord   48
John O'Groats   15, 40, 160
Johnson and Boswell   22
Johnstone, George   150
Journal keeping 10

Kansas   16
Kelso   111
Kemp, Norman   9, 193
Kenmore   25, 36
Kentucky   27
Killiecrankie   12, 137
Killin   31, 35, 154
King, J.C.   45
Kinghorn   124
Kintyre   79
Kipling, Rudyard   16, 191
Kirkcaldy   196
Kirriemuir   134, 138
Knox, John   31, 34
Kyle of Lochalsh   159
Kyles of Bute   107

Lakes (English)   35, 51, 127
Lanarkshire   37
Lands Valuation Court 16–17
Landseer, Sir Edwin   135
Largo   16, 49
Largs   69, 70, 180, 188
Laurencekirk   26
Leicester   140, 143
Leipzig   184
Leith   47, 69, 150
Leven   15, 194, 196
Leyden, John   35, 39
Linlithgow   62, 144
Liverpool   54, 68, 82, 142
Llandudno   173
Loch Achray   153
Loch Eck   57

Loch Katrine   4, 35, 48, 56, 59, 137, 153–154, 184–185
Loch Leven   111
Loch Linnhe   32
Loch Lomond   48, 143, 185
Loch Maree   11, 163
Loch Ness   152
Loch Tay   25, 182
Loch Vennachar   152
Lochearnhead   53
Lochgilphead   164
Lochgoilhead   74
Lockerbie   161
Logie, D.W.   154, 157
Londonderry   60
London   40, 95, 117, 142
Lossiemouth   67, 80
Lovat, Lord   118, 164
Lubbock, Geoffrey   174
Luggage 3, 9, 82
Lundin Links   125
Lunn, Sir Henry   110, 175
Luss   25, 29
Lyall, J. Watson   116

Macalister, Sir Donald   175
Macbraynes   51, 130, 157–158, 162
Macdonald, Alexander   17
MacDonald, Sir John   164, 169–170
MacDougall, Captain   75
McFadyen, John   11
McGonagall, William   83–84
MacGregor, Malcolm   4
MacKay, Daniel   131
MacKenzie, Evan   117, 121
MacLachlan, John   116
MacLaren, Ian   119
MacLaren, John   142
MacLeod, Dr Norman   102–103
MacPherson, James   39
MacTaggart, William   79
Machrihanish   195
Malcolm, George   112
Malloch, Elizabeth   189
Malmesbury, Earl of   114
Malvern   88, 102
Manchester   144, 157

Mandler, Peter   8
Margate   37
Martineau, Harriet   139
Mawman, Joseph   40, 90
Maxwell, Helen   167
Maxwell-Scott, General   196
Meikle, Dr Thomas   103
Melford   150
Melrose   12, 14, 101, 139, 140, 182, 193
Mendelssohn, Felix   10
Mentone   88
Millais, Lady   16
Millais, Sir John Everett   135
Millport   2, 73, 163, 193
Milne, Mrs Malcolm Bruce   176
Mitchell, Joseph   154
Moffat   40, 87, 89–91, 102, 180, 182, 186–187, 190
Monifieth   124
Mont Blanc   129
Monte Carlo   5, 88
Montrose   130
Montrose, Duke of   154, 185
Morison, Dr   87
Morpeth   139
Morris, Tom   99, 126
Motoring 164–168, 170, 183–184, 195
Muirfield   123
Mull   22, 34, 116
Munsell, Walter   163
Murdoch, Mrs   89
Murray, Sarah   22–23, 29–30, 32–33, 40
Murthly Castle   28
Musselburgh   123

Nairn   65, 78, 80, 83, 87
Naismyth, Alexander   26
Nenadic, Stana   21
New Lanark   15, 26–27
New Zealand   108
Newburgh   132
Newcastle   102, 144, 176
Newhaven   49, 190, 192
Newman, John Henry   146
Nightingale, Florence   119
Nodier, Charles   25

North America   108
North Berwick   14, 74, 81–83,
   123, 128, 132, 173, 194
Norway   176
Notman, George   103

Oakley, Ollie   173
Oban   2, 46, 50–51, 73, 81, 111,
   116, 131–132, 137, 151, 152,
   157–159
Oldham   10
Ousby, Ian   27
Owen, Wilfred   181
Oxford   53, 81, 159

Paisley   61
Pankhurst, Christabel   18
Pankhurst, Emily   15
Pannanich   89
Paris   115, 145, 182
Paterson, Dr William   101
Paul, Dugald (innkeeper)   55
Paul, William   114
Pease, Edward   63
Pease, Henry   52
Peden, George   1
Peebles   86, 100, 135, 155, 168,
   175, 178, 180, 194
Pennant, Thomas   22
Penney, Scott Moncrieff   47
Perth   13, 29, 63, 117–118, 123,
   156, 165
Peterhead   40, 66
Pettie, Mr John   79
Philp, Andrew   17, 104, 141
Pitkeathly (Bridge of Earn)   89
Pitlochry   16, 29, 102, 110, 164
Platt, Col. Henry   159
Plummer, Dr   89
Plumptre, James   27
Police regulations - payment of
   bills 9
Porter, Anne   56
Portnacroish   32
Portobello   12, 67, 70, 72, 81, 83,
   155, 190, 194
Portpatrick   152, 179
Portree   143, 158
Portrush   173

Postcards 16, 148
Potter, Beatrix   16
Prestonpans   67
Prestwick   194
Priessnitz, Vincent   88, 101
Publicity 90, 98, 130–131, 153–
   154

Queensferry, North   34
Queensferry, South   40, 67, 74

Railways 60–63, 82, 141–144,
   150–156, 173, 195–196; early
   excursions 61–62, 155; sporting
   traffic 114, 177–178; golf 5,
   124; light railway schemes 152;
   station organisation 152, 156–
   157; receipts at Elie 125;
   closures 169 195–196
Rattray, Wellwood   79
Resorts – artists' colonies 79
Rest and Be Thankful   18
Riviera   3
Roads 31–33, 164–168
Rochefoucald, La   30
Rogers, (Dr) Charles   53, 98–99
Rome   145
Roslin   39, 52
Ross, Horatio   121
Rothesay   10, 45, 65, 68, 73, 76,
   80, 83, 86–87, 101, 155, 186,
   188
Rumbling Bridge   143
Ruskin, John   135
Russell, Thomas   25

St Andrews   47, 49, 69, 73, 123,
   134, 194, 196
St Boswells   12
St Fillans   44
St Fond, Faujas   27, 30, 33
St Kilda 157
St Kilda   157
St Mary's Loch   15, 111, 161
St Ronan's Well   89
Saltcoats   188
Sassoon, Siegfried   181
Scarborough   65–66, 186, 192,
   196

Schinkel, Karl Friedrich   50
Schmoll, P.   17–18
Scott, Walter   45–46, 50, 83, 113
Scottish Automobile Club   165
Scottish Club of America   196
Scottish Tourism Development
   Association   197
Sea-bathing 49, 66–71, 82–83,
   187–188; mixed 73–74; dress
   72–74; bathing machines 66–67,
   83
Seamill   101
Senex   68
Shandon   107, 190, 192
Shanks, John (guide)   23
Shetland   157, 162
Shipton, E.R.   161
Simmons, Jack   7
Simpson, Eric   88
Sinclair, Catherine   110, 121
Sinclair, Sir John   146
Skye   44, 58, 83, 137, 172
Sladden family   159
Slessor, Mary   105
Smart, R. N.   138
Smith, Alexander   81, 137
Smith, George J. Cayley   35
Smollett, Tobias   35
Smout, T.C.   34
Snaefell   152
Snowdon   152
Snowie (gunsmith)   115–116
South Africa   108
Southport   173
Southwold   182
Souvenirs 24
Spas 40, 88–90, 195; Bridge of
   Allan 95–100; Moffat 89–91;
   Strathpeffer 91–95
Speed, James   27
Sport - deer 122–123; fishing 100–
   102; golf 83–84, 105, 190;
   grouse 40, 112–122, 123–128,
   178; mountaineering 110;
   yachting 109–110, 159
Stables, Dr Gordon   162
Staffa   22, 34, 39, 50, 54, 158
Steamships 47–55, 59, 63, 83,
   157–160, 180

Stevenson, Robert Louis   93
Stewart, John   67
Stewart, W. Grant   120
Stirling, Margaret   90
Stirling   8, 13, 31, 54, 63, 98,
   100, 137
Stoddart, Thomas   22, 111
Stonehenge   87
Stornoway   159
Stowe, Harriet Beecher   3, 146
Strathpeffer   44, 89, 91–95, 151,
   177, 195
Strathspey   14, 110–111
Strome Ferry   162
Stronachlachar   184–185, 190
Student reading parties 53
Sturrock, John   12
Sunday observance 72, 74–77,
   105, 163
Sunderland   146
Sutherland, Duke of   92
Swimming pools 194
Switzerland   87, 127, 175

Talbot, Henry Fox   139
Tarbert   164, 167, 175
Tarbet   48, 57, 75
Taylor, Roger   138
Taymouth   25–26, 193
Taynuilt   36
Tennyson, Lord   133
Thomson, Prof.   98
Thornton, Colonel   113
Tobermory   53, 190
Torquay   72, 87
Tourism fluctuations 147, 171–
   172, 178, 196; models 17–18
Townshend, Chauncy   53, 58–59
Travis, John   72
Trollope, A.   117
Troon   124, 188, 194
Trossachs   44, 46, 57, 135, 152–
   153, 157, 174
Troup, William   97
Trouville-sur-Mer   86
Turnberry   124
Tweedie, Mrs   112
Tweedside   110
Tyndrum   30, 164, 167

Tynemouth 66

Uig 83
Uist 124
Valentine of Dundee 135, 137
Vandalism 59, 75–76
Venice 145
Verne, Jules 10, 72–73
Vichy 88
Victoria, Queen 18, 33, 115, 132
Visitors' Books 8, 25–28, 177, 184;
 Abbotsford 139–140; Birnam
 Institute 15–16; New Lanark 26–
 27
Visitors' Lists – general 14, 78–82;
 Bridge of Allan 94–96; Dunoon
 80; Shandon 107

Wade, General 31
Wade, Rev. W.M. 69–70
Wales, North 23, 27, 35, 42
Wales, Prince of 121
Wales, South 72
Walker, Adam 36
Walker, Fraser & Steele 116
Walker, Fred 49
Walker, George and Jane 105,
 139
Wallace Monument 8, 99, 100,
 135
Walton, John 71
War and tourism 45, 171–172,
 174–180, 192

Warrington 50
Warwick Castle 3
Watson, Jennifer 80
Watt, A.P. 191
Watt, James 27
Weld, Charles 54, 58
Wemyss Bay 106
Westward Ho! 124
Whistlefield 155
Whitbread, Samuel 112
Whitby 186
Whitley Bay 196
Wicks of Baiglie 46
Wight, Isle of 38
Wigton 162, 194
Wilde, Oscar 139
Willis, N.T. 114
Willis, R.L. 32
Willoughby, Lord and Lady 59,
 133
Wilson, George Washington 130,
 135–140, 148–149
Wilson, James 158
Wilson, McGregor 79
Winans, W.L. 122
Worcester 56
Wordsworths, Dorothy and
 William 31–32, 34, 36, 40
Wye Valley 58

York 105
Young, John 12
Ypres 192

A SHORT HISTORY OF
THE POST WAR WORLD
1945-1970

By the same author
LIVING IN ENGLAND

Chaucer's England
The Elizabethan Age
Fielding's England

DUNCAN TAYLOR

90

*A Short History of
the Post War World
1945-1970*

London
DENNIS DOBSON

To Ralph

First published in Great Britain in 1977
by Dobson Books Ltd, 80 Kensington Church Street, London W 8
Printed in Great Britain by
Weatherby Woolnough, Weilingborough, Northamptonshire

Hardcover ISBN 0 234 77667 6
Paperback ISBN 0 234 77856 3

Contents

		Page
1945	. . . .	7
1946	. . . .	16
1947	. . . .	23
1948	. . . .	28
1949	. . . .	35
1950	. . . .	40
1951	. . . .	48
1952	. . . .	56
1953	. . . .	64
1954	. . . .	70
1955	. . . .	78
1956	. . . .	85
1957	. . . .	94
1958	. . . .	101
1959	. . . .	108
1960	. . . .	116
1961	. . . .	126
1962	. . . .	136
1963	. . . .	145
1964	. . . .	155
1965	. . . .	164
1966	. . . .	173
1967	. . . .	187
1968	. . . .	199
1969	. . . .	212

1945

NEW YEAR'S DAY was bright and cold throughout Britain. You could skate outside, on frozen ponds and flooded fields. But what 2 January would be like was an official secret. Neither the thin, eight-page newspapers, nor the two BBC radio programmes (there was no television) provided a weather forecast. It would have been too useful to the Germans who, together with Austria, Hungary, Bulgaria and Romania, were at war with the Allies – the British Commonwealth, the U.S.A., the U.S.S.R. (Russia), China, France, Norway, Denmark, the Netherlands, Poland, Czechoslovakia, Yugoslavia and Greece. The national anthems of the Allies were played through before the nine-o'clock news on Sunday evenings.

Since 1943 the Italians had been for the most part out of the war. Italy was occupied by the Germans in the north and by the Allies in the centre and south.

Britain and the U.S.A., allied with China, were also at war with Japan.

Asked why he was fighting, a British soldier would probably have said: 'To stop Hitler', 'To stop Mussolini', 'To stop the Japs'. In the case of Germany and Italy the war was thought of as against two cruel, boastful, near-crazy dictators – Hitler and Mussolini. In Japan there was no single person whom people thought of as the enemy, and the Japanese did not organise mass murder, as Hitler did against the Jews. But they had committed others acts of inhumanity, particularly against civilian as well as military prisoners.

By now the Allies expected to win the war. On 6 June 1944, 'D-Day', they had landed on the Normandy coast, under the supreme command of the U.S. General Eisenhower, and had advanced against strong opposition. In August support came from landings in the south of France. Paris was entered on 25 August. The next objective was the Rhine.

In Italy Allied armies, which had entered Rome on 4 June, were now north of Florence. Resistance fighters helped them, behind the German lines.

In Greece resistance fighters had helped to clear the Germans from their country, but were about to embark on a long and pitiless struggle among themselves.

7

On the eastern front the Russians were advancing into Poland, Czechoslovakia, Hungary and Yugoslavia.

In the Far East, although the Japanese still occupied large parts of China, the British were ready to advance into Burma, and the Americans had recaptured the Marshall Islands and the Philippines.

So on that sunny, frosty New Year's Day of 1945, the British people, who had been at war since 3 September 1939, expected to win. Their mood was optimistic, but their life was 'austere'. 'Austerity' was a word everybody knew. Clothing, textiles, furniture, fuel and many foodstuffs were rationed. There were no luxury goods in the shops. If you wanted to buy a 'wireless', as radio was then called, there was no choice to make. Only one type of set was manufactured for civilians. You had to have that, if you could get it.

Nevertheless, nobody starved, everybody worked, thirty-six London theatres were open, and at Dumbarton Oaks, in the U.S.A., a conference had laid the foundations of a new organisation, which was to keep the peace, when it came – the United Nations.

Or would Hitler produce another secret weapon? London and southern England had been attacked since the summer of 1944, first with flying bombs (V.1's), known to the public as 'doodle-bugs' or 'buzz bombs' (you could hear them coming), and then with long-range rockets (V.2's). But the launching sites of most of these weapons had now been overrun. The Germans had no more surprises for us, except their tenacity. They supported their unconventional air weapons with a daring conventional counter-attack on the ground. This was in the Ardennes, the hilly forest of southern Belgium. It was still a threat at the end of 1944 and Belgium was not liberated until 4 February 1945.

Had the Allies a secret weapon? The most spectacular attempt to put a quick stop to the war had been made by the Germans themselves on 20 July 1944, when high-ranking officers tried to murder Hitler with a bomb. The plot failed. The officers were tortured and hanged. The Allies had nothing to do with this; but they had a secret weapon and it was a bomb too. Luckily for the Germans, it was not ready yet.

Early in February 1945 the papers announced that Winston Churchill, President Roosevelt and Marshal Stalin had met 'in the Black Sea area'. A few days later the name of the meeting-place was revealed – Yalta, in the Crimea. There had been much to discuss – what to do with Germany, as soon as she was defeated, and what to do with the countries which were now being freed from German occupation. You might think that being freed would result in freedom. Not at all. In Greece it had resulted in a bloody civil war between Left and Right, in which Churchill himself had intervened by visiting Athens at Christmas 1944. A settlement (in favour of restoring the monarchy, under King George) was not reached until 1946, and the communists fought on in the mountains until 1949.

Poland and Yugoslavia also presented problems. Poland had a right-wing government in exile in Britain. Yugoslavia had an exiled King. But Poland was being liberated from the Germans by Russian troops and the communist Marshal Tito had led the Resistance in Yugoslavia. At Yalta the Western powers realised, though this was not actually stated, that both these countries could not be prevented from turning communist. They also accepted the fact that the boundaries of pre-war Poland would not be restored. The Russians insisted on keeping part of eastern Poland, though offering part of eastern Germany to Poland in return.

In the statement issued after Yalta, the fate of Germany was only described in general terms. She was to be divided into four zones occupied by the three Great Powers and France. And then what? 'It is our inflexible purpose,' the statement went on, 'to destroy German militarism and Nazism and to ensure that Germany will never again be able to disturb the peace of the world . . . It is not our purpose to destroy the people of Germany, but only when Nazism and militarism have been extirpated will there be hope for a decent life for Germans and a place for them in the comity of nations.'

This 'comity of nations' was already being planned. A conference met at San Francisco in April to prepare a charter for the kind of international body which had been discussed at Dumbarton Oaks (Washington) in 1944. By the end of June it had done so, and the United Nations Charter was signed by 50 nations. The United Nations Educational Scientific and Cultural Organisation (UNESCO) and the Food and Agriculture Organisation (FAO) were also established this year. The World Health Organisation (WHO) followed in 1948.

How did 'Hitler and his Nahzees', as Churchill used to call them, react to the news of their impending extirpation? Hitler himself never wavered. He would not think of surrender and had plans for a fight to the death in the mountains of Bavaria. The mass murders in the concentration camps went on. Prisoners of war, weakened by years of captivity, were marched into the interior to prevent their liberation by the Allies.

The first crossing of the Rhine was made by the Americans on 9 March, while the Russians were approaching Berlin from the east and had entered Austria.

On 26 April Russian and American troops met on the River Elbe.

1945

Nothing more was heard of Hitler's intended fight to the death in Bavaria. The Russians took Berlin on 1 May. Germany and Austria were overrun.

On 2 May papers carried the headline: HITLER DEAD. The news had been broadcast by Hamburg radio, which had played Wagner recordings before making the following announcement:

> It is reported from the Fuehrer's headquarters that our Fuehrer [leader], Adolf Hitler, has fallen this afternoon at his command post in the Reich Chancery, fighting to the last breath against Bolshevism and for Germany.

Admiral Doenitz had been nominated as Hitler's successor. He said:

> Our Fuehrer's battle against the Bolshevist flood benefited not only Europe, but the whole world.

The facts about Hitler's death were not established until later. At the time it still seemed possible that he had made his escape to South America. Nobody has been found who saw him die, but the evidence leads to the conclusion that on 30 April he shot his mistress, Eva Braun, whom he had married on the previous day. He then shot himself. The two bodies were burned in the garden of the Chancery.

'Hitler's jackal', Mussolini, was caught trying to escape with his mistress from Italy to Switzerland (28 April). The Italian partisans into whose hands they had fallen acted quickly and with an eye for spectacle. They shot the pair and later displayed their bodies in Milan – upside down.

On 7 May Germany surrendered. 8 May was celebrated as VE Day. (Victory in Europe. Victory over Japan was still to come.) An IMMEDIATE signal was sent from the Admiralty to the Royal Navy: 'Splice the main-brace' (Issue rum). Londoners danced in the streets. King George VI and Queen Elizabeth (now the Queen Mother) appeared on the balcony of Buckingham Palace. Churchill spoke from a balcony in Whitehall. Searchlights lit up St. Paul's.

But cheers for victory after a long war have tears mixed up with them. Too many friends are dead. Many who mourned private losses on that summer evening thought also of a friend of Britain who had died only three weeks before. Already ailing at Yalta, Franklin D. Roosevelt had died on 12 April at the age of 63.

The news reached London at midnight and Moscow in the early hours of the morning. Roosevelt had led the country which was then Russia's most powerful ally. *The Times* reported:

Mr. Molotov (the Foreign Minister) called on the U.S. Ambassador soon after 3.00 a.m. to present the Government's condolences. Muscovites on their way to work stood hatless for a moment and went on subdued. Housewives on early shopping missions spread the sad news. Some wept openly. Today in Moscow it is as if some great light had suddenly been dimmed.

'What an enviable death was his.' Churchill, destined to live another twenty years, in which he would experience disappointment and failing health, was speaking in the House of Commons. 'He had brought his country through the worst of its perils and the heaviest of all its toils . . . For us it remains only to say that in Franklin Roosevelt there died the greatest American friend we have ever known, and the greatest champion of freedom who has ever brought help and comfort from the new world to the old!'

It was the hottest April for forty years. On the 18th, St. Paul's was full for the memorial service to President Roosevelt. While the Last Post sounded and the congregation streamed out into the sunshine, the citizens of Weimar, in Germany, were also thinking about death. On that warm spring day the American commander who had recently taken over, ordered a thousand of them to march six miles to the newly liberated concentration camp of Buchenwald. They were conducted by American military police on a tour of the crematorium, outside which two piles of thin dead bodies were stacked. They passed through the living quarters, where prisoners still lay on their three-tier bunks, too weak to move. They saw the stables, where thousands had been shot, and the research block, where doctors had used human beings to experiment on. All this had been happening within six miles of these people's homes. Some of the women of Weimar burst into tears.

Buchenwald was only one of a number of hideous camps to which Jews and opponents of the Nazis were sent, either for extermination in gas chambers, or for the most brutal imprisonment and slow starvation. Himmler, the man chiefly responsible, was captured by the British two weeks after the armistice. He had a blue capsule concealed in his mouth. It contained cyanide of potassium. He bit on this and thus slipped out of the noose which would doubtless have awaited him after trial as a war criminal at Nuremberg.

Lesser men were being tried all over Europe, wherever their brutalities had been committed. The Danes had to look around for an executioner. They had not hanged a man for fifty years.

But were *all* Germans guilty? This had been a question often asked during the war. Were we fighting the Nazis or Germany? When no great anti-Nazi movement emerged, the feeling grew that there was no point in trying to distinguish. British troops entering Germany were forbidden to 'fraternise'. 'Germans,' said General Montgomery, 'must learn their lesson – that they are guilty.' On the other hand non-Nazis or less virulent Nazis had to be found to carry on government and administration, in addition to which we were pledged to try and re-educate, which is difficult if you are at the same time keeping people at arm's length. Above all the troops wanted German girls. The Russians, less weighed down by principle in this respect, soon had a club going in Berlin where German girls danced with them. Before very long the anti-fraternisation regulations were relaxed.

Meanwhile another form of fraternisation was coming to an end in Britain. There had been a coalition government throughout the war, with Mr. Attlee and a number of Labour ministers serving under Mr. Churchill, a Conservative. Not long after VE Day it was made known that the Labour party were not prepared to remain in the coalition till the end of the war against Japan; so Parliament was dissolved and polling day fixed for 5 July, though, because of the enormous postal vote from members of the Forces, the result would not be known until the end of the month.

Churchill toured the country and was everywhere acclaimed for his war leadership. But not all who cheered the war leader were confident that he would make an equally good peace leader. Churchill himself was sure. He said: 'Now someone has to bring the ship into harbour, and I am willing to carry on at the helm.' People shouted 'Good old Winnie', but when the results were announced on Thursday 26 July, 393 Labour seats had been won, as against 198 Conservative. Only 12 Liberals and 2 Communists got in. Churchill's wife said to him, by way of consolation, 'It may well be a blessing in disguise.' He replied: 'At the moment it seems quite effectively disguised.' He resigned and Clement Attlee became Prime Minister, with Hugh Dalton as Chancellor of the Exchequer and Stafford Cripps as President of the Board of Trade. Herbert Morrison was Leader of the House of Commons and Lord President of the Council.

The Labour government lost no time in making a start on their policies of nationalisation, improved social services on the lines of the Beveridge Report (published 1942) and colonial freedom. They had also to represent Britain in international affairs, where their ideas differed little from those of the Conservatives.

The last conference of war leaders opened at Potsdam, near Berlin, on

17 July, when Churchill was still Prime Minister and went himself to meet Stalin, and Truman, who had risen from Vice-President to President of the U.S.A. after Roosevelt's death. The conference adjourned for a few days so that Churchill could be in Britain when the election results came out. When it resumed on 30 July Attlee and Ernest Bevin, the new Foreign Secretary, were the British representatives. The Conference agreed to the Oder-Neisse line as the provisional eastern frontier of Germany, which was to be controlled 'as an economic whole'. Peace would be made with Germany when eventually a central German government was established. As this would have to be a government which both the Russians and the Western powers approved of, the word 'eventually' was a wise insertion. No treaty has yet been made.

Russia had not declared war on Japan, but Truman and Churchill took advantage of their meeting at Potsdam to send an ultimatum, to which Chiang Kai-shek, at that time President of China, was a joint signatory. The Japanese were offered a choice of surrender or prompt and utter destruction. This was published in the newspapers of 27 July. It has been argued that if this message had been sent through diplomatic channels, instead of being announced to the world in a way which made it difficult for the Japanese to accept without 'losing face', the war might have been ended without resort to the atom bomb. The atom scientists, although they had worked on the bomb for years in the U.S.A., would have been deeply thankful for a decision against dropping. The argument used by the American government was that the explosion of the bomb would save the enormous loss of American lives which would have been incurred in a conventional attack by landing troops; but if a little more discretion and patience could have avoided both methods of attack, should they not have been exercised? Many wish they had been. Truman, however, had received news on 16 July, while on his way to Potsdam, that an atom bomb had been successfully tested in the U.S.A. and he had decided to use one, if the Japanese held out after the ultimatum of 27 July. Churchill had agreed to this and, when Attlee arrived, he did not dissent.

The Japanese did not surrender, so on 6 August an atomic bomb was exploded in the air above Hiroshima, a city of 360,000. There had been devastating raids on German cities with 10 ton conventional high explosive bombs, but the atom bomb had two thousand times the destructive power of one of these. (This was only the first bomb, apart from the one used for the test. There have been enormous developments in the twenty-five years since it was exploded.) This first atom bomb killed 90,000 in Hiroshima and destroyed everything within half a mile of where it burst. Since the

Japanese still did not surrender, a second bomb was exploded over another of their big cities – Nagasaki – killing 40,000, on 9 August. On the same day Russia declared war on Japan and advanced into Manchuria. This was a very short war indeed. Two days later, on 11 August, Japan offered to surrender. And on the same day a correspondent wrote to *The Times:*

> Does the decision to use the atomic bomb mean that because of the goodness of the Allied cause there are no limits to what it is right to do for the sake of speedy victory?

From then until now nuclear weapons, referred to in official language as 'deterrents' and by ordinary people simply as 'the Bomb', have been the subject of international negotiation. In countries where argument and demonstration are allowed, people have argued and demonstrated. Meanwhile more and more nuclear weapons have been made. The Russians exploded their first bomb in 1949. The British Commonwealth, which had co-operated with the Americans on the first atom bomb, now developed their own, and tested it successfully in Australia (1953). Under de Gaulle the French produced a bomb. Now China and India have done so too.

After the Japanese were defeated, some Europeans assumed that the colonies they had occupied would return to their pre-war status. The Dutch were the first to be disillusioned. In their former possessions – the East Indian islands which included Sumatra and Java – the Indonesian nationalist Ahmed Sukarno declared a republic as soon as the Japanese surrendered. A 'people's Defence Army' became active in the autumn of 1945. The turn of the French in Indo-China was to come later, but they were already being driven from Syria, which they had governed before the war.

European countries also had plenty of problems in Europe. Belgium's King Leopold was suspected by some of collaboration with the Germans. Were the Belgians to have him back? In France there was no doubt at all that Marshal P´etain had collaborated. The French tried him and condemned him to death, but did not shoot him. Who was to rule France now? General de Gaulle, leader of those French who had fought for the Allies, had been in charge since the liberation. He resigned on 1 January 1946. The Communists, though the strongest party, were not strong enough to form a government on their own. France was to suffer constant changes of government for years.

In Yugoslavia a communist government under Marshal Tito was already established and laid claim to the Italian port of Trieste and the district adjacent to it. This was difficult. The West no longer thought of

Italy as an enemy. A temporary solution was reached in 1947 by creating a 'Free Territory' consisting of two zones. Zone A, under British and United States government, contained Trieste itself; Zone B was to be governed by the Yugoslavs.

Some twenty million people had no political problem, because they had no country. These were the Displaced Persons, most of whom had moved west out of areas occupied by the Russians. They included Jews from concentration camps who hoped to begin life again in Palestine. They lived in camps organised by UNRRA (United Nations Relief and Rehabilitation Administration) whose most immediate anxiety was whether an epidemic would break out in the camps during the winter.

Britons celebrated 'VJ' (Victory over Japan) Day on 16 August. Now the war really was over. The government promised that there would be a million releases from H.M. Forces before the end of the year. What were we to do with our gas masks? Could not the rubber be put to some good use? Little boys were using it for catapults. Big boys, and girls, learned that from April 1947 they would have to stay at school till they were 15 – an extra year.

In October there was a dock strike. In the same month 'Lord Haw-Haw' was hanged. He was William Joyce, who had broadcast treasonable propaganda from Germany during the war in the slightly supercilious tone which earned him his nickname. He had been tried in Britain. On 21 November the trial of major war criminals began at Nuremberg.

Many Britons were full of hope. The war was won. The Labour government promised fair shares and equal opportunities.

There seemed a chance that the wartime friendship with Russia would last. Moscow Dynamos, the most famous Russian football team, came over and played Chelsea – result, a draw. In this atmosphere someone remembered that in 1951 it would be a hundred years since the great Crystal Palace exhibition, when Britain was the leading industrial nation of the world. Why not celebrate? Why not somehow, in spite of the inevitable austerity of post-war Britain, save enough to stage an Exhibition in 1951 which would show Britain's peacetime achievements and cheer people up?

They were going to need it.

1946

'DESPITE THIS SOCIALIST Utopia, I still cannot purchase a pair of braces with elastic.' That was one newspaper reader's reflection at New Year 1946 – the dawn of the first peacetime New Year in Britain since 1939. The writer was probably not one of the thousands of men recently demobilised from the Forces, since a pair of not altogether inelastic braces was part of the outfit supplied to all on their release. At that time most men still kept their trousers up with braces and shirt collars were detachable. You got one shirt in your demob outfit, two collars, and a pair of links to secure the turn-back cuffs. There were also a suit, hat, raincoat, tie, two pairs of socks (except for the Navy), a pair of shoes and ninety clothing coupons to meet any other requirements. Women members of H.M. Forces were provided with coupons to buy clothes of their own choice.

New clothes could only be bought if you had enough clothing coupons. Peace had brought quick and efficient demobilisation – it had 'unrationed' men and women; but it had not unrationed goods. Compared with North America and Australia, Britain was still in a period of 'austerity'. Viewed from Europe, however, our position was enviable. Everyone could be sure of getting his rations without turning to the 'Black Market'. Nobody starved. And, at least among the under-forties, there was great hope for the future – for a better planned Britain and for a continuance of friendship with all our wartime Allies, in particular with Russia.

People talk of 'cementing' a friendship; but in fact friendships never set hard like cement. Perhaps 'lubrication' is a more appropriate metaphor. The apparatus for lubricating the friendship of the Allies and ultimately admitting to it the peoples whom they had conquered, was to be the United Nations. This body had as yet no permanent home; so in January 1946 it met in London. The General Assembly, consisting of delegates from 51 nations (there are now about 130), began work on 10 January. One decision easily arrived at by the Assembly was the exclusion from the United Nations of Spain, which, under Franco's dictatorship, had been friendly to Hitler and Mussolini, though remaining neutral. The Assembly instructed the Security Council to take 'adequate measures' if the Franco regime did not end in a reasonable period. jthis however did not discourage Peron,

16

elected President of the Argentine in February, from establishing an authoritarian regime there, aided by his wife Eva, who died in 1952. Peron was not overthrown until 1955. He then lived in Spain but enjoyed a brief return to power from 1973 until his death in the following year.

The Security Council consisted of five permanent members (U.S.A., U.S.S.R., China – still under Chiang Kai-shek – Britain and France) and six non-permanent (Brazil, Egypt, Mexico, Poland, the Netherlands and Australia). Spain was to be one of many problems which the United Nations failed to solve, usually because of disagreement between Russia and the Western Powers.

The first appeal to the Security Council was by Iran (Persia), against occupation of part of the country by Russian troops. Russia replied that there were British troops in Greece and Indonesia. The dispute was settled later in the year by direct negotiations.

While supporting the United Nations Organisation, Churchill, at Fulton (U.S.A.) in March, demanded in addition a 'special relationship' between the British Commonwealth and Empire and the United States, in the face of Russian domination in central Europe. 'A shadow,' he said, 'has fallen on the scenes so lately lighted by the Allied victory. From Stettin, in the Baltic, to Trieste, in the Adriatic, an iron curtain has descended across the Continent.' Stalin of course remembered that Churchill had supported intervention against the Bolsheviks after World War I and that in spite of British and American admiration for Russia's performance in World War II, his two great allies were on the whole anti-communist. Less than a year after VE Day what came to be called a 'Cold War' was developing between Russia and the West.

The U.N. Assembly agreed on the setting up of a commission to make recommendations for the control and peaceful development of atomic energy. On the same day it was announced that the United States would test bombs in the Pacific during the spring and summer. During March Bikini atoll, a ring of coral islands was evacuated and on 30 June an atomic bomb (this was before hydrogen bombs) was dropped on it, successfully. The public became familiar with the mushroom-shaped cloud created by the explosion. '£8,000,000 goes up in smoke,' ran a headline. The bomb, it seemed, was expensive. For only £3,000,000 more you could have a battleship. H.M.S. *Vanguard*, which had started her trials in May, had cost £11,000,000.

However, the English language was enriched as a result of the tests with the word 'bikini', now applied to scanty bathing suits and underwear, usually female. It struck someone that a woman with very little on was comparable in her effect to the impact of an atomic bomb. Be that as it may, the idea caught on and the word found its way into the dictionary. Bikini itself was used for bomb tests until 1958 and could not be lived on again until 1969.

As scientists worked on the assessment of the Bikini bomb, there was an old-fashioned explosion on the other side of the world, the results of which did not take long to calculate. Jews blew up the King David Hotel in Jerusalem, killing ninety-one people (22 July).

Jerusalem at that time was the capital of Palestine, the territory between the river Jordan and the Mediterranean, known to Christians for centuries as the 'Holy Land'. Although the ancient home of the Jews, it had been ruled by Arabs and later by Turks for over a thousand years, and finally 'mandated' to Great Britain by the League of Nations after World War I.

The Balfour Declaration of 1917 had promised Jews a national home in Palestine, and this did not create serious problems during the 1920's. Groups of Jews from Poland and Russia had been returning to Palestine and making a living with difficulty on agricultural settlements since the 1850's, and though the Zionist movement (founded in 1897) encouraged this, immigration after World War I was not heavy. Thus in the early years Palestine was not a particularly troublesome territory for the British to govern. It was only when Hitler came to power in Germany in 1933 and began his systematic persecution of Jews that what has been called the Exodus began.

The first Exodus, described in the Bible, had been a mass movement from Egypt to Palestine. The second Exodus was from Germany and countries which the Germans occupied. Unlike the tribes which Moses led, the exiles began their journeys in ones and twos; but thousands eventually reached Palestine, where the Arab population began to fear that it would be outnumbered. Though the British had had to suppress an Arab revolt between 1936 and 1939, they had then met Arab demands to some extent by declaring that Jewish immigration should be restricted to 75,000 between 1939 and 1945 and that thereafter there should be no more immigration without the consent of the Palestine Arabs.

A prime consideration in this last apparently heartless measure was to insure against loss of support by the Arab world in the war with Germany, which was then foreseen. During the war terrorism ceased. Numbers of Jews and Arabs enlisted in the Allied forces. On the other hand, the Mufti of Jerusalem, leader of the Palestine Arabs, took refuge in Germany. But after the war the problem was more serious than ever. Though the whole world was horrified by the fate of the Jews in central Europe, no country was willing to accept unlimited numbers of survivors, many of whom turned to Palestine, which they felt to be their home. The numbers trying to gain entry were far greater than the 75,000 agreed for the period 1939-45.

When Bevin became Foreign Minister in 1945 he thought that the whole business could be straightened out by getting the Arabs and Jews together round a conference table. 'If I don't get a settlement, I'll eat my hat,' he said. In August 1945 he refused a request from President Truman that 100,000 admissions should be allowed. Thus the possibility of Anglo-American co-operation in solving the problem was lost, while Bevin's hopes of solving it on his own were not realised. By 1946 the British were blockading the coast, intercepting immigrant ships (though some managed to slip through) and transferring those on board to camps in Cyprus, while Jewish terrorist organisations made it their aim to get rid of the British and set up an independent Jewish state. The King David Hotel was a British military headquarters, and that was why the terrorists blew it up.

A week later (29 July) the Peace Conference opened in Paris, but although twenty-one Allied nations were represented, the Conference did not hold the centre of the stage as the Versailles Conference had done after World War I. Only treaties with Italy, Hungary, Romania and Finland were under consideration. It was too early for the Allies to agree on how the two occupied countries, Germany and Austria, were to be dealt with. An Austrian treaty was finally signed in 1955. No German treaty has yet been signed, since most of the Allies, of which the U.S.A. is much the most powerful, do not want Germany permanently divided, while the Russians feel that reunification would be dangerous to them, since a Communist government would be unlikely to result.

One place where, on the whole, the Allies did agree, was Nuremberg in Germany. In November leading Nazis began to stand trial there for 'crimes against humanity' – the enslavement and mass murder of millions of Europeans, in particular the Jews. The judges were British, American, Russian and French. Hitler and Goebbels (Nazi Minister of Propaganda) had committed suicide; Martin Bormann had escaped, probably to South America (it is still not known whether he is alive or dead); but after a trial which had begun in November 1945, death sentences were pronounced on eleven leading Nazis (12 October 1946). Goering managed to take poison – a phial of cyanide; how he got it, at 10.45 p.m. on 15 October, has never been explained; but between 1.0 and 3.0 a.m. on the 16th the other ten were hanged. The Jew-baiter Streicher shouted, 'The Bolshevists will get you!' but the others gave no trouble.

There were seven long prison sentences, which were served in the inter-allied prison in Berlin. Rudolph Hess, Hitler's deputy, who had flown solo to Scotland during the war, with peace proposals, finally remained there alone.

In courts all over Europe other 'war criminals' were still being tried for committing atrocities or collaborating with the Germans, and there were similar trials of Japanese and their friends in the Far East. In Britain the news that the Yugoslavs had shot Mihailovitch at dawn on 17 July was of special interest, since in the early stages of the war he had been treated as our ally. Later he had helped the Germans, while Britain backed Tito and his 'partisans'.

Italy, after a referendum (5 June), had become a republic. The Greeks, on the other hand, voted in September for the return of their king.

At home in Britain, March saw the rowing of the first post-war Oxford v. Cambridge boat race. A reporter commented: 'Food rationing is possibly responsible for the Oxford crew this year being one of the lightest on record.' People were not in fact under-nourished and even after bread rationing was introduced on 21 July (it lasted until 25 July 1948) everyone still had enough, from the child under 7 years with 2 oz. per day to the male manual worker with 15 oz. But it was one more colossal bore for housewives and it was depressing that bread rationing, which had been avoided throughout World Wars I and II, should have been found necessary in peace, only a few weeks after the great Commonwealth Victory parade through London (8 June) and the first post-war garden party at Buckingham Palace (9 July).

Rationing was a bore, but a good housewife could manage, and many of her family had meals at school or in factory and office canteens. However, the best of housewives cannot manage without a home. It was lack of housing, not lack of food, which led to a flare-up. Homeless people began moving into unoccupied army camps during the summer and were left undisturbed, but when blocks of luxury flats in London, standing empty after being released from wartime use by the government, were taken over by 'squatters' (a new use, now well established, of an old word), the government had to act. It was Aneurin Bevan, Minister of Health and Housing, hitherto a champion of the oppressed, who now had the unpleasant duty of turning the squatters out. He managed to do so by agreement, without using the police. At the end of November it was announced that aircraft factories had produced 10,000 aluminium houses. These were the 'pre-fabs' (made of pre-fabricated units) with an official life of ten years, some of which are still in use.

Perhaps the action of the squatters frightened the Government into getting the pre-fabs more quickly off the assembly lines. Ministers had certainly set themselves an enormous task. There had never before been a Labour government with a working majority. So, in addition to adapting the country to peace-time conditions the government had to launch long-planned and long-promised socialist measures – nationalisation, and the repeal of the Trades Disputes Act – together with other measures establishing new social services, which had been agreed by the coalition government during the war.

Some people no doubt took heart when H.M.S. *Vanguard* sailed down the Clyde in May for her trials. She was a 42,500 ton battleship which had cost £11,000,000, but during the 1950's she and all other battleships became obsolete.

In the autumn the 'Britain can make it' exhibition drew thousands to the Victoria and Albert Museum in London, where they were willing to queue a long time in order to see a splendid exhibition of the work of British designers – scientific instruments, cameras, toys, glass, pottery, furniture, sport and travel goods, fabrics. These appeared all the more splendid because people had forgotten what bright new goods or gaily decorated shop windows looked like.

The BBC Television Service, which had enjoyed a minority audience in the 30's and been closed during the war, had reopened in June, but there were not yet many viewers. Most of them used sets they had managed to keep since before the war. The public in general depended on radio, which, beginning on 29 September, now offered them the Third Programme, in addition to the Home and the Light. 'The Third' demanded a high level of intelligence and interest in the arts. It was the envy of musical people and intellectuals all over the world and some countries imitated it. Audience figures, however, were always low. In spite of bitter protests the BBC decided to drop the name and some of the more demanding content during the 1970's. 'Woman's Hour', born in the same month as The Third, continued.

As Christmas approached, the sickly but serviceable glow of fluorescent lights lit London for the first time. No special illuminations spanned the main shopping streets. There were more civilians to be seen, but most of them were in demob suits which reflected the male fashions of 1939 – wide trousers with turn-ups and, frequently, a double-breasted jacket with wide lapels. Women's skirts were still at wartime length, below the knee. Police uniform did not yet include a collar and tie.

A coloured picture in the Christmas number of the *Illustrated London*

News showed a family celebrating round their television set ('the peep-show of to-day') with the women in long dresses, the men in tails and white ties and their boy in an Eton suit with a starched collar. This family might have had Christopher Fry's verse play *A Phoenix too frequent* on their list of Christmas treats. A reviewer had written: 'Here is wit, poetry, sentiment and misanthropy, which excites both the mind and the senses.' But a more suitable play for a family outing would probably have been *The Guinea Pig*, by Warren Chetham-Strode, which had opened in February and portrayed, not unsympathetically, the progress of a working-class boy through a traditional Public School. The Fleming Report, published in 1944 as part of the policy of planning a better post-war world, had recommended that boarding Public Schools should recruit 25% of their pupils from local authority schools. The play was therefore topical. 'I'll try . . . My God, I'll try' was its closing line, spoken by the dedicated, war-wounded young housemaster, who had married the beautiful daughter of his old-fashioned predecessor. In fact it has been the local authorities rather than the Public Schools who have prevented the Fleming Scheme from going very far. They have found it impossible to decide who should be chosen and how they could justify such enormous expenditure on only a small proportion of the boys and girls for whose education they are responsible.

There were other plans, however, which were made in 1946 and did in fact bear fruit later. The Severn road bridge was designed. With a span of 3,000 feet it was to be the longest suspension bridge in Europe. Stevenage, on the Great North Road, thirty miles from London, learned that it was to be the first of the New Towns, which were to be *planned* by the government instead of just growing. And the about-to-be-nationalised railways hoped to use less coal from the about-to-be-nationalised coal mines. A caption below a photograph read: 'Firing a locomotive by means of a tap!' Over a thousand coal-burning locomotives were to be converted to oil. But they would still be powered by steam. Diesels came later.

It was wise to think of an alternative to coal, the fuel which until the war had been so abundant in Britain. On 31 December 1946 a letter in *The Times* headed COAL STOCKS contained the warning:

I forecast a crisis by February.

1947

NATIONALISATION WAS AN important part of the policy of the 1945 Labour government. It was thought that, for instance, if the mines had belonged to the nation instead of to private owners in the nineteen twenties, wage cuts and strikes would have been avoided. So, on New Year's Day 1947, the government took over the coal mines, which became the property of the National Coal Board. There were about 1,500 collieries and 400 small mines. The Board also took over about a million acres of land, became the employer of 690,000 miners and the master of 23,000 pit ponies. Mr. Shinwell, a veteran of the Labour party, who was now Minister of Fuel and Power, presented Lord Hyndley, Chairman of the new Board, with a bound copy of the Act which had created it. He spoke of difficulties ahead; more coal was being consumed, particularly in the production of electricity and gas, and more was needed for export. On the other hand miners were anxious to have the five-day working week as soon as possible. The new board would need to recruit more men and spend huge sums on modernising the pits, half of which did not even have baths.

Mr. Attlee, the Prime Minister, said that the Coal Board was a fine team going in to bat on a sticky wicket, but he believed it would score a great number of sixes. The winter of 1947 proved an inappropriate season for cricketing metaphors. As H.M.S. *Vanguard* steamed down Channel on 1 February, taking King George and Queen Elizabeth to visit South Africa (then still in the Commonwealth), her masts and rigging were coated with icicles. For her, warm weather lay ahead. Britain, meanwhile, and much of western Europe, froze. One night a temperature of 18°F (centigrade had not yet been adopted) stopped Big Ben, which fell silent after the first stroke of twelve. Ice and snow clogged the railways, so that even such coal as was available could not be moved to the power stations quickly enough. At one time London only had enough coal for a week. There were drastic electricity cuts. Many factories had to close, and their employees were thrown out of work. BBC programmes were reduced to save power. Television, recently restarted, went off the air altogether. People lit candles, if they could get them, and wore their old service overcoats, if they had them. When the thaw came at last, in the third week of March, there were floods.

On 1 April, the school leaving age was raised from 14 to 15. The London School Plan (produced by the Labour-dominated London County Council, which governed London before the creation of the Greater London Council in 1963) laid down that all secondary education in the county should be provided in comprehensive high schools. Comprehensive schools were much criticised as being too big (they had around 2,000 pupils), but they have now become general and the dreaded selection exam which children, at the age of '11 +', used to take to decide whether they were more suitable for a 'grammar' or a 'modern' school, has been made largely unnecessary.

In May there was a tremendous fuss about plans for a new power station on Bankside, opposite St. Paul's. The winter had certainly shown that more power stations were needed, provided we could keep them supplied with fuel; but it was feared that this power station would spoil the view of St. Paul's, which at that time towered above every other building in London. The power station was in fact built and now attracts little attention, compared with the high-rise buildings which have gone up quite close to St. Paul's in the City itself.

In July people were cheered by the reappearance of Eros, the silvery statue of the god of love, which stands above the fountain in London's Piccadilly Circus. (Eros, like many other statues, had been removed during the war.) Love was in the air that summer. Our present Queen, then Princess Elizabeth, had become engaged to 'Lt. Philip Mountbatten, R.N.', and they were married in Westminster Abbey on 20 November. The Life Guards turned out in full dress for the first time since the war, but Mr. Shinwell, now the Secretary of State for War, said this was 'a special effort for a special occasion'. The Guards at Buckingham Palace remained in khaki.

Another event which cheered people up was the successful crossing of the Pacific by the raft *Kon-tiki* with her crew of six (five Norwegians and a Swede) led by the Norwegian Thor Heyerdahl, who wished to prove his theory that islands of the south Pacific could have been colonised centuries ago by raft migrations from Peru. The *Kon-tiki* sailed on 28 April and reached the Marquesas Islands on 7 August. Heyerdahl's book about the voyage (1950) was a best-seller.

Later in August the first Edinburgh Festival for Music and the Arts set a fashion which many towns have since followed; but the music which was being hummed or whistled at work or in the streets in 1947 came from the first two of the great mid-century American musicals to reach London – *Oklahoma* (Rogers and Hammerstein), which opened at Drury Lane on 30 April, and *Annie get your gun* (Irving Berlin), which opened at the Coliseum on 7 June.

It is hard to say why at this point in her history the U.S. began producing the best musicals in the world. The fact that musicals are costly to produce and that Britain was poor is not sufficient explanation.

Britain *was* poor, and so was Europe. This was the reason for the most important international event of the year – the announcement of the Marshall Plan. General Marshall was now the American Secretary of State (the equivalent of the British Foreign Secretary). In a speech on 5 June he proposed that, if the countries of Europe would unite in deciding what they most needed to hasten the recovery of Europe as a whole, the U.S.A. would give them all possible help. The offer was eagerly grasped. Sixteen nations met on 12 July 1947 (Austria, Belgium, Denmark, France, Greece, Iceland, Ireland, Italy, Luxembourg, Holland, Norway, Portugal, Sweden, Switzerland, Turkey and Britain). Czechoslovakia and Poland had intended to take part but were forbidden to do so by Russia. The Russians were suspicious of the Marshall Plan, because they thought its aim was to increase American influence in Europe.

Whatever the motives for Marshall Aid, millions of dollars of it poured into Europe during the next ten years in the shape of raw materials and manufactured goods – raw cotton, for instance, to help the German textile industry, tractors to help farmers. The idea was to set Europe on its feet again. Of course this also helped American industry; but not all purchases were made in the U.S.A. and the plan could not have been carried through Congress, which approved it in April 1948, without the support of the general public. There was a feeling that Europe had suffered and that the more fortunate U.S.A. should help.

But the help which one group of Europeans – the Displaced Persons – wanted most was a country in which to start a new life. Of those who were Jewish, thousands struggled to reach Palestine, while the British government still felt it their duty to prevent them entering. The Jewish terrorist organisations – the Stern Gang and the Irgun – felt it *their* duty to continue a ruthless campaign, aimed at ending the mandate. On the evening of 4 May a carefully planned attack on Acre gaol freed 250 prisoners. In July the illegal immigrant ship *Exodus* was intercepted. Those on board put up some resistance before being forced to land in Cyprus for internment. Not long afterwards two British sergeants were decoyed by a girl, kidnapped and hanged. Agreement was impossible. The least unsatisfactory arrangement appeared to be partition – dividing the country between Arabs and Jews. This was now planned for 1948.

To the 'Indian sub-continent' (this awkward phrase is unavoidable now that 'India' means a nation which only covers part of the huge peninsula), partition came sooner than to Palestine – on 15 August 1947. In both areas attempts were made by the British to avoid it, because you can never deal justly when you carve up a country. It never happens that all the A's are conveniently living on one side of a natural boundary, such as a river or mountain range, and all the B's on the other. There are always pockets of A's living among the B's and vice versa. So when you create A-land and B-land, you have minorities in both, and they are unlikely to be gently handled by the majorities of A-landers or B-landers, proud of their new nationhood and their A-ness (or B-ness).

Britain's Indian Empire contained people of many languages and a number of different religions, but two groups were far more powerful than any of the others – the Hindus, represented by the Congress party, and the Muslims, represented by the Muslim League. There were fewer Muslims than Hindus, so it was they who wanted liberation from British Rule to result in partition and not in a united new India in which Hindus would be supreme. How the Japanese would have handled this situation will never be known. Their wartime advance towards India had been resisted and finally stopped in Burma. During the war, in British India, as in Palestine, there was comparative calm; but as soon as the war was over, rioting broke out again and there was a mutiny in the Royal Indian Navy. The riots were between Hindus and Muslims, but both sides were anti-British.

How Churchill would have dealt with this problem is another interesting speculation. But he was no longer in power and the Labour government were pledged to help the Indians towards independence. In spite of the bitter Hindu-Muslim hostility, Mr. Attlee still hoped to avoid partition. He sent Lord Mountbatten out as Viceroy (the supreme official of British India) in February 1947 with instructions to hand over power to a united India if possible. Mountbatten (uncle of Prince Philip and now an Admiral of the Fleet) had been Supreme Commander in the Far East when the war ended.

It was very soon clear that avoidance of partition was not possible. In the north west the Sikhs were arming against the Muslims in the Punjab and violence was likely to spread to Bengal. By May Mountbatten had decided that partition was the only way to avoid civil war. And partition would have to come quickly.

On 15 August 1947 Britain's Indian Empire ceased to exist and two new states came into being – India (predominantly Hindu) and Pakistan (predominantly Muslim). Pakistan was itself divided into two parts – a larger western area containing the new capital, Karachi, and East Pakistan (now Bangladesh) over a thousand miles away. But even these two areas together made up a much smaller area than the new India.

The leaders of the new nations were Nehru, Prime Minister of India, and Jinnah, Head of the State of Pakistan. Civil war had certainly been prevented by the quick move to partition; but the immediate result was a series of massacres which appalled the world. Hindu minorities in Pakistan and Muslim minorities in India were massacred, or fled because they feared massacre. A two-way flood of migrants surged over the newly defined frontiers.

Kashmir, in the north west, was an area of special difficulty. There a Hindu Maharajah ruled a population of whom three-quarters were Muslims. He was unwilling to make up his mind as to which of the two new states to join. His country had frontiers with both. We shall hear more of Kashmir.

The post-partition massacres shocked no one more than Mahatma Gandhi (b. 1869), who dressed and lived with the simplicity of an Indian peasant and had contributed more than any other leader towards Indian independence. The British had often imprisoned him. But he was opposed to the use of violence. The sit-ins and sit-downs of to-day all originate from Gandhi's method of fighting for what one believes to be one's rights by non-violent civil disobedience.

Gandhi, though a very human person, who said that he liked to make sad people laugh, was regarded by Hindus as a kind of saint or 'mahatma'. When therefore he declared that he would fast until he died, unless the massacres stopped, the threat had a profound effect and by the end of the year the fight between the faiths had become less bloody. However, 1948 was not very old before horrifying news from India took the headlines once again.

1948

IN THE LATE afternoon of 30 January, Gandhi had come out into the garden of his house to conduct his usual prayer meeting, when an extremist Hindu stepped forward and shot him, because of his soft attitude to Muslims. Gandhi died half an hour later. Next day, as the scented smoke rose from the sandalwood pyre on which the body was burning, tens of thousands of mourners chanted, 'Gandhi has become immortal.' If this cry reflected a hope that Gandhi's non-violent, simple-life ideas would inspire the new India, the hope was disappointed. However, India is still a democracy and, far from following the trend towards military dictatorships in recently independent countries, she produced, in 1966, one of the world's few female prime ministers (Mrs. Indira Gandhi, daughter of Nehru, but not related to the Mahatma).

The partition of the Indian sub-continent was the beginning of a great movement towards independence in what had till then been the British Empire and is now the British Commonwealth – a loose union of self-governing states linked by sentiment and by allegiance to the British Crown. Burma was the next to go. She left the Commonwealth altogether – at 4.20 a.m. on 4 January 1948, the hour chosen by astrologers as auspicious for the birth of the Republic, which started life as a parliamentary democracy. This however only lasted ten years and since 1958 Burma has been a dictatorship, under General Ne Win.

Ceylon became independent on 4 February, stayed in the Commonwealth, had a woman Prime Minister, Mrs. Bandaranaike, from 1960 to 1965 and is still a democracy. It became a republic in 1972 and was renamed Sri Lanka (Resplendent Island).

In Malaya an emergency was declared. 'Emergencies' lasting for years were to be a grim feature of decolonisation during the 50's. The struggle in Malaya, against communist guerillas who used tactics similar to those of the Vietcong in the 60's, was to continue for twelve years.

Japan, not for the first time in her history, proved able to adapt quickly to ideas from the West. The Emperor Hirohito had been a god. Under the American occupation he was transformed into a Scandinavian type king-

28

without-trappings. Early in 1948 he was photographed in a lounge suit, making his first visit to a factory since his accession in 1926. The older spectators still bowed low and dared not raise their eyes; but the young kept their heads up, and some smiled.

Japan had lost the war. China was among the victors; but victory did not mean peace; it meant the revival of the civil war between the Communists, under Mao Tse-tung, and the nationalists, under Chiang Kai-shek, which had been going on during the thirties. It was now beginning to look as if the Communists would win. The Americans minded about this. Europeans were more tolerant. There had been so much cruelty and disorder in China for so long that it seemed hard to imagine how Communism could make things worse. But Communism in Europe was another matter.

People can be opposed to Communism while still finding it difficult to define. It works out differently in different countries. The plain man is usually most impressed by the authoritarianism which appears to be part of it. The Czechoslovak Jan Masaryk, who saw a Communist government established in his country under Russian pressure during March 1948, had announced: 'I want to be able to ride in a tramcar in Prague and say, "I don't think much of our present government." ' Under Communism you could not do that. Nevertheless Masaryk joined the Communist government. What was he to do? The problem faced Czechs again in 1968. Should one hopelessly resist overwhelming force, or try somehow to work with the invader and soften the blows he rains upon the people one loves? Masaryk tried for ten days; then he was found dead beneath his office windows (10 March 1948). Nobody knows how he died. The official explanation at the time was 'suicide as a result of insomnia and depression.' This was withdrawn in 1969 when Masaryk's fall was said to be the result of an accident. There is strong evidence that he was murdered.

1947 had seen the end of attempts to get 4-power co-operation in Europe. At the close of the year the conference on how to treat Germany had failed to agree. In 1948 eastern and western blocs began to form. To answer Russia's alliance of communist states subservient to her (known between 1947 and 1956 as the Cominform) Britain, France and the 'Benelux' countries (Belgium, the Netherlands, and Luxembourg) signed the Brussels Treaty on 4 March 1948. From this 'Western Union' NATO later grew.

So the two sides watched each other across a line running south through Germany and following parts of the frontiers of Czechoslovakia, Hungary, Rumania and Bulgaria. Only on the Adriatic was allegiance uncertain. Albania was still allied to Russia, but in Yugoslavia Marshal Tito, though continuing to declare his country communist, had remained independent of Russia.

In Denmark, Norway, Sweden, Finland and Italy there were parliamentary governments. These countries, except Finland, were part of the anti-communist bloc. Switzerland, though western in sentiment, always stays neutral in the international field.

Fascist Spain, under General Franco, was also of course anti-communist; but though the country had remained neutral during the war, the Spanish government was modelled on Hitler's and Mussolini's and in 1948 Spain was still outlawed by the victorious powers. She was not yet a member of the United Nations. It was hoped that Franco would soon fall.

In Greece, fighting was still going on between communist and anti-communist forces, but the communists were now confined to the mountains in the north and the Russians clearly did not plan to save them.

Austria was still divided into four zones, as was its capital, Vienna. 4-power government worked there. It still existed in Berlin too; but its days were numbered.

Russia had never liked sharing Berlin with her Allies. If an ordinary Russian looked at a map, he saw that Berlin was in the middle of the zone which his country was occupying. Why should the city be shared with British, Americans and Frenchmen whose countries, whatever their attitude during the war, had been opposed to Russian communism ever since its birth in 1917? To Russia's Allies – or should one now begin to refer to them as 'former Allies'? – on the other hand, Berlin was the capital of the country they had defeated, a country in which they now planned to revive parliamentary democracy. For the sake of their image throughout the non-communist world and in particular for the encouragement of parliamentary government in their part of Germany (the British, French and American zones were now united), they had to stay in Berlin. So when an argument arose over the new currencies being issued in the two parts of Germany, and the Russians blocked rail and road access to Berlin, from midnight on 19 June, 'to safeguard the currency of their zone', her former Allies had to decide quickly what to do. They were not prepared to surrender West Berlin (their part of the city); but, if they did not send in supplies, the 2 million inhabitants of West Berlin would starve. They would also be without fuel. Should the Allies try to force their way in along the road or the railway? That would have meant war – only three years after the defeat of the common enemy. But there was a third way into Berlin – by air. Certain 'air corridors' into West Berlin were guaranteed in the Occupation Agreement and to block them would have been a great deal more difficult than blocking the road and the railway. Anyhow, the Russians left the air lanes open and through these West Berlin was supplied for eleven months, in an operation which became famous as the Air Lift.

Nothing very heroic happened in the course of the Air Lift, but it was superbly efficient, it kept the peace and it kept the Western powers in Berlin; though when the Russians finally agreed to reopen the road and railway in May 1949, West and East Berlin had become separate cities, separately governed, as they still are.

The Berlin policy of Bevin, Britain's Foreign Secretary, had succeeded. (Do not confuse him with Aneurin Bevan, Minister of Health and architect of the National Health Service. Bevan struggled with the doctors, while Bevin struggled with the Russians.) In Palestine, he failed. The problem was turned over to the U.N., which decided on partition, but did not decide how partition was to be enforced. So when the mandate ended at midnight on 14 May and the state of Israel came into existence, with David Ben Gurion as Prime Minister, Arab armies attacked from the north (Syria and Lebanon), the east (Jordan and Iraq) and the south (Egypt). Thus began the first of four wars, in which Israel and her Arab neighbours have been involved. The Arabs consider these as one war, which is not yet over. No peace treaty has been signed. There have however been armistice agreements. The first was arrived at in January 1949, after the United Nations had tried to keep the peace for six months and their representative, Count Bernadotte, had been murdered by Jewish extremists (August 1948).

The Olympic Games – the first since 1936 – held in London in August, passed off without any major political demonstration.

As autumn came on, the U.S.A. was absorbed by the Presidential election. Truman had never been elected. As Vice-President he had inherited the Presidency on Roosevelt's death. The polls made it seem unlikely that he would get in on his own merits. But he did.

Great Britain was not at this time involved in an election. The Labour government could still expect two years in office and they were working hard. In January the railways had been nationalised as 'British Railways', a title later streamlined to 'British Rail'. As with the nationalisation of the mines, a year earlier, the public were presented by the publicity people with a list of the property which they were acquiring. It included 20,000 steam locomotives (though nine diesel electric ones were soon ordered), 25,000 horse vehicles, 100 cross-channel steamers, 900 trams and 70 hotels. The shareholders in the former railway companies were compensated and the people who worked on the railways saw nothing particularly shameful about becoming servants of the state. On the other hand, the National Health Service was only established in July 1948 after a long and bitter struggle between Aneurin Bevan (Minister of Health and Housing) and the doctors, who said that they did not want to become salaried Civil Servants. Bevan yielded on this point and general practitioners are still paid according to the number of people who register with them.

Though the launching of the Health Service was a triumph for Bevan, it coincided with one of the bitterest and most widely quoted remarks he ever made. Speaking at Manchester on 4 July, he was reported as saying of the Tory Party: 'So far as I am concerned they are lower than vermin.' Young Tories retaliated by painting 'Vermin Villa' on Bevan's London house. On the whole however the public response was not light-hearted and most Labour Members of Parliament would have preferred that the words had not been spoken.

In their introduction of diesel electric locomotives, British Rail proved farsighted. On the other hand the faith still placed by the government in flying boats for long-range air transport proved misplaced. (One to seat 100 passengers was planned at this time.) Another experiment which did not spread was district heating – hot water piped to a whole housing estate.

A man caused great surprise by having a 'dry shave' on a train. Electric razors were new to most people. So was the New Look, obviously. The expression referred to a distinctive new fashion for women. After eight years during which little had changed, skirts suddenly became wider and reached to within 18 inches of the ground. Princess Elizabeth wore them when she visited Paris in May.

Policemen were also due for a change of fashion and were promised collars and ties, instead of high-necked tunics, for summer wear.

The harassed housewife had one burden lifted at the end of April. Potato rationing ended. And a report on supermarkets in the U.S.A., where they had flourished since the 1930's, raised hopes that we might see some in Britain. But it was 1954 before we did.

In London Grosvenor Square was laid out as a public park in memory of President Roosevelt. His statue was unveiled in April. There had been some controversy about the standing figure, since Roosevelt always sat, because he suffered from infantile paralysis (polio), a crippling disease, epidemics of which were occurring almost every year (though there were fewer cases in 1948 than in 1947). However, a standing figure was produced.

The new U.S. Embassy was not yet built and Vietnam was still part of the French colonial empire; so Roosevelt at that time looked down on a square still free of demonstrators. Standing in the square on 14 November, you could have heard 41 guns in Hyde Park, saluting the birth of Prince Charles.

Mrs. Eleanor Roosevelt, the President's widow, had taken an important part in drawing up the 'Universal Declaration of Human Rights' and in securing its adoption by the United Nations General Assembly, which met in Paris during December. 48 out of a possible 58 members voted in favour. It was useful to have these rights defined, but they are ideals rather than rules. Here are examples:

Article 1. All human beings are born free and equal in dignity and rights. They are endowed with reason and conscience and should act towards one another in a spirit of brotherhood.

Article 2. Everyone is entitled to all the rights and freedoms set forth in this Declaration, without distinction of any kind, such as race, colour, sex, language, religion, political or other opinion, national or social origin, property, birth or other status. . . .

Article 5. No one shall be subjected to torture or to cruel, inhuman or degrading treatment or punishment.

Article 18. Everyone has the right to freedom of thought, conscience and religion. . . .

Article 19. Everyone has the right to freedom of opinion and expression. . . .

Article 20. (1) Everyone has the right to freedom of peaceful assembly and association.
(2) No one may be compelled to belong to an association.

Article 23. (2) Everyone, without any discrimination, has the right to equal pay for equal work.

Article 25. (1) Everyone has the right to a standard of living adequate for health.
(2) Motherhood and childhood are entitled to special care. . . .

Article 26. (1) Everyone has the right to education. Education shall be free, at least in the elementary and fundamental stages. Elementary education shall be compulsory.

Member countries were called upon to cause the Declaration to be 'disseminated, displayed, read and expounded . . . in schools . . .' Twenty years later 1968 was proclaimed Human.Rights Year and a world-wide publicity campaign was undertaken. But no court of appeal was set up by the United Nations. All you can do, if you feel that your rights have been infringed, is to write to the Secretary General – unless you live in Europe. There the Council of Europe not only established in 1953 a Convention for the Protection of Human Rights and Fundamental Freedoms, but laid down a system of appeal to an International Commission and in the last resort to a Council of Ministers or to the European Court of Human Rights. During 1968, boys who had enlisted in the British Navy and Army on nine-year engagements appealed, unsuccessfully, to the Commission, seeking to obtain an earlier discharge. The Commission also heard allegations of torture against the Greek regime.

Though the United Nations could not punish those who infringed human rights, the War Crimes Tribunal could punish 'crimes against humanity' and were still doing so in 1948. During December America's chief enemy, Tojo, Prime Minister of Japan from 1941 to 1944, was hanged with six other Japanese war criminals – old men (two were seventy).

In London Christmas night 1948 was the coldest for 78 years.

1949

THE YEAR 1949 produced a summer of record sunshine. June was the driest month for eleven years and by August there was a drought. The sweltering police gradually got their blue shirts, with collars and ties, but women's skirts, planned in the previous autumn, took no account of the heat and descended another 6 inches – to within a foot of the ground. Rationing of clothes and textiles had stopped in March, so there was no problem for a girl, if she had some money.

Britain was buying more from the U.S. than the U.S. was buying from Britain. The rising dollar deficit, which was beginning to worry the government, did not worry most people. Polio did though. The hot summer crowded swimming pools, which were beginning to be identified as places where the disease was caught. The number of cases reported was higher than in 1948, though still below that for 1947. The disease also struck at Austria, France, Germany, India and New Zealand and reached a peak in the U.S.A. – where 45,000 cases were reported.

For about 3 months the sky was blue. Up into it, on 27 July, shot the de Havilland Comet, piloted by Group Captain John Cunningham. 'Shot', because the aircraft was jet propelled – the world's first jet-propelled airliner. She climbed quicker than the piston-engined airliners in use at that time, and cruised at 500 instead of 350 m.p.h. It was to be three years before Comets could begin regular passenger flights (1952), but in the meantime hope rose. People felt that here was a development in which Britain was leading the world, and an export which would help to fill the dollar gap.

The Comet brought us the expected prestige and dollars, and though withdrawn in 1954 after two mid-air explosions, returned to service in 1957. But the future was not to be monopolised by turbo-jets. The jet principle had also been developed to drive propellers and the turbo-prop Vickers Viscount had already taken pressmen on a trial run in December 1948. The propellered Viscounts, later joined by the Vanguards, were to survive into the turbo-jet age, because they were more economical on shorter flights and did not need such long runways. Their Rolls-Royce Dart engines gave passengers a quiet flight. It was claimed that you could converse in an undertone on board. And flight in good conditions was so steady that a pencil could be stood on end and remain erect – an old-fashioned pencil, that is to say. They were commoner then than now. The ball-point pen, patented by Laszlo Biro in 1937, had become popular during the war, but was not yet in general use.

Flying boats were still being built for the long range flights to Africa and the East, which they had made before the war, but comparatively few places had sea or river landing facilities and it soon became unprofitable to build aircraft for these alone. As more landing-fields were built, flying boat services decreased.

Air travel was still a luxury. Transatlantic passengers had to be won over from the comfort of first-class travel on an ocean liner. The American Boeing stratocruiser offered sleeping berths, including double berths for couples who reckoned they could sleep soundly in a width of 42″. But the American aircraft that the public heard most about during 1949 was the Skymaster, which, for the first six months of the year, until the Russians lifted their blockade on 12 May, carried much of the airlift cargo into Berlin. 35 Skymasters were lost in accidents during eleven months.

Non-air transport was developing too. The new Morris Minor, designed by Alec Issigonis, had appeared late in 1948 and was to continue in production for twenty years.

A double-decker rail coach was tested on the commuter rail services of south London. A train made up of eight double-decker coaches carried 1,104 passengers, as against 772 on a single-decker train. Such coaches are used in the United States but they were not developed here.

Finally, the merchant seaman, accustomed to wretched accommodation in pre-war days, was to be better looked after. It was announced that a new 8,300 ton freighter was to provide the crew with single berth cabins, containing a chest of drawers and a built-in wardrobe.

A less spectacular technical development than those described above, but a more revolutionary one, was taking place at Manchester University. 'ENIAC', the first electronic digital computer, had been completed in U.S.A. in 1946. The public were told in June about experiments at Manchester with an automatic sequence-controlled calculating machine, 'distinguished from other automatic computing machines by its use of a memory-storage system'. This new 'thinking machine', the computer, was good material for makers of jokes. Could a computer light a pipe or fall in love? How far could it go in replacing human beings? Twenty years later we have no doubt about the answer: a very long way.

It was a good year for jokes. In U.S.A. the Hollywood film world was already being drained of talent by television, so that in Britain the films of the year were British, and three were comedies – *Whisky Galore!*, *Passport to Pimlico*, *Kind Hearts and Coronets*. But radio comedy suffered a great loss. Tommy Handley died. He had been the star in *Itma* (*It's that man again*), a weekly comedy show of unique quality which had delighted enormous audiences at home and overseas, during and after the war. In 1949 radio was still far more important than television in this country. There was no ITV, no BBC2 and no colour TV. The one BBC TV programme could only be received in southern England at the beginning of the year. But during 1949 BBC TV advanced into the Midlands. Tommy Handley's successors would have to be TV men.

Nigel Balchin's powerful novel *The Small Back Room* about World War II as waged in Whitehall, appeared as a film, directed by Emeric Pressburger, but the film of the year was *The Third Man* (directed by Carol Reed, story by Graham Greene, leading actors Orson Welles and Trevor Howard). It had some splendid comic scenes and a theme tune played on the zither which everybody hummed. But it was in fact a thriller with a serious theme – the black market in the new 'antibiotics', such as penicillin and streptomycin, precious supplies of which were arriving in Europe from the U.S.A. The film was set in post-war Vienna, during midwinter, with the four victorious powers in occupation. The background was authentic and it may well be that shipments of curative drugs did in fact go astray.

'Black marketeering' (trafficking at inflated prices in goods supposed to be rationed and price controlled) was common throughout mainland Europe during and after the war. By no means unknown in Britain, it was, however, kept well in check. The Lynskey tribunal, reporting on 25 January after a long and intimate investigation into a case concerned with the issue of permits for building materials, brought disgrace upon a Labour minister and a prominent trade unionist simply for showing favour to a very pushing applicant. They had not made any money.

The 'pushing applicant', one Sidney Stanley, was more or less called a liar in the tribunal's report. Nine months later this term was being widely applied to Sir Stafford Cripps, hitherto regarded as one of the most upright, intelligent and dedicated members of the Labour Government, who had succeeded Hugh Dalton as Chancellor of the Exchequer in 1947. What had happened was that the economic situation had become so bad that the pound sterling had to be devalued. No government likes devaluation. The point of it is to make our goods cheaper for foreign countries to buy, but it results in higher prices at home and makes touring and buying abroad more expensive.

So, up to the last minute, in order to create confidence and because he always hopes that something may turn up, the Chancellor says 'We will not devalue'. Afterwards his opponents call him a liar. This happened to Cripps when, on Sunday 18 September, he announced the government's decision to devalue the pound. The electorate, who were due to express their opinion again in 1950, were not pleased; nor were they any happier for learning, two months later, that a vast government scheme for the production of groundnuts ('peanuts' or 'monkey nuts': they provide vegetable oil) in East Africa was £23m. in debt. We would have to tighten our belts. There was talk of imposing a charge for Health Service prescriptions. The nationalisation of steel was postponed until November.

The first meeting of NATO (the North Atlantic Treaty Organisation) was held in December; the members were nine European countries: Britain, France (which withdrew in 1966), Belgium, the Netherlands, Luxembourg, Italy, Denmark, Norway and Portugal; together with Canada and Iceland, but not, as yet, U.S.A. It was hardly an occasion for rejoicing. It underlined the falling apart of Europe into western and eastern blocs, a process which had been going on since the defeat of Germany and at the time of the airlift had nearly led to war. Germany now began to develop into the two nations we know to-day.

The Western zones of Germany, though still occupied by the Allies and without their own army, became the German Federal Republic, with Bonn, on the river Rhine, as their capital. On 15 September Dr. Konrad Adenauer, a Catholic in his seventies who had not been a Nazi, became the Republic's first Chancellor. The occupation ended in May 1955, though Allied troops remained by agreement for defence.

On 10 October the German Democratic Republic, under Walter Ulbricht, was set up for East Germany, with its capital in East Berlin. It was not recognised diplomatically by Great Britain until February 1973.

While Europe split, China united – almost. The communists had captured Peking in January and Chiang Kai-shek had taken refuge in the island of Formosa (Taiwan). By October Mao Tse-tung was master of all mainland Chinese and announced the foundation of the People's Republic of China. 'Our nation will never again be an insulted nation,' said Mao. 'We have stood up.'

This would have been the moment to offer the new China the Security Council seat occupied by Chiang Kai-shek's government, but the U.S.A. were not prepared to do this. It was not until 1971 that the People's Republic of China replaced Taiwan on the Security Council.

Nor were the British public at all well disposed towards Mao. They had in August welcomed home as national heroes the survivors of the crew of the *Amethyst,* a frigate which had been fired on and severely damaged by Communist guns on 20 April, while attempting to take supplies up the river Yangtse to the British Embassy in Nanking. *Amethyst'*s commander and 21 others were killed and the Communists prevented her proceeding up or down stream. They wanted a declaration from the British that *Amethyst* had fired first. Commander Kerans, who had been sent from Nanking to take command, refused to give this; but after three months (30 July) he managed to break out during the night. Having dashed down 150 miles of the Yangtse, *Amethyst* escaped to Hong Kong.

This was the first of a number of incidents which were to prevent friendly relations developing between Britain and the People's Republic of China. Before long British and Chinese troops were face to face in Korea.

But at the turn of the year most people were still pretty vague about where Korea was and how it was governed, and what importance attached to the '38th parallel'.

In Rome on Christmas Eve the Pope delivered three blows with a silver hammer on the Holy Door of St. Peter's, and entered, holding a lighted candle. This door is normally opened only once in 25 years, though there had been an exception for 1933, the 19th centennial of the crucifixion. It would now remain open till Christmas Eve 1950; for 1950 had been proclaimed a Holy Year.

1950

WHEN THE 'Holy Year' of 1950 came to an end and someone on *The Times* had the job of summing it up in a headline, he wrote:

NOW THRIVE THE ARMOURERS

During January it had become known that the U.S.A. were interested in the hydrogen bomb, which was cheaper and more destructive than the atom bomb (made from uranium 235); but the writer who used the above quotation from Shakespeare's *Henry V* as a headline, was probably thinking of the more conventional weapons which opened fire again during the second half of the year.

In Britain, as the year began, the question most frequently asked was: What will be the date of the General Election? Four and a half years had passed since the resounding victory of Labour in 1945. Mr. Attlee would have to go to the country before his five years were up. His decision was published on 11 January:

POLLING DAY 23 FEBRUARY

Mr. Bevin, the Foreign Secretary, heard the news in Ceylon, where the Colombo conference of Commonwealth Prime Ministers was reaching a successful conclusion in its discussions about the development of agriculture, transport and communications in the Commonwealth countries of South East Asia. On an Australian suggestion funds were to be provided between 1951 and 1957 by the more prosperous members of the Commonwealth. It was an arrangement comparable to Marshall Aid in Europe and became known as the Colombo Plan. Two-thirds of the money was to go to India.

The Britain to which Mr. Bevin returned in mid-January, though well fed in comparison with eastern countries, was still not free of food rationing. However, as the electors decided whether the truth lay in Labour's manifesto 'Let Us Win Through Together' or in the Conservatives' 'This Is The Road', or in the Liberal 'No Easy Way', or in the Communist Party's 'The Socialist Road for Britain', they were able to drink more milk. This stamina-providing beverage went off the ration on 15 January. It had

40

been rationed since 1 October 1941. In May the 5s. limit on restaurant meals was lifted and 'points rationing' which had applied to tinned foods, rice and dried fruit, came to an end. Whale meat was now available off the ration as a substitute for steak, but never became popular.

Certainly stamina was going to be needed for a February election. The last had been in July (1945). Candidates of all parties in country constituencies shuddered at the prospect of campaigning in icy conditions like those of 1947. The Liberals, whose strongest hopes lay in remote and often mountainous areas, were particularly aggrieved. But the weather turned out comparatively mild.

There had been some rearrangement of constituencies, and this was the first election at which nobody had two votes. The Representation of the People Acts, passed by the Labour Government in 1948 and 1949, had abolished the business premises vote and the university graduates vote. (Twelve members had hitherto been elected by graduates of British Universities, who had also been entitled to vote for a local candidate.)

This was also the first election in which public opinion polls were prominent. (Someone said, parodying a famous line of Shakespeare, that the voters were 'more polled against than polling'.) These opinion polls had gone badly wrong during the U.S. Presidential election of 1948, when they failed to predict that Mr. Truman would get in. In Britain, in 1950, pollsters did better. They were clear that the election would be a very close thing and the results on 23 February proved them right. Labour was left with a majority of seven (84% of the electorate voted). Early in March this majority was reduced to six, when Moss Side, Manchester, returned a Conservative (voting had been postponed owing to a candidate's death). The final figures were:

Labour		315	
Conservative	298		622
		307	
Liberal	9		
Communist	0		
Labour majority		8	

But the Chairman and Deputy Chairmen of Committees, both Labour, have to be subtracted from this figure, leaving a working majority to Labour of only six. Two Irish Nationalists were also elected but said that they would not come to Westminster. Finally, the Speaker was returned unopposed. These three added to the above 622 give a total of 625 members in all. Mr. Attlee made no changes among his chief Ministers. The Chancellor of the Exchequer, Sir Stafford Cripps, continued in office. So did Harold Wilson, who had been made President of the Board of Trade in 1947. Born in 1916, he was the youngest member of the Cabinet.

No Communist was elected to Parliament. The arrest, during the election campaign, of Klaus Fuchs, a senior scientist employed in the Atomic Energy Establishment at Harwell, on charges of communicating secret information to the Russians, had not made the task of Communist candidates any easier. Another Communist scientist, Dr. Alan Nunn May, had been convicted on similar charges in 1946. Furthermore, on 9 February, the United States Senator Joseph McCarthy had made a speech in West Virginia in the course of which he said that the State Department (the American Foreign Office) was full of Communists and that he knew their names. This had started a witch-hunt which went on for five years, both during the end of the Truman regime and, from 1952, under Eisenhower, whose Vice-President was the same Nixon who became President in 1968.

The investigating committee of which McCarthy became chairman terrorised men in influential positions in the United States, by accusing them of Communist tendencies on the flimsiest of evidence. Even the admired General Marshall (of 'Marshall Aid'), Secretary of Defense since 1950, whom President Truman had referred to as the 'greatest living American', was not safe from attack. Once McCarthy had publicly accused him (June 1951) of being pro-Russian, of having failed to direct American policy against the Communist menace, his reputation was ruined and in a few months he resigned.

Hitler had come to power in a country embittered by defeat in 1918 and by years of high unemployment. America had been on the winning side in 1945-6, had suffered less than her allies and was passing through an era of great prosperity. But by the beginning of 1954 the opinion polls showed 50% of her citizens approving of McCarthy and no one, from the President downwards, had stood up to him effectively. Mercifully, as we shall see, in that year he overstepped himself.

In Britain, at his trial on 1 March, Fuchs pleaded guilty. He had made a full confession. The trial lasted ninety minutes and the maximum penalty was imposed – 14 years, for what the Lord Chief Justice referred to as 'the grossest treachery'.

Though not without sympathy for Fuchs's problems of conscience (it was never suggested that he stood to gain financially to any great extent) the public were shocked by his behaviour. But they were more worried at that time about a different type of criminal. The Criminal Justice Act of 1948 had abolished corporal punishment except for attacks on prison officers and certain Justices now felt that this was leading to an increase in violent crime. On the same day that the Lord Chief Justice sentenced Fuchs, he had before him two youths who had attacked a woman and robbed her of a wallet containing £1. 'It is not for me to criticise the wisdom of Parliament,' he said, but added, 'Eighteen months ago I could have had you well whipped.' Other judges complained that they could no longer order the 'cat' or birching. The House of Lords had a debate on flogging as a deterrent, during which, predictably, one member described his experiences at Eton.

The government stood firm. The lash, however, still had a big future in South Africa, where Dr. Malan's Nationalist government, in power since 1948, was beginning to implement the policy of *apartheid* (pronounced 'apartate'), which means the separate development of the various races in South Africa, and requires a ruthless system of fines, whipping and imprisonment to enforce it. The Nationalists began by making it compulsory to carry identity cards indicating race – White, Asiatic, Coloured (i.e. of mixed blood) or Native. Next a bill was introduced which aimed at the gradual segregation of races into defined residential areas. The Nationalist government also announced that they considered South-West Africa to be part of the Union of South Africa and no longer a mandated territory. (It had been German South-West Africa until after World War I, after which it had been governed by the Union of South Africa under mandate from the League of Nations.)

Finally, South Africa laid claim to the three British Protectorates of Swaziland, Basutoland (now Lesotho) and Bechuanaland (now Botswana). The last of these was in the news because the marriage in 1948 of a tribal chief, Seretse Khama, to a white girl, whom he had met while studying law in Britain, was thought to make him unsuitable as a ruler. In 1950 the British government compelled him to leave Bechuanaland for five years. However, when he returned in 1956 he worked for the Bechuanaland Democratic Party and was its President when it won Bechuanaland's first general election under universal suffrage in 1965. In 1966 the country became independent under the name of Botswana. Seretse became the first Prime Minister and was knighted.

A ruler whose story had a less happy ending was King Leopold of Belgium. A referendum in March showed that 57.7% of Belgians were in favour of his return. With this slender margin he decided to come back in July, but so much unrest resulted that in August he announced his intention to abdicate. Prince Baudouin, the heir, was to become King as soon as he reached the age of 21, in September 1951.

On the other side of the world, in Korea, the last monarch had abdicated in 1910. The state of his country had long belied its name, which means 'Land of the Morning Calm'. His father had misruled it before him, propped by the Japanese, and among the radical young men whom he had imprisoned, tortured and forced to leave the country for demanding democratic reforms, was one called Syngman Rhee.

After 1910 Korea was governed directly by the Japanese until 1945. They had no use for radicals either. In 1919 a non-violent attempt at independence was violently suppressed. Rhee, though elected President, never had a chance to govern, and had to remain in exile.

When the Japanese surrendered in 1945, the Russians, who have a very short common frontier with Korea, marched in from the north and the Americans landed in the south. As a dividing line, the 38th parallel of latitude was agreed. There was no obvious natural boundary and the arrangement was only meant to be temporary, as a prelude to free elections in an independent Korea. The Russians however set up their own government in the north at Pyongyang and elections were only held in the south, where in 1948 Rhee at last found himself President, with his capital at Seoul (pronounced 'Sole'). He was now seventy-three. It is true that Churchill and Adenauer were older than this, but the Koreans had been degraded by forty years of Japanese domination; those in whom the spirit of democracy survived soon found that it had withered in their President. Rhee had become a corrupt old tyrant. 'Neither a perfect democracy nor wholly pacific in temper' was probably a too charitable description of his regime.

North of the 38th parallel an equally authoritarian government had been established over a much smaller population (9 m as against Rhee's 21 m). But the north had minerals and hydro-electric power. In the south farmers grew rice and barley.

The Russians withdrew their occupation troops in 1948 and the Americans theirs in 1949, but the governments of North and South Korea remained on the alert, and each proclaimed its desire to unite the country. There were frequent border incidents and at 4.0 a.m. on Sunday 25 June 1950, Northern forces crossed the 38th parallel in strength.

This happened to be an occasion when the United Nations was able to act quickly. There were American and Australian forces in Japan and a number of Commonwealth warships were in Far Eastern waters. It remained for the Security Council of the United Nations to order action if the North Koreans refused to withdraw.

Normally it would have been unthinkable that the Council should have decided on action against North Korea, because the great powers who are its permanent members have a right of veto. The Russians would obviously have vetoed a proposal to attack the government which they themselves had helped to set up. But the Russians were not present when the Council met, on the day after the invasion, and ordered the North Koreans to withdraw; nor were they present two days later when the Council ordered the United Nations to resist. Their delegate had withdrawn in January when a vote to unseat the Nationalist Chinese delegate and replace him with a representative of the People's Republic of China had been lost (Great Britain, though she had recognised the People's Republic, abstained from voting, in order not to antagonise the United States and other anti-Mao governments). Why Russia did not return in time to veto the Korea resolution remains a mystery. But her delegate still stayed away and for the first time the United Nations found itself at war. The Americans, aided by the South Koreans, bore the heaviest load, but nearly fifty countries made some contribution in men, money or materials.

By September 1950 the North Koreans had overrun most of the peninsula, but the United Nations landing on Inchon (15 September), combined with an offensive in the south, forced the North Koreans to retreat, and the United Nations retook Seoul on 28 September.

On 7 October the United Nations General Assembly authorised the American General MacArthur to advance beyond the 38th parallel, and in November his forces reached a line forty miles from the Chinese frontier. The cold was now intense. A mug of tea put down on the ground was soon a block of brown ice. If you touched the side of a tank with your bare hand, it stuck to the freezing steel. The BBC's reporter René Cutforth wrote of the Siberian wind: 'When it blows, hope dies.' (He also reported the use of napalm flame-bombs by U.N. forces, but this news was not passed on to listeners.)

Chinese troops had now joined the North Koreans. The People's Republic of China was at this time friendly with Russia. The two powers had made a treaty in February. The Chinese soldiers were referred to as 'volunteers'. China did not declare war. Should this, it was asked, prevent the United Nations from retaliating by bombing China? General MacArthur favoured retaliation (a few years later he would have talked of 'escalating' the war, but this pompous four-syllable word had not yet been loaded into the language). It was clear to less flamboyant leaders, including, fortunately, President Truman, that this would be a likely way of starting World War III. MacArthur was ordered to exercise restraint, and for a time he did so.

Aided by the Chinese, the North Koreans now pushed south again. (The Chinese had plenty of men. In September, just before their 'volunteers' entered Korea, Chinese forces were invading Tibet.) The U.N. forces retreated and at Christmas were back on a line not far north of Seoul and the frozen Han River.

While the eyes of the world were on Korea, an independence issue arose nearer home. Early in the morning of Christmas Day, Scottish Nationalists slipped into Westminster Abbey and stole the Coronation Stone.

The Coronation Stone had been brought to London in 1297 by Edward I, who had found it in the heart of Scotland, near Perth, at the Abbey of Scone. ('Scone', the last word of the last line of Shakespeare's *Macbeth*, is there rhymed with 'one'. 'Scoon', however, is now the correct pronunciation.) At Scone Kings of Scotland were crowned for centuries before Edward's armies tramped north to hammer their country. Having hammered, he humiliated, by taking away to England the hallowed stone which had formed part of Scotland's coronation chair. At Westminster a carpenter made another chair to fit the stone and though the Scots asked to have the stone back and Edward III promised to give it up, the stone remained south of the Border. English Kings and Queens sat on it to be crowned.

From 1603 the Kings and Queens of England were also the Kings and Queens of Scotland, but the coronation was still always at Westminster and the Stone stayed there. It was supposed to symbolise the unification of the two kingdoms.

There were no Scottish Nationalist M.P.'s in the 1945 Parliament, but nationalist ideas had spread amongst the Scots since the war, and by mid-1950 half a million had signed the Scottish Covenant, pledging themselves to support a measure of self-government for Scotland. This was the atmosphere in which a Glasgow student persuaded three others (one of them a girl) to drive south and recover the Stone. They used two small cars which were unheated – heaters being a luxury extra at that time.

Money was scarce too. When the first attempt failed on 23 December the group passed the rest of the night trying to sleep in the cars. None of them knew London. They were always having to ask the way. The girl got 'flu. The police twice became suspicious. When the conspirators succeeded in removing the Stone on the following night, it was carried in one of their coats. A car key slipped unnoticed from one of the pockets and its owner had to go back again to look for it. Next a large part of the Stone broke off. The smaller part fell out of the car boot in Knightsbridge and the girl, who was alone at the time, had to lift it on board again.

Public reaction to the news was very different on the two sides of the border. The Scots on the whole were proud of what had been done, and took any discussion of the subject very seriously. The English authorities were horrified. The English man-in-the-street thought it was a good joke and why-shouldn't-they-have-their-stone-anyway? Meanwhile three of the conspirators fetched the Stone from Kent, where it had been temporarily hidden under a heap of rubbish, drove north without being questioned and crossed the border on the afternoon of 31 December. One of them, Ian Hamilton, wrote *(No Stone Unturned,* Gollancz, 1953): 'We had done something which we believed would restore our countrymen's faith in the lost ideal of their nationality.'

That night, as bells and hoarse throats welcomed the second half of the twentieth century, the Stone was home, after more than six hundred years.

1951

THERE WAS NO Christmas truce in Korea, but the front had been quiet during the last weeks of 1950. Early in January the Chinese and North Koreans continued their advance south and the United Nations retreated again. Seoul was back in Communist hands on 3 January. Refugees, whipped by the icy Siberian wind, tried to escape along roads already overcrowded with United Nations troops. Many never got south of the Han River. But this time the advance did not penetrate far into South Korea, and by March Seoul was again in United Nations hands. In April and May there was another turn of the tide, and the United Nations forces headed south once more. It was then, beginning on St. George's Day, that the Gloucesters heroically held a vital hilltop beside the Imjin river. Their commanding officer, Colonel Carne, who was finally taken prisoner with a number of survivors, was awarded the V.C.

The V.C. was also awarded to Private Speakman of the Argyll and Sutherland Highlanders. A battalion of the Argylls had been among the first British troops to land in Korea and owing to an error some of them had been attacked with napalm flame-bombs by American Mustangs. Major Muir, mortally wounded shortly afterwards while leading the remnant of the battalion, was another Korean V.C.

The spring of 1951 found General MacArthur still convinced that the only way to end the ding-dong Korean campaign was to carry the war out of the peninsula and into China. He had had things his own way for a long time and was surprised, to say the least, when during lunch in Tokyo on 11 April he received a signal from President Truman, relieving him of his command and transferring it to General Ridgway. Truman's action was not applauded by all in the United States. McCarthy said of his President: 'The son of a bitch ought to be impeached.'

However, the change appeared to be justified two months later, when the Russians, who were not militarily involved, proposed a cease-fire. On 7 July, delegates met at Kaesong, on the 38th parallel. But while the delegates argued about where the cease-fire line should run, fighting went on, and though there were no big military movements after the first year of the war, it was to be two further years before an armistice was signed.

This war, and the Cold War in Europe, had to be paid for. At the end of January Attlee announced that spending on production for the Services would be twice as large in 1951-2 as it had been in 1950-1. Reservists were to have refresher training.

The news had not been so good during January that voters were likely to accept this announcement with equanimity. In that month the groundnuts scheme in East Africa (Kenya and Tanganyika) had had to be abandoned, an attempt by the Commonwealth Prime Ministers to solve the Kashmir problem had failed, and the police were still searching for the Coronation Stone. It is true that, also in January, the Beveridge Report on the BBC had proved on the whole complimentary, but in the country's pinched circumstances the minority report in favour of commercial broadcasting was what interested the public most. Why, they asked, could we not have our broadcasting free, like the Americans – paid for by advertisements? Letters pressing this point of view began to appear in the correspondence columns.

On 9 March Ernest Bevin resigned the post of Foreign Secretary owing to ill health. Herbert Morrison, the Home Secretary, took his place and within a week found himself faced with a decision by the Iranian government, headed by Mohammed Moussadek, to nationalise their oil production, most of which was operated by the Anglo-Iranian Oil Co. at Abadan.

At the Home Office Morrison had been concerned with the removers of the Coronation Stone. They gave it back on 11 April. The Persians were to prove more intractable.

Bevin died on 14 April, aged 70, and, on the whole, deeply respected. As a Trade Union leader he had fought for the dockers at a time when their pay and conditions invited sympathy. Having served the wartime coalition government from May 1940 as Minister of Labour and National Service, he went straight to the Foreign Office after the 1945 election. There he had tried unsuccessfully to solve the Palestine problem, showing himself, it was thought, more sympathetic towards Arabs than Jews. When Russia's post-war hostility became clear, he had taken a leading part in building up the Western alliance against her. His ashes were buried in Westminster Abbey near those of the great pioneers of socialism, Beatrice and Sidney Webb. 'Few have done more to rid the land of the curse of casual labour,' said Mr. Attlee. 'He strove unceasingly for peace.'

Bevin was dead. Bevan was very much alive. In April he resigned from the government. This was a protest against a tough budget introduced by Hugh Gaitskell, the Labour Chancellor. Rearmament had to be paid for. One source of income was to be the collection of a contribution towards the cost of dentures and spectacles supplied to adults through the Health Service. Bevan wanted to keep the free Health Service which he had launched. But there was more to his decision than false teeth and spectacles. He felt that the budget did not share the burden of public expenditure fairly and that military expenditure must be cut if Britain's standard of living and social services were to be maintained. Harold Wilson and John Freeman joined Bevan in his withdrawal to the back benches.

May was a mixed month for Morrison. The death of his long-standing rival, Bevin, had left him as the most likely successor to Attlee, if the time came. Already he had stepped up into the Foreign Office where he was absorbed in juggling with the Iranian hot potato. At the end of the month he submitted the Abadan oil dispute to the Court of International Justice at The Hague. But in that black year for the Labour Party he had one moment of triumph. In 1947 he had announced that the plan for holding a Festival of Britain, which had been given publicity by Gerald Barry, Editor of the *News Chronicle,* and later Director-General of the Festival, had been accepted by the government.

Now on 3 May, at noon, on the steps of St. Paul's Cathedral, a hundred years after the first admiring visitors had entered the Crystal Palace in Hyde Park, King George VI declared the Festival open. And the centre of the Festival was not on any of London's hallowed, historic sites. It was on the South Bank, with commuter trains rumbling through the middle of it, over Charing Cross Bridge, in the non-tourist London where Morrison had been born and for which he had done so much between 1934 and 1940 as leader of the Labour-controlled London County Council.

The site – between Westminster and Waterloo bridges – had been a mess. Now it housed a great exhibition. The Dome of Discovery and the Skylon hit you first – indeed you could see them excellently from the other side of the river, without paying the 4s. entrance fee. You wondered: How do they stay up? Armed with a 2s. 6d. Guide Book inside the exhibition, you learned that you were looking at the largest dome in the world. Inside, it was rather like the Science Museum, but with escalators, which at that time were only to be found, as a rule, in the more fortunate Underground stations.

What had a pavilion called 'The Lion and the Unicorn' to offer? 'Clues to British character and tradition. The Lion symbolises action, the Unicorn imagination.' A huge effigy of the White Knight from Alice in Wonderland presided over reminders of British eccentricity, British freedom and the glories of the English language from Chaucer to contemporary cockney. (This was before the phrase 'four-letter words' came into use, or we would certainly have seen something about them.) Nobody knew quite what to make of 'The Lion and the Unicorn' and everybody talked about it. Elsewhere the exhibition's portrait of Britain was more straightforward – ships and new farm machinery and planned homes with toys and hobbies lying about – while between the pavilions were gardens and trees and places to eat and plenty of lavatories and telephones. By the end of May the millionth visitor, a girl accompanied by her fiancé, had been presented with a 5s. Festival piece – a coin specially minted for the Festival year – and the two were given a lunch of steak, strawberries, ice cream and champagne.

The South Bank was the centre, but this was not only a London festival. There were exhibitions all over Britain and the Festival ship *Campania* carried a compressed version of the South Bank story to the great seaport towns. There were local festivals of music and the arts. Everywhere, there was a clean-up. And it was not just the British looking at, and being rather proud of, the British. 'For five packed months,' read the hand-out, 'Britain will be at home to the world . . . At a time when the peoples of many nations are living behind a veil of secrecy and fear, Britain will open her doorways wide.'

When it was all over, at the end of September, and most of the fun had been pulled down or auctioned, London still had the splendid Royal Festival Hall, and part of the Pleasure Gardens which had sprouted in Battersea Park. More than that. Young designers, architects and ideas men (Hugh Casson, Basil Spence, Huw Wheldon, for instance) had had their chance, and people at home and abroad who had thought of Britain only as a battered and ageing Lion, with all the world twisting its mangy tail, were reminded that the day of the Unicorn was at hand. That barbed and graceful beast provided the image of a new Britain, galloping forward among the leaders in the fields of music, drama, art, fashion, architecture, antique marketing, and industrial design.

King George had opened the Festival, but he was now in poor health and it was Princess Elizabeth, riding the police horse Winston, who took the salute at the ceremony of Trooping the Colour on Thursday 7 June. (Nowadays the Colour is trooped on a Saturday, to avoid mid-week traffic problems.) Spectators as they waited had an interesting news story to discuss. The *Daily Express* carried a report from its Paris correspondent that the French police had been asked by the British Foreign Office to find two of their senior officials, Donald Maclean and Guy Burgess. It later became known that they had crossed to France from Southampton, leaving at midnight on 25 May, had taken a taxi to Rennes and not been seen since. It was thought that they had been spying for the Russians and had fled to

Moscow after being tipped off by another Foreign Office official – Kim Philby. It was not however until 1955, the year after the Soviet diplomat Petrov had defected in Australia, that the Foreign Office admitted that Maclean and Burgess had been spies. Their whereabouts remained uncertain until 1956, when they gave a press conference in Moscow.

Kim Philby's name was cleared by Macmillan in 1955. Philby, it appeared, had had communist associates and had been asked to resign from the Foreign Office in July 1951. But there was no evidence of his warning Maclean or Burgess. It was announced that 'while in government service he carried out his duties ably and conscientiously.' However, this estimate had to be revised in 1963 when Philby also fled to Moscow and admitted to having been a Soviet agent for about thirty years.

Burgess died in 1963; but Maclean and Philby remained in Moscow. Their story has led us away from Britain in the summer of 1951, where the Festival was still proving a great success and where, on 11 July, everyone had heard with relief of the opening of armistice talks at Kaesong.

On 12 July a summary was published, giving the first results of Britain's April census. Owing to the war, this was the first census since 1931 and in the twenty intervening years the population had risen from 46 to 50 million. Women were still the majority – 1,081 of them to every thousand males.

On 20 July Abdullah, King of Jordan, who had worked for peace between his country and Israel, was shot in Jerusalem by an Arab who did not share his views. In Iran Moussadek showed no sign of being willing to compromise over Abadan. He wanted us out.

Years later Lord Attlee was asked in an interview:

> 'Why do you think that our policy became so disastrous over Persia and Abadan?'

Attlee considered it had been a mistake on his part to yield to Morrison's pressure and give him the Foreign Office; but he did not blame Morrison for Abadan. His answer was simply:

> 'I don't think anything! You can't stop these nationalist moves.'

Nor, in the same interview, did Attlee give Abadan as his reason for deciding that October 1951 was the right time for a general election. 'There were various reasons,' he said. 'The strain was very heavy on the Party. There were a lot of old men and you had to have people brought in to the House in bath-chairs' (to vote, he meant, because his government only had an overall majority of six).

The Conservatives had their old men too. They were led by one. Churchill was 76 and far from fit. 'I doubt whether he is up to the job of Prime Minister,' wrote his doctor. King George too was very seriously ill and underwent an operation on 23 September.

Attlee announced the dissolution on 19 September, not in Parliament, but in the course of a broadcast. This was new. So was the use of television for party political broadcasts during the campaign. So was the word 'psephology' – meaning the study of election trends. Polling was to be on 25 October. The Festival of Britain closed on 30 September and citizens concentrated their attention on deciding for whom they should vote.

Bad news continued to come in from the East. Moussadek had ignored recommendation made by The Hague International Court and the last British staff were withdrawn from Abadan on 3 October. Communist guerillas in Malaya had been active since the end of World War II and a series of atrocities culminated on 6 October with the murder of Sir Henry Gurney, the High Commissioner. On 16 October the Egyptian parliament approved the abrogation of the 1936 treaty (on which Britain's right to station troops in Egypt depended) and the 1899 Sudan 'condominium' (agreement, for the joint rule of Sudan by Britain and Egypt).

Neither of the two main British political parties promised to solve these Middle Eastern problems, though a Conservative poster invited the voter to MAKE BRITAIN STRONG AND FREE, while Labour asserted PEACE THE WAY TO PLENTY. Anyway, home affairs mean⁺ more to the electorate (their meat ration cut on 13 October from 1s. 10d. to 1s. 7d. worth per head per week) than the country's misfortunes in the Middle East. They wanted a check to the rising cost of living and a policy which would produce more houses. A confident Liberal poster urged

| ower
| prices
| by voting
| iberal.

However, the Conservatives won, with an overall majority of 17, which was reduced to 16 when one of them, Mr. W. S. Morrison, was elected Speaker. Winston Churchill once more became Prime Minister.

The three men chosen by Churchill to solve the problems which had been uppermost in the election were: Anthony Eden (he got the Foreign Office and with it the Iranian and Egyptian troubles), R. A. Butler (as Chancellor of the Exchequer he would have to tackle the high cost of living) and Harold Macmillan (as Minister of Housing and Local

Government, he was responsible for building the 300,000 houses a year which his party had promised).

Churchill himself wanted to get to Washington as soon as possible. Princess Elizabeth and the Duke of Edinburgh were welcomed there early in November after a successful tour of Canada. On 8 October they had flown the Atlantic from London to Gander (Newfoundland) in a propeller-driven stratocruiser, designed for 60 passengers, which took 10 hours 20 minutes (average speed 240 m.p.h.). This was the pre-jet age; it was also the pre-anti-British-Quebec age. There were scenes of great enthusiasm in French Canada. 'La Princesse' rode beneath white banners with BIENVENUE lettered in red.

Not long afterwards, in Britain, there was news of another Princess from whom much was expected. The flying-boat of that name emerged at last from her hangar for the final stages of construction. Would she and others of her type carry their namesake on future Commonwealth tours? There were grave doubts. The children's weekly *Girl*, sister paper to *Eagle* (launched in April 1950) which first appeared (4½d.) on 2 November, with Kitty Hawke and her all-girl air crew on the front page, did not send them up in a flying boat, as the editor would doubtless have done, had it been generally believed to be the aircraft of the future.

Girl, however, was largely non-technical. Like *Eagle*, it had a Bible story on the back page, and a colour print of Princess Elizabeth was given away with the first number. Advertisements for bicycles were prominent and it included a strip cartoon in which Lettice Leafe, the Greenest Girl in the School, proved a constant source of trouble to Miss Froth, headmistress of St. Addledegga's, and her overworked assistant, Miss Tantrum. Poor Miss Tantrum was still wearing the same ankle length beltless black dress, with white collar and cuffs, when the paper ceased publication about ten years later.

In November, too, Mary Martin opened in 'South Pacific' (Rogers and Hammerstein) at Drury Lane; pedestrian crossings, marked since the 30's with 'Belisha beacons' (after the Minister who introduced them), were provided with zebra stripes; and news of a gigantic and mysterious pedestrian arrived from Nepal, where Eric Shipton's Everest reconnaissance party had photographed the footprints of what the public soon came to know as the Abominable Snowman. A scientific explanation of the footprints was provided, but cartoonists and pantomime comics preferred to accept the hulking hairy figure of Nepal legend.

As the year ended, three voyages were spoken about. The first was operatic. With his tragic musical story of Billy Budd on board H.M.S.

Indomitable, Benjamin Britten at Covent Garden added one more distinction to the Festival year's glorious record of British music. The second voyage was Churchill's. He set sail for Washington after Christmas. The third voyage was planned for King George. It was hoped that in the early spring he would be able to take a cruise with the Queen on board H.M.S. *Vanguard* and thus recover his health. This hope, however, was to be disappointed.

1952

AS CHURCHILL AND Eden crossed the Atlantic in the *Queen Mary* on their way to Washington, an east-bound freighter with a cargo of pig iron, the *Flying Enterprise,* which had been hit by a hurricane, was drifting out of control three hundred miles south west of Ireland. Her passengers and crew had been taken off and reached Rotterdam on New Year's Day, but her captain, Knut Carlsen, was still on board (reading *The Seaman and the Law* he said later). He refused to leave his ship and the world watched him. On 5 January a tug managed to put her mate, Mr. Dancy, aboard. The world then watched them both. On the 7th the tug managed to take *Flying Enterprise* in tow, but on the 9th the line snapped 57 miles from Falmouth and she was adrift again. On the 11th, at 4.10 p.m., she sank. Carlsen and Dancy managed to jump clear in time and were welcomed ashore as heroes.

Shortly afterwards an event occurred in Jamaica which is now of some interest but which at the time was an entirely private affair. Jamaica was out of the news, working to repair the devastation caused by Hurricane Charlie in August 1951. Ian Fleming, then a bachelor journalist of 43, was spending the winter in his house there. On the third Tuesday in January, according to John Pearson (*Life of Ian Fleming,* Cape 1966), after taking his early swim, dressing in white shorts, a coloured beach shirt and black hide sandals, and breakfasting, he settled down at his typewriter and began the first of the James Bond stories. For the next seven weeks he typed from 9 to 12 and in the late afternoon read through the morning's work. By 18 March *Casino Royale* was finished. An English publisher was immediately enthusiastic and the book appeared in April 1953; but three leading American publishers turned it down and James Bond's success was not at first spectacular in England. In the next ten years, however, his fame became world wide. Gaitskell wrote: 'I am a confirmed Fleming fan – or should it be addict? The combination of sex, violence, alcohol and – at intervals – good food and nice clothes is, to one who lives such a circumscribed life as I do, irresistible'; and perhaps Bond's finest hour was in 1961, when *Life* listed *From Russia with Love* as one of President Kennedy's favourite books. But in 1964, after only a few years as a world-famous writer, Ian Fleming died.

Libya was born about a month before Bond. In January she was celebrating independence, attained on 24 December 1951. Most of this former Italian colony had been under British administration since the end of World War II, during which it had been one of the main battlegrounds. The British connection remained close, despite the fact that Britain's relations with Egypt – Libya's neighbour to the east – were becoming steadily worse and that guerilla warfare between British and Egyptian troops was being waged in the Canal Zone.

Libya was very poor at that time and needed the money which British and American air bases brought in. But oil exploration began in 1955 and by 1961 export of oil had begun. Libya is now very rich – to be compared with the oil-exporting states of the Persian Gulf. In 1969 a military *coup* deposed the King. The new regime under Colonel Qadhafi, was hostile to Britain and the U.S. as being too friendly towards Israel.

The problem of Egypt figures in the speech which Churchill was privileged to make to the United States Congress on 17 January. He wanted the U.S. to share the burden of defending the Suez Canal. He said: 'We do not seek to be masters of Egypt. We are there only as the servants and guardians of the commerce of the world.' Congress admired Churchill and applauded his speech, but did not share his interest in the Canal.

Further east, there was the problem of the Malayan guerillas. Malaya had been without a High Commissioner since the murder of Sir Henry Gurney (October 1951). After his return from a tour of the Colony, Oliver Lyttelton (since 1954 Lord Chandos), the Colonial Secretary, recommended General Sir Gerald Templer. The matter was so urgent that Templer flew to Ottawa to be interviewed by Churchill, who approved of him. Templer was then appointed by the King.

Churchill had gone to the U.S.A. to ask for money, but not, as he assured Congress, 'for money to make life more comfortable for the British people'. His return on board the *Queen Elizabeth* coincided with the announcement of belt-tightening measures. There was to be a 1s. charge on Health Service prescriptions. Dental patients were to pay the first £1 of their treatment. The foreign travel allowance was to be cut to £25. Certain imports were to be reduced and the Crown Film Unit, whose documentaries had brought great distinction to Britain, was to be closed down.

There was a little piece of good news – for the blind. Surgeons had been developing a technique for removing a diseased cornea and replacing it by a healthy one taken from a dead body. Parliament now considered arrangements by which anyone who wished could have his or her cornea removed shortly after death for transfer to a blind person. Since then many people have signed forms requesting that this should be done.

Encouragement of cornea grafting was an advance. But the month of January ended with the publication of a report which supported the *status quo*. 89.2% of teachers, it was learned, favoured the retention of caning in schools as a punishment, in the last resort, for maliciousness, destructiveness, wilful disobedience and bullying.

On Friday 1 February the papers (price 1½d., except for the *Daily Worker* at 2d. and *The Times* in its last few days before advancing from 3d. to 4d.) showed an encouraging picture of King George, bare-headed, in the open air at London Airport, waving goodbye to the Argonaut aircraft which was to carry Princess Elizabeth and the Duke of Edinburgh to East Africa, on the first stage of a journey to Australia and New Zealand. The King returned to Sandringham, where he was enjoying the shooting. But on the following Wednesday, 7 February, at 11.15 a.m., John Snagge, the BBC's Head of Presentation, came into one of the news studios across the way from Broadcasting House, where a current affairs programme for schools was in rehearsal, and read a short bulletin:

'The King, who retired to rest last night in his usual health, passed peacefully away in his sleep early this morning.'

The BBC (both TV and radio) then closed down for the rest of the day except for news, shipping forecasts and gale warnings. Flags were lowered to half mast and the Lord Mayor of London ordered the great bell of St. Paul's to be tolled. At the other side of the world, in Korea, gunners fired their salute with live ammunition, because they had no blank.

Next day *The Times* appeared with thick black lines between its columns and, together with the other papers, except the *Daily Worker*, devoted most of its space to memories of the King, world reaction to his death and news of the new Queen, who was already on her way back from Kenya by air. Even King Farouk and the Egyptian Government sent messages of sympathy and said that they intended to be represented at the funeral.

All BBC schedules were revised, the two radio channels 'Home' and 'Light' were merged and all light-hearted programmes, whether in radio or television, were excluded from the air until after the funeral. At 9.0 p.m. on the day after the King's death, Churchill made a broadcast of fifteen minutes. It was not one of his great speeches, but contained the sentence: 'During these last months the King walked with death as if death were a companion, an acquaintance whom he recognised and did not fear.' These words were remembered. But in private, to his friend and doctor, Lord Moran, Churchill spoke more simply: 'It was a perfect ending. He had shot nine hares and a pigeon a hundred feet up, and then he dined with five friends and went out in the night. What more could any of us ask?'

The young King Baudouin of Belgium refused to attend King George's funeral. He felt that Britain had misjudged his father's conduct during the war. His refusal produced an odd situation in which the Belgian Opposition, which was Socialist, was the party protesting against their King's failure to attend a royal funeral. Baudouin stuck to his guns and was represented by his 18-year-old brother, Prince Albert. However, on the day of the funeral, Friday 15 February, four Kings, three Presidents and representatives of countries all over the world marched in the great procession from Westminster Abbey to Paddington station. Russians were there, but not Chinese. Sailors pulled the gun-carriage (a tradition dating from the funeral of Queen Victoria). At Windsor pipers played as the coffin was carried into St. George's Chapel. There George VI was buried.

The Scots did not like the new Queen's style – 'Elizabeth II'. They argued that the previous Elizabeth had not been Queen of Scotland. Some distinction had however to be made, and those responsible would not budge from the 'II'. Nobody, however, complained about the abolition of identity cards, another measure taken by the government during the first weeks of the new reign (they were part of the lumber of war, like ration books); and on 15 March the BBC Scottish Television Service opened, bringing BBC TV to about half the population of Scotland.

The days when 'TV' meant 'BBC TV' were now numbered. With a Conservative government in power believers in television paid for by advertisers had a much better chance of getting their ideas adopted. The argument of which they made most use was that 'sponsoring' of television programmes by advertisers need not mean that the advertiser controlled the content, any more than advertisers controlled the content of newspapers. In a letter to *The Times* Anthony Wedgwood Benn answered this by quoting the Chancellor of the University of Chicago:

> The advertiser must sell goods to stay in business. The network and station manager must sell time to stay in business. The advertising agency must present programmes that sell goods, to stay in business. All these people have managed to stay in business, but American radio is a disgrace.

Sponsored television was not a straight party issue. Plenty of Conservatives were against it. But politicians knew that attacks on the BBC were popular amongst all classes, whether the Corporation was pictured as fussy old 'Auntie' insisting on too much uplift and classical music, or as a sinister monopoly supporting what is now called the Establishment (a word not generally used in this sense until the 1950's). In May the government announced in a White Paper that they would consider allowing some form of organisation which would compete with BBC TV (the radio monopoly was not to be disturbed for the time being), and on 11 June the principle of sponsored television was approved by the House of Commons.

Churchill said, as reported by Lord Moran *(The Struggle for Survival, 1940-1965,* Constable, 1966): 'It is not a subject I feel strongly about. I do not worry about it as I do over the solvency of the country.'

It was the solvency of the country – the question of how much should be spent on defence and how much on social services which brought the great orators of the Commons, Churchill and Bevan, to their feet, though a hitherto little known Conservative, Iain Macleod, was learning to challenge Bevan in language verging on the unparliamentary. 'I want to deal closely and with relish with the vulgar, crude and intemperate speech to which the House of Commons has just listened,' Macleod enunciated, adding later, 'The Right Honourable Gentleman simply does not know what he is talking about.' The Right Honourable Gentleman was nevertheless able at this time to fight against his own party as well as against the Conservatives. With 56 Labour M.P.'s, 'The Bevanites', he withdrew support from his party's policy on defence expenditure. Their figure, he felt, though not as high as the government's, was still too high. Was he going to split the Labour party?

In this same month of May the Comet service to South Africa started. This was the first regular jet passenger service in the world and it linked us to a country whose laws were becoming less and less humane towards black and coloured people.

The end of June was very hot – 87° in London. The weather held for the last London tram journey on Saturday 5 July. Cheering crowds lined a 5-mile route from Woolwich. Next week interest turned to another south London borough – Wandsworth. There in mid-June, William Marshall had been arrested in King George's Park together with a Soviet diplomat. Marshall, a radio-telegraphist in the service of the British Foreign Office, had a confidential document on him. He had been brought up in Wandsworth, where his father, a disabled bus driver, and his mother still lived. His trial at the Old Bailey began on 10 July. He got five years, a much lighter sentence than later spies were given. The jury had asked for 'the utmost mercy'. 'We feel,' said the foreman, 'that he has been led astray.'

Marshall was thought to have acted more out of loyalty to the Communist cause then for love of money.

At the XVth Olympic Games which began in Helsinki on 21 July, British athletes were not very successful. Events in Egypt soon made much more interesting news. General Neguib led an officers' revolt and King Farouk abdicated. There was no bloodshed and on 28 July, as the ex-King with his Queen and their baby embarked at Alexandria, Neguib shook hands and saluted. He was said to be a kindly man and, unlike Farouk, he wanted to improve the lot of Egypt's 20m inhabitants, 14m of whom were villagers, often living in conditions worse than those of China or India.

But could a kindly man make much headway in such a situation? Neguib's supporters wanted him to break up the big estates, which he was reluctant to do. It was noted that amongst these supporters, a group of youngish officers (aged 30-40), the most influential was a Colonel Nasser. His was a more forceful personality.

Further south, in Africa, Kenya was now added to the troubled areas – Korea, Malaya and Egypt – where British troops were already engaged. A secret society called Mau Mau had been expanding amongst the Kikuyu, one of the largest and most influential tribal groups in Kenya. Mau Mau members took a solemn oath on joining. The ceremony was conducted at midnight with impressive and sometimes horrible ritual. Those initiated swore not to disclose information about Mau Mau to the government or to Europeans, and not to help Europeans or sell them land. Many Africans in Kenya were now being terrorised into taking this oath. Those who did not, might have their huts burned down; some were murdered. On 21 October a state of emergency was declared and early in November large numbers of Kikuyu were arrested, among them Jomo Kenyatta (born c. 1889) who had been a leading Kenyan politician since the 1920's. Oliver Lyttelton visited Kenya and promised to end terrorism there.

In the weeks which followed it was a legal battle rather than the physical struggle against Mau Mau which kept Kenya in the news. Jomo Kenyatta was put on trial for managing Mau Mau, and was defended by D. N. Pritt, a distinguished English barrister, who by the end of the year was himself accused, of contempt of court, because he had cabled to London the words: 'It amounts in all to a denial of justice.'

As Kenyatta's trial began, the long series of trials for passing atomic secrets to Russia, in which Julius Rosenberg and his wife Ethel had been involved, came to an end in the U.S.A. The Supreme Court upheld its rejection of the Rosenberg appeal. They had been sentenced in 1951. Many sympathisers hoped that their cruelly long suspense would be rewarded by a reprieve; but it was not. Seven months later (19 June, 1953) the Rosenbergs went to the electric chair.

The U.S. had on 4 November elected the first Republican President for 20 years, the wartime general, Eisenhower. His Vice-President was Richard Nixon. Eisenhower appointed John Foster Dulles as Secretary of State and although the new President had been elected on a promise of making some effort for peace in Korea, where an armistice was in fact signed on 27 July 1953, it was Dulles's obsession with 'the containment of Communism' which later led to the Vietnam war.

Eisenhower's opponent in the elections, a witty, highly intelligent and urbane Chicago lawyer called Adlai Stevenson, was not a witch-hunter, but Joseph McCarthy's witch-hunt was still on. It even penetrated the United Nations and was one of the causes which led the Secretary-General, Trygve Lie, to resign on 10 November. He had resented the American claim to investigate the political convictions of American members of his staff. But the Russians did not like him either, in particular because of his support of U.N. action in Korea. So 'in the interest of agreement among the five Great Powers' the first Secretary-General of the U.N. (born 1896, appointed 1 February 1946), the son of an Oslo carpenter, retired into private life in Norway and was replaced, after much argument (10 April 1953), by Dag Hammarskjöld a Swede.

In London, on 25 November, a thriller by Agatha Christie opened at the Ambassadors Theatre. It was called *The Mousetrap*. Richard Attenborough played the detective. Since then there have been many changes of cast, but the play was still running in 1976. It was warmly but not effusively welcomed by the critics. Next day's papers were much more interested in the coinage of the new reign, designs for which had been announced. And there had already been a rehearsal of the Coronation procession.

During December, the team for the Everest expedition was chosen (the Swiss Expedition had abandoned their attempt on 22 November, because of extreme cold and high winds).

In December 1952 you could lunch in Soho for 5s. 6d., or dine for 7s. 6d.; wines by the glass (2s. 6d.) could be ordered; and you could go on to Terence Rattigan's new play *The Deep Blue Sea*. But shortly before Christmas three days of thick fog kept many Londoners at home. It was a vile smoky fog, which killed many sufferers from bronchitis and even affected cattle at the Smithfield show. Some had to be slaughtered. People were urged to mask the mouth and nose when out of doors, and the smoky fog was christened 'smog'. Wary Londoners wore 'smog masks' as they coughed and fumbled their way towards Christmas and the dawn of Coronation Year.

1953

1953 WAS TO BE Coronation Year. Everyone knew that. Other events were only in part predictable. Churchill would be Prime Minister at the Coronation, but would he then at last retire? An expedition would definitely go up Everest; but would it reach the top? Tests against Australia were certain; but would England win? What of the 'running sores' – Korea, Kenya, Malaya? Would rationing end?

The answer to the last question proved to be 'No'. But there were advances. Sweets (4 February), eggs (26 March), sugar (27 September) were derationed during the year.

Stalin had a surprise in store. After a burst of anti-semitism in January, during which nine doctors who worked in the Kremlin – most of them Jews – were accused of being agents of the American and British Secret Services, and of having tried to assassinate Russian military leaders, he was himself attacked – by brain haemorrhage and paralysis. Soon his heart and breathing were affected and he died, aged 74, during the evening of 5 March. This was fortunate for the nine doctors, but it cannot be said that Stalin died unlamented. Despite his responsibility – in the eyes of Britain and the U.S.A. – for the Cold War, his leadership when Russia was our ally, before 1945, still ensured a certain respect for him in the West. In Russia to most people he was still the great leader, who had carried the Revolution forward after Lenin's death and had brought Russia successfully through the war against Hitler. It was not till 1956 that criticism of him came into the open. Meanwhile his body was venerated alongside Lenin's in the great tomb outside the Kremlin wall.

Tension between Russia and the rest of the world was eased a little for the next few months while Mr. Malenkov, Stalin's successor, took over as Chairman of the Council of Ministers. The danger-spot in Europe was now the Trieste area, with which Russia was not deeply concerned.

Italy and Yugoslavia both felt that the 1947 division of the Trieste area into two zones had lasted long enough. There were a number of disturbances during the year and a point was reached where both sides mobilised and moved troops up to the frontier. Early in December, however, they were persuaded to withdraw.

Anthony Eden, Britain's Foreign Minister, had gone to Belgrade in September 1952 (regretfully without his wife, because he thought President Tito was a widower. Tito's marriage to a twenty-eight-year-old major in the Yugoslav Army became known only during the visit). Tito paid a return visit to Britain in March 1953. It was a security officer's nightmare, since the exiled Peter still called himself King of Yugoslavia and was not without supporters in Britain. Furthermore, although Yugoslavia had been expelled from the Cominform in 1948, and Tito had accepted military aid from U.S.A., he was a communist and Britain was at that time fighting against communists in Korea. However, the worst that happened during the five-day visit was the throwing of a smoke bomb from Westminster Bridge (Tito arrived and left by way of the Thames), and the hospitality extended no doubt helped towards the solution of the Trieste problem. This was not reached until after a further year of negotiations in which Eden played a leading part. On 5 October 1954 Zone A, which included the port of Trieste, was handed over to Italy and the Yugoslavs remained in Zone B.

But Eden missed the Coronation. He became ill shortly after Tito's visit, underwent an operation and on Coronation Day was awaiting another, for which he was flown to Boston shortly afterwards. It was clear that Churchill would not now retire, at least until Eden was fit. On the contrary, he simply added the Foreign Office to his other responsibilities and maintained his characteristic interest in detail. A sixteen shilling charge for sandwiches was to be made to each of the 3,000 distinguished guests in the Abbey. 'I stepped in and stopped that.' Extra toilet arrangements were being provided in the parks for spectators, but not food and drink. 'Looking after their exports while neglecting their imports,' Churchill called it. So refreshments were on sale, though experienced spectators brought their own provisions. Some had already taken up positions on the pavement, during the afternoon of Monday 1 June, and even those with reserved places, including thousands of schoolchildren who lined the Embankment, had to be in them by 7.00 a.m., on 2 June.

Peers, peeresses and M.P.'s travelled on the London Underground by a special train which left Kensington High Street station for Westminster at 6.30 a.m. They had to be inside the Abbey by 8.30.

By midnight on 1 June, in spite of drizzle and cold wind, the pavements along the route were already crowded. This was before transistor radios were common (transistors had been invented in the U.S.A. in 1948); it was therefore to the early editions of the morning papers that most people in the crowds were indebted for the news:

EVEREST CONQUERED

A message from Colonel Hunt, the leader of the expedition, announced that the summit had been reached on 29 May by the New Zealander, E. P. Hillary, and the Sherpa Tensing. The two climbers did not carry radio. This accounts for the delay in transmitting the message, which had the happy result of its reaching London just in time to cheer the bedraggled crowds on Coronation morning.

Everest is the highest mountain in the world and is therefore never likely to disappear altogether from public interest. One needs to know about it for quizzes. But in the years between the wars it was much more important. As the 'allure of Empire' faded, 'Everest . . . offered a symbolic substitute for conquest,' a *Times* writer reflected some years later. The generation who fought World War II had been brought up to regard the quiet, comradely, skilled, athletic and undaunted men who tried to climb Everest, as the best kind of men. In particular they had admired Irvine and Mallory, who had set out on the last stage of the ascent, but never came back (1924). For this reason Hunt's message, ending 'All is well' was received by most people in Britain with pride and joy. Hunt and Hillary were knighted and Tensing received the George Medal. Hunt was later made a Life Peer.

The Coronation put the BBC on its mettle. In particular BBC Television, with the launch of a commercial rival growing more and more certain, was anxious to succeed. Both viewers (20 m) and listeners (11 m) were splendidly provided for in programmes running from 10.15 a.m. to 5.20 p.m., which included the whole of the Abbey service and the procession there and back. As the adult population was then $36\frac{1}{2}$ m one wonders how the few millions who are unaccounted for spent the day.

In 1953 it was still assumed that viewers preferred female announcers. 'On Coronation Day morning, Sylvia Peters, looking happy and elegantly though quietly gowned, opened the historic transmission.' 10,000 troops in a two-mile column escorted the Queen in her glass coach and her most distinguished guests through the decorated streets in the rain. The tall and smiling Queen of the Tonga Islands, a community in the Pacific whose membership of the Commonwealth had hitherto not been widely publicised, rode in an open carriage under an umbrella. The crowds adored her. And they cheered Sir Winston Churchill warmly. Since 24 April he had been a Knight of the Garter. He looked rather like an admiral in his chosen uniform, that of Lord Warden of the Cinque Ports, and he rode in a closed carriage, attended by an escort from his old regiment the 4th Hussars.

A million viewers in Europe saw all this while it happened, but since no communications satellites were yet in orbit, Canada and the U.S. had to wait for as long as it took for a Canberra jet-bomber to fly the Atlantic. These aircraft made the journey in relays.

The Abbey service lasted from 11.29 to 1.50 and the actual crowning took place at 12.30 p.m. Four television cameras were 'placed discreetly inside, occupying such small spaces that their attendant cameramen had been chosen for their slightness of build'. There was nothing slight about the commentator, Richard Dimbleby, an enormous man, who remained perhaps the most famous figure in British broadcasting until cancer killed him in 1965.

Colour films appeared later in the week. Normal TV pictures were in black and white only, but colour TV was already being tried. Three cameras on a closed circuit enabled children at Gt. Ormond St. Hospital to watch in colour everything that went on in Parliament Square.

People tried to make Coronation Day an occasion on which nobody was forgotten, and nobody who was in possession of his full faculties at the time will ever forget it. Some foreign observers, however, thought that it set us dreaming too much of past glory.

Back to hard realities. The 1952 housing figures had been published in February and showed that 45,000 more houses had been completed in that year than in 1951; but the housing problem was still acute. So was the polio problem – 3,095 cases in 1951 compared with 4,475 in 1952.

Brighter news came in April when Income Tax was reduced by 6d. and Purchase Tax (replaced, together with Selective Employment Tax, in 1973 by VAT) by 25%. And on 29 May, the day that Everest was climbed, there was comfort for the thousands who had come to Britain as victims of Nazi persecution. The West German government promised to pay compensation, and this promise was kept during the following years.

In March at Karachi and in May near Calcutta Comet aircraft crashed with heavy loss of life. All Comets were grounded while tests were carried out and it was not till 1957 that they were flying again.

Commonwealth independence in black Africa had not yet begun. In addition to Sir Winston Churchill, only ten Commonwealth Prime Ministers dined with the Queen on the eve of the Coronation. They represented Canada, Australia, New Zealand, India, Pakistan (which became a Republic in November but remained in the Commonwealth), Ceylon, South Africa, Southern Rhodesia, Northern Ireland and Malta. There was also the Chief Minister of Jamaica. But the Kabaka of Buganda (in Uganda) had been deposed by the British government and Malaya, Cyprus and Kenya were all partially in revolt. Jomo Kenyatta had been sentenced to 7 years hard labour in April.

In April, too, British Guiana was granted a new constitution, but in October it was suspended. In the same month another constitution came into force, that of the Federation of Rhodesia and Nyasaland, which was dissolved ten years later (1963). At the South African general election, the Nationalists increased their majority; while in the U.S.A., Eisenhower did little, during his first year as President, to check the McCarthy witch-hunt. The Senator launched 157 of his vicious enquiries during 1953.

From Korea there came good news, a few days after the Coronation. An agreement on repatriation of prisoners had been signed at Panmunjon. An armistice followed on 27 July. The war was over, or rather it was limited to a state in which frontier incidents occurred pretty regularly and a commission at Panmunjon argued interminably about the rights and wrongs of each. In July 1972, however, it was announced that North and South Korea had agreed to work together towards unification. A direct telephone line between their two capitals was installed.

In Russia Beria, who had been head of the secret police under Stalin, was dismissed in July and in December was shot for high treason. Subscribers to the *Soviet Encyclopaedia* were asked to cut out the article about him and replace it with one on the Bering Sea. In June the Russians had experienced their first trouble with one of their satellite countries. There were strikes and a revolt against Communist rule in Eastern Germany, where martial law was enforced until 11 July.

In the Middle East, Neguib proclaimed Egypt a republic on 18 June, while in August Moussadek, so recently responsible for seizing the Abadan oil refinery in Persia, was arrested and sentenced to three years solitary confinement on a charge of having tried to overthrow the regime.

At the end of June Britain, already without a Foreign Secretary, was for a time deprived of a Prime Minister too. He had a stroke and was ordered to rest, leaving R. A. Butler to carry on until his reappearance in August. But even now Churchill would not retire. He returned to Parliament in October and in December met Eisenhower and the French Prime Minister at the Bermuda conference, which invited the Russians to a Foreign Ministers' conference in January. On his return he gave in to a threat by railwaymen to strike over Christmas by allowing a pay rise. (Another successful strike, in June, was by extras playing knights, bishops and monks in a film at Elstree. They pushed their pay up from 2 to 3 gns. a day, on the ground that they had to wear heavy clothes and armour.)

In July steel was denationalised. In September Sqn.-Ldr. Duke set up an air speed record of 726.6 m.p.h. Lt.-Commander Lithgow then raised it to 735.7. But next month it passed to the Americans. Meanwhile Professor Piccard, a Swiss sponsored by the Belgians, had gone down 10,000 feet under water in his 'bathyscope'.

The French dived too – not so deep, but with aims more interesting to the general public (e.g. the recovery of wine jars from Greek or Roman ships, wrecked in the Mediterranean two thousand years ago) and apparatus part of which (the goggles and fins) was to be adapted for holiday use by bathers everywhere.

Jacques-Yves Cousteau, a gunnery officer in the French Navy, together with two divers, Tailliez and Dumas, first experimented with the 'aqualung' (three cylinders of compressed air carried on the back under water and joined by tubes to a watertight glass mask) in 1943. In 1945, after the Liberation of France, the three formed the French Navy's Undersea Research Group, which co-operated with Piccard on his first bathyscope expedition (1948).

The aqualung enabled a man to swim down to 300 ft., without lines to the surface, and stay under for up to two hours at a time. Cousteau in 1951 set out in the research ship *Calypso* on a voyage of undersea exploration, and his book *The Silent World* (Hamish Hamilton, 1953) was published in Britain during Coronation and Everest Year, reminding us that heroes could go down as well as up. The French produced another who went down – into caves. Norbert Casteret explored the Gouffre Pierre St. Martin, on the Franco-Spanish frontier and finally reached the bottom of it in 1962, proving it to be the second deepest cavern in the world.

But the year 1953, which had seen heroes made, also saw one dethroned. During November, poor Piltdown Man, honoured, since the 'discovery' of his skull at Piltdown in southern England (1912), as one of the primitive ancestors which perhaps link us with the apes, was exposed as a hoax. The hoaxer's identity had not been established for certain; but modern aids to archaeology, such as fluorine tests and carbon dating, had shown that the famous 'prehistoric' skull and jawbone were nothing like as old as had been supposed. Furthermore, instead of both having belonged to one primitive man, they had separate origins. The skull was human. The jawbone probably came from an orang-outang. This was highly entertaining for everyone except those who had to alter textbooks and museum exhibits. It kept most people happy till Christmas, after which December closed with the good news that Russian chess masters would compete in the next year's Hastings Congress for the first time since 1934.

1954

DYLAN THOMAS's *Portrait of the Artist as a Young Dog* had appeared in 1940. Harold Nicolson, a writer, politician and former diplomat wrote (*Diaries and Letters*, Collins, 1966-8): 'I am slightly disgusted by all the urine and copulation which occurs . . . And yet it is quite clear that this young Thomas is a writer of great merit.' Thomas was then 26. A year later he came to see Nicolson, who was not only a distinguished broadcaster, but had been on the BBC Board of Governors. Nicolson noted: 'He wants a job on the BBC. He is a fat little man, puffy and pinkish, dressed in very dirty trousers and a loud check coat. I tell him that if he is to be employed by the BBC, he must promise not to get drunk.'

On 25 January 1954 *Under Milk Wood*, a poetic account of a small Welsh seaside town, and Thomas's best-known work, was given the first of many broadcasts by the BBC. But the author heard none of them. He had died in New York in November 1953.

January also saw the publication of *Lucky Jim,* by Kingsley Amis (Gollancz, 1954). By November it was being reprinted for the tenth time. It was set in a provincial university before the days of revolt. The hero, Jim Dixon, had a low opinion of his professor, but his reaction was to try and ingratiate himself rather than to protest:

> Welch was talking yet again about his concert. How had he become Professor of History, even at a place like this? By published work? No. By extra good teaching? *No.* Then how? As usual, Dixon shelved this question, telling himself that what mattered was that this man had decisive power over his future . . . Until then he must try to make Welch like him. . . .

Jim Dixon's girls wore great wide skirts of mid-calf length. He himself wore a pretty ordinary suit with two buttons, and 18″ trousers with turn-ups. Nor was he bearded. 'Teddy boys' who had first appeared in the late '40's, were not bearded either, but they grew sideboards, and their clothes were distinctive, based on Edwardian fashions (hence 'Teddy'). They wore drainpipe trousers without turn-ups ('Do they have to unscrew their feet to get into them?' someone asked), long jackets and thin ties. Teds were working class, but their new styles gradually affected men's clothing throughout the social scale.

Published in the same year as *Lucky Jim,* the ninth volume of Arnold Toynbee's *A Study of History* took a gloomy view of western civilisation. Toynbee was 65. For those unable or not inclined to keep abreast of his great work, the point was made by the Americans, whose perfecting of the hydrogen bomb was marked by the dropping of one on Bikini in March. In June the Russians announced that they too had a hydrogen bomb. Britain's 1954 Whit Monday (in those days a Bank Holiday) was the wettest for fifty years and the, meteorologically speaking, abysmal summer that followed was attributed by some to the atomic experiments of the Great Powers. Central Europe had snow at midsummer; the Danube burst its banks; the Oval was flooded during a Test against Pakistan and in the west London suburb of Gunnersbury a tornado lifted the roof off the Underground station.

It has never been proved that hydrogen bombs affect the weather. Anyhow, the cold, wet, windy summer was not the prime worry of thinking people. Their deep unease was expressed by the philosopher and mathematician Bertrand Russell. Then aged 82, he had foreseen the dangers of atomic warfare in the twenties and had spoken on the subject in the House of Lords, soon after the two bombs were dropped on Japan in 1946. His voice was quiet and precise, yet passionate. In a broadcast on 23 December he said:

> 'Is our race so destitute of wisdom, so incapable of impartial love, so blind even to the simplest dictates of self-preservation, that the last proof of its silly cleverness is to be the extermination of all life on our planet? – for it will not only be man who will perish but also the animals and plants, whom no one can accuse of Communism or anti-Communism . . . I appeal as a human being to human beings: remember your humanity and forget the rest. If you can do so the way lies open to new Paradise; if you cannot, nothing lies before you but universal death.'

The new bomb gave Churchill another excuse for hanging on to power. Eden's illness had been the excuse in 1953, but he was now back at work and clearly better fitted for the premiership than Churchill, aged 79, with strength, memory and gusto obviously failing. There were sharp attacks in the press, and Churchill was constantly considering whether the time to hand over had come. 'I don't know why I am such a bloody fool as to want to go on,' he remarked to his doctor in a moment of exhaustion. But he managed to persuade himself that only his prestige could bring the Russians to the conference table. In the summer he paid another visit to Washington, and he hoped to arrange a meeting with Malenkov during the autumn. But this came to nothing.

The Russians however were not altogether unapproachable. Things were a little easier since Stalin's death. A party of Labour M.P.'s, including Mr. Attlee, Aneurin Bevan and Dr. Edith Summerskill, visited Moscow in August. They were given dinner on the terrace of a villa in the country outside Moscow. Dr. Summerskill wished she had brought a better dress. Malenkov and leading members of the Soviet government were present, including Khrushchev. At that time he was not yet a minister, but he was Secretary of the Communist Party and by no means self-effacing. The British Ambassador thought him like a little bull, who would charge along, knocking down anything that was in his way. After dinner Mr. Malenkov picked a bunch of phlox in the garden and presented it to Dr. Summerskill.

On the following evening the Russians dined at the British Embassy. The food was not lavish ('four courses of well-cooked English dishes') but the guests stayed till 1.0 a.m. and the party was a success, though not without incident.

For instance, the Labour delegation were on their way to China. China's seat on the Security Council was then occupied by representatives of Chiang's exiled government in Formosa (Taiwan). Aneurin Bevan suggested trying to get China put on the Assembly of the United Nations as a first step. 'At this,' writes Dr. Summerskill, 'Krushchev leapt to his feet and roared his disapproval, whether because that would be an insult to China, or for some other reason, I was at a loss to understand.'

Russian hospitality towards the Labour delegation was of course a welcome change, but Mr. Attlee and his party did not represent the British government, and agreement about limiting the production of hydrogen bombs was as far off as ever.

What about other international problems? Eden worked conscientiously at these. The conference of Foreign Ministers met in Berlin during January – Eden for Britain, Dulles for U.S.A., Bidault for France and Molotov for Russia. Their declared aim was to discuss the possibility of reunifying Germany, holding free elections and making a peace treaty with the government thus established. A treaty with Austria was also on the agenda.

It had never seemed likely that the Russians would agree to elections which would almost certainly result in an anti-communist Germany. They did not, and the conference failed in its main object. Eden however records a minor success in the social field. Molotov had provided an enjoyable evening, including a ballet, for the western delegations, who did not, however, want to give three separate parties in return. There was a discussion about who should provide what at the combined party which had been agreed upon. Eden proposed that the French should be responsible for the food and the wine, the Americans for the speeches and the British for the band. This was carried unanimously.

'The only worthwhile result of the Berlin Conference was incidental,' writes Eden. 'It called the Geneva Conference into being.' At the Geneva Conference (April-July 1954), the four Foreign Ministers who had met at Berlin were joined by a fifth, Chou En-lai, representing the People's Republic of China, and by delegates from Indo-China. The need for this conference had been agreed at Berlin, because at that time the two great communist powers were good friends and Korea had shown that the danger of war between them and the Western Allies was as real in the East as in Europe.

Since July 1953 there had been an armistice in Korea. The danger area now was Indo-China (Laos, Cambodia and Vietnam) which before World War II had been part of the French Colonial Empire. When the French returned in 1946 they found that the Moscow-trained communist Ho Chi Minh (died 1969) leader of the Vietminh party, had set up a provisional government at Hanoi, then the capital of the whole of Vietnam. The French decided to fight and had now been at war with the Vietminh for eight years. (The Vietminh party was superseded by an organisation called the Fatherland Front. 'Vietcong' was the term applied by Americans to communist guerillas operating in South Vietnam.)

'We gave up India. Why shouldn't France give up Indo-China?' Churchill is alleged to have growled in conversation with Field Marshal Montgomery, who replied with the 'house of cards' argument: 'If Indo-China goes, Siam goes too. And then Malaya would be in danger.' 'Goes' meant 'goes communist.' The U.S.A. had no possessions on or near the mainland of Asia, but most Americans were fanatically opposed to the spread of communism. At home they had electrocuted the Rosenbergs and given Senator Joe McCarthy a free rein. Dulles, whom Churchill was not alone in considering a 'dull, unimaginative, uncomprehending, insensitive man' was determined to campaign with equal vigour abroad. He was particularly interested in Asia. In December 1953 he had said he might have to make an 'agonising reappraisal' of American foreign policy, as a result of which the U.S. might have to concentrate more and more on operations in the Far East if European disunity continued – in particular if

France did not join the European Defence Community. But when, in March 1954, a large French force became surrounded at Dien Bien Phu, about 200 miles west of Hanoi, he was anxious that Britain should join the U.S. in helping them.

This was an example of 'brinkmanship', a word invented to describe Dulles's method of threatening war – standing on the brink of war but not intending to take the plunge. Eden refused to co-operate (the resulting hostility between him and Dulles influenced the latter's attitude in the Suez crisis two years later). Early in May, as the Geneva conference began, the Vietminh forced Dien Bien Phu to surrender. The French government fell and it was the new Prime Minister, Mendés France, who, aided by Eden and, according to Macmillan, 'in spite of the elephantine obstinacy of Dulles', struggled with the Vietminh delegation during the last weeks of the conference and finally, in July, arrived at the division of Vietnam near the 17th parallel with which the world has since become so familiar. In 1955 the two halves of Vietnam became republics; Laos and Cambodia became independent kingdoms.

The French withdrew all their troops from Indo-China, but in September the South-East Asia Treaty Organisation (Labour support for which had led to Bevan's resignation from the Shadow Cabinet in April) was set up, with the U.S.A. as senior partner. In this capacity Americans continued to take an interest in South Vietnam. Through the years this interest was to grow.

In Britain myxomatosis had become a serious problem. A highly infectious disease, affecting rabbits, it threatened to kill off the whole rabbit population. The author Victoria Sackville-West, living in Kent, wrote to her husband, Harold Nicolson:

> I got into such a rage. I listened to a BBC Home Service programme about myxomatosis, and it was all from the point of view of the farmer or tame-rabbit breeder whose trade might be threatened. And *not one word* about what the rabbits might suffer – just profit, profit, profit, or loss of profit.

October was a satisfying month for Eden. He was made a Knight of the Garter, the Trieste agreement was signed and on the 29th the first British ship to do so since June 1951 left Abadan. Agreement with Iran had been reached.

Moussadek's antics had pleased a section of his countrymen for a time, but he had not solved for them the problem of how to make money out of their oil after they had turned the British out. Once Moussadek himself was turned out the Iranian government was anxious to obtain revenue from its oil again. America took the lead in forming a combination of companies to help them to do this. Compensation was paid to Anglo-Iranian, who, as British Petroleum ('BP') are no longer confined to the Middle East. In March 1969 they announced a big strike of oil in Alaska.

In November Gamal Abdel Nasser replaced Neguib as Egyptian Head of State; but two years before Suez it was Churchill, not Nasser, who stood in the way of Eden's success. The Foreign Secretary was still under sixty, but he had been very ill indeed. For how much longer would he be fit to take over the Premiership?

Churchill, having recovered from a stroke and looking forward to the celebration which was to mark his eightieth birthday, had not much difficulty in continuing to persuade himself that the time for his retirement had not yet arrived. And when his birthday came (30 November), with Members of Parliament from all parties assembled to honour him in Westminster Hall, he rose to the occasion with the last great speech of his life:

> 'I have never accepted what many people kindly said, namely, that I inspired the nation. Their will was resolute and remorseless and, as it proved, unconquerable. It fell to me to express it . . . It was the nation and the race dwelling all round the globe that had the lion's heart. I had the luck to be called upon to give the roar.'

The British public were in the mood to join in the cheering, since rationing on fats and meat had been abolished in July and the ration books which had cluttered every housewife's handbag since 1940 could now be burned or preserved as curios (coal and coke, rationed till 1958, were not included in the books).

Throats grown hoarse at the Coronation had had plenty of time to recover. 1954 however was not without cheer-worthy events. For some, the visit of the American evangelist Billy Graham gave cause for rejoicing in March and in the same month hundreds queued to view the ruins of the Roman temple of Mithras unearthed during the digging of foundations for another block of offices in the City of London. In May, Roger Bannister was the first man to run a mile in less than four minutes, though he only held the record for a month, after which the Australian Landy took it from him. Christopher Chataway beat the three-mile record.

That wet summer the poor sodden citizens had been warmed and enlivened by the flash and bang of the athletes' starting gun. Another starting gun, fired in the autumn, attracted less notice. It was metaphorical. It only made a little bang, but it started a big boom – in property:

> On the afternoon of 2 November 1954, Mr. Nigel Birch, Minister of Works . . . announced to the House of Commons that building licences were to be dropped entirely . . . There were cheers from the Conservative benches. (O. Marriott, *The Property Boom,* Pan, 1967).

Looking back, we can imagine the great property millionaires – Cotton, Clore, Hyams – setting off, as it were, round the track, determined to breast a golden tape in the years to come. At the time, what most people cared about was being allowed to build a house or make conversions without a lot of fuss, provided money was available. And it often was. Production, exports and wages had risen. There was full employment. In October the foreign travel allowance went up to £100.

The television licence rose from £2 to £3 in June, but the viewer's choice was soon to be doubled. The Independent Television Authority, with Sir Kenneth Clark as chairman, was set up in August and work began on the arrangements for creating a rival to BBC television, paid for by advertisements.

In those days, before we had an Ombudsman (or Parliamentary Commissioner; the first, Sir Edmund Compton, was appointed on 1 September 1966) it was nevertheless possible to fight bureaucracy and win. Ministry of Agriculture officials were found by a tribunal to have behaved improperly over some property at Crichel Down in Dorset, which had been requisitioned by the government and which its owners now wanted back. The owners proved the justice of their case and the Minister of Agriculture followed the traditional course of a member of the government whose civil servants have let him down – he resigned.

A new safeguard of individual liberties was the Press Council, set up in 1953, which issued its first report in October 1954. To it were referred – and still are referred – complaints against newspapers, e.g. on matters of taste. Among the first complaints dealt with were the exploitation of the Kinsey Report on *Sexual Behaviour in the Human Male* (published in 1948 and in its eleventh edition by 1953), the invasion of privacy by reporters, and the right of a film critic not to have his article altered so as to express the opposite of what he had written.

Horror comics for children, printed in America, did not come within the Press Council's terms of reference, but a Comics Campaign Council had been set up in 1953 and in 1954 the National Union of Teachers arranged a touring exhibition. The following year (1955) Parliament dealt with the matter by passing the Children and Young Persons (Harmful Publications) Act.

Of the traditional British comics, *Dandy* and *Beano* each sold a million copies a week. The more recent *Eagle* stood at $\frac{3}{4}$ m and *Girl* at $\frac{1}{2}$ m. Serious readers had *The Children's Newspaper*, with a circulation of 200,000 a week. *Junior Express*, *Junior Mirror* and *Junior Sketch* appeared as twopenny weeklies in September 1954. Their titles suggested that they were newspapers for children, but they proved to be aiming at entertainment rather than information and adopted a 'Let's all be pals' approach. 'Smashing' and 'super' were popular adjectives in their columns. A critic wrote, 'One imagines the editorial staff dressing in shorts and cowboy hats to write their copy.' They did not last long. *The Children's Newspaper* outlived all three, but it too died, in 1965.

At Christmas 1954 London was still suffering from the bus strike of September-October. The pre-strike services had not been fully restored; and the whole country was threatened with a rail strike early in the New Year.

But there was good news from America. McCarthy had gone too far at last and had been condemned on 2 December by a resolution of the Senate. He was not punished but his influence ceased and he died in 1957. He never recanted or expressed regret for what he had done. If he heard it, which is improbable, he was not the sort of person likely to be moved by Bertrand Russell's appeal in that broadcast of 23 December:

> . . . remember your humanity and forget the rest.

1955

WHEN WOULD CHURCHILL go? When, for that matter, would Attlee go (he was 72 and had fainted at an official function)? Would Malenkov, Stalin's successor, stay? Would a 'Summit' meeting (between the heads of the governments of the Great Powers) be possible at last? There had not been one since Potsdam. And would such a meeting be able to do anything about 'the Bomb'? These were the questions which were being asked in Britain during the long cold winter of 1955, while the M.C.C. were successfully defending the Ashes in Australia.

The question about Malenkov was answered early in February when he was replaced as chairman of the Soviet Council of Ministers, not by Khrushchev, but by Marshal Bulganin. Stalin had not yet been denounced and his name was still officially revered. But a rather easier international atmosphere had prevailed under Malenkov and continued under Bulganin. Soviet delegations – doctors, teachers, Church leaders, scientists – visited Britain during the year. Russian oarsmen rowed at Henley. In October the British and Russian navies exchanged visits. As the cruiser *Sverdlov* sailed into Portsmouth with another cruiser and four destroyers, her band played God Save the Queen. The Russian ships were thrown open to the British public. Their crews visited Portsmouth and London.

The visit was returned by the aircraft carrier H.M.S. *Triumph*, which sailed up the Neva to Leningrad, with the band of the Royal Marines playing the Hymn of the Soviet Union. However, as we shall see, the Summit Conference in July had got nowhere and by November Bulganin, now accompanied by Khrushchev ('this fat, vulgar man, with his pig eyes and ceaseless flow of talk' as he appeared to Macmillan) undertook a 'good-will' visit to India and Burma, which owed much of its success to the anti-Western speeches of the two Russians (despite the fact that they had by that time accepted an invitation to visit Britain in 1956).

In mid-February the shivering British public (whose representatives in the House of Commons had just rejected by 245 to 214 a proposal to suspend the death penalty for five years) received two pieces of nuclear news. The first was good. Twelve nuclear power stations were to be built. By the introduction of 'automation', a word which now became familiar to the public, industry prepared to make better use of the new power when it became available. Plans were also on foot for an international conference on the peaceful uses of atomic energy and this in fact took place at Geneva during August, 60 member states and 24 non-member states of the United Nations taking part.

The second piece of mid-February news had a mixed reception – Britain was manufacturing the hydrogen bomb. Churchill explained that, while Labour was in power, Mr. Attlee's initiative had led Britain to make atomic bombs. The Conservative government were trying to live up to Mr. Attlee's high standard. Their attitude, and that of most Labour members, was that if no agreement on disarmament could be reached between the Great Powers, the Bomb was necessary as a deterrent. Aneurin Bevan disagreed and said so, forcefully. Would the Parliamentary Labour Party expel him? They took the less severe step of 'withdrawing the whip', a form of temporary exclusion which means that a member is no longer sent summonses to attend important divisions. This summons is called a 'whip'; so is each of the officials responsible for sending the summonses out. Bevan, however, was only denied the whip for about a month, since by that time an election was pending and some show of party unanimity had to be maintained.

The election was due because Churchill had at last resigned the Premiership (5 April) and Eden, his successor, wanted to start his administration with a vote of confidence from the country. This he got, on 26 May. The Conservative absolute majority rose from 17 to 58. It was ninety years since a government had increased its majority on entering its second term of office.

Harold Macmillan, Churchill's Minister of Defence, now became Foreign Secretary. He was well known to the public, since from October 1951 to October 1954 he had been Minister of Housing, and had reached his party's promised total of 300,000 houses a year. In July he went with Eden to the long-awaited 'Summit' conference at Geneva, where from 18 to 23 July the heads of government of France (Faure), Great Britain (Eden), Russia (Bulganin accompanied by Khrushchev) and the U.S.A. (Eisenhower) met, together with their Foreign Ministers – Pinay, Macmillan, Molotov and Dulles. The heads of government had not met since Potsdam and it was hoped that they would achieve a relaxation of the 'Cold War' and perhaps agree upon some measure of disarmament. Eden thought that a demilitarised strip between the Iron Curtain countries and the West might be possible. But no agreement was reached. The Western powers were not prepared to dissolve NATO, of which Western Germany had become the 15th member on 9 May. Russia had recently replied by uniting her allies (Albania, Bulgaria, Czechoslovakia, the German Democratic Republic, Hungary, Poland, Romania) in the Warsaw Pact (14 May). The four Foreign Ministers met again in October at Geneva but still could not agree.

The Summit conference provided an opportunity for discussing the situation in the Far East, where Chiang Kai-shek's government on the island of Formosa (Taiwan) was supported by the United States, which in September 1954 had formed the anti-communist South-East Asia Treaty Organisation. Chiang also had troops on Quemoy and Matsu, two islands much closer to the mainland than Taiwan, and there was at this time anxiety lest Mao's troops should attempt to seize them (they had already shelled Quemoy). Dulles made it clear that this might lead to open war between China and the U.S. (another example of his use of 'brinkmanship'). Eden, however, assured the Russians that President Eisenhower was trying to calm things down. He no doubt felt that the Russians on their side might urge the Chinese, with whom at that time their relations were still friendly, to be patient. He recorded the opinion (in his *Memoirs,* Cassell, 1960) that 'the Geneva meeting was worthwhile if only for the discreet improvement it brought about in the Formosa Strait'. To the Commons he announced: 'Geneva . . . has reduced the dangers of war.' More definite encouragement could however be derived from the news, announced a few days later, that the Austrian State treaty (signed on 15 May) had come into force, making Austria an independent state again. This has been explained as 'part of the post-Stalin thaw'; but the thaw was not general and it is not easy to say why the Russians were so lenient towards Austria at this time.

Eden's premiership had begun during a strike of maintenance engineers and electricians, which closed down all national newspapers for 26 days (25 March to 21 April) and made the public familiar with the voices of editors who spoke on the radio some of the opinions which they were unable to print. Dockers at London, Liverpool, Birkenhead, Manchester and Hull went on strike at the end of May and stayed out for six weeks. A strike of engine-drivers and firemen led to the proclamation of a national emergency on 31 May and lasted until 14 June. But on 11 June these domestic troubles were temporarily forgotten while the whole world learned of an appalling disaster in France. 77 people had been killed at Le Mans in the worst accident known to motor-racing history.

In contrast to the long, cold winter, July and August were exceptionally dry and sunny. A very slow-moving play, produced by Peter Hall, which opened in London on 3 August seemed appropriate to the hot, lazy weather. Two tramps talked on and on. Nothing much happened. The reception of the play, however, was anything but somnolent. 'Mr. Samuel Beckett's *Waiting for Godot,*' wrote one critic, 'extracts from the *idea* of boredom the most genuine pathos and enchanting comedy.' Many shared this enthusiasm; others were maddeningly bored. It was not a play about which people were lukewarm, and it settled to a long run. Nor was *Waiting for Godot* a flash in the pan. Samuel Beckett, an Irishman living in Paris and, with Genet and Ionesco, creator of the movement known as the Theatre of the Absurd, was in 1969 awarded the Nobel Prize for Literature.

Lightweight plastic records, invented in 1950, were now replacing the heavy and easily broken ones which had revolved at 78 r.p.m. The new kind revolved more slowly, at 33 or 45 r.p.m., but sold faster.

Pop music was born in 1954. It was in April of that year that the American Bill Haley made the record called 'Rock around the clock', which eventually sold 15m. The film of the same title reached Britain in the summer of 1956 and sent audiences of young people crazy. They danced in the aisles and ripped up seats. In some towns the film was banned.

Haley, born in 1927, was no longer a teenager; but a teenage star was on the way. During 1954 an 18-year-old out-of-work truck driver had gone into a record shop in his home town of Memphis, Tennessee, and asked the girl in charge: 'How d'ya make a disc?' She said: 'You pay four bucks and you do your stuff into a mike.' The driver said: 'I'd kinda like to hear my own voice – with this' (he had a battered guitar with him). 'O.K.,' said the girl. 'Name?' 'Elvis Presley.'

Suddenly, in 1955, everyone had heard of Elvis Presley. Teenagers were moved to ecstasy by his songs. He was the first of the rags-to-riches pop musicians. He had many successors, of whom the Beatles are probably the most famous, but he himself has gone on singing and making money (around 300 million of his discs had sold by 1969 and he had made 29 films).

'Pop' art (first exhibited in Britain at the Institute of Contemporary Arts in 1952) has remained a highbrow taste, never approaching the popularity of 'pop' music, although the 'father' of British pop art, Richard Hamilton, has said that it should be 'popular, transient, expendable, low-cost, mass-produced, young, witty, sexy, gimmicky, glamorous and big business.' In 1955 he was teaching in Newcastle and his work was already attracting interest in London, where he had a big exhibition in 1970. But American pop art has so far been better known than British, e.g. Andy Warhol's studies of Campbell Soup cans and, incidentally, of Elvis Presley

(Elvis I and II 1964. Silk screen on acrylic and aluminium on canvas, 2 panels 82 x 82 ins. each).

The cinema at this time offered George Orwell's *Animal Farm,* in which the cartoon technique, familiar enough as applied to short comic films, was used by Halas and Batchelor to make a serious full length one. And ten years after VE Day, with Western Germany a member of NATO, good war films could still succeed, though the accent was more on British and Allied heroism than on Nazi brutality. In *The Dam Busters,* about the R.A.F. raid on the Moehne and Eder dams, Michael Redgrave played the scientist Barnes Wallis with the 'Dam Busters March' as background. *The Colditz Story* was about life in a castle used by the Germans as a prison for particularly important and particularly escape-prone prisoners of war, a subject returned to at some length and with great success by BBC television in the seventies.

However, it was becoming less necessary to go to the cinema for entertainment. There was still only one BBC TV channel, but from 22 September viewers were offered an alternative supplied by four companies selected by the Independent Television Authority. This body had also been given the responsibility of seeing that certain standards were observed on commercial television. Advertising, for instance, was only to be inserted at a 'natural break' in the programme.

The growth of television changed habits. Publicans complained about loss of trade. Men were staying at home with their wives and children. 'If they want a drink of beer now,' said one woman, 'they go and fetch a bottle in, so they can watch the telly at the same time.'

In fact pubs survived. Many installed TV (it was cinemas which began to close). Nor did television stop people reading books, as had been feared. Two big successes were *Parkinson's Law* (the principle which it lightheartedly enunciated – 'Work expands to fit the time available for doing it' – is now as well known as the most famous laws of mathematics or chemistry) and *Roaring Boys* by Edward Blishen (the first of a number of novels written by sensitive schoolteachers who had worked in tough schools).

People also went on reading the papers. Since 1951 they had been paying 1½d. instead of 1d. for the popular dailies. In September 1955 the *News Chronicle, Daily Herald* and *Daily Mirror* increased their prices to 2d. and in October the *Daily Worker* went to 2½d.

During 1955 Cyprus became prominent in the news. The Greek part of the island's population (nearly 80%; the remainder are mostly Turkish) wanted to get rid of the British and perhaps unite with Greece. Cyprus had been a British colony since 1925. Its importance as a military base was increasing, as the situation in Egypt became more precarious, and there was also a feeling that we should not leave without obtaining from the Greeks some guarantee of security for the Turkish minority. But the Cypriot leader, Archbishop Makarios, was impatient and had the support of EOKA, the resistance force organised by Colonel Grivas. On 25 September Field Marshal Sir John Harding was sent out as Governor and in November a state of emergency was proclaimed.

Operations against terrorists in Malaya and Kenya were still going on (France was faced with similar problems in Algeria). But Kenya's neighbour Uganda presented a happier picture. Agreement had been reached with the Kabaka of Buganda, who now (17 October) returned after two years of exile. He became the first President of independent Uganda in 1963, but was deposed by Dr. Obote's government (1966) and died an exile, in an east London council flat, in 1969.

Churchill had stepped down at last. When would Attlee follow suit and who would follow him – Morrison, long the deputy leader, Bevan, or Gaitskell (aged 49, educated at Winchester and New College and once referred to by Bevan as a 'desiccated calculating machine')? Attlee resigned the leadership of the Parliamentary Labour Party early in December and was made an Earl. In the election for the leadership which followed the voting was: Gaitskell 157, Bevan 70, Morrison 40. Gaitskell thus became leader of the Labour Party – the youngest leader of any party for 60 years. Bevan, considering that he had earlier in the year been on the verge of expulsion from the Party, had done well. But for Morrison the result was a catastrophe. 'It was a bitter rebuff for one who had sat in the pavilion with his pads on for so long,' wrote *The Times*. The House of Commons did not see him at the wicket again. His remaining innings were to be played in the Lords (he was made a life peer and took the title Morrison of Lambeth), or as Chairman of the Board of Film Censors, where the wicket was to become stickier and the bowling more tortuous, in the swinging Britain of the sixties. But halfway through the decade, when nude girls and prolonged or intimate love-making were still excluded from the screen, Morrison died (March 1965).

Churchill had gone. Attlee had gone. 'Their going,' wrote *The Times,* 'set the seal of history on the war in which the one had proved himself the greatest among the leaders of free men, and on the social revolution of the next five years over which the other had presided with such a deceptive air of mildness. Everything by the end of the year appeared set for a new response to the challenge of new times. The Prime Minister had changed, the Leader of the Opposition had changed, there was a new Parliament, younger men were on the front benches. All that was missing from the transformation scene was new policies and new ideas.'

1956

FOR US THE year 1956 is the year of Suez, the year of Hungary, the year of Stalin's unmasking, the year of the play *Look Back in Anger* (by John Osborne), the year when Rock'n Roll dancing hit Britain and the teenage pop musician Tommy Steele was launched. But for the Sudan, which had been under joint British and Egyptian rule, 1956 meant independence (1 January). Egypt, though crusading in the anti-imperialist cause, had not been particularly eager to step down, when she found herself on the side of those whom she would otherwise have considered as oppressors. There had been Egyptian hopes of swallowing the Sudan and establishing a Kingdom of Egypt which would have stretched from the Mediterranean almost to the Equator. However, Egypt no longer had a King, and Nasser, her new ruler, had other ideas for establishing his country's prestige.

In China, Chairman Mao chose 1 January for the introduction of an important change in national custom. From that date Chinese newspapers were to print their contents in horizontal lines of type, running from left to right, instead of in vertical lines, read from right to left. This was part of the drive towards making it easier for illiterate people to learn to read and take an interest in the news.

The Chinese papers soon carried a story which shocked and infuriated their readers, while delighting most of the rest of the world. At the 20th Congress of the Communist Party in Moscow, on 25 February, Khrushchev denounced Stalin. Stalin had been regarded as second only to Lenin among the heroes of Communist Russia. His body had been reverently deposited close to Lenin's beneath the Kremlin wall. But Stalin, the world was now told, had been a murderer who perverted justice, a blunderer in war who would not listen to advice, a maniac whose whims were ignored at the risk of death or dishonour.

Was this the real thaw at last? 1956, which produced a black autumn, saw Britain brightened by a little optimism in the spring. (The Chinese, however, were red hot with rage and the split between Russia and China – the two great communist countries of the world – dates from this time.) On 18 April Bulganin and Khrushchev, the first Russian leaders to land in Britain since the Revolution, arrived at Portsmouth on board the cruiser *Ordzhonikidze*. On the whole the 10-day visit was a success, but it was marred by one mysterious incident. A Lt.-Commander Crabb disappeared after diving, in frogman's gear, not far from the Russian cruiser. It was generally believed that he lost his life on a secret service mission whose aim was the close inspection of the *Ordzhonikidze's* hull. Instructions from the government to the effect that the Russians were not to be spied on during the visit (e.g. that their rooms in Claridge's were not to be 'bugged'), somehow failed to reach those responsible for planning this operation. Eden was furious and announced in the Commons: '. . . what was done was done without the authority of Her Majesty's Ministers. Appropriate disciplinary steps are being taken.' A body identified as Crabb's, wearing a black rubber diving suit, but without head or hands, was washed up not far from Portsmouth more than a year later (June 1957). The affair is still in part a mystery. Did Crabb have an accident? Did the Russians kill him? Or did the Russians capture him, 'plant' a body resembling his and compel him to serve them in the Soviet navy? An accident is the most likely explanation.

The Crabb affair did not interfere with the visit. Talks and festivities went on as planned. At a dinner given for 'B and K', as the press called them, by the Labour party, hopes of a softening in the Russian attitude towards their satellites were dashed. Gaitskell had asked Khrushchev about the social democrats (i.e. the opposite numbers of the British Labour leaders) still known to be imprisoned in Eastern Europe. Khrushchev replied brusquely that their fate had nothing to do with him. To round off a prickly evening, he added that, if he were an Englishman, he would rather be a Conservative than a Socialist.

How far Burgess and Maclean had been helpful in briefing B and K before their visit is uncertain. But the defectors were now known to be living in Moscow, and early in February had been allowed to meet western journalists at a press conference in the National Hotel.

There was no thaw in Cyprus. On 9 March the tough, bearded Cypriot leader Archbishop Makarios joined the select company of great national leaders (such as Nehru, Gandhi and Kenyatta) who served a term of imprisonment or detention before their countries became independent. He was deported to the Seychelles Islands, a British colony in the Indian Ocean.

Lord Chandos, who by that time had been replaced by Lennox Boyd as Colonial Secretary, comments (*Memoirs,* Bodley Head, 1962) that it would have been better to send Makarios to Athens: 'All exiles tend to lose support, and even bonny Prince Charlie soon forfeited his influence at the

French court.' However that may be, terrorism in Cyprus continued. The last British troops were due to leave Egypt in June and the maintenance of British authority in Cyprus was therefore thought to be increasingly important.

Apart from the 'B and K' visit, the most discussed subject in Britain during April was Macmillan's introduction of Premium Bonds (he was now Chancellor of the Exchequer). This was before the more recent legislation which has brought us bingo and betting shops. At the time many people thought it immoral that the public should be encouraged to gamble, even if it was not the sort of gambling in which you could lose your money. Sermons were preached on the subject. The Archbishop of Canterbury referred to the purchase of premium bonds as a 'cold, solitary, mechanical, uncompanionable, inhuman activity.' The bonds were on sale from 1 November; £40 m worth were bought in the first month, and the computer responsible for selecting winners was built up by skilful publicity into an uncle figure named Ernie (Electronic Random Number Indicator Equipment). Ernie was part of the Civil Service, a body who in the same month had won for themselves the five-day week. Ernie was therefore one of the first of the new generation of civil servants who have never known Saturday morning work.

Nor would Ernie ever travel 3rd class. Foreigners had long been puzzled by the fact that British trains only had two classes (1st and 3rd) and that there was no 2nd. In Europe three, or even four classes had been the rule. We now fell into line (3 June) by changing 3rd to 2nd and European railways have gradually reduced their classes to two.

Those in doubt about what class they belonged to could turn to a new book by L. S. C. Ross *What are you?* in which the expressions 'U' (standing for Upper Class) and 'non-U' were employed for the first time, and there were lists of U words (e.g. pudding, napkin) with their non-U equivalents – sweet, serviette.

'He says he denies the difference of class distinctions.' Jimmy Porter is contemptuously quoting the (fictitious) Bishop of Bromley, a contributor to one of the two 'posh' Sunday papers (the *Sunday Telegraph* did not start until February 1961) which he is reading in a squalid attic bed-sitting-living-cooking-washing-room, while his wife irons. *Look back in Anger,* John Osborne's first play, had opened in London on 8 May, with Jimmy Porter as hero, or rather 'anti-hero', a word for unadmirable leading characters which begins to appear at this time. On the 9th *The Times* commented that the play 'has passages of good violent writing, but its total gesture is altogether inadequate . . . the hero regards himself . . . as the spokesman for the younger post-war generation, which looks round at the world and finds nothing right with it.' Kenneth Tynan, however had no doubts. 'It is the best young play of its decade,' he wrote.

Look Back in Anger was a tremendous success. 'Angry young men' became a useful subject for gag writers and cartoonists. But by the time that their anger took an active form, in the student riots of the late sixties, the phrase had fallen into disuse.

When Tynan himself looked back – on the drama of the 50's – he regarded *Look Back in Anger* as the break-through from the post-war period during which classical revivals and the verse dramas of T. S. Eliot (e.g. *The Cocktail Party*, 1950) and Christopher Fry (e.g. *The Lady's not for Burning*, 1948) had been popular. 'They [the verse dramas] gave us access to imagined worlds in which rationing and the rest of austerity's paraphernalia could be forgotten; they also reminded us that words could be put to other public uses than those of military propaganda, news bulletins and government regulations.' But in the spring of 1956 'John Osborne spoke out in a vein of ebullient, free-wheeling rancour that betokened the arrival of something new in the theatre – a sophisticated, articulate lower class . . . Osborne's success breached the dam, and there followed a cascade of plays about impoverished people. Such plays had existed before; the novelty lay in the fact that the emphasis was now on the people ,rather than on their poverty. For the first time it was possible for a character in English drama to be poor and intelligently amusing.' (*Tynan Right and Left*, 1967.)

During the week when Osborne's play opened, two Cypriots were condemned to death. One had shot a Cypriot policeman, the other had tried to kill an Englishman. There were protests in Britain as well as in Cyprus about the sentences, but they were carried out at 3.0 a.m. on 10 May. Both prisoners were hanged. Later in the year in Kenya, Dedan Kimathi, 'Field Marshal' of the Mau Mau forces, was captured and condemned to death.

On 20 May the first American hydrogen bomb to be dropped from the air exploded over Bikini. But in Europe and the Middle East there were as yet no obvious signs of the disasters which autumn would bring. It is true that at the end of June riots broke out at Poznan in Poland 'for bread and freedom'. But they were suppressed. Moussadek was still in prison, though near the end of his 3-year sentence. Israel and Egypt had agreed on a plan to station UN observers in the 'Gaza strip', the area where there was most risk of hostilities developing. In mid June the last British troops left Egyptian soil.

'When the July days came our thoughts turned to holiday plans.'

Quietly, Sir Anthony Eden (later Lord Avon) begins his account of the crisis which brought him down. But the chapter heading is laconic and unambiguous: THEFT. This refers to Nasser's decision, announced on 26 July, to nationalise the Suez Canal.

The Canal was due to become Egyptian property anyway in 1968. No one can say whether Nasser would have waited till then, if Dulles had not, on 19 July, withdrawn the American offer to help in financing the High Dam at Aswan, or even if Dulles had acted less abruptly. Nasser said in a BBC interview ten years later: 'I was surprised by the insulting attitude with which the refusal was declared. Not by the refusal itself.' However that may be, he saw his chance for a gesture which would strengthen his position in Egypt, bring in, from payments made for using the Canal, some of the money he needed for the dam, and mark him out as the leader of the Arab world in its crusade against Israel. This gesture he made, vociferously, from a balcony in Alexandria. The word 'imperialism' appeared three times in one sentence. Israel was vilified.

The speech was well received by the Egyptian crowd, less so by Eden, who was handed the report of it while he was entertaining King Faisal of Iraq (massacred with his family two years later in Baghdad) at a dinner party in Downing Street.

Britain, France and Germany had all been partners in the offer of assistance for the dam and though he had hoped to continue negotiations for longer, Eden was not in disagreement with Dulles over the basic reason for abandoning the scheme, which was that Nasser was now thought to be spending so much on Russian war material that he might not have the resources, or the inclination, to go ahead with the dam. Britain had a much stronger interest than America in the Middle East and Eden now saw Nasser as a Hitler who would never be satisfied and who, incidently, was providing the Russians with a foothold in Africa, on the Mediterranean and across the route to the East. He decided that it might be necessary, because of the delays likely to occur if an appeal was made to the United Nations, to use force. Attempts at settlement and military preparations proceeded simultaneously. In August a conference of 22 countries who used the Canal assembled in London. At the same time French troops were arriving in Cyprus, the nearest available base for an attack on Egypt. (The French were our allies not only because the Suez Canal had been built by a Frenchman, De Lesseps, and France was financially interested, but also because of the support given by Egypt to the anti-French independence movement in Algeria.)

Early in September Nasser rejected proposals of the London conference and soon after turned down Dulles's plan for a Canal Users' Association, which aimed at maintaining international control without the stigma of colonialism. On 23 September Britain and France referred the dispute to the Security Council; on the 24th Egypt lodged with the Security Council a complaint against concentrations of troops and threats of war by Britain and France.

In October it seems probable that we acquired another ally – Israel. This was a delicate matter, in view of our close ties with the Arab countries of Iraq and Jordan. The attendance of Selwyn Lloyd, the Foreign Secretary, and his Assistant Under-Secretary at a secret meeting with the French and the Israelis in France has never been officially admitted. True, when the Israelis invaded Egypt on 29 October in retaliation against organised Egyptian raids, Britain and France called on *both* combatants to stop fighting. Egypt, however, refused and the bombing of Egyptian airfields, which the British then undertook, prevented the air attack which the Israelis had feared. The Security Council at this stage called on all members to refrain from force, a resolution which Britain and France vetoed – not surprisingly, since in spite of a call for a cease-fire by the General Assembly, they were on the point of invading Egypt and in fact landed at Port Said on 5 and 6 November. Their declared aim was to stop the fighting between Egypt and Israel, to protect the Suez Canal and to look after the British and French people living in Egypt. However, world reaction to the invasion was so hostile and the peoples of Britain and France were so far from united in support of their governments, that by midnight on 6 November the advance had been halted and a cease-fire proclaimed.

On 7 November Egypt accepted the cease-fire. The General Assembly called on Britain and France to withdraw from Egypt and agreed to set up a UN police force for the Middle East. The British and French waited until the UN force arrived, but the last of their troops had left by 22 December.

Eden meanwhile had been advised by his doctors to rest. Ian Fleming's house in Jamaica was hurriedly prepared and the Prime Minister left for a three weeks' rest there on 23 November. But in spite of the fact that about half the British electorate was shown by polls to be opposed to the Suez landing, and that the Prime Minister was now on sick leave, the government did not fall; and when Eden finally retired, owing to ill health (9 January 1957), Macmillan, who had been Chancellor of the Exchequer at the time of Suez, succeeded him.

In retirement Eden had time to compose his memoirs. 'Suez,' he wrote, 'was a short-term emergency operation which succeeded, and an attempt to halt a long-term deterioration, whose outcome is still uncertain.' On the other hand C. M. Woodhouse, the historian, interviewed in the BBC series *Suez ten years after* (1966), said, 'For years before 1956 we no longer had any power in the Middle East. What the Suez fiasco did was to demonstrate this fact . . . Suez ended up as a resounding success for Nasser.' Interviewed in the same series Nasser agreed that 'Suez helped the Arab nation, the Arab world, to regain confidence,' and added, 'I think Suez helped many of the African countries to be sure of themselves and insist about their independence.' On the military side, however, Egypt suffered a resounding defeat, and although Israel had to withdraw from the Sinai peninsula, she had gained freedom for her shipping in the Gulf of Aqaba and a respite from Arab attacks.

Finally, the BBC had its own Suez crisis, from which it emerged victorious. Eden took the view that, once the Suez operation had started, Britain was at war and that the BBC should not allow air space to those who opposed the war. The Director-General of the BBC, Sir Ian Jacob, had started on a Commonwealth tour shortly before the Suez landings, but what one of his senior officials called his 'soldierly disrespect for all politicians' inspired those who were left behind. The opposition view was heard.

October had seen the build-up of the Suez crisis. It also saw the build-up of the Hungarian crisis, of which more in a minute. But there were other events of importance. The most hopeful was the opening by the Queen of the world's first large-scale nuclear power station at Calder Hall, Cumberland (17 October). Three weeks before, a British atomic device had been exploded in Australia. It was good news that nuclear power had other uses than the making of bombs, especially when the other use was likely to lead to fewer power cuts in the winter months, and the know-how of such power stations was likely to prove a valuable export.

For light relief there was the case of the Russian discus-thrower, Nina Ponomareva. It had been thought a happy sign of the thaw in Russo-British relations that the Bolshoi ballet were expected at Covent Garden and that Russian athletes had not only been allowed to compete in this country but were free to go shopping afterwards. Miss Ponomareva, however, chose a hat and did not pay for it. She was questioned by a perhaps over-zealous store detective and ended up in court, where she was found guilty of shop-lifting, ordered to pay three guineas costs, and discharged. In the meantime, however, the Russians had taken umbrage and proceeded to create a rumpus which made Miss Ponomareva and the hat world news. It seemed likely for a time that the Bolshoi ballet, who had arrived after a difficult flight, ending with the diversion of their plane owing to bad weather, might not be allowed by their government to dance. In the end, they did. A month later, however, the Sadlers Wells ballet cancelled their visit to Moscow. This was because of events much more serious than the peccadilloes of a lady discus-thrower on a shopping spree.

Tito's idea that a country could be communist but at the same time independent of Russia, had been ill received in Moscow (1948). Of leaders in the satellite countries thought to be tarred with the same brush, Slansky of Czechoslovakia was tried and executed in 1948, Gomulka of Poland was imprisoned in 1948, Rajk of Hungary was tried and hanged in 1949. Stalin's death (1953), but still more Khrushchev's denunciation of him in the spring of 1956, gave new hope to those in the satellite countries who wanted to be communist but independent of the Russians. The East Berlin riots and the Poznan 'bread and freedom' riots have already been mentioned. In the early autumn it looked as though the Russians might tighten their grip. But when Bulganin and Khrushchev visited Poland on 19 October, Gomulka, who had been out of prison since 1954, was elected first secretary of the Polish United Workers' Party and managed to persuade the Russians that the best way to keep Poland communist was to allow her to enjoy a measure of internal independence.

Things went differently in Hungary. Strong opposition to the Stalinist regime already existed and when news of Poland's struggle for independence reached Budapest, students demonstrated in support (22 October). In the next few days workers and Hungarian soldiers joined the opposition, the security police opened fire and street fighting began.

At first the Russians appeared to give way. Imre Nagy, a former moderate communist and strong Hungarian nationalist, who had been expelled from the party after a brief period in power between 1953 and 1955, was allowed to form a government. He promised free elections and repudiated the Warsaw Pact. Although this was going much further than Gomulka had gone in Poland, Russian troops at first withdrew from Hungary. Some of the hated security police who had supported the Stalinist regime were captured by the insurgents and hanged. But on 4 November, while their government was among the most vociferous in condemning Anglo-French intervention in Egypt, the Russian army invaded Hungary. Budapest was bombed, resistance was crushed with tanks, Nagy was deposed and later killed, 140,000 refugees left the country (11,000 coming to Britain) and an authoritarian regime, strictly subservient to Russia, was re-established. The United Nations General Assembly called on Russia to withdraw, without effect. Nor did the U.S.A., where Eisenhower had just been elected President for a second term, with Nixon as Vice-President, feel able to intervene.

In spite of Hungary and Suez, the Olympic Games were held, as planned, early in December, at Melbourne in Australia. Russia won 37 gold medals, the U.S.A. 32 and Britain 6.

Though the Suez crisis was over, tankers could still not get through the Canal, which Nasser had blocked during the fighting. Petrol rationing was therefore introduced in Great Britain on 17 December. And on Christmas Eve, at Port Said, the Egyptians blew up the statue of De Lesseps, architect of the Suez Canal.

When the Canal was clear again (1957. It was blocked again later and was again reopened, in 1975) the Egyptians proved perfectly capable of running it, so the Suez Canal Company did not get it back. They did, however, receive an indemnity of eighty million dollars and, like Anglo-Iranian, have since sought business elsewhere and prospered exceedingly under a new name – The Suez Company. It has been said that nationalisation was the best thing that ever happened to them.

1957

BRITONS ENTERED 1957 with bitter memories of Suez and Hungary, with a sick Prime Minister and rationed petrol. The Canal was still blocked by sunken shipping.

In Antarctica the *Magga Dan,* carrying Dr. Fuchs and the main team of the British Trans-Antarctic Expedition through the Weddell Sea, was blocked by ice. This expedition was part of the British contribution to 'International Geophysical Year', which was to run from July 1957 to December 1958. Sir Edmund Hillary, the Everest climber, was to start for the Pole from Ross Bay at the other side of the continent. Nevertheless, on 10 January Harold Macmillan became Prime Minister and later in the year he made the speech which contained the sentence: 'You've never had it so good.' This was to be the year in which John Stephen, aged 21, who had begun his career in menswear as an assistant at the Glasgow Co-op, rented a shop in Carnaby Street, which was then a backwater off Regent Street, where the only retail trader was a tobacconist. Those who had 'never had it so good', particularly the young, bought what they soon learned to call 'way-out gear', while music played. By the mid sixties Carnaby Street was lined with clothes shops. Its name and its merchandise were known all over the world. King's Road, Chelsea, was to become almost as famous. There John Michael opened his first shop in 1957. In 1957 too Hardy Amies, a top designer of women's clothes, entered the field of menswear with a range of ties and shirts. Men now advanced shoulder to shoulder with women in the clothing revolution. But it was the Teds who had led the way. They had been the first to show that fashion, instead of working its way down from the very rich, could work its way up (see p. 70).

Young non-professional people, who had begun to earn but had not yet started to raise families, were pre-eminently the class who had 'never had it so good'. It was worth producing records which they would want to play and clothes which they would want to wear.

January was exceptionally mild in Britain and in Antarctica. The *Magga Dan* got through. The new Forth Road Bridge was approved. France agreed with Italy on a tunnel under Mont Blanc (completed 1965).

Meanwhile petrol rationing kept private cars off the roads. More people made use of London buses and the buses ran more regularly in the less crowded streets.

February produced the warmest night for that month since weather records began in 1870. The Queen paid a State Visit to Portugal. The Duke of Edinburgh joined her there, on his return from a tour of the Commonwealth. Back in London he was made a Prince of the United Kingdom (and has therefore been referred to since then as 'Prince Philip'). At the end of the month a Scandinavian airliner made the first commercial flight over the North Pole to Japan in $31\frac{1}{4}$ hours.

In March the Treaty of Rome, signed by Belgium, the Netherlands, Luxembourg, France, Italy and West Germany established, as from 1 January 1958, the Common Market (officially known as the European Economic Community or EEC), an organisation for reducing tariffs between its members. The six countries were already co-operating successfully in ECSC (the European Coal and Steel Community, created in 1951).

Britain at this stage was not interested in joining the Common Market. It was thought that such a step would involve too great a surrender of independence and would adversely affect trade within the Commonwealth.

Ghana (until then the British colony of the Gold Coast) became independent on 6 March. At the end of World War II there were only four African states which could be called independent and of these only one, Liberia, was black. The others were Ethiopia, Egypt (with treaty obligations to Britain) and South Africa (still however within the Commonwealth). Libya had become independent in 1951, Morocco, Tunisia and the Sudan in 1956. None of these was black. The Sudan includes black Africans in the south, but power is in the hands of the Arab peoples who live in the north. Ethiopia too is not ruled by the black element in its population. Thus, at the beginning of 1957, the only independent *black* government on the continent of Africa was in Liberia.

6 March 1957 was therefore not only a day of tremendous rejoicing in Ghana itself; other black African colonies were encouraged and everybody, black or white, throughout the world, who wanted to see black people attain a more responsible position, was full of new hope. Ghana's first Prime Minister, Dr. Kwame Nkrumah, was active in the Pan-African movement and it seemed that the day might come when Ghanaians would lead a crusade to free the blacks of South Africa from the bondage imposed by apartheid.

What happened in fact was that Nkrumah soon abandoned democracy, declared Ghana a republic and set up a one-party dictatorship with himself as President, bearing the title 'Osagyefo' (Redeemer). Adulation was obligatory, opposition was crushed. Nkrumah's dictatorship could not even plead the justification of efficiency. He was more interested in prestige building than in the basic needs of the country. He also liked to visit the heads of other states, and in 1966, while he was on one of these trips, heading for Peking, the army seized power in Ghana and Nkrumah did not return. He took refuge in the former French colony of Guinea, Ghana's neighbour, and remained there.

The Greek press either ignored the granting of independence to Ghana, or treated it with contempt; for the struggle in Cyprus between Grivas's terrorist organisation EOKA and the Governor, Field Marshal Sir John Harding, was at this stage not about independence but about 'Enosis', the right of Cyprus to unite with Greece ('Enosis' is the Greek word for 'union'). The next British move was to bring Archbishop Makarios back from the Seychelles. He was not allowed to return to Cyprus but arrived, during April, at one of the big hotels in Athens.

At home the Homicide Act was passed in March. It limited the death penalty to five categories of 'capital murder' only. Previously all murderers had been sentenced to death. R. A. Butler (later Lord Butler) was Home Secretary at the time. Those who have studied the question at the Home Office and elsewhere are firmly convinced that the reintroduction of the death penalty would not reduce the number of murders. As a writer in the *Observer* put it:

> The human way in which we treat our most wicked and intractable citizens will indicate the worth of our society.

While belief in hanging as a deterrent was waning, belief in the Bomb as a deterrent persisted. In fact 'the deterrent' was now the accepted name for the Bomb, among those in favour of it. Britain's first hydrogen bomb was exploded near Christmas Island, in the Pacific, on 15 May.

On 1 May the police were empowered to remove parked vehicles. The tow-away lorry and the policeman with his bunch of car keys is now an accepted figure in crowded streets. When these powers were first granted motoring was restricted owing to shortage of petrol. But only two weeks later (14 May) petrol rationing ended. The government had agreed to use the Suez Canal again on Nasser's terms and the first British ship had passed through it in April.

What happened before the Canal existed? The clipper *Cutty Sark* was now being prepared at Greenwich for opening to the public in June. She would remind them of the alternative route to the East which she had sailed – round the Cape. Oil men, exasperated by the uncertainty of the Suez Canal, needed no reminder. They were planning to stick to the Cape route and build much bigger tankers.

The first Test match of the series between England and the West Indies was played at Birmingham in June and provided some remarkable cricket. In a partnership during England's second innings, May and Cowdrey put on 411 runs. The match ended in a draw. Plenty of West Indians were among the spectators. They had begun to come over to Britain soon after the war, in search of jobs. As Commonwealth citizens they were free to do this and the Midlands was one of the areas where work was to be found. Since 1954 much larger numbers had been arriving and there were about 90,000 West Indians in Britain by the autumn of 1957.

Housing, or rather lack of it, was to be one of the causes of hostility to immigrants. Housing is a problem every government promises to tackle. Bevan had struggled with it, Macmillan had struggled with it. By now it was considered politically safe to modify the Rent Control Acts which had kept rents at pre-war levels for those lucky enough to be living in rent-controlled accommodation. The necessary Bill became law on 6 June. Plenty of people who could well afford to pay more, did so. Others moved. Old people, who could not afford higher rent and were past the age when it is easy to start a new life in a cheaper district, were the hardest hit. Meanwhile the housing shortage continued and the poorest, among whom were many immigrants who had left home precisely because they were poor, suffered most.

Towards the end of June the Medical Research Council published a report on tobacco smoking and lung cancer. This made it clear that the chances of being attacked by lung cancer were greater if you smoked cigarettes. Further proof of the connection between cigarette smoking and lung cancer was provided by the report *Smoking and Health* in 1962, which led to the tobacco companies agreeing to restrict television advertising. Quite a number of older people have now taken to pipes or cigars or dropped smoking altogether. But the young and the improvident are not much impressed by the promise of sufferings – however acute – to be endured in middle age. A report published in 1970 stated that 42% of boys aged 16 smoked on average nearly 30 cigarettes a week. Among girls of the same age 30% smoked 25 a week.

In June too *Mayflower II*, a Devon-built replica of the original *Mayflower*, sailed safely across the Atlantic. But in September the *Pamir*, a

German sailing ship used for training, sank in a hurricane. Only six of her crew survived. Eighty were drowned.

On 1 July International Geophysical ·Year began, but as that month is part of the Antarctic midwinter, there was little to report. The main party of the Commonwealth Antarctic expedition under Dr. Fuchs did not start their 2,000-mile trek to the South Pole until late in November and their arrival belongs to the news of 1958.

Malaya became independent on 1 September. Churchill's choice of General Templer had proved wise. He had created among the Malays, the Chinese and the Tamils, who share the country, conditions which made independence possible.

When British schoolchildren returned to school for the autumn term they found that two school television services were available. Independent Television had started theirs in the summer. The BBC now joined them. Education authorities, on the other hand, were in no hurry to buy sets.

When nine negro schoolchildren attempted to enrol at Little Rock High School, Arkansas, U.S.A., they were prevented by Governor Faubus until protected by Federal troops. 'Integration' (admission of coloured children to all public schools) had been made compulsory by law, but in the South, where whites had excluded coloured people from many schools, the law needed tough enforcement.

Britain was beginning to realise that she had a colour problem, but it had not yet led to the passing of laws. Another ill-used minority was in the public eye – homosexuals. Any sex acts between males rendered them liable to prosecution. The Wolfenden Report (5 September) proposed that no penalties should be imposed for sex acts between consenting adults.

On 1 October the charge for sending an ordinary letter by post was increased to threepence. There was no 'two-tier' system then, but for printed matter and postcards the charge was less. This increase would normally have kept the public growling for a week or two; but after 4 October there was only one great story in every country of the world. The Russians had put a satellite into orbit. They called it 'sputnik'.

The sputnik, a sphere 23 inches in diameter and weighing 180 lb., had been fired by rocket to a height of 500 miles, into an orbit that took it round the world once every ninety-five minutes. This came as a shock to the Americans, who had intended to launch satellites in International Geophysical Year and hoped that they would be the first to do so.

Britain was to have no part in the great space adventure which was just beginning, except as an observer, through the radio telescope at Jodrell Bank. The space explorers club only had two members. But the Bomb club at that time had three. Britain was the third. Should she opt out? Should she stop making hydrogen bombs? There were a number of people who answered 'Yes' to these questions and Aneurin Bevan had been amongst the most influential of them. It had been possible to be Minister of Health or Minister of Housing and oppose the Bomb; but now that Attlee and Morrison had moved on (to the House of Lords) Bevan had hopes of becoming Foreign Secretary, if Labour were to come back into power. At the party conference he therefore made it clear that he was not in favour of unilateral renunciation of the Bomb. Without it, he said, a British Foreign Secretary would go naked into the conference chamber. He had some hard things to say about those who still thought otherwise. *The Times* commented: 'His allies of yesterday felt the lash of his scorn.'

But amazement, not scorn, was the ruling emotion in the autumn of 1957. While the sputnik still circled the earth the Russians, on 3 November (just in time to celebrate the 40th anniversary of the Revolution), sent up another one, weighing half a ton, with a dog, or rather a bitch, on board.

The Russians had underestimated world interest in this poor animal and for a time there was even uncertainty about her name. 'Fluffy', 'Curly' and 'Little Lemon' all appeared in different reports. It was then announced that she was a Husky – 'laika' in Russian – and Laika became the accepted name. The headlines, however, stuck to DOG.

At first it was announced that the dog would be catapulted back to earth. It had travelled a million miles by 5 November and on 6 November its condition was announced as satisfactory. On the 7th, however, Moscow was silent about the dog. And on the 8th a headline read: DOUBTS ABOUT SURVIVAL. Then we had:

11 November DOG'S DEATH DENIED

12 November SATELLITE DOG RIDDLE

and finally

14 November NO INTENTION OF BRINGING DOG BACK

Bulganin was quoted as saying: 'We don't want to make much fuss about a dog.' A Russian professor added: 'I think she is dead.' So the story came to an end, leaving, as one more headline put it:

U.S. SMARTING UNDER THE SATELLITES

What was the matter with America? Her most successful launching in 1957 was a book, *On the Road* by Jack Kerouac (who died aged 47 in 1969). The sort of people who are now called 'hippies' were then known in the

U.S.A. as 'the beat generation' ('beatniks' or 'beats' for short). *On the Road* is the most famous of Kerouac's novels about them. Whatever their merits, they were clearly not the type which would get Americans on to the moon.

In December the Americans tried to launch a satellite and failed. Their interest in NATO revived. President Eisenhower attended a conference in Paris at which it was decided to have nuclear rockets ready in Europe.

In Britain the Bank rate leak enquiry made fascinating reading for those who like to look behind the scenes into the lives of powerful men. (The tribunal reported in January that no leak had occurred.) A small item of news was the discontinuation of the Queen's Bounty for triplets, which had been established in 1849 – an extravagance perhaps but one would like to have known just why December 1957 was chosen as the month in which the axe should fall. An item which no one could ignore was the railway accident at Lewisham in south London in which ninety people lost their lives.

A few days before Christmas the first British airliner went into service over the North Atlantic. She was a Bristol Britannia, which took twelve hours forty minutes to make the outward journey and eight hours forty-six minutes to come back.

On Christmas Day the Queen spoke as usual to the people of the Commonwealth; but this year, for the first time, she was televised.

1958

ON NEW YEAR'S DAY 1958 Sir Edmund Hillary and his party were reported 120 miles from the South Pole. His three farm tractors, drawing five sledges, were pushing slowly ahead through deep sticky snow at a height of 10,900 feet. They had been in low gear for thirteen hours, during which time they had covered thirty-six miles. Fuchs's party, travelling from the other side of Antarctica, were further from the Pole than Hillary.

The two operations had not been planned as a race, but Hillary and his New Zealanders were obviously keen to be the first home. They reached the South Pole, where an American base had been established, on 3 January – the first party to arrive by land since Scott's in 1912. Fuchs's part of the expedition joined them on 20 January. Fuchs then continued his journey to Scott Base, which he reached in March, having travelled across the Antarctic continent. In May he was knighted.

The battle against Mau Mau continued in Kenya; in April a state of emergency was declared in Aden; and although a truce was supposed to have existed in Cyprus since the return of Makarios to Athens in March 1957, the island was still in a state of unrest. Sir Hugh Foot, the Governor, on a visit to London in January 1958, said that everyone was 'fed up with the situation and anxious to get out of it.' Even Malta G.C. (the island had been awarded the George Cross for its heroic resistance in World War II) was seething with discontent. The scaling down of British naval activity in the Mediterranean had resulted in massive unemployment among Maltese shipyard workers. The Labour leader, Mr. Mintoff, appeared to want Malta to leave the Commonwealth. In April his government resigned, the opposing party refused to form a government, and the Constitution (granted in 1947) was suspended. Malta finally became independent in 1964.

How were other Commonwealth islands faring? Chinese interest in certain offshore islands later in the year set people wondering when they would claim Hong Kong. But Hong Kong was a useful outlet for Chinese trade with the rest of the world, and there was no powerful movement on the island for reunion with the mainland, comparable with the movement in Cyprus for reunion with Greece. So the Chinese left Hong Kong alone.

In the South Atlantic the Falkland Islands were claimed by Argentina and when, as a result of International Geophysical Year, a treaty was concluded (December 1959) between·Argentina, Australia, Belgium, Chile, France, Japan, New Zealand, Norway, South Africa, the United Kingdom, the U.S.A. and the U.S.S.R., establishing peaceful scientific co-operation in Antarctica and suspending all territorial claims, it only applied south of latitude 60°, thus excluding the Falklands.

The West Indian islands showed no desire to unite with the U.S.A. They wanted independence. But this did not lead to large-scale violence. Emigration to Britain siphoned off many of the most active citizens. The Federation of the West Indies was established in January 1958 and in April Princess Margaret opened its first parliament. However, Jamaica, by far the biggest member of the Federation, left it in 1961 and became independent the following year. Others followed – Trinidad and Tobago in 1962, Barbados in 1966, and in the latter year federation was finally abandoned.

Federation and defederation were not confined to the British Commonwealth. Four Arab countries tried the experiment of uniting in pairs. The republics of Egypt and Syria formed the United Arab Republic (1 February), but Syria left it in 1961. The kingdoms of Jordan and Iraq formed the Arab Federation (14 February), but Iraq ceased to be a kingdom in July, when King Faisal II was assassinated. In August 1958 the Arab Federation was suspended.

The Great Powers were passing through one of those periods when tension was less acute. The Soviet leaders, Voroshilov (the President), Khrushchev and Bulganin had at New Year wished the Queen 'a tranquil, peaceful life and fruitful co-operation'. But the great questions still remained unanswered – How could agreement be reached about the Bomb? How could its development be restricted? Could its use not be renounced altogether?

In 1957 Bertrand Russell had written an open letter about the Bomb to President Eisenhower and Premier Khrushchev. Khrushchev replied, Eisenhower did not; but two months later John Foster Dulles, the American Secretary of State, replied for him. Russell comments: 'The righteously adamantine surface of Mr. Dulles's mind as shown in his letter filled me with greater foreboding than did the fulminations and, sometimes, contradictions of Mr. Khrushchev.' These forebodings, followed by a discussion with Kingsley Martin, editor of the *New Statesman and Nation*, led to the launching of CND (Campaign for Nuclear Disarmament) with Russell as President and Canon Collins of St. Paul's as Chairman, at a public meeting on 17 February 1958. The CND was not united on methods. Those who believed in marching as well as meeting and who were prepared to consider civil disobedience, formed the Direct Action Committee, which organised the first Aldermaston March at Easter 1958. The March started on Good Friday from the gates of the Atomic Weapons Research Establishment at Aldermaston, Berkshire, and ended on Easter Monday in Trafalgar Square. It was orderly and in subsequent years became an accepted CND activity. But Russell writes: 'Later the marches seemed to be degenerating into something of a yearly picnic. Though individual marchers were as sincere as ever in their endeavours and as admirable, the march was quite ineffective in achieving their aim, which was to call serious attention to and spread the movement.' The last of these four-day Aldermaston marches (apart from a revival in 1968) was in 1962.

Protest and terrorism make news. It is easy to forget the practical achievements of Britain during these years. In March construction of the London-Birmingham motorway (the M1) was begun. (It was to be our first *long-distance* motorway. Work was already in progress on our first motorway, the Preston by-pass, which was opened in December.)

In May the atomic reactor at Dounreay began to produce power. In June the extended Gatwick airport was opened.

Life peers and peeresses are perhaps not classifiable as 'practical achievements', but they were a very good idea and the first of them were named in July. After ten years they numbered more than 150 and enriched the House of Lords with talented people from many different fields.

August's achievement was the Litter Act, which imposed a maximum penalty of £10 for leaving litter in a public place; but it was not practical, since we still have a great deal of litter and very few prosecutions.

In September, it was announced that three million permanent houses had been built since the War. In November, work started on the Forth Road Bridge. Throughout the country new schools had been built, and built well.

Building supplies had been concentrated on schools, houses and factories. But since the lifting of controls other types of building had become possible. Supermarkets, for instance, had begun. There were already 175. By 1961 there were 572; by 1967, 2,800.

Green Shield Trading Stamps began in 1958; the idea had been brought from Chicago by Richard Tompkins and made him a millionaire. And 1958 was the first year in which a million cars were produced in Britain.

During a miserable summer, including the wettest June since 1912, many cricket clubs lost money. But rain was not enough to save cinema audiences, which had more than halved since 1946. In that year there were 31.4 million attendances a week; now, largely because of TV, this figure had dropped to 14.5 million. Nevertheless, stupendously successful films could still be made, as was shown by *.The Bridge over the River Kwai* (directed by David Lean, leading actor Alec Guinness) which was released in 1958. Some theatre shows too were doing very well. *The Mousetrap* was in its seventh year; *The Boy Friend* and *Salad Days* were in their fifth.

Dr. Zhivago, by the Russian Pasternak, was the novel of the year, and many people derived a great deal of pleasure from Iris Murdoch's novel *The Bell.* For medium-serious teenagers the Career Novel had arrived to sugar with fiction the hard facts about jobs. Girls could be found buried in *Sue Takes up Physiotherapy* or *Molly Qualifies as a Librarian,* while their brothers were reading *The Lamberts choose the Law.*

For those who went abroad that summer, the Brussels international exhibition was a major attraction. It was dominated by the enormous 'atomium', a construction of nine aluminium spheres almost as high as St. Paul's Cathedral (at that time, though now no longer, the most prominent feature on the London skyline). Escalators inside the connecting tubes could accommodate 3,000 visitors per hour. For those impatient to reach the top the ascent could be made by lift in 23 seconds. This, it was claimed, was the fastest vertical trip then obtainable in Europe – 16.4 ft. per second. Twenty-two people could get into the lift at the same time.

It was a good summer for the Belgians. Strife between the Flemish-speaking and the French-speaking parts of the country was less bitter than it has since become, and in a world where empires were dissolving, Belgium still had the Congo. It was said that this was due to the Congolese having been denied secondary, let alone university, education and being therefore free from the evil influence of intellectuals, urging them to revolt. Not many years later events proved this view naïve, but in the summer of 1958, to the more conservative classes in France, Belgium's colonial position appeared enviable.

The French had lost Syria and Lebanon during World War II, they had lost Indo-China after a savage and costly struggle which had ended in 1954. Since then they had been faced with a rebellion in Algeria, which was the oldest of their African possessions (acquired in 1830) and had a large French population.

Frenchmen who had themselves struggled heroically against the occupying Germans, now found themselves in the position of their late oppressors. They were regarded as an occupying power by the Muslim F.L.N. (National Liberation Front) whose underground campaign was met with the same methods as the German Gestapo (secret police) had used in wartime France. It was hard for a French soldier not to be either sickened or brutalised.

The French at home were split. By May 1958 it looked as if their latest government (the 26th since September 1944, in what was called the Fourth Republic) would come to terms with the Algerian nationalists. French settlers and army leaders in Algeria, together with their supporters at home, now turned to General de Gaulle, who had been in retirement since 1946. They wanted a strong government, and they got it. The Fifth Republic, based on a new constitution which gave de Gaulle wide powers, was established on 4 October 1958.

From 8 January 1959 de Gaulle was President and his moderately authoritarian rule continued in France for ten years. He surprised many people often. One of his earliest surprises was for the French Algerian settlers. Th y had hoped that their strong man would crush the Muslim Algerian nationalists. In fact, as we shall see, he lost very little time in offering Algeria an opportunity for self-determination.

De Gaulle, though a General, in fact *prevented* power being seized by the army. But military dictatorships were established in three countries during the year – Iraq (after the murder of King Feisal in July), Pakistan (October) and Sudan (November). In Pakistan General Ayub Khan made himself President (and a Field Marshal) and declared martial law. After 1962 the constitution gave him dictatorial powers. But this move away from democracy did not take Pakistan out of the Commonwealth. Ayub resigned after a period of disorder in 1969 and was succeeded by General Yahya Khan.

The military revolution in Iraq was immediately followed by attempted revolutions in Lebanon and Jordan, the governments of which invited the Americans and the British respectively to help them. Both sent troops and there was considerable anxiety that this might result in the Cold War becoming a hot war in the Middle East, but the Americans withdrew from the Lebanon in October and the British from Jordan in November. Anxiety had by then shifted to the Far East, where the Chinese government once again appeared to be threatening the American-protected island of Formosa. On 23 August they bombarded Quemoy. As on the last occasion when this had happened (1954), hot war was feared, but after discussions between the Americans and the Chinese the bombardment stopped and there has been no sign since then of an attempt to re-conquer Formosa.

During August the Americans had another failure in space, but scored an undersea success. A rocket, intended to go into orbit round the moon, exploded at 60,000 ft. (a second failed in October, after travelling 71,000 miles from the earth). But the atomic submarine *Nautilus* made a successful voyage beneath the Arctic ice and passed in the course of it under the North Pole.

The wet summer in Britain had been made more depressing for Londoners by a bus strike from 4 May to 21 June. A result of this was that more people became accustomed to using cars, fewer people used buses when they came back on the road and in consequence there was an excuse for a reduction in services. This was carried out in August and again in the autumn.

The worst home news of the summer came from Nottingham. There, on 23 August, whites fought blacks. Bottles were thrown. Knives were out. This was the beginning of the end of unrestricted immigration from the Commonwealth. *The Times* of 27 August carried the headline: NOTTINGHAM M.P.s URGE CURB ON ENTRY OF IMMI-GRANTS, CRITICISE 'OPEN DOOR' POLICY. A Labour member had said that free entry, practicable in the 19th century, was 'completely impossible under modern conditions'. A Conservative had 'believed for some time that there ought to be something in the nature of a quota'.

On 28 October Pope John XXIII was elected (Pius XII had died on 9 October). The new Pope was a big kindly-looking man of 77, the son of a peasant. Much was hoped from him.

Much was hoped from V.S.O. (Voluntary Service Overseas) which this year sent its first 18 volunteers to work in African countries of the British Commonwealth. There were 1,500 volunteers abroad in 1969.

Much too was hoped from UNESCO, whose new building was opened in Paris in November. This building was certainly a fine example of international co-operation. It was designed by a team of architects – Breuer (U.S.), Zehrfuss (France) and Nervi (Italy). Walter Gropius, a distinguished exile from Hitler's Germany, and a pioneer of functional architecture (died 1969), was on the guiding committee. Picasso and Henry Moore contributed large works. It was not far from the Eiffel Tower and gave pleasure to many visitors to Paris, where there had been little new building sce the War.

UNESCO is one way of spreading enlightenment. But there are circumstances in which some people think it has to be fought for. Since November 1956, Fidel Castro and his lieutenant Che (i.e. 'Old man', a friendly form of address) Guevara had been fighting a guerilla campaign to free Cuba from the rule of the dictator Batista. They felt that they were fighting to free minds as well as bodies, against ignorance as well as poverty. They had now reached Havana, the capital of Cuba, just too late for a merry Christmas, but with every prospect of a happy New Year.

1959

THE YEAR 1959 was remembered for its fine summer. The winter in Britain was not unusually cold but the frost was sufficient to crack the new Preston motorway and close it for a month of repairs. M1 was still being built. The Preston by-pass was at that time Britain's only motorway, and a bit of frost put it out of action. The public were not pleased. Later in the year the *fine* weather was blamed for the fact that the first Mini-Minor cars had not been sufficiently tested in rain before appearing on the market. They were made by B.M.C. (the British Motor Corporation, later British Leyland) which had been formed by merging Morris and Austin (1952). When the Mini's initial faults had been corrected it emerged as perhaps the most remarkable British achievement of 1959. The transverse engine and small wheels provided the easy-to-park car which everyone wanted, and the price was low. Incidentally, the car added a new word, or at any rate a new prefix, 'mini-', to the language; and 'mini-' soon bred 'maxi-'.

Alec Issigonis, who designed the Mini, had also designed the Morris Minor; but it was only on the arrival of the Mini that someone had the idea of building up a car designer into a public figure. The name of Alec Issigonis thus became one which Britons learned to be proud of in the 1960's. They also heard of Christopher Cockerell (knighted in 1969) who had been experimenting on how to get boats to travel faster by overcoming wave resistance. His Hovercraft was neither aircraft, ship nor land vehicle, though it could travel over land, ice or water. It rode on a cushion of air, sometimes as high as 6 ft., supplied by a large fan, and made its first test run on water at Cowes in June.

Another name of which more would be heard in the 60's was Cuba. Cuba to most people had meant sugar and cigars and the place where Winston Churchill had had some of his early experiences as a war correspondent. On 1 January 1959, the forces of the right-wing President Batista finally yielded to those of the leftist Fidel Castro, now Prime Minister. Though not at first a communist, Castro found that the U.S.S.R. was the country most ready to help him. Cuba thus became a Russian satellite off the eastern coast of the United States, providing a disturbing example for other Central and South American countries.

On the same day on which Dr. Castro entered Havana, General de Gaulle was installed as the first President of the Fifth Republic of France. How long would this last? Few would have betted on the sixty-eight-year-old general ruling for a decade (till 1969), fewer still on Castro's outlasting him.

Everyone usually agrees that the Swiss are wonderful, but until recently they had a skeleton in the cupboard. Women had no vote in Federal elections. This surprisingly reactionary state of affairs was the subject of a referendum on 1 February 1959. But the proposal to give votes to women in Federal elections was lost (not till 1971 were women allowed to vote). Next day, however, in Virginia, U.S.A., where reaction surprised no one, a shred of light shone through. Schools which had been closed since September 1958 because of white opposition to integration, now re-opened and admitted negro children.

And suddenly there was good news about Cyprus. The terrorist activities of Colonel Grivas and his underground army had been directed against the British and the world had derived a picture of Britain, in order to maintain her military base, holding down a people struggling to be united with their mother country, Greece. 'Enosis' (Unity) had been the aim. The fact that nearly one fifth of the islanders were Turks, whose rights the British were bound to protect, had received less publicity.

Now however the Greeks and Cypriots changed their attitude. 'Enosis' was dropped. An independent Cyprus had become the goal. After a conference in London an agreement was signed on 19 February by the Prime Ministers of Britain, Greece and Turkey, as a result of which Cyprus was to become a republic with a Greek President and a Turkish Vice-President. The House of Representatives was to be 70% Greek and 30% Turkish. These arrangements came into force in 1960. Archbishop Makarios became President and Dr. Kutchuk Vice-President.

Though there were many moves towards independence in 1959, it was the only year between 1956 and 1967 when no British colony was freed. The year's sole declaration of independence was in Tibet; but it was crushed by the Chinese and on 31 March the Dalai Lama took refuge in India.

'Moves towards independence' may seem too mild a term. At the end of February there were riots in Malta dockyard, following the dismissal by the Admiralty of 6,000 workers (a loan was made to the dockyard later in the year). Early in March there were riots in Nyasaland, in protest against that country's inclusion in the Central African Federation. In Kenya the deaths of eleven Mau Mau prisoners (in 1958) were found to have been caused by violence on the part of the guards and although Jomo Kenyatta's term of imprisonment ended in April, he was still restricted in his movements and could not take part in politics. Nevertheless in November the seven-year state of emergency in Kenya ended and arrangements were being made for a constitutional conference in London early in 1960.

1959 looked a likely year for a General Election. The 1955 Parliament would have run four out of its permitted five years, and Macmillan's government was popular. The public was relieved at the Cyprus settlement and found Mr. Heathcoat Amory's budget pretty palatable, when it appeared in April. Income tax was down from 8s. 6d. to 7s. 9d., beer duty by 2d. a pint; there was to be no limit on foreign travel allowances after 1 November. More than this. Macmillan, accompanied by his Foreign Secretary, Selwyn Lloyd, had in the last week of February paid a visit to Moscow. This was a step towards 'the Summit' and a 'Summit meeting' seemed to many people at that time the only way of reaching a settlement with Russia and bringing the 'Cold War' to an end.

Who were the political mountaineers to be? Only the top people of the top nations would do ('top people' was a phrase adopted from a series of posters captioned: 'Top people read *The Times*'). Eisenhower (U.S.A.), Khrushchev (Russia), Macmillan, perhaps de Gaulle, perhaps Adenauer (West Germany). All these heads of government travelled widely during the year without all meeting together; only in December was a date finally agreed for a Summit meeting. It was to be in Paris, on 16 May 1960.

In May 1959 a conference of the Foreign Ministers of Britain, the U.S.A., Russia and France, at Geneva, succeeded in keeping Berlin from again disturbing the peace. One figure, familiar since 1953 at all such gatherings, was absent. John Foster Dulles, Eisenhower's trusted Secretary of State for over six years, had resigned owing to ill health and died on 24 May. The Geneva conference adjourned to enable Ministers to attend his funeral. Would Gromyko go? Did Russia want to be represented at the graveside of the world's leading anti-Communist? Apparently, yes. When politicians and diplomats from all over the world packed Washington Cathedral for the funeral service, Gromyko was there too.

In Britain, during May, the long hot summer had begun. Throughout England and Wales it lasted until October. Male city-dwellers became interested in the light-weight suits which were becoming available in new crease-resisting materials. Perspiring dons filed into the Senate House at Cambridge and abolished the regulation which made Latin or Greek a compulsory subject in the entrance examination (Oxford, a year later, made a similar concession). Perspiring actors opened Bernard Miles's Mermaid Theatre in the hitherto theatreless City of London, with *Rape upon Rape,* an 18th century comedy. This kept the theatre open, in spite of the heat, and the Mermaid has since become almost as much a part of the City scene as the Monument or the Mansion House.

The Queen and the Duke of Edinburgh missed some of the fine summer. They left for Canada in June and on the 26th, together with President Eisenhower, the Queen opened the St. Lawrence Seaway, a system of locks and canals linking navigable stretches of the St. Lawrence in the area where it forms the boundary between Canada and the U.S.A. Meanwhile a new Canadian newspaper tycoon was establishing himself in London. Roy Thomson (now Lord Thomson of Fleet) who had already become known to the public as the man who had said that running the commercial Scottish Television station was 'like having a licence to print money', bought Kemsley Newspapers, including the *Sunday Times,* in July, and the organisation was renamed Thomson Newspapers before the year's end.

All newspapers, however, were not in empires and the *Manchester Guardian* chose mid-August as the moment to drop its allegiance to the north-west. The Manchester label had not prevented the paper becoming known throughout the world during the first half of the twentieth century, but apparently it was felt that simply as the *Guardian* it would fare better in the fiercer competition of the 1960's.

During this sweltering August, coincidence brought into force two Acts of Parliament about sex, one restrictive, the other permissive. The Street Offences Act made soliciting in public places by prostitutes illegal. They disappeared from Piccadilly and Hyde Park, or at any rate had to indicate their calling very unobtrusively. Some of the trade went to 'call girls' who could be booked by telephone. The Obscene Publications Act changed the standard of obscenity in regard to publications. The work as a whole was to be taken into account, and whether it was a work which the public were likely to read. It was not long before the Act's effect was to be tested in the 'Lady Chatterley' case (1960).

Paradoxically, by far the most important event of that hot month was the discovery of a prodigiously rich new source of natural gas, which most people consider as a substance which makes you or your meals hotter, though salesmen will be quick to point out its other uses, including refrigeration. Years of drilling for oil in Holland had produced little result. Now, in the northern province of Groningen, the drill struck gas in a sandstone foundation two miles down, and in the months which followed tests showed that the Dutch were in possession of the second largest supply of natural gas ever discovered.

Natural gas was not new. The oil-producing countries had been wasting enormous quantities of it for years. (What was wasted in one year in Venezuela would have more than covered Britain's needs for the same period.) The U.S. and Russia have long made use of it. But until recently there has been no economic means of transporting natural gas. A solution was on the way in 1959. If you freeze natural gas, it becomes not solid but liquid. The first experimental crossing of the Atlantic with a cargo of liquefied gas was made in February 1959 and in October 1964 three specially constructed tankers began to make regular trips carrying liquefied gas from Algeria to France and Britain. Meanwhile however the Groningen discovery made long-distance transport of natural gas seem much less important. The hope now was that there might be enormous supplies under the North Sea.

This hope was realised. Drilling for gas in the North Sea is difficult and dangerous. The first drilling platform, B.P.'s *Sea Gem*, which made the first discovery, collapsed during a storm and others have had to be withdrawn owing to damage sustained in heavy weather. But plenty of gas has been found by the oil companies. They bring the gas ashore, and the British Gas Council distribute it.

Nuclear power will play an increasingly important part in the supply of energy. Meanwhile oil is the great rival of coal and this was already clear by the late 1950's. During its first ten years the National Coal Board had had to struggle to maintain supplies. Coal even had to be imported. But in 1957 demand for coal began to fall off and by the end of 1959 36 million tons remained unsold.

The record-breaking fine weather continued through September 1959; but for politicians in Britain this was not to be a holiday month. The General Election was to take place on 8 October. For the Conservatives it was essential to remind voters that, in Mr. Macmillan's words, they had never had it so good. 'Don't let Labour ruin it' was their message.

The space race made more interesting reading. In May two U.S. monkeys had been fired to a height of 300 miles and returned safely; in September a Soviet rocket hit the moon, and on 4 October another encircled it, transmitting photographs of the other side, which nobody had yet seen.

But on 8 October in Britain the other side was unlucky. The Conservatives not only won their third election running but once more increased their majority. No party had ever before won three general elections in succession with an increased majority each time. The figures were now:

Conservatives	365 (including the Speaker)
Labour	258
Liberal	6

The Conservatives thus had a majority of 100 over the other two parties combined. The Liberals fought 217 constituencies to win their six seats. The Communists (18 candidates), the Scottish and Welsh Nationalists, and the Sinn Feiners won no seats.

The *Daily Worker* (3d.) blamed Gaitskell's 'right wing policy' for Labour's failure:

> The fight for peace was surrendered to the Tories. Macmillan was able to pose as the champion of the Summit and of understanding with the Soviet Union.
>
> Labour did not reply by exposing Tory policy on West German rearmament, NATO, the Cold War, the arms race and the insane policy of using the H-bomb first. On all these issues the Labour leaders declared their agreement with the Tories.
>
> Labour's policy boiled down to the claim that they would run capitalism better than the capitalists. It is not surprising that many electors should draw the conclusion that in that case the job could well be left to the party of the capitalists – the Tories.

Was more nationalisation, was unilateral abandonment of nuclear weapons a policy which would win the next election? These were to be the big questions within the Labour party in the early '60's. The party's Constitution, dating from 1918, insisted in its fourth clause, that the party should aim at 'the common ownership of the means of production' (i.e. nationalisation). Gaitskell had given much thought during the 1950's to the question how far nationalisation should go and at the Labour Conference at Blackpool in November 1959 he suggested that Clause 4 should be revised. He said: '. . . we regard public ownership not as an end in itself, but as a means – and not necessarily the only or most important one – to certain ends, such as full employment, greater equality and higher productivity.' But the Blackpool Conference was against revision.

The 1960 Conference, at Scarborough, passed a resolution which went some way towards supporting Gaitskell's views on Clause 4, but this time successfully attacked his anti-unilateral disarmament policy and his support of NATO. It was not until the Blackpool Conference in October 1961 that he had the party's full support.

A Londoner looking round towards the end of the year, which was also the end of the decade, saw that two new features were likely to multiply – parking meters and high rise buildings. Meters had come to Britain in 1958. They first appeared in Mayfair and were now to be introduced in St. Marylebone and a number of cities outside London. St. Marylebone also had the new high Castrol building. A mile to the west was Cecil Elston's group of high and low office blocks in Eastbourne Terrace, Paddington. The Carlton Tower Hotel was being built in Kensington. Thorn House had risen not far from Trafalgar Square. And in November planning permission had been granted for 'Centre Point', the tall office block at the junction of Oxford Street and Charing Cross Road. It is now finished. The developer has embellished a previously drab corner with fountains, and the windows of the block are an interesting shape. But it is still empty (1976). And what will be the effect on traffic when it is let and full of office workers? That same November (1959) the opening of the M1 slashed the driving time between London and Birmingham, but once vehicles had left the motorway at either end they were liable to find themselves bumper to bumper again.

The West End theatre was enriched during 1959 by Arnold Wesker's *Roots* from the Royal Court (where the English Stage Company's productions, begun in 1955, had been attracting attention since *Look Back in Anger* in 1956) and by two plays from Joan Littlewood's Theatre Workshop, a company formed in 1945 and based for some years after 1953 at Stratford in East London – Shelagh Delaney's *A Taste of Honey* and Brendan Behan's *The Hostage. The Boy Friend* had been taken off after 2,084 performances; but *Salad Days* and *My Fair Lady* soldiered on into the sixties, and *The Mousetrap* into the seventies. The Guards outside Buckingham Palace did not. The manners of tourists in London had deteriorated. They could not leave the Guards alone. So the red coats and bearskins withdrew to a more sheltered position within the gates, and there they have stayed.

Cider with Rosie by Laurie Lee, looked back, but not in anger, at life in a Cotswold village during the early 1920's. The blurb said that it put on record 'the England we've traded for the petrol engine.' It became a best-seller.

In the Vatican John XXIII also looked back without anger and wrote in *Journal of a Soul* (Chapman, 1964):

> The experience of this first year gives me light and strength in my efforts to straighten, to reform, and tactfully and patiently to make improvements in everything.

Above all, I am grateful to the Lord for the temperament he has given me, which preserves me from anxieties and tiresome perplexities. I feel I am under obedience in all things and I have noticed that this disposition, in great things and in small, gives me, unworthy as I am, a strength of daring simplicity, so wholly evangelical in its nature, that it demands and obtains universal respect and edifies many.

1960

EARLY IN 1960 two Harolds visited South Africa – Macmillan, the Prime Minister, and Nicolson, the writer and former diplomat. Nicolson wrote home to his son:

> I cannot describe to you the horrors of Apartheid. I asked an Englishman how one pronounced the word, and he said 'Apart' – pause – 'hate'. And by God, hate it is! It is far, far worse than anything I had supposed.

He found all seats on the esplanade at Durban marked 'For Whites only'. At the Cape Town Post Office whites and negroes were served at separate counters. And these of course were comparatively small examples of the indignity and terror to which black people and whites who supported them were subjected. An example of the extreme ferocity with which South African police could act was soon to be provided.

Meanwhile Macmillan arrived in South Africa in the course of a tour which took him also to Ghana, Nigeria and the Federation of Rhodesia and Nyasaland. (The Federation still existed, uneasily.) He was invited to address the South African Parliament and did so on 3 February. He said that it was impossible for Britain to support South Africa in her racial policies. It was the British government's aim 'not only to raise the material standards of life, but to create a society which respects the rights of individuals – a society in which men are given the opportunity to grow to their full stature, and that must, in our view, include the opportunity to have an increasing share in political power and responsibility.' After saying something of developments in other parts of Africa he ended with the words: 'The wind of change is blowing through the continent.'

The members of the South African Parliament listened in silence and some did not even applaud at the end. But the world was listening and 'The wind of change is blowing . . .' became the second of Macmillan's pronouncements to be long remembered and often quoted. (The first was 'You have never had it so good'.) His speech was one of a number of factors which give 1960, as we look back upon it, the flavour of an African year. Another was the large number of colonies (18), mostly French but including Nigeria and the Congo, which became independent, bringing the number of U.N. African members to 26, with territories covering about half the continent. Another was the struggle which followed Congolese independence. Another was Sharpeville.

The story of Sharpeville is short. South African blacks have to be in possession of passes and carry them at all times. In March there was a demonstration at Sharpeville against the pass laws, during which, as *The Times* put it, 'by mischance, miscalculation, fear or fanaticism,' the police fired into the crowd of Africans and sixty-seven were killed. Of course cries of horror and indignation were raised all over the world; but although Macmillan had dissociated Britain from South Africa's racial policies, neither he nor the Labour government which succeeded him considered it practical to take any action against that country, except for the ban, imposed by Labour, on the sale to it of certain armaments. As for the recently independent African states, they are still too poor, or too absorbed by internal quarrels, to become crusaders. It was not until the 1970's, after Mozambique and Angola had rid themselves of Portuguese rule, that the wind of change showed signs of rising.

Most of the new African states started peacefully and with democratic governments; some of them in time became 'one party' states – i.e. dictatorships of a sort; in Nigeria there was a long and bloody civil war, but it broke out some years after independence. Only in the Congo was independence immediately succeeded by chaos.

The Belgian Congo became the Congolese Republic (do not confuse it with the formerly French 'Republic of the Congo') on 30 June 1960. How far were the Belgians to blame for what followed? From their first ruthless acquisition of the territory in the 19th century they had not been enlightened colonisers and since they provided no higher education for the Congolese, it is clear that they were not intent on guiding them towards independence. When they granted it, they did so in a hurry (there had been riots in 1959). Having granted it, they were anxious not to lose the wealth of the Katanga mines.

There had been elections earlier in the year as a result of which Joseph Kasavubu and Patrice Lumumba took over as President and Prime Minister respectively on 30 June. They had in fact been political rivals and were unlikely to form a successful coalition. No system of training Congolese officers for the army had been introduced. All the officers were Belgians. There they all were still. To the Africans in the ranks this did not look like independence. On 6 July they mutinied. The consequent disorder gave Moise Tshombe, soon to be elected President of Katanga, the excuse to declare Katanga independent, and the Belgians the excuse to send troops to Katanga for the protection of the mines. On 15 July United Nations troops arrived to preserve order in the Congo as a whole, but not at that time to oppose the secession of Katanga, which Mr. Hammarskjöld, U.N. Secretary-General, ruled was an internal matter in which the U.N. should not become involved. Lumumba therefore asked Russia for help and received some. This brought the Cold War into the Congo. The Russians declared that Mr. Hammarskjöld and the U.N., with U.S. backing, were unwilling to oust the Belgians from Katanga.

Strong action by the U.N. could quickly have restored order in the Congo; but with the Great Powers split, the country remained in a state of civil war and U.N. troops were there until 1964.

Lumumba was an early casualty. By September Congolese N.C.O.'s had been turned into officers and the most forceful of them, Colonel Mobutu, declared that the army would now take charge. Lumumba was arrested and, in February 1961, murdered. He is likely to be remembered as a patriot. Tshombe, who served the Belgians, is not. He ended as a prisoner in Algeria after his plane had been hi-jacked, and he died there in 1969.

Should Hammarskjöld have acted differently? Unfortunately the man who brought the U.N. into the Congo war did not survive to write a book about it. He was killed when his plane crashed in the Congo, early in the morning of 18 September 1961, while he was on his way to a meeting with Tshombe. Sabotage was suspected, but has not been proved.

Hammarskjöld, so far as is known, did not keep a diary, in the usual sense of the word – i.e. records, descriptions and comments entered day by day. He did however write down from time to time his reflexions upon the nature of life, together with favourite quotations, poems written by himself and passages of self-examination. This manuscript, written in Swedish under a title whose literal translation is 'Signposts', was called *Markings* when published in English (1964). Readers derived from it the picture of a lonely, acutely conscientious and intensely hard-working man. Born of a distinguished Swedish family in 1905, he had devoted himself to public service and never married. He was appointed Secretary-General of the United Nations in 1953 and reappointed in 1958. He once jokingly described his position as 'like being a secular Pope'. He believed in God and wished that more people did so. 'On the bookshelf of life,' he wrote, 'God is a useful work of reference, always at hand but seldom consulted.' And he did not regard himself as infallible. One of the last entries in *Markings* (8 June 1961) is his poem, which ends:

Sleepless questions
In the small hours:
Have I done right?
Why did I act
Just as I did?
Over and over again
The same steps,
The same words:
Never the answer.

The answer provided in *Murderous Angels* (1969) by Conor Cruise O'Brien, an Irishman who played a prominent part in the United Nations Congo operation, is as follows:

> In part, the very violence of the Soviet polemic, and the staleness of its rhetoric, defeated its purpose. Hammarskjöld had earned too much respect ... for anyone outside the Communist organisations to acquiesce easily in the Soviet Government's labelling of him as 'a sorry lackey of the colonialists.' Yet it is clear ... that there was much more force in the Soviet contention about Hammarskjöld's role in relation to Lumumba, than appeared at the time ... United Nations officials, covered by Hammarskjöld's authority, helped to secure Lumumba's political destruction, and deliberately refused to prevent the arrest which led to his physical destruction.

It was not until 1965 that a government established control over the whole country, including Katanga. The name of the capital was then changed from Leopoldville to Kinshasa. The name Congolese Republic was changed to Republic of Zaire in 1971. The Republic took over the Katanga copper mines and the Belgian company which had owned them was compensated.

Africa in 1960 provided grounds both for hope and for despair. Half of it was free, but the free half did not include any of the areas where there was a strong white population. South Africa remained a police state; the Federation of Rhodesia and Nyasaland, since it included the intransigent white-dominated Dominion of Southern Rhodesia, was clearly not going to work (though the Kariba Dam opened by the Queen Mother on 17 May provided both Zambia and Rhodesia with electric power). In Kenya there had been some improvement; the state of emergency was over; but in January-February a constitutional conference, held in London, was boycotted by African elected members and made no progress. In July there were signs of renewed Mau Mau activity, and the Governor replied by ordering the detention of subversive elements.

The struggle was fiercest in Algeria, where the French army in January rebelled against de Gaulle's moderate policy and its leaders were forced to surrender. On the other hand de Gaulle was not prepared to accept the demands of the Algerian National Liberation Front (F.L.N.) and their representatives came home without a settlement, after a conference in France in July. This however was the moment which de Gaulle chose to grant independence to the French West and Central African colonies. Wisely. Of the neighbouring British colonies, Ghana was not only independent but had just become a republic (with Nkrumah as President) and was about to contribute troops to the U.N. force in the Congo; Nigeria's independence was due in a few months and Sierra Leone's in 1961.

At the granting of Nigerian independence (1 October), Princess Alexandra officiated. The Queen's own children were still too young. The youngest, Prince Andrew, had been born on 17 February, four days after de Gaulle had exploded France's first atomic bomb in the Sahara.

By exploding his bomb de Gaulle, as it were, put his thumb to his enormous nose and extended the fingers towards nuclear disarmers the world over. But the 3-power conference on ending nuclear weapons tests, which had begun in 1958, continued at Geneva throughout the year and in Britain the Campaign for Nuclear Disarmament (C.N.D.) with its atom bomb badge, attracted more and more support, particularly from young people, though one of its leaders, Canon Collins of St. Paul's, was in his fifties and Bertrand Russell, the President, was eighty-eight.

On the afternoon of Easter Monday, C.N.D. supporters, many of whom had marched from Aldermaston, packed Trafalgar Square. There was no disorder. A choir sang:

> Men and women, stand together,
> Do not heed the men of war,
> Make your mind up now or never,
> Ban the bomb for evermore.

The band carried a placard:

DON'T BOMB THE BAN, BAN THE BOMB

Speakers included Labour M.P.s from the left of the party, Trade Union leaders, the Bishop of Southwark and the Moderator of the Church of Scotland.

Bertrand Russell however felt that even a demonstration of this size would not influence the government. It certainly did not prevent Macmillan announcing in November that a base for American Polaris submarines, equipped with nuclear weapons, was to be established in Holy Loch, on the Clyde. Nor did it sufficiently impress Gaitskell, the Leader of the Opposition, who, when an A.E.U. motion for unilateral disarmament was passed at the Labour Party Conference in October, announced that he would 'fight, fight and fight again' to get Conference to adopt a different policy.

Russell therefore wanted to develop civil disobedience, which Gandhi had used as a weapon in the struggle for Indian independence. His proposals met with strong opposition within C.N.D. and in October he resigned the Presidency, though continuing to support the campaign. His civil disobedience movement came to be called the Committee of 100. Its activities began early in 1961.

One hope which the Trafalgar Square crowd shared with the government and with the majority of the Labour Party, was that the Summit meeting, which was due to take place in Paris on 16 May, would succeed. Some optimism was justified. It was only slightly clouded when on 5 May Khrushchev announced that a U.S. plane had been shot down over Russian territory.

What most people were thinking about on 5 May was Princess Margaret's wedding on 6 May to a distinguished professional photographer, Mr. Anthony Armstrong-Jones (Lord Snowdon 1961). Princess Margaret was popular and thought to be keener on the arts than on sport, which was on the whole unusual in the Royal Family, although her grandmother, Queen Mary, had been an enthusiastic collector of antiques. There had also been sympathy for her a few years previously when she had decided not to marry a man whom she had known for some time, because he had been divorced. So on 6 May crowds gathered along the wedding route, radios and television sets were turned on, the bells of Westminster Abbey rang out and a vast public was able to enjoy the event.

Next day however attention returned to the Summit. The U.S. admitted that a very high-flying aircraft, a Lockheed U-2, had been engaged on an intelligence mission over Russia. What next? In the atmosphere created by such an incident, could any positive result be hoped for from the conference? Only if one side made a gesture of unusual magnanimity. Neither did. Khrushchev came to Paris and demanded an apology for the U-2 incident. Eisenhower came and refused to accept what he called Khrushchev's 'ultimatum'. Next day it was announced that the conference had broken down.

The pilot of the U-2, Gary Powers, had been captured by the Russians, who later exchanged him for their agent Colonel Abel, whom the Americans had caught. But there was no question of an exchange for the Nazi, Adolph Eichmann. A group of Israelis had tracked him down in Argentina and kidnapped him. They announced on 23 May that he was in their hands and would be tried as the man responsible for the deaths of thousands of Jews during World War II.

In this crowded month the European Free Trade Area came quietly into existence. An organisation never likely to hit the headlines, it was a union of seven countries who were not members of the Common Market – Austria, Denmark, Norway, Portugal, Sweden, Switzerland and the United Kingdom.

'A BUSY MONTH' headlined *London Transport Magazine* (2d.), looking back on the events of May. For London Transport the handling of crowds bound for the F.A. cup final and Princess Margaret's wedding procession presented the month's major challenges, and they were also busy instructing staff in the operation of the new 'all-silver' trains which were to come into service later in the year on the Central Line. For the wedding, London Transport's gardening superintendent, an official whose work is little known to travellers in central London, canopied the entrance to Tower Hill station with flowers. The honeymoon was to start in the royal yacht *Britannia,* which was lying off Tower Pier. Study of the sepia photographs accompanying the story show all women's skirts reaching below the knee. Numerous members of London Transport staff are shown, but none are black. (In pictures taken over a year later in October 1961, there are still only a very few black faces to be found.)

There is nothing in these London Transport magazines about passengers' manners, but letters in the press about this time show that the custom of men giving up seats to women and the young to the old was still much more general than it has since become. However, 'Eighteen-year-old, Handsworth, Birmingham' complained to the *Daily Mirror* about the manners of the older generation:

> I stood up on a crowded bus to let a woman have my seat and she said: 'I should think so too.' I sat down again and told her that if that was her attitude she could stand.

It is doubtful if readers of the *Daily Mirror* paid much attention to 'Eighteen-year-old, Handsworth', on that day. It was 7 July and the front page carried only one photograph – a speaker vigorously gesticulating with his clenched fist, his tie flapping loose over the lapel of his jacket. The headline read:

NYE BEVAN DEAD

He had died in the afternoon of 6 July after a six-month illness, aged 62. His greatest achievement had been the National Health Service, but members of all parties, however bitterly he had opposed them, honoured him most for being the kind of man he was. 'A great and courageous fighter,' said Macmillan. To Gaitskell he was '. . . a warm-hearted friend, above all a man of force and power, a man of strong and independent mind, a man of compelling and magnetic personality, a man who counted – a big man.'

Who would succeed Bevan as Deputy Leader of the Labour Party in Parliament? George Brown was elected, but this did not make him next in succession for the leadership. It was Harold Wilson who challenged Gaitskell's position as leader later in the year, but he only received 81 votes against Gaitskell's 166.

In August the state of emergency in Malaya, declared in 1948, came to an end.

While United Nations troops established themselves in Katanga and Russian propaganda writers abused the west, Russian athletes came out well ahead in the Olympic Games at Rome, with 43 gold medals against 34 won by the United States. Britain won two, the 50 km walk and the 200 m women's breast stroke. And in spite of the state of the world, 84 countries took part.

It was the right year for a bonanza in Rome. An Italian film, Fellini's *La Dolce Vita*, had won first prize at Cannes. It showed that there was plenty of money about, much of it ill spent, despite the restraining influence of Pope John. Italian post-war industrial expansion was at its height. AGIP, the Italian state petrol enterprise brought to life by Enrico Mattei, was now a serious competitor against the long-established firms. The south however did not yet share in this prosperity and Danilo Dolci from his home in the sultry little Sicilian town of Partinico waged a lonely campaign against poverty, ignorance and graft.

Sicily at least had no race problem. In the southern states of the U.S.A. they had all Sicily's problems – poverty, ignorance, graft – and race discrimination as well. A breeding ground for violence? You might have thought so; but in 1960 it was still non-violence that was tried. At Nashville, negro students sat firmly at lunch counters where café proprietors refused to serve them. They did not reply to insults or return blows. When arrested and convicted for 'disorderly conduct' they refused to pay fines and went to prison. These were the first 'sit-ins'. They worked. The lunch counter proprietors found themselves forced to abandon segregation in their cafés.

In November the Americans elected a new President, John F. Kennedy. He was a 'Democrat'. Eisenhower had been a 'Republican' and, incidentally, the oldest President in American history. The two parties do not correspond to radicals and conservatives, but on the whole the more progressive and humane voters are likely to be among the Democrats. As well as being a Democrat, Kennedy was comparatively young (born 1917) with a young wife and family. He appealed to people's hearts. The word 'charisma' hitherto confined to the vocabulary of sociologists, came into general use during the sixties to describe this quality. Kennedy, de Gaulle, Khrushchev – all had 'charisma'.

However, charisma is not enough. You need a policy. In December 1960, just before Kennedy took office, Ho Chi Minh announced in Hanoi that he was setting up a National Front for the Liberation of South Vietnam. This was the origin of the 'Vietcong', which means 'Vietnamese Communists'. Since the departure of the French, the South Vietnamese had been receiving equipment and training from the Americans. This aid Kennedy, advised by Dean Rusk, whom he had made his Secretary of State, ordered to be increased in 1962.

In 1960 the first report of a working laser (Light Amplification by the Stimulated Emission of Radiation) was made. A laser produces a light beam which does not diffuse (unlike the beam produced by an electric lamp). It has many uses and possibilities (e.g. in ultra-accurate measurement, communications, machining of metals, and surgery).

British Rail now said goodbye to the manufacture of steam locomotives. The last was named in March, and by 1968 all had been withdrawn from service.

Goodbye to battleships too; H.M.S. *Vanguard*, the Navy's last, came out of commission in June. Goodbye to four newspapers – *The Bulletin* (a Glasgow illustrated daily), the *News Chronicle* and the *Star* (the Liberal London morning and evening dailies), and the *Sunday Graphic*. ('The death of the *News Chronicle* is the biggest journalistic tragedy for many years,' wrote James Cameron.) Goodbye too to the long respected and war-hallowed Nine o'clock News on radio. Too many people were viewing TV at that hour (the BBC's new Television Centre had opened in June). We got 'Ten o'clock' instead, and comment as well as news (a former journalist, Hugh Greene, had become Director-General in

January, the first member of the BBC staff ever to reach that position).
Goodbye finally to the farthing, which was withdrawn on 31 December
(the halfpenny survived until 31 July 1969).

Welcome, however, to the Royal Shakespeare Company, who from
December made the Aldwych Theatre their London home. And welcome
to *Lady Chatterley's Lover,* the novel written by D. H. Lawrence and first
printed in the twenties, which Penguin Books were able to publish in
November, after a six-day trial. Under the Obscene Publications Act
1959, the book was no longer, in the opinion of the jury, obscene. Sales
were brisk. One Cambridge bookshop sold 700 copies before 11.00 a.m. on
publication day.

On the first day of the Lady Chatterley trial the prosecution had referred with distaste to certain words which occurred frequently in the book
and 'no doubt would be said to be "good old-fashioned Anglo-Saxon
four-letter words" '. The expression 'four-letter word' became current
thereafter and the words themselves began to be considered occasionally
permissible in print during the 60's. The *Penguin English Dictionary*
(1965) broke new ground by including two of the commonest. Africa was
not the only part of the world where the wind of change was beginning to
blow.

1961

'WE WERE ABSOLUTELY swooped on. At that time I could not imagine what it was. I thought they were Teddy boys.'

'Teddy boys' was by this time becoming an old-fashioned expression. Anyway, 'they' in the above quotation were not Teddy boys but Special Branch officers. The lines are from Miss Gee's description of her arrest, on 7 January 1961, in Waterloo Bridge Road, together with Houghton and Lonsdale. Miss Gee, a civil servant employed by the Royal Navy at the Portland centre for counter-submarine research, and Houghton, another civil servant, who had formerly been in the navy, had obtained highly secret material which was in Miss Gee's shopping bag at the time of her arrest. She was just handing the bag to Lonsdale, a Russian agent.

The arrest of Gee, Houghton and Lonsdale was followed, shortly afterwards, by that of Peter and Helen Kroger, whose bungalow in Ruislip was found to contain vast quantities of incriminating material, including a short wave radio, a seventy-five-foot long aerial in the attic, and cypher packs. Concealed in a Ronson lighter were schedules for broadcasts to Moscow. These five agents, known as the Portland Spy Ring, were tried in March and found guilty. There was some surprise at the length of Lonsdale's sentence – twenty-five years. The Krogers got twenty, Houghton and Gee fifteen.

The press and the public were highly critical of the security arrangements, or lack of them, which had made it possible for Houghton and Gee to behave as they had done. Another shock however was on the way. Two months after the Portland trial, in May, George Blake, a Foreign Office official, was convicted after a trial to which the press and the public were not admitted, of offences against the Official Secrets Act. These were found deserving of forty-two years' imprisonment. Rebecca West, whose book *The Meaning of Treason* deals with all the cases of treachery and spying which created sensation after sensation in the post-war years, states that Blake's was the longest term of imprisonment imposed in a British court for a hundred and fifty years. Blake however escaped from Wormwood Scrubs in October 1966. Lonsdale was exchanged in 1964 for Greville Wynne, a British businessman convicted of spying by Russia

The Krogers were exchanged in 1969 for Gerald Brooke who had been convicted in Russia for distributing subversive literature (p. 170).

Murder worries people more than spying. The Criminal Justice Act 1957 had introduced a category of offences called 'non-capital murders' which were not punishable with death. As a result people were once more asking: 'Are we being too soft with criminals?' There had been 144 cases of murder in England and Wales during 1960, with an alarming increase towards the end of the year. Seven murderers had been hanged. Should there be more hanging or none? In the first issue of the *Sunday Telegraph*, a new 'quality' Sunday paper which appeared on 5 February, the leading article stated:

> The feeling grows that there would be something to be said either for making hanging the standard punishment for murder, as it used to be, or for abolishing the death sentence altogether, but that there is nothing to be said for the law as it stands at present . . . Sooner or later Mr. Butler the Home Secretary must make up his mind.

A Criminal Justice Bill was in fact before Parliament during 1960-61 and became law in July 1961. It was concerned with Young Offenders and lowered the minimum age for a Borstal sentence from 16 to 15. What it did not do, in spite of pressure from some M.P.s and members of the House of Lords, including the Lord Chief Justice, was to reintroduce corporal punishment. The cane up to the age of 17 and the birch for those between 17 and 21 had been proposed.

When so many 'popular' papers had died, it was a bold move to add a third to the two 'quality' Sunday papers. How did the *Sunday Telegraph*, the first new national Sunday paper for 40 years, hope to attract readers? Not by a novel format. It looked very like the *Daily Telegraph*, even preserving the gothic lettering of the title. The best way to answer this question is to look through the paper. In doing so one can get an idea of what educated citizens were interested in towards the beginning of 1961 and what opinions might have appealed to some of them.

The leader writer had not sought to make up the minds of his readers on hanging. He had urged Mr. Butler to make up his. A neighbouring article however took a definite line about the Congo. Under the headline 'Time for retreat from the Congo quicksands', Mr. Hammarskjöld was urged to withdraw the U.N. force from the Congo and allow it to work out its own destiny as one state or several, perhaps with the aid of the Belgians. (The article included a plea for the release of Lumumba, but, as already related, Lumumba was murdered a few days later.)

In a section of short paragraphs headed 'To the point', the British motor industry received a rap over the knuckles. There had been a decline in North American sales during 1960, partly owing to the fact that 'compact' cars manufactured in the U.S. made Americans less dependent on Europe for small cars. Nevertheless, the *Sunday Telegraph* pointed out, while British North American sales declined, Volkswagen sales in the same area were up 38%.

Another paragraph expressed the hope that the all-African jazz opera *King Kong*, which had been permitted in South Africa and was about to visit Britain, would be as popular as the Springboks had been. The Springboks were a white South African rugby side who had just completed a tour with only one defeat. Feelings about apartheid, in spite of Sharpeville, did not yet run high enough to lead to demonstrations. *King Kong* played for some months and in 1964 the South African revue *Wait a Minim* had a successful run. It included some moderately anti-apartheid jokes. Supporters of apartheid claimed that this showed the leniency with which the apartheid policy was operated.

Still on the centre page of the new paper, we find Mr. Enoch Powell referred to as 'dedicated', 'a Tory Minister of first-class intellectual calibre and of proved integrity.' But Powell had not yet taken up the subject of immigration. He was Minister of Health and as such had had the unpopular task of increasing charges in the Health Service (1 February). Dentures and spectacles would cost more and the prescription charge would go up from 1s. to 2s.

Finally an article entitled 'They grow up so quickly' reminded readers that the age of puberty among girls and to some extent among boys was becoming lower, that fifty years ago menstruation had begun on average at the age of 15½, but that now it was probably 13½ or even 13, and that in spite of this, young people were staying longer at school. 'No one really knows how big a problem this presents,' the writer went on. There was certainly a movement during the 60's towards treating the upper forms of schools less as children and more as adults, and the movement towards 'student power' has spread to sixth forms.

On 6 March the price of most morning papers went up from 2½d. to 3d. (which was also to be the price of an ordinary letter after 10 October. There was no 'two tier' system as yet). The *Guardian* went from 3d. to 4d. and *The Times* from 4d. to 5d. *Daily Mirror* readers had the consolation of hearing that the paper would now be produced from, to quote Cecil King who was then the proprietor, 'the finest newspaper building in the world, a Taj Mahal'. Opposite Gamages (now demolished) in High Holborn it impressed the passer-by as the *Express* and *Telegraph* buildings had impressed him in Fleet Street during the thirties. Anyway, whatever your chosen newspaper, it was going to contain plenty of interest during March and April 1961.

On 8 March the first Polaris submarine arrived at Holy Loch. On the 13th the trial of the Portland Spy Ring began. Next day the *New English Bible* was published. This translation by a group of scholars was soon a best-seller, but a controversial one. Many people who had learned from childhood to enjoy the resounding prose of the Authorised Version (1611) did not take kindly to the new translation, 'this Hansard type of Bible' as Harold Nicolson called it.

On 15 March, Dr. Beeching, a director of Imperial Chemical Industries, was appointed Chairman of the British Transport Commission. (From 1962, when the British Transport Commission ceased to exist, he was Chairman of the British Railways Board.) His salary of £24,000 attracted attention. (The Prime Minister, for instance, was earning £10,000.) It proved however to be hard-earned money. Beeching's job was to streamline British Railways (now called British Rail). This necessitated the closure of numerous uneconomic branch lines. Those who used the lines and failed, as most did, to get Beeching's proposals rescinded, remembered him only as the source of their woes, while those who benefited by improved services resulting from the Beeching economies quickly forgot him.

The day after Beeching's appointment (16 March) South Africa withdrew from the Commonwealth, becoming a republic on 31 May.

April too was eventful. On the 11th the trial of Adolf Eichmann began in Jerusalem. He was accused of killing millions of Jews in gas chambers, by torture, by starvation and by persecution; of deporting Slovenes and Poles; and of exterminating thousands of gypsies. The trial went on until August and made a new generation aware of what Hitler's policies had meant twenty years before. The verdict, not announced until 11 December, was: Guilty. Eichmann was sentenced to death, appealed, had his appeal rejected and was hanged on 31 May 1962.

On 12 April 1961, a Soviet cosmonaut called Yuri Gagarin was wakened at 5.30 a.m. and learned that he had been chosen out of a final short list of three to be the first spaceman. He was launched into an elliptical orbit with a greatest height of 187 miles and came down safely about an hour and three-quarters later, having circled once round the earth. (Four months later the second Russian astronaut, Major Titov, was up for 24 hours and went round the earth seventeen times.) The whole world saluted

Gagarin and later in the year he made a successful tour of Western countries. His smile won many hearts, but we shall not see him again. He died in an aircraft crash in 1968.

While honouring Gagarin personally the Americans could not but regret that the Russians had once again got in, or rather got up, first. There had been the Sputnik, then the dog, and now it was a man. In May the U.S. did succeed in getting Commander Alan Shepard 116 miles high, but he did not orbit the earth and was back in 15 minutes. Captain Virgil Grissom made a similar ascent in July. These were remarkable achievements, only marred by the fact that Russia seemed at that time to be doing better.

The U.S. had no need to be ashamed of her astronauts. When, later in the year, Harold Nicolson wrote of America as 'still blushing scarlet . . .' he was not referring to the space programme, but to the 'Bay of Pigs' incident. April was only President Kennedy's fourth month in office. Had it been his fourteenth, things might have happened differently. Nevertheless he bore the ultimate responsibility for the American support given to this abortive invasion of Cuba on 17 April. 1,500 Cuban exiles, opponents of the Castro regime, organised by the U.S. Central Intelligence Agency, set out from Florida and landed in an area called the Bay of Pigs, where Castro's forces were ready and took 1,200 prisoners. Castro proposed to exchange these men for 500 bulldozers or tractors but the negotiations broke down. In the end food and medicines were sent, and the prisoners were released by Christmas 1962.

De Gaulle also had a revolt to deal with. On 19 April units of the French Army once more seized power in Algiers. Once more de Gaulle asserted himself and General Challe, who had led the revolt, surrendered on 25 April. Talks with the F.L.N. again broke down, on 18 July.

It is important to remember that France is separated only by the Mediterranean from Algiers, which was then a part of France, just as Northern Ireland is part of the United Kingdom. But the peculiar danger of France's position was that a military dictator who seized power in Algeria would not have expected to stop there. He would have wanted to rule the mother country as well and, in view of the unsettled state of France since the end of the war, might have had a reasonable chance of succeeding.

De Gaulle formally assumed dictatorial powers in times of crisis, and at other times he was in a position to get a good deal of his own way. But he was not a dictator. Creative artists, for instance, were not stifled. In this anxious year French films once more regained the lead in the international festivals. *Last Year at Marienbad* and *Hiroshima mon Amour* won prizes at Venice and Cannes respectively.

Hollywood this year showed signs of recovery from Joe McCarthy's throttling paws and produced *Spartacus,* which was the story of a slave revolt in the last century of the Roman Republic. It was made quite clear that the 'goodies' were Spartacus and the slaves, a fair number of whom were crucified in the final sequences, while the 'baddies' were Crassus (played by Sir Laurence Olivier) and the Roman army. Any decent guy seeing the film identified himself with Spartacus; the suggestion that Mao Tse-tung or Castro might be analogous figures in modern times would have shocked him profoundly, as would any analogy between Spartacus's followers and the blacks in the southern states, whom this year 'Freedom Riders', mostly white students from the North, were helping by non-violent methods in the struggle against segregation, often being beaten up by southern whites in return.

However, it was people *not* being shocked which was to be one of the leading characteristics of the sixties. In Britain *Lady Chatterley* had let in the four-letter words and now Mr. Butler had let in bingo and betting shops. These had been made legal by the Betting and Gaming Act (1960). One of the objects of the Act was to legalise betting for people outside the class who ran accounts with bookmakers. Such people had previously had to place their bets with men who collected them at street corners – an illegal practice, but hard for the police to prevent. The first betting shops were allowed and appeared on 1 May 1961, since when they have multiplied.

The 'gaming' sections of the Act gave many cinemas (languishing under the competition of television) a new lease of life as bingo halls, where the housewife could 'have her flutter' (the expression had been used in official circles before, when Premium Bonds were introduced), but the extent to which this and other forms of gaming would develop, making London into one of the leading gambling centres of the world, was pro-bably not foreseen.

To sex shocks and gambling shocks were now added the shocks of near-blasphemy and near-libel, in what Kenneth Tynan (born in Birmingham in 1927 and by this time a drama and film critic of repute on both sides of the Atlantic) called 'the funniest revue that London has seen since the Allies dropped the bomb on Hiroshima'. This was *Beyond the Fringe,* an expanded and revised version of a revue which had been one of the unofficial or 'fringe' items in the previous summer's Edinburgh Festi-val. It had opened at the Fortune Theatre (one of London's smallest, next door to Drury Lane) in May.

There had been comic clergymen on the stage for centuries, but they were usually portrayed off duty. A parody of a sermon was new. So, in a

West End theatre, was a parody of the Prime Minister. Hanging had usually been dealt with sentimentally on the stage. Now we had a monologue in which a condemned man kept asking himself the obvious yet normally avoided question: Will it hurt? More shocking perhaps than any of this to the over-forties was a 'send-up' (an expression which about this time began to be used instead of 'parody') of the conventional heroic account of the Battle of Britain. (In *Oh! What a Lovely War* – see 1963 – contempt was concentrated on the generals and the audience was allowed to retain the traditional admiration for the men in the trenches.)

The cast of *Beyond the Fringe* were, in alphabetical order (as described in *Tynan Left and Right*):

> Alan Bennett 'with his kindly, puzzled face, he resembled a plain-clothes friar, badly in need of a tonsure.'
> Peter Cook 'like a well-kept minor poet, all lanky elegance.'
> Jonathan Miller 'gawky and angular, with large feet and carrot coloured hair. "I'm not a Jew," he explains. "I'm Jew-*ish*. I don't go the whole hog." '
> Dudley Moore 'a smaller young man with twinkling dark eyes and twinkling dark hair.'

Beyond the Fringe did not start a tradition of satirical revue, nor did *That Was The Week That Was,* by which late Saturday evening viewers of BBC Television were first delighted in November 1962. But Peter Cook's *Private Eye,* first published on 25 October 1961, was still entertaining many and infuriating a few in the seventies. Up to a point public men like to be made fun of and the most famous are the subject of cartoons almost every day. But when *Private Eye*'s columnist Lunchtime O'Booze wrote about them, they did not always see the joke.

There is a census in the first year of every decade (except that none was held in 1941). Householders had filled in forms during April and by midsummer the first figures were published. We learned that there were rather more than $52\frac{1}{2}$ m of us in the United Kingdom – an increase of about $2\frac{1}{2}$ m over 1951.

There we were, $52\frac{1}{2}$ m. Ought we to enter the EEC ('Common Market')? Gaitskell said: 'No'. The government had finally decided: 'Yes'. Would the EEC members have us? The government now opened negotiations. They wanted a form of membership which would provide for the interests of both Commonwealth countries and of members of EFTA and also for the interests of British agriculture. This sounded quite a tall order, but in fact it was de Gaulle and not the impossibility of arriving at satisfactory terms of membership which kept us out. Nobody would have predicted then that by the end of the 1960's we would still be knocking at the door.

Only after de Gaulle had died and been succeeded by Pompidou did Britain at last gain admission to the Common Market (Jan. 1973). Opposition then came from this side of the Channel where many Labour and some Conservative M.P.'s were anxious to pull us out again, or at least to renegotiate the terms of entry.

In the late summer and autumn Yuri Gagarin's engaging smile was forgotten (he had been with us in July) and the Cold War was back. On 13 August the East Germans stopped the hitherto easy movement between the two halves of the city and erected barriers which were soon replaced by a wall. The excuse given for this was the shortage of manpower in East Germany (the German Democratic Republic). 103,000 people had arrived in West Berlin from the East during the first half of 1961. During early August the number mounted to 2,000 and then 3,000 a day.

On 1 September the Russians made their first nuclear test since 1958 and exploded a bomb of over 50 megatons. The U.S. resumed tests with an underground explosion on 15 September.

On 17 September an anti-nuclear demonstration held without permission in Trafalgar Square resulted in 1,000 arrests. Bertrand Russell had meanwhile served a prison sentence – two months commuted to one week, in view of his failing health – he was 88 – for inciting the public to civil disobedience. The Committee of 100 had started their activities in February with a Trafalgar Square meeting, a march down Whitehall and a sit-down of about 5,000 outside the Ministry of Defence. This was orderly and the sitters went home at 6.00 p.m. But an attempt on 9 December to penetrate the Wethersfield air base led to several of the Committee of 100 receiving sentences of 18 months.

The Cold War was meanwhile in evidence in the Congo, where the efforts of United Nations troops against Katanga were being made without Russian support and where Hammarskjöld met his death on 18 September (p. 118). In October he was awarded a Nobel Peace Prize and on 3 November U Thant (b. 1909), a Burmese who had been a headmaster before the war, Director of Broadcasting after it and from 1953-7 Burma's permanent representative to the United Nations, was unanimously elected acting Secretary-General. His appointment was confirmed in November 1962.

In addition to the Congo problem U Thant now had to deal with Goa, the small Portuguese colony on the west coast of India which the Indian government had been claiming since independence. On 11 December Mr. Nehru used a phrase which Hitler had been fond of and announced that India's 'patience was exhausted'. Indian troops invaded on the 18th, there were few casualties on either side and the Portuguese surrendered next day. U Thant could not prevent this and in fact Portugal's failure to grant independence to her two African colonies made protests against Indian 'aggression' in Goa sound hollow.

Goa was not the only small place which sent people to their atlases during the autumn of 1961. In October an erupting volcano devastated the island of Tristan da Cunha, a lonely British dependency in the South Atlantic. The whole population of 260 was brought to Britain in November, and in January 1962 they were housed at Calshot, Hants. Jobs were found for most of the able-bodied. During the year however it was found that the island would be habitable again and the exiles voted to return. This they did in 1963, though some came back to Britain again in 1966.

At the end of October most people learned with surprise that, in spite of the denunciation of Stalin in 1956, his body still lay beside Lenin's in the revered mausoleum beside the Kremlin. Streets, cities, whole regions, still bore his name. News now came from Russia that all this was to be put right and that the body had been moved.

From 1 November, Scouts were allowed to wear long trousers, one of a number of changes in their uniforms and those of the Girl Guides, which were designed to bring them up to date. The long trousers came just in time to help Scouts to withstand the rigours of one of the coldest Christmases of the century. Housewives, however, were more in need of help to withstand the rigours of the pre-Christmas shopping spree (advertising expenditure had been bigger than ever during the year – £490m, compared with £453m in 1960). The far-sighted were already subscribing to *Which?*, the organ of the Consumers' Association. The C.A. had started work in 1956 and *Which?* first appeared in 1957. In 1963 the government recognised the importance of the consumer movement by setting up the Consumer Council, but this body was disbanded in 1970, as an economy measure, just as it had become established and respected.

For Tanganyika, still full of the joys of independence gained on 9 December, it was a happy Christmas. In addition to freedom the country had gained the distinction of having harboured the earliest human remains yet known. These had been discovered during the year by Dr. L. S. B. Leakey in the Olduvai Gorge and had been declared, after testing by the recently developed potassium-argon dating process, to be 1¼m years old. (The potassium-argon method is useful for determining ages greater than a million years. For ages measured in thousands and tens of thousands the longer established radio-active carbon method is employed.) The remains were those of an 11-year-old child and parts of an adult. The child had been murdered by a blow on the head.

Tanganyika became a republic in December 1962, with Julius Nyerere as President. Zanzibar became independent in December 1963 and in April 1964 the two countries united to form the state of Tanzania.

Further north, at Christmas 1961, Kenya was not yet free, and Jomo Kenyatta, though out of prison since August, was still restricted under the Emergency Regulations.

For members of the Commonwealth who wanted to move to Britain, the prospects were not good. The Commonwealth Immigrants Bill had been published in November. The Labour Party at that time opposed the restriction of immigration from the Commonwealth, but in April 1962 the Bill became law. It introduced a system of admission by employment vouchers issued by the Ministry of Labour.

On 21 December, the first American soldier (known at that time as an 'adviser') was killed in Vietnam.

1962

ON 15 JANUARY 1962 the daily weather reports were broadcast for the first time with temperatures in centigrade as well as fahrenheit. That year, however, after the cold Christmas, temperatures were not exceptionally low. The French struggle in Algiers, rather than the weather, made the front page news, though what was still referred to as 'the Bomb' was never far off. On 29 January the 3-power conference on nuclear weapons tests, which had opened in October 1958, collapsed. A month later the British exploded a nuclear device underground in Nevada (U.S.A.).

On Sunday 4 February readers of the *Sunday Times* were offered relief from the grimmer aspects of world news in a 'Colour Section'. 'Authorised delivery charge 3d. per month' read the small print. There had been some argument about problems of distributing this 40-page magazine together with the other Sunday papers. It was the first of the colour supplements (later called 'magazines') which were to accustom readers to brilliant colour photography and give young photographers their chance during the 60's. The centre spread of this first number was devoted to Mary Quant clothes. She and her husband had opened Bazaar, a Chelsea dress shop, in 1955; they had now started mass-production. 'The success of their second wholesale collection,' read the caption, 'will spread the Bazaar Look past Chelsea and Knightsbridge into the hitherto more conservative provinces.' The photographer was David Bailey, then in his early twenties and at the beginning of a spectacular career, which had begun when he taught himself photography as a hobby while doing his National Service with the R.A.F. in Malaya.

On 20 February Col. John Glenn orbited the earth three times in the U.S. spacecraft *Friendship VII*. The arrival in Vietnam during the same month of the first U.S. Special Forces attracted much less interest. There were fewer than 1,000 Americans in Vietnam at that time and they were said to be acting only as advisers. The Special Forces, all parachutists, in their green berets, were later built up as the heroes of the war. John Wayne directed and starred in a film about them, which reached Britain in August 1968. Much of their activity is secret. In 1969, when their commander was charged with the murder of a Vietnamese, the public expected to learn more of what was going on. But the charge was dropped.

Although on 19 March the civil war in Algeria, which had begun in November 1954, officially came to an end, the O.A.S. (Organisation de l'armée secrète), an ultra-right-wing body founded in 1961 by General Salan with the object of keeping Algeria French, did not observe the cease-fire for some months. General Salan was arrested in April and on 23 May was found guilty on five capital charges, but the Military Tribunal which tried him would not impose the death penalty. When the sentence 'criminal detention for life' was announced, defending lawyers sang the Marseillaise and spectators shrieked 'Algérie Française!'

Next day interest shifted to the U.S.A., where Carpenter took off to orbit the earth three times; and in Britain, at the end of the week, on Friday 25 May, the new Coventry Cathedral was consecrated in the presence of the Queen.

Coventry had been heavily bombed on the night of 14 November 1940 and the German attack had been concentrated on the centre of the city. The Cathedral, except for the tower, was gutted. It had not been one of the great English cathedrals; in fact it had only become a cathedral in 1918; but it had been a noble 14th-15th century parish church and after the raid the Provost said: 'We will rebuild.'

Rebuild? Did this mean restore the Gothic ruins, as the French and the Belgians have done after two World Wars, and as we did in the case of the Gothic-revival House of Commons? Or did it mean build a cathedral of twentieth century design? In that case, what was 'twentieth century design'? Something traditional, or something fresh? Anyway, why build a cathedral at all in a country increasingly pagan and desperately short of houses and schools? Answers to these questions had to be found.

No time was lost in making a start. Late in 1944 Sir Giles Gilbert Scott, architect of the modern-Gothic Anglican cathedral in Liverpool, produced a design, which was not accepted. In 1947 it was decided to hold a competition. At first one of the conditions was that the new Cathedral should be in the Gothic style, but when instructions were finally prepared for the competitors (any architect in the British Commonwealth or the Republic of Ireland was eligible) the condition about Gothic style had been dropped. The winner, announced in Festival of Britain Year (1951), was one of the Festival of Britain architects, Basil Spence, then in his forties.

In the post-war years a licence was necessary before any building work might be undertaken. This was to ensure that scarce materials and labour were used in the main for housing, for schools, and for factories likely to help the export drive. It was not till May 1954, only a few months before the licensing system was dropped for good, that a licence for the new Coventry Cathedral was granted and work could start on the execution of Spence's highly original design, which at that time had numerous critics, including the Coventry City Council. Spence writes: '. . . many people had got into the habit of saying "that concrete monstrosity" without knowing much about the design or indeed caring very much.'

The 'concrete monstrosity' (it is in fact of stone) which the Queen saw consecrated in 1962, turned out to be one of the great churches of the world. Spence's instructions had been that the building should seize on the truths of the Christian faith 'and thrust them upon the man who comes in from the street.' This he did, aided by the greatest artists of the day – Graham Sutherland, who designed the huge tapestry above the altar; Jacob Epstein, whose St. Michael grows triumphantly from the eastern wall; John Piper, whose stained glass colours the baptistry; John Hutton, who engraved the glass of the great west screen; and many others.

The keynote of the opening celebrations was reconciliation. The West Germans had contributed to the new Cathedral and a West German, Dietrich Fischer-Dieskau, sang in the performance of Benjamin Britten's *War Requiem* in the Cathedral on 30 May. A Russian soprano, however, withdrew and the Archbishop of Moscow, who had promised to preach at a lunchtime service, later declined. A Czech organist, who was to have given a lunch-time recital, gave illness as his excuse for staying at home. But the Russians sent a gift of books to the library of the Cathedral's International Centre and an icon came from Stalingrad.

There were three government representatives at the consecration of Coventry Cathedral. One was Profumo, the War Minister, who was to become known to the whole world in the following year. He was apparently giving satisfaction at this time because, when Macmillan decided to reconstruct his cabinet on 13 July and ministers' heads rolled, in what the *Daily Mail* called 'the biggest wave of political executions in peacetime history', Profumo's remained on his shoulders. The list of seven dismissed cabinet ministers began with the name of Selwyn Lloyd, Chancellor of the Exchequer, who was replaced by Reginald Maudling, then aged 45. Selwyn Lloyd had not succeeded in establishing a wages policy. Maudling, it was thought, would do better, and would supply the vigour and sense of purpose necessary to bring success to the Conservatives in the next election. At the foot of the list of new appointments appeared a name, which, like Profumo's, was as yet little known – Enoch Powell. Aged 50, he was already Minister of Health; but he was now to be a member of the Cabinet. The Commonwealth Immigration Act came into force that month, but Powell still had not gained a reputation for holding exceptionally strong views on racial questions.

Algeria too was soon to be engaged in cabinet-making – for the first time. On 3 July France had handed over power. On 26 September Ben Bella was elected by the Algerian National Assembly as Algeria's first Prime Minister. The war for independence had been bloody and destructive, but had not prevented the development of oil and natural gas. Oil had first been struck in 1955 and the new government now enjoyed profits from a thriving industry.

In East Africa Uganda gained independence during October. A year later a republic (within the British Commonwealth) was declared and the Kabaka of Buganda became the first President.

On 6 August there were independence celebrations on the other side of the Atlantic, in Jamaica. Here independence had not been preceded by years of violence, but there had been a great disappointment. The Federation of the West Indies, set up in January 1958, had come to an end in May 1962. By federating it had been hoped that the ten British West Indian colonies would achieve greater economic prosperity and carry more weight politically. Jamaica would have been the largest unit in the Federation, but Jamaica wanted to be on her own. Sir Hugh Foot, a former governor, wrote (*A Start in Freedom,* 1964):

> When I went back to Jamaica for the Independence Celebrations in August 1962, I wandered out of the State Ball to watch the people dancing outside the big new hotel. They were dancing to a new calypso called 'Jump up for Independence'. I have forgotten exactly what the words were but they were a rejoicing to be free from association with the rest of the West Indies – a cheap scoffing at the small islands. I felt suddenly alone and utterly wretched. A fine idea was being ridiculed. A great conception had failed. The forces of isolation had won . . . Jamaica had chosen a selfish second best.

Trinidad and Tobago were declared an independent state on 31 August. The remaining eight colonies formed a new West Indies Federation, with the Federal Capital in Barbados. There was no racial issue, such as disrupted the Central African Federation; but the problems of uniting widely separated islands with poor communications are great. Not everyone would blame Jamaica for the course she took.

Communications, though under-developed in the Caribbean, were making advances of varying degrees of importance in other parts of the world. Telstar, the first communications satellite, was launched from Cape

Canaveral and at 1.0 a.m. on 11 July the first picture was transmitted through it to Britain.

It was fortunate that Telstar had not been launched a week earlier. Satellites already in orbit for other purposes were said to have been affected by the explosion of a United States nuclear device in the Pacific on 8 July, which penetrated to a height of 200 miles and was seen in New Zealand, 4,000 miles away.

In the field of air travel, Britain this year made two contributions and promised a third (Trident's maiden flight in January, VC10's in June, and agreement with the French in November on co-operation over the supersonic Concorde). Should journeys by Hovercraft be included under 'air travel'? In that case Britain made a further contribution in 1962 – the world's first Hovercraft service, which opened in July, between Rhyl in North Wales and Wallasey in Cheshire.

On the railways the picture was gloomy. Rationalisation recommended by Dr. Beeching meant, at this stage, closures of small lines and workshops, with consequent disquiet among passengers and railway employees. But there was good news for Londoners. On Monday 20 August the *Evening Standard* (price 3d.) carried the headline:

NEW VICTORIA TUBE:
IT'S GO AHEAD

Work was to start at once.

Above-ground transport was also being rationalised. The last electric trolley buses left the London streets in May. They had run since the early thirties and were a form of transport which, after an initial jerk, gave a very smooth ride. But the fact that they picked up electricity from overhead cables by means of a 'trolley' made them less manoeuvrable than buses, and the cables involved maintenance costs. Glasgow, where trams had continued, said goodbye to the last of them with some ceremony on Saturday 1 September. There were processions containing trams of every period – single-deckers, double-deckers and one drawn by horses.

For the private motorist B.M.C. announced in August their revolutionary hydrolastic (water and rubber) suspension Morris 1100. More visitors than ever crowded into the Earls Court Motor Show in October, but the state of the motor industry was not happy. Manufacturers had been beset by labour troubles as well as by stiffer American competition. Motorists, though promised 1,000 miles of motorways by 1970, were oppressed by the road congestion of 1962. Parking meters were spreading (they had reached the seafront at Brighton) and although the 70 m.p.h. speed limit had not yet been imposed, a 50 m.p.h. limit had been tried at week-ends. There was talk of making the fitting of seat belts to front seats compulsory.

But there was plenty of petrol. Esso launched an impressive promotion campaign. It took the form of a precise instruction, with an appropriate illustration, on hoardings throughout Britain and Europe. The English version read:

· PUT A TIGER IN YOUR TANK

Tigers are of course untouched by fashion. Advertisers who had to portray men now had to decide whether a sober executive type should still be shown with turn-ups on his trousers. A BOAC advertisement settled for turn-ups and a trouser of about seventeen inch width. On the other hand a chewing gum firm, in a famous series of advertisements which began 'Certainly not . . .' and, only after explaining where chewing would not be appropriate, went on to plug the product, showed at least one respectable character in narrow trousers with no turn-ups.

Men, with or without turn-ups, were not only consuming more petrol. They were drinking more beer. World consumption reached the record level of 9,308 million gallons in 1962.

By mid-March four million people had bought the New English Bible, during its first year of publication. Production of other books was mounting too, in spite of predictions that television would kill reading, and in spite of the fact that the average price of a book had already reached 23s. 3d. 25,079 titles were published in Britain during 1962; 1,179 were children's books (253 more than 1961), 600 were technical books (140 more than in 1961), 2,328 were fiction (29 more than in 1961).

Plenty of beer, plenty of Bibles, plenty of other books, plenty of petrol, increasing electricity supplies (in October the reactor at Dounreay, in Scotland, began to generate electricity for the national grid), but still not plenty of houses and flats. In November at Kidderminster a block of prefabricated flats was opened. It had been completed in seven months, with, it was claimed, a quarter of the labour normally required. A hopeful sign; but looking back today, one can see how few of those hopes were realised.

The Russians put two men in orbit on 12 August and they communicated in space. On 27 August the U.S. sent Mariner II on a voyage to Venus, and contact between Venus and Earth was established on 14 December. On 1 November Russia launched a spacecraft on a seven-month journey to Mars. Science could do all this; but housing and feeding the world remained intractable problems, and science, we now realised, could make horrifying mistakes. A drug called Thalidomide, which had been taken by pregnant women as a remedy against morning sickness, had been found to lead to horrible deformities in their babies. 329 cases were reported in Britain during 1962. In Germany the situation was even worse.

In July China had attacked India's north eastern frontier and fighting went on intermittently until a cease-fire in November. The U.S. sent aid to India. Pakistan was not prepared to help unless India agreed to a plebiscite in Kashmir. While the two greatest nations of Asia thus found themselves on the brink of a war likely to be fought with conventional weapons, Russia and the U.S.A. came nearer to a full-scale nuclear war than they had ever been. This crisis arose over events in Cuba.

Since the Bay of Pigs fiasco in the previous year relations between Cuba and the U.S. had been tense. Castro turned to Russia for arms and got more than he probably expected, since Khrushchev seized the opportunity to install launching sites for ballistic missiles capable of carrying nuclear warheads as far as Washington or the Panama Canal. The Americans had nuclear bases in Turkey and although Kennedy had ordered them to be dismantled some months previously, because they were obsolete, his orders had not been carried out.

Security in Cuba seems to have been remarkably good. The Russians admitted no Cubans to the area where they were building the sites and no spy apparently managed to infiltrate. The Americans only realised what was going on when a U-2 aircraft brought back photographs on which the sites could be identified. These were shown to the President on 16 October. He discussed the problem with his advisers for six days, during which the world knew nothing about the sites. He was not prepared to accept the view that Russian missiles in Cuba were no more outrageous than U.S. missiles in Turkey. The missile sites must go. That was certain. On the other hand, he was not prepared to order immediate bombing of the sites and another invasion of Cuba. He realised that one false step might lead to war and therefore settled for the mildest course which could achieve the desired ends. A blockade of Cuba would be imposed. To make it sound less high-handed it would be called a 'naval quarantine'. Ships suspected of carrying missiles from Russia would be stopped and searched.

The 'quarantine' plan was introduced and the world heard about the missiles for the first time on Monday 22 October. The week which followed was one of intense anxiety. If a Russian ship refused to stop and was fired on by the U.S. Navy, what then? World War III seemed very near that week. While Russian ships sailed on towards Cuba, Adlai Stevenson put the U.S. case at the United Nations and U Thant urged restraint.

Bertrand Russell (who died in 1970) sent telegrams to U Thant, Kennedy, Khrushchev, Macmillan and Gaitskell.

The 'quarantine' went into effect on Wednesday 24 October and for the next three days there was intense anxiety in case the Americans should have to use force. But the Russians ordered a number of ships to turn back and the Americans let through ships which they had no reason to suspect of carrying missiles. It was not until Friday that the first vessel was stopped and boarded. She was not Russian, carried no contraband and was soon allowed to proceed. It was clear that Khrushchev was not pressing his right to take missiles to Cuba.

But the danger of war existed until the missiles already in Cuba were removed. After several messages had been exchanged with Kennedy, Khrushchev finally agreed, on Sunday 28 October, to dismantle the sites and remove the remaining missiles. In return Kennedy guaranteed that the United States would not invade Cuba. Nothing was announced about the missile sites in Turkey but, as noted above, Kennedy had intended them to be removed anyway.

The world sighed with relief, and a period of better relations between the U.S. and Russia began. The 'hot-line' (direct teletype link) between Washington and Moscow was set up in August 1963. Both Kennedy and Khrushchev had gained prestige in their respective countries and could therefore afford to be more conciliatory without being labelled weak by their political opponents.

For viewers of BBC television who were willing to sit up late on Saturday nights, the end of the year was enlivened by a new topical revue: *That Was The Week That Was*. The producer was Ned Sherrin and the introductory paragraph on the *Radio Times* page which listed programmes for 24 November was unobtrusive. It was:

> David Frost will lead Millicent Martin, Kenneth Cope, David Kernan, Roy Kinnear, Bernard Levin, Lance Percival and William Rushton through about sixty minutes of material, some of which will be written during the week, some on the day, and some as they speak.

'TW3', as it came to be called, shocked some, delighted others, and surprised everyone, since the BBC had never before presented biting personal satire and jokes about religion and the monarchy. Politicians who were already getting rough treatment from *Private Eye,* now found themselves guyed on the television screen, in front of an audience which before long reached nine million.

Snow, however, began to fall before Christmas 1962, and the public which was warming to Frost at their firesides or, increasingly, in their centrally heated houses, was soon being chilled, delayed, inconvenienced and endangered by a record-breaking frost out of doors.

Nor was the year without its treason trial. Spending his first Christmas in prison, at the beginning of an eighteen-year sentence for spying on behalf of the Russians, was William John Christopher Vassall.

1963

JANUARY 1963 WAS even colder than the historic February 1947. The Thames froze right across in places; there were ice-floes near Tower Bridge; even on the sea there was ice from East Sussex to the Thames Estuary. Women in Cambridge were given special permission to wear trousers with their undergraduate gowns.

February was bitterly cold too. Records could not produce a comparable winter since the eighteenth century. The rarity of such severe weather was, predictably, produced as an answer to complaints about delays on railways, and blocked roads. Was the public prepared to pay for defrosting devices on the railways and road-clearing equipment, together with the necessary maintenance charges and additional staff, simply in order to avoid inconvenience every few years? Local authorities and those in charge of railways in fact do a great deal, and winters during the next decade were less severe than that of 1963.

There was also the question of domestic heating. The amount of gas and electrical heating devices sold had not been kept in line with the amount of gas or electricity available. Not enough power stations were finished yet and there was no North Sea gas.

During that icy January the British public heard two pieces of sad news. The first was that General de Gaulle had vetoed our entry into the Common Market. 'Britain is insular, maritime . . . linked to distant countries,' he complained. Britain was by no means unanimous about the benefits of entry, but the government had decided to apply, and even people opposed to the government and to entry into the Common Market did not relish being snubbed by de Gaulle.

Gaitskell would have had something to say about this, but he was acutely ill in hospital and on the evening of Friday 18 January he died. He had been Leader of the Opposition for seven years and Chancellor of the Exchequer during the last year of the post-war Labour government. As the next General Election drew near, many Labour supporters, though not those who believed in unilateral disarmament, had looked forward to his becoming Prime Minister. Now they could only read the obituaries. One colleague regarded Gaitskell's life as a standing contradiction to those who believed that only 'men with cold hearts and twisted tongues' could succeed at Westminster. Another wrote: 'He took the cynicism out of politics.'

Who was to succeed Gaitskell? In November 1962 George Brown had defeated Wilson in the vote for Deputy Leader of the Parliamentary Labour party. This did not mean that he was heir to the Leadership. Wilson had been on a lecture tour in America, and arrived back a few hours after Gaitskell's death. L. G. D. Smith writes (*Harold Wilson. The Authentic Portrait,* Hodder and Stoughton, 1964):

> In the car from the airport the silence was eventually broken.
> 'I suppose you're going to stand for the Leadership?' asked his secretary.
> 'Yes, I expect so,' Wilson replied, adding: 'And if I'm elected, the first thing I'll do is to recommend Dora Gaitskell for a life peerage.'

The three candidates were Wilson, Callaghan and Brown. Wilson won. Dora Gaitskell was created a Life Peeress in 1964.

The Queen and the Duke of Edinburgh left on 31 January on a tour of Fiji, New Zealand and Australia. While they were away unemployment in Britain rose to 878,356, the highest since February 1947; Profumo, Secretary of State for War, made a statement in the House of Commons which he was later to confess had been misleading; and on 27 March, the day before the royal party's return, Dr. Beeching's *Reshaping of British Railways* was published.

This report was the final depressant of a grim winter. Its positive aspects – improved inter-city services for both passenger and freight – were less easily visualised than those which involved the closure of about 5,000 miles of track and 2,000 stations, with 70,000 railwaymen becoming redundant as a result. A strike was threatened, but was called off when better terms for redundant men were promised. Local committees were formed all over the country with the object of saving branch lines. Some concessions were won. A body called the 'Branch Line Reinvigoration Society' included in its propaganda a plea for close co-ordination between the planners of bus and rail services. If buses were to replace branch lines, railway and bus timetables would have to interlock.

Trains, however, still remained unchallenged as transporters of visiting heads of state (except in the case of Tito who, it will be remembered, for security reasons, was disembarked at Westminster Pier). The cream and chocolate Pullman cars with their glistening brass door furniture, sliding up to the red-carpeted platform of beflagged and beflowered Victoria or

Waterloo stations, gave an appropriate start to what were usually happy occasions.

On 14 May King Baudouin of the Belgians at last paid us a visit, with his Queen, Fabiola. Everything went smoothly. A wreath was laid on the Tomb of the Unknown Warrior in Westminster Abbey, there were banquets, and a visit to Covent Garden. The visit ended on 17 May.

The visit of King Paul and Queen Frederika of Greece (9-12 July) followed a similar time-table but was very differently received by the public. Frederika (mother of Constantine, then heir to the throne) had belonged to a Nazi youth organisation and the Greek government, though not yet turned into a dictatorship by the Colonels (1967) was ferociously anti-communist; it still held a number of political prisoners, among them Tony Ambatielos, whose British-born wife lived in London and was trying to do all she could to secure her husband's release.

When Queen Frederika came to London privately in April, for Princess Alexandra's wedding, she was chased outside Claridge's Hotel by a crowd seeking sympathy for Mrs. Ambatielos's cause. During the official visit, as the Greek and British royalties left the Aldwych Theatre after a performance of *A Midsummer Night's Dream* (10 July), they were booed. Next day a crowd gathered outside Claridge's, and arrests were made.

King Paul, who died on 6 March 1964, went home with his Queen. Ambatielos was later released, though he had to leave Greece when the Colonels came to power. In London the visit produced a shocking aftermath – the Challoner case.

Four youths, who had been playing tennis, were among the prisoners arrested on 11 July and taken to West End police station, where they were examined by a Sergeant Challoner and three police officers. Pieces of brick were found on them and they were charged with possessing offensive weapons. But they were ably defended and after almost a year of investigation, by which time Sergeant Challoner had been declared insane, the three police officers were convicted of 'planting' the bricks and, in certain instances, of obtaining convictions by perjured evidence. The judge said (23 June 1964): 'Dishonest, perjured police officers are like an infernal machine, ticking away to the destruction of us all.'

Another case which caused anxiety to persons interested in the working of British justice was that of Chief Enahoro of Nigeria. Faced with a charge of treasonable felony in his own country, he had taken refuge in Britain. After six months of legal argument and appeals by members of the public, he was sent back (16 May) by the Home Secretary, Henry Brooke, to be tried in Lagos. There (7 September) he was sentenced to fifteen years' imprisonment, but he was freed when Gowon came to power in 1966.

As Enahoro flew back to Nigeria under arrest, representatives of his and 30 other independent African countries were about to start for Addis Ababa where, on 22 May, Emperor Haile Selassie of Ethiopia ópened the four-day conference at which the Organisation of African Unity was formed. The Organisation pledged support for the liberation movements in South Africa and Portuguese Africa. President Kwame Nkrumah of Ghana felt that this did not go far enough. He wanted a political union of all African states, along the lines of the U.S.A. or the U.S.S.R. But President Nyerere of Tanganyika said: 'What is "going far enough"? No good mason would complain that his first brick did not go far enough.'

Eight months before (October 1962) another attempt to achieve unity of purpose amongst a diverse and intractable assembly had been set in motion at the Vatican by Pope John. This was the Second Ecumenical Council (1962-5). 'Ecumenical' or 'Oecumenical' means that it was drawn from the whole inhabited world. The Pope looked eagerly forward:

> ... everyone was convinced that I would be a provisional and transitional Pope. Yet here I am, already on the eve of the fourth year of my pontificate, with an immense programme of work in front of me to be carried out before the eyes of the whole world, which is watching and waiting.

The Council recessed in December and before it reassembled in 1963, Pope John was dead (3 June). He was succeeded by Cardinal Martini as Paul VI (30 June). But the 'watching and waiting' world was not disappointed. The Ecumenical Council continued in its efforts to adapt the Roman Catholic Church to the modern world, which was the purpose for which Pope John had called it together. Cardinal Heenan, Archbishop of Westminster, explained in an *Observer* article (January 1970): 'Before Pope John's Vatican Council all members of the Catholic Church below the rank of bishop belonged to the Light Brigade.' Now they were beginning 'to reason why'.

Rethinking was not confined to Roman Catholics. The Church of England, proud of its now world famous Cathedral at Coventry, was stirring too. On 19 March *Honest to God* by the Bishop of Woolwich, Dr. John A. T. Robinson, was published as one of a series of Student Christian Movement paperbacks. It proved unique. A serious theological work, it immediately sold like James Bond. The *Observer* introduced it under the headline 'Our Image of God Must Go'. The former *Sunday Pictorial,* in its first number after changing its name to the *Sunday Mirror* (7 April), asked

Dr. Robinson to present the theme of his book. In the course of his article he wrote:

> The traditional imagery of God simply succeeds, I believe, in making him remote for millions of men today.

While the Bishop of Woolwich sought to bring God down out of the sky and 'put him back into the middle of life', Russia was filling the vacuum with astronauts. Her fifth, Colonel Bykovsky, was launched on 14 June and made 82 orbits. On 16 June Miss Valentina, the world's first woman astronaut, took off and made 49 orbits.

During this month, when Catholic eyes were wet with sorrow and Russian eyes with joy, Londoners began to laugh and cry in Wyndham's Theatre, near Leicester Square Underground, over a musical show which opened on 20 June. It had been transferred from Joan Littlewood's Theatre Workshop, where it had been running since 19 March.

> When we're gassed,
> We're sick as we can be,
> 'Cos phosgene and mustard gas
> Is much too much for me.
> They're warning us,
> They're warning us,
> One respirator for the four of us;
> Glory be to God that three of us can run,
> So one of us can use it all alone.

Charles Chilton's sardonic musical *Oh! What a Lovely War,* inspired by a visit to Arras, where he had found his father's name inscribed with 35,000 others on a monumental wall devoted to those who 'died in the battle but had no known grave', took Londoners back to the horrors and the stoic bravery of 1914-18. The songs were those of the time, when words were often made up by marching troops to fit tunes – sometimes hymn tunes – which they already knew. Thus to the tune of 'Onward Christian Soldiers' they sang:

> Forward Joe Soap's Army
> Marching without fear
> With our old commander
> Safely in the rear.

Joe Soap had been brought back to life in a world of synthetic detergents. By 1962 these were 78% of the total soap and detergent market in U.S.A.

and 56% in Britain. As to the old commanders, they had received pretty rough treatment in *The Donkeys* by Alan Clark (1962). At a time when one might have expected books critical of World War II to be prominent, it was Haig and other generals of World War I who were attacked. Two years later (1965) BBC TV attracted enormous audiences, both at home and overseas, with a long series of World War I programmes called *The Great War.*

In June 1963, however, attacks on 'old commanders' suddenly became much less important than attacks on the old man who was then commanding the country – Harold Macmillan. Kim Philby, who had been suspected of complicity with Burgess and Maclean (1951), who had been cleared by Macmillan in 1955 and then became a newspaper correspondent, had disappeared from Beirut during the spring of 1963. It was now announced (1 July) that Philby had in fact been the 'third man' and before long he was known to have escaped to Moscow. But it was the Profumo case which shook the government most severely.

In March Profumo, the Secretary of State for War, had made a statement in the House of Commons, denying rumours about himself and Christine Keeler. Miss Keeler was known to associate with a Soviet officer in London, Captain Ivanov. Obviously there might be a security risk; but Profumo denied that there was anything more than an innocent social relationship between himself and Keeler.

Enquiries proceeded. On 4 June Profumo admitted that he had misled the House of Commons and resigned his office. Later in the month Lord Denning was asked to conduct an enquiry into the security aspects of the affair. His report, published in September, sold over 100,000 copies in a few days. It said there had been no security leakage and it attached no blame to the security services. But confidence in Macmillan's judgment had been shaken. He had trusted a man who was not only capable of lying to the House of Commons but who, it now appeared to the public, associated with a disreputable collection of people, in particular a Dr. Stephen Ward, who was found guilty of immorality and died from an overdose of drugs on 3 August. Rachmann, whose name later added the word 'rachmanism' (ruthless behaviour as a landlord) to the English language, was also connected with the group.

Profumo left public life and devoted himself to social work. Keeler served a prison sentence for perjury and came into the public eye again during 1969, when the *News of the World* printed her memoirs, amid considerable expressions of disgust from other papers.

On 8 October Macmillan had to go into hospital for an operation on the prostate gland. This illness, following the Philby and Profumo affairs, led him to look for a successor. It was not then the practice of the Conservatives to choose their leader by voting. A number of conversations therefore took place at Macmillan's bedside and elsewhere. Mr. Butler and Lord Home (pron. Hume) emerged as the most likely candidates. After the Queen had visited Macmillan in hospital on Friday 18 October, it was announced that he had resigned and that Lord Home had been invited to form a government. Home gave up his peerage in order to be eligible for a seat in the Commons and, as Sir Alec Douglas-Home, was elected M.P. for Kinross on 8 November. He was 60 – by no means too old, according to the standards of politicians. Adenauer, German Chancellor since 1949, had resigned on 15 October at the age of 87, and de Gaulle was 73.

Home's sudden rise to fame corresponded in time with that of the Beatles, the Liverpool group consisting of John Lennon, Paul McCartney, George Harrison and Ringo Starr, who were managed by Brian Epstein until his death in 1967 at the age of 32. By September 1963 'Please Please Me', 'Twist and Shout' and 'She loves you' were all top sellers.

> But it wasn't until the night of 13 October 1963 that the Beatles stopped being simply an interesting pop music story and became front page hard news in every national newspaper.
> This was the night they topped the bill at the London Palladium on a show which was televised as 'Sunday Night at the London Palladium'. An estimated audience of 15m viewers watched them that night. (Hunter Davies, *The Beatles: the authorized biography*, Heinemann, 1968.)

In July over 1000 died in an earthquake which destroyed much of the town of Skopje in Yugoslavia.

On 8 August the Scotland-London Post Office express was ambushed as it passed through Buckinghamshire. £2½m were taken, only a fraction of which has been recovered. Any tendency to regard the robbers as gallant highwaymen has been checked by the knowledge that their attack on the 57-year-old driver of the express, Jack Mills, reduced him to a state of disablement from which he never fully recovered. All the robbers received long prison sentences. Two escaped. One of these, Wilson, was recaptured in Canada in 1968. The other, Biggs, escaped in 1965 and was seen (he was photographed with his wife in a night club) but not recaptured in Australia during 1969. In 1974 he was in South America but attempts to bring him back to Britain failed.

Reports that Mrs. Biggs had been paid £30,000 for her story by a newspaper moved the members of the N.U.R. Branch to which Driver Jack Mills belonged to raise a fund for him in 1969. £34,315 was subscribed, but Mills did not live to enjoy it. He died (though not from the head injury sustained in the train robbery) in February 1970.

Post Office trains had been running for 125 years and none had been robbed before. The scale of the crime appeared to be unique. It was referred to as The Great Train Robbery. How was the money spent? In an article in 1969 *Time* reckoned that even the men who remained at large for some time had enormous expenses. Payment for blackmail, plastic surgery, false passports, an organised escape and subsequent travel made deep inroads into the stolen money. No one settled down to a life of luxury.

As often, the good news during that summer was less spectacular than the bad. By the end of July agreement had been reached in Moscow between Russia, Britain and the U.S.A. on the banning of all except underground nuclear tests. The announcement of this was one of the last made by Macmillan as Prime Minister and one of the rare ones on which all parties joined in congratulation.

Just before and just after Macmillan's resignation, the Newsom and Robbins reports were published. 'Newsom' recommended the raising of the school leaving age to 16 (this was done in 1972) and a variety of improvements in secondary schools. 'Robbins' recommended an expansion of Higher Education, which has been one of the major developments of the 60's.

On 22 October the Old Vic reopened as the National Theatre with *Hamlet* as its first production.

Back in May the magazine *Vogue* had for the first time published a photograph in which the model was a coloured girl. Peter Rand had taken the picture and the garment shown was a 'peignoir in sheer linen, as plain as a snowdrop and crusted with cotton lace. 19½ guineas.' That same month, in Birmingham, Alabama, U.S.A., a non-violent demonstration against segregation was violently broken up. Martin Luther King was arrested. Sympathy for the Civil Rights cause increased, a mass march on Washington was organised, and on 28 August 200,000 demonstrators gathered at the Lincoln Memorial. There were whites, including rabbis and clergymen, among the marchers; and there was no disorder. Why were they all there? Martin Luther King, in his deep, melodious voice, answered this question from the steps of the Lincoln Memorial.

The negro is still sadly crippled by the manacles of segregation and the chains of discrimination . . . he finds himself an exile in his own land. We have come to dramatise this shameful situation . . . we have also come to this hallowed spot to remind America of the fierce urgency of now. . . .

There was further trouble at Birmingham in the autumn, when Governor Wallace resisted attempts to desegregate schools. Four negro schoolgirls were killed by a bomb planted in a church. ('Negro' rather than 'black' was at that time the acceptable term.) It looked as though a showdown between the Federal authorites, instructed by President Kennedy, and Governor Wallace was imminent. But events took a different turn. In Dallas, which is not in the 'deep south' and where racial problems are less prominent, Kennedy was shot on 22 November. His presumed murderer, Lee Oswald, was white and Jack Ruby, the man who shot Oswald two days later, as he was about to be transferred from Dallas police headquarters, was white too. The spectators were mainly white. One thing is certain about this mysterious crime. Race had nothing to do with it.

The race struggle and the Cold War were forgotten while the President's body was flown back to Washington and the great gathered from all over the world for his funeral. An old Pope and a young President (46), from both of whom much had been hoped, had died within six months of each other.

If Lee Oswald shot Kennedy, was he alone, and what was his reason? The enormous Warren Report (26 volumes) on the affair, made public in September 1964, was at first generally supposed to have arrived at the truth. More recently, criticisms of the report have been made, e.g. in Mark Lane's *Rush to Judgement* (1966) which became a best-seller.

The Vice-President, Lyndon Johnson, a 55-year-old Texan, was sworn in as the new President. He served the rest of what would have been Kennedy's term and was then elected President for 1964-8. In 1969, in retirement, he said:

> It's been very clear to me that I had certain disadvantages . . . in general, summed up in one sentence – a general inability to stimulate, inspire and unite all the people of the country, which I think is an essential function of the presidency.

On 12 December Kenya achieved independence. Jomo Kenyatta had been finally released early in 1963, in time to lead his party (KANU – Kenya African National Union) to victory in the June elections. He became Kenya's first Prime Minister and when the country became a republic a year later he was also made President. Both offices he still holds.

Kenya was a country where permanent white domination seemed likely; but this was prevented and a large white population was able to live on under black rule. The Asian population, however, suffered cruelly. They were settlers of long standing, like the whites. The first of them had arrived in 1896 to work on railway construction, and later much of the country's trade came to be in their hands. Several Asian lawyers had helped Pritt to defend Kenyatta during his long trial. But Kenya's Africanisation policy made it impossible for Asians to earn a decent living there.

Some political opposition was allowed. In the 1969 elections (the first since those of 1963) only KANU candidates stood; but among these voters could choose. A number of ministers lost their seats and the country's first woman M.P., Mrs. Grace Onyango, was elected. The opposition party (KPU – Kenya People's Union) was banned.

Tribal rivalry was still important. Tom Mboya, a prominent member of the KANU party, was murdered in July 1969. Mboya's tribe were the Luo, most of whom were in the KPU led by Oginga Odinga. When Kenyatta went electioneering in Luo territory, he was jeered at during a meeting. He turned on Odinga and his KPU followers and said: 'We are going to crush you into flour. Anybody who toys with our progress will be crushed like locusts.' As he drove away spectators threw stones and the police fired at them. Nine people were killed. Two days later Odinga was arrested.

Nyasaland (now Malawi) had become independent in February, with Dr. Hastings Banda as Prime Minister. It became a republic in 1966. On 31 December the Federation of Rhodesia and Nyasaland ceased to exist and, in October 1964, Northern Rhodesia became the independent republic of Zambia with Dr. Kenneth Kaunda as President. Further east the Federation of Malaysia was set up in September 1963 with Tunku Abdul Rahman as Prime Minister. Singapore was at first part of the Federation but left it in August 1965 to become an independent state, with Lee Kuan Yew as Prime Minister. On the other hand Sabah and Sarawak, areas in the island of Borneo which are about 1000 miles from the Malaya peninsula, remained within the Federation.

After 1963 the independence movement which attracted most attention in Africa was not black or brown, but white. Its members lived in Rhodesia.

1964

'THAT WAS THE year that was,' sang Millicent Martin on the evening of Saturday 28 December 1963. That was also the end of the adventurous TW3 programme, which had reappeared in September. Hugh Greene, the Director-General, said (*The Third Floor Front*, Bodley Head, 1969): 'It was in my capacity as a subversive anarchist that I yielded to the enormous pressure from my fellow subversives and put TW3 on the air; and it was as a pillar of the Establishment that I yielded to the fascist hyena-like howls to take it off again.' In an address at Birmingham University ('not a student hooted') in 1968, six months before his retirement, he quoted the above remarks and added:

> I do not need to go over the subsequent history of the so-called satire programmes. Inspiration seemed to fade. Times changed. Perhaps the mood of the nation changed. In any case, none of them came up to the first sparkle of TW3. None the less, this vein of programming undoubtedly influenced the flavour and content from then onwards of some of our plays, some of our light entertainment and some facets of our approach to current affairs. (Should we have had Alf Garnett without TW3?) Nothing could ever be the same again.

Where was joy to be found in January 1964? Maybe you had been given *The Group* by Mary McCarthy for Christmas and could become involved in what the blurb called the 'sad-funny' story of eight Vassar girls from the class of 1933. You had surely been given or bought some discs. Not only the Beatles. The Rolling Stones were to have their first American tour during the year; the folksinger Bob Dylan was acknowledged as the voice of teenage discontent everywhere; Cliff Richard's 'Bachelor Boy' had sold more than a million; and 'Dominique', sung in French by a Belgian nun, had been at the top of the Hit Parade for most of December.

You could dance the twist or the shake. You could, if they came your way, see some very good films from 1963 – *Tom Jones* with Albert Finney, *This Sporting Life*, the first feature film to be directed by Lindsay Anderson, *The Servant* with Dirk Bogarde giving, according to one critic, the performance of his life. You could also see a film which had taken a long time to make and had cost a great deal of money – *Cleopatra* with Elizabeth Taylor, Rex Harrison and Richard Burton.

Technical progress had provided two most acceptable Christmas presents – the 'pyrosil' dish and the transistor radio. Pyrosil ware looked like china, but could stand the severest thermal shock. You could take it out of a refrigerator and put it straight on to a naked flame. Transistors – well, there is now no need to explain what transistor radios are. What does need explaining is that at this time, when they first became popular, the only pop music within their reach came from Radio Luxembourg. There was no BBC Radio 1, no BBC local radio, and no commercial radio. To fill the gap and make money for their owners and for advertisers, 'pirate' radio stations began to be set up during 1964.

On the mainland of Britain all wireless transmission must be licensed by the Minister of Posts and Telecommunications, and until 1972 the BBC was the only body allowed to be licensed for general radio broadcasting. How were the pop merchants to get on the air?

If anyone had set up an independent broadcasting service on land they would have been detected and prosecuted before very long; but broadcasting from a ship at sea, if the ship were outside the three-mile limit, along which an imaginary frontier is assumed to run, was thought at this time to be within the law. The Swedes, the Danes and the Dutch, however, had all had some success in suppressing such activity, which had begun in 1958.

Until 1964 no one had thought it worth while to invade Britain with pirate transmissions, but on 29 March that year 'Radio Caroline' began to broadcast programmes from a ship, moored off the Essex coast, just beyond the three-mile limit. In December a 'Radio London' opened, on board a ship in the same area. Meanwhile two other stations had begun to transmit from disused World War II forts in the Thames estuary and Radio Caroline (North) had begun operations off the Isle of Man.

By 1966 Radio Caroline and Radio London each claimed over eight million listeners and there were more than a dozen pirates in business. A third disused fort in the Thames estuary had been brought into use and Radio Scotland was afloat, first off Dunbar, then in the Firth of Clyde. The story is told by Paul Harris, in his pro-pirate book *When Pirates Ruled the Waves* (Impulse Publications, 1968).

Pirate operators hoped that the great success of their programmes would frighten the government out of taking any action against them; and in fact it was not until 1967.(after Labour had achieved a working majority in the 1966 election), that the Marine Broadcasting Offences Act made the activities of the pirates illegal as from 15 August. Most of them closed down, but Radio Caroline carried on in defiance of the law until March 1968. By that time the BBC's pop channel, Radio 1, was well established. It had been opened on Saturday 30 September 1967 by Tony Blackburn, a former pirate disc jockey, and a number of other ex-pirates had joined it.

What with pop from the pirates and trad from the BBC, the air of 1964 was full of music. Love, as always, was a popular subject of song. Venereal disease statistics, however, made less good listening. Between 1958 and 1965 the cases of syphilis reported from clinics trebled in men and doubled in women.

Shakespeare was to be 400 years old on 23 April. The question whether he, or Bacon or Marlowe or Queen Elizabeth I had written the plays was again getting an airing. Accommodation for the study of these and all other problems connected with Shakespeare was provided by the Shakespeare Birthplace Trust, whose fine new Shakespeare Centre was opened on 22 April, as part of the 400th birthday celebrations at Stratford-upon-Avon. This was one of many exciting new buildings which were appearing, now that building licences had been gone for a decade.

The poet would have been pleased that this elegant and inspiring provision for studying his works (an interior dominated by cherrywood is reached through glass doors decorated by John Hutton) went forward simultaneously with provision for the performance of plays, from his own to the most recent. These were now appearing not only on radio and television (on 21 April BBC2,swith Michael Peacock in charge, had opened, though not broadcast, owing to a power failure), but also in new theatres. The Belgrade at Coventry had been completed in 1958. Other new theatres opened in Leicester, Chichester, Middlesbrough and St. Helens, and at Southampton University. These were now joined by Peter Moro's Nottingham Playhouse, planned to take both proscenium and open stage productions and including a large workshop for stage designers. Its productions have made it probably the best-known theatre outside London, apart from Chichester, which was linked with the National Theatre.

Among other interesting new buildings this year were the Post Office Tower (London's tallest building – 580 ft. / 176.3 metres), the Bull Ring at Birmingham (one of Europe's largest air conditioned shopping centres) and two restaurants in London's Royal Parks. London also needed a third airport and Stansted, Essex, was provisionally chosen as its site (24 March). But furious opposition arose, and other sites had to be considered. Maplin, on the Thames estuary, was finally chosen; but before work was started the project was abandoned (1974).

New housing was under construction all over the country, though never quickly enough. One of the most distinguished schemes was in Sheffield, where the Park Hill redevelopment rose near the city centre on a hillside which had previously been occupied by a slum. The new towns, 13 of which had been founded between 1947 and 1950, were all making progress. The largest was Hemel Hempstead (63,000), followed by Harlow (61,200), Basildon (60,500), and Crawley (60,000). Cumbernauld, near Glasgow, which had not been founded until 1956 and later won a design award, now numbered 10,000.

Housing went ahead, but not enough. Roads and bridges went ahead, but not enough. The M2, starting near Canterbury and running halfway to London, had been opened on 29 May 1963. The tunnel of the year 1964 was on the continent, under the Great St. Bernard Pass, linking France and Italy; but the bridge of the year was in Scotland, carrying a road across the River Forth.

The Queen opened the Forth Road Bridge on 4 September 1964. It had taken six years to build. The weather had caused delays and now marred the royal visit. Assembled dignitaries and the splendid bridge were hidden by sea mist, which only cleared partially when the band played 'All the world is waiting for the sunrise'.

On 15 September the *Sun* rose in Fleet Street – neither its own subeditors, nor those of its rivals, could resist the obvious pun. It was not the tabloid *Sun* of today, which only dates from 1969, but a full-size newspaper, costing 3d., which aimed at filling the gap left by the failure of the Labour-supported *Daily Herald*. On its front page the *Sun* announced the date of the General Election – 15 October. Inside, as part of a feature called YOUR PLACE IN THE SUN, appeared a selection of answers to a reporter's question: Why do you think young men are growing hair down to their shoulders?

It was not, however, the length of young men's hair but the rowdiness of their habits which was raising most questions in 1964. The trouble occurred particularly at the Bank Holiday week-ends when groups of 'Mods' and 'Rockers' descended on seaside resorts and frequently came to blows. Mods and Rockers had succeeded the Teddy boys. Mods were less tough than Rockers and went to dance halls more. One said: 'Mods can talk among themselves. Rockers just say: "Huh, gimme a cuppa tea"; that sort of thing.' Rockers were devoted to their motor bikes. Mods rode scooters.

During the Easter week-end, more than 100 youths were arrested at Clacton. During the Whitsun week-end, there was trouble at Margate, Brighton and Bournemouth. On August Bank Holiday (the last, incidentally, to be held on the first Monday in the month) there was grave disorder at Hastings.

New Society, a periodical launched in October 1962 and aiming 'to mirror, to analyse, to understand, not to exhort or moralise', carried out a survey of 44 youths arrested at Margate and sentenced on Whit Monday to fines, detention centre or prison. A Rocker explained:

> I met up with some of my old mates in Margate. The police kept moving us on, which we didn't like. One of my mates said to one of the police: 'That uniform bothers me.' We both had a go at the copper and my mate was arrested. Later on, I was arrested when I was trying to resist being pushed around by the police. Earlier on, we had had a few bundles with Mods.

The *Weekend Telegraph* appeared for the first time on 25 September. In the same month the *Observer* had introduced a colour magazine and the third 'quality' Sunday paper had to have one too. The *Telegraph* people, however, chose to bring theirs out with the Friday number of the *Daily Telegraph,* promising '. . . a different style of description and discussion. Strong pictures light up the scene and the writer can act out the story in greater depth and in greater detail than is palatable in the greyer pages of a newspaper.' Just how a writer 'acts out' a story was not explained. It was the pictures which mattered. The lead story, 'The small but ugly war' was illustrated by colour photographs of South Vietnamese torturing captives, a dreadfully burned child, a parcel containing a dead child in the arms of its father, and a beaten-up member of the Vietcong. 'Behind Washington's talk of vigorously carrying on the war against the Vietcong is the bitter conviction among many that it cannot now be won,' read the accompanying text. Another feature, also on an American subject, pictured Harlem and discussed 'what it feels like to be a Negro'. A British Army advertisement reminded readers that we too had jungles to patrol ('Carrying the imperial burden without enjoying the fruits of empire,' *The Times* called it). In January British troops had helped to quell mutinies in Tanganyika (which in April united with Zanzibar to form Tanzania), in Uganda and in Kenya. They had intervened between Greeks and Turks in Cyprus. Now they were active in the part of the island of Borneo which, having joined the Federation of Malaysia, was under attack from Indonesia. On 2 September Indonesian landings had been made, without success, in Malaya itself.

On 21 September Malta G.C. became an independent state within the Commonwealth. Elections had been held in 1962, after which G. Borg

Olivier had become Prime Minister. He continued in that post after independence.

October was to be a memorable month. To have an election campaign
and the Olympic Games and a royal visit to Canada, running simultaneously, was interesting enough, but the middle of the month produced
some surprises.

On 13 October a Russian spacecraft, with three men on board, landed
after making 16 orbits in just over 24 hours.

On 14 October the black American clergyman Dr. Martin Luther King
was awarded the Nobel Peace Prize. This was in recognition of King's
non-violent desegregation campaign, which, so it seemed at the time, had
succeeded, with the passage of the Civil Rights Bill on 2 July. Yet by the
end of 1969 a Washington report stated that about three-fifths of the black
schoolchildren in the United States still attended schools which were
virtually all black.

On 15 October (polling day in Britain) Khrushchev, who had been
First Secretary of the Soviet Communist Party, as well as Prime
Minister since 1958, was replaced in the first post by Brezhnev and in
the second by Kosygin. Khrushchev had turned seventy in April and
had 'requested to be relieved of his duties in view of his advanced age
and deterioration of his health'. As noted on page 151, seventy was not
so very old for a politician. It seemed possible that Khrushchev had in
fact been dismissed. It was said that he had encouraged the 'personality
cult', which means that he had put himself too much in the limelight.
Very little was heard of him after that. He lived in the country near
Moscow and died in 1971.

Another septuagenarian politician was Nehru, Prime Minister of India
since independence (1947) who died on 27 May, 1964, at the age of 74. He
had spent two years at Harrow, three at Trinity College, Cambridge, and
nine (for political reasons) in prison; he had thus had plenty of time for
self-examination and, unlike Khrushchev, was critical of himself. He felt
that one could not get things done quickly enough in a democracy and was
afraid that he might become too dictatorial. *The Times,* on the other hand,
took a different view. Drawing upon the rich and sonorous vocabulary
which it has since abandoned, it commented, in its obituary, that Nehru,
when he assumed power, 'was culpable more for vacillation than for
Caesarism'.

It was hoped that Khrushchev's successors would stop the wrangle
between Russia and China. 'CHANCE FOR MAO TO MAKE IT UP'
read a headline on 15 October. On the 16th China exploded her first

nuclear device, an atomic bomb, thus becoming the fifth of the world's nuclear powers. The *Daily Worker* (3d.) explained:

> China is a Socialist Power, and has developed nuclear weapons for defensive and not offensive purposes.
> Nevertheless, most friends of the Chinese people will regret that this step has been taken . . . The nuclear strength of the Soviet Union is sufficient to shield the Socialist camp.

As Khrushchev stepped down, Russian after Russian stepped up on to the place of honour in the Tokyo Olympic Games (10-24 October) and was decorated with a gold medal. This happened forty-one times. When silver and bronze medals were added, Russia had a total of 96 and the U.S.A. 90. This repeated the pattern of the 1956 and 1960 games, in each of which Russia collected the largest number of medals and U.S.A. the second largest number.

Britain had won a gold for bobsleigh in the winter games. At Tokyo we had four golds. Two went to women. Mrs. Mary Rand, who won the long jump with 22 ft. 2 ins., a world record, was the first British woman ever to win an Olympic gold for athletics; Miss Ann Packer, a 22-year-old London schoolteacher, who won the 800 metres, was the first British woman ever to win an Olympic gold in a track event. The men's long jump also went to Britain (L. Davies). Our other gold was won by K. Matthews in the 20 km walk. The Japanese made it all into a film of exquisite beauty – *Tokyo Olympiade.*

De Gaulle had meanwhile staged a marathon of his own and was touring South America on the longest foreign visit ever made by a French Head of State (20 September-16 October). His praise of nationalism and support for the right of self-determination was not lost on the French Canadians. Queen Elizabeth, whose fourth child, Prince Edward, had been born on 10 March, was booed as she passed through the flagless streets of Quebec on Sunday, 11 October. Things had changed since her warm reception in 1959. It was estimated that soldiers outnumbered spectators in the streets by 8-1.

On the 13th the Queen was back in London. On the afternoon of Friday 16th Sir Alec Douglas-Home arrived at Buckingham Palace at half-past three. He had been Prime Minister for a year, less one day. He had come to offer his resignation, which the Queen accepted. Shortly after four Harold Wilson arrived with Mrs. Wilson, their two sons and his father. When the family drove away again, he was Prime Minister – the youngest (48) of the twentieth century (in Britain, that is to say. Ian Smith, Prime Minister of Rhodesia since 13 April, was 45).

Labour was in again, with an overall majority of five after thirteen years in opposition. They had 317 seats, the Conservatives had 303 and the Liberals 9. What had caused the swing? Neither party had aroused much enthusiasm. Both supported NATO. Neither supported unilateral renunciation of nuclear weapons. Both favoured a further attempt to enter the Common Market, though Conservatives were likely to make it sooner. Which would really be able to increase productivity, and reduce the number of strikes?

The Conservatives, having been in power, were more easy to criticise. There had been the spy cases, the Profumo case, the Beeching Plan (it was noted that about a dozen Labour gains were in places where railway stations had been threatened by the much-abused Dr. Beeching) and then, during Macmillan's illness, the shilly-shallying over the choice of a new leader.

But the decisive factor seemed to be that, after the shilly-shally, the wrong man was chosen. Home had not been keen on the job. His brother, William Douglas-Home, wrote a successful play called *The Reluctant Peer*. 'How happy would an ex-14th Earl feel on the hustings on a rough wet night in Wigan?' the *Evening Standard*'s lobby correspondent had asked. He now wrote: 'Sir Alec was just out of his depth in the hurly-burly of campaigning.' The point was made again as a caption under a photograph of Home: 'Out of his depth in the hurly-burly of campaigning.' Beside it was one of Wilson captioned: 'Suddenly people he wanted to like him were liking him. . . .'

George Brown (aged 50) was immediately given the job of devising and operating an incomes policy. Increases in incomes and prices were to be checked unless they reflected an increase in productivity. A new ministry was set up, and Brown took charge, with the title of First Secretary of State (indicating that he was Wilson's deputy) and Minister for Economic Affairs.

Patrick Gordon Walker had been 'shadow' Foreign Secretary, while his party was in opposition, so Wilson now gave him the Foreign Office. But Walker had lost his seat. At Smethwick in the Midlands, where he had had a majority of 3,544 in 1959, the Conservatives had concentrated on the immigration question. Gordon Walker's more humane approach did not commend itself to the electorate, who returned a Mr. Griffiths with a majority of 1,774 (Andrew Faulds regained the seat for Labour in 1966). On 21 January 1965 Gordon Walker fought a by-election, lost and had therefore to resign his office. Michael Stewart replaced him as Foreign Secretary.

James Callaghan was Chancellor of the Exchequer; Lord Gardiner, Lord Chancellor; Denis Healey, Secretary of State for Defence; Richard Crossman (died 1974), Minister of Housing and Local Government; and Barbara Castle, Minister of Overseas Development. These were all in the Cabinet. Roy Jenkins, Minister of Aviation and faced with the question whether to continue support of the Concorde project, was not. Jennie Lee (Aneurin Bevan's widow) was Parliamentary Under-Secretary at the Ministry of Public Buildings and Works, but moved before long to the Department of Education and Science, where she was influential in launching the Open University and in securing generous expenditure on the arts. The Arts Council grant, which had been less than £3m in 1963, was over £8m in 1968-9.

Three weeks after our election the Americans had theirs. Lyndon B. Johnson (Democrat) defeated Barry Goldwater (Republican) and became President of the U.S.A. for the next four years.

On 15 December Wedgwood Benn, the new Labour Postmaster General, announced that in future the Post Office would issue more cele-bratory stamps. This was not just a bid for the philatelic vote. People like gay stamps, especially at Christmas, and they were not then soured by the knowledge that the charge for a letter would be going up from 3d. to 4d. in April 1965. But some no doubt included in their Christmas prayers an item to the effect that, in addition to celebratory stamps, we were in need of achievements worth celebrating.

1965

'I AM READY to meet my Maker. Whether my Maker is prepared for the great ordeal of meeting me is another matter.' Thus Churchill, replying on his 75th birthday (1949) to the question: Have you any fear of death?

At that time he still had four more years as Prime Minister before him (1951-55), including Coronation Year (1953), during which he was made a Knight of the Garter, and 1954, when the last volume of *The Second World War* was published and Parliament honoured him on his eightieth birthday. The last two volumes of his *A History of the English-Speaking Peoples* were published in 1957 and 1958 and in the latter year he headed the Trust which was to found Churchill College, Cambridge, as a tribute to his work. But by the end of the 50's he had become an invalid and was seldom seen in public. On his 90th birthday, in November 1964, congratulations poured in from all over the world, but he could not enjoy the occasion. On 10 January he had a stroke, but even that did not release him from the life which was now so burdensome. He lay there, absolutely still, while day after day reporters stood outside his house in Hyde Park Gate, waiting for news. It was not until Sunday 24 January that they got it. Sir Winston Churchill had died shortly after 8.0 a.m.

The Prime Minister and the party leaders, whose tributes were broadcast that evening, found it hard to match the eloquence of the man they were mourning. They were at their best when they used his own words. Macmillan quoted: 'In war, resolution; in defeat, defiance; in victory, magnanimity; in peace, good will.'

Even de Gaulle wrote, with feeling, both to the Queen and to Lady Churchill.

Throughout Wednesday, Thursday and Friday, thousands filed past Sir Winston's body, as it lay in state in Westminster Hall, and on the Friday night crowds waited in the cold on the pavements for the funeral. This was an occasion so moving and so lit with unpretentious splendours, that Churchill himself had clearly given some thought to the planning of it.

All who watched the funeral have their memories of Saturday 30 January 1965. Churchill had described himself as 'impatient for the morning' of his first day as Prime Minister in 1940. Not long afterwards, as

Germany occupied Europe, he had said in one of his greatest broadcasts: 'The morning will come.' There were many in the all-night crowds who could remember that.

Morning did come and the coffin, wrapped in the Union Jack, was carried from Westminster Hall at 9.45 a.m., as Big Ben struck. The great bell was then silenced for the rest of the day – one tremendous Westminster voice paying tribute to the other.

At a royal funeral your eye can be caught and held by the splendour of the uniformed mourners. Churchill had no lack of these. But the kings, queens, princes, presidents and premiers were waiting, with the British royal family, in St. Paul's. Only the Churchills formed part of the long funeral procession – the ladies in black, driven by a coachman in scarlet; the men, very unmilitary in top hats, walking behind the marching sailors who drew (100 in front) and braked (40 behind) the gun-carriage which carried the coffin.

Though the wind was bitterly cold, there was no frost; but the streets had been sanded, so that no man or horse would slip. From high above the procession the sand looked like a carpet of gold dust, lighting an occasion from which the sun had withdrawn. Below, on the pavement, it was the *sound* of the coarse sand, rhythmically trodden by the sailors, which remained with you. The rest of the troops all wore heavy greatcoats, but not the sailors, crunching in precise long files beside the thick white tow-ropes. They passed very close with their gun carriage; if you cried then, nobody minded.

After the service in St. Paul's the coffin was taken by launch from Tower Pier to the Festival Hall Pier, and thence to Waterloo Station where it was put on board a special train. That was the end of the state funeral. Churchill was buried during the afternoon beside his mother in Bladon Churchyard, Oxfordshire, not far from Blenheim Palace, where he had been born.

Hundreds of cameras, both professional and amateur, had clicked and whirred during the funeral. Expenditure on photography had reached £69m in 1964 – £4m up on 1963. Not only were more people taking more photographs, but they wanted more of them in colour. In 1955 one picture in twenty-two had been in colour. Now, ten years later, the figure was one in three (but colour TV, though developed by BBC and ITA, could still only be seen on experimental transmissions).

The photomicrograph (photograph of a magnified object) was in general a tool used by scientists, but it was now realised that a magnified photograph of, for instance, a snow crystal could be considered as a work of art. The Op art painters (e.g. Victor Vasarely, Bridget Riley), whose work was introduced to the public at the Museum of Modern Art in New York during 1965, were influenced by microphotography. They were abstractionists, quite different from the Pop artists. Though their pictures did not become widely known, their influence could soon be seen in dress and curtain fabrics.

Photography of dresses, or rather of girls modelling dresses, had become an extremely attractive career. Clothes with the Quant look (for a time known as the 'Cookie' look) called for a dynamic type of photographer like David Bailey, and this new way of working so impressed the Italian film director Antonioni that he now came to Britain and made *Blow up* (released in 1967). That the athletic technique of the photographer hero of this film (played by David Hemmings) was not entirely a caricature, is suggested by a description of Bailey at work given, surprisingly, by Cecil Beaton, in *Vogue*. The great older generation photographer 'sat', if that is the word, to the great younger generation photographer. 'He came storming in here, knew exactly what he wanted to do, and created such a feeling of enthusiasm! While he was taking his pictures he kept up a continuous stream of encouragement – "Marvellous, super, super, a bit to the left, Chief, great, marvellous, marvellous. . . ." '

Beaton, however, was anything but a back number. He was a dress designer as well as a photographer. Towards the end of 1964 his photographs of the costumes he had designed for Audrey Hepburn in the film of *My Fair Lady* were published in his book *Cecil Beaton's Fair Lady* (Weidenfeld and Nicolson, 1964) and the film opened in London on 21 January.

Would these glorious frothy dresses, reaching to the ground, affect current fashion? Would skirts get lower? The *Daily Worker* had warned in the autumn of 1964:

> If you are buying a new coat this year and it will have to last you through the 1965-66 winter as well, don't get it too short or without possibility of letting down.
>
> I would be willing to bet that this time next year will see hemlines going down again.

Hemlines, however, for younger girls, began to climb and by 1966 the miniskirt was in, rising to 4, 5, 6 or even 7 inches above the knee. With the Beatles, and Carnaby Street, it formed part of the image of 'swinging London'. One feature of swinging London, however, was a French import. In 1965 the discotheque arrived. Here minis flickered to pop on a small floor under exotic lighting patterns.

The non-pop-loving public welcomed the arrival from U.S. of the musical *The Sound of Music*. Richard Lester's film *The Knack* with Rita Tushingham won the grand prize at Cannes, but it seemed that what people wanted most was sophisticated, sexy violence. The James Bond story *Goldfinger* made the film of the year.

Not that the world was starved of violence. British troops were still helping in the defence of Malaysia (where Indonesians made landings during January) and in maintaining order in Aden, during the period leading up to independence. India was twice at war with Pakistan during the year (9 April to 30 June in the Rann of Kutch; 5 August to 23 September in Kashmir). In Bolivia, where since November 1964 a military government had been in power, there was a general strike in May. Fighting broke out in La Paz and a state of siege was declared (Che Guevara left Cuba in April but did not reach Bolivia until November 1966. See page 188). In May, too, China exploded a second nuclear bomb.

It was, however, the Americans who found themselves most involved in violence, owing to their support of the South Vietnamese, to their intervention (April) during a rebellion in the Dominican Republic and to the continued harassment of blacks by whites in the southern states of the Union.

1965 was a decisive year in Vietnam. The sudden death of Adlai Stevenson in July prompts one to ask whether, if Stevenson had defeated Eisenhower in 1952 or 1956, American policy in South-East Asia would have been less aggressive. But Stevenson did not become President. Dulles had organised SEATO after the French defeat (1954) and, as soon as the French had left, American 'advisers' had begun to take their place.

When Kennedy succeeded Eisenhower, amid high hopes, he had showed no intention of pulling out. In 1960, the year towards the end of which he was elected President, there were 785 American 'advisers' in South Vietnam; in 1962 there were 11,000; by the end of 1964, a year after Kennedy's murder, there were 23,000.

In 1965 President Johnson turned the U.S.A. into the ally instead of the adviser and trainer of the South Vietnamese. In February U.S. aircraft began to bomb targets in North Vietnam. In March marines were landed. From now on it was a bigger war. It occupied more time on American television screens and now it was not only South Vietnamese whom you saw killing, wounding, wounded, dying – it was Americans. Could be your own cousin in Milwaukee, your daughter's fiancé from Detroit.

On TV the younger generation saw what they were in for. Parents saw what was going to happen to their sons. They were not cowards, but they asked: Is the cause worth such sacrifice? 'Teach-ins' were held to discuss the war. Student protest began. 'Draft cards' (the cards summoning conscripts to report for their period of service) were ceremonially burned. 'Vietnam' replaced 'the Bomb' as the target of protest, in Britain as well as the U.S.A., although Britain was not directly involved (Australia, however, and New Zealand sent small contingents).

Shortly before Christmas it was announced that during the first 11 months of the year, 1,100 Americans had been killed. But they had been more than replaced. There were now 165,000 American troops in Vietnam. By March 1966 this figure had risen to 235,000.

Black Americans were drafted, trained to fight, watched on television, killed, or brought home as seasoned campaigners to the U.S.A. This toughened the colour war in later years.

It was not just a matter of denial of Civil Rights in the South. Throughout America blacks were worse off. Their average income was 55% of a white's? Their unemployment rate was double. Their infant mortality rate was almost double. More than a quarter of their teenagers had no jobs.

Already in 1965, Stokely Carmichael was shouting: 'We want black power.' Between 11 and 15 August, there was rioting in the Negro area of Los Angeles, and, on the 18th, police and National Guardsmen fought a gun battle in the streets against the Black Muslims, a black-power movement whose one-time leader, 'Malcolm X', had been shot dead in New York on 21 February.

Non-violent protest was still being tried in the South. Freedom marchers on their way to Montgomery, the capital of Alabama, were violently attached by police and 57 blacks were said to have been injured (7 March). Two days later a white clergyman who had come from Boston to join the protest was clubbed to death. The demonstrators could claim success in so far as President Johnson succeeded in rushing through Congress a bill designed to protect the Negro right to vote; but this was not enough to convince the majority of black Americans that non-violent protest was the best way to gain their ends.

In Britain meanwhile people were saying: 'We don't want race riots here,' and views on immigration were changing. Controls had been tightened in February and when a White Paper *Immigration from the Commonwealth* was published in August, *Punch* wrote:

> An immigration policy *is* needed, but what has happened to convert the Socialists from the bold, generous gesture-making integrationists of 1964 into the narrow, colour-bar-conscious opportunists of 1965?

Nevertheless the Race Relations Act 1965, which came into force on 8 December, aimed at making life less difficult for immigrants who were already in Britain. It prohibited 'discrimination on racial grounds in places of public resort' (e.g. pubs) and penalised incitement to racial hatred.

Britain's was not the only race problem with which Wilson was faced that autumn. Rhodesia (there was no longer any need to say 'Southern Rhodesia', since Northern Rhodesia had become Zambia) wanted independence. Why should she not have it? The reason was that 'independence' in this case meant independence of a white minority government which was known to be opposed to the political ambitions of the black majority. It seemed certain that without the restraint exercised by London, Rhodesia would gradually go the same way as South Africa.

One of Wilson's first duties on becoming Prime Minister in 1964 had been to warn Rhodesia's Ian Smith that a unilateral declaration of independence (UDI) would be an act of rebellion against the Queen. A year later (12 October 1965) the UN General Assembly called on Britain to prevent UDI in Rhodesia by all means. The Organisation of African Unity, meeting at Accra on 22 October, called on Britain to use force if necessary. On 5 November the UN General Assembly reiterated this plea.

Wilson had meanwhile flown to Salisbury but failed to reach agreement with Smith, who declared UDI on 11 November. Force was not used but 'sanctions' (restrictions on imports) were later imposed. Considerable evasion of these was possible, partly because Rhodesia had common frontiers with South Africa and Portuguese Mozambique. (Until their revolution in 1974, the Portuguese shared the Rhodesian and South African belief in white supremacy. After the revolution Mozambique and Angola achieved independence.) Sanctions did not succeed in bringing down the Smith Government and Rhodesia remained in a state of rebellion against the Queen. A republic was declared in 1970.

While the wind of change fanned flames or vainly buffeted brick walls throughout Africa, it swept unnoticed over Dr. Albert Schweitzer's hospital in Lambarene, in the formerly French territory of Gabon. Author, musician, composer, scholar, and humanitarian, winner of the Nobel Peace Prize (1952) and honorary member of the Order of Merit, he was probably by far the most distinguished citizen of the continent where he had made his home since 1913. But he was not cast for the role of prophet or reformer; he remained a recluse within his small circle at Lambarene, where he died (4 September).

One of the films of the year was the comedy *Those Magnificent Men in their Flying Machines.* But serious flight was also in the news. Up the spacemen went again. The Russians and the Americans both achieved a walk in space – Colonel Leonov from Voshkod 2 on 18 March, Major White from Gemini 4 on 3 June. Gemini 3 had made the first American pilot-manoeuvred, two-man flight on 23 March (Grissom and Young). With Gemini 5, in August, the Americans took the space endurance record (5 days) from the Russians – Cooper and Conrad stayed up for nearly eight days. In December Gemini 6 (Schirra and Stafford) and Gemini 7 (Borman and Lovell) made the first rendezvous in space, approaching to within 6 feet of each other 185 miles above the Pacific.

The most successful unmanned flight was that of the American Mariner 4. Launched in November 1964 it passed on 15 July 1965 within 7000 miles of Mars and sent back photographs. The Russian Zond 2 also came close to Mars but power supply trouble resulted in loss of radio contact.

The Russians paid a good deal of attention to the moon. Their Zond 3 in July sent back photographs of the reverse side. After that they had a run of bad luck in attempts to 'soft land' an unmanned spacecraft (i.e. land it with instruments undamaged). Luna 5 (May), Luna 7 (October) and Luna 8 (December) crashed on the moon, while Luna 6 (June) missed it altogether. But on 3 February 1966 Luna 9 made the first successful moon landing and within minutes was transmitting back to Earth the first pictures ever taken on another world.

Early Bird, the world's first commercial communications satellite, was launched from Cape Kennedy in April. The first TV programme to make use of it was seen in 24 countries on 2 May.

Admiration of American achievements in space was mixed with criticism of the cost, at a time when negro poverty was contributing so much to unhappiness and disorder, and public transport was neglected. Cynics therefore had a field day when an electric power failure blacked out New York and parts of New England on 9 November. It took 12 hours to make the necessary repairs.

On 25 April Gerald Brooke, a lecturer in Russian at London University, was arrested in Moscow for subversive activities. The severity of his sentence – 5 years' detention – made it seem probable that the Russians were exaggerating his offence in order to negotiate the release of the Krogers (p. 127). Brooke was in fact exchanged for the Krogers in 1969.

The award of the M.B.E. to each of the four Beatles in June angered many, not least the members of the Order to which the group were being admitted, some of whom returned their insignia to Buckingham Palace (one of the Beatles, John Lennon, returned his in 1969). In recommending to the Queen that these M.B.E.s should be awarded, Wilson was no doubt thinking that teenagers would be voters at 21 (from 1970 the age has been lowered to 18), but he was also anxious to emphasise the value of dollar-earners to the economy. He had to preserve the parity of the £ – to avoid having to devalue. His surcharge of 15% on imports, one of his first measures in the autumn of 1964, had infuriated otherwise friendly countries with a considerable volume of exports to Britain, but it did lead to an improvement in trade figures.

Important figures which did not improve were those of prices and incomes. 'Improvement' here meant staying the same, or, better still, incomes rising while prices stayed the same. This they were not doing; but on 1 May the new Prices and Incomes Board (PIB) held its first meeting under its Chairman, Aubrey Jones, and thereafter proposed rises were referred to it. In September, George Brown, Minister of Economic Affairs, produced his National Plan, which aimed at a 25% growth in output by 1970.

With their very small majority of 5, which made another election likely before long, Labour had to preserve a glowing image. Health Service prescription charges were removed on 31 January. Business entertainment allowances, except for overseas buyers, were disallowed in the April budget. These were both popular measures among Labour supporters. How were the Conservatives to convert enough of them to ensure a return to power? They decided on a change of leader and – for the first time in the party's history – democratic election of a new one. Sir Alec Douglas-Home resigned and in the vote for his successor (28 July), Edward Heath had a majority of 17 over Reginald Maudling.

The transformation of the old London County Council into the Greater London Council (GLC) on 1 April was the result of a law passed under the Conservatives in 1963. The GLC, drawn from 32 boroughs, covered a much wider area than the LCC; but the LCC Education Authority survived as the Inner London Education Authority (ILEA).

Again this year disturbances were caused by young people at seaside resorts during the Easter and Whitsun weekends.

In May Bossard, a civil servant, was sentenced to 21 years for selling secrets to Russia; Staff Sergeant Allen received 10 years for selling documents to Middle Eastern countries.

On 1 August the government had the courage to raise the combined radio and television licence fee from £4 to £5 and the licence for radio alone to £1 5s. At the same time a ban on the advertising of cigarettes on television was introduced. Neither of these moves was a vote-catcher. Nor, perhaps, was the Murder (Abolition of Death Penalty) Act, passed in November. This act abolished capital punishment for murder and substituted life imprisonment for a trial period ending in 1970 (the abolition has now been made permanent, unless of course a future Parliament passes a law reintroducing it).

On 9 August Singapore seceded from Malaysia and became an independent republic within the Commonwealth (see p. 154). Lee Kuan Yew, Prime Minister since 1959, continued in office.

In December Roy Jenkins became Home Secretary and thus a member of the Cabinet. Barbara Castle, already in the Cabinet, became Minister of Transport. Her predecessor, Thomas Fraser, had just introduced a 70 m.p.h. speed limit on all unrestricted roads. This was to last experimentally until Easter 1966 but when the time came it was not rescinded.

Wilson's first year in power had ended in October. Kenneth Harris interviewed him for the *Observer* on such questions as the balance of payments crisis and how he got on with President Johnson. (The Rhodesian crisis had not yet broken at the time of this interview.) At one point he asked: 'Have you felt sad, bowed down, about anything in the last year?' Wilson began his reply with the words: 'Yes. Vietnam.'

1966

'AND THEN INDIA and Pakistan,' the Prime Minister went on. Their war was another of the sadnesses over which he admitted to having felt bowed down during 1965. The turn of the year was cheered by the news that peace talks between the two countries were taking place in Tashkent with Kosygin (Chairman of the Council of Ministers of the U.S.S.R.) as mediator. On 10 January Lal Bahadur Shastri, Prime Minister of India, and President Ayub Khan of Pakistan signed an agreement in which they undertook to observe their obligation under the U.N. Charter not to use force to settle disputes, and to withdraw their troops to positions held before 5 August 1965. But later on the same day Shastri died. On 19 January Mrs. Indira Gandhi succeeded him as Prime Minister. She is the daughter of Nehru, but her late husband was not connected with Mahatma Gandhi.

On 11 January cameras, microphones and reporters' notebooks had moved to Lagos, where Wilson attended a two-day Commonwealth Conference on Rhodesia. He was urged to use force, but was still unwilling to do so. A ban on all trade with Rhodesia was the most that the conference could agree to impose.

How many pressmen stayed on in Nigeria, expecting another story to break? There were straws in the wind. On 1 January the formerly French Central African Republic had suffered a military *coup d'état*; Upper Volta followed suit on 4 January. On 15 January it was Nigeria's turn. Army units rebelled and next day placed General Ironsi in power. Parliamentary government, bequeathed by Britain at the independence ceremonies a few years before, was abandoned.

A military *coup d'état* does not necessarily mean bloodshed. Nigeria's did. Sir Abubakar Balewa, the Federal Prime Minister, recently host to the Commonwealth Conference, was killed; so were the Prime Ministers of the Northern and Western Regions; so were a number of senior officers. Nor was this all that Nigeria had to suffer in 1966. On 29 July the army mutinied. Ironsi fled and Colonel (later General) Gowon took his place as head of state (the office of President had been abolished in the January *coup* and has not been revived).

General Ironsi was an Ibo, and the group of disgruntled army officers which put him in power included a number of young Ibos. After Ironsi's removal by Gowon (a Northerner) in July 1966, hostility against the Ibos flared up in the north and during September-October thousands of Ibos were killed. Of those who survived, over a million moved back to the Eastern region – their traditional homeland, which was now, under its military Governor Colonel Ojukwu, less than ever disposed to accept control from the Federal Government in Lagos.

In Ghana it was against Nkrumah's authoritarian rule and, to use a favourite Russian expression, 'personality cult', that the military, aided by the police, rebelled. General Ankrah seized power on 24 February, when Nkrumah was in Peking. Ministers were put in prison; political detainees were let out. Nkrumah's statue was pulled down and the head broke off. Civilian rule was introduced in October 1969, with Dr. Busia as Prime Minister, but abolished in 1972 by an army coup, led by Colonel Acheampong, who became Head of State.

On 12 March Sukarno of Indonesia delegated most of his powers to the anti-communist Suharto, with whose coming to power the 'confrontation' (a war in all but name) between Indonesia and Malaysia came to an end. A peace agreement was signed in August. Next year Suharto replaced Sukarno as President and Prime Minister of Indonesia. Sukarno was held under house arrest until his death in 1970.

One-man rule was becoming the fashion in much of black Africa. Dr. Obote, the Prime Minister, suspended the Constitution of Uganda on 24 February and in April had himself made President as well as Prime Minister. The deposed President was the Kabaka of Buganda, who still hoped for a measure of independence in his own part of the country. Obote however attacked and captured his palace, and the Kabaka had to leave for a second period of exile in Britain, where he died in 1969 (see p 83). In 1971 Obote's government was replaced by the much more dictatorial rule of General Idi Amin.

Sierra Leone, independent since 1961, substituted military for parliamentary government in March 1967.

Britain however remained faithful to the parliamentary system. Since Labour's return to power everyone had been wondering how long Wilson could carry on with such a small majority. During much of 1965 the opinion polls had favoured the Conservatives, in spite of the dissatisfaction with Home and the change to Heath in July. Labour's refusal to build a new aircraft carrier, cuts in defence orders to the aircraft industry, threats to withdraw from the Concorde project, threats to denationalise steel and a severe budget had all contributed towards reducing the party's popularity. On the other hand Wilson's cool handling of Rhodesia's UDI, an issue on which the Conservatives were divided, increased his prestige towards the end of the year and Labour entered 1966 with the opinion polls in their favour. The death of one of their M.P.'s in February reduced the overall majority to 3 (a Labour member had become Speaker earlier in the year and therefore no longer had a vote in the Commons). Wilson decided that the right moment had come. The date of the election – Thursday 31 March – was announced on 28 February.

Of the three election addresses which came through one north London letter-box during March, the Liberal's, on good quality glossy paper, is much the most attractive in format. The Liberal is the only one of the three candidates who does not smile, at any rate on the front page. He just looks calm and serious. On the inside pages, in a smart, narrow-lapel, one-button jacket, he smiles beside a beautiful blonde wife in a simple frock (skirt length not shown) and again with his arms round three smiling children.

The Conservative smiles on the front of his address. His wife, on the back, friendly, wearing pearls, urges the reader to 'reject the tinsel attractions of Socialism and decide for the solid sense of the Conservatives.' The Labour man, in a sporty looking tie, is laughing confidently. He does not tell us anything about his wife and family. He prints very prominently the party's election slogan: 'You *know* Labour government works.'

All three addresses mention Britain's economic crisis. This was the main issue in the election. Which party could improve the balance of payments position and avoid devaluation of the pound? Each was of course confident that it was the best qualified to do this, but economics is a complicated subject and the three addresses do not enlarge upon their parties' economic policies, which are therefore difficult to compare. For comparisons one has to turn to the various subheads. Under DEFENCE, for instance, the Conservative promises a new aircraft carrier. The Labour man says simply: 'Defence costs reduced.'

What about the Bomb, the nuclear deterrent, as it is called officially? Only the Liberal mentions it. He thinks we would do better to concentrate on conventional forces. He is also the only one of the three to mention immigration, calling for a 'more open' policy, and the only one who, under 'Education', says he wants to reduce the size of classes as well as ending the 11+. The Labour man says: '11+ to be ended. No more selection.' The Conservative says: 'Pursue an education policy free from party dogma.' On EEC (the Common Market) he is more definite: 'Work energetically for entry at the first opportunity.' The Liberal too is keen to get us in.

Labour refuses to be drawn. Their candidate makes no statement about EEC; but he makes promises about matters of more immediate interest to the man or woman in the street – pension increases, rate rebates for those in need, a chance to buy the lease of your house and become a freeholder, tax-free grants and training schemes for redundant workers; finally 'Consumer Protection', a subject also given prominence by the Liberal, who calls for 'protection against shoddy goods and misleading advertising'.

As it happened, American consumers, in particular consumers of motor cars, also found a champion at about this time – not a political party but a man. Ralph Nader had written *Unsafe at Any Speed,* criticising the built-in dangers of American cars, in particular the General Motors Corvair. On 22 March the President of General Motors appeared before a Senate hearing to apologise to Nader because an investigator had been hired to unearth details of his private life. Sales of *Unsafe at Any Speed* rocketed, sales of the Corvair fell by 70% within a year. Nader, aged 31 at the time, continued to champion consumers' rights. He found plenty to do.

Nader was not front page news, but several events in March took the public's attention from the election campaign for a while. On the 11th Princess Beatrix of the Netherlands was married in Amsterdam to a German, Claus von Amsberg. The marriage had been criticised by many in Holland, where the Nazi occupation had left acutely bitter memories. In addition the Dutch had nurtured one of the earliest of the protest movements, which were to become common throughout Europe and the United States in the next few years. These were the Provos. Usually they provoked their elders, but the Princess's choice of husband threw a temporary bridge over the generation gap. Protests were heard from every age-group. The older generation, however, showed their disapproval by staying away from the wedding procession. The crowds were thinner than had been expected. The Provos turned up, shouted 'Out with Claus!' and threw smoke bombs. Near the church where the couple were married is the house of Anne Frank which is kept as a memorial to her sufferings during the Occupation (she finally died in a concentration camp) and also houses an organisation devoted to the promotion of international understanding.

Another result of the Occupation could perhaps be seen in de Gaulle's desperate striving to make up for France's humiliation by carving out a special position for her in the post-war world. He was due to visit Moscow in June and it was no doubt with an eye towards this that he chose the month of March for his announcement that France would withdraw her troops from NATO and that all NATO military installations must be off French soil in twelve months (NATO HQ subsequently moved from near Paris to Brussels). On a visit to Cambodia in August de Gaulle called for an American withdrawal from Vietnam.

The World Cup, of solid gold, worth £30,000 and due to be competed for in July, was at this time on exhibition in the Central Hall, Westminster, whence it was stolen on 20 March. It was found in a south London garden a week later. England won it on 30 July by defeating West Germany 4-2.

Meanwhile the Archbishop of Canterbury had visited Rome, embraced Pope Paul and exchanged the kiss of peace with him (23 March). This was the first official meeting between the heads of their Churches for 400 years (i.e. since the reign of Mary Tudor, our last Roman Catholic monarch).

The election campaign was a quiet one. It was affected by the fact that the last election (1964) had been held only seventeen months before. Only 75.8% of those entitled to vote did so, although it was a calm, mild day. The polls closed at 9.0 p.m. Just over an hour later the first result (Cheltenham) was declared. In the final result Labour had 363 seats, Conservatives 253, Liberals 12 and 'Republican Labour' 1 (the member for Belfast West). Add the Speaker's seat (he was elected with a big majority, being opposed only by an independent) and you get 630, which has been the total number of M.P.'s since the 1955 election. Labour's overall majority was 97.

For the Liberals and the smaller parties the election was disappointing and expensive. A candidate forfeits his deposit of £150, if he fails to obtain more than one-eighth of the total votes cast in his constituency. Deposits were forfeited in 1966 by 104 Liberals, 57 Communists, 18 Plaid Cymru (Welsh Nationalists), 10 Scottish Nationalists, 9 Conservatives, 3 Labour and 36 others. Among the 'others' was D. E. Sutch who polled 585 votes against the Prime Minister's 41,122 and the Conservative's 20,182 at Huyton (Lancs.). This was 'Screaming Lord' Sutch, the pop musician who had for a time run one of the Thames estuary pirate radio stations.

When the new Parliament was opened by the Queen on 21 April, the ceremony was televised for the first time. Wilson had made a number of changes in his Government, but the chief posts were held by the same people. Stewart was still at the Foreign Office, Callaghan at the Exchequer, Brown in charge of Economic Affairs, Healey in charge of Defence. A month later (3 May) Callaghan produced the budget which introduced Corporation Tax and Selective Employment Tax (SET), a tax intended to decrease the number of non-productive jobs (e.g. hairdressing, garages, entertainment) and thus make more people available for industrial work. One criticism of the tax was that Government employees were exempt; but it brought in £600m in its first year, proved comparatively easy to collect, and had the desired effect of getting more people into manufacturing. However SET and Purchase Tax were replaced in April 1973 by VAT (Value Added Tax) in order to bring Great Britain into line with the practice of other EEC (Common Market) countries.

The Times (6d.) chose budget day to appear for the first time with news, instead of small advertisements, on the front page. The popular press had been doing this since around 1900 and even the *Manchester Guardian* had moved news on to the front page in 1952. A few days earlier (Monday 25 April) Dame Sybil Thorndike, a distinguished actress who also took an interest in politics, had set the presses rolling to produce the first issue of the *Morning Star* (4d.), which was the *Daily Worker* reborn.

Both *The Times* and the *Morning Star* carried protests about the bombing of North Vietnam. The Vietnam war was also the subject of an impressive play produced in 1966 – *US. The Times* had a leader 'Students out for change', which referred to disturbances at universities in Italy and Spain. The girl on the new *Times* fashion page had a skirt about two inches above the knee and older women were advised not to worry about the modern tendency to use young-looking models: 'Take no notice of the face, if it is not your age group. Just look at the clothes in a detached way.' The *Morning Star* also remembered that it was talking to two generations, and therefore, in addition to its Pop Pickings column, devoted in this first issue to Jimmy Smith, it reported a jazz concert – the Thelonius Monk Quartet, at the Royal Festival Hall. Sadly, however, the reviewer asked: 'Am I unreasonable in expecting fresh and challenging material?' Such material was certainly around. 1966 was the year in which the guitarist Eric Clapton formed the group called Cream, which had a sensational career in Britain and U.S.A., cut the single 'I feel fine' and in 1968 disbanded.

The government's Prices and Incomes policy continued to meet with strong opposition from the Trade Unions. It was admitted that there should be some exceptions (e.g. for 'lower paid workers') to the general limit of $3\frac{1}{2}\%$ for wage rises in one year. But which were the 'lower paid workers'? The National Union of Seamen claimed that they were; in addition they had not yet been granted the 40-hour week. These grievances were heightened by the feeling that the sacrifices of Union members during the war had not received sufficient recognition, and there was resentment at a number of the regulations under which crews at sea had to work. The owners' final offer was not considered acceptable by the delegates at the Union's annual conference and on 16 May all British seamen were on strike for the first time since 1911. To safeguard food supplies a state of emergency was declared on 23 May. The dockers were not on strike, so food supplies carried in foreign ships went on coming in. But 900 British ships were tied up, 27,000 men were affected and the loss to industry was estimated at tens of millions of pounds. It was the biggest strike in Britain since the war and went on for 47 days, by which time the Union had spent half a million on strike pay and agreed to a return to work from midnight on Friday 1 July. The 40-hour week was to be introduced after 12 months, but this and other concessions had been gained earlier. The prolongation of the strike was less rewarding than the seamen expected.

One of the steps Wilson had taken in the hope of making the Prices and Incomes policy more acceptable to the Trade Unions was to make Frank Cousins Minister of Technology after the 1964 election and find him a safe Labour seat (January 1965). Cousins had been General Secretary of the powerful Transport and General Workers Union. But he now felt that he could not support Part IV of the Prices and Incomes Bill, which gave the government power to freeze wages, and he resigned on 3 July. Wedgwood Benn succeeded him as Minister and Cousins resumed his post as General Secretary of the T. and G.W.U., later also resigning his Parliamentary seat.

A further worsening of the economic situation, partly caused by the seamen's strike, led to the introduction of additional restrictive measures into the Prices and Incomes Bill on 20 July (which also happened to be the date of the first riots in Belfast). The government measures included the reintroduction of currency regulations affecting foreign travel. No one was to be allowed to take more than £50 out of the country, once a year, to spend on a holiday outside the sterling area. (This remained the law until 1970.) Compensations however were available for those who stayed at home. Britain's (and Europe's) first Playboy Club had just opened.

George Brown had hoped to solve Britain's problems by a policy of greater productivity. The restrictive measures, which the Cabinet had felt were necessary, if devaluation was to be avoided, distressed him. On 20 July he threatened to resign from his post of Minister of Economic Affairs, but decided not to later in the day. In August however he changed places with Stewart, the Foreign Secretary.

Space fiction was already imagining men on the moon. A story in *Look and Learn* (1s. 3d.), an informative weekly for girls and boys, told how a group of good Russians together with Americans and British, defeated a gang of bad Russians, who had also managed to land:

Eric looked out to where the [bad] Russians had been standing. The dust was spilling down in a colossal vortex into an underground cavern that had been opened up by the landslide, and as it slid down it left the ridge exposed where the Russians had made their way towards the ship. The crater was being drained of its dust. The Moon had opened up its bowels and sucked them down.

In fact the Russians, though still very active in space research, attempted no manned flights this year. The Americans, aiming at a moon landing before 1970, went ahead with their Gemini programme. Armstrong and Scott succeeded in linking Gemini 8 with a rocket while in flight. Gemini 11 reached the record height of 853 miles on 12 September; Richard Gordon climbed out of the spacecraft and for a time rode astride its nose. Gemini 12 was launched on 11 November and during this flight Major Aldrin remained outside the spacecraft for 2 hours 9 minutes. The unmanned Lunar Orbiter I, launched in August, circled the moon and took photographs, indicating that the Americans had now caught up with the Russians in this branch of space exploration. Lunar Orbiter II, launched on 23 November, photographed the landscape from 284 miles above the moon's surface.

Francis Chichester set out to circle the earth alone, in a sailing boat. He left Plymouth in *Gypsy Moth IV* on 27 August and reached Sydney via Cape Town on 12 December. He left again on 29 January and returned to Plymouth, via Cape Horn, on 28 May 1967. The Queen knighted him at Greenwich, where Queen Elizabeth I had knighted Drake when he returned from sailing round the world four hundred years ago.

The Chinese have a much longer history than ours and put it to different uses. Four hundred years ago in their country an official called Hai Jui was dismissed from office. His memory was now revived for the following reasons.

After Stalin's death, in 1953, Mao Tse-tung (born in 1893), was the most venerable figure in the communist world. When Stalin's memory was vilified by Khrushchev in 1956, Mao did not approve. He had no use for Khrushchev and his visit to Moscow in 1957 was his last. China remained Stalinist and throughout the sixties became increasingly hostile towards Russia, which, Mao felt, was becoming more and more like a western country and therefore betraying communist ideals. He was anxious to prevent this happening in China. He therefore, in the movement called 'The Great Leap Forward' (1958), organised China into thousands of units called communes, which enjoyed a considerable degree of self-government. During the next three years bad weather ruined the harvests, the communes were not sufficiently successful, some Party members were dismissed, and there was much criticism. From 1962 Mao was occupied with the problem of getting rid of what he called right-wing criticism and of restoring to the Party the enthusiasm which had kept it together during the 30's and 40's and finally brought it to power.

Some of the criticism was veiled. This is where Hai Jui comes in. A play called *Hai Jui Dismissed from Office* was written, and, although the dismissal had taken place 400 years ago, it was clear that spectators who thought the dismissal unfair might carry their feelings over into the 20th century and look askance at some of the recent dismissals of party members. Mao called the author of the play and those who shared his views 'bourgeois rightists', 'right opportunists', or 'revisionists' (i.e. people who wanted to 'revise' traditional ideas of communism). His own supporters were 'the revolutionary masses', 'the workers, peasants and soldiers' or simply 'the proletariat'.

On 10 November 1965 an article was published by a Shanghai newspaper, savagely attacking the author of *Hai Jui Dismissed from Office* as a 'lackey of U.S. imperialism', who had distorted history to satirise the present. A flood of similar articles followed in the first half of 1966 with titles such as 'Capture the positions in the field of historical studies seized by the bourgeoisie', 'A great revolution that touches the people to their very souls'. The 'revolution' which Mao now fomented, within the already 're-volutionary' (i.e. communist) China, was called the 'Cultural Revolution', because it sprang from disagreement over a 'cultural' question – the interpretation of history.

The Cultural Revolution began with the closing of many schools and universities, not, as one might have expected, with the expansion of them. It was an exciting time for young people. They were organised in a movement called the Red Guards, who were encouraged to demonstrate against their teachers, many of whom were physically maltreated as well as being made the object of contempt. Nor, in spite of the attempt to decentralise and to encourage local democracy through the communes, were the energies of the Guards confined to their own localities. From all over China they converged upon Peking to attend demonstrations (the first was on 18 August) and catch a glimpse of Chairman Mao (he is Chairman of the Chinese Communist Party – not Prime Minister, nor Chairman of the Republic; but he is the most important person in China).

Somehow the railways carried about 11m Red Guards to Peking. Both there and when they returned to their home districts, the Guards were occupied in the denunciation by speech and posters of people thought to be bourgeois. And all this denunciation was not only a student activity.

Typical captions to photographs in a propaganda magazine are: 'Angry automobile plant workers write one poster after another, opening fire on the sinister anti-Party and anti-socialist gang', 'Commune members, who are taking an active part in the great proletarian cultural revolution, hold a discussion in the fields', 'Going into battle against the black anti-Party, anti-socialist line, soldiers write articles and blackboard newspapers expressing their resolve to crush all enemies both with and without guns'.

Everyone studied and discussed the *Thoughts of Chairman Mao,* which had been published in a pocket-size book, bound in red plastic. (There is an English edition.)

J. S. Horn, an English doctor resident in China, wrote (*Away with all Pests,* Hamlyn, 1969):

> Here in Peking, China's Great Cultural Revolution is under way and hundreds of thousands of students are demanding that courses should be shortened, that examinations cease to be tests of memory and become tests of reasoning power and an aid to study, that methods of study should be revolutionised so as to link theory with practice, and that the isolation of students from the life of the people be ended by regular participation in ordinary work.

The Cultural Revolution certainly whipped up enthusiasm – some would say fanaticism – for Mao among the young. The Red Guards however were allowed to fade away and during 1967-9 universities and schools reopened. They now aimed at improving understanding between country and town. Schoolchildren and students went to the country to learn what hard agricultural labour is like and at the same time to contribute to the discussions, based on Mao's thought, which are a part of life in every sector of Chinese society.

Because of the Cultural Revolution, there were few contacts between China and the West during the late sixties; but this did not affect trade. In 1966, for instance, agreements were made with Canada and even with Australia, whose forces were supporting the Americans in South Vietnam, for the import to China of huge quantities of wheat.

India, whose quarrels with Pakistan had been settled at the beginning of the year, now had fighting within her borders. The huge Punjab state, inhabited in the north by Sikhs and in the south by Hindus, had been provided with a capital city of exceptional beauty, designed by the French architect Le Corbusier (1887-1965) and named Chandigarh. It lies at the foot of a range of hills and is surrounded by a 5-mile green belt. One point upon which the two peoples of the Punjab agreed was that both admired

Chandigarh. When, after rioting, the Punjab was split (November 1966) into two states, Punjab (Sikh) in the north and Haryana (Hindu) in the south, they still had to share the capital. Mrs. Gandhi managed to postpone for 3 years a decision on which of the new states should have Chandigarh, but after one 83-year-old Sikh had died on the 74th day of a protest fast (October 1969), and another had threatened to burn himself alive, she gave Le Corbusier's glorious city to the Sikhs, while the Hindus were given a sum of money with which to build a new capital.

In Africa, where attention had been concentrated on the revolutions in Ghana and Nigeria, it moved suddenly to the South African Republic, where the Prime Minister, Dr. Verwoerd, was assassinated on 6 September. This however appeared to be an isolated incident, not supported by a larger plot or uprising. The murderer was a Portuguese, who had been working as a temporary messenger in the South African Parliament. B. J. Vorster succeeded as Prime Minister on 13 September. Shortly afterwards Bechuanaland became independent as Botswana (30 September, see p 43) and Basutoland as the Kingdom of Lesotho (4 October). Lesotho is an enclave entirely surrounded by South African territory. In 1970 King Moshoeshoe II was placed under house arrest by Chief Jonathan, the Prime Minister, and the constitution was suspended. One more African country had gone over to a form of dictatorship.

A further attempt to solve the Rhodesian problem was made by Wilson on 2 December, when he invited Ian Smith to meet him for talks on board H.M.S. *Tiger,* at sea off Gibraltar; but the document which they prepared together was not accepted by the Rhodesian cabinet. White Rhodesians still would not accept any plan which would ultimately hand over power to the black majority.

In South America there was only one British possession – British Guiana. This country became independent as Guyana on 26 May. In February 1970 Guyana became a republic within the Commonwealth. Barbados, in the West Indies, became independent on 30 November 1966.

The U.S.A. was counter-attacking on the pop music front. American groups – the Monkees, Love, the Doors and Jefferson Airplane were becoming as well known as the Beatles and the Rolling Stones. At the same time a new recipe for living was being tried in California. Dr. Timothy Leary, 'high priest of the L.S.D. drug cult', who was sentenced to 10 years imprisonment in 1970 for smuggling marijuana from Mexico, in 1966 provided the slogan 'Turn on, tune in, drop out'. 'Turn on' was part of the new vocabulary. It meant 'to take drugs'. A 'trip' was an L.S.D. experience. A 'freak out' was an uncontrolled situation, often resulting from drug-taking. 'Hippies' were the people who adopted this way of life. They were non-violent, believed in shared possessions and gradually filled the San Francisco district of Haight Ashbury.

On the whole the new vocabulary was mono-syllabic but one of its most important words was long – psychedelic. Nik Cohn, in *Pop from the Beginning* (Weidenfeld and Nicolson, 1969) explains:

> In the dictionary, psychedelic means mind-expansion but, in practice, out in California, it only meant faking up an acid [i.e. drug] trip. Instead of just standing up there and strumming, groups took to surrounding themselves with flashing lights, back-projected films, pre-recorded tapes, freak dancers, plus anything else they could think of, and the idea was that, faced by all this, you'd be hit by a total experience, a simultaneous flowering of all your senses and you'd fly.
>
> You didn't of course. Instead you watched the legs of them sexy go-go dancers and wound up with a headache.

In Britain, during September, the prices and incomes dispute moved from Parliament, which was in recess, to the T.U.C. Conference at Blackpool, where support for the pay standstill was won by a narrow majority.

Since the shooting of three policemen in a London street during August, capital punishment had again become a subject of controversy. The risk of hanging the wrong man was shown in the Brabin report (12 October), which stated that Timothy John Evans probably did not murder his daughter, for which he had been executed in 1950. On 18 October Evans was given a posthumous free pardon; on the 19th, 170 M.P.'s signed a motion to restore hanging.

The Tay Road Bridge, opened in August, and the Severn Bridge, opened in September, were solid achievements which gave people some much needed encouragement in the gloom generated by the difficult economic situation. Light relief was provided by commemoration of the nine hundredth anniversary of the battle of Hastings (14 October 1066). The last successful invasion of our island is no longer mourned as a resounding defeat. Hastings enjoyed an influx of visitors and those who could not get there were pretty well informed by the colour magazines and the rest of the communications industry about what happened before, during and after the battle. Reproductions of the Bayeux Tapestry, particularly its more horrific sections were popular.

A week later the thoughts of everyone in Britain were concentrated on a twentieth century horror. This was not something which happened far away, in Vietnam or in Africa. It was in our own country, at Aberfan in South Wales, where, at 9.15 on the morning of 21 October a landslide from one of the 'tips' (hills of piled-up waste from the coal mines), engulfed some houses and a primary school, killing 116 children and 28 adults.

There was nothing to be done except dig, with next to no hope of getting anyone out alive. For this work and for canteen and relief services there was no lack of volunteers. The Queen, the Duke of Edinburgh, Lord Snowdon and the Prime Minister all paid visits to express their sympathy and make sure that everything possible was being done. A disaster fund was immediately opened. When it closed at the end of January 1967 £1,750,000 had been received from more than forty countries.

Why had the disaster happened? There was intense bitterness against the National Coal Board. One father demanded that 'Buried alive by National Coal Board' should be entered as the cause of death on his child's certificate. It was announced that a tribunal would enquire into the accident, but meanwhile the press, radio and television were interviewing people on the spot. The Attorney-General felt that such interviews might prejudice the tribunal. He stated in Parliament that comment was undesirable and might have legal consequences. This infuriated the press. The Government as well as the N.C.B. were now in bad odour. However there were no committals for contempt of court and the Aberfan Tribunal was thorough. Tony Austin, in *Aberfan: the story of a disaster* (Hutchinson, 1967) writes that it was the longest tribunal in British history. It took 76 days. 136 witnesses were heard; Lord Robens, Chairman of the N.C.B., did not at first volunteer as a witness, but finally appeared on Day 70. When the report was published (3 August 1967), stating that blame for the disaster rested on the National Coal Board and in particular on nine men, who were named, Robens offered to resign. But his resignation was not accepted.

The Aberfan landslide was closely followed (2 November) by flood disasters in northern and central Italy. These were less tragic from a human point of view, though immense suffering was involved, but the loss and damage amongst art treasures and manuscripts, particularly in Florence, was without precedent. Here, as at Aberfan, money and offers of help flowed in from all over the world.

On 19 December Ronald 'Buster' Edwards, who had surrendered in London on 19 September, was sentenced to 15 years for his part in the great train robbery of 1963. However Edwards's arrest was closely followed (22 October) by the escape of George Blake (p 126) from Wormwood Scrubs.

There had been many other escapes during the year and the outcry over Blake's led to the immediate setting up of an enquiry under Lord Mountbatten. Mountbatten made his recommendations for the improvement of prison security on 22 December. There were 8 more escapes on 23 December and another 8 on 26 December. Britons saw the new year in with the knowledge that 692 prisoners had escaped from prison during the year and that 121 were still at large.

Mountbatten's recommendations and the action which followed were reassuring. But four years later Tom Clayton, after a six-month study of Pentonville, wrote of the report in *Men in Prison* (Hamish Hamilton, 1970): 'it may well have reassured the public, but it has probably set back the advance to a humane and sensible prison policy some 25 years.'

1967

IN THE MIDDLE of 1967 a Zambian diplomat caused a stir by speaking of it as 'The year of the toothless bulldog.' Africans felt that Britain was only growling at Ian Smith. Sanctions appeared to be no worse than a nuisance; they did not really hurt.

But we still had the World Cup. There was a reminder of this on New Year's Day, which was a Sunday and therefore gave people more time to read the Honours List. Alf Ramsey, who had managed England's World Cup team since 1963, was made a knight. Bobby Moore, the captain of the 1966 winning team, received the O.B.E.

Next morning *The Times* saw reason for a measure of satisfaction about our economic situation:

> The battle for the pound has gone well. Inflation has been slowed down. The squeeze has worked . . . There should be no return to the traditional, wasteful, bullying free-for-all in wage negotiations.

On Wednesday 4 January Donald Campbell embarked in his turbo-jet hydroplane Bluebird on Coniston Water, determined not only to beat his own world record of 276.3 m.p.h. (1964) but to raise it to 300. On his first run Campbell averaged 297. He turned to make the return trip, gathered speed and had covered most of the course. One of the reporters who was watching described what happened next (in *Donald Campbell, C.B.E.*, Allen and Unwin, 1969):

> Then I saw the nose start to lift very, very slowly – in fact she did look just like a whacking great blue bird trying to fly off the water. Then she seemed to stand on her tail – she seemed to be in a vertical position for one or two seconds, and there was a great cloud of spray. When the spray cleared, Donald and Bluebird had gone.

There had been 'Bluebirds' tackling the land speed record since 1924. Boats of the same name started on the water speed record in the 30's. Sir Malcolm Campbell drove them and held both records until his death in 1949. His son, Donald, won both in 1964. Since his death there have been no more Bluebirds.

Two days after Campbell's death another brave man was writing *The*

1967

Complete Bolivian Diaries of Che Guevara, edited by Dan James, Stein and Day, 1970):

> I gave a talk on the qualities of a guerilla and the need for greater discipline. I explained that our mission, above all, was to form an exemplary nucleus made of steel, and in that way I pointed out the importance of study as imperative for the future.

Che Guevara, who had helped Castro to seize power in Cuba at the end of 1959, proved much less useful at running the country once peace was re-established. Castro made him Minister of Industries in 1961, but he was not a success in that post. In 1964-5 he paid official visits to a number of African countries and led a force of Cuban guerillas in the Congo. On 7 November 1966, with a false passport and under an assumed name, he arrived in Bolivia. There he and Castro hoped to start a revolution which would fire the whole of South America and be strong enough to resist the inevitable U.S. intervention. After three months, however, Bolivians had shown no sign of joining the guerillas in the hoped-for numbers. One of Che's men wrote:

> . . . there are comrades who are not guerilla material because they are dregs . . . they want to do no work; they want no weapons, they want to carry no loads. . . .

Nevertheless, for the time being, Che and his band survived. The world heard very little about them.

News about astronauts was more readily available. Everything that happened to them was known around the world pretty quickly and so far, both from America and Russia, it had always been good news. Now, suddenly, it was bad. The Americans suffered first. On the evening of 27 January three men were trapped in the capsule of a rocket which was on the ground. They were taking part in the simulation of an Apollo launching which had been scheduled for 27 February. Virgil Grissom (40) and Edward White (36) had made space flights before. White had been the first American to 'walk' in space. Roger Chaffee (31) had not yet flown in space. Tape recordings are useful to the investigators of such accidents, but horrifying. The last message recorded from the astronauts was: 'We're on fire . . . get us out of here!' But it took over ten minutes for a rescue team to unscrew the hatch. They were too late.

A 3000-page report on the accident gave a faulty electric wire as the probable cause and sharply criticised certain aspects of the Apollo project. The test flight was postponed and it seemed uncertain whether it would after all be possible to land a man on the moon by 1970.

Less than three months later (24 April) the Russian Colonel Komarov, who had taken part in the 3-man flight of Voskhod 1 in 1964, was killed when his Soyuz spacecraft crashed on landing. It was reported that the parachute used for the final stage of the descent failed to open.

Only three days before this accident (21 April) Stalin's daughter Svetlana arrived in New York. Early in March she had requested asylum at the U.S. Embassy in Delhi, after defecting from Russia. Her reminiscences were eagerly awaited and were published before the end of the year as *Twenty Letters to a Friend* by Svetlana Alliluyeva (her maiden name). The dedication was to her mother, who had committed suicide in 1932. The contents were not real letters to a particular person. They were simply chapters in a sombre but unsensational autobiography. 'It's true,' writes Svetlana, 'my father wasn't especially democratic, but he never thought of himself as a god.'

In Britain, beginning on 13 March, some students of the London School of Economics boycotted lectures and staged a sit-in (then a novelty in this country) against the appointment of Dr. Walter Adams as Principal, to succeed Sir Sidney Caine in October (Adams's previous post had been in Rhodesia). The students had other grievances too. They said that they had not enough say in the running of the School or in the planning of courses of study. Unrest spread from the L.S.E. to a number of other colleges and to universities outside London. After 1967 sit-ins became a familiar feature of student life in Britain. Inadequate student representation became a less common complaint, but others arose, such as the one about the right of universities to keep confidential files.

Sit-ins are thought to make good news stories and activities at L.S.E. were well covered. From 16 March, however, public interest was concentrated on the Liberian tanker *Torrey Canyon,* which had gone aground off Land's End. Her crew, except for one man, were saved; but escaping oil spread along 70 miles of British coast (the French suffered even more) and the government authorised the spending of half a million pounds on anti-pollution measures. Finally on 28 March *Torrey Canyon* was bombed and set on fire to prevent further dispersal of oil, though a subsequent report doubted whether this was the best way of dealing with the situation. Proceedings were taken against the tanker's owners, to obtain compensation for the damage, and in 1969 the British and French governments were paid £1½m each.

Labour were heavily defeated at the Greater London Council elections in April. They had been in power at County Hall since the thirties but now had only 18 seats against the Conservatives' 82. Huge Conservative gains followed in May, when borough elections were held in England and Wales. The Maud Report, *Management of Local Government*, published at the end of the month, suggested how the work of all these councillors might be streamlined. Changes based on its recommendations were made in 1974.

The May general election, for which preparations were being made in Greece, did not take place. Early in the morning of 21 April tanks entered Athens. As people began to wake up and turn on the radio they heard that the Army had seized power from the Conservative government and that everyone must stay at home, except for necessary shopping. At night there was a strict curfew and some firing could be heard; but on the following day life began to return to normal and very soon, though thousands of arrests had been made, there was little sign throughout Greece that a revolution had taken place. Even the Easter celebrations, which involve the gathering of large crowds who carry candles in procession, took place as usual, except that army units joined in the ceremonies and presented arms as the priest shouted 'Christ is risen', at the stroke of midnight on Easter Saturday.

As a result, tourists returned home saying 'everything is all right', and often adding that things were now more efficiently run. This is a usual reaction of unthinking and unfeeling people towards dictatorship.

The men now in power were middle-ranking army officers. Their leader, Papadopoulos (later Prime Minister) and some others were colonels, and this Greek government was often referred to as 'the colonels'. Their excuse for seizing power was that a leftist revolution would have broken out in Salonika if they had not acted when they did. No evidence has ever been produced to back this statement. Early restoration of democracy was promised but did not take place. Opponents of the regime were still held without trial in island prisons. This denial of human rights finally led to a proposal that Greece should be expelled from the Council of Europe and to avoid this the Greek government withdrew from it (1969). But Greece was still a member of NATO. Her King, Constantine, left the country with his family in December 1967. In the summer of 1974 an unsuccessful attempt by Greek officers to take over the government of Cyprus led to the fall of the dictatorship in Athens and the restoration of democracy under a former Prime Minister – Konstantinos Karamanlis.

In Nigeria at the beginning of 1967, the situation was critical, with the Ibos of the Eastern region, under Ojukwu, bitterly hostile to control by the Federal Government of Gowon. Gowon met Ojukwu in Ghana during January and it was hoped that a compromise had been arranged. But relations between the two parts of the Federation continued to get worse and on 30 May Ojukwu declared that the Eastern Region was now the Republic of Biafra. Gowon was not prepared to allow withdrawal from the Federation and fighting began on 7 July. In the next few months Federal troops captured Enugu, the capital of Biafra, and the port of Calabar. At the end of 1967 no one thought that peace was still two years away.

During the wettest May for over a century, when most areas had twice their normal rainfall, Britons could console themselves with *The Forsyte Saga*, which had started its first 26-part run on 7 January (BBC2) or with the Beatles' latest LP *Sergeant Pepper's Lonely Hearts Club Band*, which had revived British pop from the doldrums of the mid-sixties. The month ended (28 May) with Chichester's triumphant arrival at Plymouth (see p 180). But Chichester had returned at a time of deep anxiety. Once again it seemed probable that war would break out in the Middle East.

The Suez Crisis (1956) had left Nasser with enhanced prestige but a defeated army. The victorious Israelis agreed to withdraw from Sinai, but were guaranteed access to their port of Eilat on the Gulf of Aqaba. Part of a United Nations Emergency Force (UNEF) was stationed on the strait of Tiran, which joins the Gulf of Aqaba to the Red Sea. The rest of UNEF patrolled the frontier, which ran north from Eilat to a point on the Mediterranean north-east of Gaza. During the next ten years there were raids and reprisals along Israel's northern frontier (with Lebanon and Syria) and along her eastern frontier (with Jordan). But there was no major outbreak and Israel had her outlet to the Red Sea. Nasser was not in a position to be aggressive. He was busy re-equipping and training his army and air force. Russia, eager to secure a foothold in Africa, was providing material (tanks, aircraft, etc.) and advice.

Syria also received Russian supplies and in the spring of 1967 the scale of raids into Israel and of Israeli reprisals mounted. On 11 May Israel informed the Security Council that she regarded herself as 'fully entitled to act in self-defence'. Nasser at this point decided that he was ready for another show-down. On 18 May he demanded the withdrawal of UNEF (about 3,400 men). Since these men were on Egyptian territory, U Thant could not refuse. UNEF moved out, Egyptian troops moved up to the frontier, and on Monday 22 May the straits of Tiran were closed. The reactions of the Great Powers were headlined on Wednesday (24 May):

WASHINGTON CONDEMNS BLOCKADE OF ISRAEL

RUSSIA GIVES WARNING TO ISRAEL

It was announced that Britain and the U.S. might act to reopen the Gulf of Aqaba. U Thant meanwhile was talking to Nasser in Cairo, but without result.

How far were the Great Powers prepared to go?

RUSSIA TELLS BRITAIN: STOP BACKING ISRAEL

was Saturday's headline (27 May). Russian warships were on their way to balance those of Britain and the U.S. in the eastern Mediterranean.

Then there was a week of waiting. The Egyptians were confident. The Israelis had drawn little encouragement from their Prime Minister's speech on Sunday 28 May, but the appointment of Moshe Dayan as Defence Minister (1 June) put heart into them. Dayan had been the hero of the 1956 Sinai campaign.

Jewish volunteers were arriving by air in Israel to help fill gaps on the home front left by men and women who had been called up (both sexes were in the front line). There were gifts and good wishes from all over the world. But Israel had no allies. Her people knew that they had only themselves to rely on and that, unless they won, they might be wiped out.

Dayan struck early in the morning of Monday 5 June. First the Israeli air force destroyed most of Egypt's aircraft while they were still on the ground. A few hours later Israeli tanks and infantry, their air cover unopposed, advanced against the Egyptian units in the Sinai peninsula. The Israeli victory was complete. Within three days they had reached the Suez Canal.

Dayan's daughter took part in the Sinai advance. In *A Soldier's Diary* (Weidenfeld and Nicolson, 1967) she describes a conversation with an Egyptian prisoner, a doctor, who spoke English. 'Tell me,' he was asked, 'why did they run away? Why did tank crews desert their tanks? Why didn't they use their arms?' 'They were astonished,' the doctor replied. 'We didn't expect it to happen like this. Radio announcements had told us of victory and we thought you were beaten. The officers had run away a day earlier and confusion set in.' He kept murmuring: 'We were astonished, astonished.'

Jordan and Syria fared no better than Egypt. Their airfields were attacked during the afternoon of Monday, 5 June, and large numbers of aircraft were destroyed. By Wednesday the Old City of Jerusalem, Jericho, Bethlehem and other Jordanian towns were in Israeli hands. The Syrians, in a wilder area, held out until Saturday, by which time the Jordanians and Egyptians had already accepted a ceasefire proposed by the U.N. The Syrians and Israel now joined this. So on its sixth day this short war within the long war, which had begun in 1948, came to an end. Nasser offered to resign, but he was urged to carry on and ruled Egypt until his death in 1970.

Israel remained in occupation of Sinai, the entire west bank of the Jordan and an area in Syria near the Sea of Galilee. There were numerous attempts at a peace settlement, but without success. Fanned by frontier incidents and the hot breath of rival Great Powers, the long war smouldered on, until Nasser's successor Sadat reopened it in 1973 by attacking during the Jewish festival of Yom Kippur (the Day of Atonement – September).

The Chinese, though active in a number of the developing countries in Africa, had not been involved in the Arab-Israel war. They were not inclined to side with Russia in any enterprise. Earlier in the year Red Guards had besieged the Russian Embassy in Peking for six days and Russian diplomats had been assaulted at the airport. However, the war offered an excuse for demonstrating against the British and a mob duly broke into our Embassy on 8 June.

Though both the Russian and the Indian Embassies had been attacked (the Americans were not then represented in China) the attentions of the Red Guards were particularly directed against the British, because of the arrests and closing of newspapers which had taken place in Hong Kong as a result of violent communist demonstrations. In May the house of the British consul in Shanghai was sacked while he and his family were there. He was later kicked and smeared with glue at the airport. Next came the attack already referred to and on 22 August, late at night, Red Guards set fire to the Embassy in Peking and assaulted the staff. Later in the month, outside the Chinese Embassy in London, there were clashes between members of the Embassy staff and police.

Early in September the Red Guards were ordered to cease violence, but it was some time before the British Embassy staff were given visas to come home and Mr. Anthony Grey, Reuter's correspondent, was held prisoner in his house in Peking until October 1969, when the last of those arrested during the Hong Kong disturbances were released.

On the other side of the Pacific the riots were racial. They could not be turned off like a tap, as those of the Red Guards had been, and they led to many more deaths. 1967 was a grim summer in the U.S.A. The bloodiest of the riots was in Detroit and lasted from 23 to 30 July. At least 40 people died, 2000 were injured and 5000 were left homeless as a result of looting and burning. Between 12 and 17 July during rioting in Newark, New Jersey, there were 26 deaths, 1500 injured and over 1000 arrests. Many other cities were affected, including Chicago, Boston, New York and

Washington. One of the retaliatory measures taken by the government was a law making it a Federal crime 'to cross state lines to incite a riot'. It was under this law that the prisoners in the Chicago trial of 1970 were prosecuted.

There were no race riots in the Dominion of Canada, which this year was celebrating its centenary with festivals and projects across the country and with an international exhibition of great splendour (opened 27 April), built on islands in the St. Lawrence off Montreal. 'Expo 67' was the inspiration of Montreal's Mayor Drapeau, a flamboyant personality, who also provided the city with what is probably the most elegant underground railway system in the world, in preparation for the expected crowds. Expectations were fulfilled. Visitors poured into Expo and their only complaint was that the queues were too many and too long. The Queen paid a visit; so, in the last week of July, did de Gaulle.

The General was rapturously received in Quebec, the French-speaking capital of a French-speaking province. At a dinner he said that the people of Quebec wished to take their destiny into their own hands (Ojukwu was saying the same kind of thing in Biafra). There followed a triumphal progress by road to Montreal. Every village was decorated. Some had even attempted small-scale replicas of the Arc de Triomphe. Arrived at Montreal (Montréal), which has the largest French-speaking population of any city in the world, except Paris, de Gaulle was welcomed outside the City Hall by a vast crowd in which separatists – people who want Quebec to separate from Canada – were well represented. They sang the Marseillaise, and the General joined in. They shouted 'Vive la France!' and the General echoed 'Vive la France!' They shouted the separatist slogan 'Vive la Québec Libre!' and this was the point at which the General should have held his peace, because he was Canada's guest and one does not encourage the break-up of a federation whose hospitality one is enjoying. But the General too shouted 'Vive la Québec Libre!' Up there on the balcony he raised both arms in a gesture he was fond of. The crowd roared with joy.

Mr. Lester Pearson, the Canadian Prime Minister, did not share this enthusiasm. He was considered to be one of the un-charismatic figures of the post-war world (in contrast to Trudeau, his successor), but he had made a name for himself in international affairs and was widely respected outside Canada. He said firmly that de Gaulle's statement was unacceptable. 'Canada will remain united,' he asserted. De Gaulle cut short his visit. *The Times* devoted its first leader to the affair, under the headline:

NO WAY TO BEHAVE

For another charismatic and unwelcome visitor to the American continent things turned out very differently. Castro had misjudged the ripeness
for revolution of Bolivia. The Bolivians were not suffering under their
government as the Cubans had suffered under Batista. Che Guevara's
guerilla group did not swell into an army. It never rose above 50. By 8
October only seventeen were left and Bolivian troops had surrounded
them in the mountains. A battle began at 1.30 in the afternoon:

> Che was wounded in the leg. A Bolivian comrade dragged him up a
> hill, where he clung to a tree and went on giving orders to his men.
> Then the Bolivian was killed, Che's gun was shot out of his hand and
> four soldiers surrounded him. Next day (9 October) he was executed.

His body was laid out in a village wash-house for people to come and
have a look.

What meanwhile of the so-called 'toothless bulldog'? Apart from Rhodesia the areas where Britain was directly involved overseas were Aden,
Hong Kong and Gibraltar, Aden, where 53 British servicemen had been
killed and 669 wounded since the emergency began at the end of 1963,
attained independence as part of the People's Republic of South Yemen,
which came into existence on 30 November, and in December became a
member of the United Nations. Like so many new countries it has a one-
party system of government.

Gibraltar was a different problem. It had no independence movement.
When a vote was held in September, 12,438 of the inhabitants wanted
British rule to continue. Only 44 did not. Spain, however still claimed that
the Rock was hers.

China, which is in a much stronger position in regard to Hong Kong,
appears to find it useful commercially. The Communist riots of 1967, of
which the last and worst was in October, were a demonstration of loyalty
to Mao, not an attempt to take over the island.

In Europe the Common Market was the government's main interest.
They had now decided to apply for admission, in spite of the fact that 35
Labour M.P.'s voted against and 40 abstained when the question was
debated in the House of Commons. But what these 75 M.P.'s failed to
achieve was a simple matter for de Gaulle. He made it clear to the other
Common Market countries that he did not want Britain to be admitted, and
that was that. He never relented and it was only after his retirement in
1969 that hopes of our eventual acceptance revived.

At home the iron and steel industry, nationalised by Labour in 1949 and
denationalised by the Conservatives in 1953, was now largely nationalised

again (22 March), though a small private sector was left. This measure angered the Conservatives and evoked little enthusiasm amongst Labour supporters. The man (and woman) in the street was much more interested in the Sexual Offences Act, which came into operation on 27 July, and the Abortion Act, which was passed in October and was to become operative in April 1968. The first relaxed some aspects of the law relating to adult homosexuals; the second made it much easier for doctors to comply with a woman's request for an abortion.

The new Road Safety Act, which came into force on 9 October, introduced breath tests. These were carried out with an apparatus called a breathaliser, which was much criticised. However, there were far fewer road deaths than before during the 1967 Christmas season.

The devaluation of sterling by 14.3% on 18 November was no better received than it had been in 1949. Shortly afterwards (29 November) Callaghan left the Treasury to change places with Jenkins, the Home Secretary. Further cuts in public expenditure were made, while an additional burden was imposed by an epidemic of foot and mouth disease which had broken out towards the end of October. 346,500 animals had to be slaughtered and their owners compensated before the end of the year.

One figure, however, instead of being cut had been exceeded. The Robbins Report had set a target of 350,000 university places by 1980-81. To reach this it was considered necessary that universities should have expanded to take 197,000 students by 1967-68. In fact the figure reached was 199,400. Colleges of Education (as the former Teachers' Training Colleges were now called) and Further Education Colleges were also ahead of their Robbins targets. Everyone was eager to see whether quality kept pace with quantity in the expanding world of higher education. It had been conjectured that more might mean worse.

To form the base of the pyramid which is topped by the universities a sound primary school system was needed. Primary schools had been discussed in the Plowden Report, published in January 1967. It resulted in the selection of a number of Educational Priority Areas (EPA's) – overcrowded, poor districts in big cities – for which the government made extra money available, in order to try and compensate the children for the disadvantages of their unsatisfactory living conditions. Those who hoped that the report would come out firmly against the compulsory act of worship, with which all schools start their day, were disappointed, while two proposals which *were* made – to abolish corporal punishment and to introduce teachers' aides – were not generally accepted, because they did not have the support of the teaching profession. The Inner London Education

Authority, however, stopped the caning of primary school children from 1 January 1973.

In addition to attempts by the government to improve the educational system, there had been a suggestion that the TUC (Trade Union Congress) might improve their public image and give pleasure to many by devoting some money to the arts. The idea was to show that culture was not only for intellectuals. So in 1960 Arnold Wesker (author of plays such as *Roots* in which working-class characters were central instead of playing comic or pathetic bit parts) founded Centre 42. The Centre provided six festivals in different parts of the country during 1961 and 1962 but it was then clear that without subsidies and a permanent home no further progress could be made. Jennie Lee interested Wilson, who was the Leader of the Opposition, and the gift of the Round House, a huge disused stable for steam locomotives in North London, was secured. Not enough money to convert the place into a full-scale artistic centre could be raised; but in 1967 the Round House did get started as a theatre and a number of impressive productions (e.g. Dennis Potter's *Son of Man,* 1969) were staged there. There were also pop concerts, food, drink and other goings-on.

Polo-neck sweaters had become fashionable for men. It was a sensation when Lord Snowdon was refused entry to a restaurant when he wore one with a dinner-jacket. The most interesting fashions during the summer of 1967 were to be found in California, where the hippies, dressed in a rich variety of clothes and hung with beads and bells, were now celebrating Flower Power. Surprisingly, this peak year for violent race riots in the United States was also the year in which some young people really believed in gentleness and really did hand flowers to policemen. In Britain the Beatles, who had given up touring in 1966, now became interested in the Maharishi's transcendental meditation movement. They wrote 'All You Need is Love' and gave up taking drugs. Mick Jagger, of the Rolling Stones, whose prison sentence on a drug charge had been quashed by the Court of Appeal at the end of July, was also among those interested in the meditation movement. When the Maharishi held a conference at Bangor in August, Jagger, Marianne Faithfull and the Beatles attended it. Perhaps a movement towards gentleness was appropriate, if this really was the year of the toothless bulldog.

What *was* it the year of ? Take your choice from the preceding pages and add two new plays – *Rosencrantz and Guildenstern are Dead* by Tom Stoppard, and Peter Nichols's first – *A Day in the Death of Joe Egg.* Until 'Joe Egg' no audience had ever rocked with laughter at a play about life with a dreadfully handicapped child. People were suspicious at first, and thought it must be in bad taste. But it was not. Laughter helped those who knew real Joe Eggs, children for whom doctors had found no cure.

Doctors nevertheless were conducting remarkable experiments. The first heart transplant, carried out by Dr. Christiaan Barnard in Cape Town on 3 December, received tremendous publicity, as did later transplants in South Africa and other countries. These operations, like the space programme, fired the imagination of mankind, but did little to assuage current suffering. As the first coughs and colds of winter were caught and the expected fog or frost hold-ups began, admiration for scientific achievement was once more mixed with hopes for its extension to a hundred unspectacular human ills.

1968

THE YEAR 1968 began and ended with events which directed the world's attention towards the United States – the boarding of the *Pueblo* and the voyage of Apollo 8. During the year two assassinations (of Martin Luther King and Robert Kennedy), followed by a violent presidential election (won by Nixon), were world events. It is therefore convenient to begin this short account of 1968 by looking at the American contribution to it.

The *Pueblo* was a U.S. Navy ship engaged on intelligence duties (e.g. the interception of signals sent by radio) off North Korea. It has to be remembered that although the Korean War ended with a cease-fire in 1953, troops remained at the ready along both sides of the frontier and there were incidents from time to time.

Normally, of course, the *Pueblo* kept clear of North Korean territorial waters, but it now seems pretty clear that on 23 January she went closer to the shore than she was entitled to do. The North Koreans boarded her, arrested her crew and took her into port. Dean Rusk, the American Secretary of State, maintained that *Pueblo* had been in international waters when she was boarded, and said that the North Korean action could be considered as an act of war. President Johnson called up U.S. reservists. An aircraft carrier and other warships were ordered to the area where the incident had occurred. Nevertheless the North Koreans kept *Pueblo* and her crew. It was eleven months before the latter were released (23 December), some of them to face a Court Martial on their return. The picture of American naval administration which emerged during the trial of these unfortunate men was far from exemplary.

The prospect in Vietnam appeared to be a little brighter. A few days before the *Pueblo* incident Johnson had declared the U.S.A.'s goal in Vietnam to be 'peace at the earliest possible moment'. But fierce fighting continued and on 31 January the American Embassy in Saigon was occupied for a time by Vietcong guerillas.

In February Johnson was visited by Wilson and again asserted that he was ready to end the war, if this could be done without abandoning America's allies.

On 1 April there was general astonishment when Johnson announced that he would not stand for re-election as President and would thus be free to give his undivided attention to affairs of state during the last months of his term. He did in fact place a limit on the bombing of North Vietnam (about 200 miles inside North Vietnamese territory) and announced (3 April) that he was planning consultations with the North Vietnamese with a view to opening peace talks. These began in Paris on 13 May, but progress was slow and the cease-fire was not finally signed until January 1973. American troops were withdrawn and prisoners exchanged; but fighting between North and South Vietnam, also involving Laos and Cambodia, continued and American forces remained in neighbouring Thailand.

On the day when President Johnson announced his move towards peace talks, Martin Luther King arrived in Memphis to support a march of refuse collectors who were campaigning for better wages and working conditions. His plane from Atlanta had been delayed while a bomb was searched for. There was no bomb; but this was only one of many rumours that attacks on King's life were being planned. In a speech that evening he showed that he knew the risk he was running and accepted it. He said:

> Longevity has its place. But I'm not concerned about that now. I just want to do God's will. And He's allowed me to go up to the mountain. And I've looked over, and I've seen The Promised Land.
>
> I may not get there with you, but I want you to know tonight that we as a people will get to The Promised Land.

On the following afternoon (4 April), as he stood on the balcony of the small hotel where he was staying, just after he had been talking to a friend in the street below, King was shot dead. No Promised Land for him; nor, as yet, for those he left behind. Blacks rioted throughout U.S.A. In Washington, troops guarded the White House and the Capitol. A flare-up worse than that of 1967 was expected. After three days and about 7,000 arrests the atmosphere became calmer; but the peaceful protest movement with its support from white Liberals had died with King. The first Black Power conference had been held in 1967. In the big cities of the American north many blacks felt that, if you wanted to reach the Promised Land, you would have to shoot your way into it.

James Earl Ray was arrested in Britain in July by Thomas Butler, the detective who was in charge of the train robbery case. Ray was extradited to the U.S.A. and in March 1969 was sentenced to 99 years imprisonment for King's murder.

When Senator Robert Kennedy (brother of the murdered President) was shot in Los Angeles on 5 June, an immediate arrest was made, and

Sirhan Bishara Sirhan, a Jordanian immigrant, was sentenced to life imprisonment. He was perhaps making a gesture for the Arab cause against Kennedy, whom he regarded as a friend of Israel. Kennedy died on the following day. His body was flown to New York, where thousands filed past it, as it lay in state in St. Patrick's Cathedral. On the Sunday following the murder, President Johnson called for a day of national mourning.

The question whether the possession of guns should be made more difficult was now raised once again, as it had been after the murder of John Kennedy; but all that was done was the passing of a Bill which forbade the sale of hand guns by inter-state mail order. It was alleged that most mail order guns were foreign made and that American manufacturers were therefore glad to support this measure of control, which would keep people buying American guns in American retail stores.

Gun control was not a simple rich versus poor issue. The Black Panthers (part of the Black Power movement, founded in 1966), were not in favour of it, so long as the police carried guns. As Bobby Searle put it in a speech:

> I know you know no Black Panthers are going to turn in their weapons. But the thing is going across this nation, talking about gun legislation. Why in the hell isn't it that they make some gun legislation against those pigs who are brutalising and killing? Let's disarm the cops first.

That summer the nations of the world proved more amenable to arms control than the states of the American Union. In Washington, on 1 July, shortly after the members of the Poor People's Campaign (a mass demonstration of blacks, whites and Indians, led by Ralph Abernathy) had been dispersed, representatives of fifty countries arrived to sign the nuclear non-proliferation treaty, which had been endorsed by the General Assembly of the United Nations. In the same month, however, the paediatrician Dr. Benjamin Spock, who had been active in the anti-Vietnam movement, was sentenced to two years in prison for aiding Americans to avoid the draft. He appealed and the sentence was quashed.

Now that Robert Kennedy was dead, and Johnson had withdrawn, would Senator Eugene McCarthy be the Democratic Party's candidate? An economics professor, born in 1916, he had served a year as a novice in a monastery. He had been elected to the House of Representatives in 1948 and to the Senate in 1958. Liberals campaigned for him with devotion, but he was turned down by the party convention, held at Chicago in August and memorable for the brutality shown by the city's police to anti-

Vietnam demonstrators, and for a raid by police on McCarthy's head-quarters. Hubert Humphrey, Johnson's Vice-President, was the chosen candidate.

The Republicans, meeting at Miami earlier in the month, chose Richard Nixon in preference to Governor Rockefeller of New York or Governor Reagan of California. So on 6 November it was Nixon v. Humphrey, and Nixon won by a very narrow margin. Neither candidate was of the mettle to give the United States new hope. Americans badly needed the honour won for their country by Apollo 8 at Christmas. The Russian spacecraft Zond 5 had orbited the moon and returned (15-22 September), but it was not manned. The crew of Apollo 8 (Colonel Borman, Major Anders and Captain Lovell) were the first men to circle the moon. Lovell was the first to give an eye-witness account of its surface. 'The moon is essentially grey,' he reported. 'No colour.'

'If the grey laws were broken,' Tom Nairn had recently reported of events in France, 'it is because they have grown old and become breakable. To each according to his imagination . . .'

'Here, imagination rules!' somebody wrote on a wall at the Sorbonne in May 1968.

There had been student troubles throughout the sixties in Europe and the U.S.A., and they were not confined to democratic countries. Spanish and Czech students had demonstrated, and in 1968, the peak year for these activities, Belgrade University was among those which were occupied.

Nevertheless it was the French students' revolt which coloured the year. Not only was it spectacular but it led to a general strike which nearly brought down de Gaulle and certainly influenced his decision to retire in the following year. Did it do anything for the students? Are French universities less crowded as a result (overcrowding was a principal cause of discontent)?

Nobody would claim that the events of May produced important practical results in French universities. There is talk of introducing a system of selection. At present anyone who has passed the, admittedly stiff, baccalaureat is entitled to a place. Anyway, stiffer selection procedure is not a cause which inspires students to man the barricades. The fact is that, except when they had some immediate objective, like the release of arrested comrades, the students had no programme. 'The important thing is not to work out a way of reforming capitalist society. It is to create an experience which is a complete break with the society, an experience which will not last, but which will indicate a possibility. You catch a glimpse of something, and then it's gone,' said the student leader, Daniel Cohn-Bendit.

Cohn-Bendit was a sociology student at Nanterre, the new university built outside Paris to take the overflow from the Sorbonne. Born in France (1945), he was now 23. His parents had been emigrés from Hitler's Germany and he went to Germany in 1958 for his secondary schooling. By 1967 he was back in France and beginning his studies at Nanterre. He had red hair and freckles and was a brilliant student. The fame which he acquired in 1968 rated a photograph in the Encyclopaedia Britannica Yearbook. For alphabetical reasons it appeared next to one of Charles Curran, who was to succeed Greene in 1969 as Director-General of the BBC; but Cohn-Bendit's photograph was bigger.

The photograph which naturally deserves a place beside Cohn-Bendit's is that of Rudi Dutschke. A West German student leader with a European reputation, aged 28, he had taken a leading part in the anti-Vietnam war demonstration outside the American Embassy in Grosvenor Square, London, which resulted in 200 arrests on Sunday 17 March. He might have been prominent in the Paris struggle, but he was wounded by a bullet in Berlin during April. His assailant committed suicide in jail.

A few hours after Grosvenor Square had become quiet again, early on Monday morning, in an equally fashionable area of Paris, there were three explosions, each followed by the crash of glass. The small group of students who had blown in the windows of the Chase Manhattan Bank, the Bank of America and Trans World Airlines, had the same ultimate aims as the crowd in Grosvenor Square. They wanted to impress upon Americans their opposition to the Vietnam War. On Wednesday (20 March) they damaged the American Express. On Friday, the police made five arrests (three of those arrested were schoolboys).

That same Friday evening (22 March) a meeting was called at Nanterre to demand the release of the five. A group of 142 students occupied the administrative offices. They and their adherents became known as the Movement of 22 March. They were not the first students of Nanterre to revolt. The 'bedroom revolt' against rules governing boys' access to girls' rooms and vice versa on university campuses, had reached Nanterre in the spring of 1967, and in the autumn of that year 10,000 students of sociology had joined a 10-day strike, during which curriculum reform was discussed. In January 1968 there had been a battle between students and police on the campus.

Each of these earlier flare-ups died down, but the Movement of 22 March quickly gained recruits. Allied with a number of student political groups it was soon concerned with much more than the release of the five who were thought to have used explosives.

On 29 March an unauthorised meeting was held at the Sorbonne. Police were called, but did not intervene. Easter Sunday fell on 14 April that year. French universities only have a short Easter break. As soon as it was over, disturbances began again. It was not only Left groups who were prepared to resort to violence. There were Right-wing student groups who had inherited a tradition of violence from the days of the Algerian war, when they had tried to keep Algeria French. On Thursday 2 May a Right-wing group wrecked the room in the Sorbonne which one of the Left groups used as a headquarters. An attack was also expected at Nanterre, where Leftists had commandeered a lecture theatre and were showing a film on Che Guevara; but it did not materialise. On the same day Georges Pompidou, who was then Prime Minister, left with the Foreign Minister on a 10-day visit to Persia and Afghanistan. On the following day President Johnson agreed to the North Vietnam proposal of Paris as the place where peace talks were to begin later in the month (and they did).

Meanwhile, on the afternoon of Friday 3 May, Left-wing students gathered in the courtyard of the Sorbonne to protest against a summons sent to Cohn-Bendit and five other Nanterre students to appear on Monday 6 May before the disciplinary council of the University of Paris. Police were called and it was their arrest of the demonstrators which infuriated many hitherto uncommitted students and began the fighting between students and police which reached its peak on the night of 10-11 May, when barricades were raised and fought for all over the Latin Quarter. The balance sheet, provided by Patrick Seale and Maureen McConville in *French Revolution 1968* (Heinemann and Penguin, 1968), reads: '367 wounded; 460 taken into custody; 188 cars damaged or destroyed; incalculable quantities of hate.'

Pompidou came back on the morning of 11 May, checked the police and adopted a more conciliatory attitude towards the students. On Monday 13 May a tremendous demonstration marched through Paris unmolested, with the students in the lead and workers' organisations in support. De Gaulle, at this time aged 77, felt sufficiently secure to leave on Tuesday for a state visit to Romania.

But the great march was not the end; it was the beginning of stage two, in which workers followed the student lead. Students seized their university buildings; workers seized their factories. De Gaulle realised his mistake and came back a day early (18 May). By that time two million workers were on strike. By 22 May nine million had come out.

De Gaulle's speech over the radio on 24 May, proposing a referendum, failed to recreate confidence. There was fierce street fighting in a number of cities that night, and in Paris rioters set fire to the Bourse. Pay rises agreed by Pompidou and the Trade Unions during the week-end were turned down by the rank and file, when they were told about them on Monday. Cries of 'Government of the people' were beginning to be heard. By this time both students and strikers wanted to bring down the Government.

On the morning of Wednesday 29th, de Gaulle disappeared. By the evening, however, he turned up again. He had been with the French forces stationed in Germany, presumably assuring himself of their loyalty if civil war were to break out in France. As encouragement to his generals he doubtless offered to release Salan, imprisoned since 1962 for his leadership of O.A.S. Certainly on 15 June Salan and other O.A.S. leaders were freed.

The speech de Gaulle now made to the nation (Thursday 30 May) was very different from his earlier one. It was a straight call to fight against communist dictatorship and to vote for the General's supporters in a general election to be held at the end of June. It was now the Right who streamed on to the streets to demonstrate. The Left were not prepared for armed revolution and after further savage street fighting the strikers went back to work, having secured considerable wage increases and reductions in hours. When the election was held, the Gaullists won an overwhelming victory. No one would have imagined then that ten months later (28 April 1969) de Gaulle would be saying: 'I am ceasing to exercise my functions as President of the Republic.' He had said he would resign if his proposals on constitutional reform were defeated in a referendum on 27 April 1969. They were defeated and he kept his word, withdrawing with his wife for a holiday in Ireland, while Pompidou was elected to succeed him as President (15 June).

Events in Czechoslovakia were comparable to those in France only in so far as attempts were made in both countries to liberalise an authoritarian regime. There the similarity ends. While French students were striking for not very clearly defined aims and French workers for higher pay, and while everyone was wondering what de Gaulle would do, the Czech government announced a programme of reforms and abolished censorship. The government was still Communist and included Alexander Dubcek, who had become Secretary of the Czechoslovak Communist Party in January; but they were in favour of a more liberal interpretation of Communism, with freedom of the press, the broadcasting services, speech, travel and assembly. No other member of the Warsaw Pact countries adopted this view and on 20 August East Germany, Hungary, Bulgaria and Poland all supplied contingents to the Russian force which entered

Czechoslovakia, on the ground that anti-socialist forces were plotting against the Czech state. There were hostile demonstrations, but by November, although most of the foreign troops had been withdrawn, the freedoms introduced earlier in the year had been lost again. On 16 January 1969 a Czech student, Jan Palach, set fire to himself in the centre of Prague, as a protest against the suppression of press freedom and the Russian occupation. He died three days later. Demonstrations followed, culminating on 28 March 1969 in a very large one, which took place after the Czechs had beaten the Russians at ice hockey. Because of this, Dubcek was replaced as Party Secretary by Gustav Husak and was sent as ambassador to Turkey; but he was dismissed from that post in June 1970 and two days later was expelled from the Communist Party.

The crises for which 1968 is remembered were the French riots and the occupation of Czechoslovakia. Yet few lives were lost in either. In Mexico, on the other hand, where students occupied the National University and fought for several days against the army towards the end of September, 65 people were killed. Yet the Olympic Games opened as scheduled on 12 October in Mexico City, with a girl for the first time lighting the Olympic flame; and it is the Games rather than the 65 deaths which are remembered by the outside world as Mexico's event of 1968. As usual, the U.S. (46 gold medals) and Russia (34 gold medals) headed the list of winners. For Britain, David Hemery won the 400 metres hurdles, Finnegan the middle-weight boxing, Braithwaite the clay pigeon shooting, Pattison and Macdonald-Smith the Flying Dutchman class yachting, and Allhusen, Miss Bullen, Meade and Jones the 3-day riding event.

The British non-Olympic achievement of the year in the field of endurance and skill was the voyage round the world of Alec Rose, at the age of 59. He had set out in July 1967, following the same route as Sir Francis Chichester, and after more than once coming near to disaster arrived back a year later. The Queen knighted him.

It will be remembered that the Czechoslovaks had hoped for a more liberal form of communism and been disappointed. Disappointment was also in store for Roman Catholics who had hoped for revision of their Church's attitude towards birth control. The Pope's encyclical ('Humanae vitae', 28 July) forbade all artificial forms of it, together with abortion (the Abortion Act had come into force in Britain during April). Paul VI had proved a revolutionary in regard to travel. He had visited Jordan and Israel in 1964, on the first papal journey ever made by air, and in August 1968 he became the first Pope to visit Latin America. He also streamlined the administration of the Roman Catholic Church and reduced ceremonial at the Vatican. But in matters of dogma he was conservative. He reaffirmed that priests might not marry and, as noted above, that Catholic women might not take what was now generally referred to as the Pill, the oral contraceptive which women of other faiths had been taking in increasing numbers since its introduction in 1961.

In Africa, while black fought black in the Nigerian civil war throughout the year, and Rhodesia's position remained unchanged despite sanctions and despite Wilson's talks with Smith on board H.M.S. *Fearless* in October, black Malawi took the surprising step of exchanging diplomatic representatives with white South Africa. Dr. Banda felt that this was the only way his country, which is small, could escape from also being poor. He wanted money and technical advice, which South Africa was prepared to supply. Far from regarding this as a departure from the 'apartheid' principle, Vorster regarded the arrangement as an example of 'apartheid' at work – a black and a white state existing in peaceful co-operation. Militant members of the Organisation for African Unity regarded the arrangement with disfavour and Malawi's relations with the neighbouring African states of Zambia and Tanzania were strained. Even the small independent states which are enclaves within South Africa – Swaziland joined their number in 1968 – have not attempted a relationship as close as Malawi's with their powerful neighbour.

What of Britain in 1968? The Labour government found it necessary to introduce a number of economy measures. The raising of the school leaving age was postponed from 1971 to 1973, and British forces were to be withdrawn from the Far East and the Persian Gulf by 1971.

Our financial difficulties also led to the resignation of George Brown from the Foreign Office (15 March). He had not been consulted when emergency measures were taken to stop a run on gold. He felt he should have been. Michael Stewart returned to the Foreign Office to take his place. Brown was made a Life Peer (Lord George-Brown) in 1970. The Department of Economic Affairs, which he had created, was reduced in importance following further government changes announced on 5 April, when the Ministry of Labour was renamed the Department of Employment and Productivity and took over some of the DEA's responsibilities. Barbara Castle was transferred from the Ministry of Transport to take charge of the new department. It was in this same round of changes that Short joined the Cabinet as Secretary of State for Education and Science.

During April the Conservative front bench also lost Enoch Powell. Born the son of schoolteachers in Birmingham (1912), after a brilliant career at the university (he read classics) and in the wartime army, he had been elected Conservative M.P. for Wolverhampton South West in 1950. He was Minister of Health from 1960-63 and a member of the Conservative 'Shadow Cabinet' when Labour returned to power. During this period in opposition he had become increasingly extreme in his attitude towards coloured people, believing not only that entry should be severely restricted but that coloured people already here should be urged and assisted to return home. Heath had no wish to have the Conservative Party labelled racialist; so when Powell made a particularly outspoken speech on the immigration problem on 20 April in Birmingham, he was dismissed from the Shadow Cabinet next day.

Commonwealth immigration had in fact been further restricted by an act which came into force on 1 March and whose purpose was to limit the entry of Kenya Asians, some of whom held British passports. Later in the year, however, the Race Relations Act (in force from 26 November) attempted to protect coloured people already in Britain against discrimination. Complaints were to be dealt with through the Race Relations Board and its conciliation committees. But Powell did not change his mind. On 16 November the *Evening Standard* headlined:

POWELL SAYS IT AGAIN: GO HOME

Six of Britain's new towns – Stevenage, Crawley, Hemel Hempstead, Harlow, Aycliffe and East Kilbride – 'came of age' in 1968. The phrase at that time meant that they were twenty-one years old. As the Representation of the People Act, which came into force on 12 May 1969, gave votes to all British citizens over eighteen, is eighteen likely to be the age of celebration in the future? Twenty-two new towns were under construction and others were being planned (e.g. Milton Keynes, Buckinghamshire, with a target of 250,000 inhabitants by the year 2000, and already referring to itself as a 'new city'). Achievement of this sort however makes less impact than disaster, so for one person who has heard of Stevenage or Cumbernauld you may find a dozen who remember Ronan Point.

Ronan Point is a 23-storey block of flats in east London. It is an example of industrialised or 'systems' building and the system used in this case did not employ steel or reinforced concrete frames, but relied on load-bearing walls. At 5.45 a.m. on Thursday 16 May a gas explosion occurred in a corner flat on the 18th storey. This left a corner of the floor of the flat above unsupported. It collapsed, and the flats above it collapsed in turn. The weight of falling concrete then caused the progressive collapse of the whole corner of the block. Four people were killed. A 'pack of cards' disaster, long predicted in S.E. Asia, had occurred in a much less metaphorical form in S.E. London. No regulations had been transgressed, but enquiry showed that regulations had not kept pace with technical progress. A risk involved in an otherwise well-proved system had not been foreseen, with the result that enormous expense had to be incurred to strengthen similar blocks already erected by housing authorities – yet another setback in the struggle to provide the increasing population of Britain with homes.

Two buildings thought sufficiently important for the Queen to have been asked to open them were the Hayward Gallery (July), for art exhibitions, beside the Festival Hall, and the rebuilt Euston Station (September). Most art galleries are windowless; the Hayward provides beautiful views, up and down river. There were no views from the new Euston and its windows are often obscured by advertising displays. Its most obvious defect from the point of view of the traveller, train-meeter and see-er off was the lack of seating. The 'concourse' as the entrance hall was called had at first no seats at all. Later a few were installed. The area, it was explained, had been 'carefully planned to permit passengers to move about freely'.

The Times wrote of the new Euston: 'As an example of architectural design it bears favourable comparison with the standard elsewhere in London.' But it went on: 'As a piece of urban planning . . . it stands as a monument to ignorance and bureaucratic bungling.' British Railways had not been allowed to develop the site with shops and offices (as was done, for instance, over the station in the centre of Montreal). These could have been conveniently reached by commuters from the north. Meanwhile 'a commercial development . . . a few hundred yards along Euston Road, rose to the skies without interference'.

Technically the new station was described as a 'thoroughly competent job'. The same could be said of the Victoria Line, London's new tube, of which the first section was opened in September 1968. It was of course a great help and the escalators were alleged to be able to cope with stiletto heels, which, incidentally, had now gone out of fashion; but those who looked for new elegance in the stations, adequate seating on the platforms for waiting passengers, booking facilities without queues, no shouting and a general improvement in good manners, looked in vain.

September was a poor month for public services. On the 16th, in spite of vociferous protests from letter-writers, the two-tier postal system was introduced. It was to cost 5d. ($3\frac{1}{2}$p; raised to $4\frac{1}{2}$p in 1974) for a letter to be delivered the day after posting; 4d. letters (3p; $3\frac{1}{2}$p from 1974) would usually take two days. (Before the end of 1976 first class letters would cost 8½p for 60 grams and second class, at 6½p would take about three days.) Some people felt that September was also a poor month for morals, since the Act abolishing censorship of plays came into force on the 26th, and the following day (on which, incidentally, de Gaulle once more vetoed British entry into the Common Market) *Hair* opened in London with actors occasionally appearing naked.

The British Standard Time Act (27 October) which was intended to bring us more into line with the continent and certainly gave us dark winter mornings, was another cause of public protest. Unlike the two-tier postal service, it was only a trial measure for three years, after which it was not renewed.

The play *Soldiers* by the German Rolf Hochhuth, first performed in English at Toronto in March 1968, opened in London on 12 December. It roused a protest from Winston S. Churchill, grandson of the former Prime Minister, who was magnificently portrayed in the play by the Canadian actor John Colicos. 'This play is an infamous libel, especially on the dead,' wrote young Churchill. 'Herr Hochhuth infers that Churchill connived at the murder of General Sikorski, a personal friend and honoured ally.'

For industrial protests – strikes – 1968 was the worst year since 1962; 3¾m days were lost. The motor industry was particularly hard hit.

When 1968 was named Human Rights Year, this was almost an invitation for the aggrieved and the downtrodden to protest, wherever they might be. They had certainly acted upon the suggestion and nowhere more enthusiastically than in Northern Ireland where Catholics, in their centuries-old feud with the dominant Protestants, called themselves the 'civil rights movement' and protested against discrimination, e.g. in housing, which they claimed was being practised against them. On 6 October there were battles between police and crowds in Londonderry, followed by complaints of police brutality. There was further violence in Londonderry on 19 November and at Armagh early in December. On 11 December the Prime Minister, Captain O'Neill, dismissed the Minister of Home Affairs, Mr. Craig. Craig's successor, Captain Long, ended the year but not the trouble by allowing a civil rights march to leave Belfast for Londonderry.

Amnesty International, an organisation which tries to help 'prisoners of conscience' (those imprisoned for political or religious reasons) all over the world, reckoned that of 125 countries which were members of the U.N., 110 had violated the Declaration of Human Rights during Human Rights Year, while 60 had definitely been accused of imprisoning people for political or religious reasons. One Amnesty member received a smuggled reply to her Christmas card from women arrested by the Greek Colonels and imprisoned in Crete. The *Guardian* published it. The last paragraph of the Greek women's letter read:

> Please accept, dear friend, our cordial greetings and our infinite respect. The 137 political detainees of the women's camp at Alikar-nassos.

The recipient of the letter, who sent it to the *Guardian*, added:

> *They* sent *me* their infinite respect! I am speechless, with tears in my eyes.

1969

'MAN MASTERED THE moon in 1969, but was less successful on his own planet,' wrote *The Times* as the year ended. New Year's Day fell on a Wednesday and on that day a group of about 100 students left Belfast on a four-day 'civil rights' march to Londonderry. On Saturday, a few miles outside Londonderry, they were joined by several thousand sympathisers (mainly Catholics). There were clashes between the marchers and Protestant groups, and police wearing steel helmets and armed with riot shields and batons attempted unsuccessfully to restore order. Once the march entered the town it had long ceased to be a peaceful demonstration in favour of civil rights and it now developed into a series of ugly fights between Catholics and police. By Sunday there were allegations of police misconduct in the Catholic Bogside area of Londonderry, while the Prime Minister, Captain Terence O'Neill, was asserting that there were not enough police to deal with the situation. Next day it was decided to call up 'B Specials', police reservists who were even more unpopular among members of the civil rights movement than the ordinary police. There were further riots in April.

The government of Northern Ireland were most anxious to avoid calling in British troops to keep order, but even after the resignation of Captain O'Neill in April and his succession as Prime Minister by Major Chichester-Clark, who announced a general amnesty, the situation still did not improve. In mid-July there were again serious riots in Londonderry and Belfast. On 24 July civil rights marches were banned, but after more riots in August, during which petrol bombs were used, it was decided that the task of keeping order had proved too much for the Royal Irish Constabulary. On 19 August the British Army took over responsibility for police and security in Northern Ireland.

It was because of her part in the August riots that Miss Bernadette Devlin, elected to Westminster as M.P. for Mid-Ulster at a by-election in April, was sentenced to six months imprisonment; her appeal failed and she went to prison in June 1970. The militant Protestant leader, Rev. Ian Paisley, was sentenced to three months for his part in disturbances at Armagh in November 1968. His appeal too was dismissed and he went to prison on 25 March, but was one of those released under amnesty on 6 May.

On more than half of the days of January 1969 which, weatherwise, was exceptionally mild, the papers were able to find a disaster, a riot or a demonstration to make a front-page picture. The Ulster fights were followed by the crash of a Boeing 727 near Gatwick. Next day the Anti-Apartheid Movement held a torchlight vigil on the eve of the opening of the Commonwealth Conference in London, to show their opposition to the Smith regime in Rhodesia. The Queen, arriving back from Sandringham at Liverpool Street Station with her corgis, was only on page two. The day after demonstrators with placards alleging lack of freedom in Zanzibar had replaced the torch-bearers outside Marlborough House, where the Conference was taking place. They too reached the front page. On Thursday another disaster supplied the picture. A house was shown collapsing in flames during bush fires near Melbourne, Australia.

Australia's policies are rarely front-page news in Britain, still more rarely are Australians the target of demonstrators. But the *Observer* of 12 January gave prominence to a photograph of an anti-Vietnam war protest outside Australia House (both Australia and New Zealand had contributed troops to the South Vietnamese side). One placard read STOOGE, RACIALIST, MURDERER. Mr. Gorton, the Australian Prime Minister, was in London for the Commonwealth Conference and it was against him that the protest was primarily directed.

Monday's readers learned of a 'Battle of the Strand' in London. There had been attempts to occupy Rhodesia House; two men had managed to run up the Union Jack on the pole usually occupied by the new green and white of Rhodesia, and to keep it flying over the building throughout most of Sunday; windows at South Africa House nearby were broken.

By the end of the week attention had shifted to the other side of the world where the Japanese government had decided to clear students out of the Tokyo University campus, which certain groups had controlled since June. This was an operation on a scale very different from the 'Battle of the Strand'. 8,000 police were supported by helicopters spraying tear gas and by powerful jets of water. The last resisting students barricaded themselves in the main administration building, from which they bombarded the police with a variety of missiles, including petrol bombs, before they were finally dislodged, wet but with few injuries.

The student Jan Palach on the other hand had inflicted on himself more injuries than he could bear. He had set himself on fire in Prague on 16 January in protest against the suppression of press freedom, and died on Sunday, 19 January, (p 206).

On the 23rd, baton-swinging police charged stone-throwing students in

Paris, and on the 24th students at the London School of Economics tore down 'control gates' which had been installed as a result of a sit-in of October 1968. The Director, Dr. Walter Adams, closed the School, and protests against this action provided photographs for the last days of January (the School reopened on 19 February).

In February Nigerian air raids on Biafra reminded the world that the West African civil war was still going on. So was the smouldering warfare between Israel and the Arab world. On 18 February Arab extremists attacked an Israeli airliner at Zurich airport.

On the 26 February Levi Eshkol, Prime Minister of Israel, died; he was succeeded (17 March) by Mrs. Golda Meir. Other changes in governments during the spring of 1969 were the election (5 March) of the German Federal Republic's first Social Democrat President, Dr. Gustav Heinemann (in September he was joined by a Social Democrat Chancellor, Willy Brandt), the resignation of General Ayub Khan, who handed over the Presidency of Pakistan to General Yahya Khan on 25 March, the resignation of General Ankrah, head of state in Ghana (2 April), the replacement of Dubcek in Czechoslovakia by Dr. Husak and the resignation of General de Gaulle (28 April), who was succeeded on 15 June by Georges Pompidou (see pp 174, 205-6).

In addition to the Northern Ireland troubles and Rhodesia (which declared itself a republic on 1 March) the British government had to deal with a confused situation on the West Indian island of Anguilla, to which troops and police were sent, and with a steadily worsening situation between Spain and Gibraltar. The frontier between the two was closed by Spain on 8 June. At home an unofficial strike at Ford's was declared official on 26 February and continued until 20 March. *In Place of Strife*, the government's plan for decreasing the number of strikes, had been published on 17 January but was not popular. On 1 May there were widespread strikes protesting against its proposals, which included a compulsory 28-day 'cooling-off period', to avert unofficial strikes, and powers for the government to enforce a ballot before a big official strike. Later in the same month the Bill which would have given effect to the plan was abandoned.

In deference to the French, our partners in the Concorde project for supersonic passenger flight, an 'e' had been added to the English version of the name. Both Concordes now took off on their maiden flights – the French on 2 March, the British on 9 April.

On 22 April Robin Knox-Johnston arrived in Falmouth after a 313-day voyage round the world – the first *non-stop* solo circumnavigation

(Chichester and Rose had both made a stop-over in Australia).

Sailing alone around the world is an achievement which gives almost universal satisfaction. It is not costly (i.e. people can't say: 'Think of the number of houses that could have been built with the money'). It takes skill and tremendous guts. It is done by one clearly identifiable person and is highly unlikely to have sinister consequences. An achievement like the Concorde, on the other hand, was the result of team-work. There was no one to admire. There was noise and, like the space programme, it offered little hope of improvement in forms of transport used regularly by the ordinary man. What then of the announcement by Cambridge scientists in mid-February on what the press called 'test-tube babies'? Ova taken from women volunteers had been fertilised by male sperms in the laboratory. The experiment had so far gone no further than that; not till 1974 was it claimed that a living being had been created. The grave responsibilities of scientists in regard to the effect of their discoveries had once again been brought to public notice.

For some childless women however the 'test-tube baby' research brought hope. Where normal conception had proved impossible it might in future be possible to extract an egg from a woman, fertilise it and put it back to grow in the womb. The research also threw light upon why some babies are born as mentally handicapped 'mongols', but gave no hope of it becoming possible in the near future to prevent such births. Finally, it was claimed that the research would make possible a more precise study of how certain contraceptive devices work and would thus lead to important advances in contraception.

The new Cunard liner *Queen Elizabeth 2* had proved a great disappointment on her trials at the end of 1968. One of her turbine rotors had to be returned to Clydebank for repairs; but on 2 May she at last sailed on her maiden voyage. At the end of the month the British Trans-Arctic Expedition completed the first surface crossing of the Arctic Ocean. About the same time a BBC film unit was completing a film about the Royal Family which had its first showing on BBC1 on 21 June. The pending investiture of Prince Charles as Prince of Wales, which took place at Caernarvon Castle on 1 July, had increased interest in the Royal Family both at home and abroad. Produced by Richard Cawston, the film provided a behind-the-scenes view of the Queen's life, both on and off duty, throughout a whole year. It was immensely successful.

Events happen; some become news, a few find a place in the history of the countries where they happen, still fewer, like the voyage of Columbus or the discovery of steam power, become known to literate people in many countries. References by commentators to 'seeing history being made' are sometimes exaggerated, but the headline NIXON SAYS FEAT WILL STAND THROUGH THE CENTURIES on Monday 21 July was probably reporting one of the less unreliable of the President's pronouncements. At 3.56 a.m. British Summer Time on that day Neil Armstrong, with the words 'That's one small step for a man, one giant leap for mankind' crunched the first human boot down on to the inhospitable surface of the moon. Edwin Aldrin followed him down the ladder of 'Eagle', Apollo 11's lunar module. Michael Collins remained aloft in the command module, ready for Eagle's return. The landing was televised and the voices of the astronauts could be heard pretty clearly from a quarter of a million miles away.

There had been two American space flights earlier in the year. From 3 to 14 March Apollo 9 made an earth orbital flight during which the lunar module was tested. In May Apollo 10 orbited the moon, the lunar module was detached and a descent was made to within about nine miles of the moon's surface. After these two successful rehearsals it was decided to launch Apollo 11 on 16 July; the announced timetable was followed throughout and the three astronauts duly splashed down in the Pacific on 24 July (only 53% of British express passenger trains arrived on time during 1969). Television audiences had a brief glimpse of the astronauts before they disappeared into quarantine. Their well earned heroes' welcome had to be postponed until they emerged in good health three weeks later.

The voyage of the unlucky Apollo 13 attracted much attention during 1970. It is easy to forget Apollo 12, from which Conrad and Bean made the second moon landing in November 1969, and Mariner 6 and 7, which, during July and August, televised pictures of Mars over a distance of 58m miles.

What had happened to the Russians? Soyuz 4 and 5 had achieved the first docking of two manned spacecraft in January and three (Soyuz 6-8) were launched in October. They experimented with welding in space. Meanwhile Luna 15 had orbited the moon during the Apollo 11 flight and people wondered whether it might be capable of scooping a sample of earth from the moon's surface and bringing it back; but Luna 15 simply landed on the moon and remained, leaving a puzzle about what the Russians had meant her to do.

While Armstrong and his companions were on their way to the moon and triumph, another American hero became involved in a tragic accident, which was soon attracting as much public interest as the conquest of space.

Senator Edward Kennedy's two brothers (John, the President, and Robert, a candidate for the Presidency) had both been murdered. Edward, then a likely candidate for the Presidency in 1972, was driving a girl from a party on the night of 18 July. As the car crossed a narrow bridge it went over the side and fell into a river. Kennedy escaped, but the girl, Mary Jo Kopechne, was drowned. Kennedy was given a two-month suspended prison sentence for not reporting the accident immediately, but the matter did not end there. Although Kennedy made a statement on television, it was widely felt that the events leading up to the accident had not been fully explained. An opinion poll taken in June 1970 reported 55% of those questioned as agreeing that Kennedy 'panicked in a crisis and showed that he should not be given high public trust'. It remains to be seen whether Kennedy will ever again be regarded as an acceptable candidate for the Presidency.

Three weeks after the death of Mary Jo Kopechne there occurred one of the most horrific murders in the history of California. The actress Sharon Tate and six other people were murdered on two successive nights in early August. Charles Manson, described as the leader of a hippie clan, and four women stood trial and Manson was given a life sentence.

At the end of September eight men of the American Special Forces (the Green Berets) were charged with the murder of a Vietnamese civilian. They were released; but on 24 November, casting a cloud over Apollo 12's success as the Kennedy affair had over Apollo 11's, Lieutenant William Calley was charged with the 'premeditated murder' of 109 civilians at the village of My Lai in Vietnam.

Early in December violence broke out during a concert in California where the Rolling Stones, towards the end of a triumphal United States tour, were performing before an audience of 300,000. A 'Chapter' of Hell's Angels had been employed as guards, and the ferocity with which they behaved led to the death of one spectator.

Hell's Angels also operated in Britain. Interest in drop-out youth had been stimulated when several hundred, described as hippies, occupied a large empty house in Piccadilly, which was awaiting demolition, early in the morning of Monday 15 September, and were evicted by an agile police operation on the following Sunday. Hell's Angels were not among the squatters, but were not fiercely hostile to them, as were the Skinheads. Skinheads, successors of the Mods in some respects, were primarily interested in violence, particularly against hippies, and wore heavy boots. Their hair was closely cropped. Hell's Angels, whose lives centre round their powerful motor-bikes, are less violent in Britain than in the U.S.A., unless they are attacked. The *Daily Mail* quoted one of them as saying: 'We can and do do good.' Angels who do a good deed leave a card saying: 'When we do right no one remembers. When we do wrong no one forgets.'

One of the declared objects of the Piccadilly squatters had been to provide for some of London's homeless families, and the revival of 'squatting' in empty houses, which had first been practised during the desperate shortage of accommodation immediately after World War II, once again drew attention to the plight of the homeless and ill-housed, as the TV programme *Cathy Come Home* had done. Winston S. Churchill, grandson of Sir Winston, wrote in *The Times:* 'If an earthquake were to hit Britain and make one in 10 of the country's houses uninhabitable, it would be treated as a national disaster. Colossal resources of manpower and money would be found to remedy the situation.' But since the 2m houses in Britain officially announced to be 'unfit for human habitation' have reached this situation gradually, the situation is not attacked with the vigour which an earthquake disaster would have stimulated. 'Shelter', a charitable organisation, has done much to promote the improvement of old houses, as opposed to the policy of demolition and rebuilding, and Shelter's advertising helps to keep the problem before the public. But when the 1970 election came, although Wilson was attacked for not building as many houses as he had promised, housing was not a prominent issue and neither Labour nor Conservatives presented revolutionary policies for dealing with it.

Nor was much light shed upon the housing problem by Rupert Murdoch's reborn *Sun.* An Australian newspaper owner, he had acquired control of the *News of the World* and shocked some sections of the public by opening its columns to Christine Keeler. He then took over the old *Sun,* which had succeeded the *Daily Herald* as the newspaper of the Labour movement, and turned it into a tabloid, to compete with the *Daily Mirror.* The first issue, on Monday 17 November, showed, as had been expected, that the chosen weapon was sensationalism. *The Times* wrote: 'Mr. Murdoch has not invented sex but he does show a remarkable enthusiasm for its benefits on circulation, such as tired old Fleet Street has not seen in recent years.'

The South African rugby team, the Springboks, played their first match on 5 November, against Oxford University. Anti-apartheid demonstrations took place at this and subsequent matches, sometimes erupting into violence, in particular at Swansea on 15 November. During the same month there had been many half-day strikes by teachers and on 1 December they began an official two-week strike at certain schools. This was the first strike by members of their profession in this country and was resorted to in support of a pay claim.

1969 surpassed 1968 in numbers of days lost through strikes. It was the most strikebound year since the war. The teachers were not the only group who were unaccustomed to this method of bargaining. Airline pilots struck, ballet dancers struck, Father Christmases struck; there were even some brief strikes at the BBC, though not over the new plans for Radio, embodied in *Broadcasting in the 70's*, a document which had been causing considerable public controversy since its publication in July.

A huge volume of protest against abolishing the Third Programme and a huge volume of protest against the introduction of the 50p piece instead of a note were both ineffective in moving the authorities. The Third went (in April 1970); the 50p piece stayed. Other changes in preparation for the introduction of decimal currency were the withdrawal of halfpennies in July and of half-crowns on the last day of the year.

During the same period girls' legs disappeared into maxi-skirts and maxi-coats and some thought that the mini would suffer the same fate as the Third Programme. But the mini stayed, and so did tights. 'Tights are top of the charts with over three-quarters of the leg market,' the *Evening Standard* was writing early in the New Year.

Index

Abadan: Anglo-Iranian Oil Company's refinery nationalised (1951) 49; Attlee comments 52; British staff withdrawn 53; agreement reached (1954) 74

Abdul Rahman, Tunku (Prince): Prime Minister of Malaysia (1963) 154

Abdullah: King of Jordan, murdered (1951) 52

Abel, Colonel: captured Russian agent exchanged for Powers 122

Aberfan: disaster caused by landslide (1966) 185

Aberfan, the story of a disaster (1967) 185

Abernathy, Rev. Ralph: leads Poor People's Campaign (1968) 201

Abominable Snowman: mysterious Tibetan pedestrian 54

Abortion Act (1967) 196, 206

Abyssinia. *See* Ethiopia, Addis Ababa

Acheampong, Colonel: Head of State, Ghana, after coup (1972) 174

Adams, Dr Walter: Director, London School of Economics (1967) 189, 214

Addis Ababa: Organisation of African Unity formed (1963) 148

Aden: emergency (1958) 101, 167; independent (1967) 195

Adenauer, Dr Konrad: first Chancellor of West German Federal Republic (1949) 38

Advertising: expenditure on (1961) 134

Africa. *See* under most recent name of each country

Aircraft carrier: election issue (1966) 175

Air Lift: to Berlin (1948-9) 30, 31

air speed records: Duke and Lithgow (1953) 69

air travel: Gatwick airport opened (1958) 103; Stansted and Maplin airport proposals (1964) 157. *See also* stratocruiser, Comet, flying boats

Alaska: oil discovered (1969) 113

Albania: still allied to Russia (1948) 29; signs Warsaw Pact (1955) 80

Aldermaston: marches by campaigners for nuclear disarmament (1958) 103, (1960) 120-1

Aldrin, Edwin: with Armstrong at first moon landing (1969) 216

Alexandra, Princess: at Nigerian peace celebrations (1960) 120

Algeria: rebellion starts (1954) 104-5; affects French policy over Suez (1956) 89; natural gas

112; French army rebels (1960) 120, (1961) 130, 136; civil war officially ends (1962) 137; France hands over power (1962) 139

Allen, Staff Sergeant: secrets charge (1965) 171

Allies: against Germany, listed 7

All you need is love (1967) 197

Ambatielos, Tony: imprisoned in Greece 147

Amethyst, HMS: attacked by Chinese communists, escape down River Yangtse (1949) 39

Amies, Hardy: enters menswear field (1957) 94

Amis, Kingsley: author 106

Amnesty International: 210

Amory, Heathcoat: Chancellor of the Exchequer (1958-60) 110

Anderson, Lindsay: film director 155

Andrew, Prince: born (1960) 120

Anglo-Iranian Oil Co. 49

Anguilla: West Indian island, troops sent to (1969) 214

Animal Farm: cartoon film (1955) 82

Ankrah, General: seizes power in Ghana (1966) 174; resigns (1969) 214

Annie get your gun: American musical 25

Antarctica: explored during International Geophysical Year (1957-8) 94, 98; treaty of co-operation (1959) 102

antibiotics 37

Antonioni, Michelangelo: Italian film director 166

apartheid: South African policy 43; possible crusade against 95; Nicolson describes 116; vigil against (1969) 213; demonstrations against Springboks (1969) 218; Malawi and South Africa's relations an example of 207

Apollo. *See* space shots

aqualung: development of 69

Arab Federation (1958) 102

Arabs: in Palestine 18-19, 26; invade Israel (1948) 31; murder of King of Jordan (1951) 52; *See also* under separate countries

Ardennes: German counter-attack (winter 1944-5) 8

Argentina: claims Falkland Islands 102

Armstrong, Neil: first man on moon (1969) 216

Arts Council: 163

Aswan: America withdraws offer to help finance High Dam (1956) 89

atom bomb: first used against Japan (1945) 13-14;

220

Bikini test (1946) 17; British bomb tested (1956) 91; France's first (1960) 120; China's first (1964) 160-1. *See also* hydrogen bomb

atomic energy: Geneva conference on peaceful use of (1955) 120

Atomium: at Brussels exhibition (1958) 104

Attenborough, Richard: actor 62

Attlee, Clement (Lord Attlee 1955): end of coalition, becomes Prime Minister (1945) 12; at Potsdam 13; uses cricketing metaphors 23; announces 1950 polling day 40; no changes among chief ministers 42; announces increase in Services estimates (1951) 49; on Bevin's death 49; on Abadan 52; dissolution date announced in broadcast 53; visits Moscow (1954) 72

austerity: in Britain 8, 16

Australia: non-permanent member of Security Council (1946) 17; initiates Colombo Plan (1950) 40; Royal visit postponed (1952) 58; British atomic test (1956) 91; Olympic Games in Melbourne (1956) 93; troops sent to Vietnam 168; demonstration against Vietnam participation (1969) 213

Austria: ally of Germany 7; 4-power government 30; polio epidemic 35; treaty establishes independence (1955) 19, 80; joins EFTA (1960) 122

automation 78

Bailey, David: photographer 136, 166

Balchin, Nigel: author 37

Balewa, Sir Abubakar: Federal Prime Minister of Nigeria, killed (1966) 173

ball-point pen: patented by Biro (1937) 36

Banda, Dr Hastings: Prime Minister of Malawi (1963), President (1966) 154; relations with South Africa (1968) 207

Bandaranaike, Mrs: Prime Minister of Ceylon (later Sri Lanka) (1960) 28

Bangladesh 27

Bank rate leak enquiry 154

Bankside power station: opposition to (1947) 24

Bannister, Roger: runs a mile in under 4 minutes (1954) 75

Barbados: in West Indies Federation (1958) 102; capital of new West Indies Federation (1962) 139; independent (1966) 102, 183

Barnard, Dr Christiaan: first heart transplant (1967) 198

Barry, Sir Gerald: Director of Festival of Britain 50

Batista, Fulgencio: President of Cuba ousted by Castro 108

Baudouin: becomes King of Belgium (1951) 44; refuses to attend funeral of George VI (1952); visits Britain with Queen Fabiola (1963) 147

Bay of Pigs: abortive US-supported invasion of Cuba (1961) 130

BBC (British Broadcasting Corporation): no weather forecast in wartime 7; Third Programme (1946-70), Woman's Hour begins (1946), television reopens (1946) 21; TV closed during fuel crisis (1947) 23; TV reaches Midlands (1949) 37; Beveridge Report (1951) 49; death of George VI (1952) 58; TV reaches Scotland (1952) 59; Coronation, female announcers (1953) 66; colour TV tested 67; combined licence rises from £2 to £3 (1954) 76; Suez crisis (1956) 91; TV for schools (1957) 98; Queen's Christmas broadcast televised (1957) 100; nine o'clock radio news discontinued, Television Centre opened (1960) 124; *That was the week that was* (1962) 132, 143; TW3 ends (1963) 155; pirate radio (1964) 156 no pop music (1964) 157; Radio 1 opens (1967) 157; BBC2 opens (1964) 157; combined licence rises from £4 to £5 (1965) 171; opening of Parliament televised (1966) 177; *The Forsyte Saga* (1967) 191; Royal family film (1969) 215; *Cathy come home* (1969) 218; first strikes, *Broadcasting in the 70's* (1969) 219

Beano: comic 117

Beatles, The: rise to fame (1963) 151; MBE (1965) 170; *Sergeant Pepper* (1967) 191; at Maharishi's conference (1967) 197

beatniks 99-100

Beaton, Cecil: photographer and designer 166

Beatrix: Dutch princess, wedding protests (1966) 176

Beckett, Samuel: author 81

Beeching, Dr Richard (Lord Beeching 1965): appointed to streamline British Railways (1961) 129; threat of closures 140; report (1963) 146; effect of closures on 1964 election 162

beer: more drunk 141

Behan, Brendan: author 114

Belfast 179, 210-12

Belgian Congo. *See* Congo, Belgian

Belgium: liberated (1945) 8; King Leopold 14; Brussels Treaty (1948) 29; Leopold abdicates (1950), Baudouin succeeds (1951) 44; joins EEC 95; Brussels international exhibition (1958) 104; the Congo 117-9

Belgrade Theatre: Coventry, completed (1958) 157

Bell, The: novel 103

Ben Bella: first Prime Minister of Algeria (1962) 139

Ben Gurion: first Prime Minister of Israel (1948) 31

Benn, Antony Wedgwood: opinion of commercial television 59; Postmaster General (1964) 163; Minister of Technology (1966) 179

Bennett, Alan: author 132

Beria, Laurentia: head of Stalin's secret service, shot for treason (1953) 68

Berlin: captured by Russians (1945) 10; airlift (1948-9) 30-1; conference of Foreign Ministers (1954) 72; discussed at Geneva (1959) 110

Index

Bermuda Conference: invites Russians to Foreign Ministers' conference (1953) 68

Bernadette, Count: UN representative murdered by Jewish extremists (1948) 31

Betting Act (1960): legalises bingo and betting shops 131

Bevan, Aneurin: Minister of Health and Housing (1945), acts against squatters (1946) 20; establishes National Health Service (1948) 32; resigns in protest at rearmament budget (1951) 49; with 56 'Bevanites' withdraws support for Labour policy on defence expenditure (1952) 60; visits Moscow (1954) 72; resigns from Shadow Cabinet on SEATO issues 74; opposed to manufacture of hydrogen bomb (1955) 79; unsuccessful candidate for Party leadership (1955) 83; against unilateral renunciation of the Bomb (1957) 99; death (1960) 123

Beveridge, Sir William (Lord Beveridge 1954): report on social services (1942) 12; report on BBC (1951) 49

Bevin, Ernest: Foreign Secretary (1945), at Potsdam 13; view on Palestine 19, 31; success of Berlin policy 31; at Colombo conference (1950) 40; resignation and death (1951), assessment 49

Beyond the fringe: satirical revue (1961) 131-2

Biafra: Eastern Region of Nigeria, withdraws from Federation (1967) 191; bombed (1969) 214

Bidault, Georges: French Foreign Minister, at Berlin and Geneva conferences (1954) 72-3

Biggs, Ronald: train robber, escapes (1965), in Australia (1969), in South America (1974) 151

Bikini: atoll in Pacific used for nuclear tests (1946), hence 'bikini' bathing suit 17-18; hydrogen bomb tested (1954) 71

Billy Budd: opera (1951) 54

bingo: made legal (1961) 131

Birch, Nigel: Conservative Minister of Works, drops building licences (1954) 76

Birmingham: Bull Ring completed (1964) 157

birth control: the Pope's attitude (1968) 206; the Pill introduced (1961) 207; research 215

black market 16, 37

Black Muslims 168

Black Panthers: attitude to gun control (1968) 201

Black Power movement: first conference (1967) 200

blacks: in London Transport 122; worse off than whites in USA 168; poverty 170

Blake, George: convicted of spying (1961), escape (1966) 126, 185

Blishen, Edward: author 82

Blow up: film (1967) 166

BMC (British Motor Corporation): Mini-Minor (1959) 108; Morris 1100 (1962) 140

Bogarde, Dirk: actor 155

Bolivia: general strike (1965), Che Guevara arrives (1966) 167, 188; his difficulties and death (1967) 195

Bond, James: fictional hero, 56, 167

books: more produced 141

Bormann, Martin: Nazi leader, escapes (1945) 19

Borneo: Sabah and Sarawak in Federation of Malaysia (1963) 154; Indonesian attack (1964) 159

Bossard, Frank: sentenced on secrets charge (1965) 171

Botswana (formerly Bechuanaland): Seretse Khama compelled to leave (1950) 43; independence (1966) 183

Boy Friend, The: musical (1954) 104; taken off after 2,084 performances (1959) 114

BP (British Petroleum Co., formerly Anglo-Iranian): compensated after Abadan (1954), strikes oil in Alaska (1969) 75; North Sea gas 112

Brabin Report: published 1966, on hanging of Timothy Evans (1950) 184

Brandt, Willi: Chancellor, German Federal Republic (1969) 214

Braun, Eva: Hitler's mistress, died (1945) 10

Brazil: non-permanent member of Security Council (1946) 17

breathalizer: introduced (1967) 196

Bridge over the River Kwai, The: film (1957) 104

Bristol Britannia: first British airliner on North Atlantic route (1957) 100

'Britain can make it': exhibition (1946) 21

British Rail (formerly British Railways): nationalisation, diesel locomotives to be introduced (1948) 31; 3rd class abolished (1956) 87; accident at Lewisham (1957) 100; Great Train Robbery (1963) 152; last steam engines (1968) 124; 53% of express passenger trains on time (1969) 216

British Standard Time Act (1968) 210

British Trans-Arctic expedition: sets out (1957) 94; completes first surface crossing of Arctic Ocean (1969) 215

Britten, Benjamin: composer, Billy Budd 54; War Requiem at Coventry 138

Brooke, Gerald: convicted in Russia (1965), exchanged for Krogers (1969) 127, 170

Brooke, Henry (Lord Brooke 1966): Home Secretary, decides Enahoro case (1963) 147

Brown, George (Lord George-Brown 1970): Deputy Leader of Labour Party (1960) 123, (1962) 146; Minister for Economic Affairs (1964) 162; National Plan (1965) 171; continues as Minister for Economic Affairs (1966) 177; Foreign Secretary (1966) 179; resigns (1968), Life peer (1970) 207

Buchenwald: concentration camp, conditions at liberation (1945) 11

building licences: discontinued, start of property boom (1954) 76

Bulganin, Marshal: succeeds Malenkov, at Geneva Summit, visits India (1955) 78-9; visits Britain (1956) 85; visits Poland (1956) 92; 'fuss about a dog' (1957) 99

222

Bulgaria: allied with Germany 7; signs Warsaw Pact (1955) 80

Bulletin: Scots pictorial daily, closes (1960) 124

Burgess, Guy: defects to Russia (1951) 51; Moscow press conference (1956) 86; death (1963) 52

Burma: British advance into (1945) 8; leaves Commonwealth (1948) 28; U Thant 133

Burton, Richard: actor 156

Busia, Dr: Prime Minister of Ghana (1969) 174

Butler, R. A. (Lord Butler 1965): Chancellor of the Exchequer (1951) 53; leads government during illness of Churchill and Eden (1953) 68; as Home Secretary (1957-62) in charge of Homicide Act (1957) 96; Betting Act (1960) 131; candidate for premiership (1963) 151

Callaghan, James: defeated by Wilson for leadership (1963) 146; Chancellor of the Exchequer (1964) 163, (1966) 177; Home Secretary (1967) 196

Calley, Lieut. William: charged with My Lai murders (1969) 217

Cambodia: Geneva conference discusses (1954) 73-4; independent kingdom (1955) 74; de Gaulle visits (1966) 177

Campbell, Donald and Sir Malcolm: land and water speed records 187

Canada: Royal tour (1951) 54; St Lawrence seaway opened (1959) 111; Quebec hostility to Royal visit (1964) 161; Expo '67, de Gaulle and separatists 194

Canterbury, Archbishop of (Dr Ramsey): visits the Pope (1966) 177

capital punishment (death penalty): suspension proposal rejected (1955) 78; Homicide Act (1957) limits 96; abolished for five years (1965) 96; motion to restore (1966) 184; finally abolished (1970) 96

career novels 104

Carmichael, Stokely: 'We want black power' (1965) 168

Carnaby Street 94

Carne, Colonel, VC: commands Gloucesters in Korea 48

Carpenter, Malcolm: astronaut (1962) 137

Casino Royale: first James Bond book 56

Casson, Sir Hugh: architect, at Festival of Britain 51

Casteret, Norbert: French speleologist (cave explorer) 69

Castle, Barbara: Minister of Overseas Development (1964) 163; of Transport (1965) 172; of Employment and Productivity (1968) 207

Castro, Dr Fidel: Prime Minister of Cuba (1959) 106-8; negotiations on Bay of Pigs prisoners 130; plans for Bolivia (1967) 188, 195

Cathy come home: TV play 218

Cawston, Richard: documentary film producer 215

censorship: of plays, abolished (1968) 210

census (1951) 52; (1961) 132

Central African Republic: coup d'état (1966) 173

Centre 42: Trades Union support for the arts, founded (1960) 197

Centre Point 114

Ceylon (later Sri Lanka): independent (1948) 28

Challoner case (1963-4) 147

Chandigarh: designed by Le Corbusier, becomes Sikh capital (1966) 183

charisma 124, 194-5

Charles, Prince of Wales: birth (1948) 33; investiture at Caernarvon (1969) 215

Chataway, Christopher: beats 3-mile record (1954) 75

Che Guevara. *See* Guevara

Chetham-Strode, Warren: author 22

Chiang Kai-shek, General: President of pre-1949 China, at Potsdam 13; fight against Communists 29; takes refuge in Taiwan 38; US support 80

Chichester, Sir Francis: sails round the world alone (1966-7) 180, 215

Chichester: theatre linked to National Theatre 157

Chichester-Clark, Major James: Prime Minister of Northern Ireland (1969) 212

Children and Young Persons (Harmful Publications) Act (1955) 77

Children's Newspaper, The: ceases publication (1965) 77

Chilton, Charles: musician and radio producer 149

China: one of the Allies 7-8; permanent member of Security Council 17; revival of civil war 29; People's Republic of China established by Communists (1949), Security Council seat retained by Taiwan (Nationalist) government 38; *Amethyst* incident 39; unsuccessful application for Nationalist seat on Security Council, 'volunteers' aid North Korea 45; invasion of Tibet (1950) 46; help for illiterates, anger at denunciation of Stalin 85; Quemoy bombarded (1958) 105; frontier war with India (1962) 141; atomic bomb exploded (1964) 13, 160-1; second bomb (1965) 167; Cultural Revolution 180-2; trade with Canada and Australia 182; attack on British Embassy (1967) 193; Hong Kong useful 195

Chou En-lai: Chinese Foreign Minister, at Geneva conference (1954) 73

Christie, Agatha: author 62

Churchill, Winston (Sir Winston KG 1953): Britain's wartime Prime Minister, in Athens (1944) 9; at Yalta 8; on VE day 10; tribute to Roosevelt 11; electioneering (1945) 12; Prime Minister (1951) 53; tribute to George VI 58-9; does not feel strongly about commercial television 60; takes over Foreign Office when Eden is ill 65; Knight of the Garter at Coronation (1953) 66; indisposed owing to stroke 68; at Bermuda confer-

223

ence 68; visits Washington (1954), tries to see Malenkov about hydrogen bomb 72; views on Indo-China 73; speech on 80th birthday (1954) 75; resigns premiership (1955) 79; last years, death, funeral (1965) 164 ff

Churchill, Winston S.: journalist 210, 218

Churchill College, Cambridge 108

Cider with Rosie: autobiography 114

cinema: closures 82; fall in attendance 103; bingo 131

civil rights: in US 151, 161, 168; in Northern Ireland 212. *See also* human rights

civil servants: get 5-day week (1956) 87

Clapton, Eric: forms Cream pop group (1966) 178

Clark, Sir Kenneth (Lord Clark 1969): Chairman of ITA 76

Cleopatra: film 156

Clore, Charles (Sir Charles 1971): active in property boom 76

coal: shortage 22; less demand for 112

coalition: wartime government, ends (1945) 12

Cockerell, Christopher: Hovercraft (1958) 108

Cocktail Party, The: play (1950) 88

Cohn-Bendit, Daniel: student leader in France (1968) 202-3

coinage 125, 219

Colditz Story, The: film 82

Cold War: begins 17; British expenditure on 49; discussed at Geneva 79; in Congo 133

Colicos, John: actor 210

Collins, Canon L. J.: active in CND 102, 120

Collins, Michael: third member of Apollo II crew, first moon landing (1969) 216

Colombo Plan: aid to Commonwealth countries in SE Asia (1950) 40

colour magazines: with Sunday papers, introduced (1962) 136

Comet: first jet-propelled airliner 35; service to S. Africa opens (1952) 60; grounded after crashes (1953) 67

comics 77

Comics Campaign Council (1953) 76

Cominform: alliance of Communist states (1947-56) 29

Committee of 100: activity begins (1961) 121; members sentenced (1961) 133

Common Market. *See* EEC

Commonwealth, British: one of the Allies 7; atom bomb 13; Victory parade 20; defined 28; forces in Korea 44-5; Prime Ministers at Coronation 67; effect of EEC on trade 95; conference on Rhodesia (1966) 173

Commonwealth Immigration Act (1962) 135, 138-9

Comprehensive schools: introduced in London School Plan (1947) 24

computers: developed at Manchester 36

Concorde: supersonic aircraft, agreed with French (1962) 140, 163, 174; maiden flights (1969) 214-5

Congo, Belgian: becomes Congolese Republic (1960), disorder and UN intervention (1960-5), becomes Zaire (1971) 117-9, 127

Conservative Party: election address (1966) 175; in power at GLC (1967) 189; housing policy in 1970 election 218

Constantine, King of Greece: in exile (1967) 190

Consumer Council (1963) 134

Consumer protection: Consumers' Association (1956) 134; Liberals support (1966) 176; Ralph Nader 176

contraception. *See* birth control

Cook, Peter: in *Beyond the fringe,* founds *Private Eye* (1961) 132

Cope, Kenneth: in TW3 143

cornea: from eyes of dead person, can be transferred 57-8

Coronation: of Queen Elizabeth II 65-7

Coronation Stone (Stone of Scone): taken from Westminster Abbey (1950) 46; returned (1951) 49

corporal punishment: for crime, restricted 43; in schools, retained 58; proposal to reintroduce (1961) 127; Plowden report discusses (1967) 196; abolished in London primary schools (1973) 196-7

Cotton, Jack: property boom 76

Council of Europe: sets up Convention for the Protection of Human Rights (1953) 34

Court of International Justice: at the Hague, adjudicates in Abadan dispute (1951) 50, 53

Cousins, Frank: Minister of Technology (1964), resigns (1966) 179

Cousteau, Jacques-Yves: French undersea explorer 69

Coventry: cathedral consecrated (1962) 137; Belgrade Theatre 157

Crabb, Commander: disappearance (1956) 85

Craig, William: Northern Ireland Minister for Home Affairs, dismissed (1968) 210

Cream: pop group (1966-8) 178

Crichel Down case: improper behaviour of officials (1954) 76

Criminal Justice Acts: (1948) restricts corporal punishment 43; (1957) introduces offence of 'non-capital murder', (1961) concerned with Young Offenders 127

Cripps, Sir Stafford: President of the Board of Trade (1945) 12; Chancellor of the Exchequer (1947), devalues the pound (1949) 37; continues as Chancellor (1950) 42

Crossman, Richard: Minister of Housing and Local Government (1964), death (1974) 163

Cuba: Castro's revolution (1959) 106-8; missile crisis (1962) 142-3

Cultural Revolution: in China (1966) 180-1

Cumbernauld: Scots new town 208

Cunningham, John: test pilot, flies Comet 35

Curran, Sir Charles: BBC Director-General (1969) 203

Index

Cutty Sark: open to public (1957) 96-7

Cyprus: *Exodus* immigrants interned (1947) 25; emergency begins (1955) 82; Makarios deported (1956) 86; executions (1956) 88; base for Suez operation 89; 'Enosis' (Union with Greece) movement 96; Sir Hugh Foot Governor 101; 'Enosis' dropped, agreement reached (1959), Republic (1960) 109; Greco-Turkish rivalry (1964) 159. *See also* Makarios

Czechoslovakia: one of the Allies 7-8; death of Masaryk 29; Slansky executed (1948) 92; Warsaw Pact (1955) 80; Russians invade, Dubcek replaced by Husak (1968) 206; death of Palach (1969) 213

Daily Express: on Burgess and Maclean 51

Daily Herald: price increase (1955) 82; ceases publication (1964) 158

Daily Mirror: price increase (1955) 82; manners on a bus (1960) 122; new building (1961) 128; competition from the *Sun* (1969) 218

Daily Telegraph: 127

Daily Worker: death of George VI (1952) 58; price rise (1955) 82; Labour's 1959 election failure 113; China's atomic bomb (1964) 161; fashion note 166; becomes *Morning Star* (1966) 178

Dalai Lama: leaves Tibet (1959) 109

Dallas: Kennedy murdered at (1963) 153

Dalton, Hugh: Chancellor of the Exchequer (1945) 12; replaced by Cripps (1947) 37

Dam Busters, The: film (1955) 82

Dandy: comic, sells a million a week 77

Davies, L.: wins Olympic gold (1964) 161

Dayan, General Moshe: Israeli Defence Minister (1967) 192

Day in the death of Joe Egg, A: play (1967) 197-8

D-Day: Allies land in France (1945) 7

death penalty. *See* capital punishment

Decimal currency: 219

Deep Blue Sea, The: play (1952) 62

Delaney, Sheila: author 114

Denmark: one of the Allies 7; parliamentary and anti-communist 30; joins EFTA 122; 'pirate' radio 156

Denning Report: on Profumo case (1963) 150

detergents 149

devaluation: (1949) 37; election issue (1966) 175; (1967) 196

Devlin, Bernadette, MP: 212

Dien Bien Phu: French surrender (1954) 74

Dimbleby, Richard: broadcaster at Coronation (1953), death (1965) 67

discotheques: first in London (1965) 166

Displaced persons: 20 million homeless after the war 15; Jewish try to reach Palestine 25

district heating: 32

Dr Zhivago: novel (1958) 104

Doenitz, Admiral: succeeds Hitler (1945) 10

Dolci, Danilo: campaign against Sicilian poverty 123

Dominican Republic: US intervention (1965) 265

Dominique: Nun's pop song 155

Donkeys, The: 150

Douglas-Home. *See* Home

Dubcek, Alexander: Secretary of Czechoslovak Communist Party, replaced by Husak (1969), expelled from Party (1970) 206, 214

Dulles, John Foster: US Secretary of State under Eisenhower, 'containment of communism' 62; at Berlin and Geneva conferences (1954) 72-73; 'agonising reappraisal' 73; 'brinkmanship' 74, 80; at Geneva Summit (1955) 79; withdraws American offer to help finance Aswan High Dam (1956) 89-90; replies to Bertrand Russell 102; death (1959) 110

Dumbarton Oaks (Washington): United Nations Charter planned at 8

Dutschke, Rudi: student leader in Grosvenor Square demonstration, wounded in Berlin (1968) 203

Dylan, Bob: folksinger 155

Eagle: weekly for boys 54, 77

Early Bird: communications satellite (1965) 170

Ecumenical Council: Second (1962-3) 148

Eden, Anthony (Lord Avon 1961): Foreign Minister (1951) 53; visits Belgrade (1952) 65; misses Coronation through illness 65; at Berlin and Geneva Conferences (1954) 72-3; Knight of the Garter (1954) 74; Prime Minister (1955) 79; at Geneva Summit 79; Crabbe affair (1956) 85; Suez crisis (1956) 89; retires (1957) 94

education: leaving age raised to 15 (1947) 15, 24; to 16 (1972) 152; Comprehensives 24; supplies concentrated on school buildings 103; Newsom and Robbins reports (1963) 152; in election manifestoes (1966) 175; Educational Priority Areas (EPA's) result from Plowden Report (1967) 196; first teachers' strikes (1969) 218

Edward, Prince: born (1964) 161

EEC (European Economic Community, 'The Common Market'): established (1958) 146; de Gaulle keeps Britain out (1961) 132-3; again (1963) 145; in 1964 election 162; in election manifestoes (1966) 175-6; Britain rejected (1967) 195; again (1968) 210; VAT (1973) 178

EFTA (European Free Trade Area): created (1960) 122, 132

Egypt: non-permanent member of Security Council 17; abrogation of 1936 treaty 53; Churchill tries to interest US Congress 57; represented at funeral of George VI 58; Farouk abdicates, Neguib's policy (1952) 61; republic (1953) 68; Sudan (1956) 85; last British troops leave 87; Suez crisis 89

Eichmann, Adolph: captured (1960) 122; trial and execution (1961-2) 129

225

Index

Eisenhower, Dwight: General in command on D-Day 7; elected US President (1952) 62; fails to check Joseph McCarthy 42, 68; at Bermuda Conference (1953) 68; at Geneva Summit (1955) 79; elected for second term (1956) 92; opens St Lawrence Seaway (1959) 111; at Paris Summit (1960) 121

Elections: General, in Britain July 1945 12; February 1950 41; October 1951 53; May 1955 79; October 1959 112-3; October 1964 162; February 1966 177

electric razors: 32

Eliot, T. S.: author 88

Elizabeth II, Queen: marriage (1947) 24; Paris visit (1948) 32; Canada tour (1951) 54; Far East tour abandoned (1952) 58; Scots dislike 'II' 59; Coronation (1953) 65-7; Portugal visit (1957) 95; opens St Lawrence Seaway (1959) 111; visits Fiji, New Zealand, Australia (1963) 146; visits Macmillan 151; opens Forth Road Bridge (1964) 158; booed in Quebec (1964) 161; knights Chichester (1967) 180; at Aberfan (1966) 185; at Expo '67 194; opens Hayward Gallery and Euston station (1968) 209

Enahoro: Nigerian chief denied asylum (1963) 147

enosis: union of Cyprus with Greece 96; dropped 109

EOKA: anti-British force in Cyprus under Grivas 83, 96

Epstein, Brian: manages Beatles 151

Epstein, Jacob: St Michael statue at Coventry 138

ERNIE (Electronic Random Number Indicator Equipment) 87

Eshkol, Levi (Prime Minister of Israel): death (1969) 214

Establishment, The: in 1950s begins to mean 'upper class' 60

Ethiopia (Abyssinia): after World War II 95; Organisation of African Unity formed (1963) 148

European Coal and Steel Community: established (1951) 95

Euston: the new station (1968) 209

Evening Standard: on 1964 election 162

Everest, Mount: team chosen for ascent 62; summit reached, news reaches London on Coronation Day 66

Exodus: immigrant ship intercepted on way to Palestine (1947) 25

Expo '67: inspired by Mayor Drapeau of Montreal 194

Fabiola: Queen of the Belgians, visits London (1963) 147

Faisal: King of Iraq, murdered (1958) 89, 102

Faithfull, Marianne 197

Falkland Islands: claimed by Argentina 102

FAO (Food and Agriculture Organisation): established (1945) 9

Farouk: King of Egypt, sends sympathy on death of George VI 58; abdicates (1952) 61

fashion: skirts 32, 35, 122, 166, 178, 219; trousers 70, 141, 145; tights 219; Carnaby St 94; polonecks 197; stiletto heels 209

Faubus, Governor: opposed to integration in US (1957) 98

Faulds, Andrew M.P.: regains Smethwick (1966) 162

Fellini, Federico: film director 191

Festival of Britain: idea suggested (1945) 15; described (1951) 50-1; closes 51, 53

Finland: peace treaty (1946) 19; parliamentary government 30; Olympics at Helsinki (1952) 61

Finney, Albert: actor 155

Fischer-Dieskau, Dietrich: sings at Coventry (1962) 138

five-day week: won by civil servants (1956) 133

Fleming, Ian: creator of James Bond 56

Fleming Report: on Public Schools (1944) 22

Flower Power 197

flying boats 32, 36; 'Princess' 54

Flying Enterprise: heroic attempt to keep her afloat (1952) 56

Foot, Sir Hugh: Governor of Cyprus 101; on Jamaican independence 139

foot and mouth disease (1967) 196

foreign travel allowance: raised to £100 (1954) 76; no limit (1959) 110; £50 (1966-70) 179

Formosa. *See* Taiwan

Forsyte Saga, The: on BBC TV (1967) 191

Forth Road Bridge: planned (1957) 94; work starts (1958) 103; opened (1964) 158

four-letter words 50, 125

France: one of the Allies, liberation 7; atom bomb 13, 120; political problems 14; permanent member of Security Council 17; polio epidemic 35; Prime Minister at Bermuda Conference (1953) 68; underwater archaeology 69; reverses in Indo-China 73-4; Geneva Summit 79-80; Le Mans disaster 80; Suez crisis 89-90; tunnel under Mont Blanc decided on (1957) 94; joins EEC 95; Algeria 104-5, 120, 130, 139; African colonies independent (1960) 116; successful films (1961) 130; de Gaulle President (1959) 105; withdrawal from NATO (1966) 281; events of 1968 202-5; student riots (1969) 213-4. *See also* de Gaulle

Franco, General. *See* Spain

Frank, Anne: her family's house a memorial 176

fraternisation: forbidden in occupied Germany 12

Frederika: Queen of Greece, demonstrated against in London (1963) 147

Freedom marchers: in US 168

Freeman, John M.P.: resigns in protest against rearmament budget (1951) 49-50

French Revolution 1968 204

From Russia with Love: among President Kennedy's favourite books 56

Frost, David: presents *That was the week that was* 143

Fry, Christopher: author 22, 88

Fuchs, Klaus: arrest (1950) 42; convicted of spying 43

Fuchs, Dr (Sir Vivian 1958): in Antarctica (1957-8) 94, 98, 101

Gagarin, Yuri: first spaceman (1961) 129; visits Britain (1961) 133; death (1968) 130

Gaitskell, Dora (Lady Gaitskell 1963) 146

Gaitskell, Hugh: his rearmament budget which includes Health Service charges leads to resignation of Bevan, Wilson and Freeman (1951) 49; enjoys James Bond books 56; leader of labour party (1955) 83; questions Khrushchev (1956) 86; blamed by *Daily Worker* 113; suggests revision of Clause 4 (1959), disarmament policy dispute (1960) 113; 'fight again' speech on unilateral disarmament (1960) 121; on Bevan, challenged by Wilson (1960) 123; death (1963) 145-6

Gandhi, Mrs. Indira: Prime Minister of India (1966) 28, 173; allots Chandigarh to Punjab (1969) 183

Gandhi, Mahatma; fasts to stop massacres 27; murdered (1948) 28

Garnett, Alf 155

gas, natural: under North Sea 111-2, 145; in Algeria 139

Gatwick: airport opened (1958) 103

Gaulle, Charles de: French general and President: atom bomb 14; resigns (1946) 14; keeps Britain out of EEC (1961) 132-3; again (1963) 145; in South America (1964) 161; on death of Churchill (1965) 164; withdraws from NATO, visits Moscow and Cambodia (1966) 176; 'no way to behave' (1967) 194; twice again vetoes Britain's EEC entry (1967) 195, (1968) 210; events of 1968 202-5; resigns (1969) 205, 214

Gee, Winifred: sentenced for spying (1961) 126

Genet, Jean: French author, Theatre of the Absurd 81

Geneva: Conference on Indo-China (1954) 73; Summit Conference (1955) 80; Foreign Ministers' meetings on Berlin (1959) 110

George VI: on VE day 10; leaves for South Africa 23; opens Festival of Britain 50; death (1952) 58

German Democratic Republic (East Germany): established (1949) 38; strikes and revolt (1953) 68; signs Warsaw Pact (1955) 80; Berlin Wall built (1961) 133; recognised by Britain (1973) 38

German Federal Republic (West Germany): established (1949) 38; occupation ends (1955) 38; compensates victims of Nazism (1953) 67; joins NATO (1955) 79-80; joins EEC (1957) 95; loss of *Pamir* (1957) 97-8; World Cup defeat (1966) 177; Heinemann first Social Democrat President, Brandt first Social Democrat

Chancellor (1969) 214

Germany: surrenders (1945) 10; polio epidemic 35

Ghana (formerly Gold Coast): independent (1957) 95; Nkrumah's rule till 1966 96; contributes to UN Congo force 120; Nkrumah deposed (1966), civilian rule (1969), army coup (1972), 174, 214

Gibraltar: Spain claims (1967) 195; Spain closes frontier (1969) 214

Girl: children's weekly 54, 77

GLC (Greater London Council): formed from LCC and additional boroughs (1965) 171

Glenn, John: orbits earth (1962) 136

Gloucesters: action on the Imjin river in Korea (1951) 48

Goa: surrenders to India (1961) 133-4

Goebbels, Joseph: Nazi Minister of Propaganda, commits suicide (1945) 19

Goering, Hermann: Nazi general, commits suicide (1946) 19

Goldfinger: film 167

Goldwater, Barry: defeated by Johnson for US presidency (1964) 163

Gomulka, Wladyslaw: Polish communist, imprisoned (1948), released (1954), made first secretary of Polish United Workers' Party (1956) 92

Gorton, John: Prime Minister of Australia (1968) 213

Gowon, General: Nigerian Head of State (1966) 173; meets Ojukwu, resists Biafran withdrawal (1967) 190-1

Graham, Billy: American evangelist, visits Britain (1954) 75

Great War, The: BBC TV Serial (1963) 150

Greece: one of the Allies 7; monarchy restored (1946) 20; civil war near its end (1948) 30; 'Enosis' struggle in Cyprus dropped (1959) 109; 'the colonels' in power (1967) 190. *See also* Constantine, Frederika, Paul

Greene, Graham: author 37

Greene, Sir Hugh: Director-General BBC (1960) 124-5; on satire programmes 155

Green Shield: trading stamps, introduced (1958) 103

Grey, Anthony: house arrest in Peking (1967-9) 193

Grissom, Captain Virgil: second US spaceman (1961) 130; death (1967) 188

Grivas, Colonel: leader of EOKA 83, 109

Gromyko, Andrei: Russian Foreign Minister at Geneva, at Dulles funeral (1959) 110

Gropius, Walter: architect, works on UNESCO building in Paris 106

Grosvenor Square: Roosevelt memorial (1948) 32; anti-Vietnam war demonstration (1968) 203

groundnuts scheme, East African: in debt 38; abandoned (1951) 49

Group, The: novel (1964) 155
Guardian, The: drops *'Manchester'* (1959) 111; price rise 128, 178, 211
Guevara, Che: Cuban revolution (1958) 106-7; in Africa (1964-5) and Bolivia (1966) 188; death (1967) 195
Guinea Pig, The: Public School play (1946) 22
Guinness, Sir Alec: actor 104
gun control: lack of in US (1968) 201
Gurney, Sir Henry: murdered (1951) 53
Guyana (formerly British Guiana): constitution granted, suspended (1953) 68; independent (1966), republic (1970) 183

Haile Selassie: Emperor of Ethiopia 148
Hair: musical (1968) 210
hair 158
Haley, Bill: pioneers pop music (1954) 81
Hall, Peter: produces *Waiting for Godot* 80-1
Hamilton, Richard: pioneers pop art in Britain 81
Hammarskjöld, Dag: appointed Secretary-General of UN (1952) 62; attitude towards Katanga (1960), life, writings, death in plane crash (1961) 118-9, 127
handicapped children: a play about one 197
Handley, Tommy: radio comedian 37
Harding, Field Marshal Sir John (Lord Harding 1958): Governor of Cyprus 83, 96
Harrison, George: one of the Beatles 151
Harrison, Rex: actor 156
Haryana: Hindu area of Punjab (1966) 183
Hastings: commemorates 1066 (1966) 184
Hayward Gallery: opened in London (1968) 209
Heath, Edward: elected Conservative leader (1965) 171, 174
Heenan, Cardinal 148
Heinemann, Gustav: President of German Federal Republic (1969) 214
Hell's Angels: at Rolling Stones California concert (1969), in Britain 217
Hemmings, David: actor 166
high-rise buildings: in London 114
Hillary (Sir Edmund 1953): climbs Everest (1953) 66; in Antarctica (1957-8) 92, 101
Himmler, Heinrich: Chief of Nazi Secret Police (Gestapo), captured, commits suicide (1945) 11
hippies: their vocabulary 183-4; Flower Power 197; murder of Sharon Tate, squatting in Piccadilly house, skinheads hostile to 217
Hiroshima: first atom bomb dropped on (1945) 13
Hiroshima mon amour: film (1961) 130
Hitler, Adolph: German leader, plans fight to the death, presumed suicide (1945) 7-9
Hochhuth, Rolf: author 210
Ho Chi Minh: sets up provisional government at Hanoi (1946) 73; founds 'Vietcong' (1960) 124; dies (1969) 73
Holland. *See* Netherlands

Holy Loch: base for Polaris submarines (1961) 121, 129
Holy year (1950) 39
Home (formerly Lord Home), Sir Alec Douglas-: Prime Minister (1963) 151; resigns (1964) 161, 171, 174
Home, William Douglas-: author 162
Homicide Act (1957): limits death penalty 96
homosexuals 98
Honest to God (1963) 148
Hong Kong 101; arrests after communist demonstrations (1967) 193; useful to China 195
horror comics: legislation against (1955) 116-7
Hostage, The: play 114
hot-line: direct teletype link Washington-Moscow set up (1963) 143
Houghton, Harry: sentenced for spying (1961) 126
housing: shortage leads to squatting, prefabs introduced (1946) 20; problem still acute in spite of increase in building 67; shortage affects attitude to immigrants 97; rent control relaxed (1957) 97; 3m houses built (1958) 103; prefabrication 141; in Sheffield and New Towns (1964) 157-8; work of Shelter 218
Hovercraft: first public test (1959) 108; first service opened (1962) 140
Howard, Trevor: actor 37
human rights: Declaration of, adopted (1948) 33; violated 210; Human Rights Year (1968) 34, 210. *See also* civil rights
Humphrey, Hubert: defeated by Nixon for US presidency (1968) 202
Hungary 7-8; peace treaty 19; signs Warsaw pact (1955) 80; revolution (1956) 92
Hunt, John (Lord Hunt 1966): leads Everest expedition 66
Husak, Dr: Secretary, Czechoslovak Communist Party (1969) 206
Hutton, John: glass engraver 138, 157
Hyams, Harry: property boom 76
Hydrogen bomb: US develops 40; US tests, Russia also produces (1954) 71; Britain decides to make 79; first air-dropped US bomb (1956) 88; Britain's first exploded (1957) 96; Bevan's attitude 99; Russell's open letter 102; Russian and US tests (1961) 133; further British test (1962) 136; US Pacific test seen from New Zealand (1962) 140

Ibos: in Nigerian civil war (1966) 174
identity cards: abolished (1952) 59
immigration: increase begins (1954) 98; Nottingham race riot (1958) 106; Act of 1962 restricts, White Paper (1965) 168; election issue (1964) 162; (1966) 175; restriction on Kenya Asians, Powell's attitude (1968) 208. *See also* race relations
import surcharge (1965) 171
income tax 67, 110

India: atom bomb 13; Partition (1947) 26-7; polio epidemic 35; benefits from Colombo Plan (1950) 40; asylum to Dalai Lama (1959) 109; frontier war with China (1962) 141; two wars with Pakistan (1965) 167; peace talks, Shastri dies, Mrs Gandhi Prime Minister (1966) 173; Punjab riots and partition, Chandigarh (1966) 182-3; Peking embassy attacked (1967) 193

Indo-China: Geneva Conference (1954) 73; French withdraw (1954) 74

Indonesia: republic declared (1945) 14, 17; attack on Malaysia (1964) 159, (1965) 167; change in government, peace with Malaysia (1966) 174

Inner London Education Authority: created (1965) 71; stops caning in Primary Schools 196-7

In place of strife: government proposals for reducing number of strikes (1969) 214

integration: enforcement in US 98, 109

International Geophysical Year (1957-8) 94, 98; results in treaty for scientific cooperation in Antarctica (1959) 102

Ionesco, Eugène: author, 'Theatre of the Absurd' 81

Iran (Persia): appeals to Security Council (1946) 17. *See also* Abadan, Moussadek, BP

Iraq: forms Arab Federation with Jordan (1958) 102; becomes republic on murder of King Faisal (1958) 105

Ireland. *See* Northern Ireland

Irgun Zvai Leumi: Jewish terrorist organisation in Palestine 25

'iron curtain': in Churchill speech (1946) 17

Ironsi, General: seizes power in Nigeria (1966) 173

Israel: Palestine partitioned (1948) 31; Suez crisis (1956) 89-91; 6-day war (1967), Yom Kippur war (1973) 191-3

Issigonis, Alec: designs Morris Minor 36, Mini-Minor 108

ITA (Independent Television Authority): commercial TV favoured by minority of Beveridge Committee (1951) 49; discussed (1952) 59; set up (1954) 76; first broadcasts (1955) 82; service for schools (1957) 98; running Scottish TV 'like having a licence to print money' 111; cigarette advertising restricted by agreement 97; government ban on cigarette advertising (1965) 171

Italy: occupied by Allies and Germans (1943) 7; peace treaty 19; Trieste 14-15; republic (1946) 20; tunnel under Mont Blanc 94, Great St. Bernard 158; joins EEC 95; floods (1966) 185

ITMA (It's That Man Again): radio comedy 37

Jacob, Sir Ian: BBC Director-General 91

Jagger, Mick: pop musician 197

Jamaica: devastated by hurricane (1951), home of Ian Fleming 56; Eden convalesces (1956) 90; leaves Federation of West Indies (1961), independent (1962) 102, 139

Japan: treatment of war prisoners 7; occupation of China 8; surrender (1945) 14; Emperor no longer a god 28-9; governed Korea until 1945 44; student protest (1969) 213

Jenkins, Roy: Minister of Aviation (1964) 163; Home Secretary (1965) 172; Chancellor of the Exchequer (1967) 196

Jerusalem: King David Hotel blown up (1946) 18; Old City taken by Israel (1967) 192

Jews: mass murders by Hitler 7, 19; at Buchenwald 11; as Displaced Persons 15; in Palestine 18; Jewish doctors accused by Stalin 64. *See also* Israel

Jinnah, M. A.: first Head of State in Pakistan (1947) 27

Jodrell Bank: radio telescope 98

John XXIII: elected Pope (1958) 106; quoted 114; death (1963) 148

Johnson, Lyndon: US President (1963-8) 153, 163; allows increased intervention in Vietnam (1965) 167; protects negro right to vote (1965) 168; *Pueblo* incident (1968) 199; not standing for re-election, peace talks start 200, 204; calls for mourning for Robert Kennedy (1968) 201

Jonathan, Chief: suspends Lesotho constitution (1966) 183

Jones, Aubrey: PIB Chairman 171

Jordan: invades Israel (1948) 31; King Abdullah murdered (1951) 52; joins Iraq in Arab Federation (1958) 102; Britain helps to stop attempted revolution (1958) 105; 6-day war (1967) 192

Joyce, William: Lord 'Haw-Haw', hanged for treason (1945) 15

July plot: attempt to murder Hitler (1944) 8

Kabaka of Buganda (part of Uganda): deposed (1953) 67; returns (1955), President of Uganda (1963) 139; deposed (1966), death (1969) 83, 174

KANU (Kenya African National Union) 154

Karamanlis: Greek Prime Minister 190

Kariba: dam opened (1960) 119

Kasavubu, Joseph: first President of Congolese Republic (1960) 117

Kashmir: Muslim majority under Hindu ruler 27, 49; war with India 167

Katanga: independent under Tshombe (1960) 117-8; mines taken over by Congolese Republic (1971) 119

Kaunda, Dr. Kenneth: President of Zambia 154

Keeler, Christine: involved with Profumo (1963), writes memoirs (1969) 150, 218

Kennedy, Edward: death of Mary Jo Kopechne (1969) 217

Kennedy, John F.: US President (1960) 124; approves intervention in Vietnam (1960-3) 167; Bay of Pigs (1961) 130; Cuba missile crisis (1962) 142-3; murdered at Dallas (1963) 153

Kennedy, Robert: murdered (1968) 200

Kenya: the Queen returns from (1952) 58; emergency declared (1952) 61, 83, 101; emergency ends (1959) 110; constitutional conference boycotted (1960) 119, 135; independence (1963) 153; Asians suffer, opposition party (KPU) banned (1963) 154; mutiny (1964) 159; Asians entry into Britain limited (1968) 208. *See also* Kenyatta *and* Mau Mau

Kenyatta, Jomo: trial (1952) 61; 7-year sentence (1953) 67; still restricted 110, 135; released, Prime Minister (1963), President (1964) 153

Kerans, Commander John: organises escape of HMS *Amethyst* (1949) 39

Kernan, David: in TW3 143

Kerouac, Jack: American author 99-100

Khama, Sir Seretse: Prime Minister of Botswana 43

Khan, Field Marshal Ayub: President of Pakistan (1958-69) 105; peace with India (1966) 173; resigns (1969) 214

Khan, General Yahya: President of Pakistan (1969) 105, 214

Kind Hearts and Coronets: film comedy (1949) 37

King, Dr. Martin Luther: arrested (1963) 152; Nobel Peace Prize (1964) 160; murdered (1968) 200

King Kong: South African all-black musical (1961) 128

Kinnear, Roy: actor 143

Kinsey Report (*Sexual behaviour in the human male,* 1948): complaint to Press Council (1954) 76

Kinshasa (former Leopoldville): capital of Congolese Republic 119

Knack, The: film (1965) 167

Knox-Johnston, Robin: sails round the world (1968-9) 214

Kon-tiki: how a raft crossed the Pacific (1947) 24

Korea: past history, outbreak of war 44 ff; armistice talks open at Kaesong (1951) 48; salute fired on death of George VI 58; armistice signed (1953) 62, 68; North Korea and *Pueblo* (1968) 199

Kosygin, A. N.: Prime Minister of USSR (1964) 160

KPU (Kenya People's Union): banned (1963) 154

Kroger, Peter and Helen: sentenced for spying (1961) 126; exchanged (1969) 127, 170

Krushchev, Nikita: First Secretary, Central Committee, Communist Party of USSR (1953-64), meets Labour MP's in Moscow (1954) 72; visits India (1955) 78; at Geneva Summit 79; denounces Stalin, visits Britain (1956) 85; visits Poland (1956) 92; replies to Russell on the Bomb 102; Prime Minister (1958) 160; at Paris Summit 121; agrees to dismantle Cuban missile sites (1962) 142-3; replaced by Brezhnev and Kosygin (1964), dies (1971) 160

Kutchuk, Dr Fazil: first Vice-President of Cyprus 109

Labour, Ministry of: renamed Department of Employment and Productivity (1968) 207

Labour Party: wins 1945 election 12; policy in the 60's 113; Gaitskell's leadership challenged (1960) 123; immigration policy 135; Wilson gains leadership (1963) 146; election address, favoured by opinion polls (1966) 175. *See also* elections, names of individual politicians

La dolce vita: Italian film (1960) 123

Lady Chatterley's lover: novel, published after court case (1960) 111, 125

Lady's not for burning, The: verse play (1956) 88

Laos: Geneva conference discusses (1954) 73; independent kingdom (1955) 74

laser: light beam, first use (1960) 124

Last year at Marienbad: film (1961) 130

Latin: no longer compulsory for Cambridge and Oxford entrants (1959) 110

Leafe, Lettice: the Greenest Girl in the School 54

Leakey, Dr Louis: prehistoric discoveries (1961) 134

Lean, David: film producer 104

Leary, Dr Timothy: sentenced for drug smuggling (1970) 183

Lebanon: US helps to stop attempted revolution (1958) 105

Le Corbusier: architect 182

Lee, Jennie (Lady Lee 1970): Open University and Arts Council 163; the Round House 197

Lee Kuan Yew: Prime Minister of Singapore 154

Lee, Laurie: author 114

Lennon, John: one of the Beatles 151; returns MBE 170

Leopold: King of the Belgians, suspected of collaboration with Germans 14; abdicates 44

Lesotho (formerly Basutoland): claimed by South Africa 43; independence (1966) 183

Lester, Richard: film director 167

Levin, Bernard: journalist 143

Lewisham railway accident (1957) 100

Liberal Party: election address (1966) 175; loss of deposits (1966) 177. *See also* elections

Liberia 96

Libya: independent (1951), exports oil (1961), king deposed, Colonel Quadhafi succeeds (1969) 57

Lie, Trygve: first Secretary-General of UN, retires (1952) 62

Life peers: introduced (1958) 103

Litter Act (1958) 103

Little Rock, Arkansas, USA: enforcement of school integration 98

Littlewood, Joan: Theatre Workshop 114, 149

Lloyd, Selwyn: Foreign Secretary in Suez crisis (1956) 90; visits Moscow with Macmillan 110; replaced as Chancellor by Maudling (1962) 138

Londonderry 210, 212

Index

London School of Economics: sit-ins (1967) 189; (1968) 214; closed owing to disturbances (1969) 214

London Transport: Princess Margaret's wedding, ill-manners on a bus 122

Long, Captain: Minister of Home Affairs, Northern Ireland (1968-9) 210

Lonsdale, George: sentenced for spying (1961), exchanged (1964) 126

Look back in anger: play (1956) 87

Los Angeles: riots (1965) 168

LP's: long playing records, invented (1950) 81

Lucky Jim: novel (1954) 70

Lumumba, Patrice: first Prime Minister of Congolese Republic (1960) 117; murdered (1961) 119; *Sunday Telegraph* refers to (1961) 127

Luxemburg: signs Brussels treaty 29; joins EEC 95

Lynskey tribunal: investigates issue of building permits (1949) 37

Lyttleton, Oliver (Lord Chandos 1954): Colonial Secretary, tours Malaya (1952) 57; visits Kenya (1952) 61; comment on deportation of Makarios (1956) 86

MacArthur, Douglas: US General and Commander-in-Chief, Far East 45; favours retaliatory bombing of China, replaced by General Ridgway 48

McCarthy, Eugene: fails to become US Presidential candidate, supports victims of police brutality at Chicago convention (1968) 201-2

McCarthy, Joseph: starts anti-communist witch-hunt (1950) 42; criticises dismissal of MacArthur 48; witch-hunt penetrates UN 62; 157 enquiries in 1953 68; condemned by Senate resolution (1954), death (1957) 77; Hollywood recovers (1961) 131

McCarthy, Mary: author 155

McCartney, Paul: one of the Beatles 151

Maclean, Donald: defects to Russia (1951) 51; press conference in Moscow (1956) 86

Macleod, Ian: replies to Bevan 60

Macmillan, Harold: Minister of Housing (1951) 53; his opinion of Dulles 74; Foreign Secretary (1955) 79; at Geneva Summit 79; as Chancellor introduces Premium Bonds (1956) 87; Prime Minister (1957) 90; 'You've never had it so good' 94; visits Moscow (1959) 110; 'Wind of change' speech in South Africa (1960) 116; Polaris base 121; on Bevan 123; reconstructs cabinet (1962) 138; clears Philby 52, 150; Profumo affair 150; in hospital, choice of successor, nuclear test ban agreement, resignation (1963) 150-2; on Churchill (1965) 164

Magga Dan: in Antarctica (1957) 94

Maharishi, The: transcendental meditation 197

Makarios, Archbishop: leads Greeks in Cyprus emergency 83; deported to Seychelles (1956) 86; allowed to return to Athens (1957) 96; President of Cyprus Republic (1960) 109

Malawi (formerly Nyasaland): riots (1959) 109; independence (1963), republic (1966), 154; diplomatic relations with South Africa (1968) 207

Malaya: emergency declared (1948) 28; murder of Sir Henry Gurney (1951) 53; General Templer appointed 57; emergency continues 83; independent (1957) 98; state of emergency ends (1960) 123

Malaysia, Federation of: set up (1963) 154; attacked by Indonesia (1964) 159; (1965) 167; peace with Indonesia (1966) 174

Malcolm X: shot (1965) 168

Malenkov, Georgi: succeeds Stalin 64; entertains Labour MP's (1954) 72

Malta GC: constitution suspended (1958), riots on dismissal of dockyard workers (1959) 109; independent (1964) 101, 159

manners: on buses 122

Manson, Charles: sentenced for Sharon Tate murder (1969) 217

Mao Tse-tung: Chairman of the Chinese Communist Party 29; 'We have stood up' 38; changes format of newspapers 85; Cultural Revolution 180-2. *See also* China

Maplin: abandoned as third London airport site (1974) 157

Margaret, Princess: opens West Indies Parliament (1958) 102; wedding (1960) 121

Marine Broadcasting Offences Act (1967) 156

Marshall, General George: American Secretary of State, launches Marshall Plan (1947) 25; Defence Secretary, attacked by McCarthy 42

Marshall Islands: recaptured by Americans 8

Marshall Plan: economic aid for Europe (1947) 25

Marshall, William: sentenced for spying (1952) 60-1

Martin, Kingsley: editor, supports CND 102

Martin, Millicent: singer 143

Masaryk, Jan: mystery of his death (1948) 29

Mattei, Enrico: creates AGIP petrol enterprise 123

Matthews, K.: wins Olympic gold (1964) 161

Maude Report (*Management of Local Government,* 1967): 190

Maudling, Reginald: Chancellor of the Exchequer (1962) 138; defeated by Heath for party leadership (1965) 171

Mau Mau: Kenya secret society, their oath 61; Dedan Kimathi, their 'Field Marshal', captured and condemned to death (1956) 88, 101; renewed activity (1960) 120

maxi-coats and skirts (1969) 219

May, Dr Alan Nunn: convicted of spying 42

Mayflower II: sails Atlantic (1957) 97

Mboya, Tom: Kenyan, murdered (1969) 154

Meir, Golda: Prime Minister of Israel (1969) 214

Mendès France, Pierre: French Prime Minister at Geneva Conference (1954) 74

Men in prison: Mountbatten Report (1970) 186

231

mental handicap: *A day in the death of Joe Egg* 197-8; mongols 215

merchant seamen: better accommodation 36

Mermaid Theatre: opened (1959) 111

Mexico: non-permanent member of Security Council 17; students killed, Olympic games (1968) 206

Michael, John: first menswear shop (1957) 94

Mihailovitch, Draža: right-wing Yugoslav wartime leader, executed (1946) 20

Miles, Bernard: opens Mermaid Theatre 111

Miller, Dr Jonathan: writer and stage director 206

Mills, Jack: injured in train robbery 152

Milton Keynes: 'new city' 208

'mini' and 'maxi' 108, 219

Mini-Minor: car (1959) 108

Mintoff, Dom: Maltese Prime Minister 101

Mithras, Temple of: Roman relic excavated in London 115

Mobutu, Colonel: heads military government in Congolese Republic 118

Mods and Rockers: Bank Holiday incidents 158, 171

Molotov, N.: Russian Foreign Minister 10; at 1954 Berlin and Geneva Conferences 72-73; at Geneva Summit (1955) 79

Montgomery, General Bernard, later Field-Marshal (Lord Montgomery 1946): on German war guilt 12; on Indo-China 73

Moore, Bobby: captain of England's World Cup winning XI, OBE (1967) 187

Moore, Dudley: actor 206

Moore, Henry: UNESCO building 106

Morning Star (formerly *Daily Worker*): first issue (1966) 178

Moro, Peter: architect 248

Morocco: independent (1951) 146

Morris: Minor 36, 108; Mini-minor 108

Morrison, Herbert (Lord Morrison 1959): Labour Home Secretary, Lord President 12; Foreign Secretary (1951) 49; supports Festival of Britain 50; unsuccessful candidate for Party leadership (1955) 83; subsequent career, death (1965) 128

Morrison, W. S.: elected Speaker 53

Moscow Dynamos: draw with Chelsea (1945) 15

motor industry: 1 m. cars in a year (1958) 103; competition of American 'compacts' 128; not happy (1962) 140; strikes 210

motorways: 103, 108, 114, 140, 158

Mountbatten, Louis (Lord Mountbatten 1947): last Viceroy of India 26; enquiry into prisons (1966) 186

Mountbatten Report *(Men in prison,* 1970) 186

Mousetrap, The: starts long run (1952) 62; continues 104, 114

Moussadek, Mohammed: Iranian Prime Minister, nationalises Abadan oil refinery (1951) 49; ignores Hague Court's recommendations 53; 3-year imprisonment sentence (1953) 68; had

failed to obtain revenue from oil 74; still in prison (1956) 88

Muir, Major, VC: heroism and death in Korea 48

Murder (Abolition of Death Penalty) Act (1965): 172

Murdoch, Iris: author 160

Muslims: in India 26, 28

Mussolini, Benito: Italian Duce (Dictator) 7; shot by Italian partisans (1945) 10

My fair lady: musical 114; film 166

myxomatosis: menaces rabbits in Britain (1954) 74

Nader, Ralph: apology from General Motors (1966) 176

Nagasaki: second atom bomb dropped on (1945) 13

Nagy, Imre: forms moderate Hungarian government, deposed by Russians, killed (1956) 92

napalm: flame-bombs, used in Korea (1951) 48

Nasser, Abdul: as Colonel supports Neguib (1952) 61; succeeds Neguib (1954) 75; nationalises Suez Canal, crisis results (1956) 89ff; 6-day war (1967) 191-3; death (1970) 193

National Coal Board: takes over mines (1947) 23; Aberfan disaster (1966) 185

National Health Service: established (1948) 32; Labour introduces charges (1951) 49; Conservatives introduce further charges (1961) 128; charges removed by Labour (1965) 171

nationalisation in Britain: of mines (1947) 23; of railways (1948) 31; of steel (1949) 38; steel denationalised (1953) 69; steel nationalised again (1967) 195-6; revision of Clause 4 suggested 113

National Theatre: formed at Old Vic (1963) 152

National Union of Seamen: strike (1966) 178

NATO (North Atlantic Treaty Organisation): originates in Brussels Treaty (1948) 29; list of members 38; West Germany joins (1955) 79-80, 162; France leaves (1966) 176; Greece still a member (1969) 190

Nazis (National Socialists): final cruelties of 9; their victims to receive compensation (1953) 67

Neguib, General: leads revolt of Egyptian officers (1952) 61; proclaims republic (1953) 68; Nasser takes his place (1954) 75

Nehru, Jawaharlal: first Prime Minister of India 27; assessment, death (1964) 160

Netherlands, The: one of the Allies 7; non-permanent member of Security Council 17; signs Brussels Treaty 29; joins Common Market 95; 'pirate' radio 156; protest at wedding of Princess Beatrix 176; natural gas 111-2

New English Bible: published (1961) 129; (1962) 4 m. copies sold 141

Ne Win, General: Burmese dictator 28

'New Look': in women's fashions 32

Index

News Chronicle: price increase (1955) 82; closes (1960) 124

New Society: periodical 159

News of the World 150, 218

Newsom Report: on secondary schools (1963) 152

New Towns 22, 158, 208

New York: power failure (1965) 271

New Zealand: polio epidemic 35; Royal visit postponed (1952) 58; US nuclear explosion seen from 140; sends troops to Vietnam 168

Nichols, Peter: author 197-8

Nicolson, Sir Harold: opinion of Dylan Thomas 70; of apartheid 116; of *New English Bible* 129; of Bay of Pigs incident 130

Nigeria: 117; independence (1960) 117, 120; Enahoro case (1963) 148; army seizes power (1966) 173; civil war begins (1967) 190-1; continues (1968) 207; air raids on Biafra (1969) 214

Nixon, Richard: US Vice-President under Eisenhower 42, 62; re-elected (1956) 92; President (1968) 202; comments on moon landing (1969) 216

Nkrumah, Kwame: Prime Minister, then President of Ghana (1957-1966) 95-6; at OAU (1963) 148; deposed (1966) 174

Nobel Prizes: Albert Schweitzer for peace (1952) 169; Hammarskjöld for peace (1961) 133; Luther King for peace (1964) 160; Beckett for literature (1969) 124

non-violence: in southern USA 131

Northern Ireland: first Belfast riots (1966) 179; civil rights marches 210-12

Norway: one of the Allies 7; parliamentary and anti-communist 30; joins EFTA 122

Nottingham Playhouse 157

nuclear power stations: Britain plans twelve 78; Calder Hall opened (1956) 91; Dounreay opened (1958) 103; supplies national grid (1962) 141

nuclear weapons: 14; conference on ending tests 120, 136; US explodes device in Pacific (1954) 71; ban on tests (1963) 152; China's first (1964) 160-1; second (1965) 167; in 1964 election 162; in 1966 election 175; non-proliferation treaty (1968) 201. *See also* atom bomb, hydrogen bomb

Nuremberg trials. *See* war crimes

Nyasaland: *See* Malawi 148

Nyerere, Julius: President of Tanganyika, later Tanzania (1962) 135; at OAU (1963) 148

OAS (Organisation de l'armée secrète): founded (1961) with aim of keeping Algeria French 137

OAU (Organisation of African Unity): formed (1963) 148; urges force in Rhodesia (1965) 196; attitude towards Malawi (1968) 207

Obote, Dr A. Milton: Prime Minister of Uganda 83; suspends constitution, deposes Kabaka, becomes President (1966) 174

O'Brien, Conor Cruise: comment on UN Congo operation 119

Obscene Publications Act (1959): changes standard of obscenity 111; Lady Chatterley case 194

Observer: on *Honest to God* 148; starts colour magazine (1964) 159; Wilson interview (1965) 274, 340

Oder-Neisse line: provisional eastern frontier of Germany 13

Odinga, Oginga: leader of Kenya People's Union, arrested (1963) 154

Oh! What a Lovely War: 132, 149

Oil: locomotives converted to 22; diesels introduced on British railways 31; in Algeria 139; big tankers for Cape route 97. *See also* Abadan, BP

Ojukwu, Colonel: Military Governor, Eastern Region of Nigeria (1966) 174; declares Republic of Biafra (1967) 191; compared with Quebec separatists 194

Oklahoma: American musical 25

Olivier, G. Borg: Prime Minister of Malta (1962) 159-60

Olivier, Laurence (Lord Olivier 1970): in *Spartacus* 204

Olympic Games: London (1948) 31; Helsinki (1952) 61; Melbourne (1956) 93; Rome (1960) 123; Tokyo (1964) 161; Mexico (1968) 206

Ombudsman (Parliamentary Commissioner): Sir Edmund Compton appointed (1966) 76

O'Neil, Captain Terence: Prime Minister of Northern Ireland (1963-9) 210-11

On the road: American novel (1957) 99-100

Onyango, Mrs Grace: first Kenyan woman MP 154

op art 166

Orwell, George: author 82

Osborne, John: author 87; Tynan on 88

Oswald, Lee: presumed murderer of John F. Kennedy (1963) 153

Packer, Ann: first British Olympic gold for track event (1964) 161

Paisley, Rev. Ian: Protestant leader in Northern Ireland 212

Pakistan: partition 27; military dictatorship (1958) 105; no aid to India against China (1962) 142; peace talks (1966) 173; Yahya Khan succeeds Ayub (1969) 214

Palach, Jan: Czech student martyr (1969) 206, 213

Palestine: King David hotel 18; the *Exodus* 25; partition (1948) 31

Pamir: German sailing ship lost in hurricane (1957) 97-8

Papadopoulos: leader of 'Colonels' in Greece (1967) later Prime Minister 190

Paris: liberated (1945) 7; Peace Conference (1946) 19; Summit Conference (1960) 121; Vietnam peace talks (1968-73) 200

parking meters 114, 140
Parkinson's Law: (1955) 82
Passport to Pimlico: film comedy (1949) 37
Pasternak, Boris: Russian author 104
Paul, King of Greece: in London (1963), dies (1964) 147
Paul VI, Pope: elected (1963) 148; visited by Archbishop of Canterbury (1966) 177; travel (1964, 1968), attitude to abortion and birth control (1968) 206-7
Pearson, Lester: Canadian Prime Minister, rebuffs de Gaulle (1967) 194
pedestrian crossings: marked with zebra stripes 54
Peking: captured by Communists (1949) 38
penicillin 37
Percival, Lance: actor, singer 143
Perón, Juan: aided by wife, Eva (died 1952), sets up Argentine dictatorship (1946) 16-7
Persia. *See* Iran
Pétain, Marshal: condemned to death by French, but not executed, for collaboration with Germans 14
Peter of Yugoslavia 65
Peters, Sylvia: BBC television announcer on Coronation Day 66
petrol 93, 95-6, 141
Philby, Kim: suspected of helping Burgess and Maclean 51; defects to Moscow (1963) 52, 150
Philip, Prince, Duke of Edinburgh: marriage (1947) 24; Prince of United Kingdom 95. *See also* Elizabeth II
Philippines: Americans recapture (1945) 8
Phoenix too frequent, A: verse play (1946) 22
photography: expenditure on 165
photomicrograph: influence on op art 166
PIB (Prices and Incomes Board): set up (1965) 171
Picasso, Pablo: UNESCO building 106
Piccard, Auguste: underwater descent in bathyscope (1953) 69
Piltdown Man: exposed as a hoax (1953) 104
Piper, John: stained glass at Coventry 138
'pirate' radio: 156 ff; 'Screaming Lord' Sutch 177
Playboy Club: first in Europe (1966) 179
Plowden Report: on primary schools (1967) 196
Poland: Russian advance into (1945) 8
Polaris: American nuclear submarines to be based in Scotland (1960) 121; first arrivals (1961) 129
police: uniforms 21, 32, 35; power to tow away (1957) 148
polio (infantile paralysis): epidemics (1947-8) 32, (1949) 35; increase (1952) 67
polo-neck sweaters (1967) 197
Pompidou, Georges: Prime Minister of France during events of 1968 204; succeeds de Gaulle as President (1969) 205
Poor People's Campaign: in US (1968) 201
pop art 81-2
Pope. *See* John XXIII, Paul VI
Pop from the beginning: 184

pop music: 81; American groups 183; British pop revival (1967) 191. *See also* under names of groups
Portland spy ring: 126, 129
Portrait of the artist as a young dog: autobiography (1940) 70
Portugal: liberation movements in Portuguese Africa 148; revolution (1974) 169
postal charges: increased (1957) 98, (1961) 128, (1964) 163; two-tier service (1968) 209
Post Office Tower: (1964) 157
Potsdam: conference opens (1945) 12
Powell, Enoch: increases Health Service charges (1961) 128; joins Cabinet (1962) 138; dismissed from it for his views on immigration (1968) 208
Powers, Gary: American U-2 pilot captured in Russia (1960), later exchanged 122
Premium Bonds: introduced, criticized (1956) 87
Presley, Elvis: first teenage pop singer (1955) 81
Pressburger, Emeric: film director 36
Press Council: (1953) 76
Prices and Incomes: Board set up (1965) 171; opposed by Trade Unions (1966) 178-9; Bill with restrictive measures (1966) 179; TUC supports standstill (1966) 184; inflation slowed (1967) 187
Pritt, D. N.: barrister, defends Kenyatta and is accused of contempt of Court 61
Private Eye: satirical periodical, first published (1961) 132, 143
Profumo, John: War Minister 138, 146; Christine Keeler (1963) 150
property boom 76
Provos: Netherlands protesters 176
psephology 53
puberty, age of: becomes lower 128
public opinion polls: first British election in which prominent (1950), get Truman result wrong 41; show 50% US citizens approve of Joseph McCarthy (1950) 42
Pueblo: US navy ship captured by North Korea (1968) 199
Punch: on immigration 168
Punjab: Sikh–Muslim riots, partition (1966) 182-3
purchase tax 67, 178
pyrosil: resistant to thermal shock 156

Qadhafi, Colonel: Head of State, Libya 57
Quant, Mary: opens Bazaar (1955), starts mass production (1962) 136; 'the Quant look' 166
Quebec: de Gaulle supports separatists (1967) 194
Queen Elizabeth II: trials (1969) 215
Quemoy and Matsu: islands held by Chiang, bombarded by China (1955) 80; (1958) 105

race relations: in US (1963) 153; riots and non-violent protest (1965) 168-9; riots, first Black Power conference (1967) 193; after King's death (1968) peaceful protest declines 200; in Britain, Race Relations Act (1965) 169; Race Relations Act (1968) 208

Rachmann and rachmanism 150

Radio: Caroline, London (pirate), Luxembourg, Scotland, BBC Radio (1964) 156

Rajk, Laszlo: Hungarian communist, hanged (1949) 92

Ramsey, Sir Alf: manager of England's World Cup winning XI, knighted (1967) 187

Rand, Mrs Mary: Britain's first woman to win Olympic gold (1964) 161

Rape upon rape: Mermaid Theatre's opening play 111

rationing: of clothing, textiles, furniture, foodstuffs, fuel 8; effect on boat-race crew 20; bread rationed (1946-8) 20; meat ration reduced 53; petrol rationed (1956-7) 93, 95-6; de-rationing: potatoes (1948) 32; milk, tinned food, dried fruit (1950) 40-1; sweets, eggs, sugar (1953) 64; meats and fats (ration books end) (1954) 75; coal and coke (1958) 75

Rattigan, Terence: author 62

Ray, James Earl: sentenced for murder of Martin Luther King (1969) 200

Reagan, Ronald: Governor of California, fails to gain Republican nomination (1968) 202

Redgrave, Sir Michael: actor 82

Reed Carol: film director 37

Reluctant Peer, The: play (1964) 162

Rent Act (1957) 97

Representation of the People Acts: (1948 and 9) abolish business premises' and university graduates' vote 41; (1968) gives vote at eighteen 208

Rhee, Syngman: exiled from Korea for democratic views 44; President of South Korea (1948) 44

Rhine: Americans cross (1945) 9

Rhodesia (formerly Southern Rhodesia): 119, 154, 162; UDI–Unilateral Declaration of Independence (1965), sanctions 169; Lagos Conference (1966) 173; election issue in Britain (1966) 175; *Tiger* talks fail (1966) 183; Walter Adams 189; *Fearless* talks fail (1968) 207; Rhodesia House demonstration (1969) 213; republic declared (1969) 214

Rhodesia and Nyasaland: Federation, constitution granted (1953) 68; not likely to work 119; ceases to exist (1963) 154

Richard, Cliff: singer 156

Riley, Bridget: painter 166

Road Safety Act: breath tests introduced (1967) 196

Roaring Boys: novel (1955) 82

Robbins Report: on Higher Education (1963) 152; target exceeded (1967) 196

Robens, Lord: Aberfan enquiry (1966) 185

Robinson, Dr John: Bishop of Woolwich 148

Rock around the clock: record and film 81

Rockefeller, Nelson: Governor of New York State, fails to gain Republican nomination (1968) 202

Rolling Stones: pop group 155; violence at California concert (1969) 217

Romania: German ally 7; peace treaty 19; signs Warsaw pact (1955) 80

Rome, Treaty of: establishes EEC (1957) 95

Ronan Point: collapse of flats (1968) 208

Roosevelt, Mrs Eleanor: work on Declaration of Human Rights (1948) 33

Roosevelt, Franklin D: President of USA (1933-45), at Yalta (1945) 8; death 10-11; suffered from polio, controversy over statue 32

Roots: play (1959) 114, 197

Rose, Sir Alec: round-the-world voyage (1967-8) 206, 215

Rosenberg, Julius and Ethel: sentenced in US for spying (1951), executed (1953) 61-2

Rosencrantz and Guildenstern are dead: play (1967) 197

Round House: fund raising (1967), success as theatre (1969) 197

Royal Shakespeare Company: at Aldwych Theatre (1960) 126

Ruby, Jack: shoots Lee Oswald (1963) 153

Rush to judgement: criticism of Warren Report (1966) 153

Rushton, William: actor 143

Rusk, Dean: US Secretary of State, increases Vietnam aid (1962) 124; *Pueblo* incident (1968) 199

Russell, Bertrand (Lord Russell): unease over nuclear warfare, broadcasts a warning (1954) 71; writes to Eisenhower and Khrushchev (1957) 102; CND President (1958) 102, 120; resigns (1960) 121; starts Committee of 100 (1960) 121; in prison (1961) 133; telegrams on Cuba crisis (1962), death (1970) 143

Russia (USSR, Soviet Union): one of the Allies 7-8; at Yalta (1945) 8-9; forces reach the Elbe 9; mourning for Roosevelt 11; attitude to fraternising with Germans 12; at Potsdam 12-13; declaration of war on Japan 14; first atom bomb (1949) 14; Dynamos draw with Chelsea (1945) 15; permanent member of Security Council (1946) 17; blocks access to Berlin (1948) 30-1; occupies North Korea 44; proposes Korean ceasefire 48; Stalin's death, Malenkov succeeds (1953) 64; Beria shot 68; chess masters return to Hastings Congress 69; produces hydrogen bomb (1954) 72; Labour MP's entertained (1954) 72; Berlin and Geneva conferences (1954) 73; Bulganin succeeds Malenkov, Russian oarsmen at Henley, exchange of naval visits with Britain (1955) 78; Geneva Summit 79; organises Warsaw Pact 80; war material sent to Egypt (1956) 89; case of Miss Ponomreva 91; sputnik in orbit (1957) 98-9; dog in space 99; aid to Cuba 108; Dulles funeral 110; rocket hits moon (1959) 112; aids Lumumba in Congolese Republic (1960) 118; Paris Summit, U-2 incident 121-2; nuclear test (1961) 133; Stalin's body moved 134; mass space shot (1962) 141; Cuban missile crisis (1962) 142-3; first woman in space (1963) 149; nuclear tests ban (1963) 152; Brezhnev and Kosygin succeed Khrushchev (1964) 160; gift of books to Coventry Cathedral 138; Svetlana Stalin leaves, spacecraft crashes (1967) 189; Peking embassy attacked (1967) 193; invasion of Czechoslovakia (1968) 206

Sabah: part of Borneo, joins Malaysia (1963) 154
Sackville-West, Victoria: on myxomatosis 74
Sadat, Anwar: President of Egypt, Yom Kippur war (1973) 193
St. Lawrence Seaway: opened (1959) 111
Salan: French general sentenced (1962) for activities in Algeria 137; freed (1968) 205
sanctions: Rhodesia 169
Sarawak: part of Borneo, joins Malaysia (1963) 154
satire 143, 155
school buildings: supplies concentrated on 103
schools: leaving age raised to 15 (1947) 15, 24; to 16 (1972) 152; Newsom report (1963) 152
Schweitzer, Dr Albert: assessment, death (1965) 169
Scotland: Stone of Scone (1950-1) 46-7; support for measure of self-government 45; protests at Queen Elizabeth numbered II 59; Scottish BBC Television Service opened (1952) 59; Forth Road Bridge decided on (1957) 94; work starts (1958) 103
Scott, Giles Gilbert: design for Coventry Cathedral not accepted (1944) 137
Scouts: long trousers (1961) 134
Searle, Bobby: Black Panthers and gun control (1968) 201
seat belts: proposal to make compulsory (1962) 141
SEATO (South East Asia Treaty Organisation): set up (1954) 74; leads to US presence in Vietnam 167
Selassie, Emperor Haile: opens first OAU conference (1963) 148
Selective Employment Tax (1966) 177-8
Servant, The: film (1963) 155
Severn Bridge: planned 22; opened (1966) 184
Sexual behaviour in the human male: Kinsey Report (1948) 76
Sexual Offences Act (1967) 196
Shakespeare: 400th anniversary (1964) 157
Sharpeville: demonstrating Africans fired on (1960) 117
Shastri, Lal Bahadur: Prime Minister of India, dies (1966) 173
Sheffield: Park Hill redevelopment 158

Shelter: charity devoted to housing improvement 218
Shepard, Commander Alan: first US spaceman (1961) 130
Shinwell, Emmanuel: Labour Minister of Fuel and Power 23; Secretary of State for War 24
Short, Edward: in Cabinet (1968) 207
Sicily: poverty 123
Sierra Leone: independent (1961), military government (1967) 174
Sikorski, General: portrayed in *The Soldiers* 210
Silent World, The: undersea exploration 69
Singapore: independence (1965) 154, 172
Sirhan, Sirhan Bishara: sentenced for murder of Robert Kennedy 201
sit-ins: first in USA (1960) 123-4; at LSE (1967) 189
skinheads: violent anti-hippy youths 217
skirts: New Look (1948) 32; within a foot of the ground (1949) 35; below knee (1960) 122; miniskirt (1966) 166; 2 inches above the knee (1966) 178; maxi (1969) 219
Skopje earthquake (1963) 151
Skymaster: American aircraft on Berlin airlift 36
Slansky, Rudolf: Czechoslovak communist executed (1948) 92
Small Back Room, The: novel and film 37
Smith, Ian: Prime Minister of Rhodesia (1964) 161-2; warned by Wilson (1965) 169; talks in HMS *Tiger* (1966) 183; sanctions not hurting (1967) 187; talks in *Fearless* (1968) 207
smoking: and lung cancer, *Smoking and Health* (1962), teenagers' smoking (1970) 97; cigarette adverts banned from TV (1965) 171
Snagge, John: Head of Presentation, BBC Radio, announces death of George VI 58
Snowdon, Lord (Anthony Armstrong-Jones): marriage to Princess Margaret (1960) 121; refused entry to restaurant 197; at Aberfan (1966) 185
Soldiers: play (1968) 210
Soldier's diary, A: about 6-day war 192
Son of man: play 197
Sound of Music, The: musical 167
South Africa: "apartheid" policy implemented 43; Comet service opens 60; Nationalists increase majority 68; Macmillan's visit, Sharpeville (1960) 116-7; police state 119; withdraws from Commonwealth (1961) 129; liberation movements 148; Verwoerd assassinated (1966) 183; first heart transplant (1967) 198; relations with Malawi (1968) 207
South Pacific: American musical 54
South West Africa: claimed by South Africa 43
space shots: 99-100, 112, 129, 130, 136, 141, 149, 160, 170, 180; American and Russian accident (1967) 188; moon orbits (1968) 202; first and second US moon landings (1969) 216; Russian Luna 15, unmanned, on moon (1969) 216
Spain: not admitted to UN 16; still outlawed

(1948) 30; claims Gibraltar (1967) 195, closes frontier (1969) 214

Spartacus: film (1961) 131

Speakman, Private William, VC 48

speed limit: 50 mph tried at weekends (1962) 140; 70 mph (1965) 172

Spence, Sir Basil: Festival of Britain, 51; Coventry Cathedral 137

Spock, Dr Benjamin: anti-Vietnam movement (1968) 201

Springboks: South African rugby side 128; demonstrations against (1969) 218

sputnik: first satellite, Russian (1957) 98-99

squatters: (1946) 20; (1969) 217-8

Stalin, Joseph: Head of Russian Government and Commander-in-Chief, at Yalta, (1945) 8; at Potsdam 13; death (1953) 64; denounced (1956) 85; body moved (1961) 134

Stalin, Svetlana: in New York (1967) 189

Stanley, Sidney: criticised by Lynskey Tribunal (1949) 37

Stansted, Essex: provisionally chosen as third London airport (1964) 157

Star: closes (1960) 124

Starr, Ringo: one of the Beatles 151

steel industry: nationalised (1949) 38; denationalised (1953) 69; nationalised again (1967) 195-6

Stephen, John: rents Carnaby Street shop (1957) 94

Stern gang: Jewish terrorists in Palestine 25

Stevenage: first New Town 22; 'comes of age' (1968) 208

Stevenson, Adlai: Democratic presidential candidate in USA (1952) 62; at United Nations 142; death (1965) 167

Stewart, Michael: Foreign Secretary (1964) 163; (1966) 177; Minister of Economic Affairs (1966) 179; Foreign Secretary (1968) 207

stiletto heels: out of fashion (1968) 209

Stoppard, Tom: author 197

Stratford-upon-Avon: new buildings 157

stratocruiser, Boeing: provides berths on pre-jet Atlantic flights (1949) 36; takes Princess Elizabeth to Canada (1951) 54

street lighting 21

Street Offences Act: soliciting in public illegal (1959) 111

Streicher, Julius: Jew-baiter, hanged (1946) 19

strikes: dock (1945) 15; railwaymen's averted, film extras (1953) 68; London buses (1954) 77; maintenance workers' closes newspapers, dockers, engine-drivers and firemen (1955) 80; London buses (1958) 106; seamen's (1966) 178; 3¼m days lost (1968) 210; reaction to *In place of strife* (1969) 214; teachers' first, others, most strike-bound year since the war (1969) 218-19

student protest: LSE and other British (1968-9) 189, 214; France (1968-9) 202-5; Japan (1969) 213; Czechoslovakia (1969) 214

Study of history, A 71

Sudan: joint rule with Britain abrogated by Egypt (1951) 53; independent (1956) 85; power in Arab hands 95; military dictatorship (1958) 105

Suez Canal: Churchill tries to interest US Congress in (1952) 57; nationalised, resulting crisis (1956) 89-90; blocked (1956), in use again (1957), blocked again (1967), reopened (1975), Suez Company formed 93; Israelis reach in 1967 war 192

Suharto: takes over most of Sukarno's powers (1966), President and Prime Minister of Indonesia (1967) 174

Sukarno, Ahmed: declares Indonesia a republic (1945) 14; delegates powers to Suharto (1966), deposed (1967), death (1970) 174

Summerskill, Edith (Baroness Summerskill 1961): visits Moscow (1954) 72

Summit conferences: Geneva (1955) 79; Paris (1960) 110, 121

Sun: rises (1964) 158; as tabloid (1969) 218

Sunday Graphic: closes (1960) 124

Sunday Mirror (formerly *Sunday Pictorial*) 148

Sunday Telegraph: first appears (1961) 128

Sunday Times: bought by Thomson (1959) 111; colour magazine (1962) 136

supermarkets: reach Britain from USA (1954) 32; increase of 103

Sutch, 'Screaming Lord': stands for Parliament (1966) 177

Sutherland, Graham: Coventry Cathedral 138

Swaziland: claimed by S. Africa (1950) 43; independent (1968) 207

Sweden: parliamentary and anti-communist, 30; joins EFTA 122; 'pirate' radio 156

'swinging' London 166

Switzerland: 30; no votes for women 109; joins EFTA 122

syphilis 157

Syria: French driven out 14; invades Israel (1948) 31; joins UAR (1958) 102; 6-day war (1967) 191-2

Taiwan (Formosa): seat of Chiang Kai-Shek's government 38; islands of Quemoy and Matsu 80, 105; off Security Council (1971) 38

tankers: bigger for Cape route 97

Tanzania (formerly Tanganyika and Zanzibar): independence, prehistoric discoveries (1961), becomes a republic (1962) 134-5; mutiny (1964) 159; relations with Malawi 207

Taste of Honey, A: play (1959) 114

Tate, Sharon: actress, murdered (1969) 217

Taylor, Elizabeth: actress 156

Tay Road Bridge: opened (1966) 184

Teddy boys (Teds) 70, 94, 126, 158

television. *See* BBC, ITA

Telstar: first communications satellite, launched 139-40

Index

Templer, General Sir Gerald (later Field-Marshal): High Commissioner in Malaya (1952) 57
Tensing, Sherpa: climbs Everest 66
terrorists: at Zurich (1969) 214
'test-tube babies' 215
thalidomide 142
Thant, U: Secretary-General of UN (1961) 133; Cuban crisis (1962) 142; 6-day war (1967) 191-2
That Was The Week That Was (TW3): satirical TV revue (1962-3), 132, 143, 155
Theatre of the Absurd 81
theatres: in London 8; new 157; Theatre Workshop 114; Belgrade, Coventry 157
Thelonius Monk Quartet 178
The Times: price rise 58; mourning for George VI 58; price rise 128; 'rich and sonorous vocabulary' 160; news on front page (1966) 178; comment on (1969) 212
Third Man, The: film (1949) 37
This Sporting Life: film (1963) 155
Thomas, Dylan: author, dies (1953) 70
Thomson, Roy (Lord Thomson 1964): buys *Sunday Times* (1959) 111
Thorndike, Dame Sybil: actress 178
Those magnificent men in their flying machines: film (1965) 169
Tibet: invaded by China (1950) 46; Dalai Lama takes refuge in India (1959) 109
tights 219
Tito, Marshal: claims Trieste 14; independent of Russia 29-30; visits Britain 65
Titov, Major: second man in space 129
Tojo, Hideki: Prime Minister of Japan, hanged as war criminal (1948) 34
Tokyo Olympiade: film 161
Tom Jones: film (1963) 155
Tonga, Queen of: at Coronation 66
Torrey Canyon: aground, resulting pollution (1967) 189
Toynbee, Professor Arnold 72
Train Robbery, The Great: Biggs (1963) 152; Edwards (1966) 185
trams: last in London (1952) 60; in Glasgow (1962) 140
transistor radios 65, 156
Trident: maiden flight (1962) 140
Trieste: rival claims of Italy and Yugoslavia 14-15; disturbances and final settlement 64-5
Trinidad and Tobago: leave West Indies Federation, independent (1962) 102
Tristan da Cunha: population evacuated (1961), return (1963) 134
trolley buses: last in London (1962) 140
trousers 70, 141, 145
Truman, Harry S: President of the USA (1945-52), at Potsdam 12; view on Palestine 19; election (1948) 31; polls get results wrong 41; restrains General MacArthur (1951) 48

Tshombe, Moise: declares Katanga independent of Congolese Republic (1960), death while prisoner in Algeria (1969) 117-8
TUC (Trades Union Congress): Support for the arts 197
Tungku Abdul Rahman. *See* Abdul
Tunisia: independent (1956) 95
tunnel: under Great St Bernard (1964) 158; under Mont Blanc (1965) 94
Turkey: Cyprus agreement (1959) 109; US missile bases 142
Tushingham, Rita: actress 167
Twenty letters to a friend: book by Stalin's daughter (1967) 189
Tynan, Kenneth: on *Look back in anger*, on Eliot and Fry 88; on *Beyond the Fringe* 131

'U' and 'non-U' words 87
U-2: US plane shot down over Russia (1960) 188
Uganda: independent (1962) 139; mutiny (1964) 159; Obote suspends constitution (1966) 174. *See also* Kabaka
Ulbricht, Walter: Chairman of Council of State, German Democratic Republic 38
Ulster. *See* Northern Ireland
UN (United Nations): planned at Dumbarton Oaks (1945) 8; Charter signed (1945) 9; Assembly in London (1946) 16; Security Council 17; Korea 44 ff; Suez crisis 89-90; Hungarian crisis 92; 26 African members (1960) 117; troops in Congo (1960-4) 117-20; Cuban crisis (1962) 142; Rhodesia (1965) 169; emergency force (UNEF) guards Gulf of Aqaba (1967) 191; endorsement of nuclear non-proliferation treaty 201
Under Milk Wood: radio play (1954) 70
unemployment: rises (1963) 146
UNESCO (United Nations Educational, Scientific and Cultural Organisation): founded (1945) 9; Paris HQ opened (1958) 106
United Arab Republic: formed (1958) 102. *See* Egypt, Syria
UNRRA (United Nations Relief and Rehabilitation Administration): organises camps for Displaced Persons after World War II 15
Unsafe at any speed 176
Upper Volta: coup d'état (1966) 173
US: play 178
USA: one of the Allies 7; Rhine crossing, meeting with Russians on Elbe (1945) 9; permanent member of Security Council 17; Marshall Plan (1947) 25; polio epidemic, dollar deficit 35; Korean War starts (1950) 44; Geneva Summit (1955) 79; Suez crisis (1956) 89-90; 'smarting under Russian satellites' 99; intervenes in Lebanon (1958) 105; atomic submarine *Nautilus* passes under North Pole (1958) 106; Paris Summit, U-2 incident (1960) 121-2; nuclear tests (1961, 1962) 133, 140; Bay of Pigs (1961) 130; Special Forces reach Vietnam (1962) 136;

238

Venus space shot (1962) 141; aid to India against China (1962) 142; Cuban missile crisis (1962) 142-3; nuclear tests ban (1963) 152; John F. Kennedy murdered (1963) 153; Apollo launching accident (1967) 188; race riots (1967) 193; *Pueblo* incident (1968) 199; Vietnam peace talks (1968-73) 200; murders of Martin Luther King and Robert Kennedy (1968) 200; Poor People's Campaign (1968) 201; Nixon elected President (1968) 202; first moon landing (1969) 216; Edward Kennedy, Manson, Calley, Special Forces trials (1969) 217. *See also* Olympic Games, space shots, names of Presidents etc.

USSR. *See* Russia

✓ 1's ('doodle-bugs') 8
V2's (long-range rockets) 8
Vanguard: turbo-prop passenger aircraft, developed by de Havilland 35
Vanguard, HMS: 17, 21; leaves for South Africa on royal tour 23, 55; out of commission (1960) 124
Vasarely, Victor: painter 166
Vassall, William: convicted for spying (1962) 144
VAT: replaces SET and purchase tax (1973) 178
VC 10: maiden flight (1962) 140
VE Day (1945) 10
venereal disease 157
Verwoerd, Dr: Prime Minister of South Africa, assassinated (1966) 183
Victoria Line: work starts on (1962) 140; first section open (1968) 209
Vietnam: Dulles's policy leads to war 62; Geneva Conference discusses 73; Vietminh provisional government at Hanoi (1946) 73; division at 17th parallel into two republics (1955) 74; Vietcong set up (1960) 124; first American killed (1961) 135; American aid increased by Kennedy (1962) 124; US Special Forces ('green berets') arrive (1962) 136; 'small but ugly war' (1964) 159; US activity stepped up, draft cards burned (1965-6) 167-8; Wilson's reference to (1965) 172; de Gaulle urges withdrawal (1966) 177; protests on bombing of North Vietnam 178; Vietcong in Saigon (1968) 199; peace talks begin (1968), agreement (1973) 200-204; Grosvenor Square demonstration (1968) 203; Australia and New Zealand involved 213; murder of civilians at My Lai (1969) 217
Viscount: turbo-prop passenger aircraft, developed by de Havilland 35
VJ Day (1945) 15
Vogue 152, 166
Vorster, Balthazar: Prime Minister of South Africa (1966) 183; relations with Malawi (1968) 207
voting age: lowered to 18 (1969) 171
VSO (Voluntary Service Overseas): begins (1958) 106

Wait a minim: South African revue (1961) 128
Waiting for Godot: play (1955) 81
Wales: Welsh Nationalists 113, 177; Prince of Wales investiture 215. *See also* Aberfan, Dylan Thomas
Walker, Patrick Gordon: not re-elected (1964 and 1965) 162
Wallace, Governor George: opposes desegregation (1963) 153
war crimes: trials and executions at Nuremberg (1945-6) 19; Japanese hanged 34
Ward, Dr Stephen: Profumo affair (1963) 150
Warhol, Andy: artist 125
Warren Report: on John F. Kennedy murder 153
Warsaw Pact: signed by allies of Russia (1955) 79
weather 7, 23, 34, 35, 60, 71, 75, 78, 80, 81, 94, 95, 103, 108, 110, 111, 112, 134, 136, 143, 145, 191, 213
Weekend Telegraph: first appearance (1964) 159
Welles, Orson: actor and film director 37
Wesker, Arnold: author 114, 197
West Indies: immigrants from 97; Federation of (1958-66) 102; independence of Jamaica (1962) 139; Anguilla trouble (1969) 214
Wheldon, Huw: at Festival of Britain 51
When pirates ruled the waves 156
Which?: founded (1957) 134
Whisky Galore!: film comedy 37
Wilson, Harold: President of the Board of Trade and youngest member of Cabinet (1950) 42; resigns in protest against rearmament budget (1951) 49-50; challenges Gaitskell for leadership (1960) 123; Leader of Labour Party (1963) 146; Prime Minister (1964) 161-2; Rhodesia (1965) 169; import surcharge (1965) 171; MBE's for Beatles (1965) 171; reference to Vietnam (1965) 172; on India and Pakistan (1965), at Lagos (1966) 173; policies in 1965 175; promotes Cousins (1966) 179; talks in HMS *Tiger* (1966) 183; at Aberfan (1966) 185; the Round House (1967) 197; talks in *Fearless* (1968) 207; housing (1969) 218
Wolfenden Report: proposes change in homosexuality law (1957) 98
Woodhouse, C. M.: on Suez 91
Woolwich, Bishop of (1959-69), Rev. John A. T. Robinson: writes *Honest to God* (1963) 148
World Cup: stolen, won by England (1966) 177; Ramsey and Moore honoured (1967) 187
World Health Organisation: established (1948) 9
Wynne, Greville: convicted of spying by Russians (1963) 126

Yalta (in Crimea): Churchill, Roosevelt and Stalin discuss future of Germany (1945) 8-9
Yugoslavia: 7-9; Trieste claimed 14-15; 29-30; 65; Skopje earthquake (1963) 151. *See also* Tito

Zaire: Congolese Republic renamed (1971) 119

Zambia (formerly Northern Rhodesia): republic
(1964) 154; relations with Malawi 207
Zanzibar 135, 213

Zhivago, Dr: Russian novel (1958) 104
Zionists 18